Dossier Secreto

New Providence Memorial Library
377 Elkwood Avenue
New Providence, NJ 07974

DOSSIER SECRETO

Argentina's *Desaparecidos* and the Myth of the "Dirty War"

Martin Edwin Andersen

Westview Press

BOULDER • SAN FRANCISCO • OXFORD

Cover design by Polly Christensen incorporates *The Surprise Search,* a watercolor sketch by Alexander Deutsch, who was a political prisoner in Cordoba's notorious La Perla during the "Dirty War." The sketch of a detention line-up in a secret military camp was painted on the back of a cigarette package during the artist's imprisonment and smuggled out, for a fee, by a visitor to a nonpolitical prisoner. (*The Surprise Search* used courtesy of the artist.)

All rights reserved. No part of this publication may be reproduced or transmitted in any form or by any means, electronic or mechanical, including photocopy, recording, or any information storage and retrieval system, without permission in writing from the publisher.

Copyright © 1993 by Westview Press, Inc.

Published in 1993 in the United States of America by Westview Press, Inc., 5500 Central Avenue, Boulder, Colorado 80301-2877, and in the United Kingdom by Westview Press, 36 Lonsdale Road, Summertown, Oxford OX2 7EW

Library of Congress Cataloging-in-Publication Data
Andersen, Martin Edwin.
    Dossier secreto : Argentina's Desaparecidos and the myth of the
"Dirty War" / Martin Edwin Andersen.
        p.   cm.
    Includes bibliographical references and index.
    ISBN 0-8133-8212-2. — ISBN 0-8133-8213-0 (pbk.)
    1. Argentina—Politics and government—1910–   2. Argentina—
Military policy—History—20th century.   3. Political persecution—
Argentina—History—20th century.   4. Human rights—Argentina—
History—20th century.   I. Title.
F2848.A6   1993
982.06—dc20   92-33310
                                                                                          CIP

BRODART 17.95 12/93

Printed and bound in the United States of America

 The paper used in this publication meets the requirements
of the American National Standard for Permanence of Paper
for Printed Library Materials Z39.48-1984.

10   9   8   7   6   5   4   3   2

To Patt Derian,
Emilio Mignone,
and the memory of the late bishop of La Rioja,
Monsignor Enrique Angelelli,
three people who spoke out and made a difference

Document Discloses Alleged Conspiracy

According to a secret document that is in the hands of government officials, an alleged conspiracy known as the "Spring Plan" was to have begun on 31 August 1990 with an incident at an Army unit, followed by a "symbolic seizure" of the Army Staff Headquarters with the objective of installing a new chief of staff.

As is common in this type of case, the document bears no identification imprints, seals, or signatures. Analysts believe that this proves the authenticity of the document, because false documents bear many imprints and authentic official seals.

Noticias Argentinas, July 24, 1990

The struggle of man against power is the struggle of memory against forgetting.

Milan Kundera, *The Book of Laughter and Forgetting*

Contents

Illustrations

****

New Providence Memorial Library

7/11/2016 8:40:22 PM   1 908 665 0311

****

Title   Dossier secreto : Argentina's
               Desaparecidos and the myth
               of the "Dirty War"

Item ID   39050001684508
Due: 8/8/2016

Acknowledgments

The reconstruction of a nation's past is an enterprise fraught with dangers even for the citizen-historian of the country under study. The risks increase exponentially for foreigners, particularly those whose understanding or hypotheses put their interpretation at odds with conventional wisdom. I was fortunate to count on the generous support and insights of many Argentines, some of whom shared my perspective, many others who did not. The fact that people were so giving to such an enterprise is one of the main reasons I remain convinced this undertaking is worthwhile—that there remains in Argentina a profound need to understand that nation's tragic recent past.

Inevitably, in the process of acknowledging the contributions of so many—and this book is the result of more than 1,000 interviews conducted in seven countries—the help of all cannot be mentioned. I hope that those who helped me and are not mentioned here will find that the book itself was worth their effort.

In Argentina, a country I consider a second home, I would like to give special thanks to the following people: María Laura Avignolo, Ailsa Berzon, "el Cabezon," Jorge Silvio Colotto, Carlos Delía Larroca, Mario Diament, Daniel Frontalini, Rogelio García Lupo, the late Pablo Giussani, Fernando Hevia, Guillermo Patricio Kelly, Alberto Kohan, Nina Lindley, José Lagomarsino, Santiago Mellibovsky, Horacio Méndez Carreras, Mario Benjamín Menéndez, Emilio Mignone, Héctor Ruiz Núñez, Oscar Serrat, Brian Thomson, José Manuel Ugarte, Horacio Verbitsky, Julio Villalonga, Rogelio Villareal, and La Rioja bishop Monsignor Bernardo Witte. All were generous with their time, insight, and, in virtually every case, affection and friendship.

In the United States, several people deserve special mention as well. Larry Birns and Patt Derian, two magnificent human rights crusaders and friends of Argentina, offered a treasure of archival material without which this book would be noticeably poorer. Joseph Eldridge and Mark Schneider had important insights to give, and I am in their debt for giving them to me. Sheryl Walter, general counsel for the National Security Archives in Washington, D.C., gave me valuable technical advice on making the federal Freedom of Information Act (FOIA) work for the purposes of this book. Riordan Roett, James R. Wacht, and George Rogers and Deborah Benchoam offered me places to stay and encouragement during uncertain and difficult times. Several career State Department officials offered critical confirmations of some of the most important discoveries of this book, and I thank them for their help while respecting their request for confidentiality. And "Sam," who cannot be identified by name, deserves enormous thanks for helping recover and restore some of the most important pieces to the turbulent mosaic called Argentine history.

Several people went to great lengths to make my manuscript both readable and more factually precise. They are David Corn, Mario del Carril, Judith Evans, Tomás Eloy Martínez, Juan Méndez, Wayne Smith, Eric Stover, Alan Thomas, and George Vickers. A special thanks also goes to my longest-term, and longest-suffering, editor—my father, Edwin M. Andersen.

At Westview Press, I would like to thank Barbara Ellington, Michelle Murphy, Shena Redmond, and Mary Bahmer. I also wish to acknowledge gratefully a grant from the Allen Hilles Fund and particularly Judith L. Bardes for her cheerful help.

Juan de Onis and the late Penny Lernoux offered their support and their help and have been important role models and friends. In whatever is good about this work, they played a part.

To my wife, Laura; my daughter, Carla Thais; and my mother, Angeline—my love and gratitude for putting up with what I thought was a magnificent obsession, although I'm sure I gave them lots of reasons to think otherwise.

Unfortunately, several people who are main characters in this book did not accede to requests for an interview. They are Henry Kissinger, Mario Firmenich, Jorge Videla, Roberto Viola, Emilio Massera, and Albano Harguindeguy. Their testimony would have been valuable because all controversies have two sides, and theirs might have shed light on one of the most tragic events in the post–World War II Western world. Until they answer the hard questions still pending, we can only evaluate their acts and try to interpret their silence.

Any and all errors found in this book are of course the responsibility of the author. Having counted on the substantial assistance of so many people, there can be no other excuses.

Martin Edwin Andersen

Prologue

In modern times few events in our hemisphere have had as devastating an impact on democracy and human rights as Argentina's so-called "dirty war." The secret repression unleashed by Argentina's generals against leftist insurgents and other dissidents in the period from 1976 to 1983—touted by the military as "the opening battle of World War III"—became a sinister and tragic model in a hemisphere wracked by political violence.

Examples of the impact of the "dirty war," and the influence of the military who "fought" it, abound. Argentine army intelligence officers schooled in disinformation, torture, and murder were the first instructors of Nicaragua's Contras—Ronald Reagan's "freedom fighters." Salvadoran military and death squad bosses responsible for the gangland-style deaths of tens of thousands also looked to Buenos Aires for guidance and support. Argentine army Col. Mohamed Alí Seineldín, a confidant and top aide of Panama's drug-running dictator Manuel Noriega, came honestly to the strongman's table, having served as a liaison between the death squads and his army superiors in Buenos Aires. And even in the 1990s Peruvian military officers facing the lunatic Sendero Luminoso guerrillas wistfully invoke the possibility of employing an "Argentine solution" against a nation of suspects.

In the aftermath of the "dirty war," when civilian rule and civility itself returned to a Latin American nation that has long prided itself as a pacesetter for its Spanish-speaking neighbors, Argentina became a model of a different sort. The brave saga of Argentine human rights groups, particularly the Madres de la Plaza de Mayo (Mothers of the Plaza de Mayo), was admired and their organizations imitated around the globe—in Guatemala and El Salvador, Peru, and the Philippines.

Argentina's democratic institutions also came under the spotlight. Never before in Latin America had former military rulers been brought to trial before fair and impartial courts to face judgment for crimes committed against those over whom they were once masters. In Uruguay, Peru, Nicaragua, Salvador, Panama—and Brazil and Chile and Honduras, too—the myth of military omnipotence, and the reality of military impunity, began to crumble before the spectacle of an

1

Argentina taking its tormentors to task fairly, impartially, and with a firm determination that military rule—left-wing or right, populist or conservative—be banished forever.

The context in which these changes have occurred has been only imperfectly understood, however. The news from Argentina has often been dramatic, the stories—of rampant inflation and soaring debt, of fabulous fortunes and labor unrest, of bloody political clashes and official repression—a jarring symphony of the violent, the exotic, and the bizarre. Yet in examining Argentina and the reasons for its misfortunes and its triumphs, one also captures some of the most important themes and issues of our time. The quest for development and participatory democracy in the Third World; the impact of cold war ideologies imported from Italy and France, the United States and Cuba; and the role of the military in societies virtually without external enemies—all these came into play, in the most devastating way, in Argentina.

Nothing captures the limitations to contemporary understanding of the news from Buenos Aires as well as the use of the misnomer "dirty war." Argentina in the mid-1970s was wracked by political instability, civil strife, and a growing body count of victims whose deaths only occasionally made sense to average Argentines, in whose name the various factions fought. The term "war," however, implies that the casualties were more likely to come from the ranks of two real armies rather than those of noncombatants.

After democracy returned in 1983, an important part of the "dirty war" story was told when President Raúl Alfonsín empowered a blue-ribbon commission to investigate the whereabouts of the more than 9,000 people who were missing. Its report unmasked the military's secret campaign of terror, torture, and death against those who opposed them and against those who were merely in the way— a campaign that contravened virtually every norm of civilized conduct. A word, *desaparecido*—the disappeared one—entered into the Orwellian lexicon in its original Spanish, a sad tribute to the efficiency with which the generals kidnapped and tortured their victims, then made them vanish without a trace.

Even after a decade of sensational revelations, trials, and public debate laying bare the generals' murderous methods, however, a larger myth remains—that of a "war." In Argentina, the military misrepresented the nature and size of the threat posed by leftist insurgents as a way of justifying their own illegal repression and their seizure of power from a corrupt and inept but also lame-duck elected government. The generals' claim that a "war" was taking place—and their extraordinary efforts to bamboozle public opinion both at home and abroad that "war" it was—sought to mask the massacre they perpetrated in the name of "Western, Christian civilization." Torture and death were meted out not only against those guilty of some crime but also against those who questioned the military's concept of what society should be like and who should be in charge.

Even when faced with overwhelming evidence about a slaughter that they had denied for years, the military continued to perpetrate a Big Lie. The guerrillas' clandestine, cellular structure and the number of armed militants—tens of thousands, the military said—required brutal countermeasures. Civilians were not qualified to dispute questions of methodology with those trained in these matters—themselves. Although the methodology was unsavory, in the mind of the military the portrayal of an unconventional "war" served as a justification. Civilians, they said, that weak and fickle class, owed them a debt of gratitude for what they had done.

Mass murder was reduced to an argument over methodology. Yet a basic question remained unanswered—was there a "war"?

As part of my responsibilities as a special correspondent for *Newsweek* and the *Washington Post*, I covered the 1985 trials in Buenos Aires of the nine military commanders charged with responsibility for the "dirty war." As a result of that experience, and the frustration of being unable to put the story in its real context in dispatches of 1,000 words or less, what had begun two years earlier as a book on the plight of the missing grew to address the larger questions that the trials—and months of investigation and exposés—could only imperfectly suggest. In place of an imperfect and misleading journalistic shorthand replete with terms such as "near civil war," or "dirty war," or "campaign against leftist guerrillas and other dissidents," this book offers the singular context in which this euphemism-ridden tragedy was played out. It will show the extent to which assassinations attributed to one side (the guerrillas) of the "dirty war" were in fact carried out by the other (the military and their death-squad allies). It will put into context the hundreds of "clashes" between guerrillas and their military foes that were really faked "battles" between the latter and already-dead detainees. (A former U.S. intelligence agent told me of having arrived at the scene of a supposed "shoot-out" between the security forces and leftist guerrillas in 1976 to find the former splashing chickens' blood around the locale before admitting local reporters and photographers.) And finally, it will show that the guerrillas' ranks themselves were infiltrated—as they were in several other Latin countries and even Italy—in such a way as to call into question the true purposes of several of their most violent acts and the authenticity of the threat they posed.

In 1984 two young Argentine human rights activists, Daniel Frontalini and María Cristina Caiati, opened the debate this book seeks to address when they published a slim volume entitled *The Myth of the Dirty War*. Limited at the time to material already in the public domain, the pair laid out the framework of what is the most damning indictment of the military, one framed in their own terms—the "war" they claimed they were fighting was largely a fraud. The guerrilla threat to Argentina was never more than a serious problem of terrorism, one that could have been handled better, and with a lot less bloodshed, by the police. *Dossier Secreto* seeks to lay to rest the argument that the "dirty war" was dirty but necessary.

How did this violence become endemic to Latin America's most cultured and economically advanced society? In Part One Argentina's transformation from a vast colonial agricultural economy to that of a booming industrial state is explored. The controversial rise of Col. Juan Domingo Perón is traced, as the leader of Argentina's emerging working class, his ascension by free and fair election to the presidency, the development and eventual decline of Peronism's state-led economic model, and the often-undemocratic ways that Perón—to some a closet Bolshevik, to others a crypto-Nazi—met the challenge of real or purported opponents.

Perón's overthrow by the military in 1955 was followed by nearly two decades of unpopular ham-handed regimes alternating power with weak civilian governments, elected only after the exiled Perón and his party—still empowered with the banners of social justice—were banned. The 1960s also saw the exponential and sinister growth of the Argentine military intelligence services, a parallel rise in military McCarthyism fueled by U.S. counterinsurgency doctrines, a crisis of purpose and mission within the armed forces, the emergence of the Cuban revolution as an attractive—to some—alternative to the continent's weak civilian political leadership and continuing economic underdevelopment, and the repression and decline in well-being of the Argentine middle class.

The growing radicalization of an important segment of Argentina's students and workers was accompanied by an increasing weariness among the people, and within large sectors of the armed forces as well, of rule from the barracks. The emergence of Marxist and Peronist guerrilla groups signaled that the military no longer held a monopoly on the means of force, and even groups historically antagonistic to Perón began to look in anticipation to the return of the *caudillo* (leader) from his exile in Madrid. Perón's return to Argentina and the presidency in 1973, however, could not contain the furies unleashed during his long absence, a power struggle exacerbated by far-right elements in his own inner circle.

Although Perón sought to bring unity to Argentina, both the far left and the far right were unwilling to renounce violence as a means of political competition. Meanwhile, the military intelligence services' own efforts to play a political role, including the penetration of the leftist Peronist Montoneros at the highest levels, brought new levels of death and destruction to Argentina, an orgy of violence that grew following Perón's own death in 1974.

Perón was replaced as president by his widow, Isabel, but it was a bizarre Perón aide named José López Rega who took power. With the help of Italian neofascists, the Rasputin of the Pampas launched a systematic campaign of terror against both his opponents and others—Jews, left-wing Peronists, and, sometimes, guerrillas. The army's internal security mission, and a relentless campaign against the military by the armed Marxist left, edged them back into a political role. After launching a highly publicized, well-orchestrated campaign against a largely nonexistent guerrilla "army" in Argentina's northwest—done, they claimed, to protect democracy—the generals focused their efforts against Isabel's corrupt and incompetent regime. Using the antiguerrilla struggle as a pretext, and with the backing of Argentina's upper and middle classes, the generals took power in March 1976.

In Part Two the dark recesses of the "dirty war" itself are penetrated. The practices and techniques used by the generals are explained, and a look at the people against whom the military's repression was directed is offered. Ostensibly a fight against violence from the far right as well as the far left, the military never punished what little was left of the independent neofascist right; rather it incorporated that element into its ranks. Meanwhile, the junta's terror tactics went far beyond pursuit of the guerrillas or even their sympathizers. Labor, universities, and progressive religious activists—bishops, nuns, and laypeople—were priority targets for the repression. More than 300 secret detention centers held thousands of people seized from their homes and workplaces and off the streets. These people were tortured and secretly murdered, their bodies thrown into the ocean, buried in mass graves, or used as "stuffing" in staged shoot-outs with the "security" forces.

In Part Three the political development of the military regime is traced from the time it took power in March 1976 to the time the generals retreated to the barracks in 1983. Although both of Argentina's two most important guerrilla groups were decimated by mid-1976, the repression continued full-blown for more than three years. At the same time, infighting between the military and their civilian allies took a growing toll—violence and death that were almost always attributed to the guerrillas. Italian neofascists, Chilean right-wing terrorists, and other murderers and ruffians who served as intelligence operatives from several parts of the globe found in the military's Argentina a hospitable place to ply their trade.

Meanwhile in Washington, a revolution was taking place—a human rights revolution. No longer content to define U.S. interests within the narrow confines of anticommunism while turning a blind eye to the brutality of client regimes, Jimmy Carter's government put the Argentine generals at the top of its list of human rights pariahs. The Carter policies saved lives and won credit with those who would one day lead Argentina back to civilian rule and democracy.

Yet the Carter period can be seen only as an interregnum in a shocking tale of U.S. complicity with Argentina's murderous generals. Despite their human rights record and despite the fact that only a year before, in 1980, the Argentine army had organized the overthrow of Bolivia's civilian government and replaced it with a military regime that not only employed a major Nazi war criminal but was steeped in cocaine trafficking as well, the junta in Buenos Aires became the toast of the Reagan administration. No longer pariahs, Argentina's "dirty warriors" became U.S. proxies in Central America, a partnership that lasted until a drunken general named Leopoldo F. Galtieri, who called himself the *niño mimado* (favored son) of Washington, invaded a group of South Atlantic islands held by NATO ally Great Britain.

The quick but bloody defeat of the Argentines by Britain sounded the death knell for military rule. A charismatic, dynamic leader named Raúl Alfonsín emerged from the shadows of military rule and prepared to lead his country back into the ranks of civilized nations. Yet U.S. enthusiasm for Alfonsín was muted at best and—particularly in the beginning—the Argentines were forced to face their tragic past without important help from Washington. Not a few noted that U.S. support for Alfonsín's Argentina never reached the level of interest and commitment offered to, and ultimately misunderstood by, that of the generals under Galtieri.

After World War II the world documented the horrors perpetrated by the Germans and their allies. Now, as "Holocaust revisionists" seek to absolve the Nazis of responsibility for camps that destroyed millions of lives, a fire wall of fact makes such ideas impossible to entertain.

In 1992 in Argentina, the virus of militarism seems to have finally ebbed from the body politic. Yet a generation of soldiers schooled in the belief that torture was a legitimate weapon still hold the highest ranks in the Argentine military. Although some admit that "excesses" occurred, hardly anyone will admit that the "war" they "fought" was largely a myth. The military still insists, as do some in the Pentagon, that it deserves thanks and praise from the rest of society. For the many revanchists who still remain, who demand medals for conduct from which the rest of the world recoiled in horror, the largely unexamined question of whether a "war" occurred in Argentina leaves them an argument to make and a case to press in the future. And there have been other times in Latin America that commentators have proclaimed the twilight of the tyrants—only to be proven wrong with almost insolent speed.

This book—like the work of those who documented the Holocaust—is meant to ensure that the fictionalized account left by the military as their official record of events in the 1970s and 1980s will not be allowed, sometime in the future, to replace fact.

PART ONE

1

The Sad Privilege
of Being Argentine

History is a pack of tricks that we play on the dead.
—*Quoted in John Morley,* Voltaire, *1828*

A ripple of excitement raced through the wood-paneled room in the majestic eighty-one-year-old federal courts building. In the packed press boxes, reporters craned their necks and attacked their notepads with pens and pencils. In the balconies, the public waited expectantly. The buzzing voices soon gave way to a tense silence. At the front of the courtroom, the sad-eyed federal prosecutor with a bushy mustache sat on the edge of his chair. His voice rose to an eloquent tenor. The Argentine people, long at the mercy of violent captors, would receive their day in court.

For six days prosecutor Julio César Strassera and his young assistant, Luis Moreno Ocampo, had plowed through their often tedious oral summations. There were 709 individual cases of human rights violations to be reviewed, assayed, and in some instances discarded for lack of evidence.[1] Throughout Strassera's summation, the nine former military commanders sat in the dock, listening impassively to his charges. Only former president Gen. Roberto Viola made use of the blocks of paper spread out on the table before him. The nine officers, Strassera charged, were responsible for the "worst genocide" in Argentine history. They alone were the architects of a policy of murder, torture, enslavement, and kidnapping that characterized the military's fight against leftist guerrillas and other dissidents during the 1970s.

For five months the testimony of hundreds of victims, family members, and public figures had been a civics lesson for Argentines. The country had been denied the truth about the military's so-called dirty war while the disappearances and murder of political opponents became an open secret the world over. Officially, nearly 9,000 people were missing.

9

It was September 18, 1985. Twenty-one months earlier, newly installed civilian president Raúl Alfonsín had promised a return of the rule of law. During that hot December 1983, Argentines' delirious celebration of democracy was mixed with dismay and horror as dozens of unmarked mass graves were unearthed around the country. Backed by a growing public consensus, Alfonsín moved quickly. He sent a raft of human rights bills to Congress, including one making torture a crime with the same penalties as first-degree murder. He established the Comisión Nacional sobre la Desaparición de Personas (CONADEP; National Commission on the Disappearance of Persons), popularly known as the Sábato Commission (for its chairman, novelist Ernesto Sábato), to look into the fate of the thousands who numbered among the missing during the military-sponsored repression. He also ordered the prosecution of the nine military men who presided over the "dirty war," as well as that of guerrilla leaders still at large.

In his closing remarks, Strassera accused the nine military men of having taken power "by assault" in overthrowing the previous elected government. They had, he charged, responded to a challenge by leftist guerrilla groups with a "fierce, cowardly and clandestine" repression that "produced the same evil they said they were combating." As he spoke, former President Leopoldo Galtieri chain-smoked nervously, his bulky body chafing in his chair and his legs in constant motion. Gen. Jorge Rafael Videla, the head of the first military junta, read religious tracts, looking up occasionally to stare, as if transfixed, at the cross behind the judges' bench. Some of the nine accused looked older than the public remembered them.

As Strassera wound to his valedictory finish, the audience began to stir. "In my task today," the prosecutor said, "I am not alone, but rather accompanied by 10,000 *desaparecidos* [disappeared ones]." He asked the court to give life sentences to army Generals Videla and Viola, retired Admirals Emilio Massera and Armando Lambruschini, and retired air force Brigadier Orlando Agosti. He demanded penalties of between ten and fifteen years for the other four defendants, including a fifteen-year sentence for Galtieri. "Your honors," he said, "I wish to use a phrase that does not belong to me, but rather to the Argentine people. Your honors, *'Never again!'*"

The audience rose to its feet. Above the din of thunderous clapping, cheers of "bravo, bravo" could be heard. Viola was clearly rattled. Looking up at the galleries, he began to curse: "Sons of bitches! Sons of bitches!" Jeers of "assassins, murderers" rained down on the uniformed general and the eight other defendants who began to file out of the court. Videla looked as if he had been slapped in the face. Clasping his portfolio protectively to his chest, he stared uncomprehendingly at the crowd. Presiding Judge León Arslanian ordered the courtroom cleared. The people had had their day in court.[2]

Three weeks later Adm. Emilio Massera took the stand. Massera once dreamed of being the Líder (leader), a second Juan Perón—the military man who had dominated Argentine political life for three decades. Had not the general himself affectionately called him Masserita (little Massera) when talking to his navy chief?

Was it not Perón who used to joke that if the admiral had joined the army, he would have some day been president of the Argentines? Had not the square-jawed, darkly handsome navy man always risen to the public occasion, his adrenaline and ambition pulsing to the roar of approval that once rang in his ears?

By his own admission, the aging playboy who took the stand did so not to offer a defense. His eyes dark and glowering, Massera declared, "No one who has won a just war has to defend himself. ... However, I stand here accused because we did win that just war. If we would have lost, none of us would be here—not you, not us—because the esteemed judges of this chamber would have been long ago replaced by turbulent peoples' tribunals, and a fierce and unrecognizable Argentina would have replaced the old Fatherland."

Massera accused his accusers of trying to sow discord among the military in order to dominate them. "To divide is to conquer, but what they are really betraying is fear, a lot of fear," he said. "Because the enemy knows today's armed forces are as capable of defeating them as were the armed forces of yesterday"—a veiled but obvious threat. "I'd almost say that I'm lucky I have no future. My future is a cell. It was since this incredible trial began, and there I will pass the rest of my biological life, being as how the other—creative life, the life of intelligence, the life of the spirit—I have already voluntarily given to this fickle and beloved nation."

The Sábato Commission Report

"During the decade of the 1970s Argentina was convulsed by a terrorism that came both from the far left as well as the far right, a phenomenon similar to that occurring in many other countries," read the CONADEP report. The blue-ribbon citizens' commission appointed by Alfonsín to investigate the disappearances had issued its findings the year before Strassera's summation.

When Aldo Moro, the leader of Italy's ruling Christian Democratic party, was kidnapped, the report noted, a member of the Italian security forces proposed to Gen. Carlos Alberto Dalla Chiesa that a detainee who appeared to have vital information be tortured. "Dalla Chiesa," the CONADEP report recalled, "responded with the memorable words: 'Italy can permit itself to lose Aldo Moro. What it cannot allow is the practice of torture.'"

That principle was not the case in Argentina. Faced with terrorist crimes, the military "responded with a terrorism infinitely worse than it was fighting," because from the day of the takeover—March 24, 1976—the generals counted on "the power and impunity of the absolute State, kidnapping, torturing and killing thousands of human beings."

Almost all the abductions had evidenced a similar modus operandi, sometimes occurring in the victim's workplace, at other times on the street in broad daylight. In most instances, the government security forces ordered a "free zone" from the corresponding police commissaries, so they could carry out their work unmolested. If they kidnapped a victim at night in his or her own home, armed commandos surrounded the entire block, entered the dwelling by force, terrorized parents and children, often gagging them, and obliged them to watch as they overpowered their prey. Often the victim was brutally beaten, a hood placed roughly over his or her head, before being dragged off to a waiting car or truck, usually without license plates. The rest of the commando group might then sack the home or loot what they could carry. "From there they would go toward a cavern in whose door could have been written the words that Dante read on the gates of Hell: 'Abandon all hope, all you who enter.' In that manner, in the name of national security, thousands and thousands of human beings, mostly young and even adolescents, came to join that gloomy, phantasmic category: that of the *Desaparecidos.* A word—such a sad privilege for Argentina—that today is written in Spanish in the world press."[3]

Dirty Secrets of a "Dirty War"

Argentina is a land of stunning paradoxes. A country of vast but mismanaged natural wealth and industrial potential, Argentina has seemingly lurched backward, away from the path of development. A place of vibrant cultural and intellectual traditions, it appeared incapable of nurturing tolerance or political stability. A society both sophisticated and more civilized than most of its neighbors, Argentina in the 1970s became South America's most efficient and brutal police state.[4]

By March 1976, the month it launched its sixth coup against a constitutional government in less than fifty years, Argentina's military clung to the threat posed by the armed insurgents as a precious—but phony—causus belli. The generals had convinced themselves they were on the front lines of the struggle against world communism, where the annihilation of the insurgents was a mere first step in a much more ambitious effort. Beyond the guerrillas lay the power base and influence of organized labor, which reached its zenith during the years immediately preceding the coup, as well as a broad, all-encompassing cast of "ideological delinquents"—liberals and libertarians, socialists and social workers, those who disturbed the generals' sense of order.

The military knew that world opinion, already outraged by public executions in Francisco Franco's Spain and mass murders in Augusto Pinochet's Chile, would not tolerate the open torture and death of those who opposed their rule. Needing a threat so pervasive and insidious as to justify their state-sponsored terror, the military invented another kind of war, a "dirty war." There was a dirty little secret, however. The "dirty war" was not a "war" at all, at least not as most understand the word.[5]

When the generals took power in March 1976, the military threat from leftist guerrillas had been effectively broken, their operational capacity limited to random, if sometimes spectacular, acts of terrorism. Even before seizing power, the generals knew the guerrillas' true strength—or lack of it. At no time did the insurgents pose a real threat to the state. By the end of 1975, the Ejército Revolucionario del Pueblo (ERP; People's Revolutionary Army), the smaller if more virulent irregular force, had been decimated. And by that time, the two top leaders of the purportedly powerful leftist Peronist Montoneros were actively—and secretly—collaborating with Argentine army intelligence, one voluntarily, the second after being captured. Not only were the guerrillas' numbers greatly exaggerated; it was as if Hermann Goering and Heinrich Himmler had been double agents for the Allies throughout World War II.[6]

The military did not simply keep this information from the public. Its intelligence services' propaganda departments were given the task of fabricating a shadowy, omnipresent terrorist threat. Not unlike magicians, the generals exploited people's expectations, presenting what people expected to see, with the result that they believed they were seeing it. Hundreds of phony terrorist acts, including scores of "armed confrontations" or "battles" between the military and already-dead guerrillas, were reported. Many occurred at night in outlying districts. Stage-managed by the "security forces," the incidents added to a sense of insecurity and fear. Many of those "killed" in these fictitious battles had been abducted, unarmed, from their homes or workplaces or off the street.

The purposeful distortion of the threat posed by the guerrilla groups went even further. Of the nearly 700 assassinations attributed to the guerrillas during a ten-year period, about a quarter were the result of unrelated common crimes, intraservice military rivalries, and accidents. Even before the March 1976 coup, the number of murders, kidnappings, and robberies by right-wing death squads—a loose federation made up of union thugs, military officers, and police—greatly outnumbered those committed by the mostly urban leftist terrorists. A former CIA station chief in Buenos Aires said that it was a desire for vengeance—not the military threat of the guerrillas—that led the generals to launch the "dirty war." The ERP was seen as a more important target than the larger, less-organized Montoneros. "The military was embarrassed because the ERP made them look like ... incompetents."[7]

The origin of the violence was also misunderstood. Power coming from the barrel of a gun may have been a popular leftist slogan. Yet in Argentina its reality predated the guerrillas' emergence. The military had been at odds with civilian society since its first successful putsch in 1930. In 1955 a group of generals ousted Juan Perón and then persecuted his followers with unprecedented harshness, ushering in a bloody factionalism within the military. The emergence of the guerrilla groups a decade later—armed organizations with usually limited popular support—was a tragic but entirely foreseeable imitation of such examples.

The corruption of Argentina's political system ran deep. In 1981 Townsend B. Friedman, a political attaché with the U.S. embassy in Buenos Aires, reviewed official American documents concerning the abduction-disappearance four years earlier of Argentine newspaper publisher Jacobo Timerman. In a confidential report to Washington, Friedman noted:

The whole saga ... goes far beyond Timerman. It is the story of political, economic and moral debasement of Argentina's political, economic and labor leaders, and it must be concluded, important elements of Argentina's upper and middle classes. They all play in the same park, and by the same rules or lack of rules. Torture and corruption—violence and degradation—seem finally to be at the heart of Argentine political life. The military, the terrorists, the politicians, the industrial leaders and the journalists are all aware of this condition and accept it. The exceptions to this blanket indictment are many—but they have not written the sad tale known as Argentine history.[8]

The responsibility for what occurred rests primarily but not exclusively with the Argentines. An international network of Nazi terrorists contributed to the tragedy, as did foreign banks and much of the U.S. foreign policy and security establishment, more preoccupied with profits, order, and internal security than with development and democracy. Moreover, U.S. intelligence officials knew early on the real size of the guerrilla threat and the stunning degree of Argentine military penetration in the leftist groups but remained silent and did nothing to bring the phony "war" to a halt. Unlike Chile in 1973, there is no evidence that the CIA played a key role in events leading to the 1976 military takeover. Yet when U.S. officials had their best chance to stop the bloodshed—in 1976—they did not do so.

Jimmy Carter took office in January 1977, bringing a breath of humanism into a stale, cynical U.S. foreign policy establishment. By then, however, U.S. officials could only try to stanch the bloodshed in Argentina. (Alfonsín, Timerman, and others later praised the Carter policy, saying it saved hundreds of lives. When Carter visited Argentina in 1984, the respected English-language *Buenos Aires Herald* noted: "It was Jimmy Carter's government that did more than any other group anywhere for the cause of human rights in Argentina." The editorial was entitled simply: "Thank you, Jimmy.")[9]

Carter's activist approach was sharply criticized by the men and women who made foreign policy in the Reagan administration. Once they were in office, human rights concerns were all but swept off the policy map while the Argentine military were transformed into close friends and allies. "I was in jail when Reagan won," recalled future Argentine president Carlos Saúl Menem, the man who succeeded Alfonsín in the first transfer of power from one elected civilian to another in Argentina in half a century. "And those who held me captive jumped for joy."[10]

In mid-1980, barely six months before Reagan took office, Argentine generals working out of the notorious 601 army intelligence battalion in Buenos Aires had directed the coup by Bolivian military officers against that country's constitutional government. Aided by fugitive Nazi war criminal Klaus Barbie and Italian ultra-right-wing terrorists, the colonels quickly turned cocaine production into Bolivia's primary state enterprise. Yet even as T. B. Friedman was writing his report detailing the profound moral corruption that resulted from years of de facto rule, the Reagan administration rolled out a red carpet for then army chief Gen.

Leopoldo Galtieri. Administration officials began to use the generals controlling the 601 unit as U.S. proxies in Central America, carrying out policies Reagan could not get the U.S. Congress to approve. In Washington U.S. Secretary of Defense Caspar Weinberger and National Security Adviser Richard V. Allen took turns lavishing praise on Galtieri, calling him "impressive" and "a majestic personality."[11]

Daniel Barjacoba Deserved a Trial

When Elena Corbin—a small, determined woman—took the stand on June 14, 1985, her day in court counted for two: for herself, the victim of kidnapping and torture, and for missing Daniel Oscar Barjacoba, her only child.

Barjacoba, a Peronist University Youth activist, was abducted by Argentine security forces near the river port of Rosario in early October 1976. A few days later Barjacoba—a short, red-haired, freckle-faced young man—and seven others were reportedly killed in a roadside "shoot-out" with security forces hundreds of miles away in Los Surgentes in the province of Córdoba. In truth, they had all been summarily executed.

Thirteen days earlier Corbin's home in the Atlantic resort city of Mar del Plata had been raided. Corbin herself was "disappeared." Her captors took her to a room somewhere where she was forced to undress. There they tormented her with electric prods. The barrel of a revolver never seemed to leave the base of her neck. "They talked to me about the Bible, they asked me about my son's last name—Barjacoba—if it was Jewish," she testified. "My son is the grandson of Spaniards; our family is a mixture of Spanish, Italian and English descent," she clarified without having been asked.

It wasn't until three years later, in 1979, that Corbin heard that her son's body had surfaced in Los Surgentes and had been buried with seven others in the San Vicente cemetery in Córdoba. The first time Corbin visited the graveyard, a workman there told her that he had to watch over the bodies at night, as neighborhood dogs came to eat them. "We began to step on craniums and femurs lying at the surface," she recalled. "It was terrifying. ... My husband and I were paralyzed."

Later Corbin's husband, Eugenio Capisano, told the court about the couple's search for his stepson. They did not find Daniel Barjacoba's body at San Vicente, he said, but there were others. A policeman had told him he had seen the body of a woman "without eyes."

"A blind woman?" Capisano asked. "And, tell me sir, how can a blind woman be a guerrilla?"

"No, señor, she wasn't blind," the policeman replied impassively. "They ripped out her eyes before they killed her."

In court the irony that the generals accused of mass murder were getting a fair trial while thousands of their victims had not, was not lost on Elena Corbin. "My son deserved a trial like this one, didn't he?" she cried out, her voice dissolving into sobs.[12]

One hot summer day in 1984—fifteen months before she appeared in the Buenos Aires court—Elena Corbin had returned to the San Vicente cemetery. The blazing sun played off the shovels of the gravediggers as they burrowed farther and farther into a hillside. Wooden markers traced out a mass grave, more than 80 feet long and 16 feet wide. As many as 1,000 people were estimated to be buried there. In and around the cemetery, some seventy uniformed policemen patrolled the area, with plainclothesmen lurking nearby. Some of the uniformed detail were on horseback; others led snarling German shepherds on their rounds. The road running in front of San Vicente was sealed off at one end by a patrol car and a police van. The tight security was said to be part of the investigating judge's orders to keep both photographers and the curious at bay.

The exhumation was not the first time the San Vicente cemetery had come to the public's attention. In June 1980, the staff of the Córdoba judicial morgue sent an administrative complaint to then President Jorge R. Videla. The workers requested extra pay. They wrote:

> It is impossible, Mr. President, to describe a real picture of what we had to put up with. Upon opening the doors of the rooms where the bodies were kept in the depository thirty days without any type of refrigeration, we were met by a cloud of flies and the floor was covered by a layer about 10.5 cms. deep of worms and larvae, which we had to remove with buckets and shovels. Our only clothing was trousers, overalls, boots and some had gloves; others had to carry out this work in their street clothes— masks and caps were provided. ... Despite this we did not have any type of compensation for carrying out the job as requested; it should be noted that the majority of these cadavers were those of subversive delinquents.[13]

From the morgue the bodies were sent to San Vicente, where they were buried at night under the watchful eye of the police.

* * *

In March 1984 Corbin and others gathered at San Vicente watched as a worker carefully unearthed a skull, lifting it out of the pit with his shovel into the waiting hands of a forensic doctor dressed in a white gown. The physician rubbed his fingers around the hole above the eye sockets. "Bullet," he said.

The scrabbly earth yielded another skull, this one wrapped in rotting cloth. It, too, had been perforated by a bullet; the slimy material was identified as a blindfold. A little while later a blue-uniformed worker unearthed a third cranium; this one had a tuft of reddish hair dangling down from one side. Nearby, the aunt of Daniel Barjacoba brought her hand to her open mouth in a gesture of horror. Frozen in her own thoughts, the woman remained there, her eyes staring at the ground where the workers scraped with rakes for more bones. "This is all very sad," said Elena Corbin. "Until you see the body, until you can give it a decent burial, how can you admit the death?"

The investigating judge, hair slicked back and dressed in a shiny blue suit, had been appointed three years earlier by the military. He was highly critical of the human rights groups. "Don't forget many of these 'kids' weren't little angels," he said. The police looked nervous. The judge ended the probe after less than 5 percent of the total grave area had been uncovered. Later, amid the jumble of skulls and bones, a team of American forensic specialists were able to identify the remains of one young woman killed in the "shoot-out" at Los Surgentes.[14]

Daniel Oscar Barjacoba was still missing.

Wounds That Will Not Heal

Two Argentine researchers, Moises Kijak and María Lucila Pelento, investigated the effects of the generals' policy of mass disappearances and later presented their study, "Situaciones de Catástrofe Social" (Social catastrophic situations), to the World Congress on Psychoanalysis in August 1985. They noted that all societies share common points of griefwork: the possibility of accompanying and attending the deceased—or at least having news about the date and circumstance of the death; the possibility of keeping a vigil over the dead and of burying him or her; the possibility of locating and/or visiting the tomb, and the possibility of the mourner to express his or her sorrow supported and sustained by society. The researchers pointed out that in natural catastrophes such as floods and aviation and maritime tragedies, official institutions seek to provide information about the moment and circumstance of death. Even in wartime, those in power are expected to give information about the dead. When it is impossible to conduct funerals, there are commemorative occasions and monuments that allow for a certain expression of grief.[15]

The social circumstances of the military's policies of forced disappearances, Kijak and Pelento noted, "not only serve to obscure and hide the truth, but the search for information itself becomes the source of threat and danger." They found that the mourners-in-waiting created by the military often "find themselves submerged in a situation of panic, impotence and abandonment." The need for survivors to try to accept the possible death of a loved one while holding out hope that he or she will reappear alive "operate violently simultaneously or successively, exposing the psychic apparatus to a high degree of disintegration." The conflict creates intense feelings of guilt, "greatly magnifying the feeling that by giving the person up for dead, the mourner is somehow killing him."

Doctors Who Heal, Doctors Who Make Pain

On August 7, 1985, a tall, middle-aged man made his way to the witness stand. Norberto Liwski, a doctor who worked for the Alfonsín government, had long combined medicine with social activism, having worked in the sprawling slums of Buenos Aires. Later he became a pioneer in the investigation and treatment of physical and emotional problems of the children of the missing. Liwski himself had been a *desaparecido*.

On April 5, 1978, Liwski was abducted by a heavily armed, civilian-dressed commando squad as he entered his Buenos Aires apartment. The kidnappers had opened the door from inside the dwelling as Liwski began to enter. Then they shot him in both legs at point-blank range.

Liwski was taken to a secret detention center, in police slang a *chupadero* (the word comes from the verb "to suck"), in Buenos Aires province. There, as he was placed on a table to be tortured, a physician working with his captors counseled Liwski not to resist, given the gravity of his wounds. During the interminable sessions of electric prods and whippings that followed, Liwski frequently heard the voice of the physician, whom he later identified as Dr. Jorge Vidal. At one point, his captors told Liwski that one of his small daughters was going to be tortured along with him. One of them turned to Vidal and asked what was the minimum weight a child had to have before he or she could be tortured. "Vidal replied, his voice full of conviction, that beyond 60 pounds it was possible to use electric prods." Vidal's comments, Liwski said, showed a detailed knowledge that could only have come from experiments on other prisoners.

Earlier, before the Sábato Commission, Liwski testified: "For days I was tortured with electric shock applied to my gums, chest, genitals, abdomen and ears. Then they began with a systematic and rhythmic beating with wooden rods on the shoulders, buttocks, calves and soles of my feet." Adding to his plight were worries reflecting Liwski's own medical training. He wondered about the possible consequences of muscle contractions caused by electric shock, followed by muscle relaxation caused by beating. ("The heart cannot always resist such treatment," he said.) Liwski was hung with hooks to the jail wall and tortured with a device that seemed to crush his testicles. When, after a month in captivity, Liwski's blindfold was removed,

> I finally saw the damage they had done to me. I remembered when I studied medicine there was a photo in a textbook of a man who, because his testicles had grown so large, had to carry them in a wheelbarrow. Mine were of a similar size, colored an intense blackish-blue. Another day, despite the size of my testicles, they put me face down again. They tied me, and without hurry, they raped me with a metal object placed in my anus, purposely ripping my insides as they went. Afterward they used the object as a conductor for electric shock, still placed as it was. I cannot describe the sensation of being burned all inside.

Liwski was later brought by his captors before a "war tribunal," which declared itself incompetent to judge him as no charges had been brought. When he was hauled in front of a civilian court, Liwski was absolved without ever having been charged with a crime.[16]

U.S. Policy: Between Complicity and Condemnation

When Patricia ("Patt") Derian, the Carter administration's former assistant secretary of state for human rights, entered the Buenos Aires federal courts building the night of June 13, 1985, all but one of the defense attorneys got up to leave. As they went across the street for coffee, one of the defense lawyers shouted: "Why don't you ask Ronald Reagan what he thinks about that woman?"[17]

The man had a point. Derian had carried Jimmy Carter's human rights crusade to the far reaches of the globe. Reagan, then still a radio commentator and aspiring presidential candidate, told his listeners that Derian "should walk a mile in the moccasins" of Argentina's generals before she criticized them. Shortly before Reagan took office, Derian debated Jeane Kirkpatrick, the incoming U.S. ambassador to the United Nations and a harsh critic of Carter's activist human rights policies. The United States should not openly criticize rights violations in friendly "moderately repressive autocratic governments," Kirkpatrick said. Distinctions between "totalitarian" leftist governments and "authoritarian" rightwing regimes were lost on Derian. "What the hell is moderately repressive—that you only torture half the people, and that you only do summary executions now and then?" And on the eve of Alfonsín's inauguration Derian's successor, Elliott Abrams, responded to her criticism of the Republican administration's promilitary stance in Argentina by ridiculing her views as "romantic, sentimental and silly."[18]

In her testimony before the court Derian, an iron-willed woman tempered in the civil rights battles in her native Mississippi and the segregationist South, recalled a 1977 meeting with navy chief Massera. The interview did not take place, as protocol would have it, in the Liberator building—the military's towering headquarters in downtown Buenos Aires overlooking the presidential palace. Instead, at Massera's insistence, it was held at the Escuela Mecánica de la Armada (ESMA; Navy Mechanics School), which, Derian had been told, housed a secret concentration camp. Massera denied that his navy tortured prisoners. That, he said, was done by the army and air force. Derian pressed the point, insisting that as they talked, "down below they might be torturing somebody." Massera replied by smiling broadly, making a gesture as if washing his hands: "Remember what happened with Pontius Pilate?"

The first time she met Videla, then president and head of the army, the neatly groomed general told Derian he was having trouble keeping the lower ranks under control—because so many of their comrades had been killed by subversives. "I replied that if he was chief executive he was responsible for what was happening, above all being a military officer and having the reins of command." On their second meeting, Videla did not use the same excuse.

Eighteen months before she was to appear in court, Patt Derian was invited by Raúl Alfonsín to attend his inauguration. No one missed the significance of the gesture. Presidential candidate Alfonsín had criticized what he called the abandonment of human rights by the Reagan administration. The activist policies of Derian's former boss—Jimmy Carter—had saved lives and brought honor to the United States, he said.[19]

On inauguration day an enormous, friendly, and mostly middle-class crowd jammed around the Casa Rosada presidential palace to get a glimpse of their new president. Only three visiting dignitaries were roundly booed. Two were the representatives of the neighboring military dictatorships of Chile and Uruguay. The third was Vice President George Bush.

Kissinger's "Green Light"

The Carter administration policies were a radical departure from those that preceded it as well. Robert Hill, a conservative businessman-diplomat, had been appointed by President Richard M. Nixon as U.S. ambassador to Argentina in 1973, the year Juan Perón returned in triumph from his Spanish exile. To his many critics, Hill fit the stereotype of the Ugly American. He married into the W. R. Grace fortune, which included a company with extensive holdings in Latin American and a reputation for ruthlessness. As ambassador to Costa Rica in 1954, Hill was involved in the overthrow of left-leaning but democratically elected Jacobo Arbenz in a CIA-sponsored coup in Guatemala. Although he served as an envoy to five Latin nations—Mexico, El Salvador, and Spain were the others—Hill never mastered Spanish.[20]

Like many others, Hill greeted the 1976 coup in Argentina with relief. Not only was Isabel Perón's government incompetent and corrupt, her inner circle shielded important fugitives from prosecution on narcotics charges in the United States. Early that year a siege-like mentality had descended on U.S. embassy personnel in Buenos Aires. Hill's own residence was heavily guarded, and he shuttled back and forth to work under an escort worthy of Al Capone. Two years before, in 1974, an American diplomat stationed in Córdoba had been severely wounded in an attack by Marxist guerrillas. The following year, a retired U.S. businessman who served as an honorary consul in the same city was kidnapped and murdered by leftist Peronists.[21]

Fearful of being kidnapped for ransom or even killed, most American businessmen by the time of the coup had already moved to Montevideo, across the wide Río de la Plata, or flew in for business from São Paulo. "There are difficult days ahead," Hill warned the National Security Council in a secret "Country Analysis and Strategy Paper" the day before the coup. "The strategy [set out in this paper] is essentially one of protecting our people and property from terrorism and our trade and investment from economic nationalism during this trying period."[22]

The isolation imposed by security concerns did not keep Hill from soon realizing what was happening. The military was on a rampage. The former Dartmouth football player became increasingly worried as specific human rights cases were brought to his attention: three Palatine priests and two seminarians were murdered in a revenge killing by a government death squad; an American priest and the daughter of a U.S. missionary were brutally tortured; a progressive Catholic bishop was killed in a staged auto accident.

"Hill was shaken—he became very disturbed—by the case of the son of a thirty-year employee of the embassy, a student, who was arrested, never to be seen again," recalled former *New York Times* Buenos Aires bureau chief Juan de Onis. "Hill took a personal interest. He went to [Interior Minister Albano] Harguindeguy, who he knew, saying 'Hey, what about this? We're interested in this case.'" Hill talked personally to the foreign minister, Adm. César Guzzetti, and finally, to President Videla himself. "All he got was stonewalling, he got nowhere. Hill's last year [in Argentina] was marked by increasing disillusionment and dismay, and he backed his staff on human rights to the hilt."[23]

It was a much-changed Hill who met with Patt Derian in early 1977. Only weeks before, President Carter had pledged that human rights had been moved to the forefront of American foreign policy. Hill was deeply troubled. He wanted to talk about what he knew concerning former Secretary of State Henry Kissinger's role in Argentina's rights situation and why the generals were only partly to blame for the slaughter taking place.

In June 1976 Kissinger had met with Foreign Minister Guzzetti while both were attending a meeting of the Organization of American States (OAS) in Santiago, Chile. Ironically, the meeting took place in the Hotel Carrera, later immortalized as the Hotel "Cabrera" in *Missing,* Constantin Costa-Gavras' chilling tale of disappearance and murder in Augusto Pinochet's Chile. "The Argentines were very worried that Kissinger would lecture to them on human rights," according to a memorandum, prepared by Derian's staff, covering the conversation held by Derian and Hill in Buenos Aires:

> Guzzetti and Kissinger had a very long breakfast but the Secretary did not raise the subject. Finally, Guzzetti did. Kissinger asked how long it would take ... to clean up the problem. Guzzetti replied that it would be done by the end of the year. Kissinger approved.
>
> In other words, Ambassador Hill explained, Kissinger gave the Argentines the green light.[24] Within two weeks after the June meeting, de Onis knew what Kissinger said. He asked the ambassador for confirmation. The ambassador could not reply. No one told the embassy of Kissinger's statements. Later ... the ambassador discussed the matter personally with Kissinger. ... Kissinger confirmed the Guzzetti conversation. Hill said that the Secretary felt that [incumbent President Gerald] Ford would win the election. Hill disagreed. In any case, the Secretary wanted Argentina to finish its terrorist problem before year end—before Congress reconvened in January, 1977.
>
> In September, Hill prepared an eyes-only memorandum for the Secretary, urging that the U.S. vote against an [Inter-American Development Bank] loan on [human

rights] grounds. Hill felt that it would strengthen his hand in dealing with the Argentines. The memo was given to Assistant Secretary [Harry] Shlaudeman. The latter asked the ambassador personally if Hill really wanted to send the memo to the secretary, who had already decided to vote for the loan. Shlaudeman suggested that the secretary might fire Hill. Hill told Shlaudeman to send the memo.

Hill returned to Argentina around early September. The Argentine press had been saved for him and he sifted through stacks of newspapers. He saw that the terrorist death toll had climbed steeply. The ambassador said that he wondered—although he had no proof—whether the Argentine government was not trying to solve its terrorist problem before the end of the year.[25]

2

Perón and Argentina's Golden Era (1930-1955)

> The failure of Argentina, so rich, so underpopulated is one of the mysteries of our time.
>
> —*V. S. Naipaul*[1]

In many respects Argentina's destiny resembled what might have been the fate of the United States if the South had won the Civil War. A fertile, sprawling land ruled by a genteel and vacuous oligarchy, Argentina had leadership incapable of transforming it into a modern, capitalist state. For decades Argentina has been held up as the premier example of failed national promise.

Unlike Brazil to the north, Argentina boasts a homogeneous, literate population. Ninety percent of its people are of European descent—mostly Spanish and Italian. Vast tracts of richly productive agricultural land and a sometimes glittering cultural life—Buenos Aires is still often called the Paris of Latin America—gave Argentines a standard of living well above that of their neighbors. At the turn of the century Argentina ranked higher than Canada and Australia, later reaching seventh place in the world, in economic power.

There were three benchmarks in Argentina's inexorable slide toward underdevelopment. Two were military coups: the 1930 overthrow of reformist President Hipólito Yrigoyen and the coup twenty-five years later that toppled Juan Domingo Perón. The third benchmark came as a reaction to the Great Depression—an increasing state role in the economy, which contributed to growing external account imbalances, accentuated sectorial disequilibrium, and encouraged inflation-spurred growth.[2]

By the end of the last century political power had been concentrated in the hands of large landowners and merchants. The emergence of this ruling elite coincided with a deep penetration of British commercial and banking interests and the centralization of power in the booming metropolis of Buenos Aires. Although not formally a part of the Crown's far-flung overseas possessions, the country was frequently referred to as "British Argentina."[3]

In 1912 the ruling conservatives were pressured into enacting a new election law that provided universal and compulsory male suffrage. Four years later their principal opponents, the Unión Cívica Radical (UCR; Radical Civic Union), swept to victory in Argentina's first unquestionably fair presidential election. Despite the party's name, the Radicals' program was mildly reformist—one of its strongest planks concerned education. The coming of the Radicals—Argentina's first successful nonaristocratic political party—to national leadership marked the entry of the emerging middle class, composed of immigrants and their offspring, into the mainstream of decisionmaking.

In 1930 the government of Radical party leader Hipólito Yrigoyen was overthrown in an obscurantist military coup backed by the country's powerful landowning interests. Decades of institutional order came to an end. The new divorce of legality and power in Argentina was symbolized by the fact that the Supreme Court chose to recognize the legitimacy of the regime that took power in 1930 instead of resigning or seeking to protest publicly.

The military ruled for less than two years. The reins of government were then handed to the conservatives by means of fraudulent elections. Despite an enormous leap in urbanization and the coming of age of hundreds of thousands of voters whose parents had recently immigrated, the social and economic demands were expressed through a creaky and dishonest political system. Noted American historian Peter G. Snow: "The period between 1932 and 1943 is frequently referred to as the 'era of Patriotic Fraud.' According to the conservatives, it was their patriotic duty to engage in electoral fraud, for otherwise the Radicals would hoodwink the immature voters, return to power, and once again lead the country down the road to ruin."[4]

Officially organized right-wing nationalist paramilitary groups conducted a violent campaign against leftist parties and labor unions. Even Radicals and moderate Socialists were tortured by the new Special Section of the Federal Police. Despite military claims that the Yrigoyen government was riddled with corruption, the regime that replaced it became mired far deeper in irregularities, graft, and patronage. In 1933 the government gave humiliating commercial concessions to Britain in order to avoid losing to trading rivals within the Commonwealth the right to export to the British Isles.

As World War II ended in Europe, an obscure army colonel elbowed his way to power using a standard of nationalist populism, displacing but not disinheriting the mean-spirited and fatuous oligarchy and rescuing a tattered military establishment with its thinly veiled Axis sympathies from the blind alley into which it had driven itself. Juan Perón had served as an Argentine military observer in Benito Mussolini's Italy at the beginning of World War II. He left Europe in 1941 still favorably impressed with the social structure—Il Duce's "organized community"—of Italian fascism. ("I will do what Mussolini has done but without his mistakes," he boasted in 1943.)[5]

Perón's return to Argentina paralleled a vast transformation beginning in the economy, as gold reserves began to swell from burgeoning agricultural exports to a beleaguered Europe. The breakdown of supply of manufactured goods from the Old Continent at the same time gave impetus to domestic industrialization and a rapid expansion of the urban labor market. The boom brought with it a revolution of rising expectations for Argentina's mostly unorganized and poorly protected workers whose demands coincided with those of a reformist middle class, already made expectant by the specter of the defeat of the Axis and growing weariness of military rule.

In June 1943 Perón took part in a nationalist military revolution. At the time he was a leader of the Grupo de Oficiales Unidos (GOU; United Officers Group), one of a number of secret lodges that came to dominate the Argentine armed forces. Much has been said and written about the GOU, with many of Perón's foes maintaining the group was a many-tentacled Nazi network meant to aid a hard-pressed Hitler in conquering all of South America. In fact, the lodge was composed of a loosely organized band of younger high-ranking officers who professed worry over the growing indiscipline and immorality within the ranks resulting from the military's political alliances. The officers were also preoccupied by a generalized social corruption that they believed would become a breeding ground for a Communist takeover.[6]

Perón had a canny intuition about the social and political changes taking place. The energetic colonel with a brilliant smile in no time had himself named secretary of labor and social welfare. Later he became vice president and minister of war. In a regime noted for its lack of polish, the eloquent, cultured Perón soon became the real power in the government of General Edelmiro Farrell, a man more at home at the horse races than grappling with the reins of government.

It was while Farrell was still in office that Perón began to harness the political strength of the growing working class. As labor minister he pushed for higher wages and social reforms for the *descamisados* (shirtless ones), who made up Argentina's urban proletariat. Under Perón's direction, for the first time the country's labor legislation was enforced, shifting the workers' allegiance decisively in his favor. Meanwhile Perón co-opted some of the best minds of the well-meaning but politically ineffectual Socialists. Perón, recalled one historian,

> was more conscious than any other military man of the explosive character of the Argentine social situation. The great changes in the world of work, probability of an economic crisis, and the existence of strong and demanding unions linked to leftist parties seemed to him the portents of a revolutionary threat. ... Social justice, control of the working class and depoliticization of the unions were the three foundations upon which his political project rested. ... The passionate colonel's imagination, dynamism and speaking ability contrasted with the sad circumspection and empty rhetoric of his comrades-in-arms.[7]

New Providence Memorial Library
377 Elkwood Avenue
New Providence, NJ 07974

9410306

Perón's social reforms did not sit well with all sectors of society. Middle-class reformers were hungry for a chance to overthrow the Axis-sympathizing regime and smelled blood. They worried that the colonel's social program was nothing more than an attempt to establish a Mussolini-style fascist beachhead in South America. Leftist union organizers found opposition to Perón was a quick ticket to jail. No group, however, opposed the army colonel with more bitterness than the rural aristocracy. These men were accustomed to running their vast holdings—and the lives of their peasant workers—like feudal lords. They were livid when Perón set down a minimum labor rights law covering agricultural workers.[8]

Some of the military grew uneasy with Perón's politicking. They worried about his alliance with the workers. Their fear of social chaos and a pronounced antimilitary feeling within the general population, however, worked to Perón's advantage. Many closed ranks around him. Egged on by the upper classes, Perón's military opponents finally moved against him. He was packed off under arrest to an island off the coast of Buenos Aires. In response hundreds of thousands of worried, angry laborers put down their tools and swarmed to the city center. It was, said writer Ernesto Sábato, as if "an enormous and silent force, almost sub-terranean, had been put into motion." Many converged on the Plaza de Mayo in front of the presidential palace, demanding Perón's return. It was October 17, 1945.[9]

When he was freed, Perón returned to the capital to virtually dictate terms to the government that had jailed him. It may not have been, as one Peronist general called it, "the popular revolution of October 17." It was, however, a clear sign that Perón had forever altered Argentina's political equation. No longer was all power in the hands of a small, reactionary elite. From October 17 the Plaza de Mayo became "Perón's plaza." On February 24, 1946, Perón captured the presidency with 55 percent of the vote in one of the cleanest elections in Argentine history.

The Perón Presidency

Perón's first term was characterized by rapid industrialization and impressive gains for Argentina's workers, who organized into labor unions and became the backbone of the Peronist movement. Meanwhile, the military was given an un-precedented role in the growing number of state industries and in the bureau-cracy in general.

During the first years of his rule, a bullish economy appeared to reflect Perón's own boundless vitality. Scores of new factories signaled the emergence of infant industries protected by high tariffs and generous subsidies. Argentina soon boasted a national airline and an expanded merchant marine. It was Perón's government that built the natural gas pipeline—in its time the world's longest—that served Buenos Aires for several decades. Hospitals and schools, military barracks and highways, nursing homes and soccer stadiums sprouted up around the country. Low-cost public housing offered the poor, especially rural migrants, a chance to escape the grinding poverty that had persisted in Argentina despite its great natural wealth. As union coffers swelled, organized labor was able to purchase or build resort hotels around the country, renting or raffling their units to their membership.

As Perón embarked on an ambitious effort to incorporate the *descamisados* into political life, decreeing sizable social welfare benefits and giving the previously disenfranchised majority limited access to the anterooms of power, he was ably aided by his second wife, a former actress named Eva Duarte.

It is hard to overestimate the role played by Evita, as she was known to the masses who adored her. "She supplied the magnetic current that linked the leader to his mass, that infused Peronism with soul, that lent a unique quality to the charismatic glow of the conductor," wrote Perón biographer Joseph Page. "She complemented him exquisitely, her violent rhetoric enabling him to play the unifier, her contact with the people freeing him for more elevated matters of state, her manipulation of the bureaucracy shielding him from the unpleasantness of imposing discipline."[10]

Evita was shrewd and vivacious. A hint of a melancholic vulnerability only increased her rapport with the dispossessed. She worked tirelessly to bring Perón's message of hope to the downtrodden, larding the appeal with her own role as benefactress to the needy. It was largely due to her prodding that Perón introduced women's suffrage. Although she was snubbed by the perfumed parlors of Buenos Aires because of her humble beginnings and her earlier career as an actress, even her enemies had to admire her stamina and physical courage. "Peronism will be revolutionary," Evita proclaimed, "or it will be nothing."

To the anglophile landed aristocracy, Perón's program was the antechamber to the "sovietization" of Argentina. Other critics, including those on the left, just as insistently maintained the Peronist agenda was "Nazi-fascist." In its most abstract and colorless presentation, most observers agree that Perón's program was a mixed bag of nationalism and social welfarism, articulated politically in a strong leader and structurally in a strong central authority. An advocate of a "Third Position" between capitalism and communism, Perón put forward a program that became synonymous with social justice at home. Meanwhile he steered an independent course on foreign policy and appealed for Latin American political and economic unity.

Perón, said one observer, was a man "more complicated than marble, and the carefully cultivated Perón myth, although it is even larger than a big man, reflects his complexities and contradictions." Bankers and sportsmen, authors and adventurers, economists and shop stewards all fell under Perón's spell. Years later left-wing Peronists and Marxist-oriented guerrillas claimed Peronism's mantle for their own. They pointed to the revolutionary changes Perón made during the time he ruled with Evita, his self-proclaimed friendship with Mao Tse-tung, and his professed admiration for Argentine-born Cuban revolutionary Ernesto ("Che") Guevara. Right-wing nationalists and avowedly fascist groups countered with Perón's favorable impression of Mussolini's Italy and his friendships with notorious Nazis such as Hermann Goering's personal pilot, Hans-Ulrich Rudel, and Luftwaffe ace Otto Skorzeny. They also noted the countries in which Perón chose to weather his exile after being overthrown in 1955—Alfredo Stroessner's Paraguay, Marcos Pérez Jiménez's Venezuela, Rafael Trujillo's Dominican Republic, and Francisco Franco's Spain.[11]

Few issues reflected Perón's complexities and contradictions as sharply as the issues of anti-Semitism and the postwar Nazi migration to Latin America. Argentina is home to both the largest Jewish community in Latin America *and* the largest number of Axis war criminals on the continent. One of the most important outbreaks of anti-Semitism in Argentina came in the wake of the 1943 military coup. The regime's nationalist ethos had a clearly pro-Axis taint, and it identified Jews and Communists as public enemies. The military also appointed the notorious anti-Semite Gustavo Martínez Zuviria as head of the Ministry of Justice and Public Instruction. Martínez Zuviria, a novelist who used the pen name Hugo Wast, promoted bizarre theories about an alleged "Jewish-Capitalist-Communist" conspiracy. Jewish schools and newspapers were subject to temporary closures; kosher slaughter in Buenos Aires municipal stockyards was banned; and efforts to revoke the citizenship of naturalized Jews were begun, although never implemented.[12]

Both then and later as president, Perón personally helped hundreds of former Nazi officials immigrate to Argentina. According to Nazi hunter Simon Wiesenthal, Perón authorized 7,500 blank passports to aid the escape of those fleeing their own defeat in Europe. By his own admission, the *caudillo* authorized the entry of 5,000 Ustachis, Hitler's murderous Croatian proxies.[13]

Among the German war criminals who came to Argentina were Edward Roschman, better known as "the Butcher of Riga"; Adolf Eichmann; Klaus "the Butcher of Lyon" Barbie; and Josef Mengele, the concentration camp doctor known as "the Angel of Death." Ante Pavelic, the unbelievably brutal one-time Ustachi *poglavnik* (führer), later led a bloody international terrorist campaign against the government of Marshall Josip Broz ("Tito") from his exile in Buenos Aires. His lieutenant, Stejpan Hefer, the "model" fascist bureaucrat whose ruthlessness during the war had led even Mussolini's army to protect Jews and Serbs from his Ustachis' predations, also found refuge in Argentina.[14]

In part, Perón's willingness to play host to the fleeing Nazis was apparently based on his belief that they could help in industrialization and in making good on his commitment to refitting a military institution restless about its own deficiencies. Argentina needed technicians, Perón said later, to help build Argentina's new merchant fleet, establish arms and aviation factories, and speed up the development of its incipient oil industry.[15]

Perón was convinced that the onset of the cold war foreshadowed violent confrontation between the superpowers. He also was worried about the prospects for civil war if Argentina did not progress rapidly. Like policymakers in Washington,

Perón had concluded that the defeated Nazis were less dangerous than the Communists who celebrated victory in Eastern Europe. (Both the British and the Americans were more selective, affording refuge generally only to the most important technocrats and intelligence specialists of the Third Reich. Both, however, had much more traffic with former Nazis than they admitted at the time.)[16]

Argentina was also a place where the "national question"—or search for identity—was still being debated 130 years after Argentine independence. Many theorists claimed the answer lay in the "whitening" of Argentina's mostly southern European and vaguely mestizo population. Perón—like many of his military colleagues, with their Prussian training and traditions—at times appeared to believe in the superiority of the German intellect. And the fleeing Germans were mostly educated and largely Catholic. His essential pragmatism, some historians concluded, led Perón to judge that there were overriding national imperatives that justified his actions or, in his own words, required him "to know how to use what is usable."[17]

"Look, the British Empire was built by good men and pirates," Perón once told an intimate who complained about the growing corruption in the general's inner circle, using an argument that lay at the heart of his views of the Nazi migration, "and I'm going to build the Argentine empire with good men and pirates."[18]

"In spite of his association with these polices, the Perón presidency represented a sharp break with the past," wrote one top Jewish scholar.

> From the beginning, Perón and Evita made it clear that anti-Semitism had no place in their movement. In 1948, Evita stated the official position: "In our country, the only ones who have separated us by religion have been the representatives of the ... oligarchy. ... Those who caused anti-Semitism were the rulers who poisoned the people with false theories." After 1948, Argentina supported Israel in the United Nations. And while he admitted many Nazis into Argentina, Perón also made room for thousands of Jewish refugees.[19]

The ultra-right-wing nationalists who supported Perón in his first presidential campaign were not rewarded with important government posts. Nor did Perón use anti-Semitism as a political tool, as did anti-Peronist sectors of the military and the upper classes. His policies of development and industrialization inaugurated a period of unprecedented social mobility, which had an invigorating impact on the Jewish community. A Jewish middle class sprang up, and not a few fortunes were made as the country seemed poised to win permanent status as a developed nation. A community of tradespeople, industrial workers, and small shopowners watched as their children attended university and then became part of a dynamic new professional class.[20] There was also some evidence that the tendency, particularly in the United States, to reflectively lump Peronism with fascism was a reflection of lingering geopolitical antagonisms. "In Washington's simplistic view," said one Israeli diplomat, "Perón would be only either a Nazi or a Communist."[21]

Historians never found credible evidence to corroborate one of several "black legends" that grew up around Perón—that European Nazis later worked as "advisers" to the police or armed forces. Nor was there any proof offered by his enemies to substantiate the claim made by the *New York Times* and *Fortune,* among others, that Perón and Evita had skimmed millions of dollars in fees from refugeseeking Nazis.[22]

Still, one historian of the period did find a subtle but pernicious effect resulting from the social relationships developed between the former SS men and other Nazi sympathizers and officials of the Argentine air force and army. "The entire Nazi past permeated little by little into the Argentine present, converting a society that at the beginning of the century tended to be open and liberal into a convent more and more walled up in authoritarianism and repression."[23]

Perón's Balancing Act

Evita died a slow, tragic death from cancer in 1952. She was only thirty-three. Her death forced Perón into a dangerous balancing act. Now he had to continue to be his movement's master strategist while trying to fill Evita's role as people's tribune. A profound change set in, as a deep-set decadence in his personal style replaced the neorevolutionary ardor symbolized by his revered Evita. Even people who had supported Perón became bored, then disillusioned, by the personality cult that had been carefully nurtured, embodied in the marching song *The Peronist Boys* with its refrain, "Perón, Perón, how great you are," blaring from public squares across the nation.

Confronted with impossible wage demands, Perón allowed the printing of millions of rapidly devalued pesos. As Europe recovered from its postwar prostration, demand for Argentine products fell sharply. Perón's ambiguous wartime stand on European fascism continued to alienate the U.S. government, which prohibited European countries from using U.S. aid money to buy Argentine agricultural products. Inflation soared, production fell off, labor unrest erupted, and political repression increased. Curbs on press freedom reached new levels, the judiciary and universities were purged, parliament was emasculated, and opposition leaders were imprisoned. The head of the State Intelligence Agency (the Secretaría de Informaciones de Estado [SIDE]), Col. Jorge Osinde, a U.S. embassy document noted, had a "gestapo-like" reputation.[24]

Critics would later claim that Perón had badly allocated the $1.4 billion in reserves his government had inherited in 1946. Some noted that Argentina's highly protected industries had lost their competitiveness. As the state bought up money-losing foreign-owned public services and stimulated light consumer industries, it created others in the public sector, often under military control. Others questioned why the state, rather than market forces, should direct development. Still, there was more than a measure of truth in the angry retort of leftist nationalist historian Juan José Hernández Arregui, who admonished: "When, after 1946, a better distribution of riches improved the lot of the common man, that infertile and perverse class [the rich] saw demagoguery and plundering just because the people were eating."[25]

The ravages of inflation gave military officers a common cause with middle-class opponents of Peronism, who were worried not only by their diminished buying power but also by the narrowing gap in social prestige between themselves and the workers. Nor did it go unnoticed by the military that the man who promised to put an end to class struggle seemed to be leading Argentina into a period of growing social unrest.[26]

Perón found a fight he did not need when he took on the powerful, highly conservative Roman Catholic church. He had enjoyed church support in the election of 1946 and again in 1951. However, church leaders condemned his proposals to legalize divorce and prostitution. They were also angered by the attempts of his movement to curb the church's organizing among the workers and by Perón's own increasingly strident antichurch rhetoric.

Although the church hierarchy moved cautiously against the government, the same could not be said for lay groups. Millions of pamphlets cranked out on clandestine presses attacked Perón, his high school–age mistress, Nelly Rivas; his business associates; and even his physical features, which were said to show his innate criminality. Mass rallies became contests between Peronist and church groups to prove who could put more partisans on the street. Perón counterattacked by ordering the forcible "deportation" of two Catholic bishops, both Argentine citizens. The move, in turn, caused the Vatican to excommunicate those involved.[27]

"My Life for Perón"

On June 16, 1955, a naval air squadron was scheduled to make a flyover of the Plaza de Mayo in a ceremony honoring independence hero Gen. José San Martín. Instead it swooped down on the waiting crowd. Opening fire with machine guns, the planes dropped 9.5 tons of bombs in the bustling area around the presidential palace. The attackers' poor aim added to the number of casualties: a trolley filled with people was hit with a bomb. No one escaped alive.[28]

The attack was meant to kill Perón and most of his key advisers. However, the president had been forewarned and had gone into hiding in the basement of army headquarters. From there the army minister directed operations to crush the rebels. The Confederación General del Trabajo (CGT; Peronist General Workers Confederation) rallied its forces around the ministry to protect Perón. The president, sensing the danger, tried to warn the unions not to send their members, but it was too late. The workers were slaughtered by the insurgents, who made a second attack some three hours after the first. An official report said some 355 people had died; other versions put the total at 2,000.[29]

The airborne rebels flew to exile in Montevideo, Uruguay (to be reincorporated, after Perón's ouster, with honors into the military's ranks). Meanwhile,
their earthbound compatriots were imprisoned. The workers, rallying under the
slogan "My life for Perón," were denied arms by the Army Ministry.

The frustrated rebellion might have changed the country's political course had
not a group of firebrands supporting Perón taken measures into their own hands.
In an early evening radio broadcast Perón claimed victory over the insurgents. He
urged his supporters to remain calm. However, a mob set fire to the office and
headquarters of the archbishop in the Plaza de Mayo. The cathedral was sacked
by angry gangs of young people, and a dozen other churches in and around Buenos Aires were torched. An eighty-year-old priest who tried to hold back an angry mob was hit on the head. He later died.

In a country where more than 90 percent of the people are Catholic, the
antichurch crusade was destined to fail; the sacking of the churches brought a
swift rebuke from the ranks of Peronism itself. "The psychological impact of the
charred churches was devastating to Catholics with memories of the atrocities of
the Spanish Civil War," Perón biographer Page noted. "By permitting the holocaust, Perón forfeited the political gain to be made from popular reaction to the
casualties of the navy bombing."[30]

Three weeks later a dispatch written from the U.S. embassy in Buenos Aires offered a precise view of how Argentina reacted to the bloodshed:

> This sort of thing is entirely foreign to modern Argentine history. ... The bombing of
> June 16, 1955, burst with cataclysmic force, therefore, upon a population conditioned
> by a century of peace to the confirmed belief that such things do not happen in Ar-
> gentina. One detects in the people a sense not only of shock, but of shame, that such
> a slaughter of innocent civilians could have happened in the heart of Buenos Aires.
> ... They have recoiled with alarm, almost with consternation from this sudden ex-
> plosion of violence. ... When to this is added the almost simultaneous burning and
> destruction of the nation's most sacred and ancient religious monuments and
> churches, the result has been an emotional shock of great disruptive force to the po-
> litical and social fabric of the nation.[31]

Perón Capitulates

Early in September 1955 a retired general traveled 600 miles overnight in a bus to
encourage military units in the provincial capital of Córdoba, an anti-Peronist
bastion, to stage another uprising. He traveled with his uniform and his saber in
his suitcase and without enough money to pay for a ticket back to Buenos Aires if
he did not succeed.[32]

On September 16 Gen. (ret.) Eduardo Lonardi's revolt against Perón met at
first with only limited success. At the beginning of the uprising Lonardi's forces
were strong only in the western region running parallel to the Andes. Additional
support came from scattered army units around the country, as well as two naval

bases. Militarily, victory once again appeared to be Perón's. But when a coconspirator, Adm. Isaac Rojas, announced he was about to bombard Buenos Aires from the cruiser *17 de Octubre,* Perón unexpectedly announced he was resigning.[33]

Why Perón decided to give up the presidency became the subject of years of debate. His enemies, and some of his friends who felt betrayed by his capitulation, charged he was a coward. Others point to his almost pathological fear of civil war, recalling the devastation of Spain in the 1930s. In fact, Perón personally was never much given to violence. "My fighter's spirit," Perón said, "pushes me toward the fight, but my patriotism and my love for the people induce me to give up all personal considerations."[34]

Still other accounts suggest Perón realized that Argentina's economic situation made it ungovernable. Thus he was content to sit it out on the sidelines while his enemies took on an impossible challenge. "They're not going to be able to govern," Perón told one associate, "and we're going to drive them crazy."[35]

Perón spent the next eighteen years in exile, mostly in Spain. His enemies had sent him packing. However, they could not destroy his legacy—however they might try. In the city of Salta, in northwest Argentina, the young novelist Ernesto Sábato, whose talent had already drawn favorable comment from Albert Camus and Thomas Mann, drew a vivid portrait of the division of Argentine society that became a permanent fixture with Perón's overthrow. Sábato, a scathing critic of the Perón government's insensitivity to liberty, had lost two professorships owing to persecution by the regime and was later condemned to months in prison for "disrespect":

> While we doctors, farm-owners and writers were noisily rejoicing in the living room over the fall of the tyrant, in the corner of the kitchen I saw how two young Indian women who worked there had their eyes drenched with tears. And although in all those years I had meditated upon the tragic duality that divided the Argentine people, at that moment it appeared to me in its most moving form. ... Many millions of dispossessed people and workers were shedding tears at that instant, for them a hard and sober moment. Great multitudes of their humble compatriots were symbolized by those two Indian girls who wept in a kitchen in Salta.[36]

Perón's quest for a front rank for Argentina among nations and the strongman's emphasis on social justice remained firmly embedded in the body politic and tied to his name. From 1955 on, vital domestic and international issues were often left unattended, as one government after another sought to hold a grip on power. Perón's gamble was that time was on his side. From the safety of a Paraguayan gunboat docked off Buenos Aires, his first stop en route to exile, Perón wrote to Nelly Rivas, his sixteen-year-old mistress: "For now, the best thing to do is hide yourself, stay calm until everything passes. And it will pass. There will be time for everything."[37]

With its slogan "Neither victors nor vanquished," Eduardo Lonardi's government was perhaps the last chance for what was broken to be repaired and for a return to the rule of law. Lonardi, whose ideas were of a Catholic-nationalist stripe, had few political skills. Supported by the church, he did not try to impose profound changes on the social and economic system established by Perón. Instead he focused on fighting what he said were his reasons for removing Perón—inflation, corruption, and parasitic bureaucracy. In some respects his government was the first attempt at "Peronism without Perón"—a formula that would be tried, unsuccessfully, several times. Lonardi's refusal to take repressive measures against Peronism and to dismantle the social gains it left behind caused him to fall victim to his own allies. He was overthrown in a palace coup little more than fifty days after taking power.[38]

Victors and Vanquished

The Liberating Revolution of 1955 was led by Gen. Pedro E. Aramburu and Adm. Issac Rojas. The new president and vice president had other ideas about victors and vanquished.

The General Workers Confederation was taken over by military officers. Some 150,000 shop stewards were stripped of their right to act as union representatives. Dozens of investigating commissions obliged thousands of citizens to prove their honor after having merely served in the former government. Thousands more were imprisoned. Even uttering Perón's name was prohibited—official communiqués called him the "deposed tyrant"—as was exhibiting Peronism's party symbols. The fury unleashed against the poor extended to bulldozing municipal swimming pools that Perón's government had built for the workers.[39]

Fearing that the body might become the center of a Peronist cult, the military government stole Evita's embalmed corpse from its resting place in the labor confederation headquarters. It was at first kept in a building controlled by army intelligence. Aramburu reportedly wanted the body taken out of Argentina and turned to the Vatican for help. Pope Pius XII reportedly gave his personal permission for the body to be buried with a fictitious name in a small cemetery outside of Milan. There it remained for some sixteen years.[40]

The Valle Revolt

On June 9, 1956, nine months after having been toppled from power, the Peronists made their first serious attempt to retake the country by force. Generals Juan José Valle and Raúl Tanco led the attack, supported by a small number of military men and counting on an undetermined amount of civilian help, perhaps 500 people in all.The uprising had been detected weeks earlier by the military intelligence services. "Even the children knew what was happening," said one rebel. A lack of coordination, desertions, and the overly optimistic view that it would take just a spark to set alight the fury of the *descamisados* condemned the conspiracy to failure.[41]

The rebellion foreshadowed the tragic events that wracked Argentina a quarter of a century later. "The triumph of Valle's movement," wrote Rodolfo Walsh, an Argentine novelist and social critic, "would have saved the country from the shameful period that followed."[42] The repression of Valle's revolt left thirty-four dead, only seven of whom died in combat. The others were killed by illegal firing squads or simply murdered. Said one historian, "In the previous decade citizens had been arbitrarily detained, there had been torture, and free speech made vulnerable in the name of social justice; now firing squads were used in the name of liberty." According to a U.S. embassy dispatch from the period: "Executions for revolt have been few and far between in Argentine history. It had become a sort of tradition that one was not shot in cold blood for participation in revolutionary movements. ... Those who are opposed to the executions wonder where this development will lead and whether, once executions are begun, they can be readily brought to a halt."[43]

On June 12 Valle, shocked by the slaughter of his subordinates, gave himself up in order to stop the killing. Once defeated, Valle might have sought refuge in an embassy, as others had done. Minutes before his own execution he told his teenage daughter Susana that, if he had, "How could I keep my honor and look at the face of the wives and mothers of my murdered soldiers? I am not a cafe-side revolutionary."

A priest recalled Valle's last moments with Susana. It was already 9:15 P.M. when she entered the gray prison yard on Las Heras Street in Buenos Aires' chic Barrio Norte. "A few moments later she saw her father arrive amid a group of helmeted navy men who walked alongside him, pointing at him with their machine guns. In a nearby room a male nurse stood by with straightjackets, in case either the girl or her father broke into a nervous fit."[44]

"I got to see him twenty minutes before he was murdered," Susana Valle said later. "He kept an extraordinary spirit. When Padre Devoto entered, weeping, my father told him, 'Don't you see, you guys are a bunch of charlatans. Aren't you always proclaiming the other world is better than this one?' To me he said, 'You're crying because you're going to remain in this mess, while I'm leaving happy.' He was able to speak very little. He was surrounded by navy infantrymen. I was sitting on his knees in a chair." A few of those who had been aiming their rifles at the pair supported themselves with their weapons, unable to withstand their own emotions. Others swooned or broke down and had to be replaced. The tension made minutes seem like hours. An officer announced: "It's time."

Even calmer than before, Valle took off his ring and put it into his daughter's hand. He gave her a few letters and then kissed her hard on the cheek. Making a slight gesture that meant "farewell," he disappeared into the hallways of the prison, still surrounded by a halo of machine guns.

The Massacre of José León Suárez

In the aftermath of Valle's revolt, the death penalty for political crimes—abolished by the constitution—was applied. Although many conspirators downed their arms at the first sign of conflict, that circumstance was not accepted as mitigation of responsibility. More bullets were used by the firing squads that followed the arrests, one critic wrote, than were fired during the rebellion itself.[45]

In June 1956 Carlos Lizaso was barely twenty-one years old. His father had been a Radical in his early years but later converted to Peronism. By 1950, however, the elder Lizaso became critical of the Peronist government, and by 1955, the year Perón was overthrown, he had almost moved into the opposition. The brutality of the "Liberating Revolution" reawakened the senior Lizaso's Peronist sympathies. His sons shared his views.[46]

The afternoon of June 9 Carlos Lizaso left his girlfriend a short note: "If all goes well tonight … " Lizaso did not know how to use weapons. He had never carried a pistol. At 11:00 that night Lizaso and some friends were detained by the police. Almost all were unaware of Valle's conspiracy. Only the owner of the house where the group was visiting and another person were conspirators. Lizaso, vaguely compromised, was unaware of the details.

The officers who conducted the raid were led by Lt. Col. Desiderio Fernández Suárez, the head of the Buenos Aires provincial police. Lizaso tried to escape but failed. Meanwhile, two other Peronist conspirators, Julio Troxler and Reinaldo Benavídez, arrived at the house and were arrested without offering resistance. The detainees were transferred to a police station in the Buenos Aires provincial town of San Martín. All, conspirators and innocents, were unaware that the revolt had failed. That same night, in the industrial suburb of Lanús, eighteen military men and two civilians faced a summary trial. Six were shot. ("Shoot them first and interrogate them later" was Fernández Suárez's mordant order.) They had been judged under the terms of a martial law that would only be decreed hours later; it was signed by Aramburu, Rojas, and three other top military men. (Aramburu reportedly wept when he signed the execution order for Valle, his one-time friend and Military College classmate.) At 5:00 A.M., June 10, Fernández Suárez barked to a subordinate: "Take those from San Martín out to a field and shoot them, too."[47]

Lizaso and the other twelve or thirteen prisoners—of whom only four or five were part of the revolt—were carried off into the night in a paddy wagon. Arriving at a field, some were forced to get out. Benavídez, Troxler, and Lizaso remained in the paddy wagon. The police vehicle stopped in front of the José León Suárez garbage dump. "We're not going to do anything to you," their captors told them as they moved them to the back of the dump.

Taking advantage of the tense seconds before the execution, Troxler bolted from the paddy wagon with Benavídez, who tried to drag Lizaso along by his hand. A shot rang out. In the confusion the police commissioner shouted: "Shoot them." A volley of gunfire crackled in the night air. Troxler, Benavídez, and two others succeeded in escaping. Lizaso, however, remained in the hands of the police. Other prisoners hid in the dump, pretending to be dead, or dove into a nearby ditch and escaped. The majority were machine-gunned to death. One, barely wounded in the arm, was shot again in the face. His mouth filled with blood. His would-be executioners left him for dead. He survived.

Lizaso was left for last. A terrifying cry punctuated the night. Angry at their own clumsiness, Lizaso's assassins riddled him at point-blank range with machine guns. His chest destroyed by bullets, Lizaso was left half sprawled over the roadway.

The Massacre of José León Suárez had ended. Valle's insurrection had been crushed. It marked the first time Peronism tried to regain power by the force of arms. It was the beginning of the Peronist Resistance, limited at first mostly to strikes and industrial sabotage. The electoral road to power had already been foreclosed. It would be reopened only in 1973. By then it would be too late.

3

Barracks Politics (1956-1963)

Since the [Reporting Officer's] knowledge of Panamanian geography is limited he could only answer that to the best of his knowledge Perón was in Panama and living at the Hotel Washington. ... At this juncture another officer interjected that the future of Argentina would benefit greatly if Perón were done away with and that the life of the assassin would be a small price to pay.

—*Information Report, U.S. Office of Naval Intelligence.*
Subject: ARGENTINA—Navy—Plotting Against Perón[1]

At sixty-four, Marcos Satanowsky, a Kiev-born Jewish immigrant, had made it to the very top as a respected lawyer for some of Argentina's most prominent families. His ascent was so spectacular that he rated special mention in the classic *Those Who Rule,* a study of Argentina's upper classes by sociologist J. L. de Imaz. Given the rampant anti-Semitism of his country's upper crust, de Imaz marveled at "this extreme case, in which [Satanowsky] has scaled all the steps of economic power until he reached the summit."[2]

Satanowsky was even more unusual in that although he assimilated the tastes and touches of gilded society, he did not turn his back on his own heritage. He didn't have to. His Aberdeen Angus were formidable competitors in the annual contest sponsored by the Sociedad Rural (Rural Society). By the standards set during the Libertadora (the Liberating Revolution), he and his family were politically "correct," opposing the general even before Perón became president. In early 1957, Satanowsky traveled to Europe and to Israel. The sojourn mixed promising business contacts with tours of art museums in Rome and Venice, haute cuisine in Paris, and forays into antique shops and perfume boutiques.

Early on June 13, 1957, Satanowsky invited three strangers who visited his law firm into his small, comfortable office in downtown Buenos Aires. Despite the discontent twenty months into Aramburu's rule, there was little in the air that warm, wet morning to suggest that the protests by the Peronists reached Satanowsky's second-story office. Non-Peronist political parties vied for power in an upcoming constituent assembly. More than 40 percent inflation since the military coup, compounded by a yawning fiscal debt, made the economic crisis felt in other sectors but only rarely in that which Satanowsky shared with his clients. A bitter showdown during the months before, pitting eighteen generals against the war minister—on issues of retirement and the merits of seniority versus "revolutionary" anti-Peronist commitment in deciding promotions—had been met with a shrug by most Argentines.[3]

Satanowsky's visitors used the pretext that they wanted him to autograph his two-volume work, *Studies in Commercial Law*. In fact, the trio sought to prevail in a dispute between the state and the owner of the afternoon newspaper *La Razón*—Satanowsky's client—concerning the daily's ownership in the post-Peronist era. Aramburu's regime wanted to put to an end the claim by the daily's former owner—himself a political chameleon—to the newspaper.[4]

Satanowsky's work on behalf of his client had already cost him his professorship at the law faculty of the state university. A scurrilous article called "Communism in Argentina"—written under an assumed name and printed in a U.S. State Department–sponsored series, *Studies in Communism*—accused Satanowsky of being a crypto-Communist infiltrated in the school. Meanwhile his client was subjected to an effort at extortion in which the head of the state intelligence agency, known by its acronym SIDE, took part.

No one knows what happened behind the closed doors of Marcos Satanowsky's office. There was a muffled sound of struggle, a gagging noise on the interoffice intercom, and the report of a gunshot. Blood gushing from his heart, Satanowsky lay, glassy-eyed, near death, attended by stunned aides. Pistols drawn, his guests covered their retreat.[5]

Subsequent investigations established that the trio who murdered Satanowsky were hired thugs employed by Gen. Juan Quaranta, who staffed the SIDE with rabid anti-Peronists, agents provocateurs, and common criminals. One of Satanowsky's assassins was Marcelino Castor Lorenzo. A pimp, strikebreaker, and bodyguard, by the time of Satanowsky's murder Castor Lorenzo was said to have killed between eight and nineteen people. Influential friends had kept him from serving more than fifteen days in jail. His two companions in Satanowsky's studio were also underworld figures whom, according to one account, Quaranta had used to try to murder Perón in Paraguay and later in Venezuela. One of the men had also served as Quaranta's bodyguard.[6]

Events surrounding Satanowsky's murder foreshadowed the techniques used in the "dirty war": anonymous anti-Semitic pamphlets, extortion attempts against Satanowsky's client and against the lawyer's family, a judicial system that responded with indifference. Even the police worked to cover up, rather than clear up, an assassination executed from the shadows of respectability.

Just as important were efforts to pin the blame for the murder on interservice rivals. Army General Quaranta hinted to Satanowsky's family that the killers might have been navy agents—a charge later shown to be false. Even so, rival military men who hated and plotted against each other eventually closed ranks in a conspiracy of silence and enforced forgetfulness.

No one was ever convicted of the crimes committed against Satanowsky and his family. Potential witnesses were jailed on the slightest pretext while the criminals remained at large. After Satanowsky's death, the formal award of *La Razón* went to his client, but its shares landed in the safe of those who coveted them from the first—the Argentine army. "From 1957 on *La Razón* was absolutely faithful to its real owner—the army—especially the army intelligence services," wrote social critic Rodolfo Walsh. "Peralta Ramos [Satanowsky's client] finally found the stable factor in Argentine politics, transcending its ephemeral governments, the permanent boss he was looking for since his days of flirting with Hitlerism."

Walsh's solitary exposés in the case, like those he did on the massacre at the garbage dump in José León Suárez, bore witness to a truth that the justice system refused to recognize. Years later *Operación Masacre* and *El Caso Satanowsky* still stood out as investigative and literary masterpieces, and their restless author moved beyond denunciation to a political commitment that cost him his life. "In each political crisis," Walsh wrote, "in the preparations for each coup, the army commander in chief sent envelopes to *La Razón,* which published their contents without modification. The oft-praised editorial talent ... was limited to choosing a catastrophic type face, its placement on the front page, or picking an unsettling headline."[7]

The mantle of silence that shrouded the Satanowsky case was left undisturbed by the mainstream press. Like *La Razón,* the press was prisoner to political commitments, social bigotry, or opportunism.

Re-Peronizing Argentina

Aramburu's regime was incapable of restoring Argentina's sense of economic and social well-being. By 1957, it was clear its laissez faire economic policies had not arrested inflation or balanced lopsided trade ledgers. Greater austerity was politically impossible. Instead of "de-peronizing" Argentina's workers, the Libertadora's harshness made them look to that earlier time as a "Golden Age," "re-peronizing" the many who were—like the father of Carlos Lizaso, the youth killed at José León Suárez—disillusioned by Perón's second government. The bloody suppression of Valle's revolt spawned a growing, distinctly antimilitary sentiment.[8]

The problem, wrote military historian Alain Rouquié, was that the armed forces took on greater responsibilities "at the exact moment their internal cohesion was weakened." Officers were tempted by the allure of "illegal enrichment," expropriations, and other activities probed by the Libertadora's "investigating commissions." Slow and inefficient, the commissions operated as if the accused were guilty until proven innocent.[9]

Factionalism grew within the services, particularly the army and air force. The proliferation of the intelligence services, said Rouquié, "truly a parallel police force run by groups within the armed forces, also contributed to demoralize those officers dedicated to their specific military tasks." French instructors schooled in "dirty war" doctrines from the bloody theaters of colonial struggle in Indochina and Algeria gave courses in Argentina's Superior War School.[10]

Perón kept a careful watch on developments in Argentina from his consecutive places of exile. He began to manipulate events back home, while keeping alive the hidden hopes of many of his compatriots. Directing his movement and the labor organization that was its backbone through hundreds of letters, written orders to supporters, and later, tape recordings, he also communicated with his followers through a series of delegates, numbering thirteen by the time he returned to Argentina seventeen years later. These delegates varied both in style and in their position on the ideological spectrum—from moderate to revolutionary left—according to Perón's political needs of the moment.

After spending less than two months in Paraguay as the guest of Alfredo Stroessner, Perón made an equally brief stay in Panama City. Despite the Libertadora's propaganda that he and Evita had stashed millions of dollars in Swiss banks, impartial observers noted that Perón lived with considerable frugality early in his exile.

It was in Panama City that Perón, at sixty still fit and amazingly well preserved, met the twenty-four-year-old Argentine who would soon become his third wife. Using the stage name Isabel, María Estela Martínez worked as an exotic dancer at the Happy Land cabaret when she met Perón two days before Christmas 1955. Shortly after meeting the general, the native of La Rioja province in Argentina's northwest abandoned the troupe and became his secretary. By mid-January they were living together. Isabel's appearance in the general's small circle added a sense of stability and domesticity to what had been an uncomfortable period of transition. Wrote Perón to a friend: "She plays the piano, dances, sings, cooks, administers the household and makes life more pleasant for us. I wouldn't trade her for the world."[11]

The Frondizi Presidency

In February 1958 the military held national elections. The Peronists were prohibited from fielding candidates. Legislator Arturo Frondizi, at the head of the Intransigents, a progressive faction of the Radical party, won the presidency with Peronist votes.

Before Perón's overthrow, Frondizi, an articulate lawyer of a nationalist tint, had been one of the few opposition politicians willing to dialogue with the Peronists. In the run-up to the election, Frondizi sent an emissary to Caracas, where Perón had taken up residence, to hammer out a pact with his old adversary. In exchange for Perón's endorsement, Frondizi promised to legalize Peronism. In the election, Frondizi's opponents, the conservative People's Radicals led by Ricardo Balbín, represented a continuation of efforts to "cleanse" the system of Peronism's influence.

Frondizi's presidency seemed to promise a respite from the arbitrariness of military rule. The new president issued a general amnesty for local Peronist leaders; allowed the general's followers to retake possession of the powerful General Confederation of Labor; and aggressively wooed labor leaders and others, trying to persuade them that his nationalist rhetoric and "identical national views" made it possible to have "Peronism without Perón." Like Perón, Frondizi rejected as obsolete the agricultural export model of development favored by the landed aristocracy and reinstated by Aramburu. Instead, like the Peronists, the Intransigents promoted an ambitious project of industrialization, although this time based on heavy industry.

To avoid resorting to huge increases in public spending, however, sustained foreign investment was needed. Frondizi's government played an active role in the stimulation of domestic savings, encouraged foreign investment, set investment priorities, established fiscal and monetary policies that furthered development, and promoted a foreign policy that would bring Argentina new markets. Exchange controls were lifted and loans contracted from the International Monetary Fund.[12]

The frondicistas could point to several areas in which their economic policies appeared to be working. They were particularly successful in refurbishing Argentina's tattered infrastructure. Yet the glimmer of prosperity was never bright enough to sustain a real national reconciliation. Key elements of Frondizi's program—its efforts to encourage outside investment, periodic attempts to impose austerity, and its reluctance to take on a large and enormously inefficient landowning class—smelled of a sellout to many former allies. A perceived process of economic concentration and an accentuation in the drift of control of the domestic economy into foreign hands added to their arguments.

Emblematic of this dispute was Frondizi's stand on foreign oil companies investing in Argentina. Despite his vigorous opposition on the issue both before and during the 1958 election, Frondizi—the author of a nationalist tract, *Petroleum and Politics*—signed controversial contracts with eight foreign oil companies. In 1959 he also "denationalized" the Lisandro de la Torre meat-packing plant, a move that led to an attempted "revolutionary general strike" by left-wing Peronists in January. In that year nearly 1.5 million workers took part in more than forty-five labor disputes in Buenos Aires alone.[13]

From his exile in Santo Domingo Perón fretted about Frondizi's efforts to woo away labor supporters, such as metalworkers' boss Augusto T. Vandor. Then, as conditions in Argentina worsened, the pragmatic Perón unhitched his political fortunes from those of Frondizi.[14]

Labor militancy and resurging violence led Frondizi to cave in to pressure from the military and impose a state of siege. By means of the bitterly controversial Conmoción Interna del Estado (CONINTES; Internal Commotion of the State) plan, those accused of "terrorism," including industrial sabotage, were subjected to military courts. The working-class cities of Berisso, La Plata, and Ensenada in Buenos Aires province were declared military zones; overseers were appointed for scores of unions, and strikers were arrested.

At the helm of a government constructed on borrowed votes, Frondizi found he could neither satisfy the Peronists nor placate rabidly conservative military officers. Emboldened by their return to the fore in public life, the military divined in Frondizi's every step the hidden designs of Juan Perón or, worse, the Communists. The Peronist Resistance, limited mostly to industrial sabotage and raids by propaganda teams, was associated by the generals with the victorious entry into Havana late that same year by Fidel Castro and his ragtag revolutionary army.[15]

The military's self-concept as "guardians of the national essence" was part of its view that the army came *before* the country, literally. Military historians point out it was the army that liberated Argentina from Spanish rule, created its first national institutions, and freed up the great, grassy pampas for settlement by first slaughtering their aboriginal inhabitants.[16]

The fight against "Communist subversion," with its focus on internal security, gave the generals a new lease on their political franchise. The line between national defense and barracks politics blurred and appeared in danger of being erased altogether. The military reserved for itself the power to patrol what they called Argentina's "ideological borders," that is, to act as unelected tribunes sitting in judgment on the thoughts and deeds of their fellow citizens. Said one general: "There exist internal borders that we must defend in full-blown Cold War."[17]

There were between thirty-two and thirty-four *planteos* (minicoups) by military factions against Frondizi's government as well as a seemingly endless chain of institutional challenges—the random insubordination of single generals and occasional efforts at putsches by discontented Peronist officers. Each threat voiced by the generals, already resentful of Frondizi's having come to power with Perón's support, undermined his fragile legitimacy and his capacity to lead.[18]

Frondizi's reputation for Machiavellian maneuver and double-dealing appeared to be confirmed by his own, often unfathomable negotiations and manipulation. Faced with a military rebellion, the president shunted aside or even punished officers who remained loyal to him while promoting the rebels. Still, his military critics were not placated, such actions serving only to erode Frondizi's already slender authority.[19]

Despite the setbacks, the frondicistas continued to seek Peronist support by promising political liberalization. Meanwhile, they presented themselves to anti-Peronists as the only alternative to Perón's return. In early 1962, Frondizi decided to put his strategy to the test in upcoming nationwide elections in which the Peronists were allowed to participate.

In March, the gamble proved to be a losing hand. The Peronists won nearly a third of the vote, outpacing the Intransigents by 700,000 votes and capturing nine of twenty-two governorships, including that of Buenos Aires, the richest and most populous province. Hard-line sectors of the army were livid, and eleven days later they overthrew Frondizi, who himself had annulled the Buenos Aires elections in an attempt to stave off the inevitable.

On April 9, the various army attachés of diplomatic missions established in Buenos Aires were called to a meeting convened by the army commander in chief at army headquarters. In the section of the report to the foreign military representatives entitled "The Present Argentine Crisis: The Mission of the Army and Revolutionary Warfare," the army outlined its thinking about the new enemy within:

> The studies made by the Argentine Armed Forces, particularly by the Army, on revolutionary warfare and on the development of Marxist action in the world, are well known. ... For their part the Armies of the free countries of America have taken part in studies of this nature in the Inter-American Course on Counter-Revolutionary Warfare, thereby strengthening the close bonds of friendship of those responsible for joint Continental Defense. These joint studies ... bring out clearly that the principal enemy of our civilization and way of life is to be found in the very heart of our national communities.
>
> That is why the enemy is tremendously dangerous. We are not attacked from outside, regardless of the enemy strength, but subtly undermined through all channels of the social organization. It poisons the minds, it weakens the spirit, it fabricates pharisees and false prophets, and distorts everything in an imperceptible process of time. Its action is similar to that of a termite. The structure appears while they undermine the foundations. One day everything collapses over our heads. ...
>
> The Argentine Armed Forces are fully aware of their duty, which ranges from the enlightening task in the field of thought in the face of the present ideologic-religious warfare which is shaking the world, to the field of actual deeds, singling out at the right time the Marxist virus carriers, and especially those responsible. ...
>
> There are many people in the country and abroad who, erroneously interpreting the sense of counter-revolutionary warfare, have believed that this action is directed against the people or against important sectors of the population. ... Nothing is further from the truth. ...
>
> Counter-revolutionary warfare is mainly intended to prevent mass contamination of the people and to prevent the seizure of basic organizations of the country by Marxist ideologists and their agents. The purpose of this counter-revolutionary warfare is to preserve the national ideological sovereignty. This must be achieved preferably through the laws of defense of democracy and through the soundness of the institutions which must be capable of generating the necessary antibodies to combat the evil. However, sometimes the combination of certain factors may call for the timely intervention of a surgeon to eradicate the evil before the body becomes too weak and is totally diseased.[20]

The year 1962 was not just the year the military ended Frondizi's tattered democratic experiment. In June, a wave of anti-Semitic activity, including physical attacks against Jews, was carried out by two fascist groups, the Guardia Restauradora Nacionalista (Nationalist Restoration Guard) and the Tacuara (named after the heavy bamboo cane used by Indians and gauchos as a spear). Both were made up largely of youths from Argentina's "best families," and both maintained fluid contacts with sectors of the armed forces, particularly the intelligence services. That year, too, Argentina experienced its first two "disappearances"—the kidnappings of rank-and-file metalworkers' leader Felipe Vallese and union member Héctor Mendoza. In joining the list of Peronism's martyrs, Vallese became a symbol of the Resistance.[21]

Uncivil Wars

Nominally headed by a civilian, the regime that ruled the rest of 1962 and the early months of 1963 was one in which the hapless citizenry played spectators to military factions engaged in their own internal cold war. Sometimes that war turned hot.

By early 1962, two distinct factions had formed within the military. Using the terminology of war games, one faction called itself the Blues (Azules); its opponents—vociferous anti-Peronists—were called Colorados (Reds). Ironically, most of the latter had been latecomers to the plotting against Perón. Many were members of the infantry. Practically the entire navy—whose officer corps was peopled by the rural oligarchy and wealthy urban classes—belonged to the Colorados.[22]

Within the ranks of the Blues were most of Perón's earliest uniformed foes. Many came from the elite cavalry. Among their leaders were officers who had been part of the dismally unsuccessful putsch carried out against Perón in 1951 by Gen. (ret.) Benjamín Menéndez, an excitable reactionary from Córdoba. A few, such as then Col. Alejandro Lanusse, had forged close ties during four difficult years in military prison after joining Menéndez's revolt. At the time Frondizi was overthrown, the Blues, although highly conservative, were seen as less intransigent on the "Perón question."[23]

In the last months of Frondizi's presidency, the anti-Peronist Colorados seemed to gain the upper hand within the military. Peronist victories in the March elections, particularly the victory in Buenos Aires province, was the last straw in their no-holds-barred opposition to the government.

Frondizi's ouster led to a government run not by a general but rather by the civilian president's constitutional successor, José María Guido. In part, this was due to the military's own internal disorder. For several months after Guido's inauguration, infighting within the armed forces appeared to be at the point of blowing up into full-scale warfare.

On August 8 the head of the IV Army Corps, in the northwestern province of Salta, rose up, demanding the resignation of the secretary of war, a partisan of the Blue faction. The rebels claimed the secretary ignored army tradition in filling the post of commander in chief. They also felt he had betrayed the principles of the Libertadora by entering into a political dialogue with the Peronists.

When the head of the III Army Corps joined the revolt, Guido was forced to relieve his war secretary. As his replacement the president named Gen. Eduardo Señorans, who was supported by the influential cavalry. The Colorados, however, decided not to obey Señorans. Instead they proposed their own candidate, the former war minister in Aramburu's regime. Their insubordination was meant to force a situation whereby they would take control of the government.

When the navy announced it was supporting the rebels, a showdown appeared imminent. Troops were deployed throughout Buenos Aires. Twenty-seven Sherman tanks from La Plata, part of the Blue forces, marched on the federal capital. They were to meet up with three tank regiments under the command of Gen. Juan Carlos Onganía. In all, Señorans counted on the support of some 300 vehicles and several thousand troops.[24]

When the military situation appeared overwhelmingly in favor of the Blues, Guido suddenly called the two factions to parley. Señorans resigned in protest. Meanwhile the Colorados maneuvered their own men into the three top army posts.

The Blues did not wait to respond. In late August, Onganía sent the new army chief a bitter memo complaining about a lack of discipline created by Colorado men at the service's top ranks. Onganía decried the fact that the Colorados were in control of the army's senior command posts, after having insubordinated twice. Worse, from a military point of view, the Colorados had even gone outside the service—to the navy—for support in an internal army matter. Early the next month, Gen. Julio Alsogaray followed Onganía's lead, complaining that Guido was "held prisoner by a band which does not allow him any liberty of action."[25]

By mid-September, the rumor circuit was aboil with reports of discontent and rebellion within the military. The expected insurrection came on September 18 at the powerful Campo de Mayo army base outside Buenos Aires. Later the same day, the revolt spread throughout the country, with the Blue rebels demanding the heads of the Colorado army leadership. The influential afternoon newspaper *La Razón,* tied to the army since Satanowsky's murder, hedged its bets in classifying the armed competitors for its readers: "It is difficult to know who among the 'legalists' and the 'rebels' is correctly using the term." A key rebel complaint involved rules about military retirement and promotion—not most people's idea of a matter of state.[26]

Early on September 19, civilian commandos supporting the Blues took over a number of radio stations. The action was key to their efforts to rally the population through a carefully crafted campaign of "psychological action." The incorporation of sociologists and mass communications experts into the ranks of the rebels led Alain Rouquié to call the Blues' revolt "the first 'scientific' coup" in Argentine history.

From the radio stations they sent out communiqués every half hour designed to create the right psychological climate; using rotund slogans they sought to give the image of a legalist, democratic army, at the service of the people. One heard, among others: "We're prepared to fight so that the people can vote," and "After Batista came Fidel Castro—dictatorship always leads to communism." The slogans were meant for rival officers, the communiqués were directed to public opinion.[27]

As rebel tanks began to move on the provincial capital of La Plata, the War Ministry ordered two bridges blown up to halt their advance. On September 20, twenty armored vehicles supporting the Colorados moved toward downtown Buenos Aires. Former president Aramburu, with an eye to his own entrance into electoral politics, called for national elections. The Argentine University Federation issued a statement of "repudiation" of military groups "who play with the country's destiny and submit the people to permanent threats and dangers." Meanwhile barricades were thrown up throughout the city center. The federal capital began to resemble a metropolis at war.[28]

The skirmishes between the contending factions included the blowing up of two more bridges and firefights around the capital. Finally, on September 22, the Colorados surrendered. Onganía, a leader of the faction that claimed to represent order and legality, was appointed army commander in chief. Through it all the president, Guido, was relegated to the same spectator's role shared by the rest of civil society. Meanwhile the armed forces battled among themselves to determine who would serve in his cabinet. Some 140 high-ranking officers were forcibly retired.[29]

Six months later, the battle between the Colorados and Blues was repeated when the navy rose in rebellion. The opening shot was a fiery proclamation by the veteran coup plotter Benjamín Menéndez. This time, however, an assassination attempt was also carried out against Gen. Osiris Villegas, a Blue leader, by one of fifteen civilian commando squads participating in the revolt.[30]

Put down after three days, the uprising cost nineteen lives and fifty-seven wounded, as well as the destruction of two army tanks and fourteen navy planes. Its suppression changed the balance of power within the military. For more than a decade the navy languished. When the admirals made their comeback, their weight was felt on land, not on the high seas.[31]

4

Winds of Discontent (1963-1969)

> Within the Peronist movement I have a mission: to lead, but to lead everyone.
> Because in politics he who wants to lead only those who are good ends up sur-
> rounded by very few. And in politics, with very few you can't do very much.
> —*Juan Perón*

National elections were called in 1963, a year after Frondizi was overthrown.
Despite its earlier, more tolerant posture concerning the Peronists, the now-
dominant Blues prevented them from fielding candidates. When the votes were
counted, the People's Radical party, led by a soft-spoken country doctor named
Arturo Illia, won the presidency with only 23 percent of the vote. Aramburu, in
his first try for elective office, came in third with 7.7 percent.

By 1963, the two factions of the Radical party had switched spots on the ideological continuum. Frondizi's term had shifted the Intransigents to the right,
away from nationalist politics. In his campaign, Illia made rejection of financial
conditions imposed by the International Monetary Fund a cornerstone of his
platform. He also attacked Frondizi's foreign petroleum contracts.

Civil-military relations under Illia showed the perverse strength of old anti-
Peronist alliances. Throughout his term, the government—with its emphasis on
tolerance and electoral fair play—would get a measure of support from its old
anti-Peronist allies, the retrograde Colorados. The constitutionalist Blues, in control of the army, were linked to Frondizi and other Illia opponents. Many Blues
greeted Illia's victory with studied hostility.

At the beginning of Illia's term, Argentina appeared poised for an impressive
comeback. GNP grew rapidly, the foreign debt shrank, and reserves in the Central
Bank reached levels not seen since the early years of Peronism. Education was a
special priority, receiving 23.2 percent of the national budget. Illia's personal style,
his moderation, and faith in the healing effects of time appeared to be just what
Argentina needed to retake the road of development.

The government's minority origins, however, proved to be its Achilles' heel. The powerful Peronist-controlled General Workers Confederation launched a so-called fight plan of protests, strikes, and industrial sabotage. The campaign came after two years of recession; during 1964 alone, more than 11,000 factories were occupied. In some cases, the strikers took corporate board members or top management personnel hostage in demand for their back salaries.

The union leadership, headed by metalworkers' boss Augusto Vandor, had an air of scandal about it and was engaged in skirmishes with the exiled Perón for control of the movement. The unions, like the leaders of the Blues and sectors of the business community tied to Frondizi, sought to destabilize Illia's government at any cost.

A split was also growing in the ranks of Peronism. The workers' dreams of a Peronist restoration kindled the flame of ambition among several of the movement's local leaders. Although a public utterance would have been considered heresy, these bosses began to think the unthinkable: Perón would not live forever. As the quiet succession struggle began, little thought was given to sustaining a government that had been elected behind their backs.

For most of the general staff, dominated by the Blues, Illia's presidency carried with it the threat of the restoration of the Colorados. His refusal to send troops to the Dominican Republic in 1965 to support the United States during the crisis there also irritated many officers. Some, seeing their traditional role of protecting Argentina's physical borders as anachronistic, sought to define a new mission. Their view drew closer to that of the Pentagon, with its focus on internal enemies, ideological frontiers, and the "Communist menace."[1]

Illia's determination to move from laissez-faire economics toward a fairer distribution of wealth meant an increase in taxes and a cut in subsidies. In response, businessmen trotted out complaints about state "inefficiency," political "demagoguery," and "a discouraging investment climate." The Rural Society even blasted as "totalitarian" a modest effort at price controls.[2]

For local Peronists, the issue was more complex. Some saw Illia's government as illegitimate and unsatisfying. Dreams of Perón's retaking power and a return to the Golden Years flourished among left-wing Peronists and the working rank and file. But despite their combativeness, Illia used legal means to end the agitation and sought systematic negotiations with the union leaders.[3]

Led by Augusto Vandor—known as El Lobo (the Wolf)—some labor bosses had already moved their bets to another type of agreement. A pact with the military, they reasoned, would best guarantee their positions and pave the way for a "Peronism without Perón." Vandor had been one of the architects of an ill-fated attempt by Perón to return to Argentina in December 1964. By showing that Perón could not come home, Vandor hoped that his supporters would cast about for a replacement. Vandor's plan, however, backfired. Although he was turned back during a stopover at the Rio de Janeiro airport, Perón had shown the faithful he was unafraid to return, despite the opposition of both the government and the military.

Vandor, who ran both the 62 Peronist Organizations (the labor movement's political arm) and the CGT, then upped the ante. In local elections held in Mendoza province in April 1966, the union boss ran a slate of candidates against that recognized by Perón. In response, Perón, by then living in Madrid, had to send his young wife to Argentina. There Isabel sought to ward off the challenge from Vandor by acting as her husband's personal representative.

When the smoke cleared, the victory was Perón's. The vandorista candidates placed a poor third, running behind both the winning conservatives and the general's own slate. In his defeat, Vandor realized that although he controlled the unions, the general was king in electoral politics. If he was to prevail, Vandor had to move the contest away from the ballot to a terrain onto which Perón could not step. A deal with the military was on its way to being born.[4]

López Rega—From the Shadows

It was during her visit to Argentina that Isabelita Perón met former police corporal José López Rega. Brandishing an old picture of himself as part of Perón's bodyguard—riding on the running board of the president's automobile—López Rega convinced retired Major Bernardo Alberte, at the time Perón's official delegate, to present him to the future first lady and president. According to one version of their meeting, López Rega, a practitioner of the occult, handed Isabel an astrology chart. Attaching himself to her retinue as it made its way back to Madrid, López Rega bode his time as a valet in the Perón household. The cloying sycophant was able to establish a bizarre relationship with Isabel, becoming her "spiritual master."[5]

A manipulative apparatchik, López Rega would become known to the public as El Brujo (the Sorcerer) and run one of Argentina's most powerful ministries. His lust for power brought with it terror and death. López Rega, manservant, would preside over the destruction of the Peronist dream.

Arturo Illia: Minority Democrat

The fate of the Illia government proved to be a milestone in the increasingly sophisticated assault on power by the generals. Its narrow electoral base crippled the elected leadership's capacity to govern. Illia's People's Radicals were only a minority in parliament. In 1966, they were for months unable to report a budget for executive approval. Illia appeared at times incapable of making compromises. Good governance did not guarantee popular support. In the March 1965 elections, the People's Radicals increased their support but saw the Peronists' strength grow even more.

The military, anxious to return to power, launched a carefully orchestrated propaganda offensive against Illia and against democracy itself. With each attack, Illia's helmsmanship grew more unsteady, softening the system up for another blow. In his last nine months as president, it was hard to know the real state of things in Argentina, as the doomsayers worked feverishly to make their own predictions a reality.

From September 1962 on, the army used sociologists specializing in mass communications to present a new image of the armed institution to the public. Gone was the time when an austere, determined general like Lonardi packed up his personal effects and traveled long miles at his own expense to rouse the ranks to rebellion. Two of Argentina's three newsmagazines, *Primera Plana* and *Confirmado,* formed part of the heavy artillery in the psychological warfare against Illia. Linked to the Blues, *Primera Plana* was a newsweekly established in late 1962 by Jacobo Timerman, a savvy, ambitious journalist, after talks with a group of army colonels. Patterned after *Newsweek,* it sought a readership of executives and businessmen. In May 1965, at the request of Gen. Osiris Villegas, a leading Blue, Timerman created *Confirmado* for the express purpose of promoting a coup. Timerman joked about renting himself out like a Xerox and how he manufactured "democratic" generals.[6]

Another key actor was an archconservative Catholic lawyer named Mariano Grondona. In 1955, Grondona was one of the anti-Peronist civilian commandos prepared to swing into action during the naval bombing of the Plaza de Mayo. During the confrontation between the Colorados and the Blues, Grondona helped the Blues carry out their sophisticated propaganda blitz. Now, from the pages of *Primera Plana,* he worked to overthrow the constitutional regime. "A tyrant is a monster; a dictator a functionary for tough times," he wrote. Argentina, Grondona claimed, "is waiting for Moses because it had been shown the Promised Land."[7]

The magazines were the cutting edge of a smear campaign against Illia. Cartoonists transformed him into a slow-witted, addle-brained turtle. The public was told that a coup was inevitable. Each error made by officials was magnified, and frequently a whisper of scandal was added. The government's "inefficiency" was compared to the always brisk, effective functioning of the military machine. Political parties were termed antiquated and obsolete. Parliamentary democracy, as understood in the Anglo-Saxon world, was said not to fit the peculiar context of Argentine public life. It was unsuited, the argument ran, to usher in the structural transformation needed to carry Argentina forward to its appointment with destiny.[8]

An article entitled "Predictions: What Will Happen in 1966?" published by *Confirmado* in late December 1965 was typical of the campaign against Illia. It read:

> On July 1, 1966, at eight o'clock in the morning, several army vehicles full of troops stopped at strategic points in the center of town. Access to the Plaza de Mayo had al-

ready been cut, and the last inhabitant of the executive mansion had left tranquilly an hour earlier. At eleven o'clock a proclamation was issued: "Confronted with the inefficiency of a government which had led the country into its gravest crisis, which promoted social chaos and broke national solidarity, the armed forces have taken power in order to assure the continuance of the nation itself." Finally, at two in the afternoon, the public was informed that a prestigious general, who had been retired from active duty for only a few months, had been invited by the military leaders to become the new chief of state.[9]

Six months later the coup came, only two days before the date the article had predicted, and the time Illia was turned out of office was off by a mere twenty minutes. Propaganda concerning the inevitability of the coup helped to make such predictions self-fulfilling.

Instead of a democratic government that, its enemies ceaselessly pointed out, was supported by only 23 percent of the voters, Argentina was now in the hands of Onganía, a retired general chosen by the heads of the three armed forces. This time there was no ringing commitment to restore civilian rule as quickly as possible. No limit was set on the time the generals said they needed to transform the system. From Washington, President Lyndon B. Johnson issued a statement of regret over this new incident of military intervention into politics. Briefly diplomatic relations between the two countries were severed. Meanwhile Onganía—using rhetoric resembling that meted out in U.S. counterinsurgency training programs—took office promising to combat "ideological infiltration, subversion and chaos."

* * *

The changing of the guard in Argentina was the object of intense interest in one capital on the other side of the Atlantic. From his austere and orderly exile in Madrid, Perón had kept up a voluminous correspondence with his followers. He played host to legions of well-wishers, historians, politicians, and others. He also penned volumes on his own favored theme: leadership.

On the eve of the coup, Perón expressed his sympathy with the seditious military. He also called on Argentines to unite and regroup in clean, free elections. "The time has come for Argentines to reach an agreement," he warned. "If not, the time will come to take up arms and fight. The path of unity is increasingly difficult; the path of arms increasingly easy."[10]

Combative Versus Collaborationist Unionism

When the Onganía regime came to power on June 28, 1966, it had two clear objectives. It sought to restore the confidence of the business sector. And it also tried to outflank Perón with an offer of participation for "collaborationist" sectors of

Peronist labor. To some, Onganía's regime heralded an Argentine version of a Nasser-style nationalist revolution. The state and industry would march lockstep toward modernization orchestrated by a set of reciprocal relationships between nationalist, proindustry military men; members of the local manufacturing community (many of whom had grown fat on state subsidies); and the working class, represented by a cooperative and quiescent leadership. As it turned out, however, Onganía's corporatist style resulted in a static, stultifying conservative regime. Although resembling Franco's Spain in political terms, it was far too close to foreign capital to suit the nationalists.

Two months after the coup, Argentina's workers began paying the price of their leadership's courtship of the military. Even as he was moving from a corporatist to a free-market economic model, Onganía decreed an obligatory arbitration law that made any labor conflict subject to mandatory litigation by the government, without recourse to the courts. Under the guise of national defense, all sectors of the labor forces were subject to military-style mobilization. Heavy-handed labor policies—such as the placing of unions into receivership—strengthened more militant sectors within the working class. "Collaborationist" labor bosses—themselves frequently on the take—worked with the regime to bust strikes by other unions.[11]

Discredited among many workers for his pact with the military, in March 1968 Vandor used his contacts within the regime to oust graphics worker Raimundo Ongaro, a combative Peronist strongly influenced by progressive church thinking, as head of the CGT. Ongaro responded by creating the CGT de los Argentinos (CGT of the Argentines), composed of the most militant Peronist unions, a few organizations headed by leftist labor leaders, and the leadership of unions put into receivership by the military. Vandor continued to control the other unions, headquartered in the old CGT building.

Despite the regime's severity, large sectors of organized labor kept up the pressure. On May Day, 1969, Ongaro's CGT issued a statement that reflected the growing resentments of large sectors of the population, particularly students and workers:

> For years they have asked us only for sacrifice.
> They've counseled us to be austere; we've been so to the point of hunger.
> They asked us to "pass the winter"; we've put up with ten.
> They've asked us to ration, and in doing so we've lost gains made by our grandfathers. And when there is not one humiliation we haven't suffered, nor single injustice that hasn't been committed against us, they ask us with irony to "participate."
> We say to them: We've already participated, not as executioners, but as victims, in the persecutions, in the tortures, in the mobilizations, in the firings, in the appointing of "overseers," in the lockouts.
> We no longer want that kind of "participation."[12]

The Cross and the Sword

The coup that brought Onganía to power pushed two tendencies within Argentina's Catholic church into open conflict. One was that of progressive Catholics in tune with a new, liberating message emanating from Rome; the other, the traditional hierarchy that supported the military. The clash between the two would not be resolved until a decade later, when the traditionalists threw in their earthly lot with the "dirty warriors."

Both Onganía and the man who occupied the Casa Rosada presidential palace five years later, Gen. Alejandro Lanusse, participated in the Cursillos de Cristiandad (Christian Catechists), a Catholic moral-rearmament movement that grew up in Franco's Spain. The Opus Dei, a worldwide network of conservative technocrats, provided ideological support for the regime. (Onganía took power after coming back from a retreat sponsored by the Opus Dei.) The president frequently attended public events with Cardinal Antonio Caggiano, a close friend of the actively anti-Semitic priest, Julio Meinvielle.[13]

From the time of Perón's overthrow, some Catholic groups—inspired both by nationalism and by the social teachings of the church—reached out to the workers and to the poor. A few even sided with the Peronist Resistance. But it was during the first years of the 1960s with the papacy of John XXIII that the Catholic church marked a new era. The prelate called on the church to break away from its secular isolation. Shortly before he died, John XXIII called on Catholics to redeem those positive aspects "for the just aspirations of men" that formed part of democratic socialism. His leadership brought a vigorous renewal in the Latin church, especially in Argentina.[14]

The influence of the Second Vatican Council, 1962–1965, was decisive in Argentina. The aggiornamento (doctrinal updating) suggested the possibility of breaking up the old alliance of the cross and the sword: the ties between the religious hierarchy, the economic elite, and the reactionary military. Thousands of young people flocked to this new and progressive church.

In "getting nearer to the world," as expressed by Pope John and his successor, the Catholic University Youth and other groups joined "base communities" and participated in factories, peasant villages, and slums. There they came to know a Peronism held dear by the poor. Finding its attractiveness enhanced by its very proscription, the youth became "peronized." A few also became enamored by the example of the late Colombian guerrilla-priest Camilo Torres.

Inspired by a document written in 1967 by fifteen Asian, African, and Latin American bishops, a group of Argentine priests created the Movimiento de Sacerdotes para el Tercer Mundo (MSTM; Priests Movement for the Third World), declaring themselves "in favor of the oppressed and the condemned of the earth ... adhering to a revolutionary process of radical and urgent change of structures ... condemning capitalism and in favor of a national, Latin American, humanistic and critical socialism." More than 400 priests joined the movement, and 500 others from the rest of the continent expressed their solidarity.[15]

The priests' movement drew sustenance from the conclusions drawn at the Latin American bishops' conference in Medellín, Colombia, in 1968: "If they jealously retain their privileges and, above all, defend them by using violent means, they make themselves responsible before history of provoking revolutions of desperation."[16]

Subterranean Warfare

Competing factions of the military did not always meet on the battlefield or plot against each other in secret barracks meetings. Throughout the 1960s, as during the "dirty war" that followed a decade later, there were threats, frame-ups, extortive kidnappings, and attempted murder carried out by rival groups within the military. Jorge Vago, a journalist linked to navy intelligence, published a broadsheet called *Prensa Confidencial*. Onganía's regime shut down Vago's publications several times; his printing press was busted up by police. Vago spent three months in jail, accused of attempting to rape a seventeen-year-old maid at his office. He denied the charge. It was later dropped.[17] In April 1969, the guard of army chief of staff Alejandro Lanusse was abducted. Upon the release of the men, they blamed other army officers for carrying out the attack.[18]

Few episodes, however, matched those involving the veritable mafia that grew up around Gen. Francisco Imaz. In 1955, Imaz had led a pistol-waving commando group demanding Perón's removal into talks between legalist military officers and anti-Peronist rebels who were negotiating the terms of Perón's resignation. During the 1960s, the general served twice as the military-appointed overseer of Buenos Aires province before moving to occupy the Interior Ministry portfolio under Onganía.[19]

Imaz belonged to an ultra-right-wing Catholic sect, Cité Catholique, along with several other ranking members of Onganía's government, such as SIDE chief Gen. Eduardo Señorans. In 1966 Imaz returned to the Buenos Aires governorship. He appointed Maj. (ret.) Hugo Raúl Miori Pereyra, a former cavalry officer and member of the Cursillos de Cristiandad, as head of military intelligence of Argentina's largest province. (Other cursillistas included Onganía and army chief Lanusse.) The group met at a retreat in Buenos Aires province known as La Montonera.[20]

In 1963, shortly before retiring as the appointed overseer of Buenos Aires province, Imaz had returned a former provincial police officer, Luis Salvador Botey, to the force. Botey had been suspended from service after having been named as responsible for the 1962 kidnapping of contraband kingpin Alberto (alias El Jaileife [High Roller]) Fleitas. Fleitas, in turn, was a one-time bodyguard for underworld boss Vicente Adolfo Ernesto ("Cacho") Otero, whose contraband operation was so extensive it counted on its own fleet of airplanes. On the take from Otero,

Botey was charged with kidnapping Fleitas, "passing him through the machine" (police slang for torture), then demanding a huge ransom from Fleitas's common-law wife. Botey eventually released his prey.

Less than three months later Fleitas's shoeless body was found in a field in Buenos Aires. A .45-caliber bullet had destroyed his head; his face and hands were burned with acid. His killer was a Federal Police officer, Juan Ramón Morales. At the time of his death, Fleitas was challenging Otero for supremacy in the contraband racket. He was also a prime witness in the criminal complaint against Botey lodged against the officer by Fleitas's wife.[21]

In June 1966, with Imaz again at the helm in Buenos Aires province, Miori Pereyra became head of the new "information secretariat," or intelligence service. Miori, who according to the general himself was "spiritually linked" to Imaz, then put Botey in charge of security of the government house in La Plata. In turn, Botey put together a network of corrupt cops, including a former bodyguard of the vicious Venezuelan dictator Marcos Pérez Jiménez. The result was an endless number of extortive kidnappings and shakedowns. Most of the victims were businessmen. Several were members of other intelligence services.

On November 23, 1966, a businessman with a long-standing civil suit concerning property that once belonged to Imaz's daughter was kidnapped as he left his house en route to his lawyer's office. Held incommunicado by police for two days, he missed his court date. Upon his release, he was told by his captors he had not been detained. He had merely been their "guest."[22]

The owner of Mustafá, the King of Transistors, located in the heart of Buenos Aires, was also abducted by two of Botey's group, tortured, and his apartment looted. Other kidnap victims included a rancher from Necochea, a contraband artist, a businessman from suburban Martínez, and the fence used by the gang to sell the radio shop's wares. A family that had won the provincial lottery was subjected to threats and attacks by the group, who demanded the winnings.[23]

The list went on. The crimes had three common denominators. The culprits were all Botey cohorts. They all belonged to Imaz's staff. And none of them was ever convicted. Among the gang's victims was army intelligence informant Tomás Agustín Alvarez Saavedra, a friend of Evita's late brother, Juan Duarte, and the owner of an extensive chain of assignation hotels. A second abductee was an unidentified friend of Marcelino Castor Lorenzo—the SIDE thug who helped murder lawyer Marcos Satanowsky. Upon leaving a casino at the ocean resort of Mar del Plata, he was mistaken for Castor Lorenzo, kidnapped and severely beaten. Still another was Onganía foe and naval intelligence confidant Jorge Vago. He was abducted and forced to publish certain articles in *Prensa Confidencial* in exchange for his well-being.[24]

A Death in the Jungles of Bolivia

The news of the death of Argentine-born Cuban revolutionary Ernesto ("Che") Guevara—killed while trying to incite an insurrection in the jungles of eastern

Bolivia—sent a tremor throughout Argentina. Coming after a quixotic effort to win the peasantry of Latin America's poorest nation to the cause of revolution, Guevara's death added to the romantic aura already surrounding his life. He became a role model for many young Argentines.

A physician by training, Guevara witnessed the CIA-directed overthrow of Guatemala's leftist but democratically elected president, Jacobo Arbenz in 1954. In Mexico, he met a group of Cuban exiles plotting the liberation of their own country and later became one of the leaders of the insurrection against dictator Fulgencio Batista, who was overthrown in 1959.[25] In 1965, Guevara mysteriously dropped out of sight. When he finally surfaced, it was at the head of a small band of armed, mostly foreign insurgents seeking to topple Bolivia's U.S.-backed military regime. (The CIA considered using former Gestapo leader Klaus Barbie, a longtime La Paz resident with excellent military contacts, in the effort to track down the guerrilla. The idea was abandoned after the agency calculated that the risks of public exposure outweighed the benefits.)[26]

Guevara meant to make "one, two ... many Vietnams" in the Americas. Yet his plans ran contrary to regional Soviet designs at the time. The Bolivian peasantry had also been the beneficiaries of an extensive land reform in the 1950s. And the military regime, which had toppled a democratic government in 1964 with the support of peasants won over by U.S.-designed civic action programs, had used the rural poor to offset the influence of Bolivia's left-wing miners. A critical examination of Guevara's failure was not forthcoming, however. For many Latins, Guevara—a charismatic figure whose chivalry had charmed even a U.S. presidential speechwriter—evoked admiration.[27]

"Comrades—it was with great pain that I received the news of an irreplaceable loss for the cause of peoples fighting for their own liberation," wrote Juan Perón from Madrid in an open letter to his followers upon hearing of Che's death in October, 1967.

> The most extraordinary young figure the Latin American revolution has to offer has fallen like a hero: Comandante Ernesto Guevara has died. ... His death tears at my soul because he was one of ours, perhaps the best of us, an example of behavior, of selflessness, the spirit of sacrifice. ...
> The majority of Latin America's governments will not resolve their nations' problems because quite simply they do not represent their nations' interests. For that reason I do not believe verbal expressions of revolutionary fervor are enough. It is necessary to enter into revolutionary action.[28]

The Night of the Long Sticks

Although a law barring persons declared "Communist" from a variety of positions, including teaching, was instituted, at first the Onganía regime appeared sensitive to issues of basic liberties. The right of habeas corpus was respected and freedom of the press was treated with caution. Soon, however, it launched an assault against free expression that extended far beyond what most people define as "politics."

With a decades-long tradition of autonomy, Argentine universities enjoyed the reputation as being the finest in Latin America. The University of Buenos Aires in particular enjoyed worldwide fame for scholarship and applied research. On the night of July 29, 1966—later known as the Night of the Long Sticks—assemblies were being held on the campus to protest the regime's efforts to curb academic freedom. The debate was cut short by a police raid. In one building, students, professors, and a visiting scholar from the Massachusetts Institute of Technology were rounded up. Forced to put their faces against a wall, they were methodically beaten for twenty-five minutes. In another area, police cleared a hall using tear gas. More than 150 people were arrested. Forty-nine were injured.

Within a month more than 1,400 professors and teachers had resigned, protesting the raid. Scores of Argentina's research elite went into exile, worsening a chronic brain drain and adding to the country's ostracism in international academic circles. Subsequently the regime went after movies, newspapers, plays, and every other form of expression. Youths with modishly long hair were given public haircuts. Federal Police Commissar Luis Margaride ordered nightspots to use bright lights to dampen enthusiasm for open displays of affection. When an American newspaperman visited Onganía on behalf of the Inter-American Press Association, he urged greater freedom for the media. The president replied: "If a free press would make it possible for Communists to take over Argentina, then I would be proud to say there is no free press here."[29]

By 1969 all that was needed was a spark for the country to go up in flames. The government did not appear to notice, but it sat on a powder keg. The abrupt police dispersal of a student meeting called to discuss the transfer of the Corrientes University student dining hall to a private concessionaire and a subsequent eleven-cent price rise for meals provided that spark. A chain reaction flared throughout the country. In Corrientes the police killed a demonstrating student. In the port city of Rosario two more died. Workers and students joined together to wage pitched battles against the police in Santa Fe, Tucumán, La Plata, and Córdoba.

On May 29, Army Day, the workers of Córdoba took over the city. To some, the Cordobazo resembled the worker-student riots in Paris the year before. Nearly all the local political parties took up the protest, which spread even to the city's most affluent neighborhoods. The insurgents took control of 150 city blocks, setting up roadblocks and barricades. For two days, the rebels, aided by rooftop snipers, held off army paratroopers backed by air force planes. It was, said one U.S. embassy cable,

a wave of nation-wide violence such as has not been seen in Argentina for fifty years. After two weeks of riots and the most successful national general strike in over ten years, the toll was twenty dead and hundreds injured. States of emergency had been declared in several major cities and accompanying military tribunals distributed sentences ranging up to ten years. Labor was unified for the first time since the 1967 split of the CGT and, for the first time in Argentine history, labor and students made common cause in the streets.[30]

Although blaming "Castroite elements, Cubans and Central Americans" for the uprising, the regime announced a complete reorganization of the cabinet. The revolt marked the beginning of the end for the Onganiato.

5

Aramburu's Murder— The "Argentine Z"? (1970)

In the air, from the very first, was a feeling of skepticism about the capacity of justice—often impotent—to clear up what the political morass wants to keep in the kingdom of shadows.

—Confirmado, *November 25, 1970*

The Cordobazo sparked a sense of expectation and unease. On June 4 Onganía replaced Economy Minister Adalbert Krieger Vasena. In buttressing their case against Krieger Vasena, the nationalists had pointed to the results of a confidential investigation conducted by the head of the national police. The probe revealed the pervasiveness of foreign intervention in Argentina's economy. (Few appeared to question the intervention of the police in what would seem to be an area outside its competence.) Worries about the "denationalization" received even greater currency, however, after it was shown that more than 250 high-ranking military officers belonged to the boards of foreign corporations operating in Argentina.[1]

On June 26 left-wing nationalists bombed nine Buenos Aires supermarkets owned by the Rockefeller family. The violence was part of a protest against a planned visit to Argentina by New York Governor Nelson Rockefeller. (Argentine labor was split, once again, over the trip, with Raimundo Ongaro endorsing the protests, while Vandor worked hard to keep union participation to a minimum.) Seven of the stores were gutted in the fires. Damages were estimated at nearly $3 million. Part of a fact-finding mission to Latin America on behalf of newly elected President Richard Nixon, Rockefeller's visit had set off similar, if less costly, protests across the continent.[2]

Four days after the bombings, Augusto Vandor was murdered.

Until eight months before, when the repentant metalworkers' chief traveled to Madrid to reestablish his relationship with Perón, El Lobo had been one of

Perón's favorite targets in correspondence with followers in Argentina. When he was killed, Vandor was poised to lead a new political and union offensive on Perón's behalf. Key to the plan was the reunification of the two CGTs and an offer of a truce with the regime in exchange for a return to collective bargaining talks. At the same time, contacts with disgruntled military officers were to be intensified.

On the morning of June 30, as Vandor was busily hammering out details of the offensive in his office at the heavily guarded metalworkers' headquarters, five men forced their way into the building after having identified themselves as Federal Police, then rounded up the union employees at gunpoint. "Where is Vandor?" shouted one of the intruders. "Where is El Lobo?" Aroused by the racket, Vandor bolted out of his office and was met by a hail of gunfire. As he lay dying, a bomb was placed between his legs. It would explode, one of the assailants said, in three minutes. Pulled out of the building by aides before it was partially destroyed, El Lobo arrived dead at a local hospital.[3]

The murder stunned the country. Onganía declared a state of siege; Interior Minister Imaz ordered mass arrests. Many detainees were labor leaders linked to the militant CGT of the Argentines, which was ordered disbanded. Ongaro was charged with responsibility for Vandor's death. Placed in "protective custody," he spent the rest of the year in jail.

The stepped-up repression was accompanied by new divisions within the armed forces. The army general staff resented the fact that Onganía made all final policy decisions, often without consultation. Personal relations between the president and army chief Alejandro Lanusse were increasingly tense, as the latter let it be known he favored a political solution to the crisis. Meanwhile the nationalist military officers who had ushered in Onganía's "revolution" grumbled that a coterie of nonnationalist conservative officers, invariably from the elite cavalry and frequently linked to multinational interests, had been put in control.[4]

By 1970 it was clear that the succession of military regimes and weak civilian governments that sought to rule by proscribing Peronism had run their course. In September the port city of Rosario was again the site of riots. The army occupied it for a second time. Last-minute concessions by the regime narrowly averted a general strike. The middle class fumed over restrictions in education and culture and worried about the regime's failure to protect local industry. Their calls for an electoral opening were ignored. Even Onganía's supporters began having doubts. What use was a strongman president if he could not impose his will?

As if to confirm such worries, 1970 began with the eruption of activities by Argentina's first urban guerrillas. In the early 1960s two attempts to spark a Cuban-style rural insurrection in the impoverished northwest had been quashed, and the tiny armed bands rapidly eliminated. In mid-1968 police raids had uncovered arms caches and suspected guerrilla bases in several parts of the country. There had been confusion about what the discoveries meant. No one knew, Malcolm W. Browne reported in the *New York Times,* "the extent and size of the suspected guerrilla network … [or] whether the guerrillas represent the far right, the far left, isolated groups of bandits, or some combination of the three."[5]

Argentines found that "armed politics" was no longer a military monopoly. The Fuerzas Armadas Peronistas (FAP; Peronist Armed Forces) sent a column brandishing weapons into a slum to engage in what became known as "armed propaganda." They distributed toys and candy to local children. A few days later a band attacked a guardpost at Campo de Mayo, the country's most important military base, stealing arms. A consul from Paraguay was kidnapped by a tiny Marxist group. There were also attacks on a coast guard post on the Río Paraná delta and police stations in Rosario, Córdoba, and Buenos Aires. To the booty of stolen weapons and uniforms was added another essential ingredient—money—as the number of bank robberies surged.[6]

The armed groups were not Onganía's only worries. Talks on issues dealing with a return to civilian rule had begun between Perón, in Madrid, and the deposed president's erstwhile mortal enemy, Gen. (ret.) Pedro Aramburu. Tensions mounted in the army. The rumor circuit buzzed with reports that Aramburu was preparing a coup, with Perón's support and that of as many as ten active-duty generals. It was, from all accounts, a time for decision.[7]

* * *

"Inexplicably, the French movie *Z*, an attack on military totalitarianism, got by Argentina's censors," wrote Browne in the Sunday *New York Times* "Week in Review" in late May.

> Crowds of Buenos Aires residents packed the street waiting to see the film and cheered the downfall of the movie's main villain, a general who bears a striking physical similarity to Argentina's interior minister [Imaz].
>
> Cheering in movies seems to be one of the few remaining forms of free expression in Argentina, and even that is threatened. A tear gas bomb was thrown two weeks ago into a theater where *Z* is showing. Totalitarian government seems to fit Argentina like an old shoe.

Quis Custodiet Ipsos Custodes? (Who Will Guard the Guards?)

Argentine military officers believed that they were different from and better than their civilian counterparts, and thus they did not owe any loyalty to civilian institutions. "In Argentina," the army high command said in one confidential document, "the Armies preceded national organization. It was they, through the sacrifice and hardship of their soldiers and the self-denial of their commanding officers, who gave birth to the Nation."[8]

As the inheritors, the direct descendants of those who gave birth to the nation, the Argentine army believed it could continue to serve as Argentina's spiritual guardian, the keeper of the "national essence." In the 1960s possibilities for the role grew, as military thinkers began to see the army's traditional functions—protecting Argentina's physical frontiers—as obsolete.

One of the most powerful influences on the thinking of Argentine military officers was French general André Beaufre. In his book, *Introduction to Strategy,* Beaufre maintained that twentieth-century man was obsessed by the senseless destruction of the two world wars. The futility of global conflict, he argued, was accentuated by the advent of atomic weapons. But just as true warfare seemed to be on the eclipse, so too did true peace. The future would be one marked by low-intensity warfare. A permanent war between East and West had been unleashed in which winning was defined as the shrewd engagement of forces short of nuclear war. Beaufre insisted that the Soviet Union was winning this conflict because the political debate in the United States was naively framed in outmoded terms of war and peace.[9]

Argentine officers also borrowed heavily from other French counterinsurgency strategists, particularly the ultra-right-wing veterans of the brutal colonial wars in Indochina and Algeria. In 1962 in his book *The Crisis of the Army,* Col. Mario H. Orsolini wrote that the French theories "filled the gap produced by the almost complete disappearance of the possibility of war between our country and its neighbors." A memorandum of conversation from July of the same year written by U.S. Agency for International Development (USAID) contract employee James D. Theberge is also revealing. Its subject was Gen. Carlos J. Rosas, at the time the commander of the 3d Infantry Division at Paraná and a man who "has frequently been mentioned as the potential leader of a military coup d'état."[10]

In 1955 Lieutenant Colonel Rosas returned from France, where he had graduated at the top of his class after two years at the War College, to take the post of subdirector of the Argentine War College. He brought two French lieutenant colonels along with him as instructors. They taught counterinsurgency doctrines to young officers who, two decades later, would carry out the "Dirty War." Theberge reported that

> General Rosas does not believe Argentina needs a conventional army to fight foreign wars. The period in which Argentina needed an army to protect its frontiers or repulse attack in international wars is past. In a world war its army would be useless.
>
> He advocates training the army for defensive counter-revolutionary warfare developed by the French in Indo-China and Algeria … [and] believes that the Argentine military must understand the social, economic and psychological problems of the country in order to prevent the conquest of foreign-inspired ideologies. He believes that dealing with the Communist threat is the most important problem facing the military.

Theberge also noted that Rosas had been much influenced by U.S. General Maxwell Taylor's book *The Uncertain Trumpet.* The embassy's evaluation: "It would appear that General Rosas is a military man of very advanced ideas who has made a correct assessment of the true role of the Argentine army. ... General Rosas' interest in anti-guerrilla warfare is one which we propose to cultivate."

As early as 1950 the United States foresaw an important role for the Latin American militaries in suppressing internal subversion. However, the idea became particularly prominent during the Kennedy presidency, as romantic notions of counterinsurgency captured the hearts and minds of policymakers. The threat of armed revolution in Latin America—or "more Cubas"—came to dominate strategic thinking about hemispheric defense.[11]

American officials used several justifications for stepping up U.S. military training and aid. The most realistic was that the relatively small investment would increase U.S. influence with groups destined for high leadership roles in their own countries. Some argued that exposing Latin military men to their U.S. counterparts would help instill in them an American-style world view and a greater willingness to submit to civil authority. During the Kennedy administration, U.S. counterinsurgency plans also began to stress a broader military role through "civic action" programs. Latin officers received high-level training in areas as diverse as fiscal planning, development policy, and public administration.[12]

"The U.S. has maintained its post–World War II position as the predominant foreign military influence in Argentina," wrote Ambassador Edwin Martin in a secret April 1966 dispatch from Buenos Aires:

> The Argentine armed forces have not turned away from us and toward third countries for their doctrine, equipment and training. On the contrary, they have concentrated on modernization and professionalization under U.S. guidance. ... What is less favorable is the possibility that the military, in spite of its generally "legalist" stance, might seek to usurp civilian powers. ... The Argentine military have not in general been amenable to U.S. concepts of what the missions of the Argentine armed forces should be, except in the area of civic action. Nor have they achieved optimum coordination with the police forces of the nation ... with respect to the maintenance of internal security.[13]

By 1969 Nelson Rockefeller, the head of the Presidential Mission for the Western Hemisphere, hailed the nation-building potential of the Latin military as "the essential force for constructive social change." He contended that massive police and military aid to Latin America was necessary to prevent a repetition of the Cuban experience. The military was seen as the only force capable of maintaining internal security. Despite the region's striking social and economic inequities, Rockefeller betrayed a notorious bias for the status quo. "The question is less one of democracy or lack of it," he reported, "than it is simply of orderly ways of getting along."[14]

The question, however, *was* democracy. U.S. training programs fostered the politicization of the military by indoctrinating it with a broad-brush anticommunism and by casting it as the guardian of national security and foreign investment. According to a RAND Corporation study authored by Luigi Einaudi and Alfred Stepan III in the early 1970s:

> A rationale sometimes used for certain U.S. military assistance programs is that "professionalism" contributes to lessened political involvement on the military's part, and to their concentration on exclusively military affairs. Logic, however, suggests that to the extent that military expertise, or professionalism, is increased in areas of counter-insurgency, nation-building and multi-sector development planning, the military would tend to become *more* rather than *less* involved in politics.[15]

Who Killed Aramburu?

May 29, 1970, was Army Day, and the first anniversary of the Cordobazo. Early that morning an army captain and a first lieutenant dropped in at the home of former President Aramburu, located in a fashionable district in downtown Buenos Aires. The general was in the shower. His wife played hostess, offering the pair coffee. She then left, saying she had a few errands to run.[16]

According to one account, when Aramburu appeared the captain told the retired general they were there to offer him an army bodyguard. Only a few days earlier, the Onganía regime had withdrawn his police protection. The three men chatted for a few minutes. Suddenly, the lieutenant flashed a submachine gun from underneath his raincoat, announcing: "General, you're coming with us."

Aramburu left without offering resistance, perhaps believing the military men would do him no harm. What he didn't know was that the "captain" was civilian Emilio Maza, who was putting his years at the military academy to use in a special performance that day. The "lieutenant" was another civilian, Fernando Abal Medina. As they made their way to a waiting Peugeot seven floors below, the trio was joined by a youth in mufti with close-cropped hair named Mario Firmenich. Dark-eyed Norma Arrostito, disguised as a flashy blonde, and two others—dressed as a priest and a police corporal—prepared to follow Maza's car in a pickup. Machine guns and hand grenades lay on the seats.

A few blocks away, the Peugeot was abandoned and the group squeezed together in the truck. Taking off their disguises, Abal Medina, Arrostito, the "priest," and the driver of the Peugeot left the pickup and prepared a dramatic announcement: A new revolutionary Peronist group, the Montoneros, had kidnapped Aramburu. The name Montoneros was taken from the ragtag armies that fought in the War for Independence and later against domination by the Buenos Aires elite. The commando headed by Maza was named after Juan Valle, the brave general executed by Aramburu and the Libertadora. In a "revolutionary trial" Aramburu was charged with the murder in 1956 of the Peronist rebels, the desecration and disappearance of Evita's corpse, the "theft" of gains made by workers during Perón's rule, the restoration of the oligarchy, and the selling out of Argentina to foreign interests.

At first the government seemed to discount the risk run by Aramburu. A police hunt was delayed for several hours. A few officials, including Imaz, claimed Aramburu's kidnapping was a publicity stunt or a diversionary tactic while he went underground to prepare a military rebellion. Imaz later reversed himself and said the abduction was the work of international extremists who had recently met in the Uruguayan town of Canelones. The claim was denied by that country's interior minister. An Imaz aide said Aramburu had landed at an airport in Montevideo, the Uruguayan capital. The report was false.[17]

On June 1 the local press received a communiqué that read:

> Perón returns. 1st June 1970. Handbill No. 4. To the People of the Nation: The Montonero command informs that today, at 07:00 hours, Pedro Eugenio Aramburu was executed. May God have mercy on his soul. Perón or Death! Long live the Fatherland! Montoneros.

Aramburu's Parker pen and wristwatch were returned to the family. His body, covered with lime, was found June 16 in a farmhouse in Buenos Aires province.

Aramburu's inner circle charged that members of the Onganía regime were behind the murder. First they claimed that the Montoneros were set up as scapegoats. When that argument collapsed, they implied the group had collaborated with, or was infiltrated by, the regime. They pointed out that a number of the Montoneros had been activists in far-right nationalist groups, such as the Tacuara, and as such were easy converts for Onganía's nationalist supporters.[18]

For a while the conspiracy theory gained widespread support among the country's conservative, antinationalist elite. It was eloquent on several points. In the months prior to the abduction several flyer-style "newspapers" began a vociferous campaign against Aramburu. With wide distribution and no visible means of support, the publications had palpable connections to the state intelligence services. A few days before Aramburu was kidnapped, Imaz's Interior Ministry had sent out a warning to public figures about the risks posed by "subversive" groups. It included detailed recommendations on how to avoid kidnapping. Aramburu's friends said that not only did he not receive the missive, his own police protection was taken away.[19]

Other details cast further doubt. Aramburu's telephone was out of order during the hours of the abduction but neither before nor after. Government officials had been informed of the crime by Aramburu's friends within an hour of the kidnapping. Yet the former treated the matter with skepticism. There were no bloodstains on Aramburu's shirt, but his hands and feet were bound. How was it possible that the former president was executed with gunshots to the neck, head, and chest, but his shirt remained clean? Also, Salvador Botey, the corrupt cop who had belonged to Imaz's staff, was not at work the day of the kidnapping. He was said to have been on a cattle-buying mission in Buenos Aires province, not far from where the general's body was later found.[20]

Finally, according to the newspaper *La Vanguardia*, Mario Firmenich—one of the Montoneros with a right-wing, nationalist past—visited Imaz's Interior Ministry twenty-two times during April and May 1970, that is, in the month and a half before the abduction. Although it was not uncommon for urban guerrillas to do a great deal of intelligence work through personal contacts and family ties, the commonality of interests between Imaz and the guerrillas was nonetheless apparent.[21]

By the end of the year the Montonero organization, composed of little more than a score of activists, had been decimated. Fernando Abal Medina, Emilio Maza, and Carlos Ramus—whose family owned the farmhouse where Aramburu's body had been found—were killed in shoot-outs with police. Five others accused of participating in the crime were tried in the first public trial in Argentina. The group included Norma Arrostito's sister and brother-in-law and a Catholic priest, whose typewriter had been used to write the Montoneros' communiqués in the days after the kidnapping. A number of others, including Firmenich and Arrostito, remained in hiding.[22]

In the years to come the regime's possible complicity in the murder was a matter of some debate. "Important" Peronist leaders privately told U.S. Ambassador John Davis Lodge that Aramburu's murder "was carried out by 'para-government' right-wing, Catholic, nationalist forces trying to prevent Onganía from reaching an accommodation with the Peronists, as advocated by Aramburu." Subsequent regimes stonewalled on the demand that an independent investigating commission be established. A former police chief during the Libertadora who was one of Aramburu's closest friends wrote an accusatory tome, *The Argentine "Z"—The Crime of the Century.* And a Federal Police officer, Alberto Villar, who played a key role in the search for the former president, also remained unconvinced by the evidence presented in the case. He began his own private inquiry.[23]

"All the elements of high drama were present—political passions, hints of torture, and the 15-year-old division of Argentines into Peronists and anti-Peronists," recalled Andrew Graham-Yool, a young reporter for the English-language *Buenos Aires Herald,* in a year-end wrap-up of the Montoneros' appearance in court. "But … in no way did the trial give the answers—it could not—to the questions still asked by the population: Who kidnapped Aramburu? Who killed him? Why?"[24]

6

Armed Politics (1970-1972)

Opportunism is the art of being opportune.

—*Juan Perón*

The military should be willing to leave the government; they'll still control the economy.

—*Alfredo Gómez Morales,*
former Peronist Economy Minister[1]

Even before Aramburu's body was found, Onganía's political future was extinguished—a point some suggested showed his government was not involved in the general's death. The man who planned to rule unchallenged for a decade was overthrown in a palace coup on June 8, 1970. The *New York Times* summed up Onganía's legacy: "All political groups were outlawed. The members of the Supreme Court were replaced. Congress was dissolved. Trade unions were suppressed. Harsh economic policies were imposed, which slowed inflation and restored stability to the peso. But the price in resentment was high."[2]

The change was meant to put an end to what army chief Lanusse called the regime's "sterile and exhausted corporatism." The challenge was reaching a broadly acceptable political settlement—with its implicit recognition of Peronism—that did not go beyond the limits of military tolerance.[3]

The armed forces commanders chose colorless Gen. Roberto Levingston as the country's leader. Picked nearly three weeks after Onganía's removal, Levingston was working in Washington as military attaché and head of Argentina's intelligence community. Mindful of their experience under Onganía, the service chiefs limited Levingston's power. Major legislative decisions and the appointment of ministers were subject to ratification by the heads of the three services.

Levingston began changing the regime's economic policies. A social "decompression," he reasoned, was needed before tackling the intractable political question. Gone were the days of austerity and open courtship of foreign companies.[4]

Levingston's moderately populist program found little popular support. The general was suspected of seeking to create his own political base, trying to bypass free elections and the agreed-upon consultation with his uniformed peers. Resistance from labor, a lack of military support, the political violence, and a surge in inflation conspired to make Levingston's term in office—just 248 days—little more than a footnote. History was being made elsewhere.

Chile: The Left Comes to Power

In neighboring Chile, a Marxist physician stunned local and international pundits by winning the presidency with a plurality of votes in elections held in early September 1970. Nowhere was the shock more strongly felt than in Washington. The victory by Salvador Allende infuriated President Nixon and National Security Adviser Henry Kissinger. Leftists had come to power in elections in a country where, as in Guatemala two decades earlier, U.S. companies had vast interests. Yet Chilean politicians, steeped in their country's democratic traditions, refused to deny Allende his victory. Although Allende's victory was cause for alarm for some, the armed forces, with a history of scrupulous respect for constitutional rule, refused to act to prevent his inauguration.

Into the breach went a team of CIA operatives known as "false flaggers"—for their phony Latin passports—to Santiago. There they met with a group of right-wing terrorists linked to a general who wanted to stage a "preventative" coup before Allende took office. Among the plotters was a small group called Patria y Libertad (Fatherland and Liberty). Nazi-sympathizing fanatics, they had begun dynamite attacks against electrical towers, shopping centers, and other targets across Chile in an effort to swing public opinion against the left. Enrique Arancibia Clavel, a Fatherland and Liberty paramilitary commander who later was involved in a spectacular assassination in Argentina, issued communiqués claiming credit for the attacks in the name of a phantom Peasant-Workers Brigade.

On October 17 the CIA promised the plotters 3 "clean" (stripped of all identification) machine guns, 6 tear-gas grenades, and 500 rounds of ammunition. Their target was army chief Gen. René Schneider, who both the agency and the coupmongers believed was a key roadblock in their efforts to put the military behind a coup. Because military esprit d'corps and respect for Schneider were so great, the dirty work was left to Fatherland and Liberty.

Schneider was to be kidnapped as he left an army dinner on October 19 and the incident made to look as though it was the work of leftists. He was then to be flown to Argentina, while the current president resigned and one of the conspiring military leaders took office. However, the attempt that night failed, as did a second the next day. "On the 22, the sterile machineguns—shipped by diplomatic pouch—were delivered to Valenzuela [a conspiring general]," *New York Times* reporter Seymour Hersh later wrote. "General Schneider was assassinated that day by a group of military officers and thugs, who did not use the American-supplied machineguns."[5]

The murder backfired. A broad spectrum of Chileans rallied to support their democratic institutions—if not their new president. Allende was inaugurated November 3. By year's end the plotters had found that the heat from Chilean authorities had grown too intense. Fatherland and Liberty's Enrique Arancibia Clavel crossed the Andes to bide his time in Buenos Aires.[6]

Perón or Death!

Representing a bygone, partly mythical Golden Era, Perón found that, in exile, he could be all things to all people—the persecuted tribune of an overwhelmingly dissatisfied Argentina. Many students, too young to remember his reign, found even more cause for their identification with him, as Perón's military successors were inexorably linked to worsening economic conditions. The generals sought to stifle dissent by suppressing politics; a generation of young people fought back. Some took up arms.

Ironically, the growing fealty to Peronism among students came in a sector that—a generation earlier—had been in the forefront of the struggle against Perón. The left, traditionally anti-Peronist, also saw that its future, if separated from the country's large working class, was bleak. From his post as editor of *CGTA*, the rebel labor confederation's newspaper, writer and social critic Rodolfo Walsh, a meditative figure with an infectious laugh, encouraged an alliance between the restless students and the more left-wing labor unions.

Onganía's "Argentine Revolution," noted one historian, had reduced governing

> to producing the necessary levels of repression, [that is] the disarticulation of the practices of all classes and groups that might question the strategy of development adopted by a minority. The military suppressed politics. Yet to suppress does not mean to annul. On the contrary, by eliminating politics' "natural" place, it became ubiquitous. There emerged new antibureaucratic and antiauthoritarian social antagonisms that shattered illusions about imposing military order.[7]

For two years, 1968–1969, small groups of young people joined together in various teams to form an incipient guerrilla movement. Armed bands took actions meant to provide weapons, financing, and recruitment. The following year they began imitating the Robin Hood–style tactics used by the Tupamaro guerrillas in neighboring Uruguay and by the followers of Carlos Marighela in Brazil. Among the factors they believed counted in their favor was the lack of an intelligence network within the student groupings, the demoralization of police forces "humiliated" by their subordination to the military in internal security, and the growing popular sympathy created by their actions.[8]

The year 1970 marked the reappearance of the Peronist Armed Forces, which had already tried to launch a rural insurgency. Two of their leaders, Carlos Caride and Miguel Domingo Zavala Rodríguez, were arrested and later joined the Montoneros. The Fuerzas Armadas de Liberación (FAL; Liberation Armed

Forces), a tiny, avowedly Marxist group also made its appearance, although it had little impact. Almost simultaneously four other groups emerged: the Argentine Revolutionary Movement, which quickly disappeared; the Fuerzas Armadas Revolucionarias (FAR; Revolutionary Armed Forces); the People's Revolutionary Army; and the Montoneros. In their first year, the organizations were responsible for more than 240 acts, most of which fell into the category of "armed propaganda."[9]

The ERP, whose leader was Mario Roberto Santucho, emerged from a decision taken in July at the Fifth Congress of the Marxist-Leninist Partido Revolucionario de los Trabajadores (PRT; Workers Revolutionary Party), held in an abandoned farm near the industrial city of San Nicolás in Santa Fe province. Frankly Trotsky-ite at the beginning, the ERP guerrillas held up the example of Che Guevara as their model. In keeping with the left's traditional distrust of Perón, who had sponsored strict anti-Communist measures in the mid-1940s, the ERP kept at arm's length from the other, Peronist-inspired groups. The parents of several ERP activists, including Santucho and Enrique Haroldo Gorriarán Merlo, were local Radical party leaders. A few had turned to armed struggle after Illia's overthrow.[10]

The first important military exploit of the FAR was the takeover of the Buenos Aires provincial town of Garín a month after a July 1970 commando raid and occupation of the small Córdoba provincial town of La Calera by the Montoneros and barely two weeks after the appearance of Aramburu's body. Led by Roberto Quieto and Marcos Osatinsky, the FAR was composed of a number of former Communist party activists, and its relationship to Peronism was more tentative than that of the Montoneros. Admirers of Che, FAR members were neither uncritically reverent about Perón's appeal nor his political machinations.[11]

The Montoneros and the FAP defined themselves as Peronist, identifying themselves with the years of the Resistance. Both emphasized their Christian background. With the notable exception of working-class Peronist José Sabino Navarro, who led the Montoneros in the period from the death of Abal Medina to his own in late 1971, almost all the first Montoneros came from the middle class and were, for the most part, linked to the Catholic church. (A U.S. embassy analysis from the period noted the difference between the Montoneros and their revolutionary peers. The FAP was described as "revolutionary Peronist," the FAR as "Marxist-leaning Peronists." The Montoneros, however, were "Peronist, ultra-Catholic nationalists.") Fernando Abal Medina and Carlos Gustavo Ramus came from religious families and were former Tacuara members who later joined the Catholic Student Youth (Juventud Estudiantil Católica). Right-wing activist Mario Firmenich, a Catholic nationalist of Croatian descent, had been hand-picked by Cardinal Caggiano to be president of a religious student group. Emilio Maza was a rightist leader of the Catholic University of Córdoba. However, two of the original group, Abal Medina and Norma Arrostito, received military instruction in 1967–1968 in Cuba.

The Montoneros appeared to represent something new in Argentine politics. Their earliest political involvement was traceable to the "direct action" groups of the far right such as the anti-Semitic Tacuara, whose inspiration came from the fascist Spanish Falange and which enjoyed close ties to the military intelligence services. Few of the first Montoneros came from the left. Almost none traced their own roots to Peronism. Yet curiously, as time went on, once hostile right-wing Catholic nationalist activists found common cause with the secular, pro-Castro left under the banner of Perón. How this transformation took place created some of the period's angriest polemics. Was the alchemy of change producing a new form of armed political movement? Was the transformation real, or was it merely a tactical alliance between competing groups trying to use one another for their own purposes? The remarkable longevity of at least one of the Montoneros' earliest militants, Mario Firmenich, who throughout his ascent as a guerrilla leader showed little affinity for the more poetic aspects of the struggle for social and political justice that characterized many Latin revolutionaries, suggested still another—largely overlooked—possibility. Were a few Montoneros—whose favored slogan was "Perón or Death!"—participating in a sinister sting operation run by one or more intelligence services?[12]

Aramburu's execution marked the Montoneros' first application of what they called "popular justice." The raid and occupation of La Calera signaled a taste for military tactics. The Montoneros betrayed an affinity for showy displays of military organization even when, as in late 1970, they could claim just a score of followers. Nonetheless, they boasted of having established "departments" of war, psychological action, maintenance, and documents. As the expanding and confused rebellion flourished, its resonance blurred the fact that the armed actions were those of small groups. Even the Montoneros, who later on demonstrated an impressive capacity to mobilize their sympathizers, were never able to translate that backing into effective irregular military support.[13]

In February 1971 the Montoneros sent Perón a letter explaining why they had murdered Aramburu. Aramburu's ambitions, they said, provided the system with an "escape valve." Things would only have appeared to change. "We are worried about a few reports reaching us, saying that with this act we have ruined your immediate political plans. We believe it is necessary, not only for us but for the entire movement, that you clarify this hypothetical contradiction between your plans and our actions."

The Montoneros also wanted to let Perón know the truth about another assassination being attributed to their group—that of textile union boss José Alonso. In the 1960s Alonso had opposed the political predations of El Lobo Vandor. However, left-wing Peronists viewed the textile leader as just another labor "bureaucrat." Alonso's murder, the Montoneros told Perón, was

committed by a commando group calling itself "Montonero Maza." This commando uses the name of our organization and the surname of our first comrade killed in combat; yet it does not belong to our organization nor do we know who they are. What is certain is that the people have joyously attributed the act to us. ... Given the consummated action, and seeing the people's satisfaction with the killing, we believe it is necessary to support it by maintaining our silence. In this way we accept the authorship of an act which the people attribute to us.[14]

Bonfire of Verities: The "Real" Perón

In replying to the Montoneros, Perón reassured them that their actions had not jeopardized his own plans. The campaign against the military, he said, needed to be waged on many fronts.[15]

The guerrillas' concern that their leader would give them a dressing down, or worse, read them out of the movement, was based on a misreading of Perón's history in exile. It was a mistake that reflected their own newcomers' status to Peronism. "The experience of the past fifteen years indicated Perón usually only disowned losers, or leaders who seemed to be gaining too much of a following in their own right," wrote historian Eduardo Crawley. "In late 1970, the Montoneros and other 'special formations' did not fit either category."

> This hardnosed, cynical approach to Perón's overlordship was never voiced in public, and only rarely in private. It was papered over with two myths. One, shared with the guerrillas' rivals within the peronista movement, was that of Perón's tactical genius. And there was some substance to it: Perón defined himself as a "conductor" rather than a politician; unencumbered by the principles that limit the actions of ideologues. Perón had proved himself a master of "the art of the possible," if only by keeping himself and his movement at the very centre of Argentine politics for a full decade-and-a-half after being ejected from power.

Another myth grew up that was peculiar only to the left:

> That there actually was a "real Perón" behind all his confusing, often contradictory moves. And this "real Perón," they claimed, was the revolutionary. ... That he did not voice this commitment more openly and wholeheartedly was due, they explained, to the fact that he was constrained by the nature of his movement, with the union and political leaders it had inherited. Perón's true nature was conditioned and distorted by the "circle of traitors" who hemmed him in. The *peronista* Left needed this myth, both to justify their declared allegiance to Perón and to rationalize their attacks on *peronista* union bosses and political chieftains. And many, if not all of them, came to believe it.[16]

Perón's ability to recast himself politically had been served by years of distortion of recent history by his enemies. By winning over a youthful vanguard, Perón gave his movement a dynamism that had flagged in the years of political wilderness. (A poll commissioned by the regime in early 1971 showed that in Buenos Aires, Rosario, and Córdoba—Argentina's three largest cities—49 percent of the respondents clearly affirmed their support for the guerrillas.)[17]

The faith of the young, their willingness to put the old slogan "My life for Perón" into practice, was in part based on the general's own hard sell. Perón claimed a return to Peronism would usher in a national, humanistic socialism equidistant from what he called "reactionary obstinacy" and the "influence of dogmatic international communist socialism." The struggle was a two-step process, with active opposition to the military regime preceding national reconstruction. "The armed forces' usurpation of power can only be resolved if action capable of dismantling that force is developed."[18]

In a message to the National Students Federation in 1971, Perón warned that the military regime was capable of violence "and for that reason we must prepare ourselves and act before whatever eventuality." Drawing the students into a web of alliances spanning the ideological spectrum, he ordered a two-track policy to be put into effect. Normal political tactics were to be used at one level and "special formations ... capable of confronting the cruel forms of dictatorship" at another. "Among the current forms of struggle it is necessary that our aboveground organizations work as energetically as possible in defense of our legal recognition, without which the country will march to a cruel struggle for which we must also be prepared," Perón added. *"For that reason, the importance of our special formations and their way of operating, as well as their slow predominance, the closer we come to violent struggle."* (Italics added)

Stefano Delle Chiaie: Black Terrorist

The tragedy about to befall Argentina was in some ways paralleled by events across the Atlantic in Italy—and for good reason. Not only were terror tactics used in one country perfected in the other but many of the terrorists knew each other and worked together.

As a parade of distinguished guests, longtime supporters, and hangers-on trooped to Perón's residence in the *madrileño* neighborhood of Puerta de Hierro, José López Rega, the Peróns' personal secretary, did his own form of networking. Many of his contacts were with a shadowy community of German Nazis, Italian and Yugoslavian Fascists, veterans of France's dreaded l'Organisation de l'Armée Secrète (OAS; Secret Army Organization), and other assorted right-wing terrorists. One López Rega visitor may have been a short (barely over five feet tall), wiry Italian named Stefano Delle Chiaie.[19]

Delle Chiaie was forced to flee to Madrid after participating in a murky coup attempt on December 7, 1970, against Italy's unstable center-right Christian Democratic government. The failed takeover was the work of Italian Fascists led by Junio Valerio Borghese, "the Black Prince." Delle Chiaie was also rumored to have been linked to a powerful radical right-wing cabal known as the "Rose of the Winds" that plotted to overthrow Italy's constitutional government in the 1960s.[20]

An exceptional organizer, Delle Chiaie's formative experiences included busting up Communist party headquarters, desecrating Jewish cemeteries, and torching union offices. By joining the neofascist Ordine Nuovo (New Order), Delle Chiaie sought a bigger stage. Using as its symbol a two-edged battle-ax, the group drew its ideological inspiration from Julius Evola, an SS collaborator during World War II. However, Ordine Nuovo's preference for talk over action soon led Delle Chiaie to found an offshoot, Avanguardia Nazionale (National Vanguard). The militants of Avanguardia Nazionale, one of its broadsheets declared, were for "man-to-man engagements. ... Before setting out our men are morally prepared, so that they learn to break the bones even of somebody who kneels down and cries."[21]

In the 1960s the Italian Communist party began shedding its postwar Stalinist image and made increasing gains at the ballot box. Delle Chiaie's shock troops found the direct action they were craving. The tightly disciplined group, never numbering more than 500 members, worked in league with the Italian intelligence services in infiltrating leftist organizations.[22]

Explosions at Padua University and at the Milan industrial fair in early 1969 were the work of Delle Chiaie's goons, although they were blamed on Italian anarchists. On August 8, eight trains were wracked by bombs. Dozens of lesser attacks were carried out in the same manner. As unease began to border on hysteria, cries sprang up for a law-and-order crackdown.

Three months after the train attacks, the demands grew to a crescendo, when a massive explosion tore through the Banca del Agricultura in Milan's historic Piazza Fontana. Fifteen people were killed. A bomb in Rome wounded fourteen others, and two more artifacts blew up in Piazza Venezia, causing extensive damage. The Servizio Informazione Difesa (SID; Defense Information Agency), Italy's main intelligence unit, knew within five days that Delle Chiaie's group was responsible for the attacks. It remained silent. Meanwhile, scores of leftists were arrested.[23]

Lanusse Takes Power

In March 1971 another uprising in Córdoba led the military junta to replace Levingston with Gen. Alejandro Lanusse, the army commander in chief. Lanusse had been a spokesman for ultraconservatives within the military. Once in power, however, he moved quickly toward the center in an effort to lessen political support for the insurgents. Ten days after becoming president, Lanusse lifted the ban, already widely ignored, on political party activity. The lieutenant general met with Chilean president Salvador Allende, defying U.S. efforts to isolate the Marxist-led government. Two unsuccessful revolts by hard-line sectors within the army allowed Lanusse to position himself as a "moderate" seeking to stave off the worst of the military reactionaries. The one-time anti-Peronist plotter eventually allowed Perón to visit Argentina. Evita's still-hidden remains were returned. And for the first time in eighteen years, free elections were promised.

Lanusse sought to create a broadened conservative consensus and tried to cajole the major parties into approving a single military-supported candidate—barely concealing his own desire for the nod. Lanusse also tried to guarantee the military a permanent voice in the new government, while ensuring that no "indiscriminate" amnesty of political prisoners be made. Implicit in this new political opening was an effort to resuscitate right-wing Peronist labor, in order to isolate the Montoneros and more radical leftist groups. This task was the job of Radical politician and Interior Minister Arturo Mor Roig.

In December 1970 Perón had undercut Levingston's political pretensions when the Peronists and other nominally banned parties issued a joint manifesto demanding an immediate return to civilian rule. By uniting Argentina's most important parties around a minimum program, Perón prevented the military from co-opting any of the parties for its own electoral purposes.

Perón then turned his attention to Lanusse. Although he talked about national unity, Perón avoided renouncing the use of violence, as Lanusse urged him to do. Instead, Perón used his "special formations"—the armed organizations—to trap the regime in a war of nerves. The armed forces could respond only with the shopworn device of proscription, this time using the transparent ruse that presidential candidates had to reside in the country before August 25, 1972.

Perón's temporizing on the issue of "armed politics" could not be attacked by opponents as mere opportunism. The appearance of the leftist guerrillas marked a growing counterterror carried out from the shadows of the military intelligence services. Leftist and Peronist students and union militants, some guerrillas, others not, were abducted—and usually tortured—with alarming frequency. Nearly a score simply "disappeared."[24]

Although their fate was a mystery to other Argentines, the U.S. embassy in Buenos Aires often knew the real story, as in the case of a FAR chief the military suspected of masterminding the assassination of an army officer. "On July 13, FAR leader Juan Carlos MAESTRE and his wife were abducted by Army officials in the Belgrano section of Buenos Aires," read a secret "Summary of Terrorist Activity—May 1–August 31, 1971," prepared by the U.S. embassy in Buenos Aires.

> Maestre was accidentally shot during a scuffle with his abductors and subsequently died. His body was discovered a few days later. … Mrs. Maestre has also been killed. … The Maestre case made headlines for several weeks and is still the subject of demands by leftist intellectual and political groups. It is widely believed by the public that the authorities were involved in the abduction. While the public does not have the whole story, it is generally known that Maestre was involved in subversive activity.
>
> Marcelo Aburnio VERD, a San Juan dentist, and his wife disappeared from their home on July 1. It is widely suspected that Verd was abducted by authorities, but thanks to public declarations by the FAL, it is also clear that he was active with subversive groups.

"Several kidnappings and an attempted kidnapping of suspected guerrilla leaders occurred during the period," noted another secret embassy "Summary" that covered activities between September 1 and November 30, 1971. "The most publicized kidnapping was that of Luis Enrique PUJALS who, [delete] was detained by Federal Police plainclothesmen on September 17, and later turned over to Army intelligence. The police and GOA officials have steadfastly publicly denied involvement or knowledge of his whereabouts but [delete] he was executed on October 23. Pujals was the top ERP leader in Santa Fe Province."[25]

A good part of Perón's strategy rested with the Peronist Youth, a group that had burst upon the national scene with unexpected energy and devotion. The young people turned out huge, enthusiastic crowds in the campaign for free elections and Perón's return. In recognition of their effort, Perón gave two youthful representatives seats on the prestigious Peronist Superior Council. His choices were themselves a message: Rodolfo Galimberti was linked to the "special formations." In early 1972 Galimberti warned old-style labor bosses they would be crushed "like cockroaches." Julián Licastro, an army lieutenant and the second choice, had left active service after having protested the repression during the Cordobazo.[26]

Perón offered the youths an honored place at his table, holding out the promise of *trasvasamiento generacional* (generational transfusion). Meanwhile he blasted the military and the labor "bureaucrats" within his own movement. "These military aren't soldiers, they're a bunch of gangsters," he taunted. "The only thing a military man is good for is to fill the space between the cap and the horse. ... What are officers but secondary students with four years of gymnastics?"[27]

The CGT leadership was called to Madrid for a tongue-lashing, with corrupt construction workers' boss Rogelio Coria singled out for abuse. "In union action there's a lot of bureaucracy," Perón complained. "I have seen them, the union leaders, defect at the most decisive moments of our political history. They have the illusion that they run the show, but this is not so: union activity only serves the defense of professional interests and cannot go any further. Politically there is very little they can run."[28]

Torture: The Only Alternative?

"The arrest without judicial charges and the frequent torture of persons suspected of left-wing subversive activities or contacts had been commonplace in Argentina," noted *New York Times* correspondent Juan de Onis in a May 1972 article entitled "Torture of a Woman Shakes Argentina."

Norma Morello had worked for eight years with Catholic groups urging social reform and organizing poor peasants and slum dwellers in the tobacco-growing province of Chaco. The teacher and rural activist was detained by the army on December 1, 1971. "Disappeared" for a month, Morello said she had been tortured for three days with electric shock and forced to go without sleep for more than two weeks. During that time, SIDE interrogators questioned her about "subversive activities" she said she knew nothing about. "Nothing has brought home the problem of political torture to Argentines more forcibly than the experiences of Norma Morello," de Onis wrote, describing her return to Chaco after months of imprisonment. "It was an extraordinary homecoming. A caravan of 100 farm trucks escorted Miss Morello from the city limits, where police checked documents, and 1,500 people attended a mass of thanksgiving for her release."[29]

"It can be said that the 'laboratory' for what occurred concerning the antisubversive fight in the second half of the 1970s (1975–1979) took place in those years (1970–1973) and that the methods and plans that the Army used in the first period were an extension and intensification of those it used a few years before, also with success, in the specifically military or police aspect of the problem," noted Argentine military historian Rosendo Fraga. "This type of doctrine ... had as a priority the obtaining of information as the only alternative to penetrating the rigid cellular organization of the terrorist organizations, the reason it became inevitable in operational and in military terms to oblige the prisoners to offer such information."[30]

A Chronicle of Two Assassinations

In 1972 the urban guerrilla groups carried out a series of daring kidnappings, bank robberies, and the occasional assassination of senior army and police officials. The surge in violence was not, for the most part, met with popular outrage because it was directed at sectors that were themselves unpopular. Even the ERP, the most potent of the insurgents, made the most of public sentiment, carrying out scores of Robin Hood–style "armed propaganda" operations in which multinational companies were obliged to make charity "donations" in slum areas in return for kidnapped executives. The Montoneros also capitalized on the prevailing mood, carrying out showy but often bloodless operations. They were careful not to attack military garrisons or to deliberately do battle with the army or police. "Favorite Montonero targets," noted British scholar Richard Gillespie, "were symbols of oligarchic privilege and opulence, such as the numerous Jockey Clubs, golf course buildings, and luxurious country clubs which were blasted."[31]

On April 10, 1972, two killings carried out by Marxist guerrillas shook the country's political establishment, providing, like that from the wide end of a telescope, a compact but sweeping view of the growing violence. That morning in Rosario, Gen. Juan Carlos Sánchez, the head of the country's powerful II Army Corps, was murdered as he was being driven to work. A fifty-two-year-old woman, who had momentarily replaced a relative who worked as a newspaper vendor at the scene of the attack, was also mortally wounded by the guerrillas. Sánchez was the third Argentine general to be killed by armed assailants this century—the others were Valle and Aramburu. In a communiqué left by the attackers, a joint commando group made up of the ERP and FAR claimed credit for the killing. The missive called Lanusse's electoral gambit a "farce." It blasted the military for keeping Argentina "under the rule" of the multinationals. It also named army and police stations where detainees were allegedly tortured.[32]

In at least one respect, Sánchez had been in agreement with his executioners. He, too, had opposed Lanusse's political program. Sánchez had carried out a ruthless but effective campaign against the insurgents. At the time he was killed, the general was reportedly readying a coup against Lanusse, whom he considered "soft" on subversion. According to one account, Lanusse's hurried pledges to bring the killers to justice and a personal trip to Rosario within hours of the murder reflected his determination to avoid the cloud of suspicion that hung over Onganía after Aramburu was kidnapped and killed.[33]

A few hours after Sánchez's murder, Oberdan Sallustro, the head of Argentina's FIAT subsidiary, was killed after being held nineteen days by ERP guerrillas. An Italian national and an admirer of Benito Mussolini, Sallustro was in charge of the automotive giant when FIAT plants in Córdoba and other cities were the centers of bitter labor conflicts.[34]

In exchange for Sallustro's life, the insurgents demanded the massive distribution of school supplies for needy children and the release of imprisoned guerrillas. Both the Italian government and top FIAT executives asked that negotiations be undertaken with the ERP. The Lanusse government refused, saying it would not parley with "common criminals." Spectacular dragnet operations were launched, unsuccessfully, across the country.[35]

Sallustro was killed when a police patrol happened upon a "people's prison" in the working-class neighborhood of Villa Lugano. As the civilian-dressed cops approached the house, they were met with a hail of gunfire. Half an hour—and more than 500 gunshots—later, three of the four ERP members inside had escaped. One of the police was critically injured. Sallustro, his hands tied behind his back, had been shot twice in the chest and once in the neck, apparently killed by police bullets.[36]

In Madrid news of the assassinations caused Perón to worry about the effect Sallustro's death might have both on European investment in Argentina and on the talks with the military about elections. Asking supporters to refrain from violence, the seventy-six-year-old general expressed his "deep sorrow" over the deaths. "What's happened pains me very much," he said, "although I'm not surprised that such a level of violence has been reached, given the state the country is in."[37]

Massacre at Trelew

The Lanusse government's last-ditch effort at building a consensus with which to isolate the Peronists fell apart on August 22, 1972. The week before, twenty-five political prisoners from the Rawson prison in desolate, wind-swept Patagonia— all members of armed organizations—had broken out of the maximum security institution, despite the refusal of Mario Firmenich, by then a Montonero leader, to cooperate outside the prison. Six, including Santucho and Gorriarán Merlo of the ERP and Osatinsky and Quieto of the FAR, succeeded in boarding a hijacked airliner and fleeing, first to Allende's Chile, then to Cuba. The rest, victims of a snafu in making a planned rendezvous, were recaptured and placed under the custody of the navy.[38]

On August 17 the Peronist party demanded that Interior Minister Mor Roig take steps to ensure that no harm came to the prisoners. Irritated by what he interpreted as Peronist propaganda, Mor Roig brushed off the request. Five days later sixteen of the detainees held at the Admirante Zar navy airbase in the southerly city of Trelew were executed, including Santucho's wife and the girlfriends of Gorriarán and Montonero leader Fernando Vaca Narvaja. The military claimed they were killed while trying to escape. However, three leftists survived—thanks to the arrival on the scene of military men who did not take part—and later recounted what the public suspected. (The regime did not help its case when it sent a detachment of Federal Police to steal three bodies lying in state in a local Peronist party headquarters in Buenos Aires in order to keep autopsies from being performed. Advised by a former head of the French OAS, a group of *federales* led by antiguerrilla specialist Alberto Villar used an armored car to batter down the door of the Peronist office. The bodies were spirited away for immediate burial.) For many, the killings—known as "the massacre of Trelew"—became a rallying cry.[39]

From his Spanish exile Perón condemned the deaths. So, too, did a young Radical politician and lawyer from the Buenos Aires provincial town of Chascomús, who was making human rights and the respect for legality his standard. "The deaths of sixteen young Argentines imprisoned for political reasons," said Raúl Alfonsín, a parliamentary deputy under Illia, twice imprisoned by Onganía, and in 1972 the leader of a left-wing reform faction within the Radicals, "is an insult to the public's conscience and demands that all civic groups speak out urgently. The constitution of a citizen's commission ought to be demanded without delay, in order to investigate these grave deeds that tear at the nation's soul."[40]

The Long Trip Back

Two months after the events at Trelew, Perón began the long trip from Spain to Argentina, by way of Rome. He gave a fair appraisal of his continuing popularity: "It's not that we were so good, but those who came after us were so bad that they made us seem better than we were."[41]

While in Italy, Perón met with Premier Giulio Andreotti. He also sought to see Pope Paul VI in an effort to formally repair the damage done by the church-state conflict in 1955. The Vatican put Perón off, wary of awarding him the political capital such a meeting might have meant. Perón's entourage was chauffeured around by Giancarlo Elía Valori, an Italian influence peddler close to Greece's ruling colonels. Officially described as the Argentine's "spokesman" in the country, Valori, who had written an article in López Rega's far-right magazine *Las Bases*, extolling the internal security functions of the military, was recommended to Perón by French-Italian industrialist Luchino Revelli Beaumont. The latter was in turn a front man for an Italian named Licio Gelli, a shadowy figure with an ascending star in Italian Masonry.[42] Perón arrived in Argentina aboard a chartered Alitalia flight. More than 35,000 troops, along with tanks and artillery, had been deployed around Ezeiza International Airport. Their presence impeded Perón's being welcomed by throngs of well-wishers who had turned out despite a pouring rain. Hundreds of thousands of Peronist loyalists were not to be put off, however. In the following days and nights they trooped before Perón's home in suburban Vicente López. The climate of exultation portended their coming electoral triumph.

7

Perón Returns (1973)

> With a generally acceptable cabinet and a policy of national reconciliation the
> Cámpora government shows encouraging signs of following a moderate
> course and respecting individual liberties.
> —*Report by U.S. Ambassador John Davis Lodge, May 1973*

For nearly a month, from November 17 to December 14, 1972, myriad public
and private efforts were made on Perón's behalf to lift Lanusse's residence requirement. The Frente Justicialista de Liberación Nacional (FREJULI; Justicialist
[Peronist] Front for National Liberation), the political front controlled by the
Peronists, threatened to abstain, as the Peronists had done in 1963, if Perón's
name was kept off the ballot. But when the Radicals announced that they planned
to participate in the election, Perón found he had won the war but risked losing
the most important battle: He was too old to watch another candidate win the
election with 23 percent of the vote, as Illia had done.[1]

Unable to change the residency law, Perón designated a presidential ticket
made up of his personal delegate, Héctor Cámpora, an avuncular former president of the Chamber of Deputies, and Popular Conservative chief Vicente Solano
Lima. (As in 1951, the Radicals were led into battle by Ricardo Balbín, a tired hack
who had just trounced reform candidate Raúl Alfonsín in a battle for control of
the party.) In choosing Cámpora, Perón picked a man of unquestionable loyalty
but few political skills. One joke had Perón calling out to Cámpora from the
shower, asking what time it was. "Any time you wish, my general," came the reply.

Jokes about Cámpora's loyalty were somewhat unfair. "Whoever was the candidate and later president would have obeyed Perón's orders to the last detail,"
said Juan Manuel Abal Medina, the young secretary-general of the Peronist
movement and the brother of the late Montonero founder. "The degree of adhe-
sion to Perón personally is difficult to understand if you didn't live it. ... There
were such extremes in many sectors of the movement that a casual word [by
Perón] about an author determined the literary tastes of entire sectors."[2]

Despite such unconditional loyalty, Perón found he lacked a political apparatus that he could count on. The burden of organizing for the elections fell to a

tiny group of aides led by Abal Medina, who was not a Montonero. Candidates for 3,600 posts were selected in just fifteen days.[3]

Cámpora's platform was one of industrial reactivation, an increase in the workers' wages, and freedom for political prisoners. Although other sectors begrudgingly aided Cámpora, it was the Peronist Youth that provided his campaign with verve and energy. The chance that Perón would die with the Peronist left in power worried labor bosses and orthodox Peronists, under attack for years of corruption and connivance with successive military regimes.[4]

López Rega Rising

It was López Rega's fortune that no one was ever quite able to explain how the cloying sycophant had scaled so far. If the former police corporal later behaved as if his power emanated from an unseen source, his pretensions were honestly held. Like Perón, he was a devotee of the spiritist Anael, the Masonic name of the Brazilian Menotti Carnicelli. Perón, who maintained an ambiguous interest in the occult, had been a friend of Anael's since the early 1950s.[5]

López Rega's involvement with the cults and a letter from Anael later helped him meet Isabel Perón and, in 1966, gain entrance to Perón's residence in Madrid. López Rega published several works on the occult, all characterized by their dense, mostly unintelligible prose. *Esoteric Astrology: Secrets Unveiled* was the longest of his books. In it he claimed the book was written by God and that the Archangel Gabriel had descended from the heavens to help him—López Rega—put the words to paper as he slept.

Isabel had quickly adopted the valet with cold blue eyes as her spiritual mentor. Perón, however, alternately treated him with tolerant amusement and open disdain. Sometimes his mood turned to fury as when, in 1967, Perón discovered that López Rega was selling a "rejuvenating tonic" in Brazil with the general's picture on its label. In 1972 a series of articles written by López Rega in his magazine, *Las Bases*—"the official organ of Peronism"—caused a brief scandal. The magazine, which boasted of having Perón as a "special contributor," praised Hitler in veiled language and sought to refurbish the image of Nazism.[6]

López Rega's ambitions seemed to cause him no lasting harm, perhaps because no one took him seriously. But as Perón's health began to fail, a physical and psychological dependence common to many elderly and their nurses developed between the general and his valet. According to Abal Medina, Perón's physical state rapidly declined between December 15, 1972, the day he left Argentina, and March 1: "We had working sessions that didn't go beyond two hours, at the end of which he was tired. In that time ... López Rega and Isabel began taking on roles they did not have until 1972. Neither had participated in any political meetings held in the general's house. But from March on, Isabel and López Rega became part of every meeting. So much so that it powerfully called our attention."[7]

An Unholy Alliance

In March 1973 the Cámpora–Solano Lima ticket won more than 49 percent of the votes, far outdistancing their nearest rivals, Balbín's Radicals, and was declared victorious. In the next two months hard-line military officers toyed with the idea of a coup. U.S. Ambassador John Davis Lodge in a confidential report to Washington (later partially released in an excised form) wrote that "ironically," these hard-liners "became more uneasy as election day approached, and, at times, appeared to have formed an unholy alliance with the terrorists by perpetrating, (delete) several strikes against political leaders and security forces during the campaign period in an effort to force the cancellation of elections and thereby prevent an increasingly probable Peronist victory." A separate cable by Lodge took note that, "in a number of cases of bombings and at least one kidnapping, (*Crónica* publisher Héctor GARCÍA), intelligence reports suggest the guilt rests more accurately on the shoulders of hardliners within the military government" seeking to force cancellation of the elections. (In 1974 the leftist magazine *Liberación* carried a two-page article claiming the kidnapping, code named Operación Poniatowski, was the work of the ERP–22 de Agosto [August 22] splinter faction.) The high command, however, understood that by annulling the election results they risked provoking an open insurrection.[8]

The leftist armed organizations, too, continued their onslaught. On May 22 mechanics union leader Dirk Kloosterman was murdered by a faction of the FAP. On May 23 two businessmen—a lumber dealer in the Río Paraná delta and the head of Coca-Cola in Córdoba—were kidnapped, though the latter abduction for ransom may have been the work of labor elements unconnected to the guerrillas. On May 24 an attempted kidnapping of a Swift executive was foiled, and a Ford Motor official was nabbed in La Plata. After an ultimatum was allegedly issued by ERP–August 22, Ford handed out $1 million dollars in food and clothing to slum dwellers. The guerrillas later denied responsibility for the kidnapping.[9]

Cámpora was inaugurated on May 25, 1973. More than 1 million people turned out to give a raucous farewell to what most hoped would be Argentina's last military government. Although the crowds were large and mostly friendly, some in the crowd attacked military men waiting to parade with cans of spray paint, and other officers were bathed in spittle. The crowd also kept U.S. Secretary of State William Rogers and Uruguay's right-wing autocratic president Juan María Bordaberry from getting to the presidential palace. Chile's Salvador Allende and Cuban President Osvaldo Dorticos were met with wild enthusiasm.[10]

Without waiting for an amnesty bill to receive final sanction by a willing Congress, youthful leftists took several jails by storm, seeking to liberate their guerrilla comrades. Three charter airliners brought former prisoners from the Patagonian prison of Rawson to Buenos Aires. "There weren't any problems," said one defense lawyer who accompanied the former prisoners, "except for those caused by a military man named Galtieri, who tried to put a few conditions on the release of our comrades."[11]

The proposed amnesty enjoyed broad political support. In several provinces right-wing Peronist governors treated the freed prisoners as liberated freedom fighters—which to many people they were. Nevertheless the precipitate action by the leftists proved to be a boon for the Peronist right and their allies in the military, who portrayed the event as emblematic of the chaos and lawlessness that seemed to play midwife to the birth of Cámpora's government.[12]

During the next twenty-five days there was a lull in the violence. Most remaining members of the oldest guerrilla group, the Peronist Armed Forces, laid down their weapons forever; the larger Montoneros and Revolutionary Armed Forces refrained from most armed actions for more than a year. The Peronist Youth concentrated on its own controversial, though mostly nonviolent, brand of activism and upheaval. Officials seen as collaborators with the ancien régime were ousted. Colleges, universities, and factories were occupied. Meanwhile the unions, led by CGT chief José Rucci, tried to regain the initiative lost to the Peronist Youth during the electoral campaign. The right staged its own takeovers, often of radio stations.

The Peronist right's fury was also stoked by a speech made in mid-June on national television by the Marxist ERP. Ignoring the government's obvious legitimacy, a masked Mario Roberto Santucho declared that Perón was old, doddering, and nonrevolutionary—reasons enough for his guerrillas to press ahead in armed struggle.[13]

Argentina was paralyzed, its government—pushing ahead with a mildly reformist agenda—a spectator to the conflict among the political and social forces which claimed Peronism's mantle. Peronist secretary-general Abal Medina called on the feuding factions to put an end to the takeovers but was ignored. So was a plea from Cámpora's interior minister.

In one of his first acts after taking office, the new minister had sharply criticized the Federal Police for its brutality and announced the force's political police unit would be disbanded. The flawed intelligence reports prepared by his security services in the following weeks kept the minister in the dark about the difficult days ahead.[14]

A Violent Homecoming

Although the historical record about Perón's plans for the presidency is murky, it is hard to believe he anointed the malleable Cámpora as anything other than a caretaker. It is likely that, because Perón did not want to fall prisoner to one of the Peronist factions, he shied away from directly taking power in a palace-type coup. New presidential elections would catapult him into the Casa Rosada, but through the front door. By the time Perón shut his suitcases in Madrid, however, plotting by right-wing Peronists was already under way. A five-man commission had been given the task of mobilizing the well-wishers for the homecoming. Four were from Peronism's hard right: José Rucci, Jorge Osinde, metalworkers' boss Lorenzo Miguel, and neofascist Norma Kennedy; the fifth was Juan Abal Medina.[15]

The security detail was left in charge of retired Lieutenant Colonel Osinde. Once counterespionage chief of the army intelligence service, Osinde later won fame as a torturer with the Special Section of the Federal Police. In 1971 Perón named Osinde his defense liaison; as such Osinde handled the exile's contacts with the military. Lanusse, meanwhile, had entrusted the secretive hard-liner to convince Perón to opt out of the elections in return for economic favors.

Cámpora had named López Rega to the post of social welfare minister, a position rich with symbolism from the days of Evita. In turn, El Brujo named Osinde secretary of sports and tourism. As Perón prepared his return, Osinde, who exchanged ten telexes a day with López Rega, organized the minister's armed guard. He included two former cops, Juan Ramón Morales and Rodolfo Almirón (the former the murderer of crime boss El Jailefe Fleitas in 1962), into the ministry's detail. He also planned for June 20.[16]

Osinde's plan was simple. The police were displaced from their task of providing security. In their stead, López Rega and Osinde organized a private army of more than 3,000 men. The podium from which Perón was to speak was occupied by members of the far-right Concentración Nacional Universitaria (CNU; National University Concentration) and the Alianza Libertadora Nacionalista (ALN; Nationalist Liberating Alliance). They carried machine guns, carbines, sawed-off shotguns, and rifles with telescopic sights. Right-wing Peronist shock troops from the Juventud Sindical Peronista (JSP; Peronist Labor Youth) and the Organization Commando (C de O; Comando de Organización) also took part, as did the "hawks"—civilian members of the police intelligence services.[17] By taking charge of security, López Rega and Osinde turned the tables on the left. The armed organizations and the Peronist Youth had planned to occupy the front ranks near the podium in order to impress Perón with their massive numbers of supporters.[18]

On June 20, Flag Day, millions of supporters—perhaps as many as 3 million— flocked to Ezeiza airport to welcome Perón. It was the largest rally in Argentine history. People poured in from the federal capital and the sprawling industrial neighborhoods ringing Buenos Aires and from far-flung provinces. Many spent the night in sleeping bags or huddled around campfires, trying to get a good spot from which to catch a glimpse of Perón. When the sun broke through the clouds shortly after noon, spirits soared even more.

At 2:30, the area around the airport was a festive sea of banners and flags. Musicians from the National Symphony Orchestra played the Peronist March from the rostrum. A column bearing posters and banners announcing themselves as members of the FAR and Montoneros approached the podium. Suddenly, they were met by a hail of machine-gun fire.

Many of the leftists had come armed with chains, a weapon used in the fights that sometimes broke out at Peronist rallies; a few, in charge of peripheral security for the columns of marching people, carried guns. Nevertheless, the gunfire continued intermittently for two and one-half hours. The scene was one of pandemonium: Bodies dropped from trees, and the master of ceremonies, on the verge of tears, pleaded for calm. People ran for cover or fell—dead, wounded, or terrorstricken—to the ground. In the confusion, the rightists fired on one another. Meanwhile someone released doves from the podium.[19]

One gang leader, the brother of an army colonel, later bragged he had lynched "two or three lefties" at Ezeiza. Rucci's chief bodyguard participated in the torture of "captured leftists" in the Ezeiza International Hotel. There, in room 118, municipal physicians found the walls splattered with blood. A business partner of Osinde directed the firefight from the podium, as well as the torture later in the hotel.[20]

At least 20 people were killed and 400 people wounded in the melee. Perón's Boeing jet was diverted to the Morón air force base west of Buenos Aires. That night, appearing on nationwide television and radio, Perón "begged a thousand pardons" from his supporters. He decided to avoid the mass rally, he said, in order to prevent further disorders.[21]

Osinde's men had been instructed to stage a shoot-out, then blame "Trotskyite infiltrators" who were planning an attack on Perón. Osinde's troops were then to try to rally part of the multitude to the Plaza de Mayo, in front of the Casa Rosada, in order "save" Perón and force Cámpora from office. Nostalgia had given way to the preposterous. The plotters wanted to replicate the events of October 17, 1945, when the workers "rescued" the jailed Perón and carried him to the presidential palace.

Tapes of monitored radio conversations held by SIDE and the Federal Police on June 20 confirmed López Rega's devious invention. There was never any plot to kill Perón. Nor was there an effort by the ERP and Montoneros to take over the presidential palace, as Osinde and his followers later alleged. The Peronist left had come to Ezeiza expecting a bloody rumble; the right had come armed for war.[22]

"Commander" Licio Gelli

When Perón returned to Argentina, Italian Masonic lodge master Licio Gelli came with him to a homecoming of sorts, too. Gelli had lived in Buenos Aires, a postwar haven for Italian Fascists, between 1946 and 1948. Among the circles in which he moved was that of the men of Mussolini's secret service, protected in Argentina by the local FIAT subsidiary. Gelli himself had joined Franco's fascist forces as a volunteer during the Spanish civil war before becoming a minor official in Il Duce's Italy.[23]

In the 1950s and early 1960s Gelli made his fortune in the Italian textile industry. He also spun a web of contacts within Italian Masonry that put him at the center of a huge, hidden network. A maniac for order and neatness, Gelli had an obscure, ambiguous way of talking—almost esoteric, with frequent metaphors about "the Spirit" and "the Light"—that shielded a cunning and zeal for power. Petroleum, arms trafficking, and high finance were special interests.

By the time he began helping Perón, Gelli was intimately involved with Italian military and intelligence officers suspected of allowing the untrammeled flight of neofascist terrorists from the peninsula. The terrorists, and their military protectors, were persistently tied to conspiracies against Italian democratic government. Later, when Gelli's secret empire came crashing down, Italy's press would speak— with reason—of a veritable "state within a state."[24]

There are various versions of when and how Gelli met Perón for the first time. The general's extended visit to Rome before his 1972 homecoming to Argentina had been conducted with Gelli's patronage. A close relationship grew between Perón and Gelli—and even more so between the Italian and López Rega—in the months before Perón's final return.[25]

Shortly before the March 1973 elections Perón, Isabelita, Cámpora, and López Rega traveled to Rome, where they stayed in suites reserved by Gelli at his own posh hotel, the Excelsior, on the Via Veneto. Aided by Gelli, Perón and Cámpora made numerous political and financial contacts. "It is advisable that you prepare lists of names of magistrates, military men, and doctors, enrolled or not in our institution," wrote Gelli in a letter to a key confidant, an Argentine diplomat, in Buenos Aires. "I am now beginning to see the possibility of placing us even further in the heart of the government, with a greater number of posts."[26]

A month after the Rome meeting Cámpora and Gelli met in Buenos Aires. In letters to his key Argentine contact, Gelli claimed both Perón and Cámpora asked of the lodge "future collaboration, for the duration of the government." Later the names of eight people were suggested by the lodge for top posts in Perón's third government, including that of foreign and social welfare ministers and Federal Police chief. Among the names offered were those of a rear admiral (Juan Questa) and a notoriously anti-Peronist army general (Carlos Suárez Mason). Only one— Air Force Brig. Osvaldo Cacciatore—was turned down.[27]

In 1973 alone, members of Gelli's Propaganda Due (P-2) Masonic lodge or men enjoying his confidence took posts as the head of the Social Welfare Ministry (López Rega) and the Foreign Ministry (Alberto Vignes), as the president of the Argentine Chamber of Deputies—and later provisional president of the republic (Raúl Lastiri)—as ambassadors at the heads of several embassies (Uruguay and Italy), in top judicial offices, and in important military positions.[28] There was also speculation, never proven, that at year's end, Gelli and López Rega were also able to pressure Perón into picking Rear Adm. Emilio Massera as naval commander in chief. The unusual selection of Massera, an intelligence officer and a P-2 member, for the post meant the forced retirement of six senior admirals and eleven vice and rear admirals.[29]

In López Rega, Gelli found a willing partner. The Italian was initially deferential to the point of effusion when dealing with the new social welfare minister. ("I would be pleased to be your 'Kissinger,'" Gelli said in a June 3 letter to El Brujo, "hoping my work will be useful.") His voice soon changed to one of authority, if not command. The Grand Master even counseled Perón on matters of state. In a July letter, Gelli suggested strong control of leftist activities and close collaboration with paramilitary groups to maintain public order. Perón, either in amusement or in earnest, called Gelli "mi comandante" (my commander).[30]

A Coup from the Right

As most of the press blamed Cámpora and his young assistants for the tragedy at Ezeiza, the plotting by López Rega gained urgency when, on June 28, Perón suffered a slight heart attack. The public was told only that he had a bad case of the flu, but among his inner circle doubts grew about Perón's chances of living out a presidential term. Nevertheless, by July 6, Perón and López Rega had pressured Cámpora and his vice president, Vicente Solano Lima, into resigning. The influence of El Brujo and Isabelita, the former cabaret dancer he held under his spell, increased exponentially.[31]

The constitution stipulated that the Senate president, Alejandro Díaz Bialet, was next in line for the presidency, and it was he who should have organized new elections, as Perón had wished. However, with Perón's acquiescence López Rega forced Díaz Bialet to take an unscheduled trip abroad. Chamber of Deputies President (and P-2 member) Raúl Lastiri—López Rega's son-in-law and a man who seven years before worked as a waiter in downtown Buenos Aires—provisionally replaced Cámpora.[32]

Cámpora's forty-nine days in power were portrayed as a necessary prelude to Perón's return to the presidency. Yet the crude manner in which he was dumped contradicted the official version. Cámpora had always been ready to resign the presidency; his public humiliation gave lie to the sanitized story. The left could hardly conceal the rout when Cámpora's cabinet presented its pro forma resignation. Only the offers by leftists Esteban Righi, the interior minister, and Foreign Minister Juan Carlos Puig were accepted. The defeat was ratified when Perón picked Isabelita, a favorite of orthodox labor, as his presidential running mate.[33]

"How was it that Cámpora and the youth miscalculated the situation?" asked the Catholic magazine *Critério*.

> In believing that the group surrounding Perón was using him, and not the other way around; in believing that Perón is a prisoner forcibly isolated from "his people"; in believing that, in Perón's eyes, López Rega is a traitor and Osinde a murderer; in believing, finally, that they (Cámpora and the youth) were called to administer the leader's charisma. In a movement that professes "verticalism," that sort of mistake is paid for dearly. But here it was not only an internal faction of Peronism that lost; the country lost too, because institutions cannot be played with as unscrupulously as this.[34]

Among those who saw the power play for what it was, was Raúl Alfonsín. The maneuver, he said, was "a coup from the Right."[35]

* * *

Mid-1973 was a time of confusion for some and of definition for others. Was it, for example, mere disinformation reports the U.S. embassy received from "reliable embassy labor sources" that claimed Cámpora had given a green light to metalworkers union leader Lorenzo Miguel to organize "an all out anti-terrorist and anti-trotskyite campaign" run out of the union's headquarters and with former Peronist Youth leader Rodolfo Galimberti at its head? Where did the loyalties of each of the armed forces lie? At the head of the army was Gen. Jorge Raúl Carcagno, an officer whose loyalties to the constitutional order were unquestioned and whose sights were trained on foreign economic enemies rather than internal political foes. Montoneros and army troops joined together to carry out civic action tasks in Buenos Aires province. Yet the Defense Ministry had changed little, if at all, since Lanusse surrendered power. Control of the military rested with the generals, not civilians. And what did it mean that while Carcagno was extending a hand to the Peronist left and ordering an end to internal surveillance, army intelligence insisted that the Montoneros were more dangerous than the ERP, given their greater popular support, and began to prepare for what it considered an inevitable confrontation?[36]

Allende Falls

On September 11, 1973, less than three months after the military brought the curtain down on Uruguay's long period of democratic rule, another of Argentina's neighbors succumbed to a military coup. Aided by the hostility of the Nixon administration and the covert action of the CIA, officers led by Gen. Augusto Pinochet overthrew Socialist President Salvador Allende. Hundreds of Allende supporters and others were hunted down and killed. Many detainees were tortured and executed in Santiago's National Stadium. Except for Argentina, from Colombia south the entire continent became a wall of military regimes, mostly of a brutal right-wing stripe.

American intelligence agencies themselves admitted that Allende's government posed no threat to U.S. national security. Within three days of his election, the CIA told the White House the United States "had no vital interests within Chile; [that] the world military balance of power would not be significantly altered by an Allende regime, and [that] an Allende victory in Chile would not pose any likely threat to the peace of the region."[37]

Nixon would hear none of it. Weapons ranging from a nearly airtight economic embargo to the bribing of journalists to giving a sympathetic wink to anti-

Allende terrorists were unsheathed. One Kissinger aide said that because Allende's was both a democratically elected and leftist government, the secretary of state viewed it as all the more dangerous. If Communists in Chile peacefully participated in government and then accepted their being voted out in a subsequent election, he reasoned, the example could serve as a dangerous precedent in a country like Italy, where the Communist party was growing.[38]

Shortly before Allende was overthrown, a delegation of Chilean military officers had secretly let Perón know of their coup plans and received his tacit approval. "What happened in Chile shows that Allende fell victim to his sectarianism, to policies which tended to excesses," said Perón a few weeks later. "We apply the law of counter-weights." Asked about the guerrilla threat in Argentina, Perón said he was confident it would be controlled. "Chile has taught us many things— either the guerrillas stop perturbing the country or we will be obliged to make them do so with all the means at our disposal, which are not a few, believe me."[39]

Montoneros, FAR Merge

Perón's return and his landslide victory in the presidential race in September had given rise to hopes that years of political instability and economic decline were at an end. On August 30 more than one million people rallied in support of the Perón-Perón ticket. The demonstration, called by the CGT, went off without incident. Columns of Peronist Youth and union supporters paraded by Perón's viewing stand in apparent harmony, if not unity.

During the first days of September Roberto Quieto, chief of the Marxist-oriented FAR, and Mario Firmenich, head of the more nationalist Montoneros, met with Perón and promised their continuing allegiance and an end to paramilitary operations. On October 12 the two groups merged under the name Montoneros, with Firmenich and Quieto its principal leaders. Although the FAR had fewer members, the merger signaled a political shift to the left by the Montoneros. Yet, recalled one Montonero leader, the merger gave a greater impression of unity between the two groups than actually was the case, the result being syncretism rather than fusion.[40]

For many Argentines the signs portended the country's restoration to what they considered its rightful place among the front-ranking nations of the world. Events soon overshadowed such optimism. Parapolice squads stepped up their campaign of intimidation and murder against progressive and leftist politicians and activists. Following its decision to continue the armed struggle against the constitutional government and a violent, if unsuccessful, attack on a Buenos Aires military installation, the ERP was declared illegal. The Marxist guerrillas kept up their own campaign of violence. And—two days after the ERP was banned— José Rucci was killed.

Perón: "Cut Off at the Feet"

By the time of his death one of the most powerful men in the country, the diminutive Rucci had come up in labor politics the hard way—through the Resistance and up through the ranks. A one-time aide to Augusto Vandor, metalworkers union loyalist Rucci became CGT secretary-general after El Lobo was murdered in 1970.[41]

Rucci's selection to the top post marked the beginning of the metalworkers' dominance of labor. Unlike many of his peers, Rucci was unconditionally loyal to Perón. Like a grainy daguerreotype, Rucci's image was forever burnished in the public's mind in a photo taken that rainy day in 1972 when Perón returned to Argentina for the first time since 1955. Bolting from the crowd of well-wishers, it had been Rucci who gave the returning legend a bear hug, while hastening to cover him protectively with an umbrella.

Profoundly nationalist, Rucci promoted "direct action" by armed groups. Internal elections, labor conflicts, run-ins with left-wing unionists—all required what he termed definitive solutions. Two weeks before Cámpora's election, he organized his own shock troops, the Peronist Labor Youth (JSP), complete with its own shooting range in the CGT headquarters. When Alfonsín criticized the dumping of Cámpora, he called the Radical a "Trotskyite."[42]

Federal Police chief Miguel Angel Iñíguez attributed Rucci's assassination to the ERP, which reportedly had sent him death threats in the months before his murder. The ERP, however, normally "signed off" on their killings with communiqués. They also almost always avoided attacks on labor leaders, no matter how conservative. They denied killing Rucci.[43]

At first the Montoneros publicly lamented Rucci's death. Inside the organization, however, Firmenich put out the word that the group was responsible for the killing, a claim made public a year later when the Montoneros "assumed" responsibility for Rucci's death—echoing the stance they had taken in 1970 when textile union boss Alonso was killed. "The most important thing so far as Montonero-labour relations were concerned," noted one historian, "was that the Montoneros were generally believed to be Rucci's assassins."[44]

A few high-ranking police officials later privately cast doubt on theories of guerrilla involvement. For them the "hit" seemed too sophisticated. Shortly after his death the army intelligence service and the Federal Police told a top U.S. intelligence agent that Rucci had not been killed by the Montoneros. He was, they said, the victim of rival "orthodox" Peronists who wanted to disburse his "empire." The Federal Police had recovered a .357 Smith & Wesson magnum dropped by one of Rucci's assassins. The FBI traced the weapon from the Smith & Wesson factory to a gun dealer in New York, who had sold it to an Aerolíneas Argentinas stewardess who had bought the weapon for a friend in the military. The Federal Police ran up against a stone wall in their investigation and were apologetic for not solving the murder.[45]

"They've cut me off at the feet," Perón croaked sadly as he viewed Rucci's body at the CGT headquarters. In many people's minds, and perhaps in Perón's, *they* were the Peronist left.[46]

No one gained more from Rucci's murder than López Rega. The killing stiffened Perón's resolve to put an end to the "special formations." The day after Rucci's assassination anonymous "anti-Marxist commandos" killed a Buenos Aires university professor and Peronist Youth member with ties to the armed left. Later that same month a leftist lawyer in Rosario was murdered. In Resistencia the Organization Command, led by a parliamentary deputy, attacked a university dining hall.

On Tuesday, October 1, provisional President Lastiri and Interior Minister Benito Llambí called a meeting of Peronist provincial governors. There a "reserved document" from Perón was distributed. An "order" for the rank-and-file, it declared that "Marxist terrorist and subversive groups have declared war against our organization and our leadership" and demanded that all those claiming to be Peronists participate in the counterattack: "All methods that are considered efficient will be utilized, in each place and opportunity." To carry out the struggle, the faithful were to use "all the elements available to the state, in order to foil the enemy's plans and punish him to the fullest."[47]

In the Buenos Aires provincial town of Santos Lugares, the Peronist Youth Superior Council office was destroyed by the Organization Command. The Nationalist University Concentration and other far-right Peronists sacked the University of Buenos Aires law school offices. Among the attackers was Alejandro Giovenco, one of the rightist thugs at Ezeiza.

A left-wing Graphics Federation worker was wounded and "disappeared" after having been abducted before witnesses in a Ford Falcon belonging to an official of López Rega's Social Welfare Ministry. A husband-and-wife team of defense lawyers had recently denounced Isabel Perón's brother as the founder of a clandestine repressive unit. The couple, left-wing Peronists and counsel to many political prisoners, were machine-gunned to death soon after at a railway station. When the assassin was apprehended by two policemen who happened upon the scene, he admitted being linked to the metalworkers union as well as to working for the Social Welfare Ministry. "I've been following him [one of the victims] since yesterday," he declared, "and received orders to kill him because he belonged to the ERP."

After such an explicit confession, the killer was released.[48]

Perón Inaugurated

Eighteen years and eighteen days after being forced into exile, Perón—just shy of his seventy-eighth birthday—was returned to the presidency. His vindication came in a landslide—62 percent, or more than seven million votes. Yet the *New*

York Times noted that Perón faced a "classic" dilemma—"Frankenstein's monster threatens to run out of control":

> Last year, when his return to power ... was not at all certain, [Perón] justified guerrilla action by saying that if he were fifty years younger he too would probably be a bomb thrower. ... But now that he is only a step away from formal as well as effective power, his views appear to have changed. He scoffed at the young lawyer who was Interior Minister during the shortlived government of Dr. Héctor Cámpora, his stand-in. The minister told police that he wanted them to be more human and less repressive. Mr. Perón observed, "that's what police are for: to repress."[49]

On October 12, Inauguration Day, other discordant notes were sounded, heralding the dark days ahead. His military rank and privileges recently restored, Perón chose the event to appear in his lieutenant general's uniform for the first time in almost two decades. Left behind, almost as if they were the part of someone else's past, were jokes about the worthlessness of the Argentine military. The loyal Cámpora was not even invited to attend the ceremony.[50]

One person who did attend was Giulio Andreotti, the veteran Italian politician. On October 12 "I was in Buenos Aires representing Italy," recalled Andreotti:

> When the ceremony was over we all went over to shake his hand. Perón asked me if I was free that evening and I replied yes, obviously. He replied, "Come over to the house and we can chat a while ... " I told the ambassador, thinking it was a cocktail party for the various delegations. ... The ambassador did not want to come because he hadn't been invited, and I told him: "He invited me as the head of the Italian delegation, not personally ... "
>
> We went to Perón's house and there we found only three people: the general, Isabel and Gelli, before whom Perón did everything but genuflect. His attitude really made an impact on me.

Six days later Perón decorated Gelli with the nation's highest honor, the Great Cross of the Order of San Martín. Gelli won the honor, Perón declared, "for having made himself worthy of the Nation's recognition."[51]

The Emergence of the Triple A

A month after Rucci's death, a shadowy right-wing death squad made its first public appearance with an attack on leftist Radical party Senator Hipólito Solari Yrigoyen. A bomb wired to the starter of his car nearly destroyed his left leg. A patrician lawyer and relative of former president Hipólito Yrigoyen, Solari Yrigoyen was counsel for many political prisoners. The day before the attack he had received a short mimeographed message that said: "Warning! The Argentine Anti-Communist Alliance (AAA)."

The Triple A was a phantom organization created by López Rega and his cronies in the Social Welfare Ministry. Its activities were carried out by a wide spectrum within the police and military, as well as certain elements of the Peronist government—in particular, López Rega. One of the most important Triple A operations was run out of the Social Welfare Ministry itself. Some 200 men from different sectors of the ultraright and the security forces were recruited for "special tasks." The basement of the Social Welfare Ministry became a modern arsenal. Most of the weapons were purchased in neighboring Paraguay, but some came, via Gelli's contacts, from Libya. Tens of thousands of dollars in reserved funds left the ministry, which ran Argentina's lucrative but legal gambling industry, in payment for the weapons.[52]

"López Rega and the thugs who worked for him in the Ministry of Social Welfare were conducting extensive extortion and drug operations," recalled one U.S. diplomat. "When the target of the extortion or the drug trafficker refused to pay off, he was eliminated by the Social Welfare Ministry people and the assassination attributed to the Montoneros."[53]

Victor Samuelson

Victor Samuelson was the thirty-six-year-old general manager of Exxon Corporation's Campana refinery located north of Buenos Aires. The morning of December 6, 1973, the Harvard business school graduate was working on contingency planning for pulling Exxon's foreign managers out of Argentina. A sense of danger was in the air. Nine foreign businessmen had been kidnapped that year. Two weeks before, a Ford Motor Company official was murdered.[54]

Samuelson entertained corporate guests at a luncheon held during a balmy summer afternoon. After the lunch he strolled around the club's grounds with one of his guests, an Exxon official visiting from the United States. Suddenly, as the duo neared the swimming pool, a voice cried out in Spanish: "Don't go any further; the place is surrounded. Go back inside."

Inside were a dozen armed ERP guerrillas, some wearing stocking masks. The rebels grabbed Samuelson. Kicking him in the ribs, they shoved him into a car waiting outside, then sped off.

Samuelson's first stop was a "people's prison" that resembled a gas-station grease pit. Five days later, *El Mundo*, a newspaper linked to the guerrillas, published their ransom demands. As the *Wall Street Journal* noted, the fact that Samuelson was captured by the ERP had both positive and negative connotations, as the group "had a reputation for carefully selecting its targets, for knowing the finances of a selected company, and for making huge inflexible ransom demands. The group also used automatic rifles and was 'trigger happy,' as one Exxon man put it. But the ERP also had a track record of returning hostages alive if ransoms were paid."[55]

The guerrillas demanded a $15 million ransom. Over the next five months, negotiations took place between Exxon officials and the ERP. An Exxon intermediary was threatened with death, and the guerrillas warned that the company would be "brought to its knees" if the ERP publicly threatened to plant bombs at service stations around the country. When Exxon officials suggested a ransom of $2 million, Enrique Haroldo Gorriarán Merlo, an ERP hard-liner in charge of the negotiations, warned that Samuelson's body might be returned "wrapped in an American flag." (Although it was not made public at the time, in 1974 Santucho removed Gorriarán from the insurgents' political bureau after the latter—suspicious about a possible infiltration within the ERP—conducted a brutal counterintelligence operation within its ranks that left one person dead.)[56]

Samuelson, meanwhile, was drugged with a hallucinogen and was later moved to a basement cell, where he spent the next four months. Exxon eventually agreed to pay $14.2 million. The news came not a moment too soon. Samuelson's captors learned of the capitulation as they were preparing a firing squad and were just minutes away from carrying out their threat. Several weeks later $14.2 million in $100 bills was flown from New York to Buenos Aires, then delivered to a guerrilla contact in six suitcases. Samuelson was later released.

Juan Perón and his second wife, Evita. Her revolutionary appeal remained an article of faith for several generations of Peronists. (Courtesy Archivo General de la Nación)

Perón and U.S. boxing champion Jack Dempsey. Although some intimates found him cold and unsentimental, the Argentine's mass appeal was undeniable. (Courtesy Archivo General de la Nación)

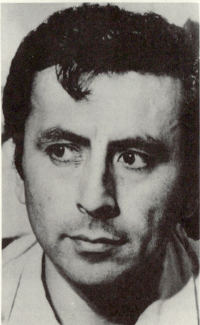

(*Above, left*): The success of Gen. Juan José Valle's failed pro-Peronist revolt, said one social critic, "would have saved the country from the shameful period that followed." (Courtesy Archivo General de la Nación) (*Above, right*): The excess of Gen. Pedro E. Aramburu's anti-Peronist "Liberating Revolution" unleashed forces that ended up in his own kidnapping and murder, perhaps at the hands of Argentine military intelligence. (Courtesy Diario Clarín) (*Left*): To Mario Roberto Santucho's followers in the People's Revolutionary Army (ERP), "Robi" Santucho was an almost mystical figure; to his enemies he was a dangerous and deadly fanatic.

Right-wing militants on the podium during Perón's marred June 1973 homecoming. The Peronist left came expecting a rumble; their rivals came armed for war. (Courtesy Editorial Atlántida)

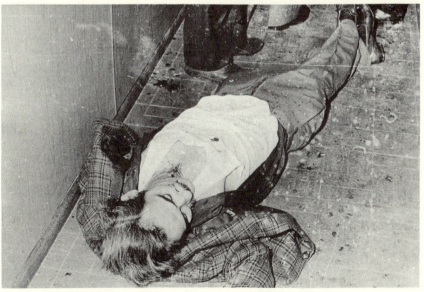

Although the Montonero guerrillas claimed credit for labor leader José I. Rucci's murder, U.S. intelligence laid the blame for Rucci's assassination on minions of Perón aide José López Rega. (Courtesy Federal Police of Argentina)

Defense minister Angel Robledo (*left*), Perón, army commander Leandro Anaya, and navy chief Emilio Massera (*far right*): The return of constitutional rule did not mean effective control of the armed forces by the civilians. (Reprinted by permission of the Associated Press)

After Perón's death, José López Rega, the "Rasputin of the Pampas," served as the sinister power behind Isabel Perón's shaky throne. (Reprinted by permission of the Associated Press)

The 1974 murder of the exiled Chilean constitutionalist officer Gen. Carlos Prats dealt hopes for democratic renewal there a brutal blow. (Courtesy Diario Clarín)

June 1973 press conference in Buenos Aires of principal PRT-ERP leaders (*from left to right*): Mario Roberto Santucho, Benito Urteaga, Enrique Gorriarán Merlo, and Jorge Carlos Molina. (Reprinted by permission of the Associated Press)

"Death's General" Acdel E. Vilas was trained in U.S. military schools. He drew his inspiration from French colonial counterinsurgency theorists. (Courtesy Página 12)

Montonero chief and 601 army intelligence informant Mario Firmenich: a modern-day Pied Piper who led a generation to their deaths. (Courtesy Página 12)

8

López Rega— Rasputin of the Pampas (1974)

José López Rega is one of those fighters who, in general, receive the ingratitude of the system they protect. ... At the president's side, López Rega takes care of the unpleasant tasks, becoming the lightning rod for criticism. Today it would be risky to forgo that service.

—*Mariano Grondona,* Carta Política, *December 1974*

Where a government has come into power through some form of popular vote, fraudulent or not, and maintains at least an appearance of constitutional legality, the guerrilla outbreak cannot be promoted, since the possibilities of peaceful struggle have not yet been exhausted.

—*Che Guevara*[1]

On January 19, 1974, ERP guerrillas undertook their most ambitious operation ever, making a nighttime assault on an army tank garrison at Azul, in Buenos Aires province. The battle raged for seven hours, with the army limiting its defense to the base's territory while the federal and the Buenos Aires provincial police carried out the main tasks of suppression. Army commander Col. Camilo Gay and his wife were among the dead. A lieutenant colonel was taken prisoner and later killed after spending ten months in a "people's prison."[2]

Appearing on television the next night, a grim, uniform-clad Perón blamed provincial authorities for tolerating "subversion." Vice-Governor Victorio Calabró, an orthodox metalworkers union leader, was tapped to replace Governor Oscar Bidegain, who was seen as too close to the radical youth of the Peronist left. Calabró quickly began to purge suspected leftists from the provincial government. "Though Perón and his orthodox followers lumped all Marxist subversives and terrorists together," wrote Perón biographer Joseph Page,

> there is actually scant indication that the hardliners of the ERP were making common cause with the Peronist left at this time. The ERP remained clandestine and kept kidnapping foreign businessmen. Extreme rightwing Peronists could not find them, so they directed their acts of retribution against the [Peronist Youth] and other leftist groups that operated openly. Thus the ERP furnished the provocation and the Peronist Left took the punishment.[3]

In the wake of the ERP attack Perón named retired Commissar Alberto Villar to be deputy chief of the Federal Police. Perón himself had to convince Villar, in retirement since Cámpora took office, to return to active duty. "I don't need it," Perón told him, "the country does." At the same time Commissar Luis Margaride—the Onganía-era crusader against miniskirts and assignation hotels—was made chief of the SS Federal (Superintendencia de Seguridad; Argentine Federal Police Security Superintendency), the political police. His benefactor was López Rega.[4]

An exhibitionist given to wearing a chain of grenades on his belt, the French-trained Villar—whom one U.S. intelligence agent called "brutal, incompetent and corrupt to the ultimate degree"—formed a group of more than 100 men for "special tasks" against the left. He called them los Centuriones (the Centurions); they called him Rommel. Many Centurions had been dishonorably discharged from the force. A number had been involved in extortion, white slavery, and drug trafficking.[5]

The left saw Villar and Margaride as a team but, in fact, the men did not get on well. When Villar was made Federal Police chief a few months later, Margaride was given the second spot, setting up a virtual dual command. One group was Villar's and was supported by Perón; the other was that of his deputy, Margaride.

Triumph and Disunion

For many people, the return of Peronism to power had meant a certain feeling of triumph. The democratic restoration—the end of electoral proscriptions—was seen as a historic reparation for events dating back to 1955. With the end of military rule came a considerable economic expansion, supported by the growth of domestic consumption and export industries. Foreign exchange reserves grew. The workers' share of national income, which in May 1973 was 35 percent, reached 42 percent, with the expectation that it could rise to the record-breaking 48 percent reached in 1955.[6]

Such confidence did not last long, however. Oil prices shot upward owing to the Arab embargo. Agricultural prices began to fall, and by July 1974, the European Economic Community banned all imports of Argentine beef, a major foreign exchange earner. Meanwhile, important opposition to the Peronists' program started to coalesce. Perón found himself hemmed in by the demands of the Peronist Youth for power and place; the turf fight between "revolutionary" and "orthodox" union sectors, and the recalcitrance of large landowners who opposed even modest efforts at tax reform and agrarian redistribution. As the coalition that brought him to power fragmented, he found he needed all of his enormous personal popularity to keep the crisis at bay. He also threatened to resign. "I came back to the country ... to unite and not to bring about the disunion of Argentines," he said, "in order to bring about a liberating project and not to consolidate our dependency."[7]

Alejandro Giovenco

On February 24 the government news agency Telam announced the death of ultraright activist Alejandro Giovenco, who died "when a bomb he was carrying in his briefcase exploded." Giovenco had begun his career as an anti-Peronist militant closely linked to Libertadora ideologue Adm. Isaac Rojas. He later served as an informant for one of the police intelligence services.

In 1973 Giovenco worked as a bodyguard for metalworkers' boss Lorenzo Miguel. One account said Giovenco died shortly after leaving the union headquarters. The police claimed that he was killed by a grenade tossed from a passing car. The two Telam journalists who published the earlier, correct version were suspended from their jobs for ten days.[8]

A Program of Counterterror

By taking several key provinces away from left-wing Peronists, Perón showed he was content to let them feel the wrath stirred by the ERP's violence. Perón's loyalties were most evident during the controversy over the Córdoba governorship.

Córdoba, one of Argentina's most industrialized cities, had since Onganía's rule been a center of social and political activism. When democracy returned in 1973, the province elected two men who embodied the years of antidictatorial struggle. The governor was politician Ricardo Obregón Cano, a traditional Peronist who had moved left with his constituency. His vice-governor was labor chief Atilio López, a veteran of the "Peronist resistance."

Many of Córdoba's factories sprang up after Perón's overthrow in 1955, and the labor leadership of the CGT in Buenos Aires did not control most of the area's unions. The local leaders of the automobile and power and light workers were leftists who were respected as honest and effective by the rank and file. Although the Montoneros and ERP were well organized in Córdoba, the province became the site of a war of ideological "purification" whose reach extended far beyond the guerrillas.[9]

As at Ezeiza, Osinde worked furiously to organize a "state of internal commotion" needed to justify the province's intervention. In the months before the minicoup he visited Córdoba at least four times.[10] The plot got under way when, in the middle of a generalized police campaign of harassment, five agricultural cooperative workers on their way to a meeting were murdered after they allegedly failed to stop at a roadblock. The provincial government ordered the police involved to be prosecuted. Obregón Cano demanded the resignation of the chief, Lieutenant Colonel Navarro, who was already tainted by various scandals. Navarro refused. Unable to break the impasse, Obregón Cano was forced to exonerate him. The institutional conflict Osinde had sought had taken place. Navarro revolted, and his forces occupied the government house. Obregón Cano, López, and a number of provincial senators and deputies found on the premises were arrested.[11]

Like clockwork, heavily armed civilians began to patrol the streets. These gangs established "operation centers" in the headquarters of the commerce employees union and at a local radio station. From there they broadcast martial music, the "Peronist March," fiery proclamations against leftist groups, and coded messages. More than 200 illegal detentions and raids were carried out in a single day, and detainees were tortured in police stations. Several powerful bombs rocked locales around the city.

Radical reform leader Raúl Alfonsín, local party activist Eduardo Angeloz, and former president Illia were among the many who raised their voices against the revolt, the latter two condemning "seditious acts committed by police groups." When the officials Navarro was holding were released by the courts, Obregón Cano went to Buenos Aires seeking help.[12]

Perón had other plans. He already had signed an order placing the province under federal control. The Córdoba government was accused of having "tolerated and sometimes even fomented different conflictive situations that caused a growing climate of public insecurity." Obregón Cano accused Interior Minister Benito Llambí and Labor Minister Ricardo Otero—an ally of the "orthodox" metalworkers—with orchestrating his removal. Perón then ordered him to be brought up on charges. Navarro resigned, too, but was cleared of accusations of wrongdoing.

Osinde and López Rega had won a resounding victory. "The beginning of the decline of Peronism … can be traced back to the last days of President Juan Perón," a U.S. Defense Intelligence Agency *Intelligence Appraisal* noted later:

> The disintegration of the movement started when he began to disregard leftist elements such as the radical Montoneros, who were united behind his political movement, and disassociated himself from them.
>
> Leftist participation in his government had given Argentina some semblance of political unity. With the death of Juan Perón, the treatment of the Peronist left evolved into a program of counterterror which brought fear to the populace and alienated the very groups Perón had wooed.[13]

Firmenich: In the "Right Column"

During the first months of 1974 the SS Federal stepped up its antileft campaign, carrying out a series of political dragnets. In February two alleged ERP members "disappeared" after having been seen at a police station. The police denied detaining the two. A Radical party sympathizer and brother of one of those amnestied in 1973 was killed. Juan Manuel Abal Medina escaped attackers wielding hand grenades and machine guns.

Meanwhile former construction workers' boss Rogelio Coria was murdered outside his doctor's office in an attack believed to be the work of the guerrillas. Just two years earlier Coria had been close to the pinnacle of power. He resigned his union post in 1973, charged with corruption by the left and disgraced among party faithful as a "traitor" to Perón. Not a single union leader attended his funeral.[14]

On March 18 Mario Firmenich and sixteen others were detained by police in a raid on a Peronist Youth meeting hall. His arrest, noted the *Buenos Aires Herald,* "gave the police the opportunity to fingerprint a man who had never been inside previously." Upon his release Firmenich addressed 500 supporters at a Peronist Youth headquarters. He charged that the arrests were "an attempt to separate us from Peronism, and the ultra-left is as much to blame as is the ultra-right."

"Because of the need for labels, Firmenich still heads the 'left wing' of the Peronist Youth and there are many of that line in the faction," the *Herald* noted. "But his speech after his arrest made many people wonder why the right wing of Peronism felt antagonized by Firmenich."[15]

Shortly after his arrest, Federal Police chief Miguel Angel Iñíguez had differing appraisals of Firmenich and another Montonero chieftain, former FAR head Roberto Quieto. The latter was not as "open" as Firmenich, he said, and had difficulty clarifying his political line. Firmenich, the retired nationalist general affirmed, was different. "He is a nationalist, Catholic and Peronist, and though, like any young man, he may disagree with regard to forms of political action, when the time comes he'll be marching in the right column. I have no doubt of that."[16]

A Different Tune

On April 25, militant left-wing youth leaders met with Perón in the presidential palace. There they complained that Alberto Camps, one of the survivors of the 1972 Trelew "massacre," and Eusebio Maestre, the brother of the revolutionary Peronist activist "disappeared" in 1971, had been tortured by the SS Federal. Perón was told that Camps was subjected to a simulated firing squad and Maestre had been forced to watch the police rape his wife while the cops goaded him to react, seeking a pretext to kill him. "Those of us who were once delinquents,"

Perón replied slyly, "know that often a complaint is inflated in order to call attention to oneself."

The general ignored a forensic doctor's report that the two had been tortured with electric shock. Instead, Perón endorsed Villar and Margaride: "They may not be Peronists, but they're good cops. So all those who go around armed better take care of themselves. As long as the others don't change their attitude, the police aren't going to change theirs either."

Having once railed against the CGT's "defection-prone bureaucrats," Perón now played a different tune: "The CGT can rest safe and secure with the leadership it has, even though some fools say that they are bureaucrats. ... I know these leaders, not from now, but from thirty years back."[17]

The "glorious youth" who did his bidding while he was in exile were now branded as "idiots" and "infiltrators." "What are they doing in Peronism?" he asked a group of right-wing youths in February of their equally young rivals. "If I were a Communist, I would go to the Communist Party."[18] In response Dardo Cabo, the editor of the Montonero newspaper *El Descamisado,* wrote in words that could not hide the hurt: "So now we are infiltrators. Yesterday we were the *muchachos* [boys] hailed with feeling by the chief of our struggle's movement. Now ... they say there are other 'socialist' parties where we can go if we like. ... Why didn't they tell us that before, when we were fighting?"[19]

An American Visitor

In April Gen. Vernon Walters, deputy director of the CIA, made a secret visit to Buenos Aires. He said later he did so for two reasons: to give Perón his word as a soldier that rumors about the U.S. plotting to overthrow him were false and to voice American concerns over the possibility Argentina would shift to the far left.[20]

On the latter point Perón assured his visitor that his fears were groundless. A declassified State Department document, "Summary of Argentine Law and Practice on Terrorism," revealed that Perón had begun taking his own precautions and that, in late March 1974,

> Perón authorized the Argentine Federal Police and the Argentine intelligence to cooperate with Chilean intelligence in apprehending Chilean left-wing extremists in exile in Argentina. Similar arrangements had also been made with the security services of Bolivia, Uruguay and Brazil. This cooperation among security forces apparently includes permission for foreign officials to operate within Argentina, against their exiled nationals using that country as a base for insurgent operations. This authority allegedly includes arrest of such exiles and transfer to the home country without recourse to legal procedures.[21]

Perón Disinherits the Montoneros

On May 1—May Day—Perón let loose a full-scale verbal barrage against the left. He trained his sights on the Montonero, Peronist Youth, and Tendencia Revolucionaria (Revolutionary Tendency—a coalition of left-wing Peronist youth groups sympathetic to the Montoneros) wings making up fully half of the more than 150,000 people who descended on a rally at the Plaza de Mayo.

The confrontation, caused by Montonero chants against López Rega and Isabelita, was traumatic—and seemed to put an end to the idea, still held by some, that a dialogue could still take place if only Perón could be shaken loose from López Rega. Chanting, beating bass drums, and waving banners and placards expressly banned by the rally organizers, the youthful columns interrupted Perón, filling the plaza with a roaring din:

> ¡Si Evita viviera, sería montonera!
> ¿Qué pasa?
> ¿Qué pasa?
> ¿Qué pasa, General,
> que está lleno de gorilas el gobierno popular?
> (If Evita were alive, she'd be a Montonera!)
> (What's the matter? What's the matter, General,
> that the people's government is so full of gorillas?)

The Montoneros rained insults on Isabel and López Rega, Vandor and Rucci. Perón was livid. "In spite of those stupid ones who are shouting," he thundered, his face contorted with rage, "the unions have remained sound for twenty-one years—and now it turns out that some beardless youths claim more merit than those who worked for twenty years." The Montoneros did an about-face while Perón was still speaking, filing out of the plaza held dear in Peronist folklore. It was the youth who took the slogan "My life for Perón" most to heart; it was now they who turned their backs on him.

Perón made one last attempt at avoiding a final break, testing a favored slogan about using what was usable. He ordered loyalists to try to reestablish a dialogue. Juan Carlos Dante Gullo, representing the Montoneros' youth wing, participated in a number of meetings. Another channel was opened up through Economy Minister José Ber Gelbard. One account said Gelbard's efforts to repair the rift were based on his fear of a strengthened López Rega. "Gelbard saw clearly the ultra-rightist tendency represented by López Rega and Isabel's inevitable succession," Montonero newspaper editor Miguel Bonasso said. "He knew political dikes had to be constructed." Meanwhile the government closed the leftist newspapers *El Mundo, El Descamisado,* and *Militancia;* Perón formed a new intelligence commission to centralize information on terrorism and, according to the U.S. State Department's summary on Argentine terrorism, "also authorized the formation of paramilitary groups to act extra legally against the terrorists, including the utilization of abduction, interrogation and execution of terrorists."[22]

López Rega did not need to be reminded of the old Spanish saying, "al buen entendedor, pocas palabras" (to one who understands, few words are needed). He struck, and struck hard. The Peronist Youth dominated the universities. The schools became the next battleground. In Córdoba, some fifty thugs led by a top Social Welfare Ministry official occupied the School of Information Sciences. Carrying credentials stamped by the police and bearing the telephone numbers of López Rega's ministry, they shot up the locale, terrorizing professors and students. In Bahía Blanca the National Technological University was occupied by thugs from the CNU. The attacks were repeated around the country.[23]

"The Best Enemy Is a Dead Enemy"

On May 11, as talks were taking place between the government and the Montoneros, another assassination tore at the nation's conscience. Padre Carlos Mugica was cut down by machine-gun fire outside a church in the outlying Buenos Aires district of Mataderos.

The charismatic scion of an aristocratic Buenos Aires family, the fair-haired Mugica had given up a promising career in the church hierarchy. Instead, he took up his ministry at the capital's largest slum, spreading from the Retiro train station to the port. The priest's pastoral vocation and his reforming zeal put him at the forefront of the movement for social and political change. In 1964 and for several years later Mugica served as a spiritual adviser to Firmenich, Fernando Abal Medina, and Carlos Ramus, all later Montonero leaders. Together they carried out social work in northern Santa Fe province, where the youths learned firsthand what life was like for the poor.

Like other Third World priests, Mugica had condoned what was called "violence from below." He later spoke out forcefully against all violence. "I am ready for them to kill me," he often said, "but I am not ready to kill."[24]

In the weeks before his death the priest was embroiled in two controversies. One was a confrontation with his one-time protégés in the Montoneros. Mugica opposed their militarism and their clashes with Perón. In the days before he was murdered, Mugica told several associates he believed the guerrillas, led by Firmenich, were out to kill him. ("I know these people," he told disbelieving associates.) He was also wrapped up in a bitter disagreement with López Rega over policies implemented by the Social Welfare Ministry in the slums.[25]

Responding to a campaign by the government and rightist labor leaders to lay the priest's death at their feet, the Montoneros took pains to condemn the killing. Firmenich wrote four articles in the Montoneros newspaper, *Noticias,* expressing his "affection and gratitude" to Mugica. The threats the priest received, he said, were the work of "infantile, ultra-leftist" elements. He accused the far right of the murder.[26]

El Caudillo was a far-right weekly publication headed by Felipe Romeo, a former activist in the anti-Semitic Nationalist Restoration Guard and the reputed leader of a Triple A hit squad. Fully a quarter of *El Caudillo*'s advertising came from López Rega's ministry and Lorenzo Miguel's metalworkers union. In December *El Caudillo* had ended an editorial against the priest: "The best enemy is a dead enemy."[27]

Mugica's killer was a Federal Police corporal acting under the cover of the Triple A. He was part of López Rega's personal bodyguard and was sent to kill the priest to put an end to his work in the slums.[28]

Perón Falls III

In June Isabel and López Rega traveled to Europe, where the vice president was to speak before the International Labor Organization. In Buenos Aires Perón fell ill, his old bronchial ailment complicated by a pneumonia he picked up while visiting Gen. Alfredo Stroessner during a thunderstorm in the Paraguayan capital of Asunción. López Rega quickly returned to Buenos Aires and—capitalizing on his domestic role—displaced the influential José Gelbard.

There was a second, perhaps more important, motive for El Brujo's speedy return. According to the U.S. State Department cable, Perón had "expressed his displeasure with the lack of response to his orders to eliminate terrorism in Argentina and announced his intention to form a new security council." On June 6 Decree no. 1732 was issued creating the security organization whose mandate was the planning and control of domestic security efforts. The council was to be headed by the president and made up of the interior, defense, and justice ministers and the commanding generals of the armed forces. "This organization was suspended by June 28, 1974, primarily due to opposition from López Rega, who … had been supervising extra-legal paramilitary operations against the terrorists. Lacking a political base of his own, López Rega would have lost strength under this latest innovation—which placed the counter-terrorist activities under the control of the security committee. López Rega exercised major responsibility during Perón's illness."[29]

Death of a Titan

Juan Perón died on July 1 at 10:25 A.M., ending nearly thirty years of dominance of Argentina's political life. Early that afternoon his widow, calm but pale, announced his death on television. As she spoke, López Rega stood at her side, his hands on her chair. Hours later, El Brujo made another television appearance, bizzarely repeating the news.

López Rega's performance was in keeping with an earlier one at Perón's bed-side. When Perón's doctors decided they could do no more to save him, López Rega grabbed Perón by the ankles, shaking him and mumbling: "I can't do it … I can't … For ten years I did it, but now I can't."[30]

The pain of a nation was to be seen everywhere. Huge crowds waited in long lines in the cold and pouring rain to catch a last glimpse of their beloved general. The Montoneros had erred in believing that Perón was a "revolutionary" in their own image, the ERP that it could challenge a man who was still passionately loved by his country's common people.

To the end Argentines of varied political beliefs and economic groups put their faith in him. While he lived, Argentina's economic and social fabric still seemed susceptible to his magic. When he was gone, his eclectic following was left alone, to reap the whirlwind of contradictions between what was hoped for and what Perón had bequeathed.

At the Summit

One of the things Perón left behind was the person of José López Rega. On July 5 Isabel called a cabinet meeting, summoning Radical party leader Ricardo Balbín; the three military service chiefs; the leaders of the CGT and its business counterpart, the Confederación General Económica (CGE; General Economic Confederation); and the presidents of the Senate and Chamber of Deputies. Balbín, Education Minister Jorge Taiana, Defense Minister Angel F. Robledo, and fellow P-2 member Navy chief Emilio Massera all weighed in with criticism of El Brujo. Balbín even accused him of being behind the armed right-wing groups. Nevertheless, the president decided to retain López Rega as her private secretary and social welfare minister. He continued to live with her in the presidential residence in Olivos.[31]

Perón's death removed a final obstacle to López Rega's plans. Isabel's presidency meant he had arrived at the summit of power. Taiana and Robledo soon resigned and Balbín ceased to play a meaningful advisory role. And the "Rasputin of the Pampas" stepped up his bloody offensive against opponents, inside Peronism and out.[32]

López Rega Strikes Hard

The momentary unity following Perón's death was quickly shattered. Unidentified civilian-dressed men claiming to belong to the SS Federal carried out hundreds of raids without judicial warrants. In some cases, such as an attack on a Peronist Youth headquarters in Buenos Aires province, the assaults were carried out with support from armed civilian groups.[33]

Following Rucci's murder, textile workers' leader Adelino Romero had become secretary-general of the CGT. A mainstream Peronist, Romero was identified with José Ber Gelbard, a López Rega foe, and his conciliatory labor-management accord known as the "social pact." On the eve of a CGT congress that was to pick a secretary general for four more years, Romero fell ill. He was rushed to a local clinic, where a "heart-type" ailment was diagnosed and visitors were prohibited. Suddenly Romero died.

The death came at a crucial moment in union politics, as the CGT leader was locked in combat with sectors tied to Labor Minister Otero and metalworkers' chief Miguel, who was then closely allied with López Rega. Rumors reached the U.S. embassy that Romero was killed—with an injection of curare—in his hospital bed, a view shared by at least one former SIDE agent. After visiting Romero's wake, Otero suffered what newspapers called a "nervous crisis" and was hospitalized. The next day, Romero's wife demanded that several somber-faced union bosses, those "who killed my husband," be thrown out of the funeral.[34]

As labor buried Romero, Arturo Mor Roig—Lanusse's interior minister and one of those politically responsible for the massacre at Trelew—was murdered. The retired Radical was felled by more than thirty-two bullets in an Italian restaurant in Buenos Aires province. Many of the more than 100,000 people gathered at a Montonero rally a few days later cheered the mention of Mor Roig's death—the leadership having put out the word that they were responsible. Yet the assassination worked to the Montoneros' detriment. The left-leaning Radical Youth split from the Juventudes Políticas Argentinas (JPA; Argentine Political Youths), a key umbrella group—particularly in the universities—to which the Montonero-dominated Peronist Youth belonged. It accentuated the public's perception of the Montoneros as isolated from the broad currents they claimed to represent. And as in the case of Rucci, the U.S. embassy was informed by well-placed intelligence sources that López Rega, not the Montoneros, was behind the assassination.[35]

It was about the time of Mor Roig's death that Radical leader Raúl Alfonsín took stock of his own security. It was not the Triple A that, as might be expected, preoccupied him the most. Nor was he overly worried by the ERP. For Alfonsín the most convincing threat was Montonero Mario Firmenich who, he thought, was capable of taking on a "contract job" put out on him by someone else.[36]

"Made in U.S.A."

By the late 1960s the CIA was promoting greater coordination among South America's security forces. According to *Hidden Terrors,* a study on U.S. police training in Latin America, it was a CIA operative who put a top Argentine Justice Ministry official in touch with authorities in Uruguay to talk about monitoring political exiles in both countries. The agency also brought Brazilian death squad members to meet with Argentine and Uruguayan police.

The agency's involvement was not limited to arranging meetings; American field officers offered hands-on help as well. When intelligence officers from Brazil's U.S.-backed regime began using field telephones in electric torture, American advisers told them how much shock the body could withstand. Uruguayan police received improved torture equipment in Buenos Aires—wires, generators, and electric needles so thin they could be slipped between teeth—from the CIA's Technical Services Division office.[37]

Brazilians, Argentines, and Uruguayans were brought together by the agency for intelligence training such as wiretapping and to receive supplies of explosives and untraceable guns. Latin police and military were also sent to a CIA-run course sponsored by the State Department's Office of Public Safety (OPS) at Los Fresnos, Texas. There they were taught to build homemade bombs.[38]

"Except for one detail," wrote *Hidden Terrors* author, A. J. Langguth, a former *New York Times* Saigon bureau chief, "OPS could have had an unassailable explanation for sending students to Los Fresnos. By now the world had entered upon a time of bombs and bomb threats. Public opinion might have readily accepted the argument that any nation's policemen needed training in the defusing and demolition of bombs. The problem for OPS was that the CIA's course at Los Fresnos did not teach men how to destroy bombs, only how to build them."[39]

Increasing terrorist activity in Argentina was met with the creation within the Federal Police of a special Explosives Brigade, trained in the deactivation and handling of bombs. Several of the force's operatives had already received training in the U.S. schools.[40]

"Some of its members, linked to Commissar Gen. Villar, began to actively participate first in the Triple A and later in the different [military] Task Groups," recalled former police officer Rodolfo Peregrino Fernández. "These were responsible for attacks which are public knowledge, such as, for example, the blowing up of the offices of lawyers representing political prisoners; attacks against publishing houses and mass media opposed to the views of the military high command, and against activists and labor organizations."[41]

Leftist defense lawyers were a favorite target of the death squads. On July 17 a powerful bomb exploded at the headquarters of the Asociación Gremial de Abogados (AGA; Lawyers' Union Association), which defended political prisoners. Two weeks later Rodolfo Ortega Peña, thirty-six, a leftist parliamentary deputy and defense lawyer, was cut down in a hail of machine-gun fire while getting out of a taxi in downtown Buenos Aires. The day before he died, the former FAP lawyer presented a request for a report by the Chamber of Deputies on the deaths of six ERP guerrillas killed by police after having been detained.

Ortega Peña's murder was carried out by Federal Police under López Rega's command. After the execution the green Ford Fairlane used by the assassins reappeared—with weapons and explosives inside—abandoned in front of the Social Welfare ministry. At the same time communiqués supposedly issued by Montoneros appeared around the city, taking credit for the attack.[42]

The campaign did not end with Ortega Peña's death. The SS Federal raided the offices and homes of several lawyers connected to him. Within a month Alfredo

Curutchet, an ERP sympathizer and Córdoba labor lawyer, was machine-gunned to death by the Triple A near Buenos Aires. A member of the AGA, Curutchet had just visited political prisoners confined in the Patagonian city of Río Gallegos. He had scheduled a news conference for the day after he was killed—to complain about torture in the prison.[43]

With Isabel Perón in office and López Rega in power, popular television shows were censored or prohjited; newspapers and magazines were shut down; schools, universities, and labor unions purged. In August the tempo of parapolice activities quickened, reflecting the fact that López Rega's Triple A was "officially" organized under the command of Federal Police chief Villar. The murders bore a monotony of method—execution by machine gun, the bodies left along isolated roads outside urban areas. The violence had begun to leave politically active Argentines and others numbed.[44]

"The Triple A was widely regarded as sinister and fought a far dirtier war than the most unprincipled guerrillas," wrote historian Richard Gillespie.

> On several occasions wounded Montoneros were picked up off the streets by doctors, carried to waiting Social Welfare Ministry ambulances, and never reached a hospital: They were either killed in the vehicles, taken to torture centers before being finished off at rubbish tips, or hung from trees. Moreover, the Triple A enjoyed official protection and seemed immune from lawful challenges: No Triple A henchmen or "Ministry of Death" employees were arrested.[45]

On August 27 Villar personally directed the closure of the Montonero-financed *Noticias,* which had a daily circulation of 150,000 copies. The reason given for the raid was the daily's "apology for subversive activities." Newspaper authorities said it was the result of an exposé it ran about a state contract with the Italian firm Montedison, whose links to Licio Gelli were unknown at the time. The newspaper alleged that illegal financial privileges had been given for the construction of a petrochemical complex.[46]

During the operation Villar demanded to know which desk was used by Rodolfo Walsh, the social critic and detective story writer who edited the *Noticias*'s police pages. As if taking measure of an invisible enemy, Villar stared long and hard at the empty piece of furniture. "I know how to win, and I know how to lose," he boasted. "I already have a coffin prepared for when my turn comes, but I also have coffins prepared for many of you."[47]

An Execution Retold

September passed under a wave of assaults, kidnappings, and murders. There was a political assassination every nineteen hours.[48]

On September 2 Isabel signed Decree no. 735, naming Gelli an economic counselor with the Argentine embassy in Rome and authorizing his use of a diplomatic passport. He did not have to report to the Argentine envoy in the Italian capital, himself a P-2 member and a future defense minister. The passport let Gelli move unmolested throughout the world.[49]

Two days later *La Causa Peronista,* a magazine run by Montonero leader Rodolfo Galimberti, carried a lurid piece on the Aramburu kidnapping four years earlier. Entitled "How Aramburu Died," the article gave an account by Firmenich and Norma Arrostito of the "revolutionary trial" and assassination of the former president. The article turned out to be a tremendous propaganda boon—but not for those who published it.

"Another grave error," *Noticias* editor and Montonero leader Miguel Bonasso said later. "When they closed *Noticias* I went to see Balbín ... looking for support. Balbín received me with *La Causa Peronista* on his desk. I knew then there wasn't any chance Balbín would move a finger to defend the paper. The organization was already gravely isolated from the political class."[50]

Firmenich's tale showed a dignified Aramburu at the moment of his death. It also gave a furtive, sordid image of his judges and executioners. Boasted Firmenich:

> He asked that we tie his shoelaces, which we did. He asked if he could shave. We told him we didn't have the materials. We took him to a hallway inside the house near the basement. He asked for a confessor. We told him we couldn't bring one because the roads were being patrolled.
>
> "If you can't bring a priest," he said, "how are you going to remove my body?"
>
> He took two or three more steps.
>
> "What will happen to my family?" he asked.
>
> He was told that we had nothing against them, that they would receive his belongings. ...
>
> We put a handkerchief in his mouth and put him against the wall. The basement was tiny and the execution had to be done with a pistol. Fernando [Abal Medina] took the task of executing him. For him, the chief always had to assume the greatest responsibility. He sent me upstairs to hit a morse [an anvil-like object], in order to hide the sound of the shots.
>
> "General," said Fernando, "we're going to proceed."
>
> "Proceed," said Aramburu.
>
> Fernando fired the 9-millimeter at his chest. Afterward there were two shots to finish him off, with the same weapon and with a .45. Fernando covered him with a blanket. No one dared to uncover him while we dug the hole in which we were to bury him.[51]

In the furor following its publication, few paid attention to certain details and contradictions in the Montonero's tale. Firmenich claimed that Aramburu said Evita's body had been secretly buried in Rome; in fact the cadaver lay in Milan.

Both the magazine's commentary and Firmenich's account seemed to go out of their way to clear former Interior Minister Imaz of involvement in the crime. "An absurd hypothesis," said *La Causa Peronista,* "that of a link between Montoneros and Imaz." Or Firmenich: "Aramburu did not have any guard, at least outside.

Later it was said that Imaz had it withdrawn days before the kidnapping, which wasn't true." Firmenich claimed a roll of film shot to record the event broke before it was developed. It was also said he burned tape recordings "because there was no place to hide them."

One detail stood out in its improbability. Firmenich said a handkerchief was stuffed into Aramburu's mouth before he was killed. The autopsy said he was gagged and had adhesive tape wrapped around his face. How was it then that Aramburu, gagged and taped, had told a waiting Abal Medina, "Proceed"?

Mario Firmenich, Army Intelligence Agent?

On September 6, as the ERP was considering a cease-fire, the Montoneros announced they were going into clandestinity, calling for "integral armed resistance." Two weeks later they startled the nation with the bloody kidnapping, just blocks from the presidential residence in Olivos, of brothers Juan and Jorge Born, owners of a vast multinational cereal company.

The retreat into clandestinity was suicide. There was still "political space" in which to fight legally. Moreover, the Montoneros had been public for more than a year. Militants were easily identified. The call to go underground caught most unprepared. Many had nowhere to go.[52]

Just how much of the Montoneros' folly was due to Mario Firmenich's leadership would be a matter of debate several years later. What almost no one knew then, and stayed a tightly held secret, was that Firmenich had—since at least 1973—been working as an army intelligence informant. That fact would be a key to understanding the massacre that was to follow.

Suspicions that Firmenich might have been an intelligence agent date to the kidnapping-murder of Pedro Aramburu. Definitive confirmation of his activity as a double agent, however, came from a retired U.S. diplomat who lived in Argentina during most of the 1970s. The source, whom Ambassador Robert Hill had given the task of monitoring the guerrilla threat, had direct access to top Argentine army officers. The American said that Alberto Valín, a colonel who worked for the 601 army intelligence batallion in Buenos Aires, confided to him that he was Firmenich's handler. Valín, considered by the embassy to be "definitely credible," had given the Americans much "invaluable" intelligence.

The diplomat said that Firmenich began cooperating with the 601 unit in the early 1970s, as the Montoneros moved openly to the left. His help was "ideological at first, then done for the thrill," according to the American. The army handled him "very intelligently."

The diplomat, who said he filed extensive dispatches to Washington on the subject, stated that one of Firmenich's first tasks was to help discredit the Montoneros. As the left-wing Peronists had largely given up armed politics by mid-1973, it was necessary to push them away from left-wing reformism into activities, or presumed actions, that would make them political pariahs. Thus

Firmenich, either himself or through "cut-outs" (emissaries who would do his bidding while distancing themselves and their acts from him), had the Montoneros take credit for a series of spectacular, but politically costly, murders they had not committed. One was Rucci's assassination; another, that of Mor Roig.

"The claim by the Montoneros that they were involved in the murders of Rucci et al. was done to make them look more powerful. It was done to show that, 'as a leader this is what I [Firmenich] am doing.'" The diplomat said he knew of several other politically explosive murders, such as that of Mor Roig, for which López Rega or the army was responsible but for which the Montoneros took the heat. Firmenich also fed the 601 unit Montoneros who could be "turned" to work as double agents.

Key to Firmenich's revolutionary play acting, the diplomat said, was the Montoneros' compartmentalized clandestine structure. Although this web allowed some cells, particularly in Córdoba, to escape Firmenich's control, the hierarchical structure in turn allowed him to offer authentic guerrillas as little real information as necessary, claiming "need to know" criteria. "The cellular structure was a myth, and Firmenich reinforced the myth at every opportunity, saying, 'Look what we did. This is why we have to keep our cellular structure.'"[53]

Black September

The Triple A unleashed a Black September throughout Argentina. Within one week former Córdoba vice-governor Atilio López; former Buenos Aires provincial police deputy chief Julio Troxler, a survivor of the 1956 massacre at José Leon Suárez; and well-known academician Silvio Frondizi, the leftist brother of the former president, were kidnapped; their bodies were found later ripped by machine-gun fire.

On the campuses attacks by rightist groups were promoted by Alberto Ottalagano, a declared Fascist and rector of the University of Buenos Aires. The five-month-old son of Ottalagano's predecessor, who was linked to the Peronist Youth, was killed when a Triple A bomb wrecked the family's home. ("Your son is the youngest martyr in the Peronist resistance," the Montoneros said in a message of condolence.) A former University of Buenos Aires dean during the Cámpora government was forced into self-exile at the Mexican embassy. Three more cadavers surfaced in downtown Buenos Aires, bearing a warning from the Triple A: "Executed for infiltrating our universities, where they corrupt the minds of young people."[54]

The Triple A's terrorism spanned professions and geography. Journalists, actors, and singers were given seventy-two hours to leave the country. Héctor Cámpora was threatened with death.

A new antisubversive law was issued in September. It was passed in parliament by the official wing of the Peronist party, with the Radicals providing the necessary quorum. The measure sharply curtailed free expression and the right to strike. Prison terms of up to five years were set for journalists who printed or reproduced information viewed as "altering or eliminating institutional order." September was also when Chilean constitutionalist Gen. Carlos Prats, the former chief of that country's armed forces, was murdered in Buenos Aires.

Since the early 1900s, the sanctity of exile had been one of the guiding principles of Latin political life. Although political murders and disappearances of exiles in Argentina occurred as far back as the 1920s—when a number of anarchist activists were secretly murdered—the campaign against the refugees began in earnest during the last days of Juan Perón. By then Buenos Aires was a mecca for exiles ranging from centrists to the revolutionary left. More than a dozen Brazilian activists were seized in the Argentine capital by security agents from São Paulo, with the collusion of the Federal Police. One high-ranking police source said a safe house in downtown Buenos Aires was staffed by two police representatives from each nearby country—"almost always the same men to keep it a secret"—to carry out intelligence work and the abduction and deportation of troublesome exiles.[55]

Chileans made up one of Argentina's largest exile groups. The regime of Capt. Gen. Augusto Pinochet considered the 2,000-mile border running along the spine of the Andes and the guerrilla movements east of the cordillera as special dangers. Members of a small Chilean guerrilla group, the Movimiento Izquierdista Revolucionario (MIR; Revolutionary Left Movement), their Argentine friends, and the politicians he loved to excoriate as "corrupt" and "decadent" were not Pinochet's worst obsession, however. A special hatred was reserved for Carlos Prats, a fellow member of Chile's military elite.

Having preceded Pinochet as army commander in chief during the rule of Marxist president Salvador Allende, Prats moved to Buenos Aires after the 1973 coup. Imbued with the Chilean military's long constitutionalist vocation, Prats settled down in Buenos Aires with his wife to write his memoirs and to keep watch on events back home. His friend, Juan Perón, arranged a job for the Chilean in a tire factory owned by Gelbard. Like Perón, Prats moved easily in the world of arms, politics, and letters.[56]

On September 30 hopes for a democratic renewal in Chile were dealt a brutal blow. Prats and his wife died in a car-bomb explosion and commando raid outside their apartment in Buenos Aires' Belgrano district. Their killers included American-born Dirección de Información Nacional (DINA; National Information Directorate) agent Michael Townley. He was supported by Milicia, a Triple A offshoot that the SIDE used as a channel for disinformation and psychological warfare. Among those involved in Prat's murder was Fatherland and Liberty commander Enrique Arancibia Clavel and former tacuarista Juan Martín Ciga Correa, a Milicia member and head of security for the University of Buenos Aires law school.[57] The day Prats was killed the head of his Argentine army bodyguard, a colonel named Reynaldo Benito Bignone, failed to show up for work.[58]

A wave of arrests and rumors swept through the country. Often they were the work of the intelligence services. "As part of the campaign of intimidation against the population, in an effort to force certain people to leave the country and abandon their public activities," a former intelligence agent later admitted, "we put together threatening cards and letters in the headquarters of the SIDE, generally using the letterhead of the Triple A. The threats were written up in different ways and had various levels of gravity." The missives were put together by various employees in offices on the second and third floors of the SIDE building, across the street from the presidential palace. To save work, copies were standardized—only the name of the person to be threatened was missing.[59]

"In October 1974, the Argentine Government organized a clandestine security committee within the Defense Ministry," the U.S. State Department's "Summary of Argentine Law and Practice on Terrorism" stated two years later. "The AAA carries out its actions on the basis of recommendations from this Committee."[60]

Federal Police Chief Villar Assassinated

On November 1, a brilliantly sunny spring day, Federal Police chief Villar and his wife were killed in the Tigre delta district upriver from Buenos Aires.

The Villars had boarded their small yacht, docked at a recreational harbor, at 10:30 A.M. A powerful bomb had been placed underneath the floorboard. When the chief maneuvered the craft barely 100 feet from its mooring, the trotyl charge was triggered by the heat of the engine, blowing the boat apart. The blast was clearly audible at the Olivos presidential residence several miles away. The Montoneros took credit for the murders, despite Elsa de Villar's death, telling supporters the bomb had been placed under the boat by a frogman and was detonated by remote control.[61]

When Margaride replaced Villar at the head of the force, he claimed that bringing the murders to trial would be the police's "number one priority." Yet the case was never officially investigated. U.S. intelligence sources said that a sergeant on Villar's staff was fingered as a Montonero. After the assassination he had been assigned to the bodyguard of the new deputy commissar. Upon learning of his treachery, Margaride ordered the sergeant to be executed in a staged shoot-out with two already-dead Montoneros. An American intelligence operative later said that a "dozen or so" Federal Police were killed in such incidents, which were later blamed on the Montoneros.[62]

Hours after the bombing a commando squad raided Villar's home in Belgrano. Although limiting their looting to objects of minor value, they did carry off Villar's private papers on the Aramburu murder—a crime the police chief always felt had not been adequately cleared up. For months López Rega had been demanding that the chief hand the files over to him.[63]

At the couple's wake, as López Rega feuded with the military over Villar's successor, El Brujo—the former police corporal—made a showy display of his new commissar-general's uniform.[64]

"To Be with Christ"

University of Buenos Aires Dean Alberto Ottalagano was named to conduct a 100-day "purging mission" of the institution. "We Catholics and Argentines are before a test of fire," he declared. "One can either be Peronist or Marxist. The political parties—the Radicals, Conservatives, etc.—will become irrelevant, as they must choose between Peronism and Marxism. ... This is the moment to be with Christ or against him. ... They have tried a so-called 'pluralist' society, and its consequences are there for all to see. We possess the Truth and Reason; the others do not, and we will treat them as such."[65]

The Peronist right demanded that the armed forces be used to fight "subversion," that Parliament be abolished, and that Isabel head a "popular military dictatorship." In place of the parties, calls arose for "an organically functional democracy" based on the armed forces, the church, and the CGT. Mussolini's "organized community" was a model for some.[66]

During the purge López Rega found his support growing among certain elements of society. *Carta Política* was a reliable indicator of the thinking of a sizable part of the Argentine upper class. There former anti-Peronist commando Mariano Grondona warned that López Rega's fall "would carry with it many dangers. ... Firmness with the guerrillas, the deideologization of Peronism, the recuperation of the university come together in the person of the minister-secretary."[67]

The government's overall unpopularity, particularly among unionized workers, forced López Rega to make a spectacular bid to the political galleries. On November 16 Isabelita surprised the country by announcing that Evita's remains would be repatriated from Spain the following day. (A month earlier Aramburu's corpse was stolen from Buenos Aires' Recoleta cemetery by Montoneros trying to force a trade for Evita's return.) There was a touch of furtiveness in Evita's repatriation. After a brief religious ceremony the body of the woman still revered by millions was rushed to the presidential residence. The union bosses, who had hardly enough warning to stage a symbolic strike in homage, were not even invited to the mass.[68]

Meanwhile the purge continued. The day after Evita's return the bodies of two young women lawyers killed by the Triple A were found floating in the Río Paraná in Santa Fe. They had been tortured, bound, and thrown into the river while still alive.[69]

A House at 244 Libertad Street

The night of November 28 José Polisecki, seventeen, the son of a wealthy Jewish businessman, was lured by an attractive blonde woman ten years his senior for a rendezvous at a café in the capital's Belgrano district. The next morning his family began receiving the first of a series of messages from a so-called Montoneros–Ala Nacionalista (Montoneros–Nationalist Wing) group. They demanded $2 million for José's release.

For three tense weeks negotiations dragged on, first by telephone, then by letter. Then on December 19 Polisecki's body was found along the Pan-American highway just outside the federal capital. In his hands and around his cadaver were pamphlets claiming Polisecki, who was apolitical, was killed for "betraying" the ERP. Seven bullets had destroyed his brain.

Two of Polisecki's captors, Nelson Romero and his brother-in-law Rodolfo Guillermo Silchinger, were SIDE agents with extensive criminal records. Neighbors testified later that they assumed both worked at the presidential palace, as Romero had a sign in his car that read "National Presidential Press Secretariat"— the office of key López Rega aide Jorge Conti. The blonde bait, a ballerina, was also a SIDE informant.

Polisecki spent his captivity, blindfolded and chained to a wall, at a SIDE safehouse at 244 Libertad street in Martínez, a Buenos Aires suburb. The house, occupied by Romero and his wife, and another around the corner, rented by Silchinger, were used to "interrogate" illegally held leftists. Romero and Silchinger were linked to top right-wing nationalist military men. They took part in "anticommunist training" conducted by the officers, even meeting socially with them, along with their wives.

One of the officers, a National Gendarmerie commander who had used Romero and Silchinger as intelligence agents and bodyguards, interrogated Polisecki at the bungalow at 244 Libertad Street. There he questioned the teenager about Judaism, Zionism, and "training camps." He later denied knowing about the extortion connected with Polisecki's calvary. "Irregular" detentions, he said, were "routine" among the intelligence services.[70]

A Chain of Reprisals

On Sunday, December 4, in the provincial capital of San Miguel de Tucumán thirty-one-year-old Capt. Humberto Viola, an army intelligence operative, his wife, and two children arrived at his parents' home for lunch. Suddenly shots rang out from two cars stationed in front of the dwelling. When the firing stopped, Viola and his three-year-old daughter María Cristina were dead. Five-year-old María Fernanda was gravely injured with a bullet wound in the head.

The attack, the ERP said, was part of a reprisal against the army for what it charged was the "execution" of sixteen guerrillas following a foiled attack on an army base in Catamarca province. By the end of the first week in December ten officers, including Viola, were killed. The campaign was called off following María Cristina's death.

The day after Viola's murder, six youths were killed in the federal capital. Two had been thrown in front of Buenos Aires' renowned Teatro Colón, covered in an Argentine flag and bearing messages about their alleged membership in the ERP. That night a Peronist Youth activist was awakened by police at his home. He was murdered on his doorstep.[71]

9

Tucumán: A Rumor of War (1975)

> It is possible the fate of the country, and of South America itself, is being decided today here in the hills of Tucumán.
>
> —*Lt. Col. Ricardo Flouret, September 1975*

> [The Argentines] have the clearest concept of antiguerrilla warfare. Perhaps because they fought in the Tucumán mountains and won. They organized our first fighters.
>
> —*Nicaraguan Contra Commander Enrique Bermúdez*[1]

On Saturday February 9, 1980, army commander in chief Gen. Leopoldo Galtieri gave a speech at the Teniente Berdina village in Tucumán province in northwestern Argentina. It was the fifth anniversary of Operativo Independencia (Operation Independence), a massive military-led campaign against the ERP. Located on the sugarcane-growing plain that parallels the mountain range running north to south across the province, Teniente Berdina had been named after a young officer killed earlier in the antiguerrilla effort.

The choice of the spot, full of symbolism, was meant to underline the point of the general's speech. In it, Galtieri refused to admit that the military had committed human rights violations. The nature of the antisubversive fight, in which "organized homicidal deviance reached a level far beyond what the human mind was capable of conceiving ... in which the plans, faces and identities of the aggressors had been hidden in the shadows," made explanations for what was done impossible. The general lashed out at "the fistful of traitors that today try to obtain—with the conscious or unconscious complicity of their foreign sympathizers—that which they couldn't achieve in a battle the Argentine people carried out and in which it legitimately triumphed."

"With the economic resources their criminal acts have produced—robbery, kidnappings, tortures reaching the limits of cruelty—they have organized a campaign to discredit this heroic and long-suffering Argentina, accusing it of violating human rights," Galtieri said. Although he did not single them out by name during his speech, broadcast nationwide over radio, it was understood that among Argentina's enemies were the Carter State Department and international human rights groups. "Five years ago ... the Argentine army had to go to the mountains of Tucumán to detain and destroy a threat that loomed over the very existence of the country itself. ... Here there was a war. An absurd war. Unleashed with criminal and intentional barbarism."[2]

Although at one level Galtieri had chosen the village for its obvious symbolism, on another the selection of Teniente Berdina was in fact an uncanny metaphor for the charade the army had concocted around the Tucumán campaign. Hernán Berdina did in fact die a violent death but not at the hand of the guerrillas, as the official version insisted. The young lieutenant and another soldier were killed in a confused skirmish at dusk between two army units, due to a confusion over passwords. Berdina's death was seen by the general running Operativo Independencia as a threat to his own career. Officers are supposed to die in battle, not by mistake. Although his superiors knew how Berdina died, they utilized the young officer's loss by resurrecting him as one more in the military's growing pantheon of "martyrs."[3]

The military's contention that there had been a war in Tucumán, even the "absurd war" postulated by Galtieri, was part of the generals' justification of their seizure of power and the massacre that followed. By early 1975 the military had become increasingly aware of the need to refurbish their institution's image, with an eye to again providing an alternative to a troubled civilian government. A virtual news blackout and Tucumán's geographic isolation gave the generals a chance to portray a conflict that was tailored to their own political objectives.[4]

The ERP never posed a major military threat to the country. Instead, the nature of the challenge posed in Tucumán was deliberately distorted by the generals. The fighting in the province also served as a test market, particularly in the army, for the institutionalization of some of the "dirty war" techniques of the Triple A. Arrayed against 5,000 army troops, the ERP guerrillas never succeeded in putting more than 120 to 140 combatants into the field, and that only for less than two weeks. The ERP units—normally totaling between 60 and 80 men—were poorly trained and armed, counted on only marginal popular support, and suffered serious morale problems. At no time did they number anywhere near the 600 or more men the military and their allied media claimed.[5]

The guerrillas were hardly, to use Galtieri's words, "a threat that loomed over the very existence of the country itself." The military high command knew it from the start, having infiltrated the group with intelligence agents. The insurgents' real number was a closely held secret. The military used the ERP's own exaggerated propaganda as proof of the threat.[6] Some 50 military and police personnel were officially listed as killed by armed leftists in Tucumán. At least a quarter actually perished in accidents or, like Berdina, died in blind firefights between military units belonging to the same side. A few were even murdered by their own comrades in arms. The inflated body count, however, served to stoke feelings of vengeance within the ranks.[7]

The dense mountain jungles of Tucumán provided a cover for a policy of torture, kidnapping, and anonymous death. The methods first tried out there were then applied to the rest of the country. It was a witch-hunt, not a war, the military had launched in Tucumán.[8]

Survival of the Fittest

For more than five generations sugar was the center of life in semitropical Tucumán, Argentina's most densely populated province and its smallest geographically. During the harvest the labor pool swelled, as arrivals from as far away as Bolivia did *trabajo golondrina* (swallow's work), swooping down on the province to toil as cane cutters and peons. Darker skin and Indian features were cause enough to determine the type of work a migrant was given. Even in the 1960s there were many who still remembered the company store, grueling sixteen-hour days for subsistence wages, and whip-carrying foremen—swaggering men who showed no compunction in demanding that the wives or daughters of their workers submit to them sexually in exchange for the smallest consideration. In the late 1940s, during the first Peronist government, conditions slowly changed as the sugar workers were given a number of social benefits. Their union, the Federación Obrera de Trabajadores de la Industria de Azúcar (FOTIA; Sugar Industry Workers Labor Federation), became one of the most powerful labor organizations in the country and a mainstay of Peronism.[9]

Such betterment was short-lived, however. The owners of the sugar plantations had refused to invest in modernization. As the price of Tucumán's sugar rose to nearly double that of the world market, only government price supports kept many of the sugar mills running. These subsidies came to an abrupt end in 1966, as the Juan Carlos Onganía regime sought to impose survival-of-the-fittest criteria on an industry long used to the dole. The results were dramatic. In 1965 Tucumán had twenty-seven mills; three years later that number had shrunk to seventeen.

Whole villages came to resemble ghost towns. Tens of thousands of *tucumános* left the province to look for work elsewhere. Many ended up populating the shantytowns surrounding Córdoba and greater Buenos Aires. "There is a feeling of gloom throughout the province," reported *New York Times* correspondent Malcolm W. Browne, in a story published in August 1968. The headline for the dispatch was itself foreboding: "Argentine province nears revolt amid poverty and repression."[10]

Imagining Cuba: The ERP's Rural Front

That the ERP chose Tucumán as the site of its most audacious—and fatal— challenge to the Argentine state reflected both dire provincial realities and some of the left's most deeply cherished myths. To many, the rugged, densely forested mountains and the flat sugarcane growing plain that sprawled out from it evoked eastern Cuba. "For many years our countries have felt the temptation to mechanically repeat the path developed by the Cuban revolution," recalled one historian and former activist of the PRT, the ERP's parent group. "During the 1960s, the guerrilla struggle, particularly in its rural form, was seen by many Latin American revolutionaries as the magic formula that would open the doors of revolution everywhere."[11]

In 1962 Mario Roberto Santucho wrote his first Marxist tract, entitled "Four Hypotheses on Northern Argentina." In it he postulated that the sugar industry was the motor force behind the regional economy and the sugar-producing proletariat its vanguard. Santucho, who lived and worked among the peasants of neighboring Santiago del Estero, returned to Tucumán, where he had attended the university and participated actively in student politics three years earlier, already committed to Marxism-Leninism. In part his conversion was due to a two-month visit to Cuba in 1961, a critical year in which the United States had unsuccessfully invaded the island republic and Castro declared his fidelity to the ideas of Marx.

Upon his return from Cuba Santucho became one of the earliest members of the Frente Revolucionario Indoamericano Popular (FRIP; Indo-American Popular Revolutionary Front), a small, regional, university-based party. The FRIP had begun its political work among the rough-hewn railway, textile, and forestry workers of Santiago de Estero, even editing several pages of the party's newspaper, *Norte Revolucionario,* in Quechua, the Indian language spoken by most of the region's poor. Santucho, for example, "spent weeks at a time in the tropical forests, sharing the difficult conditions with workers and peasants in order to talk to them about socialism." FRIP activists also began working with the sugar workers in Tucumán.[12]

In late 1963 the FRIP joined forces with a small Trotskyite group called Palabra Obrera (PO; Workers' Word) to form the Frente Unico (Single Front) FRIP-PO. Ideological differences between activists coming from Palabra Obrera, with its emphasis on urban, trade union activism, and those of the FRIP, with its special focus on the problems of the region's peasantry, made the front an unstable one.[13]

Although it succeeded in winning a few seats in the Tucumán provincial legislature in 1965 (using the slogan "Workers' candidates to the bourgeois parliament"), the FRIP-PO's most important work was done among the region's laborers and peasants. The front played a leading role in winning back control for workers of military-intervened unions and in disputing control of these unions with management-backed labor bosses. Factories and plantations faced with closure or that owed workers months of back pay were taken over, sometimes with management personnel held as hostages. Strikes, massive demonstrations, and industrial sabotage proliferated. The workers at the San José mill, where Santucho worked as the union's accountant, occupied its factory seventeen times in one year.[14]

In May 1965 the FRIP-PO held a convention in Buenos Aires, in which the two groups formally merged to form the Workers Revolutionary Party, known by the acronym PRT. Time and Robi Santucho's own personality would eventually turn the PRT's course away from the Trotskyites' more traditional political path. Wide-eyed and simply dressed, Santucho was to his followers a charismatic, almost mystical figure. Soft-spoken, energetic, and persuasive, he seemed at times a mixture of a monk and a peasant—a youthful Western version of Vietnamese revolutionary Ho Chi Minh, whom he admired.[15]

Even in those early years, warning signs about Santucho's personalist form of leadership went unheeded. At the time, few criticized the personality cult that he allowed to grow up around him. Nor was his tendency to overly rosy political evaluations called into question, much less his rather mechanical attempts to transfer lessons learned by the Vietnamese revolutionaries to the reality of northwest Argentina. Nor did anyone seem worried by the fact that Santucho had very little tolerance for dissenting opinions once he had made up his own mind.[16]

Onganía's presidency and the closure of the province's sugar mills brought seething social tensions to a boil. The policies emanating from Buenos Aires fell heavily on two sectors that had already undergone a strong dose of radicalization—students and rural laborers. Pressure from the grass roots combined with the activism of the PRT and other leftist or Peronist groups in what increasingly looked like class conflict, becoming an open confrontation with provincial and police authorities. As local conditions worsened, the PRT edged closer to a position favoring violent insurrection. At the same time Argentine-born Cuban revolutionary Ernesto Guevara was making headlines across the nearby border, in Bolivia. "The appearance of el Che in the Bolivian jungle created great expectations among Latin American revolutionaries, and, of course, in Argentina's PRT," recalled Julio Santucho, a brother of the ERP leader. "A legendary compatriot, a hero of the Cuban revolution, he ignited a spark of hope for the liberation of the suffering Bolivian people in a zone bordering Argentina's northern provinces—where at that very time the workers' vanguard was demanding the preparation for the unleashing of revolutionary armed struggle."[17]

Open Conflict

On June 12, 1974, *El Combatiente,* the organ of the PRT, announced the establishment of the Compañia del monte Ramón Rosa Jiménez (Ramón Rosa Jiménez

Mountain Company). The military unit, named after a local ERP militant killed by the police, was based in the Tucumán *monte* (mountain region) and was meant to usher in a new stage of "open conflict" with the government. "The renovated impetus of the worker and popular struggles has already inaugurated the generalization of the war," the article proclaimed. "The rural guerrilla front ... ought to assure the existence of military units capable of disputing the territory and within a certain time period gain bases of support and, later, liberated zones."

The month before, the ERP made a more direct affirmation of its presence. Twenty guerrillas briefly overran the unprotected village of Acheral. There some of the town's 1,800 inhabitants were subjected to a fiery harangue by one of the armed leftists clad in olive green fatigues. Marching into town in parade formation, the insurgents ran up a blue and white flag with a five-pointed red star, the ERP banner, in the village square.

Although the invaders quickly dispersed, the propaganda coup had its desired effect. The Argentine news media began to speculate, sometimes hysterically, about the imminence of the establishment of a "liberated zone" in Tucumán. For the next eight months the guerrillas carried out similarly stagy attacks. They briefly overran one factory and a handful of villages and hamlets, setting up precarious base camps in the mountains and infrequently clashing with the security forces. Lacking a real military strategy, the guerrillas allowed themselves to be lulled by their own propaganda into a fatal overestimation of their own success. "In general, the perspective of 'prolonged war' was forgotten, while the concept of 'generalized combat' was accepted before we were ready," admitted one survivor of the *compañía*. "We were already talking about 'liberated zones' when we had just begun to fight."[18]

At the time of the Acheral takeover the ERP was undisputably Argentina's best-organized guerrilla force. Formed into tightly compartmentalized "cells," ERP combatants saw themselves as an ideologically pure "armed vanguard" that avoided the "right-wing opportunism" and "militaristic tendencies" they saw in their rivals on the left. "Among ourselves there are no insignias of rank," the ERP proclaimed. "Our only *comandante* is and will be Che Guevara, who retakes the emancipating tradition of San Martín and Bolívar."[19]

Although their first acts were characterized by Robin Hood–style "armed propaganda," the guerrillas quickly became specialists in ransom kidnappings of businessmen and attacks on military units. Between the time of their emergence and the opening of the rural front in Tucumán, the ERP was responsible for, among other acts of violence, the abduction of a former chief of navy intelligence, the kidnap-murder of the president of FIAT-Argentina, and the attempted armed takeovers of the 141st Army Communications Batallion in Córdoba and the 10th Armored Cavalry Regiment in Azul. A splinter group, the ERP–22 de Agosto, also murdered retired Rear Adm. Hermes Quijada, the navy's official spokesman at the time of the executions of the sixteen guerrillas in Trelew in 1972. According to one estimate, 60 percent of foreign businessmen left Argentina in 1973, the result of more than 170 business kidnappings that year. Many of these were the work of the ERP.[20]

The vortex of armed conflict, in which ERP cadres were taken farther and farther away from their political work among "the people," helped lead to two fatal misperceptions. One was seeing only what they wanted to see, or "the strong tendency to transform into massive phenomena advances that were only taking place in sectors of the vanguard." Far worse was the admission that the guerrillas had erred as to who was their enemy. "To establish the socialist revolution as an immediate objective led to the visualization of Perón as the principle enemy of the forces of progress," recalled Julio Santucho. The "real enemy," he said later, was the "financial oligarchy and its political-military instrument—the fascist tendency that gained hegemony within the armed forces." With Cámpora's election, he noted, "political conditions had modified substantially." There was a huge difference between fighting a military dictatorship and combating a government overwhelmingly chosen in free elections. The guerrillas "did not understand those changes, with grave consequences later on."[21]

Operativo Independencia Begins

Operativo Independencia began Monday morning, February 9, 1975. Four days before, the military had prevailed upon Isabel Perón to sign secret Decree no. 261, authorizing the army high command to "execute the military operations necessary to neutralize and/or annihilate the actions of the subversive elements acting in Tucumán province." A coded message from the army high command in Buenos Aires had arrived Sunday night, giving the green light for the massive operation planned by the army high command for some months.[22] The fact that there was a freely elected government in power proved to be a propaganda boon for the military, who had been massively repudiated at the polls less than two years before. Gen. Jorge R. Videla, the head of the army general staff, ensured that the army took maximum advantage of the chance for the institution to polish its image with an intensive "psychological action" campaign. In a secret document, YM-15, dated February 5, Videla ordered the service's propaganda experts to develop an intensive effort whose purpose was "to let the country know that the army's intervention grows out of a decision by the executive branch, in order to elicit a favorable response from the populace."

The document underscored that one of the most important themes of the psychological action effort would be that "the army defends the people's legitimate interests against those who deny its essential rights." Noting that "terrorism exploits the weakness of its victims," one of the military directives made explicit the propaganda pitch to be used in order to capitalize on the political legitimacy of civilian rule: "Let's show them we are not afraid, that having a people's government obliges us to defend it."[23]

The army was not the only group to smell the possibility of political capital from the antiguerrilla effort. The decree signed by Isabel putting Operativo Independencia into effect also included provisions for the inclusion of López Rega's Social Welfare ministry in the campaign. The department was given the task of carrying out "the civic action operations necessary among the population affected by the military operations." Before the end of the month López Rega himself would appear in Tucumán. There he inaugurated five social assistance centers, distributing funds and truckloads of medicine in poor neighborhoods. He boasted that if he could, he would be "the first to grab a gun to eradicate subversion."[24]

Isabel's decree also ordered that development of "psychological action" operations be run by the presidential press secretariat, headed by Jorge Conti. Reputed to be a ranking member of the Triple A, Conti was in turn to coordinate his activity with the army high command.[25]

Operativo Independencia began between 6:00 and 7:00 A.M., when 1,500 army troops were deployed by Gen. Acdel Edgardo Vilas in a rectangle 36 miles long and 24 miles wide running along Route 28, south of San Miguel de Tucumán, the provincial capital. The zone, in which seemingly endless fields of sugarcane surround the towns and sugar mills along the highway, ran parallel to the densely forested mountains to the west.

Although the ERP knew the operation was imminent, the military threw a mantle of secrecy over the effort. What information the army did allow to filter out of the so-called "operations zone" was meant to portray a picture of close combat between two uniformed and identifiable armies. The picture of conventional warfare presented to the public was in keeping with the intent of the secret directives for repression of the guerrilla challenge approved by Isabel Perón's government. The orders stipulated that suspects could be held incommunicado for only forty-eight hours, with thirty days as the maximum time period a prisoner could be detained without trial. They strictly limited the army's zone of operations and, on paper, appeared to safeguard the prerogatives of the civilian authorities.[26]

However, while the public's attention was being focused on the "theater of operations" running along the mountain range, the "war" was actually being conducted elsewhere. "From the beginning of Operativo Independencia everything was centered in the cities of San Miguel de Tucumán and in Concepción," recalled General Vilas, who, as commander of the 5th Infantry Brigade, was the man in charge of the effort. "There were four months of intensive urban struggle." The secret war, Vilas said, was necessary as the guerrillas frequently slipped out of the mountains, seeking refuge in the cities by donning street clothes and passing for civilians. The "operational advantage" of transferring the struggle to the cities, he said, made it possible to carry it out "with an economy of means and *without having suffered during 1975 one casualty among the legal forces. ... There, in San*

Miguel, the mass of the Compañía Ramón Rosa Jiménez was captured." (Italics added)[27]

But what kind of struggle was it in which thousands of army troops were deployed in the countryside to fight a wily enemy who, nonetheless, became notoriously ineffective once he reached the city limits? How was it that a group that constituted "a threat that loomed over the very existence of the country itself" suddenly allowed its ranks to be decimated, without killing a single adversary? How were the ERP guerrillas moving about in the cities detected, and how was the secret urban "war" carried out there without the rest of the country taking notice?

Acdel Vilas: Death's General

When talking among his subordinates, Gen. Acdel Edgardo Vilas liked to brag that he was *el general de la Muerte* (Death's general). He also liked to compare himself to Lt. Col. Héctor B. Varela, whose brutal strike-breaking campaign in the early 1920s—immortalized in Osvaldo Bayer's four-volume epic *Los vengadores de la Patagonia trágica*—had resulted in the massacre of hundreds of rebellious workers in southern Argentina. "I want to see the bodies of twenty subversives in front of me each day," Vilas once harangued his troops. Frequently they complied.[28]

Under Vilas's command, torture became a standard operating technique, and the general himself was no stranger to the brutal sessions. Vilas later boasted of having established Argentina's first clandestine detention center, and he operated army commando units in civilian dress out of unmarked cars. He also initiated the use of *La Capucha,* the dreaded hood worn by security personnel to prevent their identification while conducting illegal detentions or executions without trial.[29]

It was Vilas who decided which prisoners were "harmless" and therefore could be brought before a judge and which were not and for whom there awaited another fate. "Vilas had a fixation with subversion," recalled Gen. (ret.) Mario Benjamín Menéndez who, as a colonel, served under Vilas's command. "He was even worried about ideas that could be considered subversive, or those who might want to change what were considered 'traditional' values, or people who questioned how he ran things."[30]

Vilas's colleagues frequently complained that his 1974 promotion to the rank of general was based on his openly Peronist sympathies and friendship with López Rega, but even so, he was the only general in his promotion who was not put in charge of troops. His commandless condition changed only when an accidental plane crash—occurring during an aerial reconnaissance of the rugged Tucumán *monte*—killed the man who headed the 5th Infantry Brigade a month before Operativo Independencia was about to begin. (At the time the ERP–22 de Agosto claimed credit for the accident.)[31]

Among his men Vilas sparked a certain sympathy as *un general tropero,* a military man who shares the lot of his troops, an image he cultivated. For others, however, the officer was clownish and brutal. A former superior depicted Vilas as a sort of military Walter Mitty. "Vilas," he said, "is a mediocre man who always dreamed of being important."[32]

Trained in U.S. command and combat schools, Vilas nevertheless looked to the French for guidance in counterinsurgency tactics. Those he most admired were the men who led the French Secret Army Organization in a vicious but ultimately unsuccessful effort to keep Algeria a colony. In particular, Vilas was enamored with the works of French army Col. Roger Trinquier, who once purchased, without the French government's knowledge or approval, the entire opium crop of a Laotian tribe to finance the French war against the Communists. Trinquier's book, *War, Subversion and Revolution,* a long apology for the use of torture, "black propaganda," and other "special operations" in antiguerrilla warfare was, Vilas said later, his "principle guide" during his time in Tucumán."[33]

French counterinsurgency theory suggested the need for a joint political-military command. An idea antithetical to the civilian control mandated by the orders emanating from Buenos Aires, it was nonetheless embraced with enthusiasm by the ambitious general. Despite orders limiting his operations to a well-defined theater of operations in the Tucumán countryside, Vilas repeatedly extended his reach far beyond both professional and territorial boundaries. He quickly set himself up as a sort of military proconsul. His own political contacts in Buenos Aires, particularly among the right-wing nationalists associated with López Rega, insulated him from complaints made by the provincial governor of Tucumán and, later, the governor of Santiago del Estero.[34]

"My intention," Vilas later bragged,

> was to supplant, *even by using methods that I was prohibited from using,* the political authority of Tucumán province, trying to overcome, by melding civilian and military efforts, the Marxist guerrilla outbreak, which had the people of Tucumán under its spell and which threatened to expand into other provinces.
>
> Although my task was not to replace the authorities I soon realized that, by sticking to regulations ... the operation would end in disaster. The nature of the subversive war, which touched all sectors of society, required a single, coherent command. ... If I limited myself to readying, training and commanding my troops, ignoring areas—the labor scene, business, universities, social life, etc.—that on paper did not correspond to me, the enemy would continue to have the "sanctuaries" it enjoyed until that moment. (Italics added)

In Tucumán, Vilas said, "everyone understood there existed a parallel government situated in the 5th Brigade."[35]

Vilas's fascination with the ideology and methods of the OAS also put him in direct conflict with the legal framework for carrying out the repression set down in the orders signed by Isabel Perón. The general, who claimed that subversion got its start with the French Revolution of 1789, saw the antiguerrilla fight as an all-encompassing struggle between the Forces of Light and the Reign of Darkness, in which no one was beyond suspicion.[36]

"When we began to investigate subversion's causes and effects," Vilas said,

we arrived at two inescapable conclusions. One was that, among other causes, culture was really the motivating force. The war that we were fighting was eminently cultural. The second was that there was a perfect continuity between Marxist ideology and subversive practice, whether it be in its armed military facet, or in the religious, institutional, education or economic spheres. For that reason subversion had to be dealt a mortal blow in its essence, in its structure, that being its ideological sustenance.

The military "were beaten if we allowed the proliferation of dissolute elements—psychoanalysts, psychiatrists, Freudians, etc.—inciting consciences and questioning national and family roots."

The "nonconventional methods" used by his troops, Vilas said, were necessary to dismantle the ERP's cellular structure. The guerrillas had a rigorous regime of work and monitored meetings, and if one of the cell members disappeared and thus did not show up at his prearranged "date," the others escaped, usually to another province.

One ought to remember that many of the subversives were people well known in Tucumán. They were immediately able to mobilize the political parties, the courts and even the Interior Ministry to look into their fate. If the detention procedure had been carried out with my men wearing their uniforms, there wouldn't have been any alternative to handing them over to the justice system to see them released a few hours later. But if the operation was carried out by officers in civilian dress, in 'operational' cars ... then things changed.

"One had to forget," Vilas said,

the teachings of the military college and the laws of conventional war, where the formalities of honor and ethics were essential parts of military life, to get in step with this new kind of fight. ... If, out of respect for classical norms, we had abstained from employing nonconventional methods, the task of intelligence—and this was a war of intelligence—would have been impossible to carry onward. (Italics added)[37]

Lessons from "The Schoolhouse"

Vilas claimed that by December 18, 1975, ten months after Operativo Independencia began, 312 guerrillas had been killed, and 322 more had been either wounded or detained. A list prepared seven months later by the army's own intelligence services, however, showed that only 226 people participated in the Ramón Rosa Jiménez Mountain Company throughout its entire eighteen-month existence. By the general's own count, 1,507 people—"accused of maintaining close relations with the enemy"—had been held at La Escuelita (the Little School) detention center in Famaillá alone. Torture was routine at La Escuelita, which got its name from the fact that it was located in a schoolhouse. It was the first clandestine concentration camp run by the army in the country and one of a number that operated in the province beginning in 1975.[38]

Many cases of torture, disappearance, and violent death in Tucumán went unrecorded. According to the testimony of at least one former military officer who was later purged from the army for his democratic beliefs, whole villages—men, women, and children—in remote mountain areas were tortured by Vilas's special squads. Bombing sorties were frequently conducted by the air force—against a total of sixty to seventy guerrillas spread out over several hundred square miles. It was, *New York Times* correspondent Juan de Onis wrote in November 1975, "a war in which there are apparently no prisoners and in which the military make little distinction between guerrillas carrying weapons and collaborators serving as couriers or supplying the men in the hills."[39]

* * *

The official investigating commission established by the Tucumán parliament nearly a decade after Operativo Independencia began found "a grim similarity" in nearly all the crimes committed during the antiguerrilla fight from 1975 onward. "The repressive system put together had a basic objective: the mass diffusion of terror in order to paralyze any attempt at opposition," the commission said in its official report. The methods used "differed from others that were known [because of] a new repressive characteristic—the victim's kidnapping, or illegal detention."

> From this central element, kidnapping, came all the rest: the later disappearance of the victim ... his transfer to unknown and clandestine detention centers; the participation of repressive units made up of elements that hid their identity; the operation completely outside the justice system; the abandonment of the victims in the hands of the abductors, who had no legal impediments to their treatment [of the prisoners]; the discretional application of punishments that knew no limits other than the interrogator's needs, with the objective generally of extracting "information"; the refusal of any state agency to recognize the detention had taken place; the uncertainty and terror within the kidnap victim's family, and the deliberate confusion of public opinion.

Among the tortures used in Tucumán were electric shock applied to gums, breasts, and genitals; the "electric bed," a metallic bedspring upon which the victim was forced to lie as electric current was passed through the wires; and the burial of the victim's entire body except his head for several days. Detainees were also tied to the back of tractors and dragged across rocky fields and hung with wire by their arms until the skin was ripped away, leaving the victim's musculature exposed.[40]

Son of the Devil: The Return of el Familiar

Throughout the Argentine northwest the tradition of folk legends was very strong. In the province of Santiago del Estero many of the tales had a magical, benevolent twist, explaining the world of Nature in parables whose characters were creatures that thought like Man. But in sugar territory, particularly in Tucumán, where peasants believed in devils and demons, the most important local myth was sinister and threatening. It revolved around the shadowy Perro Familiar (the Family Dog), known to Tucumán's peasants as simply "el Familiar."

It was commonly believed that el Familiar was the son of the Devil and stalked its prey after nightfall. When a peasant mysteriously disappeared, sometimes to be found later with his body ripped apart, his co-workers mourned the loss. Unable—or unwilling—to explain the phenomenon, they chalked it up to the predations of el Familiar.

There are a number of social and psychological interpretations for the appearance of el Familiar in the sugar-growing region. Most have a common theme in the powerlessness felt by its peasants. Some claimed the work of el Familiar was in fact that of the mill owners and their foremen, who took advantage of the people's superstitions to rid themselves of troublesome labor agitators. Suspicious deaths remained uninvestigated, as the poor were used to living with and accepting death, even violent death.[41]

For the peasants of Tucumán the appearance of Vilas and the army in Operativo Independencia was no different than a return of el Familiar.

Juan and Francisco Aranda

At 11:30 P.M., March 23, 1975, the guests at a wedding party held at a private home in the town of San Pablo danced as they waited for the newlyweds to arrive. Suddenly a group of soldiers and civilian-dressed men carrying weapons burst into the house. They demanded that two of the guests, eighteen-year-old Juan Eugenio Aranda and his brother Francisco, twenty-one, identify themselves. The two youths were then forced into a waiting unmarked army truck.

"They identified all the wedding guests and those who didn't have their documents with them were separated out and forced to form a line," remembered the boys' mother. "Screaming, I demanded an explanation. ... Finally a man dressed in an army uniform came forward. Tall, blond, thin, looking like he was about fifty years old, he said with a firm voice, 'I am the chief of this operation.' ... On April 4, I was told my boys were killed in a shoot-out but wasn't given the place where it occurred. Already the provincial police had informed me they had been gunned down in a battle in the mountains."

Both youths had been seen by witnesses at La Escuelita concentration camp in Famaillá after their abduction. Yet on April 5, under the headline "Identity of two guerrillas killed by army confirmed," *La Gaceta* told its readers: "Juan Eugenio Aranda ... was killed in a firefight with a military patrol Thursday morning in an unspecified mountain zone. ... His brother, Francisco Armando Aranda ... is the other extremist who was killed in the confrontation."

A day later the newspaper published a communiqué issued by the 5th Army Brigade. "Investigations are taking place after the shootout that occurred April 3, 1975, between military troops and a subversive group, in which subversive delinquents Francisco Armando and Juan Eugenio Aranda died." The case was not an isolated one. It was unusual only in the number of witnesses. To those who did not know how the boys disappeared, the case appeared to be another example of the tough task faced by the military in order to eliminate a stubborn, violent—and large—guerrilla threat. For those who did know, the abduction left a feeling of impotence and terror.[42]

The Children of Manuel Antonio Mercado

At 4:00 A.M., August 23, 1975, a car, a taxi, and two small trucks made their way along a dirt road before coming to a stop in front of the home of Manuel Antonio Mercado, located in a squatters' settlement on an abandoned patch of railway on the outskirts of San Miguel de Tucumán, the provincial capital. Inside, Mercado—a cane cutter who had worked at the nearby San José plantation—slept with his wife, two daughters, and the young man who the day before became his son-in-law. It was a happy time for the family. On August 22 Mercado's daughter María del Valle had gotten married in a civil ceremony. A religious wedding was planned for the next day. María's wedding clothes were carefully laid out for the big event.

The big metal lock that provided the only security for the one-room adobe and tin hovel proved no match for an explosive charge, and three shots pealed out in the darkness. As Mercado remembered later, there were "many men," six, a dozen, how many he couldn't remember in his grogginess and confusion. The intruders wore military uniforms and hoods, except for a small man in a suit and tie who made no attempt to hide his identity. Ordering Mercado back into the house, the men carried María, twenty-one, and her twenty-seven-year-old sister Adela del Carmen, off into the night. Exactly two months later the men returned, this time taking away Mercado's son. The three remain "disappeared." María's husband was not arrested.

Mercado said he was sure the three were not guerrillas. Their only crime, said people who knew them, was that the girls had signed a petition demanding land and work. The cards they had filled out were part of a strategy undertaken by members of a guerrilla "surface" organization to "raise the consciousness" of the people by making them act on their own necessities. Whether the girls knew they had signed documents that were part of some revolutionary strategy was unclear.[43]

Two "Homeric" Battles

As the army would admit much later, there were only two real battles between the guerrillas and their adversaries in Tucumán in all of 1975. Both occurred in the countryside.[44]

The first, the Combat of Manchalá, was the result of the ERP's frustration with the army's perceived unwillingness to fight them on their own territory. On May 25 a column of some sixty guerrillas prepared to launch a sneak attack on the army headquarters located in the city of Famaillá, 22 miles south of the provincial capital. Not only did Santucho hope to capture Vilas in his own headquarters. The attack was to take place on May 29, Army Day, the anniversary of both the *Cordobazo* in 1969 and the Montoneros' kidnapping of former military President Aramburu a year later.[45]

The ERP plan was to lie low for several weeks in order to give the army the impression it was winning the battle for the countryside, later to rise up and strike at Famaillá, "crushing its task force in only one blow." Of the sixty uniformed guerrillas and a similar number of revolutionaries in civilian dress meant to provide logistical support, more than half were recruited from ERP units outside Tucumán. Nearly all returned to their bases following the attack.[46]

Word that they had been detected forced the ERP to speed up its planned assault. The insurgents' caravan of trucks and pickups advanced along an abandoned dirt road in order to avoid running into military patrols. As they approached the Manchalá schoolhouse, they were spotted by a contingent of fourteen soldiers who were painting the building as part of the military's civic action program. Taking refuge in a chicken coop, the army men took on the larger group of guerrillas, who were forced to dismount from their vehicles and search for cover along the roadside. As a fierce gun battle raged, one of the soldiers escaped and ran ten miles to Famaillá for help.

As the army reinforcements arrived, the guerrillas dispersed in disarray. In their haste they had left behind the trucks, loaded with weapons and provisions. More importantly, they abandoned mounds of internal documents that gave the army precise information about their plans, strength, and organizational structure.[47]

One guerrilla survivor later admitted that the ERP rout was followed by "a disorderly retreat ... caused in part by the lack of combat experience shared by the comrades. ... A few comrades were lost after disobeying orders; there were those who reacted individually to the attack, without obeying their commanders. ... After Manchalá, the party began to ask for volunteers to reinforce the fifteen to twenty comrades who remained in the mountains."[48]

As was characteristic of the armed confrontations, casualty reports from Manchalá varied widely. The ERP admitted suffering two deaths and three wounded while claiming, wildly, that it had killed twenty-eight soldiers. One of the guerrilla dead, known as Sargento Dago, was a Chilean military instructor and member of that country's Revolutionary Left Movement, an anti-Pinochet guerrilla group. The army, for its part, said it did not lose any men, while variously claiming to have killed seven to seventeen guerrillas.[49]

The military had succeeded in surrounding the guerrillas and could have annihilated them on the spot, one former intelligence officer admitted, but a pursuit order was delayed for hours and the insurgents escaped into the night. The delay, he believed, was due to the military not wanting to eliminate too soon an enemy whose repression had become a political asset. Said Lt. Ernesto Urien, who was later cashiered from the service for opposing the illegal repression: "When I got to Tucumán and found out there were 67 of them and 4,000 of us, I said to myself, 'What the fuck are we doing here?' It was all a smokescreen."[50]

"After Manchalá," a Federal Police officer who took part in a special "antisubversive" unit in Tucumán said, "the guerrillas became more like armed bands working on their own, trying to just survive." Following the battle, Vilas later bragged (although it was not admitted at the time), the ERP's fighting capacity "was completely undermined."[51]

The second major "battle" occurred near Acheral on October 10. A group of twelve to fourteen guerrillas had descended from the mountains to meet a shipment of provisions sent by truck from Buenos Aires and stopped to rest in a large field of sugar cane. The *tablon* (stand of cane) was surrounded on all sides by already-cut fields.

The army had been tipped off to the presence of the guerrillas by Jesús ("El Oso") Rainer, an intelligence agent infiltrated into their ranks in Buenos Aires. Surrounding the guerrillas, the army set fire to the field, while helicopters bombarded the guerrillas with rockets and trotyl explosive charges. The insurgents were wiped out, while one low-ranking army officer died in the confrontation.[52]

The Death of a Soldier

The violence wracking the rest of the country frequently meant that the public's attention turned away from events in Tucumán—and the army's sanitized version of the conduct of the "war" there—to deaths that escaped anonymity and the cloak of fearful silence that dated back to the time of el Familiar. Often the dead who made the news had, in life, worn uniforms.

On August 23, 1975, the body of army Maj. Argentino del Valle Larrabure was found in the river port city of Rosario, hundreds of miles southeast of Tucumán. The officer weighed some 110 pounds less than when he was captured. He had been strangled. Military spokesmen claimed the body showed signs of savage torture.

Larrabure had been captured by the guerrillas as they tried to take over a military explosives factory in Villa María, Córdoba, twelve months before. Throughout the year Larrabure's wife tried to make contact with the officer through letters published as advertisements in the newspapers. "We have to give you some good news and some bad news," one of the missives read. "I'm doing well in psychiatric treatment. Our children are finishing school fine. Your friends support you. And something that hurts us: Your mother passed away without suffering." Another letter revealed the family's desperation: "Despite the faith the kids and I have, each day is harder without you. We need you, and for that reason I ask you not to give up."[53]

Larrabure's death, one former U.S. military attaché recalled, "deeply affected the psyche" of the army officer corps. Afterward, he said, "these guys were cocked and ready to go."[54]

The Unreported Reality

In 1975 the reality of the "war" in Tucumán so badly chronicled by *La Gaceta* also went unreflected in Buenos Aires' newspapers. In October the conservative morning newspaper *La Nación*, one of the country's most important dailies and a faithful representative of Argentina's large landowning interests, ran two stories about the antiguerrilla operation. The content of the first was reflected in its title: "Security and faith replace fear in Tucumán zone." The second was a paean to the "progress" military intervention had meant to the region: "160 days of normal harvest, without one union interruption. What last year was a strike zone is now one of uninterrupted production."

"Positive and concrete acts," the newspaper noted, "don't always have the same velocity as bad news."[55]

"Stalingrad" in the Semitropics

In December Gen. Acdel Vilas was transferred out of Tucumán. It was a bitter pill for the self-styled "Peronist general." Vilas had dreamed of assuming the post of Tucumán's first provincial military governor, putting an end to the guise of civilian control that was by then all but fiction anyway. While Vilas's attentions were concentrated in Tucumán, his benefactor López Rega had gone into political eclipse, as had the loperreguista faction within the army. In the meantime, Vilas's enemies within the force had put out the word, never proven, that the general had shifted the brunt of the repression away from the Peronist left—particularly the Montoneros—as part of a Byzantine interparty "deal." The Montoneros' own hatred of Vilas seemed to belie the charge.[56]

It was a melancholy farewell for Vilas, who could justly claim credit for the annihilation of the guerrilla forces in the province. The staged demonstrations of support, including pleas from the provincial parliament and the unions to the army high command that the general be kept on, went for naught. Even so, Vilas's last words to Tucumán brimmed with barracks melodrama: "People of Tucumán, a few days ago I read something that I want to express as a symbol of what I feel for all of you: You can forget those about whom and with whom you have laughed, but never can one forget those about whom and with whom one has cried."[57]

The army high command, however, was far from ready to issue its own farewell. On December 18 III Army Corps commander Gen. Luciano Benjamín Menéndez made a ringing defense of the army's antisubversive effort, saying Tucumán would be the ERP's "Stalingrad." Although the comparison with the Russians' epic battle against the Nazis was ludicrous, Menéndez's use of the future tense was no accident. The guerrillas had been effectively defeated in the province for more than six months. But the army refused to declare their politically profitable little "war" as finished.[58]

On Christmas Eve army chief of staff Videla flew to the army operations headquarters in Famaillá to issue his service's holiday greetings. In less than a year the military had succeeded in reversing its political fortunes, turning the tables on the Peronist government and clearly going on the offensive. In part, the change in the military's image was due to the successful propaganda campaign emanating out of Tucumán. No longer was there talk about how having a "people's government" obligated its common defense.

Instead, Videla complained that "subversive elements are being favored by a massive complicity" on the part of many Argentines. Putting the Peronist government on notice, the general told his audience that the politicians in Buenos Aires had just ninety days to get the Argentine house in order. "With the right of those who have shed our blood, the Argentine army demands that there be a clear definition of positions. Immorality and corruption must be suitably punished. Political, economic and ideological speculation must stop being employed as a means for adventurers to achieve their ends."[59]

10

Counterterror (1975)

There is nothing more dangerous than revolutions that do not carry out the postulates they themselves generate, and nothing more unfaithful than the public man who, when at the height of power, shows himself to be in disagreement with the doctrines that he sustained when he was in the political wilderness, and that had determined his ascent.

—Hipólito Yrigoyen

Isabel's decision to put the army at the head of the antisubversive campaign in Tucumán gave the military an opportunity denied to them by her husband. Juan Perón had refused to consider the guerrillas as anything more than a police problem. Given the guerrillas' strength, he knew Argentina's highly militarized police forces could meet the challenge.[1]

Perón's wariness was also based on his belief that a military role would compromise constitutional rule. Perón's instinct proved correct. The Tucumán campaign returned to the army its sense of mission; its restored pride put the swagger back in its step. Operativo Independencia, noted two historians of the period, "dragged out over time and instilled in the Argentine military a climate of warfare unlike anything that had been seen during an entire century."[2]

The year 1975 also marked a chilling upswing in paramilitary murders: A month's toll was no longer measured by the dozens but rather by the scores or hundreds.[3]

One of the most important paramilitary operations was that in Córdoba and was headed by retired air force Brig. Raúl Lacabanne, who had been appointed as *interventor* (federal overseer) of the province in the aftermath of the overthrow of left-wing governor Obregón Cano. (Córdoba's Radicals scored Lacabanne as "corporativist, fascist and totalitarian.") Many of the bombings, arson, extortive kidnappings, and murders allegedly carried out by the guerrillas were actually the work of Lacabanne confidants. The U.S. embassy was aware that Lacabanne's men also were deeply involved in narcotics trafficking. Several major drug figures—involved in both heroin and cocaine traffic—paid them substantial protection fees.[4]

Hitler's "Black Widow"

In a country of some 30 million people, some 300,000 are Jews. Argentina's Jewish community was by far the most important in Latin America and one of the seven largest in the world. Outside of Israel, Argentina also boasts the world's biggest Jewish religious school system.

A few Sephardic Jews came to Argentina in the early years of Spanish colonization, often trying to escape the religious persecution of the Inquisition that was in full force on the Iberian peninsula. However, the most important immigration came primarily in three later waves. The first, in the late nineteenth century, marked the arrival of thousands of Eastern European Jews. German Baron Mauricio Hirsch bought land on the fertile pampa and in Palestine, offering an escape from anti-Jewish violence in several countries. In the interwar period another group arrived, most seeking refuge from the growing shadow of Nazi Germany. The last group, coming after World War II, was swollen with Holocaust survivors.[5]

Anti-Semitism was promoted by the traditional ruling alliance of military, clergy, and the large landowners entitled by the Spanish crown. Yet Jews and "new Christians"—Jews who converted to Catholicism to escape the Inquisition—made their mark as scholars, doctors, and pioneers. With the colony's declaration of independence from Spain and the establishment of the Argentine republic, religious freedom was enshrined, although Catholicism retained its role as the official religion.[6]

Perón's overthrow in 1955 ushered in a period of conflict. Authoritarian military regimes alternated with weak civilian ones. Superimposed on worsening economic conditions, the political chaos at times gave the appearance that the country's social fabric was quickly unraveling. Anti-Semitic literature flourished on newsstands. Jewish students were beaten, and businessmen were intimidated.

One of the most violent groups was the neo-Nazi Tacuara, from which a large number of security force personnel and several guerrilla leaders emerged. "The general public feels that Tacuara's deeds go unpunished thanks to some special military immunity," noted the newsmagazine *Primera Plana*. "Those who hold that opinion cannot easily prove their claim, but certain leaders of the Armed Forces are convinced that the terrorist bands are an effective barrier against the spread of communism." The far right had other benefactors as well. One report said police had proof that the Arab League was paying most of Tacuara's expenses, a reflection, perhaps, of the fact that Argentine Jews were among the most generous groups in the Diaspora in contributing financially to Israel.[7]

Peronism's return to power in 1973 marked the zenith of social acceptance for Argentina's Jews. Perhaps no better evidence was the fact that José Ber Gelbard, a Jew and a self-made businessman, served as economy minister. However, after Perón's death, López Rega put known anti-Semites in highly visible government positions.[8]

The role played by López Rega, the Rasputin of the Pampas, is crucial for understanding the anti-Jewish violence. Under the tutelage of Licio Gelli, López Rega expanded on the contacts he made in the Arab world while working for Perón in exile in Spain. He paid special attention to cultivating relations with Muammar Kaddafi's Libyan regime. Meanwhile Gelli promoted closer ties between Italy's ruling Christian Democrats and that nation's one-time North African colony. ("When Abdullah Ben Abdid, a Libyan dissident, planned a coup against Kaddafi in 1970, Italian secret service officials warned the Libyan leader in enough time to thwart Abdid and his accomplices," *Newsweek* reported. "Rome's efforts paid off: by the mid-1970s Italian companies had won most of the work in Libya's oil-financed building bonanza.")[9]

In January 1974 López Rega had headed a week-long Argentine economic mission to Libya, accompanied by death squad leaders Morales and Almirón. The importance of the trip was underlined by the fact that both Perón and Isabel saw the delegation off at departure and welcomed it back on its return to the airport. For those unaware of López Rega's ties to the P-2, the choice of El Brujo might have seemed surprising, given his unfamiliarity with economic issues. Being Jewish precluded the chance of Gelbard's leading negotiations with an Arab country—and Libya was vociferously anti-Semitic. However, the mission could have been headed by a top Foreign Ministry official versed in economics.[10]

López Rega's Libyan trip was highly touted in the Argentine press, especially those publications linked to Peronism's internal factions such as *Mayoría, Las Bases, Crónica,* and *Gente.* Articles exalted the ideological similarities between Peronism and the Libyan regime on a broad range of Third World issues. López Rega met Kaddafi several times, the latter expressing admiration for Argentina and proclaiming Perón his master in politics. Meanwhile, the presidential press office took out large ads in the country's newspapers, headlining the trip: "Argentine Mission to Libya as a Bridge of Brotherhood between the Arab World and Latin America."

A number of accords were hammered out between the sorcerer and his Arab host, with large commissions reportedly raked off by the Argentine Social Welfare minister and his Italian Masonic benefactor. While the world reeled from the Arab oil embargo, Libya agreed to supply Argentina with 3 million tons of crude during 1974 in order to meet its needs for fuel from abroad. The Arab regime also promised to contribute to help cover the year's oil shortage in neighboring Paraguay and Uruguay, to which Argentina was to reship needed supplies. Argentina in turn agreed to sell Libyans wheat and beef, help them build a petrochemical distillery, and construct 2,000 housing units in Tripoli and 5,000 classrooms in ten Libyan towns using Argentine contractors. It promised aid in developing Libyan technology and agriculture and in the peaceful use of atomic energy.[11]

At the end of 1974 López Rega sent Gelli, then officially the Argentine commercial attaché with the embassy in Rome, on a sensitive mission. The lodge master was to try to convince officials in Bonn to allow Argentina to sell arms to Libya made under West German license, despite a fourteen-year-old treaty prohibiting such sales. "In keeping with the talks held with the Arab Republic of Libya," El Brujo wrote to Gelli, "it is necessary to obtain approval for the sale of Salta-type submarines" to be constructed in Argentina. "I found the atmosphere to be most chilly," Gelli wrote back two days before Christmas. "There is no intention to arm the Arabs there, much less the country in question." López Rega nonetheless sent sixty army colonels to Libya as part of their advanced training.[12]

Anti-Semitism surged in early 1975. *El Caudillo* was run by Triple A leader Felipe ("La Viuda Negra de Hitler"[Hitler's Black Widow]) Romeo and boasted advertising from López Rega's Social Welfare Ministry and Miguel's metalworkers union. Upon being closed by the Peronist government in March, the magazine carried an open appeal for pogrom: "Nine at night is a good hour for this ... the place you already know: the Quarter of Usury. Wave a thousand truncheons, bloody a thousand heads ... then all will be devastated."[13]

In April roving gangs in Córdoba began to attack Jewish youths, and anti-Semitic posters and magazines proliferated. The state-run Channel 11 television station carried a program on Libya in which Israel was the focus of numerous anti-Semitic comments, particularly on the part of the Syrian ambassador, Col. Jawdat Attasi. "The Jewish religion, the Jewish race," he said, "wants to run humanity's resources." The program reported the existence of "a Jewish plan to take over Patagonia or northern Argentina" to create a new state of Israel. The "Zionist plot"—the "Plan Andinia"—received wide echo in small provincial papers.[14]

April 30 was a particularly busy day for the anti-Semites. Downtown Buenos Aires appeared swathed in posters and spray-painted signs in support of *El Caudillo* and its slogan "The best enemy is a dead one." Near the offices of the publishing house Editorial Abril, leaflets from an Argentine Anti-Imperialist Alliance accused well-known actors and the owners of Abril of belonging to a "Marxist-Jewish conspiracy." Those named were told leave the country or "be executed." In the provincial capital of Mendoza the scene was repeated, with the city awash in swastikas and such threats against Jews as "With Jewish blood we'll make soap." In the port city of Rosario radio LT2 canceled a twenty-five-year-old program, "The Hebrew Hour," for "programming reasons." It was replaced with an Arab program with a marked anti-Jewish tone.[15]

In June Nazi and fascist literature in Spanish translation began to be given wide circulation on newsstands and in bookstores. Published by Editorial Milicia, the books included two by Benito Mussolini, *Fascism* and *Revolutionary Fascism;* two by Adolf Hitler, *My New Order* and *My Enemies and Yours;* and three by Joseph Goebbels, *Toward the Third Reich, The Conquest of Berlin,* and *Hitler or Lenin.* According to one writer at the time, "Milicia appears to be a phantom company and the source of its inexhaustible funds is unknown." In fact, Milicia, part of the Triple A, received funds from the SIDE, since early 1975 under López Rega's direct control.[16]

Although politicians, the Catholic Church, and other authorities at times repudiated the anti-Jewish violence, few matched the performance of Jacobo Timerman's *La Opinión*. The newspaper's crusade against the attacks resulted in a number of its reporters receiving death threats. In early November *El Caudillo*, described in one U.S. embassy document as a Triple A "surrogate," reappeared, this time bankrolled by Lorenzo Miguel. Its first new issue brought with it a thinly disguised death threat against political columnist Heriberto Kahn, himself closely tied to Massera's political ambitions: "Another time, Pen-pusher, you will run the risk of having that name of yours—Pen-pusher—changed, 'pen' [pluma] for 'lead' [plomo]. Do you understand, Pen-pusher?"[17]

Terror in a Company Town

The serpent-like Paraná is one of the great rivers of Latin America. On its western shore a veritable industrial beach links Argentina's two most populous cities, Buenos Aires and Rosario. Along its delta region to beyond the town of San Lorenzo, a distance of some 240 miles, are strung the SOMISA government steel complex in San Nicolás; the Zárate-Campana petrochemical works; Rosario's bustling port; tractor factories owned by John Deere and Massey Ferguson in San Lorenzo, and Villa Constitución, site of the country's most important metallurgical plants.

In 1975 Villa Constitución, a city of 35,000 people, was the site of a vicious repression because a local union affiliate had been taken over by a militant but unquestionably representative leadership. By the end of the struggle one worker out of eight was fired and blacklisted by factories in the area; one out of every 100 people in Villa, as it is called, was jailed; one out of every 1,000 was murdered; one out of every 2,200 remains missing.[18]

Three companies dominate the town: Acindar, Marathon, and Metcon.

A subsidiary of U.S. Steel, Acindar was a multifaceted steel producer. Its production represented 70 percent of the Argentine market for laminated steel, 50 percent of its needs for steel for construction, and one-fourth of the country's production of the laminated metal in all its forms. The interests of Acindar, a massive conglomerate, extended far beyond being one of the three most important steel industries in Argentina. From 1973 its largest shareholder, José A. ("Joe") Martínez de Hoz, served as its president. The Eton-educated scion of one of Argentina's most prominent families, Joe was also a large landowner and a member of the board of Pan American Airways and ITT. Investment banker David Rockefeller was among his close friends.

For several years Villa Constitución's metalworkers tried to wrest control of their union, the Unión Obrera Metalúrgica (UOM; Metalworkers Union), from the national leadership. The UOM, led by Lorenzo Miguel, claimed 270,000 members and was Argentina's most powerful union. Isabel's labor minister, Ricardo Otero, came from its ranks. However, after a series of strikes, factory occupations, and other actions, in 1974 a center-left coalition swept to victory in a local union election with 64 percent of the votes.

The reform fever of that long Southern Hemisphere summer extended beyond the workplace. Neighborhood assemblies sought solutions to local problems. Campaigns against shortages were organized, plans were drawn up for reopening the old municipal slaughterhouse and for housing, parks, paving Villa's mostly dirt roads, and the construction of sports facilities.[19]

In the months before March 1975 the independent workers were the object of a wave of intimidation. Anonymous death threats found their way into factory stewards' clothes lockers in the plants or were attached to the workers' time cards. The city began to awake every morning to find Villa's roads littered with pamphlets promising to "clean the city of lefties." The walls of a local cemetery were painted with huge spray-painted letters warning that "very soon they will be here."

"Months before the coup we had instructions to work the factories," recalled a Buenos Aires provincial police officer who belonged to special operations groups whose tasks were similar to those performed in Villa. "In particular, against labor leaders and activists. We received information from the businessmen, as well as from some right-wing Peronist labor leaders and intelligence personnel infiltrated into the factories. Any shop steward or worker considered bothersome was labeled a subversive."[20]

In early March 1975 Martínez de Hoz, Acindar's president, met with Isabel Perón to "let her know of his preoccupation over the events in Villa Constitución and, in particular, over the climate of insurrection." The picture painted by Martínez de Hoz was a willful distortion. The tiny contingent of guerrillas in the area were in number and actions far less than in most urban areas. While both ERP and Montoneros offered the combative workers their "solidarity," the leadership of the local unions was in the hands of rival, and sometimes antagonistic, political groups. Elections, not violent revolution, had been chosen by Villa's workers. "We didn't have any indication that subversion was rampant in Villa Constitución by any means," said one U.S. diplomat stationed in Buenos Aires. "Nor was the labor activity linked to subversive activity."[21]

"In a 1974 interview with the newspaper *Clarín* Martínez de Hoz recognized we had raised production by 2.4 percent," recalled Juan Actis, one of the metalworkers' leaders who was detained.

This increase was achieved without the company investing more capital and without hiring more workers. ... What's more, this also contradicts what Labor Minister

Ricardo Otero was saying, when he charged that the combative sectors of the union movement, with Villa Constitución as its center, were responsible for the increase in absenteeism in the country. While we ran the union, and until we were suppressed, there was not one hour's worth of strikes.[22]

On March 20, 1975, at 7:30 in the morning, a caravan of Ford Falcons without license plates coming from San Nicolás and Rosario converged on Villa. The more than 100 vehicles contained 500 heavily armed men. Many did not try to conceal their identity. Others wore hoods, dark glasses, or covered their faces with handkerchiefs. The operation was ordered by Federal Police chief Margaride and carried out by Commissar Antonio ("El Padrino" [The Godfather]) Fischetti. Civilian commandos carried SIDE credentials and ID bracelets bearing the initials of López Rega's Social Welfare Ministry.

The raiders installed themselves on the Acindar grounds and made their headquarters in the lodges used by the company's bosses. There, according to an investigation conducted later by the Sábato Commission, they operated one of the first clandestine detention centers in the country. One of those who worked in the torture chamber went on to become one of the most important of the paramilitary figures employed by the regime that took office the following year. His name was Aníbal Gordon.[23]

The assault cars and armored vehicles were supported by launches from the Navy Prefecture and helicopters of the Federal Police. A specialized repressive unit of the Buenos Aires provincial police, known as the Pumas, joined in the operation. In all, nearly 4,000 men took part in the suppression of Villa's workers. Hundreds of homes were raided and looted, and more than 300 workers were jailed.[24]

The workers struck back. For fifty-nine days, Villa Constitución was the scene of a bitter strike. On April 22 the city shut down tight. Columns of demonstrators began marching downtown. Seven thousand people defied hundreds of security personnel who took up positions in the heart of Villa. The protesters were attacked and brutally dispersed. Reporters trying to cover the story were beaten; photographers were forced to expose their film. More than 100 arrests, a dozen serious injuries, and a worker killed by a grenade were the toll of that morning's protest.

The phantom of subversion was a pretext for the imposition of a reign of terror. "The supposed plot was no more than the culmination of a hard-fought battle between labor groups," said one historian of the period, "with the government supporting its partisans—the minority—as part of a strategy of suppression of the union opposition."[25]

Throughout 1975 Villa Constitución, and in particular the workers at Acindar, continued to endure the brutal suppression. At the SOMISA works the union's shop steward network was decimated: its left-wing Peronist Felipe Vallese faction was dismantled, its secretary-general was imprisoned, and one of its members was murdered. In October a woman lawyer and two stewards were kidnapped and killed. In December two brothers shared the same fate. On January 8 three workers were abducted from their homes, to reappear later that day machine-gunned to death. All had been tortured at La Casita (the Little House), one of the lodges for top-level Acindar staff on the company grounds.[26]

On May 13 Lt. Gen. Leandro Enrique Anaya resigned as commander of the army, citing unidentified disagreements between him and Defense Minister Adolfo M. Savino, a secret member of the P-2. According to a U.S. embassy cable, one problem concerned Villa Constitución. "There, the government's own actions have brought about a strike which threatens to paralyze heavy industry in Argentina," the report said. "Apparently, López Rega and Mrs. Perón wanted to send in the army to break the strike. Anaya refused."

Anaya was replaced by Gen. Alberto Numa Laplane, "one of the few Peronist generals in the army. Indeed, he was among those who flew to Rome in 1972 to escort Perón back to Argentina. ... He is probably the only general ... who, to some extent, sympathizes with López Rega."[27]

López Rega Overplays His Hand

By early May labor conflicts throughout Argentina were on the upswing, as the chilling effects of repressive legislation passed in late 1974 began to wear off. But unlike that in Villa, most of the union turmoil was part of an offensive by the unions to gain ground for upcoming wage negotiations. Just when it appeared the unions and Isabel's government were headed on a collision course on salaries, the former appeared poised to clinch a deal with management. Then Economy Minister Alberto Gómez Morales, one of Peronism's most respected economists, resigned.[28]

On the surface his replacement, businessman Celestino Rodrigo, shared the same reputation for financial orthodoxy as Gómez Morales. Yet Rodrigo was a creation of López Rega and like him had a fascination with the occult. And although they shared a basic prescription for the ailing economy—lifting the price freeze, setting the peso at its real value, increasing agricultural prices, stimulating private investment, pruning the unions' power, and reducing the budget deficit— Gómez Morales had proposed a gradual approach. Rodrigo sought to do everything at once.

Fuel and electricity prices were doubled, and the peso was devalued by 50 percent. Fearful of yet another price spiral, housewives swarmed on local shops, buying up available stocks. In June inflation officially increased by 34.7 percent, the highest level on record since Argentina began measuring such economic indicators in 1960. For many, particularly the middle class, the specter of Weimar Germany was too real for comfort.

During the second week of June top U.S. policymakers received a secret report from the State Department's Bureau of Intelligence and Research (INR). Its findings were bleak, a reflection of the mood in Buenos Aires:

> President María Estela Perón faces the most precarious political circumstances of her 11-month tenure. ... The situation is not beyond recovery, but in the absence of corrective measures, the Government's chances of surviving until the 1977 elections continue to decline. Responsibility for the revival of old political practices rests principally with the administration. President Perón has made it clear that hers would be a "right-wing" Peronist administration with little interest in maintaining the dialogue initiated by her husband with nongovernment groups. ... There has been a marked shift away from the military's commitment to refrain from political action at almost any cost. ...
>
> Disenchantment with, and the primary threat to, President Perón's administration stems from the extraordinary influence that López Rega exerts over the President and the Government's policies. ... López Rega's charmed political performance is attributable both to his own skills as a master of intrigue and apparently to fear across the Argentine political spectrum that President Perón would resign if he were ousted. However, opposition to López Rega has become so widespread that his room for maneuver is now severely restricted.[29]

The unfolding economic disaster, popularly known as the Rodrigazo, meant the breakdown of wage talks between labor and management. Grass-roots discontent among the workers threatened to explode. The largely orthodox Peronist union bureaucracy found itself in a fight for its very existence, while trying to find a solution that would give Isabel Perón a face-saving political settlement. "The ship is sinking and we're not going down with it," one labor leader said. "There's not a single union that can ask its membership to stop the wage talks." Added another union boss: "The leftists can take advantage of the growing popular discontent, but the workers still can turn a deaf ear to them. We have to show them [the rank and file] that their leaders will fight to protect their salaries."[30]

On June 27 the CGT organized a work stoppage and a rally at the Plaza de Mayo—"Perón's plaza"—in an ostensible show of support for Isabel, while allowing the rank and file to heap abuse on Rodrigo and his political mentor, José López Rega. In an official communiqué released at 3:00 A.M., Isabel urged the workers "not to abandon the workplace and to carry on with the daily task in order to carry out General Perón's ideas." Despite her plea, and a rainy day, the work stoppage was almost total. The Plaza de Mayo was jammed. The protesters respectfully left the president out of their chants. But the significance of the unions' decision to confront a Peronist government could not be missed.

On July 2 President Gerald Ford received a copy of the *National Intelligence Daily,* a top-secret report prepared by the office of CIA director William Colby. It claimed, wrongly, that Isabel had won "a significant, although probably short-lived victory in her continuing conflict with the unions." A CIA analyst in Buenos Aires said that Isabelita's "unexpectedly strong position has caught the labor leaders off guard" and that they pledged to support her. "At the direction of chief presidential adviser López Rega, the government sought first to undermine the authority of the labor leaders and now seeks to divide the whole labor movement. … If the government wins its contest with labor, the main winner will be López Rega; his mastery of the political situation will then be virtually complete."[31]

Friday morning, July 11, the government announced the resignations of López Rega and the ministers of defense and interior. In a statement the former social welfare minister explained his resignation from "official posts" while underscoring his "unalterable friendship" with Isabelita. López Rega also remained at the presidential residence in Olivos, blocking access to Isabel who, he said, was ill. His police and bodyguards had largely displaced the army Grenadiers as the president's protectors.

Six days later Rodrigo quit as economy minister. "Argentine President Perón's political position is growing steadily weaker," the CIA reported the next day, a Friday. "Labor leaders, formerly Mrs. Perón's strongest political supporters, have now become her most persistent adversaries. … They may press for a complete restructuring of the Peronist political hierarchy in order to eliminate the influence of López Rega."[32]

That night a group of cabinet ministers tried to see Mrs. Perón. They were to tell her that the military and a number of political groups wanted an end put to López Rega's ubiquitous presence. As the politicians were trying to finesse their way into seeing Isabel, the official presidential bodyguard, the Grenadiers, overpowered López Rega's bodyguards, disarming them. Although some military men and political leaders wanted López Rega to stand trial for corruption and misconduct, on Saturday he packed his bags and led a huge caravan to a local airport. Flying to Brazil in the company of a dozen bodyguards, the once omnipotent "minister of death," the government reported, was winging his way to Europe on an "official mission," first as President Perón's "extraordinary and plenipotentiary ambassador," then as "her personal representative."[33]

"The military junta that was then preparing the coup d'état knew their task was more difficult with my being around," López Rega claimed, improbably, years later. "They tried to get rid of me any way they could. They told the president, Mrs. Perón, that they were going to kill me in the presidential palace, and she told me they'd end my life if I didn't go. Her eyes filled with tears when she told me, 'They're going to kill you.'"[34]

As López Rega left Argentina, the president appeared in a taped broadcast of a meeting she had after the showdown at the presidential residence. Speaking before several thousand women belonging to a far-right wing of the Peronist party, Isabel shouted: "The fatherland is in danger. That is the truth. But as long as there is even one real Peronist woman, those who want to destroy us will not succeed in their plans."

Pasty-faced without makeup, her hair messily combed, and her voice both weary and shrill, Isabel Perón appeared to have taken stock of just how alone she was. In tears, she stepped back from the microphone in a pathetic gesture to show her audience how much weight she had lost. "I wish I had more strength, but I don't. I never tried to defraud the country. Sometimes God places us under difficult trials."[35]

The House at 244 Libertad Street

At midday on a warm and cheerfully sunny Friday, a select group of local and foreign journalists gathered at a gray, two-story house in suburban Martínez, north of Buenos Aires. Some had shown up blindfolded. They had come for a clandestine press conference with the Montoneros' "superior command." Guerrillas and journalists were wearing patriotic badges on their lapels. June 20 was a public holiday in Argentina.[36]

As the visitors arrived at the door of the flat-roofed house, located at 244 Libertad Street, an attractive young woman in a traditional black and white maid's uniform met them at the entrance. As they waited inside after being searched, the reporters were fed *empanadas,* a meat pasty served hot, and white wine. Later they received multicolored plastic-covered press kits, which announced they would be addressed by Comandante Mario Firmenich. The kits also contained a detailed rundown of the September abduction of Juan and Jorge Born, photos of the businessmen brothers in captivity, maps of the bloody ambush in which their chauffeur and a manager of the Bunge & Born multinational were killed, and a review of other Montonero military exploits.

When Firmenich appeared, he was dressed in a tie and jacket; after slipping into an adjoining room to change, he returned to face the expectant group. He was wearing an open, short-sleeved shirt and jeans.

"The guerrilla chief spoke with controlled excitement," recalled *Buenos Aires Herald* reporter Andrew Graham-Yool, one of those who attended the clandestine event. "The press conference had been called because it was Argentina's Flag Day and the second anniversary of Juan Perón's return to Argentina from exile in Spain. The 'imprisonment' of the Born brothers was proof that 'we are now a force to be reckoned with, a political organization which cannot be ignored.' His preoccupation seemed to be with not being ignored. He was the chief."

Firmenich "denied that he was a Marxist-Leninist; he had not read either; he was a Socialist Nationalist. ... 'How much did you get for Born,' somebody asked. Firmenich smiled back and his smugness seemed to form a cloud around him, 'What we set out to get: 60 million dollars.'"

A short time later Jorge Born appeared, wearing dark glasses. "Where was his brother Juan? A guerrilla broke in ... concerned that his charge might blunder: Mr. Juan Born had been released some months ago. I asked for a date. 'One loses track of dates,' Born said. The best I was offered were guesses. 'December, or January, or maybe April.'

"A reporter admired Born's jacket. It was a good fit. Born agreed. He supposed that his captors could afford it. There was laughter; Born warmed to the people around him. It was remarked that he had a good haircut; he said that his hair had always been kept short. He remarked that he had been brought to this house in a car only a few days before."

The $60 million ransom the Montoneros claimed they had received shattered previous world records for extortive kidnappings in modern history. The military precision with which the Montoneros nabbed the two brothers, and the élan with which they held their press conference, seemed to confirm the guerrillas' claim as a force to be reckoned with, an organization that could not be ignored. And this at a time when the government couldn't seem to do anything right.

Graham-Yool escorted Born, wearing dark glasses with cotton pads on the inside of the lenses, to his release not far away. "I remembered that I had not asked who owned the house: who was in it? how had they got the house? was it rented? were the occupants captives or allies? They did not bother to answer. They were not going to tell me."

The real answers to the questions Graham-Yool had posed were revealing. The chalet was a safehouse used by security force personnel to torture illegally detained leftist suspects, both before and after Born's release. Six months earlier, SIDE operatives Nelson Romero and Rodolfo Silchinger—part of a phantom Montoneros-Nationalist wing—had held José Polisecki there for nearly a month, murdering him after their $2 million ransom demand was not met. The two agents were themselves intimately linked to a secretive group of ultranationalist Catholic military men. The guerrillas not only held their press conference in the SIDE lair; Romero and Silchinger were present when Jorge Born was released!

A neighbor, Inéz Kuzuchian de Pazo, later provided a key testimony in establishing what had actually occurred. Kuzuchian de Pazo lived in front of Romero's house, and the SIDE operative was a familiar figure. He was often seen driving a red Ford Falcon bearing a sign that read "Presidential National Press Secretariat," an organ controlled by López Rega. Silchinger, she remembered, used a blue Falcon.

Kuzuchian de Pazo said that shortly before noon on June 20, she had gone outside with her family to say goodbye to a relative. She noticed unusual movement in front of the house, where a pretty maid dressed in a classic uniform greeted a large number of guests, mostly men. Kuzuchian remembered one peculiarity among those who arrived—nearly all were wearing lapel badges. She recalled that several of the visitors carried cameras or movie equipment. About an hour later Nelson Romero arrived, accompanied by Silchinger and Romero's mother-in-law.

Sometime after the trio arrived, Kuzuchian de Pazo saw a car pull up alongside the house. A relative told her he saw two men wearing dark glasses get out of the auto; they were led by the arms into the house. "One thing that caught the eye was that the car backed up to the house. The way in which the two men were steered inside made it seem they couldn't see, or had their eyes blindfolded, or that the lenses of their glasses had been covered in some manner."

An International Brotherhood of Fear

After López Rega went into exile, Italian terrorist Stefano Delle Chiaie employed several of the Argentine's hit men, including death squad leaders Morales and Almirón, in the secret anti–Euskadi Ta Askatasuna (ETA; Basque Country and Liberty) army he ran for Gen. Francisco Franco's police in Spain. Delle Chiaie, the Spanish dictator claimed, was "one of the few men capable of putting things right in Italy." Later testimony before an Italian court revealed that, by 1974, Delle Chiaie's terrorist network was receiving financing from Gelli for weapons and training camps. In September Delle Chiaie, who had formed a working relationship with the Argentine Milicia, met with Chilean secret police agent Michael Townley. The purpose of the meeting was to plan an attack on exiled Chilean Christian Democratic leader Bernardo Leighton.[37]

The attack on the Chilean was carried out by a Delle Chiaie aide as Leighton walked down a Rome street with his wife. The couple, gravely wounded, survived the assault. A few days later a Miami-based Cuban exile group called Cero claimed responsibility for the shooting, offering as proof precise information on how the attack was carried out. Townley said later Delle Chiaie had put out the false trail by channeling the information to the Chilean DINA and from there to an anti-Castro Cuban paramilitary activist in Miami.

In November Delle Chiaie had private audiences in Madrid with Pinochet and DINA chief Manuel Contreras. The three men were in the city to attend Franco's funeral. Contreras reportedly received Delle Chiaie's pledge to step up surveillance of Chilean exiles living in Europe, using his network of ultraright political and intelligence contacts.[38]

By late 1975 some 120 Chilean exiles throughout Latin America had either been secretly killed or deported back to Chile, most of them from Argentina. The traffic went both ways. The Chilean regime also connived with elements of Isabel's government to dump the bodies of anti-Pinochet activists who died under torture in Chile on Argentine soil. The dead were then reported to have been killed in gun battles.[39]

* * *

In October, López Rega wrote Gelli a letter seeking help. "It is necessary that a few journalists or news agencies start issuing stories favorable to me or about my honesty and capability," he said.

> The FAMILY ought to show me off as a practical demonstration of support for a brother. ...
> I want to make clear I have absolutely no political ambitions. My mission ended when I achieved the return of the GENERAL, of EVA PERON, and the formation of a

democratic Peronist government, continuing through ISABEL. The rest of my work with the people was only my gift to them. ... A MAN and a WOMAN have put their face to the SUN. Tomorrow will bring what is deserved.[40]

"Face to the Sun"

With López Rega's departure the military high command ordered intelligence units to take control of the "irregular" paramilitary squads. In Córdoba they were integrated into the D-2 police intelligence unit and supervised by the 141st Army Intelligence Detachment. In Buenos Aires the army won operational control of most of the paramilitary groups cooperating in the region. Wednesday afternoons are traditionally R and R periods in the service. However, in the Campo de Mayo base outside the federal capital, Capt. Mohamed Alí Seineldín used the time to meet with Federal Police officers to "mark" targets. Seineldín, said one police source, was the "visible link" between the army and the Triple A. The Mar del Plata commando was dependent on the army intelligence detachment there and operated in and around the seaside resort town 250 miles south of Buenos Aires on the windswept Atlantic coast. Its contact was the owner of a private investigations agency, Oasis, a subsidiary of the Magister agency belonging to Gen. Otto Paladino.[41]

In early February 1976 Paladino was made head of the state intelligence agency, SIDE. César Enciso, a bodyguard for metalworkers' boss Lorenzo Miguel and Paladino's future son-in-law, and Aníbal Gordon, a neo-Nazi with a lengthy criminal record and ties to the metalworkers, became members of a "special group" organized by the general. Made up of an important nucleus of ultraright "direct action" activists and common criminals, the cell was given to Gordon to run. Among those joining the group was Eduardo Ruffo, a SIDE employee who later became Gordon's chief aide.

A few months earlier Paladino, a fervent admirer of Spanish dictator Franco and at the time the commander of the 10th Infantry Brigade, declared: "Violence is the stigma of our time. Today one no longer dies *cara al sol,* facing the enemy, because he hides in the shadows. Today the salesmen of false illusions proliferate." Despite Paladino's evocation of "Cara al Sol" (Face to the Sun), the hymn of the Falange of Spanish fascism, it was a style he himself avoided. Paladino's special group rented an automobile repair shop—Automotores Orletti—and converted it into a secret detention center. There Paladino and Gordon oversaw the torture of hundreds of people conducted under a portrait of Adolf Hitler.[42]

Impunity for the Terrorist Right

"Ex-Social Welfare Minister José Lopez Rega was widely suspected of controlling and protecting right-wing terrorists, such as those in the [Triple A], prior to his

ouster," a confidential U.S. embassy memorandum, entitled "Right-wing Terrorism Since López Rega," reported.

> What sets the present right-wing violence—especially that carried out by the AAA—
> somewhat apart from that of the past is the degree of official protection and support
> it enjoys. This support is, to be sure, surreptitious, but it is nonetheless very real.
> Government spokesmen sometimes verbally condemn right-wing terrorism, but to
> date not one single right-wing terrorist has been arrested, nor one act of right-wing
> violence seriously investigated and its perpetrators brought to justice. ...
>
> The principle targets of right-wing violence at this point are not leftist extremists;
> rather, they are those who are too outspoken against or openly opposed to Mrs.
> Perón and her entourage.[43]

A "Delinquent State"

In his book *Le Crime contre L'Humanité,* Eugene Aroneau postulated three phases
in the development of the "delinquent State." In the first stage, legal rights were
suspended for certain categories of people on the basis of race, religion, national-
ity, or political affiliation. The second occurred when public forces, "absent in the
application of legal rights, are present in the detention, transportation or execution of the victims." The last stage, said Aroneau, was the delinquent State's consolidation of power. Terror was no longer the result of excesses committed—in
the Argentine case, by the security forces or the extreme right—but rather "the
result of a defined system, previously organized and encouraged from the power
structure."[44]

By the end of 1975, all three stages were in various phases of completion at
once. A final battle was being prepared in a war in which the enemy would not
die with their "faces to the sun." Rather, thousands of people would be brutalized
by torture and then executed in obscure dungeons designed by Argentina's military intelligence services.

11

The Generals Plot
a Comeback (1975-1976)

It is necessary that in Argentina all those people who need to die do so in order to achieve the security of the country.
—*Gen. Jorge R. Videla, Montevideo, October 10, 1975*

In the early hours of November 3, 1975, Isabel Perón was taken to the emergency ward of a medical clinic in the tony capital neighborhood of Palermo Chico. The press said she was suffering from a gall bladder ailment. In truth, she was prostrate from the strains of office.[1]

Isabel's deteriorating health mirrored Argentina's own sagging fortunes. In June the unions rebelled against her government's attempt to impose wage restraints. A confrontation with army commanders had followed over the appointment of a Peronist sympathizer and active-duty colonel as interior minister. Judicial inquiries probed into corruption by high officials in Perón's government. Isabel herself was tainted by the scandal over the misuse of the funds of a Peronist charity group. Her party was wracked by internal bickering. The economy continued its downward spiral, as inflation soared and strikes proliferated. In September and early October Isabel had taken forty-five days of sick leave. More than 1,000 people had already been reported killed in political violence that year. In a twist of fortune former President Lanusse announced his own presidential candidacy, denouncing fascism and quoting Juan Perón.[2]

On October 5, the Montoneros had assaulted an army garrison, a federal prison, and an airport in the northern provincial capital of Formosa and commandeered an Aerolíneas Argentinas Boeing 737. Although the insurgents were beaten back, more than thirty people died—mostly guerrillas and soldiers. The attack, the first Montonero assault on the army, was personally planned by Mario Firmenich. It had two devastating effects on the guerrillas: It spurred mass death squad reprisals against recently registered members of the new Montonero "surface" organization, the Auténtico (Authentic) party. And in its wake, traditional conservative military officers prevailed over a more populist peruanista group sympathetic to Peru's nationalist president Gen. Juan Alvarado Velasco. The attack helped to close army ranks against the Montoneros. "The debate in the army about whether the Montos were nationalists or Marxists persisted," recalled Ernesto Barreiro, a young army officer, "until the attack on Formosa."[3]

On October 11 President Gerald Ford received a top-secret alert from the State Department. Entitled "Argentina: Military Flirts with Intervention?" it said: "In the face of Mrs. Perón's reported determination to resume the presidency, Embassy Buenos Aires has learned from several reliable sources that the military is on the verge of deciding to act against her. [The Defense Attaché Office] contacts within the military cannot confirm the rumors."

The military's restlessness seemed to grow week by week. Shortly before Perón was hospitalized, a funeral in Buenos Aires for Diego Barceló, a brutal young army lieutenant killed by guerrillas in Tucumán province, took on the characteristics of a political protest. "There are so many scoundrels in this country that will have to be shot," one colonel fumed at the burial, held in Recoleta cemetery. "Sooner or later we will have to fumigate. One of these boys is worth ten thousand of theirs." Posters, the work of a mysterious Grupo para la Acción y la Libertad (Group for Action and Liberty), sprung up around the capital, defiantly taunting: "Soldiers, how long must we wait?"[4]

Isabel's sudden hospital stay sparked rumors that she was about to resign. During her earlier sick leave Senate President Italo Argentino Luder had filled in for her. There were hopes the colorless Luder would take control, thus reducing the chance of a military takeover. Isabel, however, was determined to hold on to the presidency. "The forces arrayed against Perón could have prevented her return," the CIA told Ford on October 17. "They have chosen not to on the grounds that she is the legitimate president and most Argentines still prefer a constitutional solution." The military had "once again decided to step aside and allow her government to fall victim to its own incompetence. They expect public disenchantment to create a situation in which direct military intervention would be palatable."[5]

On November 5, as the CGT "mobilized" its blue-collar legions against the possibility of a coup, Isabel vowed from her hospital bed: "I have not resigned, nor will I resign. My temporary health problem is not cause enough for unethical groups pitted against the people's interests to try to strip authority from its legitimate holders." That same day a top-secret cable from the U.S. embassy to Ford reported that despite assurances by Interior Minister Angel F. Robledo that "Mrs. Perón would be a figurehead after her return, she has continued on a collision course, risking either a military coup or impeachment."[6]

Perón had only two real options. One, urged by some Peronists, Raúl Alfonsín's center-left wing of the Radicals, and democratic-left groups, was to bring other parties into her government in a "civic front." This action, they argued, would put a brake on military plotting. The other, favored by her aides and the general staff, was to circle the wagons and wait—a virtual invitation to the military to press ahead with their assault on power.[7]

The morning of November 6 Robledo called his fellow ministers to his office to hammer out a common strategy. The group requested a meeting, granted a week later, with the hospitalized Perón. Meanwhile, calls for the president's impeachment grew. Robledo again insisted that Isabel's resignation was imminent. This time, he said, she would ask for a long leave to take a trip abroad, a pretext that would provide its own solution. The former cabaret dancer, however, refused to act out her part in the script Robledo had written for her. "Embassy Buenos Aires reports that Mrs. Perón, having lost almost all her public support, remains virtually incommunicado in her hospital room and refuses to resign," a top-secret State Department report to Ford noted. "Civilian/constitutionalist forces are still undecided as to how to remove her ... but clearly must find a way soon or see the military take over." Four days later the CIA reported that Perón "continues to depend on López Rega ... now exiled in Spain, and has a direct phone line to him."[8]

On November 17, Isabel returned to office and announced presidential elections for October 1976, only eleven months later. Her closest advisers believed that by calling elections Isabel had stymied her enemies. At the same time the army, led by Videla, used Isabel's return in order to obtain her agreement that the armed forces officially take over the direction of the antisubversive campaign.

Although denying any interest in taking power, the military had taken a growing hand in political affairs. Army corps commanders controlled what news could be broadcast on radio and television stations and banned reports that disturbed the public order. The military also carried its antisubversion campaign to fourteen provinces and the federal capital, an effort that led to hundreds of detentions, ceaseless searches, and a watchful eye over provincial police and local political authorities.[9]

On November 24, in a top-secret article in the *National Intelligence Daily*, the CIA reported that the military's counterinsurgency effort "seems to be alleviating military pressures on Perón. ... Hundreds of suspected subversives reportedly have been arrested and some killed in sweeps that, for the first time, have been supported by helicopters and other aircraft." The new military role, it noted, "could pave the way for greater military control of national affairs. Already, the military is reportedly pressing to have its greater power formalized."[10]

The Air Force Tries to Steal a March

December proved no kinder to Isabel. An all-pervasive tension seemed to grip the political world. In the first six days of the month alone, thirty-four people were reported murdered for political reasons. In Tucumán army officers acting under the guise of paramilitary personnel provided the provincial capital with a particularly grisly scene, blowing up a car in which six prisoners lay dead or dying. The bombing, done under the cover of night, left gore spread out the length of a block. In Buenos Aires twenty-one Peronist parliamentary dissidents separated from the official bloc, forming their own caucus and calling themselves the Grupo de Trabajo (Work Group).

Meanwhile several dozen Federal Police serving as guards for top officials and political and union leaders were called to a secret meeting at the Buenos Aires headquarters of the SS Federal, the political police. They were told their jobs now required an extra duty—the filing of daily reports about who their wards saw, what they were saying in private, any break with their normal routine, and who they slept with.[11]

It was two other events, however—the revolt by a group of air force officers and an ERP attack on an army arsenal—that made Isabel's weakening hold on power palpably more tenuous.

On December 18 at 7:30 A.M. the commander in chief of the air force, Brig. Héctor Fautario, was detained at the Buenos Aires municipal airport as he prepared to travel to the provincial capital of Córdoba. The revolt was headed by Brig. Jesús Capellini, a leader of the force's far-right, Catholic nationalist wing. Capellini intended, he declared, to usher in a military regime that would lead Argentina to a "rebirth of nationalist and Christian principles."

The government, desperately trying to show its command of the situation, sought to quickly defuse the situation. It named Brig. Orlando Agosti, a candidate backed by the rebellious officers and a longtime friend of army chief Videla, as Fautario's replacement that same day.

The rebellion, however, continued. Capellini tried to force the army chiefs conspiring in the shadows to commit to his revolt. (When airplanes "bombed" the Casa Rosada with pro-Videla leaflets, a helpless Isabelita watched them float to the ground, accompanied by a few aides and La Rioja Gov. Carlos Menem, who had remained loyal to his fellow riojana even during the days of López Rega.) Capellini had two goals—to prevent the prospect of national elections from ruining the military's chances for power and to improve his force's internal position among the plotters.[12]

Despite its ambitious goals the Capellini uprising had a certain sham quality to it. "When the Argentine air force was directed to bomb the rebels, they followed their orders—with a few minor modifications," a top-secret White House report noted two weeks later. "When they arrived in the target area they established contact with the rebels on the ground, and carefully warned them away from the target area. When they finished their bomb runs they warned the rebels that their gun cameras had to show some destruction, so the rebels towed a demolished vehicle to the center of a field, filled it with gasoline and ignited it—after which the Air Force attacked the truck and 'demolished' it."[13]

Two days after the uprising began, the CIA informed Ford that the rebellion was continuing and that "the armed forces' top command has made no move to suppress the insurrection, [putting] the position of President Perón in increasing danger." Videla had "issued a veiled warning to the President and apparently hopes she will resign and spare the military the onus of ousting her to end the rebellion."[14]

The military high command wanted to leave the country struggling on the verge of collapse. "The Army could unquestionably oust Perón, but Commanding General Videla prefers to see her forced out by civilian pressure," the State Department told Ford in a top-secret morning summary, "and at the moment seems content to bide his time, neither moving against the rebels nor joining them."[15]

Isabel and her retinue closed themselves off into a self-absorbed isolation, incapable of correcting their course. "President Perón, facing the most serious challenge yet to her authority, reacted in her usual fashion," the CIA reported in a pithy page 1 article in the *National Intelligence Daily*. "Her office issued defiant statements of her refusal to step down; she remained, for the most part, secluded with a handful of supporters. Once again, she was reported ill."[16]

From their strongholds at the municipal air base and the Morón air brigade west of the capital, the mutinous officers held out until December 23, when they gave up after making a secret pact with the air force high command. Capellini was held solely responsible for the revolt, and he retired. No one else was punished. Agosti told the airmen their revolt had caused no hard feelings. "They were not defeated," said Comdr. Hugo di Ricci when he arrived by helicopter to take command of the Morón base.[17]

Monte Chingolo: The ERP's Last Stand

The same day Capellini surrendered, more than 150 ERP guerrillas attacked the 601 Domingo Viejo Bueno Arsenal, ten miles from the federal capital in the sprawling industrial suburb of Monte Chingolo. It was the seventh time since 1973 the ERP had made an important attack on a military base—all against the army.[18]

The attack began at 6:30 P.M. The guerrillas deployed several groups of combatants, some recently arrived from Tucumán. The most important column rammed a truck, followed by six cars carrying twenty-five to thirty guerrillas, through the batallion's main entrance. The guards were overpowered with the help of a soldier-collaborator.

Half of the attack force—mostly very young and including a number of women—blockaded the two access roads, overturning a dozen trucks and buses and torching them. Some thirty guerrillas breached the rear of the arsenal, protecting their flank by strewing mines around a nearby railway. The ERP high command, installed at a nearby hotel, directed the attack.[19]

The access roads blocked, the ERP fighters began to advance, their objective fifteen tons of armaments and munitions. According to an ERP communiqué, after the attack the guerrillas were to blow up "installations and matériel not seized and effect an orderly retreat." Meanwhile support groups carried out diversionary attacks on police stations in the industrial suburbs of Quilmes, Avellaneda, and Lanús and in the provincial capital of La Plata.[20]

Such feints did not work as the military intelligence services had advance warning of the attack, allowing them to set a *ratonera* (rat trap). In the days leading up to the attack, the entire batallion of the Viejo Bueno Arsenal had been confined to barracks. They had received information that the access roads would be blocked by the guerrillas in order to cut off logistical support for the batallion from the outside. On December 20, a former SIDE agent recalled, provincial governor Victorio Calabró "got word from the Intelligence Directorate about the planned assault. An agent had been infiltrated into the ERP months before and we had received instructions from the subdirector of security about the possible attack on a military unit in the region." On December 23, however, with Christmas approaching, half the troops were given leave.[21]

"At 6:30 P.M.," the intelligence official recalled, "I received a cable saying 'situation normal,' which was the code for 'alert' or 'attack.' I had received from my superiors all the documentation—maps and plans—in order to operate out of any of the bases in the region. These established where to carry out the pincer movements and how to distribute personnel in three rings around the area attacked."

During the first hour of fighting the guerrillas succeeded in breaching the outside line of defense, occupying the trenches that had been dug by the soldiers in preparation for the attack. Despite the military regime's later propaganda and a few newspaper reports at the time, the guerrillas had mostly antiquated weapons and poor logistics. "There were some who had hand grenades and FAL automatic rifles, but many of the guerrillas were armed with old shotguns and .12 calibers."[22]

Two hours into the fight, at dusk, the guerrillas were surrounded, although the combat lasted until past midnight. Irregulars given support tasks on the outside retreated into the base itself, struggling to fortify their position. The insurgents' diversionary attacks and attempts to contain the military had been quickly overcome by the latter's superior firepower and strength.

The combat zone was an ethereal no-man's-land of the sound and fury of battle. The arrival of troops in armored personnel carriers, the orders barked out of megaphones into the twilight that warm summer night, the powerful searchlights of the circling helicopters, and the beaming lanterns of the light tanks added a surrealistic touch to what would prove to be the ERP's Waterloo. In an "unprecedented" display of force the army was supported by two of its own regiments, groups from the provincial police, gendarmerie, and navy, and air force and navy planes, as well as police and military helicopters.[23]

"The attackers who hadn't been killed up to that point then massed together, suddenly breaking out of the base and firing in all directions. As they fanned out, they headed for cover in a nearby slum, thereby breaking our first line of encirclement." The ERP's vehicles, mostly late-model autos, were abandoned in the guerrillas' disorderly retreat. The former intelligence official recalled: "The helicopter gunners shot at anything that moved—you could hear shouts of 'I give up, I give up' which were answered by machinegun fire."[24]

The repression was followed by two occurrences that became characteristic of the so-called dirty war. One, the military altered the death count to justify its own excesses. And, two, their carefully choreographed presentation of the "facts" allowed them to misrepresent the size of the guerrilla threat the country faced, both before and after the battle.

Of the approximately 100 guerrillas who participated in the attack on the military installation itself, the first official statements calculated that some 50 guerrillas had been killed. (Six government soldiers were also killed in the battle.) The ERP later confirmed 45 casualties among their ranks, between the dead and disappeared. Videla himself said, "There were about 80 casualties among the subversive delinquents—both dead and wounded." In the military's *Official Report* issued a month later, however, the guerrilla casualties had risen to 200.[25]

According to the former intelligence official, the difference in numbers in the body count was a deliberate misrepresentation to cover up the size of the slaughter: "The day after the battle, when the forensic doctors from the provincial police arrived, there were about 200 dead. Some had been cut open with bayonets and were sprawled upon the grass. There were many slum dwellers among them. It was messy to heat water and soften up their hands so we could identify them, so they cut them off and shipped them to the fingerprint department."[26]

When the *Official Report* was issued on January 31, 1976, it judged the attack on Monte Chingolo to be "the most important operation planned by the guerrillas since they began operations." It also noted, with uncharacteristic candor, that the ERP had shown "great organizational and operational deficiencies that revealed little military capacity. ... Their activity is relegated to the exercise of terror, obvious evidence of their weakness."[27]

A Disputed Archipelago

On January 3 Argentina returned to the pages of the *National Intelligence Daily*. The CIA reported that

> there now appears to be little chance that the President will be ousted by parliamentary tactics. President Perón ... is steadfast in her determination to stay in office. Under these circumstances, military leaders, particularly General Jorge Videla, will be forced to play a larger role in national political decisions. Military leaders are in a good position to do so. After the air force rebellion and the victory over the guerrillas, military unity and coordination have been greatly improved, and Videla has emerged as a strong political figure.

Many Argentines enjoying summer vacations along the Atlantic or at Andean mountain resorts paid little attention to a communiqué issued January 3 by the Argentine Foreign Ministry. Grave difficulties, it charged, had developed in talks with the British over the Falkland Islands crown colony, known in the Argentine as Las Islas Malvinas. The parley, in which Argentina pressed its century-old claim to sovereignty over the windswept archipelago in the South Atlantic, had broken down. A few days later, Argentina asked for the withdrawal of the British ambassador. Perón, the CIA reported, was trying "to divert public attention from domestic strife."[28]

The Strange Fall of Roberto Quieto

On January 13 Montonero guerrillas set fire to a commuter train 20 miles from downtown Buenos Aires, destroying five cars and forcing its passengers to descend at gunpoint. A communiqué distributed to the media said the attack was a reprisal for the kidnapping and disappearance of guerrilla leader Roberto Quieto. He had been abducted, unarmed and without bodyguards, while on a family outing in a northern Buenos Aires suburb on December 28.

Quieto's kidnapping and a series of subsequent abductions in Córdoba provided the background for one of the most bizarre, and sordid, episodes of the time. It had been Quieto himself who, before Christmas 1975, had sat down to type out orders to Montonero *combatientes,* instructing them to avoid contact with their families during the holidays. Within hours of his kidnapping Montoneros launched a noisy campaign, demanding that his detention be "legalized." Overnight hundreds of slogans appeared painted on walls throughout the capital, demanding his reappearance: "QUIETO—PRISONER OF THE GORILLA ARMY." On January 3, scores of Montoneros conducted *actos relámpagos* (lighting strikes), in the federal city center. Cars were torched, fire bombs thrown at shops, and leaflets scattered demanding that the guerrilla's "physical integrity" be respected. Quieto's case also became something of an international cause célèbre, with telegrams of support from François Mitterrand, Jean-Paul Sartre, and others.[29]

At first the military and Federal Police denied they held Quieto, a former FAR leader and one of the most wanted Montoneros. Then the Montoneros' campaign came to an abrupt halt. The night of December 29 the security forces conducted two raids on key guerrilla hideouts. In the following days and weeks there was a wave of detentions and disappearances; in Córdoba some twenty students, unionists, and several members of the Authentic party were seized by armed men. Over the next three months, more than seventy people in Córdoba were kidnapped, ostensibly by the Triple A. Military and police officials told authorities the abductions were the result of "quarrels between guerrilla factions" resulting from some leftists refusing to take part in the attack on Monte Chingolo. Among the Montoneros the word was put out: Quieto was talking.[30]

U.S. intelligence sources said later that Quieto was the victim of a betrayal from within the Montonero leadership itself. Nevertheless, in February a Montonero Revolutionary Tribunal found the absent Quieto guilty of allowing himself to be captured and of "informing." The latter charge was aggravated by the speed with which he broke and the importance of the information he provided. Quieto was charged with disobeying the Montonero maxim: "Don't surrender alive; resist until you escape or die in the attempt." His guilt magnified by his rank, he was blamed for having visited the beach with his family on other occasions, for not using antisurveillance techniques, and for offering only passive resistance. There was a precedent: In August 1975, a twenty-six-year-old guerrilla was executed by Montoneros for squealing, even though he claimed that he had been tortured. The Montonero tribunal found Quieto guilty as charged.[31]

Burnishing the Military's Image

On January 7 a speech Isabel planned to deliver to the bewildered country about the "national project" left by Juan Perón was abruptly canceled. The motive: the profound differences between the president's views and the version prepared by Interior Minister Robledo. The speech written by Robledo, bearing large red X's, was returned. Robledo's fate was sealed. His fall carried along in its wake the ministers of defense, justice, and foreign affairs. Meanwhile at a ceremony at Buenos Aires' ornate Teatro Colón, Isabel Perón presided over the traditional presenting of swords to the newest officers of the armed forces. "There is a terrorist front ... meant to muddle our principles and essential values by watering our country's soil with innocent blood," she assured the military. "You are not alone in this fight."

The expected cabinet change was made nine days later. Four new ministers were appointed; right-wing Peronist José A. Deheza was tapped as the new defense minister. Five days later the army pressured the government into naming Gen. Albáno Harguindeguy as chief of the Federal Police. "If the decision depended on me, I'd name Harguindeguy," Videla told Deheza. Harguindeguy quickly reincorporated into routine police work some 4,000 agents who worked as bodyguards and drivers for union leaders. "The measure had two explosive effects," wrote one historian of the period. "On the one hand public opinion breathed easier upon seeing an end, finally, to the gangsterism of the union bureaucrats; on the other that the mini-army run by [union bosses] Casildo Herreras, Lorenzo Miguel and company would not interfere with the imminent assault on the presidential palace."[32]

On February 6 a right-wing provincial party alliance called for Isabel's impeachment, accusing her of "immorality, unconstitutionality, illegality and ineptitude." Rumors of an imminent uprising by navy men added to the uncertainty. The government was rocked by the disclosure that a retired army lieutenant testified before Congress that López Rega's former personal secretary had provided ministry funds to purchase twelve cases of British-made submachine guns to arm the Triple A. Meanwhile José Miguel Tarquini, the public relations director of the Social Welfare Ministry and a death squad leader, was murdered by Montoneros.

A week later María Caride de Lanusse, the daughter-in-law of the former military president, was killed when a bomb exploded in her home. The newspapers at the time reported that the incident was the work of leftist guerrillas. In fact, the woman had left a grenade on a nightstand to protect herself from government security forces, which were threatening her father-in-law's family. The bomb had gone off accidentally when she put it in her purse as she prepared to go out. The police announced they had begun a search for her killers. That same week leftists assassinated Col. Rafael Reyes, the commander of antiguerrilla forces in Mar de Plata, while right-wing death squads murdered a Catholic priest working in a Buenos Aires slum, and three labor leaders were kidnapped and killed in La Plata and Rosario.[33]

Meanwhile the plans put together by the army chiefs were being carried out to the letter. The coup's foremost alchemist was Gen. Roberto Viola, the chief of the army high command and the man responsible for engineering Videla's ascent to the post of commander in chief in August 1975. Since September Viola had directed the contingencies for the assault on power and resolved to use the first trimester of 1976 to give the plot its finishing touches. The strategy he pursued was simple: improve the military's image; justify the coup as filling a "power vacuum"; and organize a clandestine, efficient, repressive apparatus.

Justifying the military's bid for power as a necessary requirement of the "dirty war" was still problematic. "The guerrilla action does not have the impact on civilian life that urban violence had in a small city such as Beirut, where armed clashes paralyze all activity," noted a *New York Times* story from Buenos Aires before the attack on Monte Chingolo. "In this sprawling city of eight million, the violence is diluted by space and numbers, and most people never hear a shot fired."[34]

To give the guerrilla problem a sense of urgency, journalists linked to the military high command and, in particular, to the intelligence services were given the twin tasks of disseminating fears of chaos and improving the "image" of the coupmakers. They worked to create a few of the myths that not only helped pave the way for the coup but also gave the new regime the keys to demobilize and then destroy any civilian resistance. The impending chaos, the overwhelming power of the guerrillas, and the clash between "hard-line" officers—modeled after Chilean dictator Augusto Pinochet—and "moderate" officers—such as Videla and Massera, who only wanted the military to intervene until a "real" democracy could be established—were part of the propaganda. Rodolfo Fernández Pondal, of the restricted-circulation bulletin *Ultima Clave,* and Julio Carricar were given the task of filtering such "reports" to foreign correspondents: "If it is not the current military leadership it will be the hard-liners who will take power, the excitable ones, the real fascists, and this will end up being a blood bath."[35]

The campaign bore its fruits. When the coup finally took place, most reporting from Argentina for foreign publications overdramatized the guerrilla threat. At the same time, the incoming military leaders were bestowed with qualities that were belied by their secret plans for repression. The *New York Times,* one of the first foreign newspapers to catch on to what was really happening in Argentina, characterized Videla as "tormented by the prospect of a new military government. ... [He] has shown no personal ambition for the presidency." And in an analysis the day after the coup, the newspaper said: "Gen. Videla and Adm. Massera, both of whom have extensive civilian contacts ... are said to be sensitive to domestic and international opinion on issues such as human rights and political liberties. They have no enthusiasm for the repressive excesses of the Chilean regime of Gen. Augusto Pinochet."[36]

"Do You Have Anyone to Denounce?"

Far removed from the European stylishness and relatively comfortable living standards of Buenos Aires—surrounded by its rich and enriching pampa—is the province of La Rioja, population 200,000, located in the impoverished Argentine northwest. In 1976 La Rioja was still a backwater, a sea of flat, dusty scrubland, interspersed with the blue-pink foothills of the Andes. Peasants tended to the vineyards and walnut and olive groves in much the same way as had their ancestors during the time of Spanish colonial rule. Left-wing terrorism was virtually unknown in the province.

Unknown to most riojanos, prior to the coup plans for the local repression were drawn up in the offices of the newspaper *El Sol,* an ally of the region's landowning interests. *El Sol* publisher Tomás Agustín Alvarez Saavedra, linked to the Servicio de Inteligencia de Ejército (SIE; Army Intelligence Service), was one of those kidnapped during the 1960s amid bitter interservice rivalries.

For several days two army officers in civilian dress sat around a desk before a blackboard in the office of the newspaper's director. Each day several citizens considered "reliable" by the military authorities were called to review lists drawn up on a blackboard of members of local organizations and provincial and national government workers. "Do you have anyone to denounce?" the visitor was asked. One, who said he refused to participate in the process, reported that during his visit he recognized the names of several people who were later detained or arrested.[37]

The Axis of Stability

By early 1976, the axis of Argentina's stability, and the perceived durability of its institutions, had passed to the military. The intelligence services, anxious to polish the military's image, found both progovernment and antigovernment politicians willing to compete for the generals' favor with declarations praising the military's benign and democratic intentions. For the government it was a dangerous game, and one they were sure to lose. With each passing day the generals stepped up efforts to portray the coup as imminent.[38]

Faced with an employers' lockout on February 16, the government reacted tepidly. Two days later SIDE chief Gen. Otto Paladino told Isabel that a coup could be avoided "only if she resigned." Perón remained unmoved. "I will not resign," she told her justice minister later that day, "even if they put me before a firing squad. To do that would be to betray Perón's legacy." Her position was seconded by Italo Luder, her would-be replacement: "I am not going to move a finger to get Isabel to resign."[39]

That same day Isabel met with the military chiefs to announce she was going to finish out her term, of which only eight months remained. She promised not to accept renomination or any other candidacy. Deheza explained a package of antisubversive measures, searching for a consensus among the generals. The commanders, however, kept their own counsel. No one could miss the meaning of that silence.

Time Runs Out on a Clock Without a Calendar

The repressive laws drawn up by Isabel's advisers provided for a quick and energetic repression, a legalistic rendition of concepts very close to those espoused by the military. "Our pulse will not flutter if it comes to having to sign a 'proceed' on a death sentence dictated by the military courts," Deheza told Videla, when the minister proposed applying martial law to turbulent Córdoba province.[40]

Time, however, had all but run out. Despite a plea by the CGT for an immediate "change of course," government officials made Isabel Perón's staying in office their only objective.

Meanwhile the high command quickened its pace of meetings, hammering out the program they would follow once installed in office. Only thirty men knew in detail the commanders' secret plans. Operación Aries was rapidly becoming a reality. The final touches were made with care. The commanders, meeting in the army's Libertador building in the shadow of the presidential palace, took turns at the typewriter, trying to avoid leaks by secretaries and subordinates. The military feared that Peronism still had the capacity to turn the masses out into the streets, which would necessitate a visible and bloody repression.[41]

On February 24 a beleaguered Isabel Perón asked Deheza to demand that the service chiefs state their loyalties once and for all. Meeting in the minister's office, Videla, Massera, and Agosti chose ambiguity. The military would intervene, they warned, if the politicians left a vacuum that could be filled by "subversion." When the minister importuned Videla about when that might be, the army general would only reply, "Doctor, my watch does not have a calendar."[42]

The next day the right-wing provincial legislators renewed their calls for impeachment, and dissident Peronist deputies demanded that Isabel be put on trial. Lorenzo Miguel counterattacked with: "Some leaders, under the influence of a well-orchestrated psychological campaign, are waving flags that have nothing to do with Peronism's banners." Miguel called a parley of labor leaders for Friday,

February 27, in Mar de Plata, the first day of the long Carnival holidays. There, he hoped, the union men would announce their unequivocal support for the president.[43]

In Buenos Aires General Paladino informed presidential secretary Julio González that, given Isabel's refusal to resign, the coup would be carried out during Carnival week. When Deheza found out, he called Videla and police chief Harguindeguy to a midnight meeting at the Casa Rosada. Harguindeguy discounted the possibility of a military revolt. When Videla, in civilian dress, arrived a few minutes later he, too, dismissed the rumors.

Isabel's advisers knew their only hope was an eleventh-hour show of union support. Deheza and González traveled that same night to Mar del Plata, where they found Miguel dispirited and worried. A few hours earlier he had had a surprise meeting with Admiral Massera in the presence of CGT leader Adalberto Wimer and electrical union chief Oscar Smith. Massera told them that the only way to save the constitutional order was to force Isabel to resign and Luder to take office. Miguel had rejected the proposal but sensed the end was near.

Meanwhile Economy Minister Emilio Mondelli, a rather orthodox banker, announced a series of emergency measures to "salvage" the nation from inflation and growing debt. Never had the Peronists felt the need to show that they were in control of the crumbling economy as now.

At the Peronist national party congress, Miguel and Isabel loyalists Carlos Menem and Deolindo Bittel beat back a challenge to her, proposing a new "political dialogue" to save the country from a coup. For many Peronists it was still inconceivable that someone without the name Perón could run the movement. At the convention Isabel played on fears that without her the party was in danger of breaking apart. "What some people don't understand is that if my head rolls, they will then cut the heads off those who come behind."

But it all was too late. Backed by the military, Calabró, the anti-Isabel provincial governor of Buenos Aires, called for public resistance to the Mondelli plan. The government then decided to take control of the province in order to repress the "sedition" that Calabró's action implied. When asked for his advice, Videla refused to give the army's approval for the measure. Isabel's advisers were forced to step back, given the possible resistance by Calabró and the passivity of the generals.

On March 13 the rumors of an imminent coup buzzed through the capital's already overheated political circuits. Gen. Samuel Cáceres, one of the few remaining loyalist officers, told the government the uprising was in a matter of hours and that there was no military sector willing to resist. Deheza sought out the opinion of General Vilas, then the second in command of the V Army Corps headquartered in the southern port of Bahía Blanca. Vilas confirmed that all units were loyal to Videla.

There was nothing left to do but wait. When on March 19 a colonel was offered the post of undersecretary of defense, he declined the offer, saying "next week the armed forces will be in power." American and European television crews began combing the streets of Buenos Aires, filming the run-up to the coup everyone was expecting. Isabel told associates she was afraid she would be arrested while presiding over the celebration of the 164th anniversary of the elite Granaderos regiment the following day. Deheza attended in her absence.

Although a sense of paralysis gripped the government, there was one last desperate attempt to break through the military's encirclement. At 7:00 in the evening on March 22, Isabel called a cabinet meeting, to which were added Luder, Miguel, and three others. There the president declared it was necessary to demand, again, a definition of the service chiefs' loyalties.

"At eleven sharp the next morning," Deheza recalled, "the three commanders entered my office, taking their seats around a work table." Deheza reiterated a series of promises that catered to the commanders' smallest whims: from the reorganization of Peronism to the naming of a new cabinet; from the calling for a "national unity government" in which other parties would participate to the resignation of all members of the cabinet and even Isabel herself from any party posts.[44]

Videla, Massera, and Agosti rejoined that they had never made more than "suggestions" and never sought to impose their own views. "But at this late date, it doesn't make any sense to talk about new political formulas," Videla concluded. Deheza brandished the argument he thought would still carry the day: The subversives ought to be fought with popular support, he argued, for the antiguerrilla struggle would be imperiled if the elected government was overthrown.[45]

Deheza's entreaties fell on deaf ears. Since early 1975, when the army entered the antisubversive struggle, the military had used the Peronist government to defeat the guerrillas politically. Constitutional rule was no longer needed to complete their physical annihilation.

The commanders promised to give their response at 7:00 that evening. When they returned, Videla summed up the military's position: "The state shows itself incapable of carrying out its mission. There is generalized social indiscipline. The citizens' security is seriously threatened. The government does not control its own party. The industrial guerrillas are capable of damaging the country's productive apparatus." Deheza, getting nowhere, desperately pressed ahead to save the situation, offering a final concession. The government, he said, would move up the presidential elections and offer a candidate who would give the armed forces the guarantees they required.[46]

It was 10:10 the night of March 23. The service chiefs rose to leave. As Videla offered his hand to Deheza, he said: "Doctor, I would like you to give the government's position before the army high command, and so I would like for you to come to headquarters tomorrow at noon, where I will call all those corps commanders who are not in Buenos Aires." Massera and Agosti also agreed, then bid the expectant Deheza good night.

Deheza rushed to tell Isabel of the results of the meeting. While they met in the president's wood-paneled office, the other ministers waited anxiously in the ante-chamber outside. When the two were finished, Isabel called an urgent cabinet meeting, which lasted past midnight. Interior Minister Roberto Ares, who had just had supper with General Harguindeguy, reported that the police chief had told him there was still time to negotiate. It was already March 24, 1976.

Encouraged by the developments, Isabel adjourned the meeting until the next morning. She bid the group goodbye, announcing she was going to the Olivos summer residence to rest. Perón was joined by Julio González, her military aide-de-camp and the head of her bodyguard. The rest lingered at the Casa Rosada, re-viewing the day's events. A while later González's personal secretary, visibly upset, told the group that Perón's helicopter had not arrived at Olivos, despite having had enough time to get there.

Isabel's helicopter had landed at the metropolitan airport, 2.5 miles from the presidential palace, after its pilot complained of technical difficulties. When they disembarked, the head of the air base, a commodore, welcomed the president and invited her for a coffee in his office while, he said, another vehicle was made ready. Meanwhile, her aides were quietly surrounded by a group of officers. In the commodore's office a general, an admiral, and a brigadier told Isabel of the mili-tary uprising. They invited her to sign a document announcing her resignation. If she cooperated, they promised, a plane waiting on the runway would carry her into exile.[47]

At the presidential palace a group of soldiers led by an army officer in civilian dress violently raided the building, detaining those who remained. The group was hauled off to two navy ships, *Bahía Aguirre* and *Treinta y Tres Orientales*, docked in the port of Buenos Aires. They soon would be joined by other Peronist political and labor leaders.

The takeover was the sixth time the military had seized power in less than fifty years; thirty of the last forty-six years had been under military rule. Around the country military units occupied public offices, replacing civilians with officers from their ranks. The new junta dissolved Congress, replaced the Supreme Court, and purged judges; it abolished individual legal guarantees and decreed the death penalty for political reasons—an action prohibited by the Argentine constitu-tion. The generals baptized their rule the Orwellian-sounding National Reorgani-zation Process, known in Spanish as el Proceso.

The generals portrayed their antiguerrilla efforts as "the opening battle of World War III." For most people, who could not make sense of the subterranean logic behind the growing slaughter, the outside world became opaque—a place of danger. They were told, and many believed, that the guerrillas counted on the clandestine legions of thousands of armed militants. They were told, and many believed, that the irregular warfare waged in silence around them portended a virtual state of civil war, made all the more tragic by the insurgents' methods and the unorthodox means needed to repress them. The military had even succeeded in portraying themselves as opposed to the violence of the Triple A death squads, whose work they were about to officially take over. Virtually no one knew that the ERP had fielded less than 100 guerrillas in Tucumán and was prostrate after Monte Chingolo. And few suspected the degree to which military intelligence had penetrated the guerrillas' ranks and the frequency with which "terrorist" activities were the result of manipulation by the generals or their civilian allies.

The military's own "secret directives" for the conduct of the repression said there were three "priority objectives" in the "antisubversive struggle"—schools, churches, and factories. The military junta had barely come to power when troops took positions in the principal factories around the country. Shop stewards and union activists were detained or abducted. The machine guns mounted around the plants assured that no sounds of protest would be heard.

PART TWO

12

Priority Target: Repression in the Factories

An activist who was agitating and impeding workers from returning to their jobs in the Constitution Plaza area was felled by a security force patrol on Wednesday night.

The information was given out in a communiqué issued by the 1st Zone Command. It said that the security forces surprised an activist who was agitating for a work stoppage and tried to impede a few workers from going to work. He was felled by gunfire. The legal forces—the text ended—are carrying out their mission meant to assure the right to work.

—La Opinión, *November 7, 1977*

When Bernardo Alberte, Perón's one-time personal delegate and secretary-general of the Peronist movement, began writing his letter the day before the coup, he knew the potential cost of his act of protest. But Argentina's future was at stake, as was that of its workers and the institution the retired lieutenant colonel had belonged to for years: the army.

In the preceding days, the capital had been buzzing with rumors of the impending coup. Alberte knew, as perhaps few others could, the political ideas of those who conspired and the interests they represented. In October 1945 Lieutenant Alberte was jailed for opposing military efforts to exclude then-Colonel Perón from the government. In 1954–1955, he served as President Perón's military aide and led the defense of the Casa Rosada against the bloody though unsuccessful June 16, 1955, navy revolt. Alberte had also taken part in the long struggles of the Peronist Resistance—twenty years of fighting for social justice, frequently from a jail cell.

Only three days before the coup Alberte himself had narrowly escaped certain

175

death. A commando squad, intent on murdering him, occupied his office on the 700 block of Rivadavia Street, near the presidential palace. He had just left the building and watched from the street as three people were carried—handcuffed and blindfolded—from the premises.

Alberte addressed his letter to army commander in chief Videla. It was March 23, 1976, only hours before the military were to carry out their plan. He knew that one of the generals' primary targets would be the workers.[1]

"Throughout this century we Argentines have suffered a cruel experience," Alberte wrote. "While brandishing the argument, as it is being brandished again, of the need to defend 'a way of life'—'our way of life'—the military always takes sides against the majority." The names of places and incidents he mentioned sounded like the staccato of a beating drum: the slaughter of hundreds of striking workers in desolate Patagonia in the 1920s; the 1955 bombing of the crowded Plaza de Mayo by navy planes in the ill-fated effort, with its hundreds of casualties, to overthrow Perón; the 1972 execution without trial of the guerrillas of Trelew; the military's efforts that same year to keep people from turning out to greet Perón upon his return after years of exile. The list went on.

Alberte sensed the pattern that was about to repeat itself. He scored the meetings called by "the 'leading' industries and the most blue-blooded of the large landowners and cattlemen," who together with representatives of the armed forces debated the country's economic situation and criticized the government. "When it is announced the army will intervene against 'subversion in the factories,'" Alberte wrote, "the situation is serious, and also dramatic, not only for the workers, but for the armed forces as well, as they are being prodded into … the role of substitutes for industrial security police, until now private, and to guard the interests of only one sector—precisely that sector least representative of the general interest."

Alberte sent the letter to Videla. Early March 24, while the plotters carried out their plans, Alberte recieved his reply. At 2:00 A.M. a joint army–Federal Police unit broke into Alberte's home at 1160 Libertador Avenue and, screaming "Alberte, we've come to kill you," threw him from a window of his seventh-floor apartment.

While Alberte's body lay lifeless below, his killers busily looted his home in open view of his terror-stricken family. Before leaving, one of the intruders displayed the impunity that would characterize *el Proceso*. Identifying himself by name and rank in a telephone call to authorities at the military hospital, he ordered them to immediately fetch Alberte's body. For nearly eight years no judge would investigate the murder. (One magistrate who refused to act, Alberto Sarmiento, allegedly commented: "All Peronists like Alberte ought to fly out the window.")[2]

That same night the army unleashed a vast Pilot Operation as ordered by Secret Directive 222/76, occupying factories and union headquarters around the country. As Alberte predicted, private factory security guards were replaced by those in green military uniforms.

The day of the coup fifteen unions were taken over by the military, a number that grew to several hundred within a few days. The right to strike was revoked. The General Confederation of Workers, the 62 Organizations—the labor arm of Peronism—and all union activity were banned. The "Document of Basic Objectives and Aims of the National Reorganization Process," signed by the military junta on March 24, suspended "political activity, political parties, and the union activity of the workers, businessmen and professionals." Public employees were subject to the jurisdiction of military courts. The 6 million member CGT and its affiliated unions were placed in the hands of army colonels, navy captains, and air force commodores. The unions also lost control of an estimated $3 billion in social welfare funds. The once-powerful General Economic Confederation, a reform-minded group of small- and medium-sized entrepreneurs, was dissolved. An international arrest order was put out for its leaders. In the provincial city of La Plata the number of political prisoners held at one prison multiplied, from 130 to nearly 600, in the days after the coup, with nearly all of the newcomers being workers unconnected with the guerrillas.[3]

What the military called "subversion" included job actions and ballot-box victories. Also included were nationalist reactions to foreign economic pressures, part of a battle that had been fought inconclusively for more than a century and that had been exacerbated by fierce multinational competition in Argentina in the 1960s. Over the next seven years the means for keeping the work force in line proliferated—warnings, suspensions, disciplinary firings. Old wage gains disappeared. Regulations on health, hygiene, work safety, and job security gave way to absolute guarantees to employers for the transfer of workers and the modification of rules governing their work. The military empowered employers with the right to question potential employees about their religious, union, and political ideas; the right to fire workers for "crimes" not proven in court; and the right to eliminate profit-sharing and worker participation in management. To this was added the constant presence of police in the factories and their use to impose arbitrary company orders. Often the police and army became the virtual enforcement arm of corporate personnel policy.[4]

A few weeks after the coup educator and long-time Peronist activist Emilio F. Mignone was invited by the Inter-American Development Bank to a cocktail party held at the posh Plaza Hotel in downtown Buenos Aires. "Most of the people there were functionaries of the new administration, the majority in uniform, whom I did not know," Mignone recalled. "Upon seeing a friend I went over to him. He presented me to the person he was with. It was Walter Klein, the father of the second-ranking member of the Economy Ministry, who was also named Walter Klein. We were standing close to the door. Suddenly there entered an exultant Gen. Alcides López Aufranc—he had just been named president of the Acindar steel company, replacing the new economy czar, José A. Martínez de Hoz.

The general came over to our group to say hello. Klein congratulated him on his appointment, saying, "An energetic man like yourself was needed over there." López Aufranc smiled, pleased. Later the conversation drifted to rumors about a possible strike in the industry, with Klein saying he had information about the detention of twenty-three factory stewards. The general—thinking I, too, was part of the gang that had taken power—replied in an assuring manner: "Don't worry Walter, *todos estan bajo tierra* [they're all dead and buried]."[5]

"Purifying" the Workplace

The factories were one of the priority "objectives" in the antisubversive struggle. During the first ten months after the coup, workers' real wages dropped more than 50 percent. Guillermo Walter Klein, Martínez de Hoz's closest collaborator, was only being truthful when he said the military's program was "incompatible with any democratic system and [was] only applicable if supported by a de facto regime." Juan Alemann, Videla's treasury secretary, admitted that economics was the driving force behind the military's political repression. "With this policy," Alemann said,

> we seek to weaken the enormous power of the unions, which was one of the country's biggest problems. Argentina's unions were too strong, which made it impossible for any political party to flourish, because unions had all the power. Now, with a fluid labor market, the worker no longer goes to the union leader with his problems, because if he doesn't like his job he gets another, and that's that. ... We've weakened the unions' power and this is the basis for any political solution in Argentina.[6]

The military's campaign came after minute planning. A whole body of Directivas Secretas (DS; Secret Directives), put into practice from 1975 throughout the military period, guided the generals' actions and contained a totalitarian bent. The Pilot Operation decreed in DS 222/76 established that the army was to intervene in industry and state-run enterprises "to promote and neutralize conflictive situations of a work-related nature, provoked by or which can be exploited by the subversives, in order to impede agitation or insurrectional actions by the masses and contribute to the efficient functioning of the country's productive apparatus." The repression, said the army Secret Directive 504/77, sought an "ideologically purified" workplace.[7]

"Subversion in the workplace" became a multipurpose pretext for the ferocious repression unleashed against the workers. The military's own intelligence services reported that "the subversives have not had much success to date in the infiltration [of grassroots union groups], given the low percentage detected."[8]

A profile of political prisoners in Argentina drawn up by the American embassy in Buenos Aires in mid-1977 was revealing. In the category of "trade union activists held for union related activities which were legal until enactment of legislation [after the coup], without any associations with the subversive groups," the embassy estimated between 750 and 1,000 people were being held. Some 500 who fell into that category were "presumed killed." A second group was made up of "rank and file workers." These were "being held for participation in or association with strikes, slow downs, or other exercise of traditionally recognized trade union activities considered legal until [the coup] and intended to obtain redress for work related or salary related grievances." Between 3,000 and 4,000 ordinary workers were estimated to be in jail, with 750 "presumed killed."[9]

The guerrillas' presence in the factories was minimal. The Montoneros, with more ties to the workplace than the ERP, had fantasized that the coup signaled the opening of armed struggle between two armies, one "revolutionary," the other "counterrevolutionary." Nowhere did such hubris work to more tragic effect than in the repression unleashed against combative union leaders and delegations, the so-called "industrial guerrillas," a term coined by conservative Radical party leader Balbín and used in the military's secret directives.[10]

Efforts by the Montoneros to use workers' demands as a tool for ushering in a socialist revolution showed the guerrillas' misunderstanding of the nature of union conflict in Argentina. They aggrandized individual factory conflicts into portents of generalized class warfare. What they seemed not to understand was that their days of political extortion had quickly come to an end. No longer could the numerically weak guerrillas use high-octane—and deadly—theatrics to make the far more powerful government look impotent. The day after a guerrilla attack it was not the guerrillas who had to go to work at the same factory where it occurred. Even when not politically linked to the guerrillas, the combative labor activists were nevertheless "burned" in the military's eyes. In a country where even tepid reformism was suspect and the population at large terrorized, the activists had nowhere to turn.[11]

What's Good for General Motors

Nearly all major industrial plants were occupied by troops. In some cases, such as Ford Motors, a garrison of the I Army Corps remained for several months in the company's sports field.

The hand-in-glove coordination between the military and the Ford Motor Company management made its General Pacheco plant in Buenos Aires province the apotheosis of brutality against workers. "They surrounded the plant with trucks and jeeps, armed to the teeth, registering us one by one and detaining many comrades. They checked our trunks and locker room, making constant searches. ... About 100 delegates were detained, destroying the shop steward structure. In Ford alone more than 100 workers were abducted. Some reappeared later as detainees, others were liberated. Many never returned."[12]

Union stewards Adolfo Sánchez and Juan Carlos Amoroso were called the day after the coup to a meeting of the heads of Ford Motor's labor relations department and its stamping plant. "All of us factory stewards were present. There they notified us that they had already refused to recognize us as workers' representatives. In that meeting the boss, Galarraga, read a note a colonel had given him ... exhorting us to work, forgetting all our demands." As there were still pending negotiations requested by the stewards over an accounting matter, Amoroso asked whether those talks were going to be held. "You, sir, do not understand," the Ford boss replied. "This meeting has ended. Tomorrow say 'Hi' to Camps." When the workers asked, "Who's he?" of the man—Col. Alberto Camps—who later bragged that he was responsible for some 5,000 deaths, the Ford bosses burst into laughter. "Ya se van a enterar [You'll be finding out soon enough]," they replied.

Three days later Amoroso, Sánchez, and the other stewards were kidnapped from their homes by armed men bearing file cards taken from Ford personnel archives. On April 12 police and army troops surrounded the General Motors Barracas plant in a spectacular operation. One factory wing had refused to work after being stripped of their benefits for doing unsafe jobs. An army captain and a few of his soldiers began to interrogate the workers over the cause of the stoppage. Later they talked with the factory bosses. Army troops then entered the plant and began to push the complaining workers at rifle point back to their posts. Once the situation was "normalized," the troops withdrew, taking with them three protesting workers.[13]

Obliged to work with rifles pointed at their backs at a feverish rate of production, the labor discipline and repression made conditions unbearable. Situations similar to that of Ford and General Motors occurred at Argentina's other large automotive plants: FIAT, Renault, Peugeot, and Mercedez Benz. Not only the mechanical workers suffered the effects of the first military operations, however. Almost all the country's factories were put under supervision. This change was especially true in those companies that were deemed as vital by the military and in the leading industries in each sector or activity.

Power and Light

In spite of the repression, some in Argentina's trade union movement—for thirty years a pillar in the country's power structure—attempted to fight back. In September 1976, six months after the coup, wage conflicts broke out at General Motors, Ford, FIAT, Peugeot, and Chrysler. The government responded immediately. Law 21400 imposed a six-year prison term for participating in a strike and ten years for those judged to be "instigators."

In October the electrical workers union, Luz y Fuerza (Light and Power), one of the country's most powerful, challenged the reign of terror. The union had been taken over by the generals shortly after the coup. Some 260 employees at SEGBA, the state-run electric company, had been fired. All were shop stewards and union activists. One was the union general-secretary, Oscar Smith.

Luz y Fuerza had been a strong supporter of nationalizing the country's electrical industry. In recent years the union had carried out its own experiment in workers' self-management, unique in Argentine labor history. During that period SEGBA's productivity improved, a record supply of energy was provided, industry-wide strikes were avoided, and industrial sabotage was nonexistent. In 1973 there were 166 days in which the power produced was insufficient to meet demand, with subsequent brownouts and blackouts in Buenos Aires and elsewhere. Two years later the deficit-producing days had been reduced to 14.[14]

Once the military came to power, SEGBA's participatory system was forcibly ended. The World Bank expressly conditioned its issuing of loans to the company's privatization and the elimination of what SEGBA's military-appointed directors called the "sovietizing" experiment of workers' participation in management.[15]

The military suspended the collective bargaining agreement won by the union in early 1976. That, combined with the massive firings, caused Luz y Fuerza to launch the first job action against the regime. As the secret concentration camps swelled with prisoners and much of Argentina was swept up in an immobilizing terror, Oscar Smith began a brave and imaginative attack on the regime and its economic designs. Elected as the union's head the year before, El Negro (Blackie) Smith, as his friends called him, was used to being in the front lines. He had been one of those who led the general strike against López Rega in 1975, despite threats from the Triple A. He had even confronted Isabel Perón, desperately worried that Peronism's traditional reform program was being corrupted by the murderous social welfare minister.

"Tell Blackie to make himself real scarce," anonymous voices repeated daily over the telephone. Smith resolved to launch a frontal attack against the military's intervention of his union. By creating local labor units by zone or area responsible for negotiations with the companies, they emerged as a "phantom" union that made a mockery of the military's control of Luz y Fuerza. Such audacity did not come cheaply. On September 3 Luz y Fuerza union leader Agustín Sánchez and his wife were "disappeared" in Tucumán.[16]

On October 5 electrical workers in Buenos Aires downed their tools and rallied at the union headquarters. Acting on Videla's orders, the I Army Corps troops and navy infantry began a military occupation of electric power stations. During three days—October 7, 8, and 9—ninety SEGBA workers were detained, twenty-seven more in Puerto Nuevo, and eighteen in Pilar. Detentions were also carried out at the Italo electric company and against Luz y Fuerza workers in four Buenos Aires suburbs—Morón, Quilmes, Lanús, and San Miguel. The Central Costanera in the federal capital was also violently occupied, and Agua y Energía, the state water company, fired forty workers.[17]

Smith pressed ahead with his *plan de lucha* (battle plan) to force the junta into negotiations. In the electric plants and generators occupied by the military, the workers were obliged to work at gunpoint. On October 13 three SEGBA workers were kidnapped. The union quickly intensified the job action, a pressure credited with saving the lives of the trio but not sparing them savage torture.

Smith's combative union had delivered the regime an unaccustomed blow. On February 1, as new work rules went into effect, the personnel ignored the government's decision and went to work according to the former schedule. Videla, Massera, and Agosti met on Friday, February 4, to adopt measures meant to beat back the challenge. After a four-hour cabinet meeting, the military threatened that all the union's activity would be considered "subversive"—which could only mean greater repression and possible death for the workers.

That weekend the union kept up its pressure. The day the junta met, the capital's supply of electricity dropped precipitously. Elevators and water tanks in large buildings ceased to function. (Miriam Lewin de García, illegally detained in the Navy Mechanics School concentration camp, remembered later that her torturers had to interrupt their most vicious session when the electric prod they were using stopped working due to the Luz y Fuerza strike.) Twenty thousand disciplinary slips went out in a company that had 24,000 workers.[18]

The workers responded by launching a series of "surprise strikes." On Monday, February 7, Smith and the regional union leadership announced their opposition to the military's plan to privatize the nation's power industry. Five platforms were knocked out of service by acts of sabotage by the workers in the following days, while Smith negotiated with the military an end to the conflict and to the intervention of the union.

On February 10 Col. Américo Dahler, the army's representative at the Labor Ministry, called Smith and other Luz y Fuerza workers to a meeting at his office. Smith's intuition, tested in countless negotiations, warned him danger was near. That night Smith slept at his parents' house. According to Oscar's brother, Santo Smith, the unionist left their parents' home on February 11 about 8:30 A.M. "He climbed into a Dodge 1500 that he had on loan and took off," he said. "That's the last we heard from him." According to witnesses, the orange Dodge with a black vinyl top was intercepted by two Ford Falcons, from which spilled a number of men wearing jeans and dark sunglasses. Smith was forced into one of the vehicles.[19]

On February 18 Maxwell Chaplin, the deputy chief of mission at the U.S. embassy in Buenos Aires, sent a confidential cable about Smith's kidnapping to the State Department that underscored the extent to which the military's methods were known to the country's political and economic elite:

> There are still no concrete leads as to Smith's whereabouts or as to who has him. The consensus among trade unionists continues to be that Smith has been seized by an operations group of one of the secret services or perhaps a joint group from various of the armed forces acting autonomously. ... [name deleted] and others appear relatively confident—at least for the moment—that Smith will eventually turn up alive—that is, the perpetrators do not now intend to assassinate Smith and make it appear to be the dirty work of the guerrillas.[20]

Later investigation suggested the navy was responsible for Smith's kidnapping and murder. Some sources say Smith's independence, and Massera's fear the union leader might have cut a deal with the admiral's rivals in the army, were responsible for his death. A solution to the conflict would have provided a precedent for negotiations with other unions. This development in turn would have improved the image of ambitious army chief Gen. Roberto Viola, the head of the dialoguistas, with labor leaders. Viola's interservice rivals understood that the way to torpedo the larger political design was to kill Smith.[21]

After the abduction Smith's wife, Ana María Pérez, met with President Videla to ask his help. "He received me with a rosary in his hand. 'I've just finished my prayers,' he told me. Later he said my husband's disappearance might have been a 'self-kidnapping,' or that maybe he was held outside the country, although he admitted the possibility it might have been the work of parapolice or paramilitary forces. 'The thing is, your husband is too involved in the union.'" She also met with another junta member, air force Brigadier Orlando Agosti. "He said he couldn't understand how my husband could go out without bodyguards—'I never go out without mine,' he said. He also asked me, curiously, how old were my daughters, then nine and fourteen. 'Ah, well,' he said, 'luckily they're already older.'"

Little credible information about Smith ever came to light. One former detainee at the Navy Mechanics School claimed, years later, that the circumstances of his captivity allowed him to establish that the navy was involved in Smith's abduction. Not much else is known.[22]

Just days before Smith was abducted, four Luz y Fuerza stewards had been abducted. Not one would return alive. The kidnapping of their most important leader broke the electrical workers' fighting spirit, and the example had a chilling effect on the rest. The strike was ended the following day. The resistance appeared to be crushed.

13

Priority Target:
The Church of the People

Wars are never fought with white gloves. We have used against the terrorists the same drastic methods that they have employed.
                                                    —*José A. Martínez de Hoz*

They will not confuse us, either with their titles or their ecclesiastical robes, nor with their cunning and speculative behavior. An infinite minority cannot be allowed to continue upsetting the minds of our youths, teaching them foreign ideas and converting them into social critics, with an interpretation cunningly distorted of what Christian doctrine is. All this is subversion.
                                        —*Adm. Rubén Chamorro, Director, ESMA*[1]

The night before the coup, Adm. Emilio Massera and Gen. Jorge R. Videla met with the ecclesiastic hierarchy at the headquarters of the Conferencia Episcopal Argentina (CEA; Argentine Episcopal Conference) at 1867 Paraguay Street in downtown Buenos Aires. There they talked about the events to come and the need to save "Western and Christian Argentina." Adolfo Tortolo, archbishop of Paraná and chief vicar of the armed forces, not only endorsed and blessed the military's power grab but also allowed himself to "give advice" concerning a few aspects of the sharing of power planned by the generals. Tortolo continued throughout the regime to exercise great influence on his friends Videla and air force Brigadier Agosti, whom he knew from childhood in the Buenos Aires provincial town of Mercedes.[2]

Already in Tucumán, Monsignor Victorio Bonamín, the military vicar, had called for the coup: "The army is purifying the dirtiness in our country. Wouldn't Christ want the armed forces one day to reach out beyond their job?" Less than a month later, August 2, 1975, Tortolo praised the "clean and efficient" action of the army in the antiguerrilla campaign. The real nature of the "war" unleashed by the armed forces, with its methods of torture, rape, looting, and death, was not unknown to church elders. Even before Videla became president, Bonamín had publicly resorted to the term "dirty war" that the Argentine military inherited from their French mentors in Algeria: "I ask divine protection in this 'dirty war' in which we are engaged ... a war in which God Himself must have been interested, so that He could participate with HIS help." For some members of the church it was a "holy war," "a fight in defense of morality, of the dignity of God, most definitely a fight in defense of God."[3]

Unlike the churches of Chile, Brazil, and El Salvador, the Argentine Catholic church did little to stop the slaughter. Even faced with the vast martyrdom that claimed bishops, priests, nuns, and laymen, including more than 40 deaths, 120 disappearances, and hundreds imprisoned, much of the Argentine church hierarchy kept silent, out of fear or out of complicity. "The church always played it dumb," said Gen. (ret.) Ricardo Flouret, once a top aide to Videla. "It always looked the other way." Wrote Catholic scholar Penny Lernoux, "Because the Argentine experience so closely resembles the performance of the Catholic church in Nazi Germany, it again raises the question of whether power is more important to the church than the Gospel imperative to be a witness to the truth."[4]

Much of the Argentine church had ignored the wave of social activism that had moved the Latin American church since before the Second Vatican Council. With few exceptions the Catholic hierarchy had turned a deaf ear to Pope John XXIII's proclamation in 1963 of *Pacem in terris*, which recognized the growing participation of his fellow churchmen in social and economic reform. Pope Paul VI's proclamation four years later of the encyclical *Populorum progressio*—a vigorous attack on inequality, crass materialism, racism, and the selfishness of richer nations—created discomfort, not devotion.

Ties between the Argentine Catholic church and the military had always been strong. After Argentina's nineteenth-century liberator, Gen. José San Martín, won a major battle against the Spanish, he invested the Blessed Virgin with the rank of general. In December 1954 Juan Perón undertook an official antichurch policy, hoping to reduce the church's power and influence. When General Aramburu overthrew Perón in 1955, the papal flag was displayed next to that of Argentina, with the air force flying a cross formation followed by a *V* for *Christus Vincit*. Eleven years later, when General Onganía overthrew another elected government, he appointed several members of the secret right-wing Catholic lodge Opus Dei to his cabinet.[5]

During 1975 the progressive churchmen had faced the wrath of the right. In the naval port of Bahía Blanca a priest was murdered and the John XXIII academy where he was vice rector partially destroyed. In the Buenos Aires provincial town of Sanchez Elías the church Nuestra Señora de Carmen was leveled by a powerful bomb. The dean of humanities at the Catholic University of Mar del Plata was kidnapped—her mutilated body to be found a year later buried in the beach. Two priests, Elías Musse and Raúl Troncoso, were arrested. In the western province of Río Negro a bomb destroyed the Sierra Grande Church. In the north, in Formosa, a French priest active in agrarian reform was abducted by the army, to be expelled from the country a year later. In Neuquén province the Mamá Margarita Catholic home for the children of destitute Mapuche Indians was raided. In Goya two priests were jailed. Catholic leader Daniel Bombara was machine-gunned to death. The Argentine delegate to the Fifth International Council of Young Catholic Workers went missing. A priest in the Buenos Aires provincial town of Urdampilleta was kidnapped while in the middle of saying mass.[6]

The year 1976 opened with the New Year's Day kidnapping of Miguel Angel Urusa Nicolau, a fifty-eight-year-old Salesian priest and teacher who taught at secondary schools in Rosario and Córdoba. He reportedly died while being tortured. Brother Julio San Cristóbal, of the La Salle community, was also abducted. He disappeared without a trace in February 1976.

Perhaps the worst case was that suffered by the parish of Villa Itatí, a fetid slum on the outskirts of Buenos Aires where the *villeros* (slum dwellers) were mostly immigrants from the northeastern provinces or neighboring Bolivia and Paraguay. There the local priest, José Tedeschi, had for five years worked hard to get needed social services to the community in the form of sidewalks, electrification, running water, and a medical clinic.

At 4:00 P.M. on February 4 a group of armed men dragged the priest into their car. Cries for help and the reaction of neighbors, who themselves were beaten, did not prevent the abduction. A few days later Tedeschi's body was found on the outskirts of La Plata. His eyes had been gouged, his teeth and nails yanked from his castrated body.[7]

One of those responsible for the murder was a low-ranking army officer, Orestes Vaello, a member of a paramilitary group linked to the National University Concentration. Vaello told the Sábato commission that in November 1975 the group allegedly confirmed that the priest was linked with Montoneros, and they received the order to kidnap and eliminate Tedeschi. "In the slum we had two penetration agents [informants]. The order to kill Tedeschi finally came from the First Army Corps headquarters. He was executed outside the city of La Plata."[8]

Three days earlier, on the night of February 1, Rosa María Casariego, 25, a teacher and catechism instructor, and her husband, Luis Alberto Cabrera, were kidnapped by armed men from their home in a poor Buenos Aires suburb. A worker at the Aquamarine shipyards, which produced fiberglass boats, Cabrera served as a steward in the Sindicato de Obreros de la Industria Naval (SOIN; Naval Industries Workers Union). That same night a *patota* (gang) made up of Buenos Aires police kidnapped a friend of the couple who was also a SOIN union leader. Oscar Echeverría, twenty-six, was a steward at the Maestrina shipyards. Five days later in a field in Moreno, a suburb west of Buenos Aires, the bodies of two men and a woman were found riddled with bullets. Each was blindfolded, each with his or her hands tied to the shoulders. *La Razón,* the sensationalistic afternoon daily run by the army, dispatched the grisly news with a small article of a few lines. While Rosa María was being tortured, they had cut off one of her breasts, it reported. The medical examiner said she bled to death hours before the shooting.[9]

At her funeral on February 9 Padre Francisco Soares, a fifty-eight-year-old Brazilian priest with whom she gave catechism instruction, denounced Rosa María's assassins by name. He also denounced those responsible for the systematic attack to which workers at the shipyards and those affiliated with SOIN had been subjected. Only two weeks earlier Radical party leader Adolfo Gass had also denounced the disappearance of Carlos Asencio Alvarez, a worker at the Astarsa shipyards abducted from his home in San Fernando, in the same area. Gass demanded the urgent intervention of the Interior Ministry. Alvarez's body, partially burned and showing multiple bullet wounds, was found along the shoulder of provincial Route 6, near Campana, an industrial city 54 miles from Buenos Aires.

Padre Soares would outlive his denunciation by only six days. The night of February 15 Soares and his invalid brother were murdered—machine-gunned—in their run-down home in Carupá, a poor district north of the capital.[10]

Massacre of the Palotines

On Sunday, July 4, 1976, two days after a Montonero bombing at Federal Police headquarters in downtown Buenos Aires in which twenty people were killed, a group of parishioners queued for mass, waiting for the Palotine fathers to open the massive doors of the San Patricio (St. Patrick's) Church in the aristocratic, tree-lined Belgrano neighborhood. As the crowd grew restless, a seventeen-year-old church organist and layworker ventured into the rectory, looking for the missing priests.

Alfredo Kelly, Alfredo Leaden, and Pedro Dufau and seminarians Salvador Barbeito and Emilio Barletti lay dead in the rectory living room, their badly beaten, bullet-riddled bodies resting in a huge pool of blood that covered the floor. More than sixty bullets had shattered the furniture and left pockmarks in the walls. There, written in the victims' own blood, were the clues to the slaughter: "For poisoning the virgin minds of our youth," "For the police blown up in Coordinación," and "Curas hijos de puta" (Priests sons of bitches). During the slaughter one of the seminarians had been raped, after his death, with a church document shoved up his anus. An unexploded bomb lay nearby.[11]

The personal magnetism of Padre Alfredo Kelly had attracted groups of young people touched by the sincerity of his message. "Neither alms for the church nor snobbish charity excuses social injustice," Kelly repeated each Sunday. Businessmen, military officers, judges, and politicians were among those who heard his fiery sermons, and some demanded his resignation.

Both the papal nuncio, Pio Laghi, and Cardinal Primate Juan Carlos Aramburu had gone to San Patricio after the murders. The Palotines' own superior in Argentina, Padre Kevin O'Neill, later recalled a "revealing conversation" he had with the papal nuncio: "He told us that, after having returned from the

San Patricio church on the fourth of July, he had made inquiries at a foreign embassy. We asked him if it was the American embassy. He wouldn't say yes or no. He said that there they told him that paramilitary forces had done it."[12] In fact, a group operating out of the Navy Mechanics School headed by Rear Adm. Rubén Chamorro carried out the operation. "During working lunches," recalled Miriam Lewin de García, an ESMA survivor, before the Sábato commission, "Lt. Jorge Radice showed off his black humor, saying with a sneer that his task force had carried out the murders of [Argentine diplomat] Elena Holmberg, the French nuns—he called them his 'flying nuns'—and the Palotine priests."[13]

The Martyrdom of a Bishop

The life and death of La Rioja bishop Enrique Angelelli symbolized Argentina's "Church of the People." Known by friends as El Pelado (Baldy), Angelelli had a commitment to his diocese in the country's historically ignored northwest that made God's work be war on the province's endemic poverty. Angelelli worked tirelessly in community development. Cooperative farms were set up to cultivate vast tracts of unexploited land. Pools of trucks and agricultural tools were founded, as were peasant organizations formed to press for credit to buy seeds, to share scarce water resources, and to pressure the government into handing over virgin, untilled land to be worked by the poorest of the impoverished peasant farmers.[14]

Angelelli, the scion of a wealthy Italian immigrant family, had arrived in La Rioja in 1968 and found himself confronted with "the other Argentina"—a region of huge landholdings and Indian peons, working in a virtual master-slave relationship that hearkened back to the days of the Spanish conquest. Like their ancestors, the Indians worked as the white man's beasts of burden, tending to the vineyards and working in the walnut and olive groves.

Wealthy landowners and military men, quick to interpret any attempt at social change as "Marxist subversion," unleashed an implacable persecution against Angelelli and his followers. When in 1973 Angelelli—who was Gov. Carlos Menem's confessor—imposed ecclesiastical sanctions on thirteen large landowners who had attacked him for his support of the peasants, the *haciendados* (landowners) denounced the bishop to Rome. The ploy backfired when the papal delegate sent to investigate held that the prelate's work was consistent with church teachings and deserved "praise and support."[15]

Infuriated, the landowners labeled the bishop "Satanelli" and began to organize a more direct attack. Lay workers, religious teachers, nuns, and priests were imprisoned without motive. Many were expelled from the province for "security reasons." Others were forced to leave the country. The military high command's endgame was soon to manifest itself—assassinate some churchmen as an example to the rest.

The flash point came at a mass held at the Chamical air base a few days before the coup. There the bishop used his sermon to condemn the possibility of a military putsch and defended constitutional rule. A high-ranking officer leapt from his pew, yelling at Angelelli they were "not there to listen to politics" before storming out. The ensuing scandal obliged Angelelli to end religious ceremonies at the base. The decision was immediately reversed with an "apology" to the military by the right-wing military bishop Monsignor Bonamín, who, according to one account, gave a sermon about the "justifiable death of the anti-Christ even dressed as a bishop."[16]

Far-right Catholic groups, known as the Cruzada de la Fe (the Faith Crusaders), increased their attacks on Angelelli. In an advertisement published July 17 in the local newspaper, *El Sol,* owned by army intelligence informant Tomás Agustín Alvarez Saavedra, the crusaders declared: "His staying in the diocese makes unity impossible." The next day Chamical parish priests Gabriel Longueville, a Frenchman, and Juan de Dios Murias were murdered.

Angelelli himself chronicled the events in a document meant for the Vatican and the French embassy:

> It was 9:30 the night of July 18. The two priests had finished eating supper at the house of the Sisters of San José, nuns who helped with the parochial work at the "El Salvador" parish in Chamical, 84 miles south of the capital of La Rioja. Two individuals, dressed in civilian clothes, called at the door of the dining room and were met by Padre Carlos. They told him they wanted to speak with him and Padre Gabriel. ... Upon leaving the priests told the nuns they had to travel to La Rioja ... they had been shown police credentials. ... The priests gathered their things at the parish house, that was connected in the back with that of the sisters. ... [Later] the four got into the car, driving south. ... The sisters noted a certain preoccupation by the priests while the civilians conducted themselves with a certain military behavior and normality.[17]

Told the next day about what had happened, Angelelli made urgent inquiries before the Federal Police delegation, the provincial police headquarters, and the Army Engineering Batallion. At each he received denials of any knowledge of the priests' whereabouts. Given the seriousness of the situation, the bishop also contacted the nuncio, Pio Laghi, Cardinal Raúl F. Primatesta, and the head of the order to which Padre Carlos belonged.

That morning, railway workers who saw two bundles along the tracks had taken them for sleeping linesmen. Upon their return that afternoon, however, they found the bundles covered with army blankets. Uncovering the bodies, they found a list of names of priests. "On Tuesday, the 20th, during the afternoon," Angelelli told the Vatican, "a team of railway workers found the bodies of both priests nearly a mile from Chamical, their bodies sprayed with bullets, hands bound, and in terrible shape. Their watches indicated the deaths may have occurred around 11:00 Sunday night." (The priests, recalled Carlos Menem, "had two bullet wounds in the testicles and in the neck; they were subjected to the most atrocious violence.")[18]

The news of the murders left La Rioja stunned. On July 25 Angelelli received another blow. A group of hooded men had entered the small village of Sanogasta, looking for a priest whom Angelelli had earlier counseled to leave the area. Furious at not finding their intended victim, the men went to the house of a rural leader linked to Angelelli. Sprayed with machine-gun fire on the doorstep of his home, the man died hours later.

On the night of August 3 Angelelli had still not returned to La Rioja. He preferred to remain in Chamical to search for clues, which he promised to reveal "from the pulpit of the La Rioja cathedral if necessary." After dining with his aide, Padre Arturo Pinto, the two priests noted strange movements in the empty lot behind the parish house, where they had left their Fiat minipickup. As they went out to investigate, an auto, its headlights off, slipped away along a parallel street, disappearing into the night. The circle around Angelelli was drawing tighter.

The following day the two priests decided to return to La Rioja. They did not know that even as they were deciding to return to the capital, Adm. Emilio Massera was meeting with a "high ecclesiastical authority" in Buenos Aires. There Massera asked for the dismissal of Angelelli and two other progressive clergymen who were also frequent critics of the military.[19]

The nine miles running from the exit of Route 38 between Punta de Llanos to the provincial capital are as flat as a billiard green, and the appearance—out of nowhere—of a Peugeot 404 was therefore all the more startling. The car's occupants briefly stared at the two priests before cutting the Fiat driven by Angelelli off the road in a brusque maneuver that sent the bishop's vehicle spinning out of control along the shoulder of the road, somersaulting more than 100 feet before coming to a stop. As the mysterious car sped away from the scene, Padre Pinto lay badly wounded and unconscious, to later be taken to a hospital by an auto that happened by. Angelelli was not so lucky. The bishop lay lifeless on the pavement, his arms outstretched as if crucified, his cranium destroyed. Despite the heavy air of intimidation, 6,000 mourners turned out for Angelelli's funeral to hear Archbishop Vicente Zaspe recall that El Pelado had often confided to him, "I am ready to die, if my death will bring reconciliation to La Rioja." Months later local authorities were obliged to repave the section of the road where Angelelli was killed. In the spot where the bishop had lain dying in a pool of blood, La Rioja's poor had come to carry away tiny chunks of asphalt, which they revered as sacred relics.[20]

The "accident," as the military authorities later called it, had hardly taken place when more than fifty police and military men arrived at the scene, prohibiting anyone from nearing the spot where the bishop lay dead. The lifeless body remained there for more than six hours until it was reviewed by a local judge. A few humble workers from the district, eyewitnesses to the crash, refused to testify about what they had seen, intimidated by threats they had received from the military. However, it was later established that Angelelli was carrying with him a file of important proof about the deaths of the priests. The archive disappeared following the accident, to surface soon after in the office of Interior Minister Gen. Albano Harguindeguy.[21]

José Deheza, the former Peronist defense minister, recalled: "One day I went to see Harguindeguy to ask about some Peronist comrades. The telephone rang and his face lit up with a smile. When he hung up he said, 'Bishop Angelelli has just died in an accident.' "[22]

It was an "accident" the military knew about and had been planning. According to one testimony taken by the Sábato Commission: "During one of the interrogations, Captain Marco and Captain Goenaga told me La Rioja's bishop, Enrique Angelelli, the psychiatrist Raúl Fuentes and Alipio Paoletti were to die ... before the end of the month. Angelelli died ... Fuentes has been missing since the end of 1976 and Alipio Paoletti was intensely sought after."[23]

Eyewitnesses privately admitted to church authorities that they "saw them take the bishop from his car and beat his head against the ground." All police records on road controls operating that day and an order prohibiting Angelelli's appearance on a local radio station either disappeared or were incinerated. Armando Torralba, a reporter for *El Independiente,* said the judge who intervened in the case, despite finding the wheels of Angelelli's car were in perfect condition, nonetheless obliged him to write that "a blowout of a rear tire has been established." In June 1986 a judge found that Angelelli's death "was not due to a traffic accident, but rather a coldly premeditated homicide that the victim had foreseen."[24]

Silence of the Shepherds

What the Argentine church did in the face of the slaughter, why, and what more it might have done, are three issues destined to occupy religious historians for years. Faced with a less serious provocation during Perón's second government— only one priest had been murdered—the church nevertheless confronted the regime. During the early days of the repression, church officials, unlike much of their flock, knew what was going on—they could not help but know given the thousands who filed before each Curia asking for help. Yet—in part because they believed it more effective, in part out of fear, and in part to avoid conflict— church officials preferred private and confidential protests to the authorities, waiting a full year before making a strong public statement.

What more could the church have done?

Given the lack of effective redress to the church's private complaints, the churchmen could have refused to hold traditional Te Deum masses during national holidays and attend official acts and could have withdrawn its military chaplains from the barracks. The church could have issued a "white paper" setting out its concerns, allowing the faithful a chance to understand what was happening and giving the church the possibility of disassociating itself from the regime, at the same time putting decisive pressure on the generals. The Argentine church might also have created an institution like Chile's church-sponsored Vicaría de la Solidaridad (Vicariate of Solidarity) human rights organization, a vehicle for aiding victims of repression and their families. Not only did the Argentines not do this, but they kept private efforts, such as the Permanent Assembly for Human Rights and the Ecumenical Movement for Human Rights, at arm's length. Although progressive churchmen such as Bishops Jaime de Nevares and Jorge Novak joined such groups in their own name, the church's position limited their freedom of action and effectiveness. The lack of dynamic, public, and official leadership by church elders also served to demobilize the ranks of priests, nuns, and subordinate institutions, such as Acción Católica (Catholic Action), who felt without direction and did nothing. In addition, willing sister churches such as that in the United States found themselves hampered in their efforts in part by a lack of requests for support from the Argentines.[25]

In May 1977 the church finally found its voice—weakly—denouncing the regime's role in the kidnapping, torture, and murder of thousands. Although condemning Marxism, the bishops issued a broadside over military charges that individual bishops and priests favored communism. "The church has its own judges to pass judgment on the teaching performance of its pastors," they said. "We therefore reject the shallow judgment of some that link bishops and priests with ideologies that are incompatible with the faith."[26]

Although the declaration caused great discomfit among the military, the regime responded with silence. Videla said simply the bishops had the right to voice their concerns. The government, he said, listened to them with care, as was fitting when dealing with members of the church. The press aided the regime's strategy of limiting the impact of the bishops' message, relegating its text to the inside pages of the newspapers under headlines only vaguely reflecting its content. At the same time, comments of bishops who strongly justified the repression were given important display. The church pressed no further, and the "military's" bishops still carried the day.

Christian Torture

The commitment of certain sectors of the church went to some of the wildest imaginable extremes. There exist numerous denunciations about the participation of priests—most of them military chaplains—who participated in kidnappings, raids on homes, the illegal handing over of children of *desaparecidos,* and the torture of prisoners. There were cases like that of army chaplain Padre Francisco Priorello, denounced as a participant in torture sessions in the Campo de Mayo military base, the site of two clandestine detention centers. Iris de Avellaneda testified she was tortured by Priorello: "The person who tortured me was named Padre Francisco, who afterward put on his 'good mask' and asked us: 'They beat you, my daughter? Poor thing.'" There the victim lost her fourteen-year-old son, Floreal, who had been kidnapped with her on April 15, 1976. His body appeared later, with seven other cadavers, floating off the coast of Uruguay.[27]

In February 1977, shortly after the disappearance of one of her sons, Hebe de Bonafini, the woman who later became the president of the Mothers of the Plaza de Mayo, went to see Monsignor Antonio Plaza, the archbishop of La Plata and chaplain-general of the Buenos Aires police department, for help. The archbishop sent her to an office in the basement of the cathedral where a retired policeman named Sosa—he told her—had information about her son. There she was interrogated: "What did your son do? Who are his friends? Where do they live? Where do they work?" Hebe de Bonafini understood. She insulted the cop and ran out of the place. Later, together with other mothers who had fallen for the same trick, they investigated; Sosa was an active duty policeman working for the political section of the provincial police.[28]

Where the church elders best expressed their commitment to the military regime was in the "tranquilization of consciences" of killers and torturers and in the formation and ideological sustenance of those charged with carrying out the "dirty war." The presence of priests such as Rodobaldo Ruisánchez (spiritual adviser to provincial police chief Fernando E. Verplaetsen and professor at the Superior War School), Egidio Esparza (of the same school), or Marcial Castro Castillo allowed for the works of the military intelligence centers to pass for "Christian." Padre Sabas Gallardo, the military chaplain of the 4th Brigade in Córdoba, which participated in the unbelievable brutality committed in La Perla detention center, assumed as his own the doctrines coined by certain French officials during the occupation of Algeria: "If torture lasts more than forty-eight hours it is a sin, since torture is allowable only during that period of time, as afterward the subversive cell disperses." Concerning "Physical Integrity and Torture," Castro Castillo taught:

> Only the gravest crimes and irreparable damages can be punished with death. For lesser crimes, lesser punishments should be applied, but they should always consist of the definitive or temporary privation of a good. ... The good withheld can be liberty, through imprisonment; honor, by publicizing the crime; or even physical integrity, through corporal punishments, physical suffering or even mutilation. ... Corporal punishment is, morally speaking, as valid as ever. ... The "rack" and the "picana" [electric prod] do not differ in their moral standard.[29]

14

Priority Target: The "Cultural War"

> The least resistant died in their cells and their bodies were left there for days, as an advance notice to those who were still breathing. Others were taken to the bathroom so they could shower and shave, they were given clean clothes and then taken outside. Later the task group members returned alone and—shouting so that no one could help but hear them—commented: "What a great 'armed clash' that was."
>
> —Página 12, *May 5, 1991*

"They hadn't begun to live, and although some were aware, the majority didn't understand all the horror. They lived in a world that was still infantile, which showed when they played in the showers, their only moment of relative liberty. They thought they were living a novel, an adventure they would tell about later on. All of them were characterized by their purity, their innocence and their solidarity."[1]

Graciela Geuna, a survivor of Córdoba's La Perla death camp, recalled some of the adolescents who passed through the clandestine detention centers. Nearly 250 youths between the ages of thirteen and eighteen "disappeared" in Argentina after having been abducted by the security forces. The military high command's National Counterinsurgency Strategy (Estrategia Nacional Contrasubversiva; ENC), had made education, like factories and religion, a "priority objective" of the National Reorganization Process.

Under the military, education and culture became another front in the "dirty war." "It is necessary," an army secret document declared, "to normalize or purify those spheres, in order to act upon the philosophic-ideological bases of subversion." The military unleashed a "cultural war" in which the enemy sometimes did not know he or she was the enemy. Social conflicts, political opposition, debate, cultural and ideological nonconformity—a good part of that which makes up the most profound values of a free society—were seen as manifestations of revolutionary warfare.[2]

"In reality," said Gen. Acdel Vilas,

> the only total, integral warfare is cultural warfare. ... We do not confront an opponent who fights to defend a flag, a nation or its borders. He who attacks us doesn't do any of that. He is, simply put, part of an army of ideologues whose headquarters could be in Europe, America or Asia. He lacks a national identity. He is the product of a counterculture with a well-defined objective: to destroy the foundations of the Western civilization of which we Argentines naturally form part. ... What we create in the individual is his mind. ... The fight isn't one to conquer terrain, physically, but to conquer minds. Not to take advantageous physical positions but to mold mental structures in his favor.[3]

Vilas traced the roots of Argentina's problems to the egalitarian ideas ushered in by the eighteenth-century French Revolution. The very number of Argentine institutions of higher education raised Vilas's suspicions. The existence of the country's many colleges and universities formed part of a sinister grand design. Vilas, a graduate of U.S. army training schools, wrote:

> If we think that in Argentina we have more than thirty national universities and another thirty institutions of higher education, we will then understand why so much emphasis was put in making them proliferate and to what extent we're the object of Marxist infiltration. The new universities were created in order to cover the entire national territory.
>
> Marxist beachheads were established in some famous university centers in countries, such as France and the United States, that have a culture to which we are very permeable and receptive. These became converted into "brainwashing" centers for scholarship students or Argentine intellectuals, which began with an intense reculturalization. Upon returning to the country they ... became the fifth column in the cultural war in their own nation.[4]

"A Conflict of Civilizations"

On April 29, 1976, a month after the military coup, an army lieutenant colonel ordered the burning of thousands of books in Córdoba. The event was televised on local stations. The next day a communiqué was issued by the III Army Corps and published in almost all the newspapers in the country:

> The Third Army Corps lets it be known that it has proceeded to incinerate this pernicious documentation that affects the intellect and our Christian way of being. So that none of these books, pamphlets, magazines, etc., will be found anywhere, this decision was taken so that our youth is not to be tricked any longer about the true good that our national symbols, family and church—in short, our most traditional spiritual estate synthesized in God, Fatherland and Home—represent.

Similarly in Mendoza, virtually untouched by the guerrillas' violence, the military rector of the Universidad Nacional de Cuyo held a press conference to show some 10,000 "subversive" tracts snatched during raids on the homes of local professors and students.[5]

More than a year later junta member Adm. Emilio Massera issued his own fix on the phenomenon of cultural subversion. The ills of Western society, he said in a speech at the Universidad del Salvador in Buenos Aires, could be traced to three intellectuals: Karl Marx, Sigmund Freud, and Albert Einstein. Marx, the admiral said, was guilty of questioning conventional attitudes about private property, Freud of "attacking the sacred internal being of the human person," and Einstein of challenging existing ideas about space and time. He did not mention the fact— he didn't need to—that all three were Jews.[6]

Dissent in both public and private schools was crushed. The minister of education or a military delegate attached to the ministry was able to prevent private institutions from hiring any teacher or education professional who had been dismissed earlier for broadly defined "subversive or antisocial" activities. Private religious and lay institutions were banned even from choosing their own teacher corps. Those violating injunctions such as hiring or keeping the educational pariahs on their staff were subject to losing their state license—tantamount to a closure order.[7]

Barely four months after the coup Education Minister Ricardo Bruera claimed that some 3,000 academics, administrators, and teaching assistants in national secondary schools had been dismissed. At the same time ninety-five career fields had been eliminated by decree from universities and secondary schools. The social sciences—especially political science, sociology, and psychology—and the humanities were hardest hit, although curriculum cuts and personnel changes also deeply affected some medical and mathematics faculties. "In a word, they are universities in name only," said José Westerkamp, a well-known nuclear physicist and human rights leader, who looked at Argentina's educational system after four years of military rule. "Fear is the only thing that predominates."[8]

Of the nearly 10,000 complaints received later by a government commission investigating disappearances, 21 percent of the disappeared were students, 10.7 percent scientists and professional people, 5.7 percent teachers, and 1.3 percent workers in the cultural field. The national teachers union (Confederación de Trabajadores de la Enseñanza de la República Argentina [CTERA; Confederation of Education Workers of the Argentine Republic]) said that more than 600 teachers were kidnapped from their homes or schools and disappeared forever. (CTERA president and human rights activist Alfredo Bravo was himself kidnapped and tortured in 1977. Bravo credited President Jimmy Carter's human rights policies with his release.) The military's intention, as expressed in a secret directive, was to eliminate any and all centers of thought that "could interfere with the development" of the regime.[9]

To sustain this "normalization" effort, the high command drew up three main tasks. Spying on the intelligentsia was stepped up. Military "agents" were also to act on opinion leaders, businessmen, educational authorities, and others in order to prevent or "normalize" conflicts that could negatively affect the regime. And military and security operations were carried out against suspected dissidents.

The regime created an intelligence center in an Education Ministry building. Operated out of the office of the ministry's military liaison, the spy network lasted throughout the life of the regime. The cabinet-rank delegate supervised the collection of individual "rap sheets" on teachers who were considered "suspicious" or "unreliable." He also ordered investigations, or police shadowing of suspects, and put together a series of "legal" measures designed to ensure the sector's "ideological purity."[10]

An elaborate network of informants was established. Colleges and universities were "occupied" by members of the intelligence services, who held administrative posts ranging from secretaries and teaching assistants to professors. Armando Luchina, a young Federal Police officer, later testified about his work in infiltrating the psychology department of the Universidad de Buenos Aires. Luchina said he and others received bonuses for turning in students they considered "suspect."[11]

The task was complemented with an intense activity by military men who gave talks before teachers about the repressive action being undertaken. "The bottom line of what we want to do in the country is educate the kids and reeducate adults," Lt. Col. Federico Minicucci told a group of 110 Buenos Aires school principals. "At issue is the conflict of civilizations at the world level. The problem is not politics, not countries against countries. Rather this is a problem in which conceptions about life are at odds, one of which ought to prevail in order to organize the world."[12]

Minicucci was one of the heads of the clandestine Vesubio concentration camp, where among the hundreds of prisoners was a group of adolescents from the Carlos Pellegrini high school in Buenos Aires; they remain "disappeared." It was at Vesubio that thirteen-year-old Pablo Miguens was tortured with electric shock in front of his mother in order to make her "talk." Sixteen-year-old Alejandra Naftal was also tortured and questioned about activities at the school.

Little escaped the control of the repressive apparatus. In each university an intelligence department and a network of collaborators was organized and, in general, functioned clandestinely as the Department of Press and Public Relations. At the Universidad Tecnológica Nacional (UTN) the department was headed by an army captain and received intelligence reports put together by the regional faculties. The department itself was set up along the lines of an intelligence detachment, with three sections: an information-gathering unit, a counterintelligence section, and a registry and archives office. The information-gathering unit (mesa de reunión de información) was designed to put together reports and biographical data on students and professors. Its work did not always merely mean the end of a career; its findings could be a death sentence.

Using these departments, the ministry-level intelligence center put together a blacklist of students expelled for their political activism. The list was circulated to universities around the country, which effectively ended any chance for those named to continue their studies. The control also reached those who were at the beginning of a university career. To an entrance process made already highly restrictive by the military, an "ideological test" was added in order to ensure that only right-thinking aspirants were admitted.[13]

At the Universidad Nacional de Tucumán (UNT), not only was a security unit installed but a clandestine detention center was set up within the institution itself in the physical education school. There more than 250 students were held by the army, "listening to the nearby screams and shouts of the victims, and at night, the report of the firing squads."[14]

The repressive tasks carried out under the Orwellian heading of "normalization" were also uncommonly brutal at the Universidad Nacional del Sur (UNS), in the Patagonian city of Bahía Blanca. Remus Tetu, the university's rector and a self-professed Fascist of Romanian origin, had since the end of 1974 carried out a persecution of leftist and nonnationalist right-wing groups. A member of the paramilitary groups that operated in Bahía Blanca later testified that Tetu had facilitated the "infiltration" of those groups into the university. The neo-Nazi CNU had a "safe house" on the grounds of the university that was used to torture and assassinate its victims and a camp—on university property—located some 24 miles away used as a detention and torture center.

Witch-hunt in Bahía Blanca

Operating on the Patagonian terrain of his hero, Lt. Col. Héctor B. Varela, Vilas saw subversion where the naked eye suggested it did not exist. The UNS, he said, was "a factory of subversive elements, where public figures, former ministers and old legislators had absolute impunity in carrying out their task of ideological attraction." Saying the most important tool in the antisubversive campaign was a "realistic" intelligence unit, Vilas recalled that he "proceeded to form two special teams to operate at nighttime."[15]

At the end of June 1976, under Vilas's direction, the Federal Police began a vast investigative operation under the direction of Commissar Carlos Baldovinos and his assistant Félix Alejandro Alais, the latter intimately linked to the Triple A and the brother-in-law of Gen. Carlos Guillermo Suárez Mason. (Baldovinos was killed shortly thereafter by the Montoneros, after being betrayed by his own niece.) The investigation, Vilas said, was "designed to accumulate proof of Marxist ideological penetration in the UNS and in the secondary schools." As their work progressed, Vilas and Alais, a graduate of U.S. police training schools, counted on the collaboration of former rector Tetu and active local CNU groups and were egged on from the pages of the newsmagazine *Gente* and the local Bahía newspaper *La Nueva Provincia*.

A month later, on August 5, Vilas held a dramatic press conference in which he claimed the security forces had uncovered an "international conspiracy" of "ideological and sociocultural infiltration" at the university. In what the regime called the biggest breakthrough in the antisubversive fight in academia, seventeen professors were arrested, accused of being Marxists, and thirty others were listed as wanted.

Among those charged was Gustavo Malek, former education minister during the military regime of Gen. Alejandro Lanusse. Malek had recently been installed as regional director of the United Nations Educational, Scientific and Cultural Organization (UNESCO). When, in response to the unfolding developments in Patagonia, Malek's former boss, Lanusse, sent out an open letter asking for moderation and respect for human rights, the former president was himself sanctioned with five days' arrest. Yet Lanusse's action and growing international pressure were beginning to have their effect. Returning later from his post in nearby Uruguay, the former education minister presented himself before Vilas's superior, V Army Corps commander Gen. René Azpitarte, who backtracked on Vilas's charges.

(One of those detained, economics professor Alberto Barbeito, later defended himself with letters from famous economists attesting to the fact the curriculum he taught could not be considered "subversive." Among those he received was a letter from Nobel economics prizewinner Milton Friedman, whose free market "Chicago school" ideas were much in vogue throughout the military dictatorships of southern Latin America. "I have studied the course material of the Argentine economists at Bahía Blanca," Friedman wrote, "and it does not contain any message nor certainly could it be called 'subversive.'")[16]

In a matter of months scores of people were abducted and detained, among them former Radical party legislators Hipólito Solari Yrigoyen and Mario Amaya. Solari Yrigoyen was brutally mistreated for months before being freed largely as the result of pressure from the Carter administration, the Venezuelan government, and Amnesty International. Amaya died in detention from the effects of torture. His body was retired from the Devoto penitentiary by Radical reform leader Raúl Alfonsín, who headed the party faction to which the young deputy belonged. Many others "disappeared." A few, such as Elizabeth Fress, who was held by the V Army Corps, would later be used as *relleno* (stuffing)—a term the military used for already-dead detainees who were taken to a site in order to fake an armed confrontation with "subversive delinquents."

Personalities "Hostile to Society"

The universities were not the only educational institutions targeted by the regime. Between May 1976 and the early part of 1977 the military undertook a vast operation in the country's high schools. Scores of adolescents between the ages of thirteen and eighteen were systematically hunted down by military authorities.

Most of the victims were merely romantic and rebellious. Available evidence points to only a few who were weapons-carrying guerrillas; in most cases their participation was limited to pamphleteering and spraypainting signs on walls. Many of the victims belonged to student centers at their respective schools, and some—as members of the radicalized Unión de Estudiantes Secundarios (UES) (High School Students Union), linked to the Montoneros—had participated in a few "takeovers" of the schools during the years of agitation 1973–1974.

The military systematically misrepresented its actions against the secondary school students. "We pick up kids who were in subversive schools in order to change their minds," a colonel standing at the doorway of the Campo de Mayo army base explained to the parents of adolescent Juan Alejandro Fernández, who "disappeared" in 1977. "Probably your daughter is in a recuperation center," a military chaplain told the mother of María Claudia Falcone, a sixteen-year-old kidnapped in 1976. Neither Fernández nor Falcone ever returned.[17]

The night of July 7, 1976, eighteen-year-old Alejandro Goldar Parodi left the house of his fifteen-year-old girlfriend, Magdalena Gallardo. Parodi had planned to go to the movies with friends Carlos Marín, Hugo Toso, and Pablo Dubcovsky. In the early hours of the next day armed men kidnapped Magdalena Gallardo from her parents' home. At the same time the four other youths "disappeared." All had been students at the Colegio Nacional de Buenos Aires, run by the Universidad (Nacional) de Buenos Aires and one of the oldest and most traditional secondary schools in the country. High honors student Franca Jarach had been kidnapped shortly before. Seven other schoolmates suffered the same fate. Only Cecilia Ayerdi and Alejandra Tadei, both of whom were only fifteen, survived to tell of the horrors of the Vesubio and Quinta Seré clandestine camps. Of Magdalena Gallardo there was only one trace: a heart scratched on the wall of a cell in the SS Federal Police headquarters.

A similar fate awaited students at the Escuela Superior de Comercio Carlos Pellegrini, also run by the Universidad (Nacional) de Buenos Aires. There at least six students were kidnapped and killed, and nearly a dozen others were abducted and tortured.

"Subversive action [at the high school level]," said an army document distributed by the Education Ministry in 1977, "is carried out by trying to form in the students a personality that is hostile to society, to the authorities and all those fundamental institutions and principles that support them: spiritual, religious and political values; the armed forces; the organization of economic life, of the family, etc. This aggression aims to achieve a collective psychological transference that gradually changes the basic concepts of our society into others, completely different." In short, change was "subversive."[18]

Night of the Pencils

The youths could not imagine the depths of horror that the regime had reserved for them. In September 1975 high school students in Buenos Aires province began what eventually was a successful protest for a lower student bus fare. It was, in many cases, a demand imposed by economic necessity. The teenagers demanded a half-fare rate, which was already in existence for younger children.[19]

Shortly after the coup the regime determined to eliminate the half fare. The students, unconscious of the risk, decided to organize small protests in a few cities. Some—not all—of the organizers were Montonero sympathizers and saw the protest as a way of helping politicize their peers. The military's response was immediate. The campaign was labeled "subversion in the schools," and "punitive" actions were ordered.

On September 16, 1976, in the Buenos Aires provincial capital of La Plata, police chief Col. Ramón Camps—a man the Alfonsín government later charged was responsible for the "direct participation in the deaths of thousands of people"—ordered the deaths of those who participated in the protest. Throughout the province more than twenty adolescents were kidnapped. One of the victims, Francisco López Muntaner, was only fourteen years old. All were taken to clandestine detention centers, tortured, and put before mock firing squads. Pablo Díaz was sixteen when he was kidnapped.

"They never told us the reasons for our abduction," Díaz remembered later.

They only asked us questions like: "And, you, what do you do? What grade are you? What's the matter with you? What were you involved in? Who are you responsible to?"

I told them that I was in the students' center, that it was legal, and that I couldn't imagine [I was there] for that. Once they brought someone in who recognized me, but I couldn't see who it was because I was blindfolded. "No, it's not him," he said, "he was in the students' center, he participated in the school fare campaign." Then they took me to a room, stripped me, put me on a sort of cot, tied me down and said: "We're going to give you a session so you never forget" and began to burn my lips.

One time they told me that they were going to take me to the "truth machine." I told them "yes," to please do so, because I thought they were talking about one of those machines you see in the movies that has a register that moves when you tell a lie. But I didn't know it was, in fact, their name for electric torture. ...

They gave it to me in the mouth, on my gums and on the genitals. They even pulled out a toenail with a tweezers. Often we were hit with billyclubs, fists and kicked. ... They asked all of us about the school fare, why we participated, what motivated us to ask for the reduction, who was guiding us. ... We had to sleep on the floor. Us guys were in our underwear, because they had taken our clothes from us. Almost all of us ended up in rags, almost nude. The girls were also like that, and some didn't have bras. ...

At night, amid the screams of those who were being tortured, the girls cried. Some, like Claudia [Falcone], called for her mother.[20]

Claudio de Acha was crazy about rock music and dreamed about becoming a film director. Since she was a little girl, María Claudia Ciochini wanted to be a scientist who studies caves and caverns. ("Kill me, but don't touch me any more," the girl screamed desolately at her captors, while pounding on the door of her cell.) María Claudia Falcone was the outstanding student of her school of fine arts and a UES delegate. Her father, the former mayor of La Plata, had been sentenced to death, then pardoned, in the aftermath of Valle's revolt in 1955. Claudia's talent for painting also came from her father, who had received a national painting award years earlier. Although her older brother was a member of the Montoneros, Claudia belonged to Peronismo de Base. A detention order issued by the 601 army intelligence battalion said she was of "minimum dangerousness."[21]

Despite the desperate conditions of their captivity, the youths found ways to keep each other going and, in a sense, maintain their own illusions. "When they took us to wash, they took everyone together, men and women, blindfolded and tied up," recalled Pablo Díaz. "When we'd pass each other, we'd give the other our hand in order to keep up morale. 'We'll get out,' we told ourselves. Sometimes, at night, we'd sing with Claudia or with de Acha, trying to keep our spirits up, making jokes and seeing who sang the best."

"Through the cell wall, Claudia and I had begun a sentimental relationship," Díaz later testified.

One day I asked the guard to let me see her for just a minute, as Claudia was crying a lot. "I'll give you 15 minutes," he said. When we saw each other we couldn't speak. We were in tatters. I was in my underwear, dirty, with my eyes infected. Claudia, very skinny, scared, with her hair in a tangled mess.

When I got close to her she told me, weeping: "Don't touch me—they raped me—don't touch me. When I was being tortured they turned me around and raped me from behind, then in front."

She couldn't stop crying. I grabbed her hands and tried to calm her. "Don't worry," I told her, "we'll get out of here. We'll be able to make plans together." When on December 28 they told me I was going to get out, that they were transferring me to a legal jail I told the other kids. There was a great silence. I thought we were all getting out together. I felt badly that Claudia couldn't come with me, but I thought they were going to free all of us. We hadn't done anything.

When they came for me that night, Claudia asked me something I'll never forget: "Every New Year's Eve, raise a cup for me and for the kids. Because I'm already dead." I told her no, that I couldn't believe that. I left shouting to them that we'd all get out.[22]

When their ordeal finally ended, of the fifteen kids seized in La Plata only three survived: Emilse Moller, Patricia Miranda, and Pablo Díaz. Two of the three had important family ties with the authorities. Emilse Moller was the daughter of a police commissioner, who rescued her and her friend, Patricia Miranda, from the Pozo de Quilmes detention center. Díaz was the son of a professor at La Plata's Universidad Católica and counted among his family's friends Archbishop Plaza, one of the clergy most involved in the illegal repression. The others were killed.[23]

The massacre, known as the Night of the Pencils, not only affected the city of La Plata. In many other places high school students connected with the bus fare campaign suffered the same fate. In the Buenos Aires provincial village of Los Cardales, for example, five high school students were "disappeared" for their participation in the fare protest.

The campaign did not end with the high schools. The military also found that subversion had reached the elementary level. "Subversive actions are undertaken at this level by ideologically trained teachers who influence the minds of small students, promoting the development of rebellious ideas or behavior, apt for the action to be developed later on," said one military document. "At this level the communication is direct, through informal chats and by readings and commentaries of tendentious stories."[24]

In 1978 officials in Córdoba prohibited the teaching of modern math, arguing that it might be a subtle form of subversive indoctrination. Hundreds of children's books, too, found their way onto the objectionable list. The military banned the distribution and use in the schools of Antoine de Saint-Exupéry's *The Little Prince*, a universally acclaimed short story, and *God Is Faithful,* a book of religious instruction for children ages ten to twelve written by Sister Beatriz Casiello (and found unobjectionable even by the conservative Argentine Episcopal Conference).[25]

The terror that seized the classrooms is hard to exaggerate. Even recommending a book could be dangerous. A secret directive signed by army chief of staff, and later president, Gen. Roberto Viola, demanded that "any time subversive reading is detected" in education institutions, a full report was to be sent to the army high command, including the name of the teacher who suggested it. The Centro de Estudios Legales y Sociales (CELS; Center for Legal and Social Studies), Argentina's most respected human rights office, estimated that the number of books published in 1979 was 45 percent less than that published at the time of the coup three years earlier.[26]

Faced with the indiscriminate repression, thousands of Argentine intellectuals sought work abroad, exacerbating the country's chronic brain drain. Argentina had achieved something of a Golden Age in science during the periods of democratic rule in the late 1950s and mid-1960s. During that time Argentine universities achieved a high level of development in research in disciplines such as physics, biology, and sociology. At the same time the modern arts flourished with a particular intensity. However, the desire to change and reform society, which in those years began to combine pure research and high technology with political action, was abruptly interrupted, never to recover. Shortly after the 1966 coup Onganía's regime sent police into the universities in a bloody raid known as the Night of the Long Sticks. The action caused 300 members of the science faculty at the Universidad (Nacional) de Buenos Aires to resign in protest and began a long process of deterioration of academic standards and repression. Eight years later, rightist Peronists purged the universities. More than 400 other academics were fired.

The unceasing pattern of coups and democratic interregnum had caused many first-rate scientists—such as César Milstein, a Nobel laureate for his research in medicine—to flee. When Milstein received the prize in 1984, he already had been living in England for two decades.

Within months of the 1976 coup nearly 100 research scientists supported by the Consejo Nacional de Investigaciones Científicas y Técnicas (CONICET; National Council on Scientific and Technological Investigations) were fired, as well as more than 600 scientists from the National Research Institute for Agriculture and Cattle Breeding, the National Institute for Industrial Technology, the National Physics and Technology Institute at San Miguel, and the National Energy Committee. Between October 1976 and September 1978 fourteen physicists, engineers, and other employees of Argentina's continent-leading atomic energy commission were "disappeared" by the security forces.[27]

When César Milstein returned to Argentina for a few days in 1976, he could not bear the strain and terror in which the country was living. "I went with my family to spend fifteen days, but after four days I couldn't stay any longer, not even as a tourist. I asked myself how Argentines would be able to stand such a climate."[28]

15

The Secret Camps

They can say what they want, I was held in Germany's concentration camps, I was persecuted during the [military regime], and my daughter was kidnappped here. The only difference was that there they cremated people and here they threw them in the river.
—*José Moscovits, President, Association of Survivors from Nazism*[1]

La Perla, did it exist? Sure, it was a place to keep detainees, not a clandestine jail. ... It was more that the subversives who were there were being protected from their peers.
—*Gen. Luciano B. Menéndez*

Modeling their tactics on Hitler's night-and-fog decrees used in occupied Europe, the Argentine military practiced a forced disappearance of people that was systematic, massive, and clandestine. It required building 340 secret centers in which victims were housed and preparing mass graves for their burial. It included organizing and training of scores of "task forces" to work the streets and hundreds of people to staff the centers.[2]

During 1975 the armed forces began choosing the location of the death camps. The captive's stay was seen as a short one, as he or she was to be quickly killed. The secret camps were given the acronym LRD, for Lugares de Reunión de Detenidos (Places for the Meeting of Detainees.) By November 1975 the LRD El Vesubio had already begun to function.

El Vesubio is the Spanish name for the volcano near Naples whose eruption during the Roman empire destroyed the town of Pompeii. The name was given to the Argentine camp by the military, who joked about the black column of smoke that spiraled from Vesubio into the sky and could be seen from a distance. The effusion was caused by the constant incineration of cadavers mixed with old tires.[3]

The existence of the LRDs was repeatedly denied by the military hierarchy. The claim was part of an "anti-Argentine campaign" carried out from abroad, it said. Even in 1983, with the military in disarray, Videla told a civilian court: "During my term as president of the nation I never knew of procedures that took place outside legal norms, nor the detention of people in clandestine places. ... Concerning the existence of clandestine detention centers ... there was a sort of generalized rumor about these spread mostly from outside the country."[4]

Techniques for disposing of prisoners' bodies were meant also to do away with evidence of the crimes. Methods depended on the place and logistical capacity of each service. Sometimes mass burial as *n.ns.*, or "no-names," in common graves was used. Bodies were also burned with old tires, erasing all traces and helping cover up the stench. Prisoners who were still alive were thrown from airplanes or helicopters into the ocean. "I finally found a good way to make people disappear," Col. Roberto Roualdés, one of General Suárez Mason's closest aides, told a longtime colleague in the ornate Circulo de Armas in downtown Buenos Aires. "Cover their bodies with tires and douse them with gas oil, then light it."[5]

"The day of the 'transfer,' everything was very tense. The detainees were beginning to be called by number," recalled several former prisoners at the Navy Mechanics School, a well-tended complex of white buildings sandwiched along the Río de la Plata between two of Buenos Aires' wealthiest neighborhood. "They were taken to a nursing station in the basement, where a medical assistant was waiting to give them an injection that put them to sleep, but didn't kill them. Still alive, they were carried out and put into a truck, taken asleep to the municipal airport and loaded onto an airplane headed south, to the open sea, where they were thrown out alive."[6]

Four hundred and eighty miles west of the Navy Mechanics School, Piero DiMonte, a prisoner at La Perla camp outside Córdoba, remembered the uncertainty he and his fellow detainees felt, faced with the daily "transfers."

> None of those who were "transferred" ever returned. We prisoners were tormented by that uncertain and mysterious future. As much as we could, each one of us would ask the guards or "older" prisoners: What will happen to us? What is our future? The responses were many and contradictory. Some held we would be freed, others that we would be sent to unknown jails in the south, near the Andes. ... Some officials told us about rehabilitation or recovery centers that many detainees evaluated as "low-level subversives," or "small fry," were to be sent, to later "rejoin society."[7]

One group of officials was brutally frank with DiMonte and other prisoners, telling them the "transfers" were moved a few miles away. There awaited another group of officers:

> The prisoners were lined up or made to kneel in front of graves already dug, their mouths and eyes covered with gags, their hands tied behind their shoulders. There they were executed. The cadavers, once in the graves, were splashed with gas and pitch and burned. All the officials present participated, from junior-grade lieutenants to Gen. Luciano B. Menéndez, and Gens. [Arturo G.] Centeno, [Jorge A.] Maradona, [Juan B.] Sassiaín, [José A.] Vaquero. Capt. [Ernesto] Barreiro said "the only officials with clean hands will be those who graduate next year [1978] from the military college."[8]

Occasionally, there were unexpected witnesses to the work of the firing squads near La Perla. When democracy returned to Argentina, Juan Solanille, a plain-spoken farmer, told a court:

It was around March 24, 1976, when I was working as a day laborer at a site that abutted La Perla, that strange things began to happen at the Little Bull Hill. In May, while making the rounds of the fields I discovered a well about 13 feet by 13, and about seven deep. Shortly thereafter, I think it was a Sunday, I saw a number of cars approach the place, including two white Ford Falcons that were sandwiched in between two army trucks, one which was painted with a white cross on its canvas covering. I had to round up my animals, and while doing so I met up with a neighbor who worked the adjoining field. ... We went up a hill from where we could see. ... When we got to the top the shooting started. We could see a man with a hood over his face running, his hands tied behind his back, falling and struggling back up until he fell one last time. Farther on the shooting continued and other people, also tied up, were falling. ... Some 50 people were killed.[9]

In the following months, Solanille discovered some 500 graves while riding horseback around the Little Bull Hill, on land belonging to the III Army Corps. The testimony before the same court by 1st Lt. Ernesto Urien would confirm part of Solanille's recollection.

I worked as the chief of Company B at the General Paz military academy. As it was known that the Inter-American Commission on Human Rights was coming [in September 1979], Lt. Gustavo Gelfi received an order outside his duties at the institute. ... Gelfi confided to me that the activity, which was secret, was to dig up the bodies in the area belonging to the Third Army Corps training camp, using road equipment that he himself had to operate. The dug-up bodies showed signs of having been buried without a coffin nor even a bag. They were spread about the area, some bearing their documents. Then they were put into barrels of lime to make them disappear without a trace.[10]

In Argentina the mass graves later revealed to a horrified world were proof of the disappearances. In the province of Buenos Aires alone there were more than 200 large, illegal—and secret—burial sites.[11]

A report issued in late 1983 by the army high command recognized the existence of "detention centers throughout the country," although in a fit of bureaucratic bad memory said it could not determine where they had been. Twenty days before the return of democracy a secret radiogram had been sent from the interior ministry to military units under its control: "Classified documentation concerning the antisubversive struggle must be returned to each respective military command, which will immediately proceed to incinerate it."

The destruction of documentation was meant to eliminate evidence of crimes. The military high command told the Alfonsín government in 1984 they "could not locate" the camps. The Sábato commission found some 340 of them. The army chief of staff and the five army corps were found to possess documents that authorized the destruction of the buildings that housed the camps.[12]

Most prisoners never saw a judge. Thousands were secretly held for weeks, months, and even years. When the Inter-American Commission on Human Rights of the Organization of American States prepared to visit Argentina in September 1979, some prisoners at the ESMA were hidden in the Río de la Plata delta—a lush, semitropical area covered with thick vegetation—in order to eliminate signs of their existence. Others were killed. A few, forced to stay behind, were dressed in navy uniforms and obliged to pretend they were sailors. The military had promised the commission "its fullest cooperation."[13]

"Fish Food" and "Floaters"

One of the first recorded cases of cadavers "disappearing" mafia-style into the deep came shortly after the coup. A body, so disfigured that its identification was nearly impossible, surfaced on the Uruguayan side of the muddy, red-brown waters of the Río de la Plata. Uruguayan officials said that its features suggested it might be that of a Korean or Japanese, perhaps a sailor washed overboard in high seas in the South Atlantic.

The hypothesis did not hold up. The river continued to deposit its macabre cargo along Uruguay's Atlantic coast. Some bodies bore deep cuts, others were missing limbs, most lacked fingernails and toenails. The situation soon reached the intolerable. In the posh beach resort of Punta del Este—favored by upper-class Argentines—people began to complain that the "floaters" were ruining their vacations.

On May 14, 1976, eight cadavers appeared in Uruguayan waters. A communiqué from the Naval Prefecture noted the last of the bodies was that of an adolescent with dark brown hair and a heart-shaped tattoo on his right arm with the initials *F.A.* The boy's hands and feet were bound and his neck broken, and the body showed signs of torture. The boy, fourteen-year-old Floreal Avellaneda, had been raped and murdered by *empalamiento*, a medieval form of torment in which a thick pole was shoved into his rectum until he suffered grave lacerations and internal hemorrhaging. Avellaneda and his mother had been kidnapped a month earlier and held as hostages until his father, a labor activist, was captured.[14]

In 1985 former military President Lanusse testified about the kidnapping of his cousin, Argentine diplomat Elena Holmberg. He recalled when, in his presence, I Army Corps commander Gen. Guillermo Suárez Mason recriminated a local police official for the delay in identifying Holmberg's body, which had been found in the Río de la Plata delta. "Don't forget, general, that you people have thrown more than 8,000 bodies in the river," Lanusse remembered the policeman as replying. "How do you expect us to recognize each one?" Although the regime claimed at the time that Holmberg was killed by leftist subversives, it was later established she had been murdered by the task force that operated out of the Navy

Mechanics School. According to one top former police official, hundreds, possibly thousands, of bodies were dumped off navigation marker no. 14, just off the coast in front of the Jorge Newberry municipal airport.[15]

Former gendarme Omar Eduardo Torres, a guard, also witnessed the methods used by the regime. In Tucumán, he said, the firing squads did their grim work barely 1,500 feet from El Arsenal concentration camp. "They made the prisoners kneel on the ground next to an open grave and shot them in the head so that they'd fall inside, where they had put old tires and oil and where later they burned the cadavers," Torres remembered. "Gen. Antonio Bussi was always present in those executions." At another post Torres found that at the Morón air base outside Buenos Aires prisoners who arrived already drugged were "transferred" to air force planes, from which they were thrown into the ocean. According to Torres, those who carried out the task joked, "Now the fish will have something to eat."[16]

Bodies were even off limits to next of kin. Juan Chester, a doctor at the Posadas hospital outside Buenos Aires, was kidnapped on November 26, 1976, by an armed group. Six days later Chester's body was found floating in the Rio de la Plata estuary. A year later the authorities gave Chester's wife a death certificate. "They never turned over the body, just a piece of paper," she recalled. Elena Arce Sahores was abducted by the army and held in the city of La Plata. When her father sought out a colonel to ask that his daughter's life be spared, the officer cut him off sharply: "Don't look for her any more." When the father then entreated the military man to let him bury her, the colonel responded angrily: "Bodies don't get handed over."[17]

The Camps

The clandestine detention centers were indispensable to the policy of disappearances. In military personnel lists the torturers staffing the camps were often distinguished by an *AEI,* for *aptitud especial para inteligencia* (special intelligence aptitude), marked next to their names. The organization of the camps, their layout, and daily routine showed that their purpose went beyond the physical elimination of their captives. They sought to destroy the prisoner's identity, to alter his concept of time and space. Detainees were subjected to "experiments" of torture, resistance to pain, and psychological conditioning beyond the limits of imagination itself.

"I had a prisoner who was 'mine,'" boasted Francisco Andrés Valdéz, a police death squad member who later gave extensive testimony to the Sábato Commission. "I had him tied with a dog's chain and used to take him into the patio and walk him around on all fours, making him bark. One day he didn't want to, so I shot him in the head. He was a shithead Jew." (In 1985 Valdéz murdered his wife and was reportedly killed in a shoot-out with Federal Police a few weeks later.)[18]

Some of the camps were installed in military bases especially equipped to handle them. However, it was the nonmilitary sites that best captured the impunity with which the military regime operated. Nothing was sacred. There were camps that functioned in old rural schools (La Escuelita de Famaillá), in hospitals (Hospital Posadas), old tramway warehouses (Olimpo), automobile repair shops (Orletti), state offices (Hidráulica de Córdoba, Club Atlético, Escuela de Educación Física de la Universidad de Tucumán), old provincial radio stations (La Cacha), motels under construction (El Motel de Tucumán), in kidnapped people's own homes (El Embudo de San Roque). Guards and torturers plied their sad trade on sugar plantations (Ingenio Nueva Baviera), in summer residences outside Buenos Aires (Vesubio), in mansions donated to the state (Quinta Seré), and even in historic places such as the ancient farm once inhabited by Gen. José San Martín, Argentina's founding father and the creator of its army (Ex Ingenio Lules de Tucumán).[19]

Five large concentration camps, with a total of 14,500 prisoners, served as cornerstones for the military's illegal framework: Vesubio and Campo de Mayo outside Buenos Aires, the ESMA and Club Atlético in the federal capital, and La Perla in Córdoba.[20]

Vesubio was installed in La Tablada, near Ezeiza International Airport. Some 2,000 prisoners were lodged there, including Héctor Oesterheld, a Montonero sympathizer and the author of the famous *Eternauta* comic strip series, and writer Haroldo Conti. The camp functioned until early 1979, when it was destroyed on the eve of the arrival of the Inter-American Commission on Human Rights of the Organization of American States.

The Vesubio buildings and grounds had been used for the illegal repression since at least November 1975, five months before the coup. At first Vesubio served an operational base for paramilitary groups linked to the intelligence services and the Triple A. Then it was known as La Ponderosa, a state-owned summer home leased to the Federal Penitentiary Service. From May 1976 on, the camp was under the control of the I Army Corps headed by Gen. Carlos Suárez Mason.[21]

One of the camp's peculiarities was the existence of reserved residences in which Vesubio's masters lived. Maj. Pedro Durán Sáenz, alias Delta, lived at Vesubio during the week, forcing women prisoners to share his bed, then ordering their elimination. Married and the father of five, Durán Sáenz returned home every weekend.[22]

Inside Vesubio the walls were painted with swastikas, and the worst brutality was reserved for Jewish prisoners. Suárez Mason was a frequent visitor to Vesubio. During his visits prisoners were forced to participate in meetings and even dinners with their military captors, especially those detainees who were known for their political activity or professional achievement. Durán Sáenz's successor, Lt. Col. Crespi, alias Moreno or Teco, presided over the liquidation of hundreds of prisoners between mid-1977 and late 1978.[23]

The Campo de Mayo detention center functioned in the army base of the same name, the country's most important military unit. In March 1976 Campo de Mayo was run by Gen. Omar Riveros, who was later succeeded by Generals Reynaldo Bignone and Cristino Nicolaides. More than 3,500 prisoners were processed through the center; few survived. Locked in sheds, they were chained, hooded, prohibited from talking or moving while sitting without support or the possibility of lying down for fourteen hours a day. Campo de Mayo was also used as a location for aircraft to land and transport detainees to other locations, such as the border with Paraguay, where they frequently were killed.[24]

In Campo de Mayo both children and the elderly were forced to endure all types of punishment. One practice was the so-called *picana automática,* a cattle prod–like device that discharged electricity every three or four seconds, the charge lasting the same amount of time. The victim was tied with a wide leather belt at the base of his or her vertebrae. The prisoner remained alone during the two- to three-hour sessions, without being asked questions or maintaining any other kind of contact. Later the interrogators asked for a "confession." If none was forthcoming, the process began anew.[25]

The camp inside the Navy Mechanics School began functioning during the run-up to the 1976 coup. Operations stopped completely only days before Alfonsín was inaugurated in late 1983. The ESMA camp owed its existence to efforts by Adm. Emilio Massera to increase the navy's quota of power during the doling out of public offices to military men after the coup. As a result of a number of military crises, since 1962 the navy had been losing its role as the army's main partner in making national decisions. Massera saw the chance to regain the political initiative by putting the navy's stamp on the "antisubversive struggle."[26]

More than 5,000 people were held in the ESMA. The camp functioned in the officers' casino, a three-story building with a basement and huge attic. The officers slept on the first two floors; in the basement the torturers plied their trade; on the third floor and in the attic, the prisoners awaited their fate. During winter and summer, temperatures reached inhuman extremes. The victims suffered the limitless sadism of their captors, from hungry rats being placed inside their bodies to the mutilation of genitals with razor blades. One Montonero suspect was forced to watch as his twenty-day-old baby was tortured with electric cattle prods in an effort to make the father talk.[27]

The Club Atlético (Athletic Club) was also run in the federal capital, near the presidential palace. Its official name was the Central Antisubversiva (Antisubversive Center), but its initials *C.A.* gave rise to the name by which it was commonly known. The camp was part of the Argentine Federal Police Security Superintendency, the SS Federal, under the control of the I Army Corps. The old police supply depot was used between 1976 and December 1977, housing more than 1,500 prisoners.

Huddled in the basement of the ancient building, without ventilation or natural light, the prisoners were abandoned to the whim of two psychotic interrogators, Juan Del Cerro, alias Colores, and Julian the Turk. At night the screams of those tortured reverberated from the walls, mixing with a strident music their captors played to drown out cries for help. The bodies of a few hung from iron rings attached to the ceiling.

Those who survived the interrogations lived to confront other horrors, such as the permanent terror, silence, and impotence of the Tubes, tiny cells without ventilation or light. It was a netherworld in which prisoners tried to adapt without going insane. "They applied electric current to my entire body, especially my eyelids, vagina, breasts and eyes," remembered Ana María Careaga, who was sixteen and pregnant when she was abducted. "In those moments ... the only thing I wanted to do was to die."[28]

Headquartered in Córdoba, the mighty III Army Corps oversaw more than ten provinces and more than half the nation's territory. There, under the command of Gen. Luciano Benjamín Menéndez, functioned La Perla. Also known as "the University," more than 2,500 people were held at the camp.

Reflecting Menéndez's right-wing nationalism, La Perla was run by a group of officers—such as Maj. Gustavo Von Dietrich, alias the Lion, and Maj. Ernesto Barreiro—known for their avowedly Nazi ideas. Officers assigned to La Perla joined their superiors as members of a secret lodge, part of a nationwide military organization. The group not only sought to eliminate opponents but also conspired against the ruling military leadership, whom they accused of being tied to the economic interests of Martínez de Hoz and his plan for "colonial domination." Officers, particularly those who saw duty at La Perla, were forced to take part in a "blood pact," thus ensuring their silence.[29]

The Tortures

Torture methods used by the military were meant to produce pain, collapse, a breakdown of resistance, fear and humiliation, a strong sense of imminent death, weakness, and physical alteration. Its purpose was to reduce the detainee to the state of nearly animal existence. The prisoners faced endless acts of aggression running from blows by fists, sticks, or feet to the application of the "telephone"—repeated blows to both ears at the same time using open hands—meant to break the victim's ear drums. José Poblete, a young Chilean who lost his legs in a train accident as a youth and who was obliged to use a wheelchair, was forced to drag himself across the ground to the bathroom in El Olimpo while his torturers beat him. Karate was used to torture but also to kill. Campo de Mayo survivor Juan Carlos Scarpatti recalled seeing two new torturers "practice" on four detained railroad workers by doing karate kicks on the hooded prisoners, commenting on "the advantage of this blow or that, and whether it was mortal or not." Prisoners whose hands and feet were bound were also hung, while their captors beat them or subjected them to electric shock. The prisoner was often placed head first into tanks of stagnant water or human waste. Another form of psychological torture was simulated firing squads, sometimes done en masse, sometimes individually, subjecting the victim to stress levels that could produce serious psychic damage.[30]

After ERP chieftain Mario Roberto Santucho died resisting capture, his family became the object of military wrath. Manuela Santucho, his sister, and Carlos Santucho, his brother, were kidnapped and taken to the camp known as Automotores Orletti. "They filled a huge tank of water in the middle of the shed," remembered Enrique Rodríguez Larreta, an Uruguayan journalist who had been kidnapped while looking for his missing son.

> Carlos Santucho, who was completely delirious, kept rising, saying he didn't have anything to do with anything. ... Then they balanced themselves over him, chaining him. They had hung a harness with some rope above the tank and began to dunk him into the water. ... Santucho banged against the sides of the tank until he didn't move any more. At the same time they made his sister Manuela read the newspaper story about the death of her other brother.[31]

Another of the more common torments used was sexual torture. Rape and humiliation were a constant. Metallic objects were placed in the vagina or anus, to which electrical current was applied. This torture was used against both children and pregnant women.

Torture sometimes resulted in attacks of madness or delirium. Prisoners were constantly awakened during the night, adding to their anguish and depression, enduring the suffering with insufficient clothing or even nude. "In the Banfield investigations brigade we were in our underwear, I was in my shorts which ended up in rags," recalled one young captive. "The girls were in their underclothes, some without bras." During days, weeks, and even months, the detainees remained blindfolded or hooded, subject to constant threats and, in some camps, the unwilling listeners to music put on full blast to cover up the screams of people being tortured.

> They put a blindfold with cotton on with a piece of wide, rubbery adhesive tape. ... After some time I was able to get the blindfold loose a little. My eyes were watery because the cotton was rotting. Those days were very hot, and the tape started to melt. My eyes filled with sores. Finally, I couldn't see anything. Toward the end I thought I had gone blind. After December 28 they came for me. ... I told the doctor I had a rotten smell in my eyes, and he told me, "Just bear it, just bear it." They took me to a room. ... The doctor told me to sit, and then pulled the cotton, which was all stuck, out of my eyes. It was one big running sore. I screamed my lungs out, but I couldn't open my eyes. ... Then I heard the lieutenant colonel say, "This kid has got to be made well—look how he is. We can't take his photo this way."[32]

The victim was Pablo Díaz, the high school student detained in September 1976.

16

A Society of Fear

One of the improvements of the methods used in Vietnam and refined in Santo Domingo consists of political crimes—the assassination of real or supposed Communists—that are not blamed on the government. Rather they are committed by select military or police groups, while the president protests publicly about the crimes, at the same time letting it be known in some way that he cannot pursue their authors. In this way terror spreads because the people feel defenseless and at the same time the government is not shown to be guilty.

—Former Dominican president, Juan Bosch, 1968[1]

Fear was an essential weapon in the military's plan to seize, purge, and remold Argentina. After the coup arrogant and aggressive soldiers armed to the teeth patrolled quiet neighborhoods for no apparent reason, checking documents and making random arrests. For those who lived through it, the climate had the same nerve-racking quality of a civil war. Every day the newspapers, radio, and television brought fresh news from the "front": terse military communiqués offering hints of Homeric clashes between the security forces and guerrilla groups. Yet apart from the military's intrusion into daily life, the civilian "battlefield" seemed deathly tranquil, normally interrupted only by the "clashes" between the legal forces and the guerrilla enemy that invariably occurred along deserted roadsides in the hours of the evening.

Fear was present during the Peronist regime, too, especially as the brutal slayings conducted by the guerrillas and what appeared to be rogue right-wing death squads reached their apogee in 1975. By the time of the March 1976 coup many Argentines felt they had reached the limit to their feelings of personal insecurity. Bombings, kidnappings, and death were a daily presence, but one hard to make sense out of for the politically uninitiated, which was most people. The use of bodyguards and security agencies ballooned; paradoxically the arrogance and impunity with which these men acted generated an even greater market for their services. It was not uncommon to see unmarked Ford Falcons full of beefy security men—arms dangling out the windows, pistols in hand—cruising down Libertador Avenue, one of Buenos Aires' main thoroughfares.[2]

But those who thought they had already experienced the worst were mistaken. Flawed and chaotic as the Peronist government was, constitutional rule still allowed people full access to the courts and ample opportunity to seek redress in the press. Under the military the media was muzzled and the courts became mere window dressing—torture and death without trial reached unheard-of proportions. The very fact that no military regime had previously engaged in such a bloodletting caused those who heard rumors of concentration camps and mass executions to discount them. The reports were even harder to accept given the regime's careful identification with the Catholic hierarchy, a symbiosis nurtured by some of the cloth's leading sons.

The military seemed to leave no propaganda outlet untouched. Even advertisements for the government's tax collection office ran ads that showed a tank pursuing an evader. "The number of disappearances continues to increase," wrote Patt Derian after an official visit in 1977 to Argentina.

> The government disclaims all knowledge of the whereabouts of these people. It looks as though they're going after the thinkers, professors, writers, politically inclined people who dare, no matter how modestly, to dissent or might dissent or are thought to disagree. ... More and more parents begin to fear for the safety of their adolescent children, as increasing numbers of ordinary citizens are rounded up, detained for 24 to 48 hours and abused while in detention.[3]

The Silence of the Media

Many Argentines, weary from fear, maintained their silence and helplessly witnessed the military's coercion. Others, out of venality, economic speculation, or mere sympathy with the "national reorganization process," became transformed into active collaborators.

Journalism is the one profession where, faced with mass murder, the apology—"I didn't know"—is either a demonstration of professional ineptitude or cowardice. Yet an endless number of media members contributed to the disinformation campaign launched by the armed forces. The press, like the country's political, union, and religious leadership, knew what was going on; the failure to do its job helped ensure that the rest of the population did not.

The permanently shifting political sands in Argentina had helped to enshrine opportunism as the most common characteristic of newspaper owners. Before the coup a number of large Buenos Aires dailies, including Jacobo Timerman's *La Opinión,* were on the ground floor of the military's conspiring. One high-ranking navy officer later admitted that fully a week before the coup he had approved the page proofs for a supplement being prepared by one mass-circulation newspaper on why Isabel Perón had been overthrown.[4]

Even *La Opinión* argued that, because Argentina was at war, the press was justified in becoming a faithful propaganda instrument of the state. But even so, warning notes sent by the presidential press secretariat for having published "inconvenient" information and telephone calls to "counsel" about how to play a story or to warn about an article considered offensive replaced the military's earlier solicitousness toward the press. From April 22, 1976, all the media received "verbal instructions" from the press secretariat, "prohibiting whatever reference, information or comment about subversive episodes, the finding of bodies, kidnappings, disappearances, the death of seditious elements and the assassinations of military men, police or security agents, unless such acts are confirmed in official communiqués."[5]

From the day it took power the military junta's press policy was clear: up to ten years imprisonment for anyone who used the press to "publish, divulge or propagate news, communiqués or images with the purpose of perturbing, damaging or impairing the reputation of the activities of the armed forces, security forces or the police." The message could be even more to the point: Héctor García, publisher of the tabloid *Crónica,* was kidnapped and held with a hood over his head for forty-eight hours by military officers carrying out a "preventative warning." It was García's second abduction in less than three years.[6]

In the following months the Federación de Trabajadores de Prensa (Press Workers Federation) was taken over by the military; foreign correspondents were expelled; and scores of journalists were imprisoned, "disappeared," or killed. Official organs worked overtime to give Argentines the impression that disinterested military gentlemen were involved in a life-and-death struggle with a hidden but powerful enemy bent on the destruction of the country's way of life. The government news agency Saporiti, for example, one of two state wire services, was run by the state intelligence service. Telam, the official government news agency, brimmed with intelligence operatives doubling as journalists.[7]

With the exception of the *Buenos Aires Herald* and occasionally *La Opinión,* the privately held press acted little better. Máximo Gainza, the publisher of the right-wing newspaper *La Prensa,* admitted years later that members of his staff had received pamphlets printed in the SIDE headquarters that were "signed by Montoneros."[8]

Less than a month after the coup an important newspaper in Córdoba let its personnel know that on orders of the III Army Corps it was no longer permissible to publish stories about family members searching to find the whereabouts of people presumed detained. Publications linked to political parties or groups were closed. Others, like *Cuestionario* and *Crisis,* faced with continual threats and the disappearance of a few of their collaborators, opted for closing their doors. In May 1976 four well-known journalists were kidnapped and "disappeared" forever, and former Uruguayan education minister and journalist Zelmar Michelini was killed in Buenos Aires.

The media's performance was perhaps at its worst in the magazines in the giant Editorial Atlántida group run by Aníbal Vigil, which included *Gente,* the newsmagazine *Somos,* and the woman's magazine *Para Tí.* A former star reporter for

Gente later charged that the publishing house regularly received "information kits" in yellow envelopes, complete with photos, from the fourth-floor Department of Psychological Action of the 601 army intelligence batallion, which then were rewritten for style and published as news by the magazines. "The intelligence services were always sending us informants or packets of information," she said.[9]

Gustavo Cabezas had been kidnapped by Argentine security forces, his body later handed over to relatives by the authorities who alleged he died in a military confrontation. While he was "disappeared," his mother, Thelma Jara de Cabezas, was herself abducted after visiting her terminally ill husband in the hospital. Jara de Cabezas, who was secretary of the Comisión de Familiares de Desaparecidos y Detenidos por Razones Políticas (Commission of Relatives of People Disappeared for Political Reasons), was tortured in the ESMA. Forced to write letters that were later sent from Uruguay to Videla, French President Valery Giscard D'Estaing, and Italian head of state Sandro Pertini and to human rights groups, she denied she had been kidnapped, explaining she had fled the country to escape being murdered by the Montoneros. Recalled Jara de Cabezas:

> One night in May 1979, they took me to what appeared to be an unused office. There they introduced me to a young girl who said she was a reporter and who did an interview with me that was to be sent abroad where I was forced to say I was obliged to seek refuge with the armed forces in order to keep the Montoneros from killing me. I was also taken two times to Uruguay using a false passport with the name Magdalena Margarita Blanco. In Montevideo they forced me to make declarations to journalists from New York [working for Rev. Sun Myung Moon's *News of the World*] who were going to publish the article in the U.S. and Europe. What they made me say was meant to discredit human rights groups in Argentina and also Amnesty International. During the interviews there was an official of the Uruguayan security forces present.[10]

The complicity of Argentina's collaborationist press reached its apogee in the case of Jara de Cabezas. "In mid-August I was taken to a coffee shop where I was interviewed by a journalist from the magazine *Para Tí* and a photographer from that medium. The interview was followed from a nearby table, using a microphone, by intelligence official Luis D'Imperio, alias 'Abdala,' Julio Sarmiento and two guards." The text of the "disappeared person" interview was published by *Para Tí* later that month under the title: "The Mother of a Dead Subversive Speaks." In it Jara de Cabezas denied belonging to the Mothers of the Plaza de Mayo rights group and justified her son's death by saying he was a Montonero.

Another Vigil publication, *Somos,* ran two articles, one illustrated with pictures, claiming the military had constructed "rehabilitation camps for subversives." The stories said that priests, lawyers, psychologists, and medical doctors tended to the detainees in a familial atmosphere. The camps never existed.[11]

The Outside World Becomes Opaque

During 1978 and 1979, as the violence was slowly subsiding in Argentina, Guillermo O'Donnell, one of Argentina's most prestigious social scientists and his wife, psychologist Cecilia Galli, carried out a singular field study on fear and military rule. "It was," recalled O'Donnell, "a way to exorcize our own fear, by studying that of others. We were looking in a mirror, hoping we could find that we were not crazy."[12]

Some 120 people were asked to respond to a questionnaire. Given the times, the pair limited their questioning to people whom they could trust and who trusted them. ("Both sides needed to know they were not dealing with policemen.") A few were businessmen, a couple of others labor leaders; most were—like the O'Donnells—middle-class professional people. "Under the circumstances, we committed all possible methodological horrors, beginning with interviewing only those whom we didn't have too much fear in interviewing," O'Donnell jokingly said later. "We believe we achieved the most unrepresentative sample in the history of the social sciences."

O'Donnell and Galli found that during the worst of the repression Argentines tended to deny what was going on around them. Most said they preferred the "peace" established by the military to the chaos of the Peronist regime. Reports of massive rights violations were chalked up as unsubstantiated rumor, with respondents frequently attributing cases of repressive violence they knew about—even disappearances—to the work of a few "crazies" at the margin of government. Many seemed to identity with the aggressor, making elaborate excuses that blamed the victims for their own fate. Those who suffered losses in their own families, such as human rights leaders Emilio Mignone and Augusto Conte, both of whom had missing children, were subjected to a "double killing." Labeled as *resentidos* (people consumed by their own resentments), even their grief and anger were denied them from the outside world. As the terror worsened, "the outside world became opaque," as Argentines retreated into the family, privately attributing little authority to anyone outside its circle and viewing all others as foreign and potentially dangerous.

Yet at the same time, within the family structure, O'Donnell and Galli found that a miniregime of terror had taken root, as parents, terrified their children would become involved in "something," tried to control them, accentuating the authoritarian character of the Argentine family. A few well-publicized terrorist acts, such as the 1976 murder of Federal Police chief Gen. Cesáreo Cardozo, who was killed when an eighteen-year-old girlfriend of his daughter put a bomb under his bed, were almost always mentioned by those questioned as supporting their precaution. (The fact that the girl, who belonged to the Montoneros, had been recently released from detention through Cardozo's intercession, even though she had been accused of being a guerrilla, added a particularly sinister aspect to the case.) The other most frequently discussed terrorist act was the 1974 murder of army Capt. Humberto Viola and his infant daughter in an ambush by the ERP. Both incidents were heavily utilized by the military's "psychological action" departments to discredit the guerrillas and justify the slaughter the regime was carrying out.

Buenos Aires—"A Better City for the Best People"

In Buenos Aires "dirty war" tactics were easily transferred to attack a more visible enemy: the city's slum dwellers. As the regime completed its first year, a campaign was undertaken to eliminate the capital's slums, not by programs offering hope to the desperate, but rather by a systematic campaign of forced eradication. With martial efficiency trucks were sent in to a shantytown, usually at night or in early morning, the residents loaded up with whatever they could carry, to be finally dumped like trash on the other side of the city limits.

The military's treatment of the poor contrasted sharply with that by the deposed Peronist government. During the Peronist period the neighborhoods in which the slum dwellers concentrated enjoyed a certain municipal infrastructure. Water and electricity were provided, normally for free, by the city; permission to build schools, day-care centers, and grocery stores was granted. At the time of the coup, approximately 5 percent of the city's population lived in *villas miserias* (slums). Twenty years earlier Buenos Aires' marginal population accounted for only 1 percent of the total but in the interim had grown as Bolivians, Paraguayans, and families from Argentina's impoverished north made their way to the capital, looking for work in construction or in industry.[13]

Four years of military rule found the municipal authorities bragging that 76 percent of the city's slum dwellers had been "removed." Sniffed Guillermo Del Cioppo, head of the municipal housing commission: "Our only intention is that those who live in our city be culturally prepared for it. To live in Buenos Aires isn't for just everyone, but for him who deserves it. … We ought to have a better city for the best people."[14]

Success extracted a heavy social cost. Services to the poor were cut. Using retired security force personnel, local police, and even army troops armed with tear gas, machine guns, and dogs, the housing commission supervised the removal of entire families, who were trucked to barren land on the outskirts of greater Buenos Aires, often with only the belongings they could carry with them. Bulldozers demolished what had previously been their homes.[15]

PART THREE

PART THREE

17

The Junta Takes Charge (1976)

Gen. Videla is ... tall and lean ... with blue eyes and black hair ... a genuinely nice person, very polite, although inclined to be timid, has a spontaneous smile and handshake. Off-color stories ... are taboo with Gen. Videla. While militarily competent, Videla was not considered strong-willed. ... He was not necessarily a "yes" man, but tended to be more comfortable as the assistant to a stronger individual. This could be attributed to his religious background.
—*U.S. Defense Intelligence Agency, "Biographic Sketch," February 1979*

At the time of the coup the army counted on more than 80,000 troops and 100 French and American-made tanks and had units spread up and down the country. The army chiefs also had reserved absolute control of the "antisubversive fight" for their own service. Bitter turf battles among the three services had played midwife to the coup itself. Embarked on a huge rearmament program meant to put the navy on the same footing with the army, Massera demanded that his service be treated as a political equal. Never again, the navy men vowed, would they be relegated to the political backwaters, as had happened after the internecine strife between the Blues and the Colorados in the 1960s. The air force, too, jealously guarded its prerogatives, all the more so after Capellini's December 1975 uprising.[1]

Massera conditioned his approval of the army's coup plans to the parceling out to each of the three services equal responsibilities for governing. For the first time in Argentina's long history of coups, the army had to share power. A third of the parcel went to each service.

The regional army corps commanders also demanded their quota of power. Before the coup Videla had to promise the head of the III Army Corps, Gen. Luciano B. Menéndez, that the commanders would have more power than the provincial governors who were to be appointed. In effect, each military region—based on the "security zones" designated in 1975 for the purpose of the "war against subversion"—became a fiefdom. Provincial governments were to become mere administrative entities.[2]

The original division of territory predated the coup and was composed of four great zones, one for each army command. The federal capital, the province of La Pampa, and most of that of Buenos Aires stayed in the hands of the I Army Corps. The riverine provinces to the north were assigned to the II Army Corps; the windswept, barren reaches of Patagonia, to the south, were the domain of the V Army Corps. Menéndez claimed an immense swath of land running along the Andes that formed the III Corps, territory equaling about half of Argentina's land mass. Later a fifth zone was added and put under the command at the Institutos Militares. The new zone controlled the Campo de Mayo army base, the country's most important military installation, as well as an area around the federal capital.

The army not only tried to keep control of the conduct of the antisubversive operations. It also sought to hold on to the intelligence apparatus and its "social communication" system, commonly referred to as propaganda. The generals wanted to cede only small parcels to the other services. Concessions were merely meant "to satisfy their aspiration to intervene effectively in the antisubversive fight." The air force was given control of a tiny sliver of territory, made up of the suburban Buenos Aires districts of Morón, Merlo, and Moreno—where its principal bases were—and a zone around the metropolitan airport in the federal capital.[3]

Massera was not content to control a zone of influence in the port of Buenos Aires as well as dominion over Argentina's rivers and ocean territories, as the generals had originally planned. Pressured by the navy chief, the army had to also cede an important operational zone in the highly industrialized Río Paraná delta, as well as two of the twenty-seven military areas into which the federal capital had been divided. Eleven Federal Police precincts, more than a fifth of its jurisdictions in the Argentine capital, were also deeded to the ambitious admiral.

The doling out of precise responsibilities to each force did not alleviate interservice conflicts, it accentuated them. At first the army was resigned to accepting the system of 33.3 percent of the posts for each service. Rapidly repairing its position, it then sent the agreed-to framework tumbling into imbalance. The first step came with the designation of its commander as president and the arrogation for itself of the "primary responsibility in the war" against dissidents. The army was yoking the other forces to its operational control and thus violating their agreement. The army also retained more than 60 percent of the lesser public offices.[4]

Civilian appointments were also a battleground among the three forces. The Foreign Ministry had been given to the navy, and Massera deployed his greatest efforts at maintaining control over the bureaucratic plum. Yet Martínez de Hoz tried to place a few of his friends in important embassies. He proposed the president of the Rural Society as Argentine ambassador in Paris, a move vetoed by Videla's own people. After great jockeying Videla was able to place a few key ambassadors: in Brazil, in Venezuela, in the Vatican, and in the United States.[5]

For the United States: "No Immediate Problem"

"From the U.S. point of view, the Videla government presents no immediate problem," read a secret State Department Bureau of Intelligence and Research memorandum a week after the coup.

> Neither US embassy officials nor the US [government] … has been accused of engineering or supporting the coup. The three service chiefs who constitute the junta are pro-US, anti-communist officers who probably will identify Argentina internationally with the West and with less-developed country moderates on North-South issues. Pending investment disputes probably will be settled quickly in order to enhance the junta's chances for attracting foreign investment and loans.
>
> Human rights could be a problem areas as the military clamps down on terrorism. To date, however, the junta has followed a reasonable, prudent line in an obvious attempt to avoid being tagged with a "Made in Chile" label.[6]

Suffer the Little Children

Carla Rutila Artés was one of the littlest victims of the "dirty war." When the Argentine military took power, her mother, Argentine Graciela Rutila Artés, was working in Oruro, Bolivia, an urban hub resting along the spine of the Andes, in support of a miners' strike. Carla's father, Uruguayan-born Enrique Lucas López, was a member of the Bolivian Movimiento Izquierdista Revolucionario (Revolutionary Left Movement), a group dedicated to restoring to the presidency the left-wing populist general, Juan José Torres, overthrown in a bloody 1971 coup. Although Torres was himself no democrat, his eclectic radical reformism, based on "peoples' assemblies," had won a group of die-hard supporters in a poor, turbulent country known for its seemingly endless changes of government.

On April 2, 1976, military commandos raided Graciela Rutila's home in Oruro, wrenching the nine-month-old Carla from her crib. There Rutila was beaten mercilessly and forced to watch as the invaders held the infant, stripped naked, by the heels and whipped her. Sent on to La Paz, the lofty Andean capital, Graciela Rutila was put in the hands of the torture specialists of the Departamento de Orden Político (DOP; Department of Political Order). Five years earlier Rutila's mother, Matilde Artés Company, a leftist actress, had received similar attention from the DOP. It left her spinal cord nearly severed, her nose and jaw dislocated, and her mouth full of broken teeth.

In July an Argentine Federal Police delegation showed up for the woman. Before leaving, Rutila was subjected to electric torture, beatings with clubs and whips, and burning with cigarettes. She was also nearly drowned in a tub of soapy water. The month before Torres had been murdered in Buenos Aires; now the Argentine team wanted to know her husband's whereabouts. Lucas López was arrested in Cochabamba a few months later and tortured to death along with Torres's private secretary, Pedro Silvetti.[7]

Intelligence officials had placed tiny Carla in an orphanage in early April. In late August she was reunited with her mother and taken overland to Buenos Aires. Although Graciela was killed, the child was given to Eduardo Ruffo, the right-hand man of SIDE chief Otto Paladino. Like his boss, the darkly handsome Ruffo was an admirer of Hitler; he also had been a member of the Triple A and a follower of Aníbal Gordon, the former bank robber and notorious death squad chieftain. In October 1977 Carla was given a phony birth certificate and a new identity, that of Gina Amanda Ruffo, the daughter of Ruffo and his wife Amanda Cordero. Officially, Carla Rutila Artés did not exist for eight years.

That same month a small group of women seeking the children of their own missing children formed the Abuelas de Plaza de Mayo (Grandmothers of the Plaza de Mayo).

Licio Gelli: The Brotherhood of the Family

Despite his strong ties to the deposed Peronist regime, Italian Masonic lodge master Licio Gelli joined those who welcomed the March 24 coup. Gelli had made a special effort to court the military. In a letter to an Argentine diplomat and fellow Mason, he suggested that Isabel's fate was the result of not having followed his advice. On March 28, Gelli telephoned Gen. Carlos Suárez Mason, a lodge member and commander of the powerful I Army Corps. He was calling, he said, to convey his "sincere happiness [that] all had turned out according to plan."

A day later Gelli wrote to junta member Emilio Massera, the navy commander and another P-2 member. The coup, he said, "was foreseeable for some time. The former administration showed excessive fragility and had driven the country to extremes." A strong government, Gelli counseled, "steady in purpose, could put the nation again among the countries of prestige. That government will know how to snuff out the insurrection of Marxist-inspired movements."[8] Using his occult name, Daniel, for his signature, on May 12 López Rega wrote Gelli a letter from his refuge in Spain, asking for help. "I have served without thinking of the danger," he reminded the Italian lodge master. "A word of honor was given, the Brotherhood of the Family was talked about. I did my part without hesitation or reserve." The former social welfare minister also worried about the fate of Isabel. Since the coup, the deposed president had been under house arrest at an estate in the Andean resort of Bariloche. López Rega suggested that Gelli pay her a visit: "I think Suárez Mason could facilitate seeing the missus [señora]." A month later, the once-omnipotent Brujo penned another missive, this one more plantive in tone. "Lichio! I am very sick, tired, and filled with loathing. ... All will pay for their tremendous error."[9]

A Monopoly on Violence

In May 1976, two months after the military coup, army chief of staff Gen. Roberto Viola issued a secret order, DCJE 405/76, designed to restructure military jurisdictions and prepare the army for more intensive antiguerrilla exercises. "There has been a change in the context in which antisubversive operations can be carried out," the document noted. The coup and the approval of the National Counterinsurgency Strategy, "directed from the highest level of the State," gave the military its sought-after monopoly on violence.

The order meant the official dissolution of the "irregular groups." The military had alleged that among the reasons for the coup was the need to put an end to the "death squads" and promised to control the violence legally. Order 405/76 recognized that operations had been carried out by the military and attributed to "uncontrolled" groups, such as the Triple A. It was Viola himself who had recommended, in a secret directive for operations in Tucumán, the use of "semi-independent groups" acting as "guerrilla hunters." But now, Viola warned his generals, it was inadvisable to maintain those "groups." It was imperative "to centralize the leadership and the increase in intelligence activities" for greater efficiency. "From this point on, the restriction of unilateral actions ought to be assured."

Yet the unilateral actions continued. No longer were they the work of the "groups," now part of the intelligence services. Rather they were carried out by whatever military chief had duty linked to the repression. As mandated by secret order 405/76, the entire country had been converted into a gridwork of zones, subzones, areas, sectors, and subsectors. Each became a fief in which the military man responsible had enormous discretionary power.[10]

The complex and chaotic system came into being primarily for two reasons. One was the search for a military deployment that would give great latitude in operating by zones, in order to increase the "effectiveness" of the proposed repressive methodology. The second concerned the internal struggles among the services. This conflict was carried out by groups and secret lodges within each force. All were in search of a greater quota of power.

Enshrining Unfairness: Martínez de Hoz

A critique of the regime's economic policies made public in early May echoed that made on the eve of the coup by Peronist Bernardo Alberte. According to *La Opinión*, it was "up to this point the first in-depth criticism made against the economic policies of minister José Martínez de Hoz." A group of Radical economists led by Roque Carranza and Bernardo Grispun charged that the military's program was unfair—"more favorable to private interests than general ones"—and warned that "unemployment will increase and so too will the country's economic and social unrest."[11]

A businessman with strong connections to U.S. banking and financial interests, Martínez de Hoz had enacted an economic policy favorable to foreign investment and trade. His task was, to be sure, a tough one. The regime had inherited serious balance of payments problems, a surging inflation, growing state debt, rampant speculation, and paralyzed investment. Yet Martínez de Hoz's remedy benefited financial speculators, agricultural exporters, large industry, and international corporations—a windfall for the rich that came at the expense of both wage earners and small and medium-sized national industries. While clamping down on wages, Martínez de Hoz freed prices. Most people's purchasing power plummeted by half. Exchange rates were unified; tariff barriers were slashed. The state's economic apparatus was meant to be dismantled, and a "survival of the fittest" open-market economy installed. Social costs were ignored, except for an occasional protest by military officers worried about their possible effect on the course of the "dirty war."

As one American historian noted:

> The Army's war on subversion and Martínez de Hoz's program elicited opposite responses from outside observers, who detested the extreme brutalities of the former but generally praised the latter. In many respects, however, the two policies were complementary and inseparable. The butt for both was the urban sectors: the unions, industry, and much of the middle class. The Army's task, with the war against subversion in part as a pretext, was to shatter their collective bargaining power and their means of resistance; Martínez de Hoz's role was to weaken and ultimately destroy the economy on which they subsisted, for example, by eliminating the state as a major source of employment and the chief agent distributing resources in urban society.[12]

Operación Condor: War Without Borders

Operación Condor, the brainchild of the head of the Chilean intelligence agency DINA, had gone into effect in late 1975. Its exotic name, the stuff of spy novels, reflected its program of cooperation among the military intelligence services of six Latin countries—Chile, Paraguay, Brazil, Argentina, Bolivia, and Paraguay. Soaring airily above conventional questions like national borders, Condor was designed to locate and eliminate troublesome political dissidents and guerrillas on the run. Among its provisions was a clause that member countries issue false documentation to assassination squads from participating countries.[13]

By the time of the March 1976 coup in Argentina, the country's security forces found themselves with an almost continent-wide hunting license. Chile carried out some of the most spectacular second-country murders. Even in tiny Uruguay the military at one time toyed with the elimination of U.S. congressional critic (and later New York City mayor) Edward Koch. It was Argentina, however, that carried out the most far-flung policy of extraterritorial raids and allowed for the greatest number of detentions and killings on its territory.[14]

"The assassination of prominent Latin American political exiles and the kidnapping or disappearance of many refugees have dramatized the insecurity of the 15,000 people who have fled here in recent years," noted the *New York Times* at midyear. "There is strong evidence of close cooperation between Argentine military intelligence and neighboring countries in hunting down and abducting politically active refugees."[15]

Early on the morning of May 18 former Uruguayan senator Zelmar Michelini was abducted from his hotel room in a heavily guarded district in downtown Buenos Aires. When asked by the hotel staff for identification, his abductors replied, "These guns are our identification." About the same time, a friend, Héctor Gutierrez Ruíz, former speaker of the Uruguayan Chamber of Deputies, was also kidnapped by armed men who looted his home, carrying off the valuables in seven suitcases belonging to the family. A confidential U.S. embassy cable from Ambassador Robert Hill to Henry Kissinger, dated May 20, noted: "Such an operation would be extremely difficult if not impossible to carry out without Argentine government acquiescence."[16]

The charismatic Michelini had retired from active politics following the detention and torture in Uruguay of one of his daughters. At the time he was abducted, the father of ten wrote a foreign affairs column for *La Opinión*. In his last column he pointedly spoke of dictatorships "that wave the banner of anticommunism, while applying the worst tactics of fascism." Gutierrez Ruíz had also toned down his political activity. The week before, however, he had met in Argentina with several Uruguayan civilians and military men to discuss the possibility of a broad-based campaign to press for elections. After the abductions few friends and politicians shook off their own fears and offered the men's families support and attempted to seek information about the victims' whereabouts. One of those who did was Raúl Alfonsín.[17]

On May 21, less than a month before Kissinger's fateful meeting with Foreign Minister Guzzetti in Santiago, the bullet-riddled bodies of the two politicians and a young Uruguayan couple were found in an abandoned car. Communiqués allegedly from the ERP were scattered by the corpses and claimed the men had been killed for betraying Uruguay's Tupamaro guerrillas.

The police refused to release the bodies to relatives, claiming they were Tupamaros. Meanwhile *La Opinión*—the only Spanish-language Argentine newspaper that tried to mobilize public opinion—received several calls from top Argentine officials, including one from Videla's office. The callers expressed "their deep sorrow and regret" over Michelini's death. On May 25 the Interior Ministry issued a strongly worded communiqué announcing that the Federal Police and a judge would investigate. As *La Opinión* noted, however, the police still had not contacted the families of the slain politicians nor taken fingerprints left behind by their kidnappers. Michelini and Gutierrez Ruíz had been killed by a group operating out of the Automotores Orletti detention camp, run by SIDE chief Otto Paladino. One of those taking part in Gutierrez Ruíz's kidnapping was a former bodyguard for metalworkers' leader Lorenzo Miguel.[18]

On June 3 Argentine authorities announced that the body of former Bolivian president Juan José Torres had been found on a rural roadside. Unlike Michelini and Gutierrez Ruíz, Torres had a highly visible political presence in exile, often visiting the slums in and around Buenos Aires that were home to many of his compatriots. When Torres's wife denounced the kidnapping, Interior Minister Albano Harguindeguy suggested at a press conference that the disappearance was a "self-abduction done for publicity purposes." Two hours later Torres's cadaver appeared. He had been blindfolded and shot twice in the neck and once behind the ear. One account suggests the crime was carried out by Bolivian Rangers who counted on support from the Federal Police and that it had been signed off on by Harguindeguy himself.[19]

The murders of Torres and the two Uruguayans were part of the Condor operation. Members of the Brazilian Serviço Nacional de Informações (SNI; National Information Service) also had free reign to interfere with the activities in Buenos Aires of the dissident Paraguayan Movimiento Popular Colorado (MOPOCO; Colorado Popular Movement). The group had influence among their conationals working on the mammoth Paraguayan-Brazilian Itaipú dam, the world's largest hydroelectric project. An FBI special agent stationed in Buenos Aires said there was a camp near the border with Paraguay. There tortured prisoners were sent to be eliminated with an injection of Brazilian curare. Two American authors who interviewed the agent reported: "Soldiers took them up in army transport planes, gutted their bodies like fish, and dropped them into the Atlantic Ocean."[20]

The Uruguayan Organismo Coordinador de Operaciones Antisubversivas (OCOA; Antisubversive Operations Coordinating Organ) killed or kidnapped at least 250 exiles in Argentina. Harguindeguy's Federal Police gave the OCOA logistical support, detention centers, and even patrol cars—used by Uruguayan teams wearing *federales* uniforms. Transferring of prisoners to Uruguay required the authorization of both Uruguayan Gen. Amaury Pranti, the head of the Servicio de Informaciones de Defensa (Defense Information Service), and SIDE chief Gen. Otto Paladino.[21]

After the coup, the OCOA's primary base was the Automotores Orletti camp. More than 200 Uruguayans were held at the camp. Prisoners held there were tortured under the direction of Eduardo Ruffo, the man who became tiny Carla Rutila Artés's "adoptive" father.[22]

Gerardo Gatti Acuña

One who did not survive the torment of captivity in Orletti was Uruguayan labor leader Gerardo Gatti Acuña. Gatti, a graphics union chief, was a founder of the leftist Convención Nacional de Trabajadores (CNT; National Workers Confederation). Uruguay's largest labor group, the CNT was one of the hardest hit when the military took power in a coup led by rightist President José María Bordaberry. Following a valiant but unsuccessful CNT-led effort to paralyze the country with a general strike in support of the parliament dissolved by Bordaberry, Gatti went into exile in Argentina, where he helped organize the clandestine Resistencia Obrero-Estudiantil (ROE; Worker-Student Resistance). Meanwhile Uruguay became the world leader in number of prisoners per capita, the treatment of whom moved Manhattan Congressman Edward Koch to label the country "the Torture Chamber of Latin America."

Between May and October 1976, at least sixty ROE members were abducted in Buenos Aires. Gatti was picked up on June 8. Five days later armed men, later identified as Uruguayan army personnel, broke into the apartment of Uruguayan union leader Washington Pérez. Pérez was taken to an unidentified building, where it was explained that his captors wanted him to serve as a contact between them and the ROE. They brought him into a room where Gatti lie in agony on a bed. He had been so badly tortured with electric shock around the eyes that he was nearly blind.

According to their kidnappers, Pérez was to contact the clandestine Uruguayan resistance group and make them an offer: the lives of Gatti and nine other ROE members in exchange for $2 million. The money, they suggested, could be obtained from various human rights groups and Uruguay "solidarity" committees in Europe. Five times Pérez was kidnapped during the negotiations; the last time he was brought before another captured Uruguayan trade union leader, for whom the military was demanding half a million dollars more. When Pérez found the ROE could not meet the ransom demands, he fled to Sweden. Gatti, the father of three children, and the others remain "disappeared."[23]

A Guerrilla Retreat

On July 2 a bomb ripped through the dining room of the Coordinación Federal building, the Federal Police intelligence headquarters and a notorious detention center. Twenty-two people were killed, nearly sixty others injured. The bomb was put in the heavily fortified complex by a Montonero sympathizer inside the police. "I was there five minutes after the blast at the police dining hall, and what I saw turned my stomach," a security officer told an Associated Press correspondent. "Women screaming, pieces of bodies strewn around. You could feel the hate from the survivors. I mean, there were these hard-faced apes whom I wouldn't want to tangle with under any circumstances, and they were standing there weeping and swearing to get even."[24]

The revenge was not long in coming. The five members of the Palotine order were killed in their rectory. A teenager was taken by police from his cell at the first light of dawn. Put up against the gleaming white Obelisk, towering over downtown Buenos Aires, he was executed. Eight bodies were found, showing signs of torture and raked by machine-gun fire, in a parking lot not far away. Seven more were found in a barren field in the working-class neighborhood of Villa Lugano. After being executed, their bodies were blown apart. In all, some seventy people were killed. The bombing was only one of several high-profile Montonero terrorist attacks in 1976. Nine days before the coup, then army commander in chief Videla narrowly escaped injury from a car bomb outside army headquarters. A truck driver passing by was killed. On June 18 Gen. Cesáreo Cardozo, the Federal Police chief, died from the explosion of a bomb put under his bed by a teenage friend of his daughter. Several dozen police had been killed since the beginning of the year.

Despite their resonance the attacks signaled that the Montoneros' fighting capacity was badly damaged. By the time of the coup the insurgents had seen their sympathizers purged from public offices, the universities, and the media. Their own press organs had been suppressed or forced into clandestinity. The Montoneros' most important "military" operation—their attack on the infantry regiment in the northeastern province of Formosa in October 1975—was also its last; for the ERP, the end came at Monte Chingolo two months later. "The urban guerrillas," said one hard-line army chief, "had to retreat to terrorism as a way of combat."[25]

18

The Guerrillas and the Agony of Defeat (1976)

> General Viola ... has a slight build ... and a habit of slouching. He has brown eyes, sandy (graying) hair, and a neatly trimmed mustache. He enjoys food, especially his mother-in-law's pasta, and drinks Scotch, also wine, and chain smokes cigarettes. He is intelligent, cautious, reserved, and straightforward; does not warm to associations immediately; but enjoys general conversation and good jokes. The son of an Italian immigrant tailor, General Viola was born into the working class and shares its passion for soccer. ... Measured and serene, General Viola is nevertheless difficult to approach.
> —*U.S. Defense Intelligence Agency, "Biographic Sketch," August 1981*

Shortly before noon on July 19 army captain Juan Manuel Leonetti stationed himself in front of the door of a fifth-story apartment in a new high-rise building complex in Villa Martelli, north of Buenos Aires. Dressed in civilian clothes, Leonetti and the three men who accompanied him waited for the building superintendent to open the door.

As the man fumbled with the lock, ERP leader Benito ("Mariano") Urteaga suddenly appeared in the doorway, quickly slamming the door shut. "It's the army!" someone shouted. "It's the army!" Urteaga grabbed his machine gun. Mario Roberto Santucho, the ERP's maximum leader, drew a .45-caliber pistol. Liliana Delfino, Santucho's common-law wife, ran into the bedroom to hide with Mariano Urteaga's two-year-old son. Urteaga killed Leonetti before being himself cut down. Santucho was shot while trying to jump out the window.

In less than four months after the coup the ERP had been all but annihilated. Until the shoot-out in Villa Martelli, however, none of the ERP's all-important five-man political bureau had been killed or captured since Trelew in 1972. The year before, in 1975, the ERP counted on nearly 300 armed members in the greater Buenos Aires area. Weapons and money were no problem. However, with the defeat at Monte Chingolo in December 1975, arms were scarce. And the quality of the militants plummeted. "By January we were recruiting anyone we could get, nobody with any experience," said one ERP lieutenant.

At the time of the coup, the number of combatants in Buenos Aires had dropped to less than 100. "We didn't know any military techniques except surprise, and that was only effective in the first years," said the ERP combatant. "The enemy got used to taking precautions. Our militants began falling like flies." The policy of disappearances was sinister but effective against the guerrillas' cellular structure. If six of nine people in a cell suddenly disappeared, the remaining three had to decipher what went wrong. Who had broken under torture? Did they tell all they knew? How much did they know? Had the cell been fingered by an infiltrator? Was he one of those missing or was he one of the three who survived? The clandestine repression created a paralyzing terror. "I had to change addresses ten times in a year. There wasn't any place to feel secure. It wasn't like Vietnam, where the people offered you refuge."[1] The situation was even more desperate in other parts of the country. At the time of the coup ERP members under arms in Córdoba numbered less than a dozen. In Rosario the whole structure had been wiped out. In Tucumán maybe half a dozen still ranged in the hills. The deteriorating situation meant the militants' meager living allowance was ended, and many had to go to work. Money problems were symptomatic of the guerrillas' lack of popular support: They sustained themselves by extortive kidnappings. And even in the best of times, experienced combatants—people who could be trusted to carry out an operation—were few. "Every time we had to do something real, it was done with four or five people. The rest didn't know how to fight."

In the last months Santucho had doggedly held onto the militaristic principles outlined in his treatise "Argentines—To Arms!" But in his last internal bulletin the ERP leader eased away from his triumphal call for total war. Slowly Santucho began to tilt in favor of the dissolution of the armed groups and a return to strictly political work. Meanwhile, concerned about his safety, the political bureau urged him to go abroad. Santucho had narrowly escaped capture in March. Knowing their man, his aides argued he was needed for "solidarity" tasks outside the country, particularly with the Eastern bloc countries.

At first Santucho resisted. Finally, he relented. Latin America's most important guerrilla since the death of Che Guevara prepared his retreat. As he readied to leave, he received an invitation from the Montoneros to a summit meeting with them and a small guerrilla group called the Organización Comunista Poder Obrero (OCPO; Worker Power Communist Organization). The purpose of the meeting was the establishment of the Organización para la Liberación de la Argentina (OLA; Organization for the Liberation of Argentina). The Montoneros proposed that the guerrillas coordinate—zone by zone—armed actions. That way other groups in the area would not be swept up in the repression that followed. The Montoneros said the meeting could not be arranged until a week later, on July 19. Santucho himself convinced the ERP political bureau he should stay until then.

Santucho planned to fly out of Argentina using a false passport at 2:30 the afternoon of July 19, with Havana his final destination. At 10:00 A.M., the ERP political bureau secretary went to the meeting place arranged by the Montoneros. Santucho planned to follow later, then return to the apartment in Villa Martelli shortly after noon to bid farewell to the other four members of the bureau. When the ERP secretary showed up at the Montonero safe house, no one was there. Taking care to make sure he was not followed, he returned to where Santucho was, warning him that they had been stood up. Santucho then sent him away on other business.

Less than an hour later, Santucho and fellow political bureau member Urteaga were dead. That same day a third bureau member, Domingo Mena, was reported to have been killed. The nexus between ERP and Montoneros—and the person who asked Santucho to delay his flight—was Mario Firmenich. It was he who had arranged the meeting at the Montonero "safe house" and then did not show.[2]

Blood Relations

The military often made little distinction between the guerrillas and their families. Seven months before the coup, on the third anniversary of the flight from the Rawson prison, the parents, brother, and sister of Mariano Pujadas, one of the guerrillas killed in the massacre of Trelew, were themselves murdered by the Triple A. Two weeks before the military takeover, a former interior minister under Frondizi—the father of Montonero leader Fernando Vaca Narvaja—was "disappeared" by police. One of Vaca Narvaja's brothers was murdered in prison in a staged escape attempt. On the eve of the coup the father of the late Montonero founder Carlos Capuano Martínez was killed. Mario Roberto Santucho's wife, Liliana Delfino, gave birth in the Campo de Mayo army hospital; she was then murdered. His family was decimated in Automotores Orletti, run by SIDE chief Gen. Otto Paladino. The seventy-year-old father of montonera María Antonia Berger, one of the three survivors of Trelew, was murdered by the army in Llavallol, a suburb thiry miles south of Buenos Aires. The mother and a brother of revolutionary Peronist Dante Gullo disappeared.[3]

The heavy hand of repression fell unevenly, however. In early August, a month after the Montoneros bombed Coordinación Federal—with its sequel of deadly reprisals—twenty-seven-year-old María Elpidia Martínez Aguero was seized by the Federal Police. The wife of Mario Firmenich and two months pregnant, she was taken to Coordinación where, she said, she was tortured—a claim disputed by a U.S. intelligence agent who said he saw her there. Martínez gave birth to the couple's second child in a legal jail in western Buenos Aires. Unlike scores of cases of detainees' children born in captivity, the infant was not taken away from its mother. Nor was the baby killed, as others were, for being "contaminated" by subversion. Martínez Aguero was released from prison in 1981, before the Falkland/Malvinas war, and mother and child—bearing valid documents—were allowed to slip into exile.[4]

Firmenich's father was an engineering professor at the University of Buenos Aires. He also worked as the head of road construction for the city of Buenos Aires. At the time, the mayor of the federal capital was Brig. Osvaldo Cacciatore. (Among the people the air force general counted as friends was Licio Gelli.) Despite the witch-hunt taking place in the universities, Victor Firmenich was not fired from his teaching post. Nor did he lose his job with the road department. Neither he nor his wife were bothered in any way during the "dirty war."[5]

Rodolfo Walsh Sounds a Warning

The Montoneros welcomed the coup as a victory in the making. "Repressive military rule is viewed as the necessary precondition for the massive popular resistance that the terrorists believe will culminate in seizure of power by the revolutionary left," noted a State Department intelligence report two weeks later. "Given this perception ... the ERP and the Montoneros cannot be expected to alter their tactics. They may decide ... to weather the storm of the military's initial onslaught and await the anticipated failure of the junta's economic program. However, they almost certainly believe that their strategy is working, and that time is their ally."[6]

The quick demise of the ERP—annihilated in less than 100 days after the coup—proved the folly of the guerrillas' calculations. Although not as immediate, the Montoneros' strategy of "active defense"—quick, low-risk attacks on key enemy personnel—in preparation for an eventual counteroffensive was equally fatal. Meanwhile the military's offensive was to be absorbed due to what, in comparison with the ERP, were the Montoneros' larger numbers. The attacks were meant to show the regime's weakness, fanning the flames of resistance.[7]

During the last four months of 1976 several Montonero bombings served to obscure the magnitude of the rout of the guerrillas. On September 12 a car bomb destroyed a police bus, killing eleven police and two civilians. The next month a bomb ripped through a cinema in the Circulo Militar army officers club injuring sixty people. On November 9 a bomb shattered the Buenos Aires provincial police headquarters, killing one. On December 15 a bomb in a Defense Ministry hall during an antisubversion conference killed fourteen senior military and intelligence officers. (Each attack resulted in reprisals in which scores of detainees, in some cases totaling nearly a hundred, were murdered.)

But neither their stylized uniforms and insignias nor military manuals and precarious munitions factories had made the Montoneros an army. After the coup the guerrillas' rhetoric could not hide the fact that they lacked fighting units capable of meeting the enemy head on. Moreover, the military takeover meant the police were relegated to a second rung in the antiguerrilla operations. The armed forces no longer limited their intervention against the urban insurgents to times when the police seemed overwhelmed. Control of the state also gave the generals virtually unlimited resources, which could be mustered at will. Their control over the mass media, for example, guaranteed that the guerrillas' message was silenced. Justifications for the bombing campaign—that they struck at the heart of a repressive, torturing behemoth—went unrecorded by the general population. An order by the Montonero high command that militants carry cyanide pills, obliging their use to avoid capture, allowed them to be portrayed as fanatics. (The military began using an antidote to ensure the capture of insurgents, so they could be "interrogated." The Montonero leadership responded by suggesting the use of glass capsules that, when bitten, produced cuts inside the mouth, allowing the poison to be absorbed directly into the bloodstream. Scores of guerrillas committed suicide using the pills.)[8]

Increasing militarization of the Peronist guerrillas also meant there was even less chance for the rank and file to challenge the Montonero leadership on political issues. The rigidly hierarchical command could not have worked to worse effect, allowing, as U.S. intelligence agents learned, penetration by both the SIDE and the Argentine army at the highest levels.[9]

By late November writer Rodolfo Walsh, a top Montonero intelligence officer, warned that the the fight was lost. Panglossian evaluations were obscuring "the real gravity of our military situation, omitting vital facts for comprehension of what it really is, such as percent of losses, territory evacuated, etc." The panorama, he said, was reflected in "the retreat of the working class, the defeat of the middle sectors and the desertion of the intellectuals and professionals." The revolutionary vanguard, he said, was running the risk of becoming the "lost patrol."

Walsh acerbically punctured Montonero rhetoric that Argentines would flock to find refuge under the guerrillas' banners. "It is to be supposed," he wrote, "that the masses are condemned to using common sense. ... To assume, as we sometimes do, that the masses can retreat toward the Montoneros is to deny what is the essence of a retreat, that is, the falling out from more exposed positions to those less exposed." He scored apocalyptic predictions that Argentine capitalism was on the threshold of a "'definitive crisis.' ... Capitalism in dozens of countries has survived much graver crises than that of Argentina today."

The alternative, Walsh said, was for the Montoneros to admit they had been militarily defeated. The guerrillas faced a situation that "threatens to convert into extermination." They needed to separate their dreams of socialism from "the hard reality of today, which does not allow the masses to even think about power, but rather about resisting in order to survive." The guerrillas, he added, ought to follow the masses in their retreat to Peronism, offering to collaborate as merely a part of a larger resistance effort. Individual and collective security should be given highest priority. The record of Montonero leaders in preserving structures under their own command should be a factor in future promotions. Walsh also suggested that the guerrillas' national leadership, together with its best-known figures, go into exile, thus "denying the enemy the possibility of inflicting upon us decisive defeats by their capture or death." Of all the suggestions he offered, only Walsh's recommendation about self-exile was heeded by the guerrilla high command.

Walsh had traveled a long road. The odyssey began with his denunciations of the 1956 massacre by the military at José León Suárez and the murder by SIDE agents of lawyer Marcos Satanowsky. Walsh worked on the parliamentary commission investigating the Satanowsky case—only to see Frondizi's Radicals cave in when the military demanded that the probe be halted. In 1959 the onetime right-wing nationalist traveled to Cuba to witness Castro's revolution. There he, Colombian writer Gabriel García Márquez, and several others founded the *Prensa Latina* news agency. On the eve of the Bay of Pigs invasion, Walsh engaged novelist Ernest Hemingway in the shortest interview of his life. "We Cubans," Hemingway told the Argentine, "will win."[10]

Walsh met Perón in Spain in 1968 when he accompanied Raimundo Ongaro to the general's residence in Puerta de Hierro. Ongaro was graphics union leader and head of the militant wing of the CGT, at the time favored by Perón. "All of us Peronists are in debt to the author of *Operación Massacre*," Perón told the journalist. Walsh later headed the labor confederation's weekly, *Semanario CGT,* where he sought to unite the workers' discontent with that of the students in the fight against Onganía. A series of articles on a shoot-out involving labor leader Augusto Vandor—in which a left-wing Peronist and a Vandor rival, Rosendo García, were killed—made the case that it was El Lobo himself who shot García and served as the foundation for another classic, *¿Quién mató a Rosendo?* (Who killed Rosendo?).

As the fight against military rule quickened, Walsh made common cause with the Peronist Armed Forces and later joined the Montoneros. In late 1975 the guerrillas had not grasped the nature of the coup in the making, he wrote later. "The possibility was allowed for, but work continued as if it wasn't going to happen." One of the Montoneros' gravest miscalculations, he said, was the extent to which the press could be controlled by the military.

In June 1976 Walsh embarked on a scheme meant to break the military's embargo on information. With a handful of friends and journalists and a wide network of informants, Walsh put together the Agencia de Noticias Clandestina (Clandestine News Agency; known by its acronym ANCLA, Spanish for "anchor"). In October he distributed a pamphlet, "Historia de la guerra sucia en la Argentina" (The history of the dirty war). The report dealt extensively with the nature of the generals' antisubversive efforts, including a specific detailed report on conditions inside the Navy Mechanics School. In December Walsh added another chain of newsletters, called *Cadena Informativa.*

Foreign correspondents found the mimeographed contents of the plain envelopes routinely appearing at their offices a relief from the dry nothingness of Argentina's regular media, which ignored Walsh's clandestine denunciations. The massacre of family members of the guerrillas, the murder of children, the extortive kidnappings conducted by members of the SIDE—all found in Walsh's work—were unreported by Argentine radio, television, newspapers, or magazines. So, too, were the looting, the secret camps, the murder of detainees in scores of fake shoot-outs, and the pitching of live people out of airplanes into the ocean. Walsh's sparse, unsparing prose—so unlike the insurgents' usual florid rhetoric—put isolated incidents into a context, unmasking the regime. The response of the major media was silence.

One Wednesday in late September Walsh was monitoring a shortwave news broadcast by the BBC. The program reported that the army had unleashed a huge operation in the federal capital. Large numbers of troops had been mobilized, a helicopter was sent to patrol the area, and an undetermined number of people were killed. Nothing of the clash was reported in Buenos Aires until Friday. It was then that Walsh learned that his daughter Vicki, like her father a journalist and a montonera, had died in the confrontation.

The insurgents' national political secretariat had been holding a meeting in Buenos Aires' Floresta neighborhood. Led by Col. Roberto Roualdés, army troops surrounded the house, opening fire with a tank and bazookas. An hour and a half later Vicki Walsh—clad in a nightshirt—put down her machine gun. Standing up on an upstairs balcony, she stretched out her arms, calling out to the stunned soldiers below: "You cannot kill us ... we choose death." She and another Montonero leader then shot themselves in the temple. One account said the deaths of the five ranking guerrillas had allowed Firmenich and Rodolfo Galimberti to escape.[11]

That December Walsh wrote "A letter to my Friends." In it, Walsh the intellectual struggled with his own pain and sense of loss. The man who called on his comrades to admit defeat and help stop the massacre taking place seemed trapped by the guerrillas' own cult of martyrdom and death.

My daughter was not willing to give herself up. It was a mature, reasoned decision. She knew from infinite numbers of testimonies the treatment dispensed by the army and navy to those unfortunate enough to fall prisoner: the skinning alive, the mutilation of body parts, the torture without limit in time or method, achieving at the same time a moral degradation, betrayal. She knew perfectly well that in a war of those characteristics, the sin was not in talking, but in falling prisoner. She always carried with her a cyanide pill. ...

Over time I have reflected about that death. I've asked myself if my daughter, if all those who die like her, had another option. The response springs from the deepest part of my heart, and I want my friends to know. Vicki could have chosen other roads that were different without being dishonorable, but that she chose was the most just, the most generous, the most reasoned. Her lucid death is a synthesis of her short, beautiful life. She did not live for herself: She lived for others, and those others are millions. Her death yes, her death was gloriously hers, and in that pride I steady myself and it is I who am reborn in it.

Mario Firmenich: Survivor

Early in December, Argentina's newspapers trumpeted another success by the security forces—the killing of one of the founders of the Montoneros in the Buenos Aires suburb of Lomas de Zamora. "The terrorist Esther Norma Arrostito cut down—She was implicated in the murder of Lieutenant General Aramburu," proclaimed *La Prensa*. As if keeping score at a soccer match, *La Razón* ran a box on the front page titled: "There's still one fugitive." The survivor was Firmenich.

"The night before last the security forces struck another devastating blow against subversion by killing Norma Esther Arrostito," reported *La Opinión*. "Arrostito ignored an order to halt, trying instead to throw a grenade that, when she was struck down by the fire of the security forces, exploded by her side. She did not have time to digest the cyanide capsules she carried in her purse."[12]

In fact, Arrostito had been kidnapped and taken to the Navy Mechanics School, where—her feet shackled in chains—she was tortured and shown off as a "war trophy" to selected visitors. She was also questioned by navy men anxious to uncover evidence with which to blame Onganía's government—and the army— for Aramburu's murder. Among those interrogating her was one of the murdered president's closest associates. Arrostito was killed more than a year after her capture.[13]

19

The Price of Power (1976)

The terrorists are still able to obstruct Argentina's industrial recovery. The race is now on to see whether the police and the military will exterminate these ruthless sowers of anarchy before they bring a substantial part of industry to its knees.
  —*American Chamber of Commerce, Buenos Aires, November 12, 1976*[1]

General Harguindeguy ... is of Basque ancestry and of large build ... with gray hair and blue eyes. Direct, honest, friendly, outgoing, and endowed with a good sense of humor, he is a likable individual who can be somewhat boisterous. He projects a rigid image, but is actually very flexible, receptive to advice, and progressive in his thinking.
  —*U.S. Defense Intelligence Agency, "Biographic Sketch," June 1980*

In August Chilean intelligence agent Michael Townley flew to Buenos Aires to meet with Delle Chiaie's men. There he learned of the coup pulled off on July 18 in Nice, France, by a group of the Italian's followers. Dubbed "the Sewer Gang," the ultra-right-wing activists tunneled into the vault of the Societe Generale bank. After burrowing into the vault from the tunnel, they welded the twenty-ton door shut from inside. The group carried away more than $10 million in jewels, securities, and documents from the safety deposit boxes, leaving the cash behind. Pornographic photos found in some of the boxes were left taped to the vault walls.

Townley was in Buenos Aires awaiting his next big assignment. The following month the Iowa-born DINA agent carried his terrorist campaign to the heart of Washington, D.C. Aided by anti-Castro Cuban exiles, Townley blew up a car carrying former Chilean diplomat Orlando Letelier, who had been foreign minister and ambassador to Washington in the government of socialist Salvador Allende. Letelier and a young American woman died in the blast.

In Buenos Aires Townley met with members of Milicia, the intelligence unit that helped the DINA assassinate General Prats. He urged the SIDE subgroup to proceed with an extortive kidnapping they planned with one of Townley's Cuban exile contacts, an associate of Delle Chiaie. The victim was president of a local Dutch bank, the Banco Holandés Unido. Townley arranged to have printed up a Grupo Rojo (Red Group) letterhead, which the Argentines used to issue communiqués and ransom demands in the name of the phony leftist commando. The man was abducted and released after a ransom was paid.[2]

Anti-Jewish violence, too, mushroomed in the six months after the coup. The SIDE-funded Milicia was immune from the government's clampdown on the dissemination of ideological works. Since early 1976 its modern printing plant spewed out a Library of Doctrinary Information. The collection included bound issues of such hate tracts as *The Protocols of the Elders of Zion* and *The Ritual Crimes of the Jews*. It also reproduced the works of Hitler, Nazi chief Julius Streicher, and propagandist Joseph Goebbels.

Extortive kidnappings of Jewish businessmen and their families soared beyond the high number that took place—largely the work of rightist Peronists and the security forces—during the long death rattle of the Perón government. A top Federal Police officer estimated that more than 200 such cases took place during the life of the regime. Jews were particularly vulnerable to extortion. If the crime was denounced, the victim risked inflaming anti-Semites in the security forces, seething with notions about Jews controlling the world's finances. Yet if nothing was done, it was a virtual invitation for such crimes to continue.[3]

The military regime claimed the attacks were the work of renegade right-wing groups. The terrorism recalled Germany of the 1930s. In June a Jewish doctor was kidnapped, and three days later his bullet-ridden body was thrown from a car. Anonymous callers to Buenos Aires radio stations said the crime was in revenge for the victim's alleged role in the abduction of Nazi war criminal Adolf Eichmann by the Mossad, Israel's foreign intelligence agency, in the early 1960s. In August the attacks included sticks of dynamite placed at a Sephardic synagogue, shots fired at a school and a cooperative bank, the machine-gun strafing of a kosher butcher shop and more than twenty other Jewish-owned stores. There was also the bombing of the headquarters of the Federation of Jewish Cultural Entities of Argentina and that of two synagogues, a drug store in a Jewish neighborhood, and a Jewish cultural center. On September 3 bombs badly damaged a school and a synagogue, and other explosives were discovered at a Jewish-owned shopping mall and at the building housing *La Opinión*. An Argentine National Socialist Front, made up of Federal Police and state intelligence agents, claimed credit for many of the attacks, declaring: "Thus commences the war which will end only when the Jewish-Bolshevik plutocracy is exterminated."[4]

The myth of uncontrolled and uncontrollable death squads quickly proved to be a farce. After meetings in October between U.S. Jewish leaders and top Argentine officials and congressional hearings in the United States on human rights in Argentina, the attacks suddenly ended. In mid-September after a meeting between the Anti-Defamation League and the Argentine ambassador, the state-funded Editorial Milicia was ordered closed. Brimming with the same hypocrisy that characterized official replies to queries about the missing, the decree said that the measure was taken because *Milicia*'s books caused reactions against certain groups. Their ideology, it claimed, was incompatible with the "essential values" of the Argentine nation.[5]

Military Politics

Although President Jorge Videla was a remote figure and without doubt one of the least overtly political of the generals, army chief of staff Viola loved the backroom manuevering—a reflection perhaps of his political ties to Radical leader Ricardo Balbín. Viola was aided by Col. Marco ("Chovito") Cúneo. As head of a secret lodge bearing his name, Cúneo wielded great influence with top officials; from the army high command, he wove a network of political and union contacts on Viola's behalf.[6]

Viola initially favored six months of military rule in order to "annihilate subversion," then partially relinquishing power to a civilian government of limited authority. Rather than abolishing politics, as the hard-liners urged, Viola tried to identify the political establishment as closely as possible with the military's antisubversive efforts. The role of men like Viola in the repression became a chimera in the debate over the nature of the regime. The "moderates" were generally those who held power and/or desk-bound commands; the hard-liners were ambitious military men chafing for more power or having a hands-on role in the repression.

Viola himself was not "soft" on the methods of the "dirty war" as the more intransigent generals charged—thus offering outsiders the false hope of a rift between "moderates" and "hard-liners." He had authored many of the secret orders for the clandestine repression. Like other purported moderates, Viola backed Martínez de Hoz's economic program, dependent on the repression, particularly in the factories. But Viola understood that politics could be war waged by other means. He knew that making the politicians allies was the generals' best insurance for crushing the guerrillas, rebutting criticism abroad, and preventing a future settling of scores.

Viola's plan was rejected by the other services and factions within the army itself. Instead, an important number of generals supported the openly fascistic projects of Generals Ramón Gennaro Díaz Bessone and Ibérico Saint Jean. Generals Luciano B. Menéndez and Carlos Suárez Mason, commanders of the III Army Corps and the I Army Corps, respectively, were among those favoring the plans crafted by Saint Jean, an intelligence specialist and former head of SIDE.

Saint Jean had been made governor of Buenos Aires, the country's most important province. The post was something of a consolation prize for the general, who nurtured his own presidential ambitions. He was supported by his own secret club of military men and well-heeled civilians called the Logia Azcuenaga (Azcuenaga Lodge), named for the Buenos Aires street where they had met and plotted since the early 1970s. Among his collaborators was army Col. Ramón Camps, the provincial police chief.[7]

Massera and the Navy Mechanics School

Massera's political ambitions were developed on three fronts. The first was the direct, frontal fight for power carried out from his post on the junta; the second, the admiral's growing pretensions of international networking. A third—cunning and clandestine—was silently carried out from the basements of the Navy Mechanics School.

Massera had already aroused suspicions with his treatment of Peronist politicians and labor leaders detained for months on two ships anchored off the capital. The generals had heard stories of Massera's traveling to one of the ships, *Treinta y Tres Orientales,* on the May 25 national holiday, where he reportedly drank a toast with jailed metalworkers' boss Lorenzo Miguel. By early August vaguely populist themes were given echo in the admiral's speeches.[8]

Through his control of the Foreign Ministry, Massera wove a net of important international links. His friendship with the shadowy Italian Masonic Grand Master Licio Gelli was a font of contacts—especially business ties—that Massera did not squander. A few military sectors lobbied to rescind Gelli's designation as counselor at the Argentine embassy in Rome. Massera ordered that the gray-haired Italian be confirmed in his post and all matters relating to him be referred to the navy commander personally through Foreign Minister Guzzetti.[9]

Argentine relations with much of Western Europe were to a large extent in Gelli's hands. One top Massera aide said the admiral saw Gelli as his link to Italian leaders such as Christian Democrats Giulio Andreotti and Amintore Fanfani. "In 1978 I personally traveled to Rome to meet with Gelli in his office at the Excelsior Hotel, in order to make preparations for Massera's trip. Gelli had friends in high places all over Europe, including, of course, the Vatican."[10]

The army had been trying to break the power-sharing arrangement between the services—unprecedented in Argentina's long history of coups—from the day Isabel Perón was overthrown. The admiral knew his political future depended on his service not being seen as relegated to a secondary role in the "combat" taking place. The repression carried out by the ESMA's *grupo de tareas* (GT; task group) 3.3/2 put the navy on an equal footing with the army. More than 5,000 prisoners were held there. Few survived.

The task group unconditionally supported Massera and became his own "private army." Massera had participated in its formation and, during an inaugural ceremony for officials designated to serve in the *grupo de tareas,* he exhorted the men "to respond to the enemy using the same violence, without worrying about the means used." In order to show his own commitment, Massera personally took part in the group's first clandestine operations. He is also said to have tortured prisoners in the basement of the officers' casino.[11]

Officially the Navy Mechanics School served an important role in training programs for lower-ranking officers. The sprawling complex in the residential Nuñez district in northern Buenos Aires, far away from the salt spray of the high seas, was the navy's most important political presence in the capital. Its well-kept white buildings and brown wooden shutters reflected the navy men's self-image as a cut above their mongrel cousins in the army.

A former chief of curriculum at the ESMA recalled that the task groups worked out of stolen automobiles. Almost every night people with hoods over their heads were brought back to be tortured and killed. The order for the clandestine operations came from his superior officers, he said. "When I suggested it might be more correct to hold summary trials and even executions—if it was necessary— but making the proceedings known to the public ... I was separated from all the ESMA's antisubversive operations."[12]

Massera decided to operate the group through the ESMA's director, Rear Adm. Rubén Chamorro, and other officers who willingly shared Massera's future. Chamorro, who used the "war names" Delfín and Máximo, served as the chief of staff for the GT 3.3/2. At the beginning, the task group barely counted on a dozen officials, but after the first seven months it had not only grown numerically but had gathered its own intelligence. This development created frictions and infighting with the Servicio de Informaciones Navales (SIN; Naval Information Service). Massera's backing gave the ESMA officers a power extending beyond their rank and specific function, and they became a pressure group inside the navy itself. They not only carried out repressive tasks but served as Massera's praetorian guard and as a lobby for his political ambitions.

By late 1976 the clash with the men from the SIN caused the latter to form its own task group, unleashing a bitter internal struggle. The SIN officers felt disdain for the members of the ESMA task group, whose officers had not attended intelligence training classes. The SIN crowd, the elite of the traditionally anti-Peronist navy, also did not feel comfortable with Massera's ever more evident populism. They felt it was a mistake for the navy to yoke its future to Massera's political bandwagon.[13]

"War" Is Good Business

Military influence over society had reached new heights. Not only did the generals divvy up public posts, but hundreds of retired and active duty officers took up positions on the boards of private companies and in managerial spots in multinational corporations. Military men and civilian intelligence personnel began turning up at the homes and offices of relatives of missing people and those of imperiled dissidents. Information, passports, clues, or merely not being killed—all were possible for a price. In Buenos Aires and Córdoba military men set up furniture and appliance stores stocked with goods looted from the homes of the *desaparecidos*. In part, Massera's political pretensions were financed by what was stolen from prisoners or extorted from their families. Interior Minister Gen. Albano Harguindeguy ran an extortive kidnapping ring, staffed by police, out of his office. (Jewish businessmen were favorite targets.) Military and police officers were killed or wounded by peers in disputes over how to split up the booty. The crimes were presented publicly as the work of the guerrillas.[14]

Within six months of the coup greed had become the primary motivation for many dirty warriors. Qualms about the way the repression was carried out were salved by double pay from the state of siege. Liberal access to the illegally obtained booty was another way of persuading the reluctant to go along. "On joint operations with the army," said one Federal Police officer who went on scores of raids, "we were no sooner past the door when their guys started ransacking the place to see what they could rip off. They didn't even take elemental precautions in case a guerrilla was hiding inside. Security got so bad I threatened to pull my people out."[15]

Into the Labyrinth

A young woman was one of fifteen U.S. citizens who disappeared during the "dirty war." The woman was missing for five months; three others never reappeared. One day a young consular services officer named Jerry Whitman got a call. U.S. embassy personnel, he was told, could see her that night. "I drove for hours out in the middle of nowhere, and when I got there [a rural police precinct], all I could see in the headlights were men carrying submachine guns," said Whitman. The woman had been tortured. "She was petrified. She thought they had brought her out there to kill her. The most important thing was to act fast—to act before the prisoner got too far into the labyrinth," he said. "Once you knew where [the prisoners] were you were home free."

In searching for the Americans Whitman distributed their descriptions to key embassy personnel and asked them to mention the missing in talks with Argentine officials. He also called the jails, police stations, and the Interior and Foreign ministries. "The standard answer was: 'We don't know what you're talking about.' I always impressed upon them that the case was being looked at in the highest levels." Whitman said he used President Ford's name "pretty liberally." One girl, he said, "was kept in a basement cell so crowded that the women had to sleep in shifts. The only air came from a small transom window near the ceiling." Some prisoners were released on the condition that they leave Argentina immediately. Several Americans released, Whitman said, suffered "lasting psychological problems" due to torture.[16]

The Fourth Man

In mid-November the navy launched an offensive meant to end Videla's dual role as president and commander in chief of the army. It sought a "fourth man" for the junta. The new face would serve as president, forcing Videla to retire to his role as army commander. Massera, whose length of service made him the junta member closest to retirement, saw himself as the logical pick for the presidency. He also suggested to Menéndez that the corps commander would make an ideal candidate to replace Videla. The "moderates" supporting Viola, however, planned not only to keep the executive in the army's hands but also to increase its powers.[17]

Viola made use of the customary year-end military command changes to counterattack. By making concessions to the wing headed by Menéndez and "losing" the 1st Cavalry Brigade, Viola forced four of his fiercest ultra-right-wing critics into mandatory retirement: Generals Otto Paladino, Acdel Vilas, Juan A. Buasso, and Rodolfo C. Mujica.[18]

On November 30 Vilas was told he had been placed "in availability," the step before mandatory retirement. The "Peronist general" had already come in for heavy criticism when he launched a crusade against the academicians of the Southern National University in Patagonia. The witch-hunt put Vilas on a collision course with former president Lanusse, the bête noire of army hardliners and nationalists, who was never forgiven by them for handing power over to Cámpora. "I support even the excesses of my men," said Vilas shortly before leaving the V Army Corps, "if the result is important for our objectives."[19]

Timerman Speaks Out

In mid-November a three-man delegation from Amnesty International came to Buenos Aires. Its purpose was to probe the growing reports about an officially sanctioned "dirty war." A month earlier the generals had debated the importance of world opinion. A document, later obtained by the U.S. embassy, had been circulated that precisely outlined what the domestic and international consequences would be if the regime did not improve its rights situation. During the Amnesty visit, Rev. Robert Drinan, a Catholic priest and member of the U.S. Congress, sought out *La Opinión* publisher Jacobo Timerman.[20]

By that time Timerman had seen several members of his staff arrested or "disappeared," including Uruguayan Zelmar Michelini. Shortly after Michelini's death Timerman had lunch at the Plaza Hotel with a navy captain. The officer admitted that the repression was "irreversible." The military had come to the conclusion, the captain said, that "whoever was in any way linked to subversion—sons, parents, relatives—had to disappear. It was going to mean a great sacrifice, but it would be worth it." Timerman said later he argued that a legal repression, even with capital punishment, would be preferable. The captain disagreed. So did other military officers with whom Timerman said he brought the subject up. At the lunch someone mentioned a recent attempted poisoning of a group of navy officers. The captain said the culprit had been caught. What had been done with him? he was asked. "We threw him into the ocean."[21]

Despite the rather bald confession of what the military had been strenuously denying, Timerman seemed to give his visitor from Amnesty a differing view. *La Opinión* reported that when Drinan pressed Timerman on the "presumed" anti-Semitic campaign then under way, "Timerman said that while there had been anti-Semitic manifestations by small groups, they did not differ much from those that for years were part of an endemic problem. ... At the same time [he] said a certain utilization of the subject of Argentine anti-Semitism abroad was the result of local political necessities in the United States and France."[22]

Ismael Edgardo Bruno Quijano

On December 20 the newspaper *La Nación* ran a small story about the release of Ismael Edgardo Bruno Quijano. The lawyer and a colleague had been kidnapped two months before by what the newspaper called "a subversive group" in a downtown Buenos Aires military zone. The incident set gilded parlors throughout the capital abuzz. Quijano had been a top official in Frondizi's government and later was named justice minister by then President Lanusse. Whereas the other man was freed the day after the abduction, Quijano's liberation came only after payment of a $200,000 ransom. Quijano's captors handed the money over to their chief, Emilio Massera. The admiral had sent the navy men on the mission.[23]

U.S. Policy: Business as Usual

At year's end the State Department issued a report on human rights in Argentina, a requirement of new congressional legislation mandating its submission by the secretary of state when requested by Capitol Hill. The International Security Assistance and Arms Export Control Act of 1976 stated that it was U.S. policy not to provide security assistance to regimes engaging in a "consistent pattern of gross violations of internationally recognized human rights" except in extraordinary circumstances. Already, during a twenty-five-year period beginning in 1950, 2,766 members of the Argentine armed forces had received instruction at U.S. military schools, a number exceeded in Latin America only by Brazil, Chile, and Peru. More than 600 Argentines had attended the U.S. Army School of the Americas at Fort Gulick in the Panama Canal Zone, an important facility for teaching counterinsurgency operations.[24]

The State Department reported that the rights of life, liberty, and security of Argentines were violated regularly by terrorists from both ends of the political spectrum. Both the military and the Peronist government that preceded it had acquiesced to violations committed by people associated with the government. The security forces had reportedly killed detainees suspected of terrorism, it said, and right-wing terrorism or counterterrorism had been committed with impunity. Active duty and retired military and police personnel were members of the squads. However, it claimed that torture—cruel, inhuman, and degrading treatment or punishment—was not a general practice; such methods were used to extract information from some prisoners, "particularly suspected or proven terrorists."

The department told Congress that Argentine leaders said that they did not condone and were seeking to curb violations of human rights. "In the present atmosphere of terrorism," the State Department said it was told by the generals, "they cannot yet control the situation." Direct U.S. investment in Argentina was placed at $1.4 billion. The year before American exports were $628 million, imports $215 million. U.S. banks and financial institutions were owed about $2.7 billion, nearly $600 million of which was to the Export-Import Bank (Eximbank) and the balance to commercial banks. The report also noted that security assistance proposed for Argentina totaled $48.4 million in foreign military sales credits. Less than $700,000 more was allocated to in-grant military training. The credits were for big-ticket items, ships and aircraft having "little or no bearing on the counter-terrorist capability of the armed forces."

The arguments in favor of assistance were familiar. It would show U.S. desire to cooperate militarily with a country with 1,000 miles of coastline on the South Atlantic stretching down to Cape Horn. It would "orient the Argentine military professionally toward the United States, exposing them to our technology and our methods." The aid offered the chance for improved communication with Argentina's military, "who have always influenced events in their country and are now the dominant sector. This helps promote and protect our various interests and helps ensure that we will get a hearing on matters of concern to the United States." It was business as usual at Henry Kissinger's State Department.

20

Jimmy Carter and the Human Rights Revolution (1977)

I have the impression that finally Argentina has a regime which understands the private enterprise system. ... Not since the Second World War has Argentina been presented with a combination of advantageous circumstances as it has now.

—*David Rockefeller*[1]

Massera then told me he thought Videla was a son-of-a-bitch. I told him, "I'd have to agree with you on that, admiral."
—*From testimony by Argentine rights leader Emilio Mignone*[2]

On January 20, 1977, Jimmy Carter was inaugurated as president. "Human rights," he announced shortly thereafter, was to be "the soul of U.S. foreign policy." Carter had used a nationally televised debate with Gerald Ford during the 1976 presidential campaign to sharply question U.S. rights practices. Then he had singled out U.S. policy toward Chile. After the inauguration, the new administration picked Argentina as a priority country in applying its new rights standard. The contrast with the State Department's year-end report could not have been greater.

Carter had not invented the rights issue. Rather, events and the Georgian's reforming zeal had come together at the right time, in the right place. Vietnam had discredited conventional foreign policy wisdom. Watergate pushed decision-making away from the executive branch and toward an activist and angry Congress. The brutality of Chilean dictator Augusto Pinochet and U.S. help in his ascent to power became the focus of congressional probing. Human rights promised to add a humanitarian aspect notably absent in U.S. foreign policy. Liberal activists and conservative opponents of foreign aid were already a de facto barrier against the routine approval in Congress of State Department requests for support for Third World dictatorships. When Carter took office, there was no credible left-wing threat to regional security in South America. From Colombia southward, mostly right-wing dictatorships held sway.[3]

A month after Carter was sworn in, Secretary of State Cyrus Vance announced that the administration was reducing security assistance to Argentina for the following year from the $32 million recommended by the Ford administration to $15.7 million. He explicitly linked the decision to the military's human rights record. The junta responded by denouncing the move as interference in the country's internal affairs. It spurned the lesser sum offered. Congressional legislation underscored preoccupation in the U.S. over the rights issue. A bill introduced by Senator Edward Kennedy sought to ban all military training and assistance, pipeline credits, and cash sales after September 30, 1978. The administration eventually abstained or voted against twenty-eight of the thirty-two proposals for loans to Argentina in the World Bank and the Inter-American Development Bank. The only loans it supported were those that met basic human needs.[4]

The administration also made important gestures meant to underscore U.S. concern. State Department officials met with Argentine dissidents and human rights activists. When former Radical senator Hipólito Solari Yrigoyen was freed from prison, he was received by Deputy Secretary of State Warren Christopher. U.S. intelligence satellites combed Argentina's vast territory—unsuccessfully—trying to locate clandestine camps. Patricia Derian, the new assistant secretary of state for human rights, visited Buenos Aires several times, faced down the generals, and spoke forcefully about the need to return to the rule of law. "Patt Derian had an enormous impact," admitted Gen. Carlos Delía Larroca, who served as the Argentine regime's ambassador to Belgium, much later, "especially on the international organizations."[5]

At the signing of the Panama Canal treaty in Washington, Carter handed Videla a list of missing people, importuning him to look into the matter. One of those on the list was human rights activist and labor leader Alfredo Bravo, a friend of Raúl Alfonsín and later a top education official in the new democratic government. Two months later in Buenos Aires, Vance told Videla he brought with him a list of 7,500 missing people. Coached by Derian, Vance acknowledged a group of mothers protesting in the Plaza de Mayo, demanding news about their missing children. Old barriers were broken down, new friendships established. (Ten years later, La Perla chief torturer Ernesto Barreiro still could not hide his amusement at having been tracked down in the clandestine camp by an officer carrying a copy of a letter from Vance that had been given to III Army Corps chief Gen. Benjamin Menéndez, asking for the release of the five-member Deutsch family, whose abduction had mobilized the U.S. human rights community. The family was later freed and relocated in California.)[6]

At the U.S. embassy, a young, exceedingly tall diplomat named Franklin ("Tex") Harris worked tirelessly to aid relatives and friends of the missing. A legend among politicians, rights activists, and religious leaders, Tex Harris made his rounds in a brown Chevy Caprice station wagon, popping in to chat at the homes of rights workers at the end of a long evening or on weekends. The embassy no longer seemed an impenetrable, forbidding fortress. The .50-caliber machine guns mounted around the ambassador's residence and manned by marines were taken down. (It took months for the weapons, enough for an army, to be shipped back to the United States.) The corridors around Harris's office were jammed with people.[7]

"I remember the first time he came to my house," said rights activist Emilio Mignone, "Harris was doing advance work for Patricia Derian's first Argentina visit." One of Mignone's daughters, twenty-four-year-old Monica, had been kidnapped from his home at 5:00 one morning in May 1976. "When I was told there was this big yanqui from the embassy at the door, and that he wanted to talk about human rights, I almost couldn't believe it."[8]

Harris also put together the puzzle of the illegal repression, giving the lie to talk about "rogue" security forces. The bloodbath was part of a plan of systematic extermination of opponents. Praised by superiors for its clarity and depth, Harris's reporting was not larded with conclusions; rather, he forced others to make them on the basis of the extensive documentation he dug up. (Harris's reporting was complemented by access to the minutes of secret junta meetings, which the embassy received through unspecified channels.) "Tex demolished the myth of uncontrollable right-wing death squads right away," recalled Patt Derian aide Mark Schneider. "He had the chain of command running from Suárez Mason down to the Ford Falcon."[9]

Gutsy and straightforward, Derian—like her boss, Jimmy Carter—came to live in Washington only after the November elections. "She was an outsider, with no bureaucratic experience, and she had been made top dog in human rights," recalled Washington rights activist Joseph Eldridge. "It ruffled a lot of feathers." Nevertheless, Derian was tireless and effective. Aided by Schneider, a former Edward Kennedy staffer wise in the ways of Capitol Hill, she won wide leverage on policy, particularly on Argentina and Chile. In the sometimes ferocious bureaucratic infighting inside Foggy Bottom and with other government agencies, Derian received key support from the highly respected Christopher and from Vance himself. "What people sometimes forgot was that Patt also had the president," Eldridge said. "Every time he spoke about human rights, it strengthened Derian's position." And Carter spoke about them a lot. "The blessing was Jimmy Carter," Derian agreed. "He always put human rights in the top five of his yearly goals."[10]

Anti-Semitism: Echoes from the Past

It made for an odd moment. Miriam Lewin de García's torturers stopped their work to engage in a "philosophical" discussion. They asked her what she thought of the family as an institution; whether she believed in God. "They asked me in what era of history I would like to have lived," she said. "I told them that I would like to have lived in France during the era of the German invasion, and that I would have fought with the Maquis in the Resistance." Looking at her with disgust, they pointed out that whatever the historical period they found themselves in, she and they would be in opposing camps. "There was a swastika in the cell," she recalled.[11]

If there was a certain logic for Lewin de García, a Jew, to have chosen the French Resistance, there was also a transcendental consistency in her tormentors' choice of Nazi Germany. Had they lived in fifteenth-century Spain, her tormentors would have just as surely participated in the Inquisition. There was an archetypical familiarity between the rack, the gas chamber, and the Argentine *chupadero* and a common mind-set, a perverse logic, among those using them.

Anti-Semitism was one of the most common denominators of the security forces and their war against "the realm of darkness." About 1,500 Jews disappeared during military rule, far more than the community's representation—about one percent—within the population at large. The Mossad, Israel's foreign intelligence agency, had to intervene with a secret operation conducted out of the Uruguayan capital of Montevideo that saved hundreds of lives. Once people entered the dungeons of secret repression, however, it was virtually impossible to get them released.[12]

Posters of Hitler, swastikas, Nazi tape recordings and flags, and ritual debasement of Jewish prisoners were found throughout the state security system. Alfonsín, a leader of the Permanent Assembly for Human Rights, once complained to the Delegación de Asociaciones Israelitas Argentinas (DAIA; Delegation of Argentine Israelite Associations), Argentina's foremost Jewish group, about an army officer who was showing anti-Semitic films at a union headquarters. Government officials told the DAIA the screenings were unauthorized. The officer was Mohamed Alí Seineldín, the onetime nexus between the army and the Triple A, who frequently harangued his troops with the cry, "Remember, boys, there are no such things as green horses or honorable Jews."[13]

While defenders of the regime claimed no one went missing solely for being Jewish, a better test was that finding prisoners not Jewish was cause for better treatment and even survival. A tall blond plumber held in a secret camp in Buenos Aires province found a swastika tattooed on his arm as a child helped improve his diet. In another, a sixteen-year-old's trip to Israel, where she represented Argentina in the Chess Olympics, was cause for closer questioning. "They were very anti-Semitic," she said, adding, "I'm not Jewish." A police corporal at the SS Federal, the police intelligence headquarters, said a special Nazi lodge sprung up among the security detail. "They passed out Nazi magazines, and the people who carried out raids used green jackets, black berets, armbands and Nazi crosses," he said. "They commented that subversion would end when there were no more Jews."[14]

Il Onorevole (The Honorable) Licio Gelli

Licio Gelli pulled out all stops in his quest for influence in the Southern Cone of South America. In July 1976 the Italian had created in Rio de Janeiro the Organización Mundial para la Asistencia Masónica (OMPAM; World Organization for Masonic Thought and Help), which he hoped would give him ascendancy over world Masonry. Supported by the Brazilian Guanabara lodge, Gelli made contact with important sectors of the military. As 1977 unfolded he and his friend Umberto Ortolani established a base of operations in military-run Uruguay. There Gelli counted on the support of Gen. Luis Queirolo, the army chief of staff. Argentina's ambassador to Uruguay was also an important local member. Ortolani was president of BAFISUD, a bank that became Uruguay's largest.[15]

In Uruguay Gelli found shelter in some of the world's strictest banking secrecy laws and was aided by some of the globe's laxest currency exchange regulations. He transformed a villa in Montevideo's posh Carrasco suburb into a fortress. His dwelling was only 300 meters from Ortolani's moorish-style palace, equipped with a powerful radio transmitter.

Allied with Argentines Massera and Suárez Mason and Uruguayan officers such as Queirolo and Interior Minister Manuel Nuñez, Gelli wove a huge political and business network. Ortolani sold three newspapers he owned—*Il Corriere degli Italiani* in Buenos Aires, *La Hora de Italia* in Montevideo, and *Il Giornale d'Italia* in São Paolo—to the Italian Rizzoli group, whose executives were P-2 members. He and Gelli created more than 200 stock companies—many headquartered in Montevideo in the P-2 owned Artigas building—and bought large farms. Scores of apartments in the exclusive beach resort of Punta del Este and 1,800 lots near its tony Club del Lago, with a total value of some $80 million, were added to their empire. The BAFISUD established ten branches in Uruguay, a subsidiary in São Paolo, and offices in Rome and Geneva.[16]

Gelli did not neglect business in Argentina. By 1977 Italian investments in Argentina were greater than those of any other country; Italy also ranked a strong second in trade. And there was the prospect of more to come. Videla, Massera, and Agosti had decided to spend $6 billion on modernizing Argentina's armed forces by 1980.[17]

The Death of Rodolfo Walsh

A year after the coup Rodolfo Walsh sent an open letter to the junta, then celebrating its first anniversary. His friend, Colombian novelist Gabriel García

Márquez, called the letter "one of the jewels of universal literature." In it Walsh charged that the military had helped disgrace Isabel's government. The chance for democratic renewal, he wrote, not Perón's ephemeral presidency, was entombed by their seizure of power.

Borrowing an invective style learned by reading ancient Roman texts, Walsh took aim at the "most profound terror ever known by Argentine society." Fifteen thousand *desaparecidos,* 10,000 prisoners, 4,000 dead, and tens of thousands of exiles, he said, were the result.

> The junta's refusal to publish the names of its prisoners is a cover-up of the systematic execution of hostages in barren fields in early hours of the morning, using the pretext of imaginary combat or phony efforts to escape.
>
> Extremists who leaflet rural areas, paint [slogans on] irrigation canals or pile 10 into vehicles that catch fire are the stereotypes of a libretto that is not meant to be believed but rather to mock international reaction to the orderly executions, while internally they underscore the fact they are reprisals unleashed in the same places of, and immediately after, guerrilla actions.

The murder of prisoners in reprisals for guerrilla attacks formed "part of 1,200 executions in 300 supposed combats in which no guerrillas were wounded and forces at your command had no deaths. ... The summary execution of guerrillas wounded or captured in real combat is shown in a year's military communiqués that attribute to the guerrillas 600 dead and only 10 or 15 wounded, a proportion unknown in the fiercest of combats."

Walsh mocked

> the fiction of right-wing bands, the presumed heirs of López Rega's Triple A, capable of crossing the country's largest base in military trucks, carpeting the Río de la Plata with dead, or throwing prisoners into the ocean from cargo planes from the First Air Brigade, without the knowledge of Gen. Videla, Adm. Massera and Brig. Agosti. ... The junta on which you sit is not the just arbiter between "two terrorisms," but rather the very source of a terror that has lost its bearings and only stutters in a discourse of death. ...
>
> These acts, which rattle the conscience of the civilized world, are not, however, the worst suffering you have brought to the Argentine people nor the worst violations of human rights you have carried out. In the government's economic policies one finds not only an explanation for its crimes but a greater atrocity that punishes millions of human beings with planned misery.

The next day, March 25, Walsh was killed by members of the ESMA task group a few blocks away from the Congress building in downtown Buenos Aires. Realizing he was being followed, Walsh had begun to run, stooping to extract a gun he had hidden in his boot. (The weapon was a small-caliber pistol he had been given years before by his wife.) Walsh died in a burst of machine-gun fire. He was fifty years old.

When he was cut down, Walsh was going to meet José M. Salgado, a former police officer who had put the bomb in Coordinación Federal the previous July. Unknown to Walsh, Salgado had been caught by the police, tortured, and handed over to the navy. The ESMA group wanted Walsh captured alive. (Mutilated beyond recognition, Salgado was returned to the *federales,* who executed him. He was reported killed in a shoot-out.) Of Argentina's newspapers only the *Buenos Aires Herald* reported Walsh's disappearance.[18]

A month after Walsh was killed, three Montonero leaders—Mario Firmenich, Fernando Vaca Narvaja, and Rodolfo Galimberti—surfaced at a press conference in Rome. They announced the formation of a "Peronist Montonero movement." (Before fleeing from Argentina, Galimberti bragged to intimates, he ordered a series of extortive kidnappings in northern Buenos Aires so he could pay his personal expenses while in exile.) Firmenich, who had slipped out of Argentina in December, was tapped as secretary-general of the new party. Two Peronist governors who had been purged by López Rega—Obregón Cano of Córdoba and Oscar Bidegain of Buenos Aires—were also present. So were former University of Buenos Aires rector Rodolfo Puiggrós and some twenty foreign journalists.[19]

The Peronist-Montoneros called for immediate elections and demanded the resignation of Martínez de Hoz, the restoration of constitutional rights and guarantees, and the rehabilitation of all political parties. They also called for the restoration of the CGT, "the freeing of all political prisoners, the suppression of concentration camps, and publication of a complete list of detainees." Firmenich said his aim was to turn Argentina into a socialist state through free elections. A military rejection of their demands would result in further violence, he said.

Three days before the press conference, García Márquez published an interview with Firmenich he conducted in Havana in the Italian magazine *L'Espresso.* Entitled "Tomorrow in the Casa Rosada," it was billed: "South America's greatest writer interrogates the continent's most wanted guerrilla." In the interview, García Márquez noted that in the year they held power the generals had "exterminated" the armed resistance. "Now, you, the Montoneros, don't have anything to do, at least militarily. You're dead."

Firmenich's response, García Márquez wrote, was dry and quick. From October 1975 on, the Montonero claimed,

> we knew there would be a coup within a year. We did nothing to stop it because the coup also formed part of the battle within Peronism. We made our calculations, war calculations, and in the first year prepared ourselves for human losses of no less than 1,500 units. We figured the following: If we were able to lose fewer than that number we were assured that sooner or later we would win. And what happened? Our losses were less than we predicted. Meanwhile, the dictatorship is exhausted. It doesn't have any other escape valves, while we enjoy a great prestige among the masses, and in Argentina we are the surest political option for the immediate future.

Firmenich's "arrogant, precise and eloquent response" did not convince the novelist, who saw it as "calculated optimism." García Márquez was unable to escape the impression that—above all—he was speaking to a "man of war. In effect, Mario Firmenich has had little time to dedicate himself to anything else but war, since he was born in 1948 in Buenos Aires."

Recalling the circumstances surrounding Aramburu's murder, García Márquez continued. "When I suggested that the Montoneros lacked the capacity for political choices, that they only think of the military aspect of a problem, Firmenich reacted energetically. I insisted, repeating that a military solution seemed to be the extreme, danger-filled alternative remaining open to the Montoneros." García Márquez, the man who later won a Nobel Prize for his "magic realism"—baroque fantasies of misshapen characters peopling the continent—concluded: "Firmenich is the strangest man I've ever met in my life."[20]

Carlos Maguid

In April Carlos Maguid was kidnapped near his home in the tony San Isidro neighborhood of the Peruvian capital. He was transferred to the ESMA. Like his sister-in-law, Norma Arrostito, Maguid was a founder of the Montoneros and took part in the 1970 abduction of former President Pedro Aramburu. Freed by the amnesty decreed by Cámpora, Maguid broke with the Montoneros in 1973. Maguid's kidnapping and death were part of the navy effort to show that the Montoneros were working with army men loyal to Onganía when Aramburu was killed.[21]

The Timerman Affair

On April 15 Jacobo Timerman was abducted from his home by a civilian-dressed army commando. "Disappeared" for several weeks, Timerman was interrogated by Gen. Ramón Camps, the anti-Semitic chief of the Buenos Aires police. He later testified that he was brutally tortured. According to a U.S. embassy document, Timerman's arrest formed part of a "war plan" by army sectors led by I Army Corps commander Gen. Guillermo Suárez Mason and Buenos Aires provincial governor Gen. Ibérico Saint Jean against the Videla government. The plan, it said, included the January disappearance of labor leader Oscar Smith; a letter bomb sent to journalist and Viola ally Rodolfo Fernández Pondal; and the April 1 kidnap-disappearance of another *La Opinión* executive, Edgardo Sajón, the former press secretary to President Lanusse. The actions targeted Lanusse and those who saw him as a possible transition figure back to civilian rule. "The army has rejected General Vilas' request to convene a special military court of honor to review ex-President Lanusse's statements in connection with the disappearance of his former civilian aide Edgardo Sajón," U.S. Ambassador Hill noted in a secret cable. Lanusse "quietly let it be known to ... Videla that if he were made to stand trial he would be compelled to reveal his files implicating high-ranking ... military officers in crooked financial schemes."[22]

The weapon in the "hard-liners'" assault, the embassy said, was the financial and political scandal surrounding Argentine banker David Graiver, who died the year before in a mysterious plane crash in the mountains of Mexico. The military charged that Graiver's financial empire served as a business front for recycling millions of dollars of hot Montonero money. By 1976 he headed a booming international investment business with holdings in Argentina, Mexico, Panama, Venezuela, Belgium, and Luxembourg. But Graiver died just before two of his most important holdings—a New York bank and one in Brussels—collapsed, leaving creditors holding the bag for $50 million. (The closing of Graiver's American Bank and Trust Company was at the time the fourth largest banking failure in U.S. history.)[23]

Paunchy and simpático, the goateed financial whiz kid spun a web of connections throughout Argentina's business, political, and military establishments. A former top official of the Social Welfare Ministry during the Lanusse government, Graiver counted among his friends Monsignor Antonio Plaza, the reactionary archbishop of La Plata, and Alejandro Orfila, secretary-general of the Organization of American States. Lanusse's son and daughter had worked in his private office and Graiver had helped former Economy Minister José Ber Gelbard set up major aluminum and newsprint plants. He was also the secret owner of 45 percent of the stock of Timerman's *La Opinión*. The truth about Graiver's relationship to the Montoneros may never be known. A book written much later by a former Montonero seemed to confirm the connection, yet at the time of the scandal a top secret embassy report suggested that Argentine military intelligence admitted there was no proof to the accusations. This view was buttressed in the embassy's deliberations by the fact that they knew that Montonero leader Roberto Quieto, "disappeared" since December 1975, was still—nearly a year and a half later—secretly collaborating with the army in an attempt to save his own life.[24]

The Graiver affair created a great unease among Argentina's Jewish community. Graiver, Gelbard, and Timerman were Jews—as were nearly all the others arrested in the probe. Details of the case were leaked to Diana Julia de Massot, a notoriously anti-Semitic newspaper owner whose daily *La Nueva Provincia* worked closely with Gen. Acdel Vilas. For Camps the case was proof of an international Jewish conspiracy. The DAIA, an association of Argentine Jewish organizations, went public to condemn "dark and pogromist forces."[25]

Timerman's arrest became part of a larger polemic over human rights in Argentina. To some, military anti-Semitism and Timerman's willingness to publish a few news items about the missing were at the root of his detention. Others claimed his checkered past proved as good a case as any for giving the regime the benefit of the doubt.

British journalist James Neilson defended Timerman from the pages of the *Buenos Aires Herald* when most of his Argentine colleagues remained silent or joined the lynch mob. Nonetheless, Neilson later wrote: "Timerman ... helped make Argentina the kind of society in which thousands of people could be made to 'disappear' and prominent newspaper owners could be jailed and tortured without anyone batting an eyelid. ... He apologized for its governments, understated their shortcomings, and explained away their lapses. ... Had he been overlooked by the 'hardliners' he could easily have become one of the most effective propagandists of the 'process.' ... That, indeed, was the role he was beginning to assume when he was seized."[26]

Argentina's "Jewish Problem"

Anti-Semitism under the military was often violent, but it also could be insidious. In June *Carta Política,* edited by Mariano Grondona (who was described the year before as "well known to and well regarded by this embassy" in an American diplomatic cable to Washington), carried a cover story that proposed a solution to Argentina's "Jewish problem." It claimed that "the Jews form rich, liberal, nonconformist collectives in the world." The article called for Argentina's "Jewish minority" to be "subsumed" into the population. Saying "the Jewish problem [was] in the last analysis genetic," the magazine warned that Argentina's future was one "without genetic barriers."

"In the current atmosphere of violent repression," charged the Council on Hemispheric Affairs (COHA) from Washington, "Argentina has more political prisoners than the rest of Latin America combined—such an article can only be seen as a call for further violence. ... Editor Grondona, long an apologist for the Videla regime," COHA continued, "is well known in Argentina as a forceful opponent of organized labor. He is also highly recognized within military circles for his support and promotion of Argentina's armed forces."[27]

Patt Derian: "No More Thumbscrews"

The military greeted Patt Derian's three trips with a mixture of curiosity and trepidation. "They would sweat and their hands would tremble," she said. "Videla shook during our meeting. They were always very courteous with me, but later pretended they had been very tough." One exception was Interior Minister Harguindeguy, who, when she pressed him on the Timerman case, "acted like a big, macho character, getting louder and louder, so I talked softer." (The general later complained to Timerman: "Who is that woman, your cousin?")

At unofficial receptions officers sidled up to her. "It was like getting close to the tiger. They had the habit of blurting things out. They were nervous, itchy, and felt compelled to speak. 'No, we don't do that, but so and so does.' Specific bits of information about their service would follow. They'd say, 'No, it's [the torture chamber] down in the basement, on the bottom floor where they have all the apparatus. It's terrible. Terrible.'"

In Buenos Aires Derian's party was followed by four cars. One was from the embassy. A U.S. security officer told her the other three represented the army, the navy, and the air force. They were not so much watching her, he said, as keeping an eye on one another. "They're afraid one of them is going to do something to you, and they'll get the blame." Derian met with a broad cross section of society, an aide taking notes of what was said. U.S. businessmen noted that labor relations had improved and productivity increased since the military took power. "The American community in Argentina thought the [human rights] policy was outrageous, that repression was needed and that Argentines were used to it." Soldiers told her they were forced to kill or would themselves be killed for disobeying orders. Officials spoke of Zionist plotting against Argentina. "At first I thought it was meant to be some kind of a joke," Derian said. "At the foreign ministry I was told Israel was behind most of Argentina's problems, that the Jews wanted their land." When Derian visited the ESMA, Massera told her flatly, "The navy doesn't torture, it's the army and air force that do it."

The Argentine military were not the only ones resisting the Carter rights message. Defense attachés and intelligence operatives stationed in the U.S. embassy in Buenos Aires found it hard to get in step with the new policies. The CIA felt rights reporting was not its mandate. A U.S. diplomat claimed the agency's input went from "minimal to zero." The U.S. military, Derian recalled, "was passing the word that once Carter knew the truth, he'd lay off, that he was a kind of dumb idealist and the human rights policy wouldn't really amount to anything; and lastly, that he wouldn't be president forever."

In a meeting with U.S. embassy personnel, Derian explained the ban on aid and military sales to the regime. An older, overweight, and overwrought military attaché stood up to question her. He praised the Argentine military and its "war against communist subversion." Derian wasn't making any sense, he complained. What was this new policy about? "I'll explain it to you," Derian shot back. "We're not going to sell thumbscrews anymore. You got it now?"[28]

When Derian returned to her office in Washington she talked to the head of the U.S. military's Southern Command (Southcom) in Panama, complaining that U.S. policy was being subverted. She also wrote a twelve-page memorandum about what she had learned. One of the headings was "The U.S. military and our intelligence agencies." She wrote:

> Through these agencies the United States government is sending a dangerous and double message. If this continues, it will subvert our entire human rights policy. ...
>
> This is the signal problem our government has in human rights. The only hope we have to gain support for our initiatives and to advance the cause of human rights is to make sure that governments understand that we are serious, and committed to our human rights policies. ...

If they believe and are told by U.S. government officials that we are not serious and committed, they are going to try to wait us out and feel betrayed when we press on.

Derian also had several suggestions. "The President as Commander in Chief [should] send a message to all branches of the armed forces stating unequivocally the human rights policy of the U.S. government, outlining the duty of the military in this regard," Derian wrote.

The President [should] instruct the CIA, the FBI and all other intelligence agencies on the human rights policy of the U.S. government. ... Courses in human rights [should] be designed and implemented at once in all service academies, military training institutes and intelligence schools ... [and] those members of the armed forces and intelligence services who cannot comply with U.S. government policies on human rights [should] be immediately separated from their services.[29]

Mothers of the Plaza de Mayo Get an Audience

Amid the terror, on April 30 the Mothers of the Plaza de Mayo held their first rally in an effort to force an interview with Videla. The president ducked meeting them. On May 11 Interior Minister Harguindeguy granted an audience to a delegation of three women. One was Azucena Villaflor de Vicenti, a founder of the mothers' group. The meeting began shortly after 7:30 P.M. Harguindeguy showed the women a detailed notebook listing "priority" *desaparecidos.* They were the children of officers, public officeholders, or others who had the access to bring the matter directly to his attention. Harguindeguy led with a standard excuse. "This is the work of gangs over whom we have no control," he said. "But, sir," Villaflor replied, "if you as interior minister and as a general cannot control these groups, what are you doing here in the ministry?"

Another woman was the wife of a retired lieutenant colonel. Her husband belonged to the same class as the general, an important link in Argentina's caste-conscious, peer-oriented military. Their pregnant daughter had been missing for a year. "Your daughter hasn't reappeared yet?" Harguindeguy asked. "But I thought she had reappeared.

"Ladies, I myself had to get a niece of mine out of the country, I took her to Mexico and I'll tell you ... there in Mexico there are a lot of girls who have gone, who have gone ... and some are prostitutes, making people believe they've disappeared. But tell me, your children ... maybe the boys went off with some woman, look, kids sometimes ... "[30]

Massera Rolls the Dice

In the second quarter of 1977 a group of navy men put together a plan tailor-made for their commander-in-chief's political debut. The government, they said in a private document, "ought to create its civic movement or political party using leaders who are in full agreement with its own objectives. ... We must avoid the error of earlier military governments, which didn't publicize what had been done under their rule at the right time, out of archaic concepts concerning self-promotion and support."[31]

In substance the navy's plan differed little from that of the army hard-liners. It lamented the predominance of Marxist and old-world liberalism in Argentine politics and proclaimed nationalism to be "a permanent center of political thinking." Workers preferred authoritarian regimes, it said, and creating a political party was "the most appropriate solution as it assures, to the greatest extent possible, that the government will be its own heir."

Massera busily tried to nail down a political base. The darkly handsome playboy—who some thought resembled tango great Carlos Gardel—wanted to lead the civic movement envisioned by his admirals. The army's weakest flank was the junta's economic plan, whose financial reform had caused a sharp recession. Massera began to direct his barbs at Martínez de Hoz.

Massera sent former Peronist deputy Luis Sobrino Aranda, long linked with the military intelligence services, on a European tour. Sobrino Aranda's mission was to establish connections in social democratic circles and with the tens of thousands of Argentine exiles living there. Massera then traveled to Europe. In Paris he met with the vice president of the Socialist International, Chilean Anselmo Sule, accompanied by Sobrino Aranda. Massera told Sule that Argentina's only hope was a solution based on social democratic principles. He insisted he needed to see as many world leaders as possible, mentioning Willy Brandt, Felipe González, and François Mitterrand. Massera later met with Sobrino Aranda and four other former members of the Peronist parliamentary Grupo de Trabajo at a Madrid hotel.

According to one account, Massera said there were only two political projects in Argentina, his and Viola's. The latter, he said, consisted of putting together the greatest number of politicians. It would be to try, with old structures and old men, to give solutions that require new structures and new men. Among those sharing Viola's hopes for the future, Massera added, were Peronists Robledo, Bittel, and Luder and Radical leader Balbín.

Massera said he proposed the creation of a "great national movement," where there would be a place for an intelligent left (where Peronism would have an important role) and a controlled right. He proposed a social democratic program in all its aspects, one that would be the only alternative capable of pulling the country out of the current chaos caused by Martínez de Hoz's economic policies.

Massera charged that the economic policies of Martínez de Hoz not only had made the Argentine middle class disappear but also had brought the country to the brink of disaster, adding, "I'm going to publicly ask for Martínez de Hoz's resignation, probably in November."[32]

One of the topics that most concerned army intelligence was Massera's repeated promise that he would give out a list of detainees held by the navy. During the talks, Massera revealed that at the last meeting of the junta, he had made the suggestion to the army. The generals, he added, had the greatest need to make a clean breast of things. Videla, he said, replied: "I need that as much as you do, because I know if we don't the situation will become untenable. But I can't. It's already out of my control—without risking unleashing something worse. I hope this ends soon, but to hand out a list is for me impossible."[33]

Missing Envoy Hidalgo Solá: A P-2 Connection?

On July 18 Argentine ambassador to Venezuela Héctor Hidalgo Solá, considered by some to be sensitive to human rights concerns, disappeared. An associate of Radical leader Ricardo Balbín, he had taken the post on the advice of the older man and other conservative party leaders. His appointment had been portrayed by some as a limited opening by the Viola wing of the army to the politicians, who were then to help cover the military's flanks as they partially retreated to the barracks. A few days before Hidalgo Solá was kidnapped, his wife went to tea with Raquel Hartridge de Videla, the president's wife, at the Campo de Mayo army base. There Raquel Videla expressed concern for Hidalgo Solá's safety. Recalled Delía de Hidalgo Solá: "She told me my husband had better be wary of Admiral Massera."[34]

Hidalgo Solá was abducted by civilian-dressed men using three cars at a busy intersection outside the fine arts museum in downtown Buenos Aires. His replacement at the head of the Argentine embassy arrived in Caracas in thirty-six hours. The rapid change was unusual for Massera's foreign ministry. The new ambassador was a close friend of Licio Gelli. Like the navy chief, he was a member of the P-2.[35]

Phantom Armies

In early 1977 a top-secret U.S. embassy briefing memorandum said that the Argentine army, in a "spectacular coup," was able to recover $85 million in Montonero money secretly hidden away in Argentina and abroad. Despite the seeming propaganda bonanza, the news of the army's breakthrough was never reported in the Argentine press. In mid-July a document written by "a group of detained Montoneros" two months earlier was given to the press by the army. Given prominent display in *La Nación*, it said that "today, May 1977," the Montoneros "were close to being exterminated." The guerrillas' exiled leadership, it charged, traveled around the world "spreading a false image of Montonero strength, one completely at odds with the reality of near annihilation." These leaders were spreading propaganda that "a nonexistent Montonero Movement had reached a membership of 200,000 or 300,000, with an almanac with the photo of Mr. Firmenich publicizing 200 military operations in the first trimester of 1977, operations that existed only in the imagination of the organization's 'military chiefs.'"

The guerrilla threat had become an accordion in the generals' hands, expanding and contracting according to the tune they wanted people to hear. Four months after the captured Montoneros said the organization was "being exterminated ... near annihilation," the Buenos Aires bureau of *Time* sent a dispatch to New York: "On the admission of security force sources, approximately 12,000 members of the Montoneros are still at large, mostly tactical support groups of the 'Column-25 West' in the southern belt of greater Buenos Aires."[36]

The P-2: Multiple and Murky Relationships

Rodolfo Fernández Pondal, assistant manager of *Ultima Clave,* may have been the first journalist to be killed in Argentina after stumbling upon the secretive P-2. The weekly newsletter was linked to army sectors loyal to Videla, especially Generals Viola and Jorge C. Olivera Rovere, and to conservative Radical politicians. When Hidalgo Solá was kidnapped, *Ultima Clave* campaigned to win his release. Unknown at the time, Hidalgo Solá's replacement as ambassador in Caracas was a Gelli confidant.

"Naturally all the kidnappings carried out by the guerrillas and other subversive elements are political acts," *Ultima Clave* stated in its edition of July 26. "But the Hidalgo Solá episode has in a very direct way attacked the image of the government and the country, deepening the danger of international isolation." The regime must put an end to "direct subversion" and "illegal counterinsurgency, which is a manifest type of parallel subversion."

Reporting on another kidnapping 8,270 miles away, however, may have sealed Fernández Pondal's fate. On April 13 Luchino Revelli Beaumont, director-general of FIAT in France and Brazil, was abducted by four armed men as he left his home in Paris. He was freed eighty-nine days later. His captors received $2 million in ransom, as well as publication of full-page advertisements in major world newspapers justifying the crime. The money was paid at La Machine bridge in Geneva, the same place the Montoneros received their ransom for the release of the Born brothers. It was said to have been deposited in accounts in the same banks.[37]

Revelli Beaumont's captors called themselves the Comité de Unificación para la Revolución Socialista (CURS; Committee for the Unification of the Socialist Revolution). Before carrying out the kidnapping, the group had investigated the financial interests controlling FIAT, discovering, for example, that Muammar Kaddafi—a key figure in Gelli's web of international contacts—was an important stockholder. The CURS was made up of a small group of Argentine exiles, almost all former members of the FAP. The others did not know it, but one—Horacio Francisco Rossi—was an Argentine military intelligence informant. (Six Argentines and an Italian who waited for Rossi in Madrid's Barajas airport were arrested by Spanish police. They were later charged with complicity in the kidnapping.)[38]

Revelli Beaumont had played a key role in events in Argentina. He was Oberdan Sallustro's boss when the Italian was abducted in 1972 by the ERP and later killed in a police rescue operation. Revelli Beaumont had narrowly escaped being kidnapped the year before by a small Peronist guerrilla group. He put Gelli's front man, Giancarlo Elía Valori, as the head of public relations for Perón when the general visited Rome in 1972. He was also a friend of López Rega.[39]

On August 2, 1977, *Ultima Clave* published a cover story entitled "Perón's Gang." In the meandering fashion of Argentine newsletters, and without ever mentioning Gelli or the P-2, *Ultima Clave* traced the shadowy hand of both through the political violence that wracked Argentina. It touched upon Revelli Beaumont's ties to Perón and Valori, Perón's visit with Romanian Premier Nicolai Ceausescu (an important P-2 set piece despite being on the wrong side of the Iron Curtain), and Valori's efforts to get the exiled general an audience with Pope Paul VI. It suggested that Revelli Beaumont paid for the 1972 Alitalia charter from Rome that brought Perón home. It hinted at the "suggestive antecedents" of Rossi, the guerrilla who had been a friend of ultra-right-wing Brigadier Lacabanne and part of López Rega's custody. It revealed that the Revelli Beaumont ransom was paid at the place where the Montoneros received their millions for the Born kidnapping. *Ultima Clave* added:

> Surely the most important revelation in the whole history of the [Revelli Beaumont] kidnapping is that its thread connects people who all knew each other: the kidnappers, the victim, the intermediaries. This is what comes to the fore in analyzing Juan Domingo Perón's multiple and always murky relationships. To see it, one only has to follow the threads that tied the corrupt, now-deceased caudillo with elements of the terrorist bands on one hand, and certain influential men in the world of business on the other.

Ultima Clave tied the strings around the figure of Perón, but it had touched upon the secret world of the P-2. Three days after the story was published, Fernández Pondal disappeared. On August 20 *La Razón* reported that the kidnapping was the work of the Montoneros. Although the navy tried to keep his abduction a secret, at least half a dozen witnesses saw Fernández Pondal in the ESMA. He was later killed.[40]

"Tiger's" Lair

Capt. Jorge Acosta's alias was El Tigre (the Tiger), which he boasted was given to him by a French counterinsurgency instructor. As head of intelligence for the ESMA task group, the bilious Tiger was in charge of a "recuperation" experiment involving a small number of prisoners. Its purpose: using *desaparecidos* for a think tank and political advisory unit for Massera. A few prisoners were chosen after threats to themselves and their families.

Collaborators came in various categories. Some became partners of their captors, going out on "missions" with the task group to finger former friends and comrades. Others advised Massera on labor issues. Two even traveled with the navy chief to Europe. One worked in the Paris Pilot Center, an office dedicated to obtaining information on Argentine exiles in Europe and on human rights organizations. One woman worked, on orders from Massera, in the Foreign Ministry, after betraying many of her friends. Some collaborators did logistic and maintenance chores, and others did clerk duties, or "intelligence and counter-information tasks." These duties included the classification of books and magazines, translations, and the archiving of documents.[41]

Collaborators helping to hunt down their comrades were known as *marcadores* (markers) or *quebrados* (the broken ones). They participated in torture sessions, lived separated from other prisoners in special quarters, and enjoyed better food and treatment. Toward the end of 1977 they were granted semiliberty, laboring in the camp during the day, returning to their own homes to sleep. A few became naval intelligence informants or worked in civilian naval posts.

Some became even more intimately involved with their torturers. *Marcadora* Anita Dvatman married Lt. Jorge Radice, a task group leader and Massera adviser. Lucy Changazzo's husband died at the hands of Lt. Antonio Pernía, with whom she became involved in a prolonged relationship. Marta ("La Negra") Bazán, a hard-bitten montonera, was known in the ESMA as "Sargenta Coca." She found tenderness in the arms of the overweight but equally hard-bitten Rear Admiral Chamorro. (As Argentina neared democratic rule, Chamorro sought refuge abroad. Bazán went with him.)[42]

Bank union leader Andrés Castillo had to write a history of Argentine unions. He was told to show that labor groups had always been infiltrated by subversives. Journalist Raúl Lisandro Cubas was forced to interview César Luis Menotti, the sought-after technical director of Argentina's World Cup soccer team. Cubas's task was to get Menotti to speak favorably about the military junta. The *desaparecido* was taken from the ESMA by Lt. Juan C. Rolón to conduct the interview. A photo of the event was surreal: The missing Cubas interviewed a man sought out by the world press, under the watchful gaze of the navy man.[43]

"There Are No Rules"

Former Economy Minister José Ber Gelbard died in exile in Washington on October 5. The gruff, self-made businessman had been accused by the regime of misusing public funds. One of thirty-six Peronists charged with having brought economic chaos to the country, Gelbard was the only one whose citizenship was revoked. The military loaded their accusations with anti-Semitic innuendoes, tarring him with ties to David Graiver. The story was a familiar one: In the 1930s Gelbard and his family had fled the pogroms in Poland. "Argentine officials have acknowledged privately that Gelbard's being Jewish was a factor in the decision to lift his citizenship," *Washington Post* reporter Lewis Diuguid wrote in December 1976. "In the virtual civil war between armed extremists over the past three years, Jewish targets have been singled out by the extreme right. The government has yet to jail a single rightist extremist."

In the last months of his life Gelbard had spent much time on getting Latin American political leaders together at a conference in Washington. The subject was to be democracy and human rights. He also offered a view of doing business in Argentina that captured the essence of a country where the rule of law had been under siege for nearly fifty years: "There are no rules. Those who are in power make up the rules. So those out of favor are bound to break them."[44]

Life in the "Fish Bowl"

While Massera sought to create a Social Democratic party in the image of Willy Brandt, in the dungeons of the ESMA the image was of the "other German"— Adolf Hitler. In October the *Pecera* (Fish Bowl) came into its own. A France-Press teletype machine belonging to the Foreign Ministry was installed. A file was constructed on the basis of clippings from the old Montonero newspaper *Noticias,* which had been robbed from the house of left-wing Peronist parliamentary deputy Miguel Domingo Zavala Rodríguez after he was killed by members of the ESMA task group. Treated like trophies, the *recuperados* ("recovered" ones) worked in the glass-paneled offices of the Fish Bowl. They moved about dragging the chains of the shackles that bound their feet, under the watchful eye of closed-circuit television. The prisoners clipped and filed local and international newspapers and put together programs for the RAE, Argentina's shortwave radio network.[45]

Opposed to any projected "political opening" sponsored by the army, Massera secretly prepared his own political party. In the Pecera, a group of prisoners put together action plans and programs for use by the navy chief. Antonio Nelson Latorre, a top Montonero military leader, studied the platform of the West German Social Democratic party, from which Massera wanted to crib for his own project. A report was prepared on investing abroad, including details about banks in Panama, Luxembourg, the Bahamas, Switzerland, and Liechtenstein. Montoneros also worked on studies of territorial conflicts—with neighboring Chile and Brazil and with Britain over the Falklands/Malvinas. If the navy had conventional defense issues with which to compete with the army, they thought, it might possible to turn its attention away from the "dirty war."[46]

Alfredo Astiz: The Blond Angel of Death

In January 1977 Lt. Alfredo Astiz, the ESMA's "blond angel," shot and then abducted a seventeen-year-old girl, stuffing her into the trunk of a commandeered taxi. Later the same year the intelligence official infiltrated a group of mothers and relatives of missing people who had begun to organize. Using the name Gustavo Niño, he feigned being the brother of a *desaparecido*. With a pretext of donating money, Astiz arranged a meeting with Azucena Villaflor de Vicenti, a founder of the Mothers of the Plaza de Mayo. Boyish, blue-eyed, and full of apparent dedication, Astiz became a favorite among the women. He was a fixture at their meetings and at the lonely marches they held every Thursday in front of the presidential palace. He was often accompanied by Silvia Labayru, an ESMA prisoner who was forced to act as "Gustavo Niño's" sister.

The mothers planned an important meeting in the Santa Cruz Church in Buenos Aires on December 8. It was a particularly difficult month for the women. The holidays were approaching. Feelings of uncertainty and desperation jabbed at the heart, for some unbearably. There was a lot of work to be done. Said one participant: "We were putting the final touches on a 'A Christmas of Peace' advertisement we wanted to publish in *La Nación* on the 10th, the 'Day of the Rights of Man.' Those who weren't able to come to the marches at Plaza de Mayo or contribute before, came with money or signed their names on our petition."[47]

That afternoon about fifteen people coordinated the effort from a little room in the annex of the church. One was Sister Alice Domon, a French nun who worked with the Ecumenical Movement for Human Rights and was secretary to the bishop of Quilmes. She had already been threatened for her work with the church's Agrarian Leagues among the peasants of the northern province of Chaco. When Astiz showed up, he added his "name" to the advertisement but seemed unhappy that Azucena Villaflor was not among the group. When the meeting was about to end, he abruptly left the church. Outside Astiz signaled to the waiting ESMA task force.

Walking along a path leading across the parish garden, the mothers and their friends left by a side gate. There the kidnappers waited. Dragging her by the hair, they bound and beat Sister Alice as they threw her into a car. Most of the rest suffered similar fates. Two days later, Villaflor and sister Leonie Duquet, another French missionary, were kidnapped. They, too, ended up in the ESMA.[48]

About that time, Montonero Horacio Domingo Maggio had escaped from the ESMA and launched his own one-man campaign of clandestine denunciations before being recaptured and killed. "It was the 11th or 12th of December," he said. "Both nuns were wearing civilian clothes and were very beaten and weak. When Sister Alice went to the bathroom she leaned on two guards, as she couldn't remain standing. I asked if they tortured her, and Alice told me they had, that they had tied her to a bed, totally nude, and applied electric current over her body." The nun had been tortured by both Acosta and Pernía. "Even in the worst moments of pain," recalled three prisoners who shared their captivity, "Sister Alice, who was in the *Capucha,* asked about the others. The height of irony was that she asked about 'that blond boy'—Astiz."[49]

The regime faced anxious queries from the French government, the superior of the nuns' order, and a number of French bishops. It attributed the abductions to an "extremist fraction." The next day the military said they had been kidnapped by Montoneros. The guerrillas, they said, demanded the release of twenty political prisoners and the granting of political asylum by France for all those politically persecuted in Argentina. A photo was also released of the two nuns, their faces etched with obvious discomfort. Posed before a Montonero poster they held a copy of *La Nación* from December 14. The Montoneros denied any participation in the act, expressing their "solidarity" with the nuns. Azucena Villaflor, Sister Leonie, and those kidnapped at the Santa Cruz Church were all later killed.[50]

Junta members Emilio Massera, Jorge R. Videla, and Orlando Agosti. The U.S. Defense Intelligence Agency later called the army leader "a genuinely nice person, very polite." (Courtesy Agencia Noticias Argentinas)

Gen. Carlos Guillermo Suárez Mason (*foreground*), a rabid anti-Peronist with an appetite for illegal enrichment, was also a key asset of Licio Gelli's P-2 masonic lodge. (Courtesy Página 12)

(*Top, left*): Short-story writer Rodolfo Walsh's life of activism reflected the increasing lawlessness of Argentine society. (Courtesy Página 12) (*Top, right*): Right-wing Catholic Mariano Grondona, a U.S. embassy favorite and anti-Peronist journalist, was both a propagandist for the military and an apologist for López Rega. (Courtesy Página 12) (*Bottom*): Videla with Cardinal Juan Carlos Aramburu: The church hierarchy offered the military both aid and comfort as they carried out their "dirty war." (Courtesy Presidencia de la Nación)

The murder of bishop Mons. Enrique Angelelli in a staged auto accident was a crushing blow to Argentina's "Church of the People." (Courtesy Editorial Esquiú)

Human rights activist Emilio F. Mignone, a lawyer-educator, was propelled to the forefront of the rights struggle by the disappearance of his own daughter. (Courtesy Página 12)

A demonstration by the Mothers of the Plaza de Mayo human rights group. Their brave and lonely struggle on behalf of their missing children became an international cause. (Reprinted by permission of Del Percio, Diarios y Noticias)

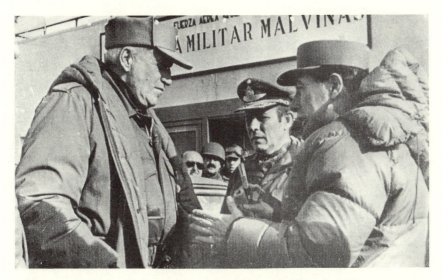

Strongman Gen. Leopoldo F. Galtieri confers with Falklands/Malvinas governor Gen. Mario Benjamín Menéndez. Against a real military foe, glory was short-lived. (Courtesy Agencia Noticias Argentinas)

An example felt 'round the hemisphere: Former military junta members Emilio Massera, Roberto Viola, and Basilio Lami Dozo enter federal courtroom during the 1985 trials of the nine former military commanders. Julio C. Strassera is at left. (Courtesy Agencia Noticias Argentinas)

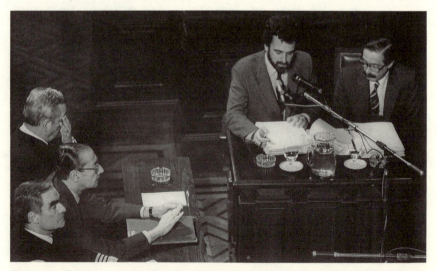

"Never again!" Former junta members Armando Lambruschini, Jorge R. Videla, and Emilio Massera listen to summation arguments of assistant federal prosecutor Luis Moreno O'Campo at historic 1985 trial, as prosecutor Julio C. Strassera observes. (Courtesy Agencia Noticias Argentinas)

President Raúl Alfonsín and reform Peronist Antonio Cafiero in Plaza de Mayo during the military crisis of Easter Week 1987. Despite showing great physical courage, the Argentine president lost crucial standing with an angry, anti-military populace. However, Alfonsín's government returned civility and the rule of law to an impoverished nation. (Courtesy Ricardo Cárcova)

Excavation of a mass grave in Avellaneda, Buenos Aires province, in 1988. (Courtesy Equipo Argentino de Antropología Forense)

21

Argentina's Killing Fields (1978-1980)

Let no one think the country is divided into private fiefdoms, let no one put the interests of a group before the interests of the country. This is a question of responsibility and therefore a question of morality.
—*Adm. Emilio Massera, June 17, 1978*

In early January 1978 the army sent an intelligence unit led by a "repented" Montonero, Tulio Valenzuela, to Mexico. Its task was to infiltrate the Montonero leadership exiled there, then kill key leaders. The plan ended in humiliating failure. For more than a year, II Army Corps chief Gen. Leopoldo Galtieri and an intelligence unit under his command had put together a staff of prisoner-collaborators. Lodged in a sprawling manor known as La Quinta de Funes outside Rosario, the detainees were mostly ranking Montoneros. By 1978 the guerrilla threat had ended. Yet in the house a printing press still cranked out Montonero newspapers and communiqués. A "Montonero documentation center" produced scores of IDs and phony credentials. Outside the camp the collaborators made contact with the few guerrillas still at large. Once in contact with the collaborators, the Montoneros were given tasks to carry out. Unknown to the guerrillas, their targets had been picked by the military. The Montoneros were later called to second rendezvous. There they were ambushed by the army. Brief military communiqués spoke of the "shoot-outs" between the insurgents and the forces of order.[1]

Valenzuela had feigned cooperation with the army in order to warn the Montonero high command of the danger. At the time he traveled to Mexico, Galtieri held his wife and son hostage. Nonetheless, once he arrived in the Mexican capital, Valenzuela blew the whistle on the unit, which was acting behind the backs of local authorities. (Contacted at the telephone number given to reporters from the Mexican newspaper *Uno Más Uno* by Valenzuela, Galtieri claimed: "I have no control over my agents outside the country.") The Mexican police arrested two Argentine army officers and a Buenos Aires police agent and promptly expelled them from the country. Like the the families of others held at the Quinta de Funes, Valenzuela's wife and child "disappeared." The Montonero leadership put him on trial for "treason." The charge: collaborating with the enemy. The same chiefs whose lives Valenzuela had tried to save stripped him of his rank. He returned to Argentina in a test of loyalty. There he was killed.[2]

Massera Cracks a Facade

The month the army sent its hit squad to Mexico, the regime rejected the arbitration findings made by England's Queen Elizabeth over a border dispute with Chile. At issue was the control of the Beagle Channel at the southern tip of South America and, by extension, Argentine territorial claims in the Antarctic. Army hard-liners joined Massera in warning that the time was running out for reaching a peaceful solution. On February 20 in the scenic southern Chilean city of Puerto Montt, Videla tried to open a new round of talks. He was rebuffed by Chilean strongman Augusto Pinochet. A few days later in Buenos Aires Massera, in the middle of a transformation from one of the foremost exponents of the antisubversive struggle to a hard-core nationalist, warned: "The time for words has ended."[3]

"The growing schism within the Argentine junta, pitting Massera and air force Gen. Orlando Agosti against Videla, is the first visible crack in the military monolith," reported the *Washington Post*. Massera's offensive, it said, included hints that the navy wanted to publish a complete list of prisoners being held. Aides said privately that he wanted those held in military camps and subject to secret trials handed over to the civilian courts. Massera, they said, wanted an early return to democracy and better relations with the United States. Carter, they said, should "see the Argentine navy as a human rights alternative." The newspaper noted that "while incidents of leftist terrorism have virtually stopped during the two years of junta rule, disappearances and allegations of torture and murder by the government have continued unabated. The elections that the junta says it eventually wants appear as far away as ever."[4]

As part of his bid for power Massera sought to widen his international contacts, particularly in Europe. Some of his trips were conducted in secrecy. Massera, said one former Argentine embassy employee, "traveled frequently to Paris without going through the embassy, which caused notice. In those trips he maintained direct contact with two officers who were part of the Pilot Center" the navy maintained in the French capital. The Pilot Center had been established the previous year by the regime in the face of the growing deterioration of Argentina's image abroad. Massera, however, had other plans. Under his direction, the center served as a base for infiltration of Argentine exile groups and the production of "psychological action" (propaganda) materials. These included the forging of letters from relatives of the missing, in order to cause confusion among the rights organizations. And there were also more personal matters. According to Ambassador Tomás Anchorena, the Argentine envoy to Paris and the creator of the center, "The center was Massera's own political propaganda and personal campaign unit."[5]

"But the ESMA's a School"

The Washington-based Council for Hemispheric Affairs had been one of the first groups to expose the massacre in Argentina. In December of 1978 a team of navy captains paid founder Larry Birns a visit. They tried to convince him that the admiral shared his concerns. In early 1978 Massera himself courted the rights gadfly. Birns met Massera in Washington at the Reservoir Road home of Associated Press correspondent Ary Moleon. There he pressed the sailor on rights issues, in particular, the detention of Jacobo Timerman. Massera called Videla a *maricón* (faggot). On human rights, however, he said the navy was "soft," whereas the army was "hard." As they parted, Massera tried slipping an expensive cigarette lighter into Birns's shirt pocket and gave him his private phone number. Birns, the scion of a wealthy family, returned to the subject of the Navy Mechanics School. "But Larry," Massera replied smoothly, "the ESMA's a school. Do you really think we torture people there?"[6]

The National Opinion Movement

On March 3, 1978, a meeting of army generals set down the "Political Bases of the National Reorganization Process." The project, which clashed with Massera's own plans, was called the Movimiento de Opinión Nacional (MON; National Opinion Movement). Although recognizing "the right to dissent in peace in a future democracy," ideologies the generals considered extremist and candidates they viewed as unfit were to be vetted. Only those who had completed a military-approved "political career" were eligible to compete. There were further limits to the generals' concessions. "In order to preserve the normal and efficient functioning of the democratic regime," they said, the political parties had to "share the national project conceived by the National Reorganization Project."

The MON was the brainchild of Viola aide Col. "Chovito" Cúneo. It had overcome strong opposition from within the army itself. Generals Menéndez, Díaz Bessone, and Riveros had opposed even mentioning "the political development of the National Reorganization Process" in the generals' meetings because they feared "a new Perón spawned from its womb." Rejecting "populist variants," they said they wanted to "return to the uncontaminated origins of the 'Process.'"[7]

Massera and the Montoneros

In April 1978 an article in *Le Monde* hinted at Massera's most secret activity in Paris—his meetings with Montonero leaders. The explosive scoop by the prestigious French newspaper was later confirmed by former Perón delegate Héctor Villalón, who said Massera "had met several times" with Montoneros both in Paris and Madrid. "I've seen them together personally." Massera, he said, had negotiated in the name of the junta a truce for the 1978 World Cup soccer games. On the eve of the games Firmenich promised that attacks would not be carried out during the event. The junta's all-out effort to turn the festivities into a propaganda boon went unmolested.[8]

Massera needed to line up a wide range of endorsements for his political ambitions. Some accord with the Montoneros was necessary in order to whitewash his own record as a dirty warrior. Massera later admitted to Máximo Gainza, publisher of *La Prensa*, he had been a part of a few conversations "with a few lower-ranking Montoneros."[9]

Kissinger Tends a Goal

The World Cup games held in June were the military's chance to show they had won popular acclaim by restoring stability and successfully repressing the guerrillas. The same day in 1976 that the junta overthrew Isabel Perón, Massera had told Videla and Agosti at a meeting that the navy considered that XI World Soccer Championship a top priority. Millions of dollars were spent sprucing up both the country and its image. Stadiums got face-lifts, color television was introduced, and suggestions made by the New York–based Burson-Marsteller advertising agency on how to combat Argentina's human rights image were carefully analyzed.[10]

Keeping a promise he made two years earlier two years in Santiago, Henry Kissinger attended the games. The presence of the generals' guest of honor was portrayed as proof of the junta's acceptance in the world. His friend Martínez de Hoz at his side, Kissinger criticized the Carter rights policies and asked for "understanding" for Argentina's military. When Argentina won the cup, the generals saw their dreams come true when wildly happy, flag-waving multitudes took to the streets.[11]

The World Cup celebration was immersed in corruption, intrigue, and violence. On August 21, 1976, the first president of the Ente Autárquico Mundial (EAM '78; World Cup Self-sustaining Entity 1978), retired Gen. Omar Actis, an army engineer known for his personal honesty, was murdered in the Buenos Aires suburb of Wilde in what was portrayed as a terrorist attack. He was replaced by Captain Alberto Lacoste, the commission vice president and a Massera intimate. Later investigations suggested that the murder had been committed by navy personnel. In 1982 the World Cup games were held in Spain at a cost of $100 million. In Argentina, four years earlier, they had cost $500 million. (*La Prensa's* Gainza estimated that Massera alone skimmed some $80 million from the production.) The EAM did not even present a final financial statement to the junta.[12]

One critic of Lacoste's stewardship was top economy official Juan Alemann. At 8:20 the night of June 21, 1978, as Argentina thrashed rival Brazil 4–0 in a crucial match, a powerful bomb exploded in front of Alemann's house. Its expansive wave extended some 150 feet, stopping just short of the 33rd Federal Police commissary. The elite army Grenadiers, rather than the police, arrived on the scene to investigate. The bomb had come from the navy.[13]

Et Tu, Licio?

Perhaps the most important of Gelli's businesses in Argentina was the locating in Buenos Aires of the Banco Ambrosiano, run by his partner Roberto Calvi. Having been set up in Argentina in 1978 as Ambrosiano Promociones y Servicios and run by a man belonging to the P-2, the bank quickly became involved in the financial black market and in arms trafficking. Massera maintained his own personal suite of offices where he would later establish his political headquarters on the tenth floor of a building at Cerrito 1136 in the elegant Barrio Norte neighborhood in Buenos Aires. Gelli's Ambrosiano occupied the ninth and eleventh floors of the same building. The bank's executive vice president, Carlos Natal Coda, was a former navy chief close to Massera. He was later named by the admiral as his point man with political and union sectors.

On May 19 Gelli wrote to a confidant that his friend Italian publisher Angelo Rizzoli—owner of the prestigious Milan-based Corrieri della Sera—had purchased 50 percent of the powerful Editorial Abril chain, which published the magazines *Siete Días, Vosotras,* and *Radiolandia 2000* in Argentina. "This is very important," Gelli said, "because 'the man of the waters' [meaning Massera] will be able to use them for his own plans." At a meeting held June 16 between Gelli, Rizzoli, Massera press spokesman Capt. Carlos Corti, and the Argentine naval attaché in Rome, the Masonic lodge leader noted that the Argentines "were sure Massera will be the next president." Corti, who was to be transferred to Rome, promised to introduce Gelli to his successor. "It will also be necessary to get to know Adm. Lambruschini, the new navy chief," Gelli noted. Rizzoli asked for advice about opening a television station in Argentina. In October 1977 Gelli had obtained an official invitation for Massera to visit La Spezia shipyards in Italy, where the Lupo frigates are made. A year later the Italian acted as the regime's intermediary in the purchase of radar and missiles from Italy's Selenia corporation. When the contract was signed, Selenia's president enrolled as a member of the P-2.[14]

Suárez Mason was active on behalf of the P-2 lodge as well. The general sent Gelli letters containing reserved information on bids for construction contracts involving hundreds of millions of dollars. "All is of interest, as there is much money involved already and you can get more and arrange things with Italian companies or with friends."[15]

Derian Fights Back

The summer of 1978 was a tough one for Patt Derian. Although she still enjoyed Carter's confidence, the human rights initiatives generated from her office collided with some hard realities. Powerful interests—both private and bureaucratic—had come together in an effort to gut the rights program. Arguments about domestic employment, balance of payments, profits, and military security were all brandished to circumvent the rights watchdogs. The Commerce and Treasury departments, the Pentagon, and private industry made their pitch in terms of jobs, trade, and overseas allies. (Low Latin labor costs, a major cause of job attrition and a result of the military's union-busting policies, were overlooked.) U.S. policy on Argentina became a prime target in the counteroffensive.[16]

In testimony before the House Inter-American Affairs Subcommittee, a defense industry spokesman bewailed sanctions against Argentina, claiming they cost an estimated $813.5 million in lost jobs. Beech Aircraft, fighting to retain a $10 million contract with Argentina—10 percent of its foreign sales—echoed the military regime's own line: "In Argentina, human rights violations are reactions by the [junta] to attempts at violent overthrow by terrorists. ... The Argentine government is gradually restoring stability." Wrote a top State Department official from the Kennedy administration: "Until the advent of the Reagan administration executives of a few banks and multinational corporations, with business groups such as the Council of the Americas, were the principal proponents of a closer relationship [between the U.S. and Argentina]. ... Since 1976 their apologies for the military regime have born an uncanny resemblance to those of their predecessors for Hitler and Nazi Germany."[17]

The U.S. Eximbank had suspended activity in Argentina. The Argentine regime informally requested $270 million in credit insurance in order to buy hydroelectric turbines from Allis-Chalmers. The Carter administration initially let it be known the request would not be approved. The ban became the focus of the attack on the rights policies. Syndicated columnists Rowland Evans and Robert Novak ridiculed Derian in a grossly inaccurate piece entitled "Undiplomatic Incident."

"The thrice-repeated but unsubstantiated indictment of Argentina by Assistant Secretary of State Patricia Derian testifying publicly before Congress reveals the shattering impact on U.S. foreign policy of human-rights crusading," they charged.

> Under questioning Aug. 9 by the House Inter-American Affairs subcommittee, human rights chief Derian responded with language seldom used by one friendly power

to another, accusing the Argentine regime of killings, kidnappings and torture. ...
Apart from being undiplomatic, there is considerable doubt of accuracy. ...

On Capitol Hill, growing attention is being paid to the imminent loss of up to $1.4
billion in sales to Argentina—including $620 million in Export-Import Bank trans-
actions. So when Derian testified ... she was asked ... why her office recommended
against the Export-Import Bank loans. ... "The reason for our advice was the continuing violation of basic human rights by Argentina. The systematic use of torture,
summary execution of political dissidents, the disappearance and the imprisonment
of thousands of individuals without charge, including mothers, churchmen, nuns,
labor leaders, journalists, professors and members of human rights organizations."
...

The tragedy is that Derian's outburst may well weaken the junta's relatively moderate elements headed by the president, Gen. Jorge Rafael Videla ...

Apart from undiplomatic ravages, was Derian telling the truth? Her office insists
the Argentine junta had "executed" 3,000 persons since seizing power ... and at least
another 5,000 persons are missing. U.S. government bureaus with vastly more experience than Derian's say the figures cannot be verified and seem inflated.

Actually, the junta, in confronting a bloody far-left revolt in 1976, used an iron fist
to prevent a communist takeover. But many killings and kidnappings are traceable to
rightist paramilitary groups not under government control and should not be
counted as government "executions."[18]

The Argentine Foreign Ministry expressed "indignation" at Derian's remarks,
saying they were "false and tendentious, an offense to the Argentine people."
Somos cited the testimony of Gen. Gordon Sumner, Jr., later a special assistant to
the secretary of state for Latin American affairs in the Reagan administration,
who charged that the Carter administration "failed miserably in applying its policy of defense of human rights in Latin America. ... Who has benefited from this
fiasco? Not the people of the Free World nor the supposed victims of the repression. Only the communists and those who promote the destruction of our system."[19]

In September Videla privately met with U.S. Vice President Walter Mondale
while attending the coronation of Pope John Paul I in Rome. The Argentine,
Mondale remembered, "looked like a whipped dog. He had a beaten look, like a
devout Catholic who had sinned, and knew he had sinned." Mondale mixed quiet
diplomacy with the leverage that came from the broad U.S. ban on aid, criticized
by Kissinger and the Republican right. The American carried away from the session Videla's promise that the Organization of American States Inter-American
Commission on Human Rights would be allowed to go to Argentina on an in-
spection visit. "There were some Ex-Im loans we were blocking and I told him if
he wanted our approval he had to allow the Inter-American Commission to go
in," Mondale said. "He said, 'Look, I can't be seen as caving in to U.S. pressure,
but if you okay the loans I promise that within two months I'll get the junta to
approve the visit.' The commission went in and produced a really tough report."[20]

The Holmberg Case: Deadly Indiscretions

Elena Holmberg, a forty-seven-year-old diplomat and a cousin of former military president Lanusse, was the only career officer assigned to the Pilot Center, serving before that as head of the press section in the embassy in Paris. The petite, dark-haired woman was scandalized by the contacts between Massera and the Montoneros. She apparently tipped off certain sectors of the army—a brother, Enrique, was a lieutenant colonel—or the regime about what she knew.[21]

Holmberg's indiscretions led Massera to demand that both she and Anchorena be removed from their posts. The ambassador survived the skirmish with the navy chief. Holmberg was recalled immediately to Buenos Aires and was given an obscure post in the ceremonial department of the Foreign Ministry. Even before Holmberg left Paris, she received a none-too-subtle warning: Days before departing, the brakes on her auto were mysteriously disconnected. Nonetheless, she believed she counted on sufficient support to confront Massera's forces. "I have to keep quiet until the end of the year," she told her brothers. "Afterward I'm going to talk." But Holmberg could not resist letting a few of her friends in on her secret. She told a fellow diplomat that she had details of meetings between Massera and Firmenich, including photos of them together.[22]

On December 20, 1978—just days after Massera went into retirement—Holmberg was kidnapped by a navy commando squad. Six days later her decomposing body was found floating in the Río Luján outside Buenos Aires. It took the authorities fifteen days to identify her body. There had never been any doubt about who killed Elena Holmberg. Anchorena, Interior Minister Harguindeguy, and a top member of army intelligence all said it had been the work of the ESMA task force. Héctor Villalón warned a friend of Holmberg's that neither he nor Elena knew what was discussed by Massera and the guerrilla leader. "You all have stuck your finger in an open sore," Villalón said. "The Montonero leadership worked from the beginning with sectors of the armed forces."[23]

Buenos Aires police chief Gen. Edmundo Ojeda told one of Holmberg's brothers: "Its very clear. This is the work of that sneaky son-of-a-bitch Chamorro [director of the ESMA]. You know what's going to happen? Now I'm going to make a telephone call and he's going to tell me he doesn't know anything. And I know they have her behind the door. ... You think the war is with Chile? Don't kid yourself. The war is with these guys—Chamorro and the ESMA."[24]

War Fever

For most Argentines the war *was* with Chile. Since early that year, when talks broke down between Pinochet and Videla, war fever pulsed through the barracks. Hundreds of millions of dollars were spent by the regime on preparations for the conflict. Rush orders were placed for the construction of fuel tanks to be scattered around Patagonia. Army units were sent to the troubled south and reservists were placed on call. Antiaircraft batteries sprouted up along the border, and by year's end blackouts and air raid drills seemed to give urgency to the military's bluster. Only the eleventh-hour intervention by the Vatican and quiet pressure from the United States, in particular by Ambassador Raúl Castro, averted a hot war.[25]

As the navy's battle with Elena Holmberg was reaching its sordid climax, Chilean Enrique Arancibia Clavel was arrested in Buenos Aires and charged with spying for the Pinochet regime, together with five other Chileans and an Argentine. When he was arrested, the thirty-four-year-old Arancibia worked as the local representative of the Chilean State Bank. A short, thin man with dark, wavy hair, he confessed that his espionage work had begun in early 1977, when regional cooperation against dissidents slackened and tensions between the two countries heated up. Arancibia said information he collected had been sent to Santiago by way of a courier system set up by secret service agent Michael Townley. Arancibia identified Juan Martín Ciga Correa, the onetime Milicia member, as one of his intelligence contacts.[26]

Arancibia said that Townley had proposed creating a multinational anti-Communist intelligence network based in Chile. Arancibia suggested Ciga Correa for membership. Later the Argentine traveled to Santiago for a series of meetings at Townley's home. The meetings were part of the groundwork for Operación Condor. Among those attending the meeting at Townley's home were representatives of Miami-based Cuban exile groups. A group of Italians, identified by Arancibia as "partisans of the late Prince Borghese," were invited but did not show up.[27]

Private Aid

David Rockefeller, the chairman of the Chase Manhattan bank, visited Argentina for two days in March. Like Henry Kissinger, he stressed that the U.S. human rights policy should not be allowed to interfere with relations between the two countries. Rockefeller praised what he called the strength of Argentina's economy, which many experts said was in the throes of crisis. As always there were warm words for his friend, José Martínez de Hoz. Rockefeller and other international bankers had lent money to the regime at several points above the prime interest rate. The loans helped finance the nearly $1 billion security apparatus, including the secret repression. U.S. banks alone had lent Argentina nearly $3 billion, of which $1.2 billion went to government or state companies. Senator Edward Kennedy charged that U.S. human rights policies were being undermined by the massive private aid to the military regimes. That support, Kennedy said, "may be what enabled five Latin American governments, whose assistance had been reduced in response to human rights violations, to reject all United States aid and continue their anti-democratic practices and violations of human rights."[28]

Timerman Released

Twenty-nine months after he was arrested, and eighteen months after he was placed in detention in his own apartment, Jacobo Timerman was stripped of his citizenship and expelled from the country. Timerman's release came only after President Videla, his justice minister, and all five members of the Supreme Court threatened to resign if the junta did not comply with the court's order that the former *La Opinión* publisher be freed. The court had ruled that Timerman's continued detention was "illegitimate" and "lacking legal foundation." He was put on an Aerolíneas Argentinas jumbo jet with $1,000 to cover his air fare, his final destination Tel Aviv. During his last hours in Argentina Timerman's own captors became his bodyguards, fearful that other military men would try to kill him.

As a Jew and a journalist in a country where both were persecuted, Timerman had become a cause célèbre. Jimmy Carter had personally intervened on his behalf with Videla; human rights and religious groups showered him with prizes while he was still confined. Said the *Buenos Aires Herald*, the only Argentine newspaper to firmly and consistently speak up on his behalf, "Timerman is now an international figure."

A day after Timerman's release, a dozen hooded commandos made an early morning attack on the two-story home of Economic Planning Secretary Guillermo Walter Klein, just blocks from the presidential residence in Olivos. The assailants gunned down two police guards and forced two maids from the home. They then dynamited the house where Klein, his wife, and four children hid on the second floor. Although the house was leveled, the family was miraculously spared when debris from the upper quarters acted as a shock absorber and cushioned them against the blast. After hearing the cries of the family from underneath the rubble, neighbors frantically dug through the debris in an effort to save them. They were freed by rescue squads two and one-half hours later. Klein's boss, Martínez de Hoz, was one of those on the scene. "It was a miracle of God," he said, tears streaming down his cheeks. "A true miracle that they were alive."

The Montoneros claimed credit for the attack. At the time of the attack, however, there were several indications the idea had been hatched elsewhere. State department spokesman Hodding Carter said the U.S. government "deplored and condemned" the bombing, an act unjustified "whatever its origin." In Argentina the *Buenos Aires Herald* had to rely on a more artful way to get its message across:

> For lack of reliable information, people are again believing what they want to believe. … They ask, for example, how it was possible for the Montoneros, who appeared to have been liquidated militarily, to stage an attack involving 14 murderers using at least four vehicles at 7:30 in the morning, within earshot of a police station and the presidential residence? The logistics involved in such an attack, say experts, would call for at least 56 people to back up the killers.[29]

The same morning Klein's house was leveled, a goon squad prowled around the apartment of Robert Cox, the crusading editor of the *Herald* and a friend of the victim. The incident was followed by threats against him made in calls to the newspaper by "Montoneros." The events were enough to persuade Cox it was time for him and his family to leave Argentina.

Two days after Timerman was freed, Gen. Luciano Menéndez led a rebellion of hardliners from his base in Córdoba. Timerman's release gave the III Army Corps commander the pretext he needed to move. Menéndez wanted to reinstate a flat ban on political activity and sought to put an end to what he saw was subversion in its newest form—the growing demand for an official accounting over what had happened to the "disappeared." Menéndez—like an uncle who had unsuccessfully tried to overthrow Juan Perón—was rabidly anti-Peronist. Convinced that the world was in the midst of World War III, Menéndez was, said one top U.S. diplomat in Buenos Aires, "a fascist."[30]

The general's putsch was quickly and nonviolently crushed, in part because expected support from Suárez Mason never materialized. An estimated 4,000 troops loyal to army commander in chief Viola surrounded the rebels' stronghold outside Córdoba. Heavily armed troops took up strategic points during the night, backed up by antiaircraft weapons, field artillery, mortars, and rocket launchers. As Menéndez's forces were surrounded, an unidentified colonel loyally defended the rebellious general. "Whatever happens," he said, "General Menéndez was one of the most upright men of the Proceso, and one of the most upright people in the Argentina army. It was Gen. Menéndez who said 'no' to Timerman's release, *he who said 'no' to the attack on Secretary Klein,* he who said 'no' to corruption." (Italics added)[31]

Two months later, on December 19, just three days after *Buenos Aires Herald* editor Robert Cox and his family had to flee Argentina because Cox's children received repeated threats from the security forces, Klein's longtime personal secretary, fifty-year-old Perla Amoroso was murdered, fully clothed, after a struggle in her bathtub. Family friends said later that one of her killers left bloody handprints around her flat, a detail Klein denies. A cloak of silence was laid over the crime.[32]

Firmenich Stays Behind: The 1979 Montonero "Counteroffensive"

The year 1979 was also the year Mario Firmenich sent more than 100 Montoneros exiled in Mexico City, Rome, Lima, and other places back to Argentina in a "counteroffensive" against the military regime. Many were discovered at the border and either were killed or committed suicide to avoid capture. Firmenich, who had taken to making tape recordings of himself in a badly performed imitation of Juan Perón and sending them to "supporters" in Argentina, had stayed behind, out of harm's way. Suspicions, wrote British historian Richard Gillespie, "even surfaced ... as to whether the National Leadership had not in fact been infiltrated. Was it pure chance that the leading former cadres of the FAR, the Montonero component most strongly influenced by Marxism, had all been eliminated?"[33]

In July Nicaragua's Sandinistas defeated the hated Somoza regime. Although Firmenich had not participated in the fighting, dozens of Montoneros had. In the wake of the Central American guerrillas' victorious entry into Managua, Firmenich—in full combat regalia—was photographed hamming it up in the dictator's bunker. The photos of him made their way onto the cover of *Somos,* a key media collaborator with the army's 601 intelligence battalion. The *New York Times* noted:

> Frustrated by the lack of progress in their own revolutions, young leftists from almost every military-ruled Latin American country volunteered to fight alongside the Sandinist guerrillas in recent months. ... The French Socialist, Regis Debray, who 11 years ago was jailed by Bolivian troops fighting the Cuban revolutionary Che Guevara, appeared suddenly on a truck bringing rebels to Managua. The leader of Argentina's Montonero guerrillas, Mario Eduardo Firmenich, joined the Sandinistas a week ago and, dressed in fatigues with a pistol at his belt, was busy giving interviews to reporters all of yesterday.[34]

The Silence Is Broken

On April 18, 1980, the results of the investigation conducted in situ by the Inter-American Human Rights Commission for two weeks the previous September were released by the Organization of American States. The commission's visit in Buenos Aires had been an event of undeniable magnitude. Local newspapers, for so long mere propaganda arms of the dictatorship, were allowed to report—cautiously—its activities. Human rights became a topic for public debate within Argentina. Political leaders broke their own silence on the rights issue to take a stand. The Peronist party charged that a senseless repression had been unleashed in the name of privilege and demanded freedom for Isabel Perón and Lorenzo Miguel.

The report confirmed that numerous and grave violations of human rights had occurred by the acts or omissions of Argentine authorities in the years 1975 to 1979. The OAS said that these affected the rights to life, liberty, security and personal integrity, and justice. It said that thousands of missing people had been killed by the security forces. The alarming and systematic use of torture was confirmed. The generals were urged to investigate, try, and punish those responsible for deaths attributed to the government. The commission suggested that the regime give detailed information about what happened to the "disappeared." It also importuned the military to reestablish labor laws and rights, halt religious discrimination, allow political parties to operate, and end the state of siege.

Bolivia's Cocaine Coup: "Made in Buenos Aires"

In June 1980 four Argentine exiles, including Mothers of the Plaza de Mayo activist fifty-four-year-old Esther Noemí Gianotti de Molfino, were abducted in Lima by the Peruvian army intelligence service (SIE). The kidnapping was made at the request of army chief of staff Leopoldo Galtieri. De Molfino's son, daughter, and son-in-law—all Montoneros—had previously disappeared in Argentina. For several days Peru's Interior Ministry held that the four had been caught conspiring with local extremists and had been expelled from the country at the Bolivian border. Meanwhile one of those abducted reportedly died while being tortured at Playa Hondable, a Peruvian army rest camp 35 miles north of Lima. The surviving Argentines were received by a Bolivian paramilitary unit under the orders of Col. Luis Arce Gómez, the head of army intelligence. Transferred to La Paz, the three were tortured by Argentine intelligence operatives, themselves part of a larger group stationed in Bolivia to oversee the overthrow of the nation's democratic government. According to one account, only Esther de Molfino survived the stay in Bolivia. She was taken out of the country in a wheelchair by a paramilitary commando disguised as a nurse. "Events surrounding the abduction and murder of the Argentines have contributed to the cancellation of an all-but-arranged trip by Assistant Secretary of State William Bowdler," reported the Council on Hemispheric Affairs. "Bowdler accompanied Rosalynn Carter to Lima for the July 28 inauguration of Peruvian president Fernando Belaúnde Terry; provisional plans had been made for him to continue to Argentina to carry on exploratory bilateral conversations."[35]

A month later police in Madrid encountered the decomposing body of Esther de Molfino. The woman had entered the country with false documents. Her body was found in an apartment rented by someone using the legal identification of one of the two Argentines with whom she had been abducted in Peru. The two men who had left her in the apartment had told the building's doorman not to disturb de Molfino. They said she was tired from a long trip.[36]

Another cause for Bowdler's aborted trip to Buenos Aires was the beginning of a new kind of Argentine extraterritorial activity. The generals no longer limited themselves to the murder of exiles in Argentina or the disappearance of Argentines living abroad. They had now put themselves into the business of overthrowing a neighboring government.

The return of democratic rule to Bolivia was a key objective of the Carter administration. In the previous two years U.S. pressure was crucial in getting Bolivia's northern neighbors, Ecuador and Peru, to hold elections. Similar suasion was applied to Bolivia, the hemisphere's poorest Spanish-speaking nation. "Mr. Carter didn't send me a letter ordering elections," admitted rightist dictator Gen. Hugo Banzer Suárez, who took office following the coup that toppled Juan José Torres. "But we could feel the pressure." The military seemed to slowly accept the election of moderate leftist Hernán Siles Zuazo, a former president and a leader of the 1952 revolution, to the presidency. On July 17, however, came confirmation of months of rumors that the military high command would not allow longtime foe Siles to take power.[37]

Even for a country that had experienced fifteen changes in government since 1964, the coup that brought Gen. Luis García Meza to power was unusually brutal. Civilian-dressed military men burst into public buildings, arresting or murdering government employees and union officials. White Toyota ambulances without license plates manned by paramilitary squads prowled city streets to round up suspected opponents. Estimates at the time put the number of political prisoners at 2,000; hundreds disappeared or were executed. On July 20 soldiers clashed with workers in the mining district of Santa Ana, 400 miles southeast of the capital, with the miners suffering heavy casualties. The Bolivian Council of Bishops condemned the military's savagery; the archbishop of La Paz said he had witnessed the execution of four youths.

The brutality of the coup fueled speculation about its deadly efficiency. Within twenty-four hours 1,000 people were detained. Although involvement in the uprising was denied in Buenos Aires, boxes of C rations and ammunition stamped "Argentine army" were found by dissident miners. Paramilitary groups involved in the violence spoke with Argentine accents. Torturers used the term *che,* a form of familiar address in Argentina. It was "absolutely certain that Argentina was deeply involved in planning and executing the coup," said a senior U.S. military adviser in Bolivia. "They did everything but tell García Meza the day to launch it."[38]

The coup had been directed by Lt. Gen. Leopoldo Galtieri. (A year later, Galtieri, by then a favorite with the new administration in Washington, boasted before his fellow generals that he told Reagan envoy Gen. Vernon Walters that in Bolivia "I decide who is put in power and when, and when he is removed.") At the time of the uprising, more than 200 Argentine military and intelligence officers and paramilitary troops were stationed in Bolivia. Intelligence and logistic support—including money, radio and other communications equipment, and arms for civilian groups—were provided by the Argentines. Among the army's contributions were several TAM light tanks, electric torture equipment—and advisers to show how to use it—and twenty white ambulances used to ferry arms to Bolivia and to carry out the abductions. The air force provided four helicopters and loaned two Pucará airplanes, painted Bolivian air force colors, which were sent in case it was necessary to bomb workers holed up in the tin mines. Propaganda also formed an important part of the Argentines' assistance. When the regime declared a state of emergency, a La Paz television station began to show "antisubversive" public advertising that had been used earlier in Buenos Aires.[39]

The Argentine regime moved swiftly to shore up García Meza's international position, exposed by an abrupt cutoff of U.S. aid. The Argentine move was something of a challenge to the Carter administration, which the military accused of leaving a strategic "vacuum" in the fight against communism. The first country to recognize the Bolivian military regime, Argentina offered the generals in La Paz $200 million in economic assistance and a $250 million advance for the purchase of natural gas. Direct grants and commercial credits from Buenos Aires reportedly brought the total in aid to Bolivia's generals to $800 million.[40]

Faced with international condemnation of Argentina's role in the coup, Videla responded: "We do not want a situation in the heartland of South America that would amount to what Cuba represents for Central America." However, at the time of the coup, Bolivia was one of the few Latin American countries with no recent history of leftist terrorism.[41]

Strategic considerations were of little concern to Argentina's military proxies, however. A senior U.S. military attaché admitted that "political ideology" was not at the heart of the Bolivian generals' power grab. "There probably isn't a communist guerrilla in this entire country," he said. The Bolivian military uprising, one joke went, was the first in history where the victors wore coca leaf clusters in their lapels. "Forget politics," advised one Santa Cruz businessman realistically. "It's really just a dogfight over who is going to control the cocaine traffic."[42]

Argentine military and paramilitary teams sent to participate in the Cocaine Coup included Lt. Colonel Mohamed Alí Seineldín, the onetime link between the army and the Triple A, described admiringly by a U.S. military attaché who knew him as "a snake eater, out-front, special forces kind of guy" and navy Lt. Antonio Pernía, one of the ESMA's most savage torturers. Also included were former members of the Triple A, including Fernando ("Mosca") Monroz, who participated in the 1974 bombing of the leftist newspaper *El Mundo* in Buenos Aires.[43]

Among the paramilitary thugs protected by Argentine intelligence chief Gen. Alberto Valín, the army's longtime liaison with Firmenich and a former adviser to Somoza's brutal National Guard, were the Italian Delle Chiaie and his vicious, movie star–handsome sidekick Pier Luigi Pagliai, described in a U.S. embassy document as a "terrorist torture freak." Delle Chiaie made his first contact with the Bolivians in late 1979 at the home of retired Argentine army intelligence officer Maj. Hugo Raúl Miori Pereyra in Buenos Aires. (A decade earlier Miori Pereyra had been the head of Interior Minister Imaz's bodyguard, and as such was responsible for the kidnapping and extortion ring run out of Imaz's office.) The Italian had recently returned to Buenos Aires from advising Salvadoran death squad leader Roberto D'Aubuisson. Miori Pereyra, whom Delle Chiaie knew from Central America, was charged by the army high command with maintaining close ties to the Bolivians, including General Banzer.[44]

After the coup, Interior Minister Col. Luis Arce Gómez was immortalized by columnist Jack Anderson as the "Idi Amin of the Andes." Arce put together a group called the Servicio Especial de Seguridad (SES; Special Security Service), headed by Delle Chiaie and Nazi war criminal Klaus Barbie. Closely linked to a goon squad under the control of narcotics kingpin Roberto Suárez called the Fiancés of Death, the team taught Bolivian soldiers torture techniques and provided protection for the booming cocaine trade, whose revenues were estimated at more than $1.5 billion annually. According to a Delle Chiaie lieutenant, the Italian served as the middleman between the Bolivia's uniformed cocaine barons and the heroin-smuggling Sicilian Mafia.[45]

The Italians bore credentials from the Argentine 601 army intelligence batallion. Delle Chiaie's contribution to the cause included the technique of early "neutralization"—by abduction or murder—of key opposition leaders. Delle Chiaie's sidekick Pagliai showed up at a torture training session wearing ballet tights, bare chested and with his torso oiled. There he killed two peasants by sticking red-hot needles into their ears.[46]

Den of Thieves

A month later the Fourth Congress of the Confederación Anticomunista Latinoamericana (CAL; Latin American Anti-Communist Confederation), an affiliate of the World Anti-Communist League (WACL), met in Buenos Aires. Chaired by Gen. Carlos Guillermo Suárez Mason, one of Licio Gelli's Argentine set pieces, the gathering received messages of support from Argentina's Videla, Chile's Pinochet, Paraguay's Stroessner, and Bolivia's García Meza. Also sending messages of support were Economy Minister Jose A. Martínez de Hoz and Lt. Gen. Luis Queirolo. (Queirolo, commander in chief of the Uruguayan army, was closely tied to Gelli and the Reverend Sun Myung Moon's Unification church.) WACL president Woo Jae Sung, a key Unification church official, also attended.

The congress secretary was retired Argentine army Maj. Hugo Miori Pereyra. Miori Pereyra was closely linked to the Moon church and one of the key figures in the recruitment of Argentine "dirty warriors" for tasks in Central America. Other participants included Salvadoran politician and death squad leader Roberto D'Aubuisson; his Guatemalan peer, the neofascist Mario Sandoval Alarcón; and a representative of the Alpha 66 Cuban-exile terrorist organization. John Carbaugh, an aide to archconservative Senator Jesse Helms (R-N.C.), and Margo Carlisle, legislative aide to Senator James McClure (R-Idaho) and staff director of the Republican Conference of the U.S. Senate, attended as observers. (Helms himself was later a key figure in trying to "sell" both D'Aubuisson and García Meza to the American public.)[47]

Delle Chiaie had returned from the Old Continent to attend the CAL convention. The Italian was part of the network of death squad activities run by the congress and was tied to a secret society named Tecos based in Mexico. During the course of the meeting, Delle Chiaie, accompanied by García Meza's personal envoy, arranged several interviews between important Bolivians and D'Aubuisson. There El Salvador's death squad chief received pledges of money and arms from the Italian's Andean patrons. U.S. columnist Jack Anderson later exposed the Tecos' dogma, which "made enemies of Jews, Jesuits, and communists—with a bit of medieval Nordic mythology thrown in for good measure. CAL-Tecos' propaganda, published in their magazine, *Réplica,* aired weird stories about Jews, witches, drug addicts and homosexuals taking over the Vatican. During his visit to Mexico, Pope John Paul II was elevated by these propagandists from a homosexual drug addict to the anti-Christ." *Réplica* had once listed *Aginterpress* as its European correspondent. *Aginterpress* was Delle Chiaie's journalistic cover.[48]

Suárez Mason admitted that the congress debated ways to carry out the anti-Communist struggle in Central America. The P-2 member played a key role in structuring future Argentine military involvement in the region. Jimmy Carter's United States, he said, did not understand the Marxist peril there. That meant "we are alone and left to make due with our own forces." The congress issued resolutions repudiating Nicaragua's new Sandinista regime and condemning "Carter communism" for having betrayed dictator Anastasio Somoza. It also demanded that the Spanish-era expulsion of the Jesuits from Latin soil be repeated, calling them "Marxist neocolonialists." Mexican delegate Rafael Rodríguez boasted of his love for the word "fascist." Salvadoran death squad leader Luis Angel Lagos vowed that "the only good communist in my country is going to be the one who is dead." Suárez Mason called on delegates to be discrete about the congress's deliberations. Its acts, he said, should speak for themselves.[49]

The ERP Kills Somoza in Paraguay

After his overthrow former Nicaraguan dictator Anastasio Somoza Debayle lived in Asunción, the capital of Stroessner's Paraguay. Exile became a life of drunken revelry. The placid local elite was scandalized by his wild parties. A highly publicized affair with a former Miss Paraguay, then the lover of Stroessner's son-in-law, was the talk of the town.

Shortly after 10:00 the morning of September 17, Somoza's limousine rolled out through the gates of his mansion and headed along Avenida España, one of Asunción's major thoroughfares. Four Paraguayan police assigned to guard him followed in another vehicle about half a block away. Three armed men, former members of the Argentine ERP, ran out of a house rented months earlier at the corner of Avenida España and Avenida América. The trio detoured traffic from the intersection, ordering neighbors into their homes. There was going to be trouble, they warned.

A stolen blue pickup with changed plates was waiting a block away from the house. Racing up alongside the limousine, it cut in front of Somoza's vehicle, forcing his driver to pull to a halt. Two khaki-clad men jumped out of the truck. Three more emerged from the rented house directly opposite. They fired automatic weapons at the two-car caravan. A man standing in the doorway of the house took aim at Somoza's auto and let loose a rocket-propelled grenade. The car rolled onto the sidewalk, its motor idling. In the street the chauffeur lay decapitated. Somoza and his financial adviser were dead inside the car. By 10:10 the killers had sped away in the pickup.

The assassination squad had been directed by former ERP leader Enrique Haroldo Gorriarán Merlo. One of his lieutenants was Hugo ("Capitán Santiago") Irurzún, the former commander of the Compañía Ramón Rosa Jimenez in Tucumán. After fleeing into exile, Gorriarán and Irurzún had put together a small group of former ERP combatants to fight with the Sandinistas against Somoza. For a brief time after the insurgents' victory, before the Cubans came in, Gorriarán helped put together the Sandinistas' security apparatus.[50]

Paraguay's borders were ordered sealed. The airport was closed, and a nationwide search began. On the night of September 18 police raided the house where Irurzún was living. They put out the story that Irurzún, living in Asunción under the protection of a top Stroessner official, was killed while trying to escape over a garden wall. He died while being tortured.[51]

"Malaise"

On November 4, 1980, Americans went to the polls. Although the gas lines of the year before had dissipated, the memory of the unaccustomed shortages lingered like a hangover. The economy wasn't mortally ill, but a chronic illness seemed to set in—high inflation and interest rates, a yawning balance of payments deficit. "Malaise" had been Jimmy Carter's diagnosis. Then in late 1979 the Soviets invaded Afghanistan. A year later, at election time, fifty-two hostages in Tehran were still held by the Ayatollah's fundamentalist militias. Neither threats, boycotts, nor a commando raid had brought them home. Many Americans were pessimistic, bewildered—and mad.[52]

Like many Latin democrats, Raúl Alfonsín, then still just the leader of a minority faction within the Radicals, had come to the United States to watch democracy work. As the election results came in, Alfonsín felt little reason to cheer. The rainy Washington weather mirrored his own gloom. Ronald Reagan had beaten his incumbent rival in an electoral tidal wave. Even the Democrats' comfortable margin in the Senate had been washed away. In Latin America it was the generals who were beaming. ("Jeane Kirkpatrick had gone all around telling these guys not to worry," Mondale remembered, "that if Carter was beaten things would change.")[53]

The day after the election Alfonsín and a small group traveling with him were invited by Jeane Kirkpatrick to a luncheon in the dining room of the conservative American Enterprise Institute. "Everyone was drinking champagne, [economist Arthur] Burns was seated at the table right behind us," remembered one of Alfonsín's friends. At some point Alfonsín gently said in Spanish: "Well, señora, there are problems in our countries' relations with the United States. You know that sometimes, particularly in the Caribbean, the U.S. position has been less than edifying." Kirkpatrick put down her knife and fork. She slowly removed her glasses. "Well, Dr. Alfonsín, let me tell you something," Kirkpatrick said coldly. "The United States has never intervened in the internal affairs of any country in

Latin America or the Caribbean, except in those cases where you have made such a mess of your own affairs that we've had to go and fix them up for you." Alfonsín changed the subject.

Later Alfonsín and his group walked to their car parked across the street. The Radical leader put his arm into that of one of his friends. Looking up at the slate-colored sky, he muttered: "Dios mío, ¿qué es lo que nos va a pasar?" (My God, what's in store for us?)[54]

22

Alfonsín and Argentina's Return to Civility (1981-1989)

Martínez de Hoz is the architect of what may turn out to be one of the most remarkable economic recoveries of modern history. ... The armed forces stepped in, as [he] explained, to bring continuity and to keep the country afloat. In this civil war atmosphere "No quarter was asked and no quarter was given," he said. "It is a sad reality that there will be a certain number of people that the government will never be able to account for."

—*Ronald Reagan*

We got along really well. We were supposed to do many things together on this continent.

—*Gen. Leopoldo Galtieri*
interview with Italian journalist Oriana Fallaci[1]

A certain thaw began to take place in U.S.-Argentine relations as the Carter administration turned its attention in 1979 to Soviet expansionism in Afghanistan and the fall of the U.S. embassy in Tehran. Gen. Andrew Goodpaster, a former Supreme Allied Commander in Europe, was sent to Buenos Aires to ask the junta's help in making a grain embargo against the Soviets effective. The Argentines—major suppliers of wheat to Moscow—refused but promised not to take undue commercial advantage. The move away from the more activist rights stance taken in Carter's first years came with a drop in the disappearances and killings in Argentina, but even the tentative renewal of ties with the generals gave Patt Derian reason to consider resigning.[2]

Nothing Carter conceived would remotely approach the bonds of friendship forged by Ronald Reagan, Jesse Helms, and the generals. With Reagan's inauguration, antiterrorism, not human rights, became the foreign policy standard in Washington. "We told Argentina that it had heard its last public lecture from the United States on human rights," Secretary of State Alexander Haig recalled in his memoirs. (Within months, however, chartered Argentine military aircraft were used to fly American-made arms to Israel and Iran in what was the forerunner to the Iran-Contra scandal.) Reagan, charged Jimmy Carter,

> condemned our human rights policy as an indication of weakness, or vacillation, or naivete. He tried to send a different signal around the world. Jeane Kirkpatrick [U.S. ambassador to the United Nations] came down to demonstrate to the Argentine dictators and to [military ruler Augusto] Pinochet in Chile that they had [a] friend in Washington. The first official visit that Reagan arranged was for the South Koreans. He did this deliberately to let the world know that my human-rights policy had been reversed.[3]

Gen. Roberto Viola, who had replaced Videla in 1980 after several days of arduous negotiations with the navy, was among the first official guests at the Reagan White House. (After a meeting in the Capitol, Viola's spokesman denied a claim by Senator Claiborne Pell [D-R.I.] that Viola had promised the publication of a list of the missing and the dead. "A victorious army is not investigated," Viola said. "If the Reich's troops had won the last world war the tribunal would have been held not in Nuremberg but in Virginia.") Argentina received goodwill visits from army Gen. Charles Meyer, U.S. Air Force Chief of Staff Gen. Richard Ingram, and Vice Admiral Charles Bagley, as well as visits from special ambassadors Gen. Vernon Walters and Gordon Sumner. Reagan also asked Congress to repeal its embargo on arms sales to Argentina. Patt Derian's replacement, Elliott Abrams, who argued that the State Department's human rights goals be "turned to our policy goals," dutifully claimed "improvement" in Argentine human rights.[4]

Reagan's first nominee to replace Derian had been Ernest Lefever, who had said that the human rights bureau should be abolished. "In a formal and legal sense the U.S. government has no responsibility—and certainly no authority—to promote human rights in other sovereign states," Lefever told a congressional committee in 1979. "It should not be necessary for any friendly state to pass a human rights test before we extend normal trade relations, sell arms or provide economic or security assistance."[5]

Although Lefever's nomination was already in trouble by the time it reached the Senate Foreign Relations Committee, the nominee did not help his case when he suggested that opposition to his appointment was part of a "Communist conspiracy." His chances were doomed after Jacobo Timerman appeared in the hearing room. Timerman had just published his riveting first-hand account of torture, death, and anti-Semitism in Argentina, *Prisoner Without A Name, Cell Without a Number,* and was himself under attack by Jewish neoconservatives such as Norman Podhoretz and Irving Kristol, part of the Reagan brain trust. Acknowledged by committee chairman Sen. Charles Percy (R-Ill.), the silent Timerman received a moving ovation. It was "the most powerful moment in the whole hearings," wrote one observer, "the appearance of someone who gave no testimony, but bore witness simply by his presence."[6]

Dirty Warriors and Freedom Fighters

The Argentine military had maintained a presence in Central America, ostensibly to keep track of Argentine guerrillas exiled in the region, since 1977. Three years later they were working as counterinsurgency advisers to death squads and right-ist regimes in Honduras, Guatemala, and El Salvador. Following the Bolivian "co-caine coup," funds received by the 601 army intelligence battalion from the Boliv-ian colonels and cocaine kingpin Roberto Suárez in payment for help in the coup there began to finance the 601's Central American operations. A civilian 601 intel-ligence operative who was later employed by the U.S. Drug Enforcement Admin-istration (DEA), told a U.S. Senate subcommittee later that much of the money was laundered through the Bahamas, then sent on to the Silver Dollar pawnshop in Miami run by Raúl Guglielminetti, a civilian 601 army intelligence agent. Guglielminetti, part of the so-called Andes Group, acted as a liaison with the CIA. His Florida base was also used to funnel weapons to ultrarightists in El Salvador and to the Panamanian military. A late 1980 attack directed by the 601 group on the Montonero-run Radio Noticias del Continente in Costa Rica reportedly re-ceived CIA intelligence and logistics support. Three Costa Ricans were killed. As the *Washington Post* later reported, Salvadoran death squad leader Roberto d'Aubuisson, a favorite of Senator Jesse Helms and the Republican right, used the Argentine dirty warriors as trainers in "interrogation techniques": "The most ef-fective method [one of the Salvadoran trainees] said, was strapping a prisoner naked to a metal bed frame set in a pool of water several inches deep. Electric cur-rent would then be run to the frame, with a special wire to the genitals. 'That was the best,' he said. 'Not even the toughest could resist that.' "[7]

The 601 batallion also began to finance the Legión 15 de Setiembre (September 15 Legion), a group of former National Guardsmen who, together with several other anti-Sandinista groups, were engaged in military actions against the new Sandinista government. The Argentines' contact with the Legion came as a result of a request by the United States and through Argentine contacts with the Miami-based Cuban exile terrorist groups Alpha 66 and Omega 7. In spring 1981 former guardsman Enrique Bermúdez traveled to Buenos Aires to meet with army intel-ligence chief Alberto Valín and received pledges of support and an attaché case full of cash. In March Reagan authorized the CIA to begin anti-Sandinista covert operations and by year's end the agency was engaged in a plan to build a 500-man paramilitary force for combat inside Nicaragua. The Argentines, aware of U.S. congressional opposition to military action there, offered to become the rebels' case officers, with Washington secretly picking up the tab. A CIA station chief later called the Argentines' participation a "fig leaf" for the United States.[8]

By late spring some sixty anti-Sandinista rebels were in Buenos Aires for intelligence and military training. The focus of the Argentines, reported the *Washington Post*'s Chris Dickey, "was always on their own great accomplishments eliminating Communists from their cities." In August the Americans and their Argentine proxies held a meeting in Guatemala City where the September 15 Legion and the other anti-Sandinista groups were merged into the Fuerza Democrática Nicaraguense (Nicaraguan Democratic Force)—the Contras. In late December, within days of retiring from the army, Valín moved to Panama City, ostensibly to serve as Argentine ambassador there.[9]

The Contra leadership soon became known from their use of systematic torture, rape, and brutalization of their own troops. The Argentine trainers, said Edgar Chamorro, an early opponent of the Sandinistas who left the Contras in disgust with their brutality, told the Nicaraguan insurgents, "We're the only people in Latin America who've beaten the communists in a war. The way to win is to fight a 'dirty war' like we did in the 1970s."[10]

Gelli's "State Within a State" Falls

In March 1981 Italian police raided Licio Gelli's villa in the Tuscan town of Arezzo searching for evidence connecting him with the fake kidnapping of Michele Sindona, a banker imprisoned in the United States who was linked to the Sicilian mafia. What they came up with turned Italian politics upside down: a list of nearly 1,000 members of the P-2, described as "a center of a huge network of subversion, tax evasion and other illegal activities." The list included three cabinet ministers, thirty generals, eight admirals, forty-three members of parliament, journalists, and scores of prominent businessmen. The mere public mention of the list was enough to cause the fall of the Christian Democratic government of Arnaldo Forlani. The head of the Office of Intelligence Coordination was forced to resign, as was the chairman of the joint chiefs of staff. New heads of the army, navy, and paramilitary police were also appointed. A senator tried to commit suicide after his name was found on the list. The *New York Times* quoted a Western diplomat as saying the P-2 had been created as a "contingency structure to prevent communists from coming to power the way Allende did in Chile." Gelli fled the country.[11]

Signs of Trouble

Despite the international outcry at the brutality of the "dirty war," the first signs of trouble for the generals came on another front: the economy. José Martínez de Hoz cut subsidies to industry and lowered the high tariff walls that had created Argentine jobs but at the cost of surplus industrial capacity and inferior, more expensive domestic goods. The repression in the workplace had severely limited wage demands and brought inflation under some control. Yet the regime failed to hold down government spending, which contributed greatly to a rapidly growing foreign debt. Whatever gains, extracted at bayonet point, there were in worker productivity were squandered by baldly political moves, such as forcing state companies to borrow from foreign banks rather than raising prices to meet current expenditures. Several spectacular bank failures underscored the fragile underpinnings of military claims of order and progress.[12]

Much of the generals' spending was on the military. The government's efforts to keep the value of the peso artificially high wound up promoting speculation on international currency markets, causing huge sums of money to leave the country. A regime that had promised to return unprofitable state enterprises to the private sector found the opportunities for patronage and corruption too tempting to resist. Fabricaciones Militares, a military-run industrial behemoth, remained the country's largest employer. The military retained control or ownership of steel mills and television stations, petrochemical complexes and electronics factories, newspapers and enormous agricultural holdings.[13]

According to *Time* magazine, by 1980 Argentina led the world in costs of bribes for doing business, with 20 percent the average required above the price of the contract. In February 1982 *Ambito Financiero* uncovered a new multimillion dollar scandal involving the adulteration of gasoline and illegal sale of petrochemical products belonging to state enterprises. At the center of the controversy was Maj. (ret.) Hugo Raúl Miori Pereyra, the former Buenos Aires intelligence chief under General Imaz, the secretary of the 1980 World Anti-Communist League conference held in Buenos Aires, and a key contact with both Bolivia's cocaine colonels and the Argentine paramilitary operations in Central America.[14]

The Falkland/Malvinas Fiasco

It was the seizure of the British-held Falkland Islands, known to every Argentine child as las Islas Malvinas, that sounded the last muster for the generals. Great Britain and Argentina had disputed ownership of the windswept archipelago for more than 150 years.

In late 1981 army chief of staff Galtieri spent two weeks in the United States, met with CIA Director William Casey, and agreed that the Argentines would organize and train the Contras with U.S. funds. Back in Buenos Aires Galtieri, who had vowed it would be a long time before Argentines were allowed to vote again, sought out navy help for a bid to push Viola aside and grab the presidency. In return, he pledged, he would invade the islands.[15]

The regime Galtieri inherited in December was a troubled one. Human rights demonstrations grew larger. The economy was listless. The new rapport with the United States had not ended the drumbeat of international criticism. On March 31, 1982, 15,000 demonstrators responded to a call by the CGT and rallied in protest in the Plaza de Mayo. The ensuing repression by the police left many wounded, but the regime was badly shaken.

On April 2, 1982, an Argentine military expedition seized the islands in an action in which only one person—an Argentine—was killed. Galtieri's decision to take the islands was rooted in a number of faulty assumptions, including the belief that the British would not fight and that Argentine sovereignty over the archipelago would bolster the regime's sagging prestige. He also believed the romance of relations with the United States, forged in the jungles of Central America, would result in U.S. support for the action.[16]

The self-styled "Argentine Patton" was wrong on all three counts. The British sent a war fleet and landed thousands of troops on the islands. (Navy Lt. Alfredo Astiz, the veteran of wars against teenage girls and nuns waged out of the ESMA, was in charge of a team of special troops, the Lagartos, in the South Georgias Islands. He surrendered without firing a shot). Despite the fact that Jeane Kirkpatrick seemed to go out of her way to signal support for Galtieri and counseled neutrality to protect the Contra program, the United States stood by its historic ally Britain when mediation efforts failed. "Argentina, taking seriously the declarations of UN Ambassador Kirkpatrick, had deluded itself that the United States might remain neutral," reported the *Washington Post*'s Bob Woodward. "So Argentine officers and officials provided a steady flow of intelligence to the CIA station and the U.S. military attachés in Buenos Aires, who forwarded it to Langley and to the State Department and the White House. It was then only a matter of who could beat a path more quickly to the British."[17]

And although Argentines did rally massively in support of the popular national cause—Raúl Alfonsín was virtually alone in calling it "military madness"—their enthusiasm was stoked by highly distorted coverage from the government-controlled media, which to the end portrayed Argentina as winning the struggle. Fed by "information kits," including doctored photos and colored drawings, from the 601 army intelligence batallion, and with *Somos* and *Gente* in the lead, Argentines learned of battles never fought, victories never won, and enemy planes and ships reported destroyed but never, in fact, even scathed. "What is at stake," claimed Mariano Grondona in a *Gente* editorial, "is the devotion of a people: its bravery, its self-esteem."[18]

The "blowback" from the military disinformation campaign—lies and distortions similar to those concocted during the "dirty war"—this time worked to the generals' disadvantage. Navy chief Jorge Isaac Anaya later testified before a military investigating commission: "I thought that in the [South Georgias Islands] they were fighting to the maximum, and it was only later that I learned this had been staged by the Navy." "Can you be more precise?" the former junta member was asked.

> I was convinced that in the Georgias they were fighting fiercely, as the result of the news I read in the newspapers. That was because I didn't really have any means of

communicating with the Georgias and, really, I was aghast when I found out they all had been detained, that there was one—accidental—death and that there had been only one wounded in combat. That after I had read that our soldiers had been all over the place. I was misled.[19]

When the Argentines surrendered after seventy-four days of conflict and the loss of about 1,000 Argentine and 250 British lives, public support for the war turned into rage and disbelief. The generals had been noticeable for their absence during the fighting.

Echoes of Dachau and Katyn

Galtieri's subsequent resignation left Argentina with a brief reign by the interior minister, Gen. Alfredo St. Jean. On July 1 a new provisional president, Gen. Reynaldo Benito Bignone—the Prats bodyguard who failed to show up for work the day his ward was murdered—took office and pledged to restore civilian rule by March 1984, the scheduled end of his term. Despite the heavy atmosphere of repression, human rights groups and labor demanded a quick return to democratic government, respect for individual and workers' rights, and a full accounting of what occurred during the "dirty war," including a case-by-case review of the fate of the missing.

Strong interservice rivalries, weariness from unsuccessful governance, and growing public pressure—in the form of taxpayer revolts, strikes, and protests—put the regime on the defensive. By September, all the officers responsible for the Falkland/Malvinas debacle had either quit or were cashiered. At a sparsely attended rally self-styled "Peronist General" Acdel Vilas announced he was seeking his party's presidential nomination. And as Bignone spokesmen were dismissing rumors of an impending coup, the rear admiral commanding Argentina's southernmost naval base was arrested—for trying to spark a rebellion.

On October 9 Massera appeared on a television show hosted by Grondona to face allegations that he had met with Montoneros, was involved in the death of Elena Holmberg, and had played a role in the kidnapping a week earlier of advertising executive Marcelo Dupont, the brother of one of his accusers, Gregorio Dupont. That night Marcelo's body, bearing signs of torture, was found three blocks from where Massera was filming the show. It had been thrown from the top of a building at about the time he appeared on television. It was later disclosed that Dupont had been killed by the 601 army intelligence batallion in a successful effort to discredit Massera.[20]

Two weeks later Emilio Mignone's Center for Legal and Social Studies announced it had uncovered the body of a labor organizer kidnapped six years earlier and the bodies of 400 others in 88 unmarked graves in the Grand Bourg cemetery near Buenos Aires. Within weeks 600 more unidentified corpses were found at six other cemeteries. "In Grand Bourg," noted the *Buenos Aires Herald*, "for most people as innocent a place name as were once Dachau, Auschwitz and Katyn, Argentina stumbled onto a past that is still, in many ways, its present." From Rome, Buenos Aires archbishop Cardinal Juan Carlos Aramburu denied what the military were incapable of covering up any longer: "In Argentina there are no mass graves, and each cadaver has its own casket. Everything is regularly registered in the appropriate logs. The mass graves are of people who died without the authorities being able to identify them. The missing? ... You know that there are missing people who are living tranquilly in Europe."[21]

November was marked by a series of death threats against human rights activists, with the army chief of staff claiming that the Mothers of the Plaza de Mayo group was "financed by terrorists." In December the first general strike under the generals shut the country down. The Rattenbach Commission began a military inquiry into the conduct of the South Atlantic war, to find later that the generals were guilty of faulty planning, limited coordination, and an embarrassing performance. In short, the military's internal security function had left it ill prepared to fight a real war. Ten thousand people joined the Mothers in their weekly protest march, and despite police repression that left one protester shot down in cold blood, more than 100,000 people rallied in the Plaza de Mayo in support of the political parties. One of the largest contingents filed into the plaza singing,

After Pocho [Perón],
After Balbín,
The leader of the people
Is named Alfonsín.

The P-2 and the Buenos Aires Connection

As Argentina reeled from its loss to the British, news from London caused a stir in several circles in Buenos Aires. On June 19 Italian financier and Gelli confidant Roberto Calvi, the head of the Banco Ambrosiano and the central figure in a $790 million bank fraud scandal, was found dead hanging from Blackfriar's Bridge in London. In September Italy began extradition proceedings against Gelli, who— on the run for more than a year—was arrested in Geneva while trying to cash a $20 million check on a numbered Swiss bank account sealed by court order. In October Italian narco-terrorist Pier Luigi Pagliai, a suspect in a 1980 bombing that killed eighty-five people in Bologna, Italy, was wounded and captured in a gun battle in Bolivia, then placed on a secret Alitalia flight to Rome, where he later died.[22]

Emilio Massera had launched his Social Democratic Party, a vehicle he hoped would catapult him into the presidency, in August. Two months later it was discovered that, prominent among the foreigners on Gelli's P-2 rolls, were two dozen Argentines, including Massera, López Rega, and Suárez Mason. Before going to press, *La Prensa*'s Máximo Gainza called Massera at 11:00 P.M. for comment. "He told me to remember that he had pardoned my life once, when I printed the story about him meeting with the Montoneros," Gainza recalled. "He said, 'Remember that I've killed three or four people with my own hands.'"[23]

Friends Like These

By the end of 1982 the world press had begun to uncover the growing U.S. involvement in the "secret war" in Nicaragua. In December a videotape of a slight, wiry man who said he was an Argentine 601 army intelligence batallion operative in Central America was given to reporters. Identified as Héctor Francés, the victim of an apparent kidnapping in San José, Costa Rica, by Nicaragua's Sandinistas the previous month, he said he was working in the region as a paymaster for Argentine military officers training anti-Sandinista rebels.[24]

In late 1980 Francés said, some fifty former Somocista National Guardsmen were trained in Argentina in paramilitary tactics. The Argentines also worked closely with Guatemalan death squad leader Mario Sandoval Alarcón and Maj. Roberto D'Aubuisson in El Salvador. One of his partners, he said, was Mariano Santa María, later identified as Juan Martín Ciga Correa, the former Milicia activist linked to the 1974 murder of Chilean General Prats in Buenos Aires. Training for the Contras, he continued, was being done in Honduras under the aegis of Honduran armed forces commander Gen. Gustavo Alvarez. A key contact, he said, was Senator Jesse Helms' close friend Nat Hamrick, who lived in Costa Rica.

With financial assistance from the CIA, Alvarez had brought Argentine "counterterrorism experts" to Honduras in 1980 to train both the Honduran security forces and the Nicaraguan Contras. He was also responsible for the introduction of Argentine-style tactics to his country, presiding over the disappearance of scores of people between 1981 and 1984. Alvarez, claimed U.S. Army Gen. Robert Schweitzer, who met him when he was working for the National Security Council (NSC), was the "one Central American general I met who had both reason and vision." Alvarez was also the godfather of the daughter of the CIA station chief in Tegucigalpa.[25]

The "Final Report"

In April the regime issued a "final report" on the "dirty war." The forty-five-minute television documentary dashed hopes that the military would give a full accounting on the fate of the missing. All those who are not in exile or in hiding are presumed dead, it said. The generals took responsibility for the actions of the security forces, explaining that the "apocalyptic" means by which the guerrillas waged war necessitated drastic countermeasures. The film's unrepentant tone was buttressed by scenes of fires, chaotic protests, and mutilated bodies. Argentina was besieged, the announcer said, by a huge and hidden army, whose soldiers wore no uniforms, carried no valid documents, and had infiltrated every area of national life.[26]

In response Italy's venerable President Sandro Pertini shot off a blistering telegram to the junta, condemning the report's "chilling cynicism … beyond human civility." The Argentine Permanent Assembly for Human Rights pointed to "innumerable proofs that 80 percent of the detained-disappeared were kidnapped from their homes, on the streets or at their workplaces before witnesses." Emilio Mignone, the dean of Argentina's human rights groups, scoffed at government claims that it had faced 15,000 armed opponents. "If Argentina had 15,000 guerrillas, today there would not be any Argentine army, given the incompetence they showed during the Malvinas war." On May 20 Adolfo Pérez Esquivel, the Argentine human rights activist who won the 1980 Nobel Peace Prize, led some 25,000 people through downtown Buenos Aires in a nighttime protest of the final report. Among those accompanying Pérez Esquivel, tired and drawn after eleven days of fasting, were dozens carrying signs protesting the abduction-murders of a Peronist activist and a former Montonero leader a week earlier.[27]

Although even Pope John Paul II strongly criticized the report, the U.S. government posted only a wan comment. Harry Shlaudeman's embassy claimed that because there were no Americans missing there was no need to speak up. In fact, at least three Americans were still unaccounted for—a fact the embassy knew but covered up in a conspiracy of silence.[28]

In June a judge ordered Massera jailed in connection with the 1977 murder of Fernando Branca, a former business associate and the husband of Massera's mistress. Massera, who went sailing with Branca on the last day he was seen alive, had returned from the outing alone. The would-be president of the Argentines stayed behind bars until the 1985 "dirty war" trial.[29]

In September 1983 the junta made a last stand by enacting a bitterly debated law granting the military amnesty from prosecution for acts committed during the "dirty war." However, the government also authorized civilian elections to be held ahead of schedule on October 30, 1983.

Raúl Alfonsín: Facing the Past Without Fear

Fifty-six-year-old Raúl Alfonsín had been a vigorous opponent of the military, literally risking his life as a member of the Permanent Assembly for Human Rights and in his unfailing attempts to seek out information about missing friends and others. He was an early critic of Martínez de Hoz and stood almost alone in his opposition to the Falkland/Malvinas war. The death of Radical leader Balbín, and the general discredit of a political class that had been silent during the "dirty war" and vocal in support of that in the South Atlantic, made Alfonsín an attractive alternative. He was helped by a women's vote that sought peace and security for their children and the vote of tens of thousands of former industrial workers who, after losing their jobs, became self-employed. No longer did these people see the state as an intrusive but beneficent and protective agent but rather as the instrument of regulations and taxes.[30]

For most of the campaign Alfonsín did not expect to win, and he geared his campaign to making the Radicals into the first viable political opposition in Argentina since the advent of Perón. The military who led the repression would be tried, he promised. The foreign debt would be negotiated on easier terms and the banks forced to share losses on that part found to be illegitimate. Prosperity would return and be shared. And Argentina would steer clear of the cold war shoals of U.S. foreign policy. In a nation weary of generals, his campaign manager explained, Alfonsín projected the authority of an elementary school principal. He often stopped in the middle of a speech to point to someone who had fainted from the heat or from emotion, asking for a doctor. The tactic became something of a joke among the press, but the message was clear: Here was a leader who would not send people to their deaths on a whim.[31]

After a failed attempt to get Isabel Perón to run, the Peronists chose as their candidate the colorless former provisional president and constitutional expert Italo Argentino Luder. Amid a wave of anti-Jewish violence Alberto Ottalagano, the former rector of the University of Buenos Aires under Isabel, was photographed giving a Nazi salute and warning Jews "not to show themselves too much." Lorenzo Miguel, back again as leader of the powerful metalworkers union, was quoted as praising Italian dictator Benito Mussolini. And after back-to-back Radical and Peronist rallies in downtown Buenos Aires, each drawing more than 1 million people, the right-wing Peronist Buenos Aires gubernatorial candidate Hermino Iglesias torched a coffin meant to symbolize the Radical party. Violence-weary voters recoiled.[32]

Luder straddled the issue of whether the military could amnesty itself for crimes committed during the "dirty war," lending credence to Alfonsín's charge that Peronist labor leaders were conspiring with the military to circumvent the democratic process in a "military-union pact." The military, Alfonsín charged, were returning union titles and property, worth millions of dollars, to the Peronists. In return, he said, they received assurances that if elected the Peronists would not call the military to account for their crimes.[33]

As the election approached, the contest grew closer. A sea change was about to take place: a return to Argentina's long-dormant civic tradition. As the polls opened, and Alfonsín's victory became apparent, the army intelligence chief charged with monitoring the election suffered a heart attack. There were some bodies that just could not resist such torture.[34]

¡Viva la Democracia!

Alfonsín's stunning triumph was a political turnabout comparable to Perón's victory in 1946. Winning 52 percent of the vote against 40 percent for Luder, Alfonsín's victory marked the first time in four decades that a non-Peronist candidate had won the presidency in a fair contest. The military ceased to be the only alternative to the Peronists.

Immediately following his inauguration on December 10, 1983—a time of wild celebration in the wide avenues of Buenos Aires—Alfonsín moved to redeem campaign promises of a return to the rule of law and peace. He quickly took steps to provide the climate and legal framework needed for democracy to survive. A major reform of the military was begun, scores of generals were forced into retirement, a civilian appointed as the head of Fabricaciones Militares, and the runaway defense budget brought under control, with the proportion of GNP allocated to the military nearly halved. The SIDE was forced to admit ownership of, and close, its Saporiti "news" agency.[35]

The Bignone junta's amnesty law was nullified and courts martial ordered for the nine members of the first three juntas on charges of mass murder. (The cases were later transferred to the civilian courts, after the military proved unwilling to try its own.) In an early sign of judicial independence, against Alfonsín's own wishes Bignone himself was indicted on charges connected with two "disappearances." The new president also ordered the prosecution of several guerrilla leaders, including Firmenich and ERP leader Enrique Haroldo Gorriarán Merlo. The last of the Argentine military advisers—a dwindling number since the South Atlantic war—officially working with the Nicaraguan Contras were called home. And a blue-ribbon commission was named to investigate the legacy of the "dirty war"; the Sábato Commission reported back that it had evidence of at least 9,000 disappearances.

Alfonsín also moved to shore up Argentina's battered international prestige, committing his government to a peaceful settlement of the Falkland/Malvinas dispute. Despite strong opposition from some sectors of Peronism, Argentina and Chile reached an agreement with the help of a Vatican mediation committee settling the Beagle Channel dispute. Argentina's nuclear program was taken out of the hands of the navy and targeted for a 30 percent budget reduction.

By the time the military handed the government over to Alfonsín, Argentina's foreign debt had quintupled, to $39 billion, from 1976, with production remaining essentially unchanged from what it had been under Peronism. By early 1984 officials estimated the foreign indebtedness of state-owned enterprises alone at more than $11.3 billion—a major drag on the economy. The blue-collar work force had shrunk to 1.3 million, from 1.8 million in 1976. Unemployment ballooned, while inflation rose to more than 450 percent.[36]

The return of democracy was also met with a change in the attitude of foreign bankers. Gone were the days of wild lending fueled by petrodollars; in their place was a new tough line for Latin creditors. Unwilling to accept their responsibility—losses—for their reckless loan policies, the banks demanded stringent economic "reforms" from countries whose new leaders were struggling to show their people that democracy meant freedom, not economic hardship. In exchange for temporary fixes of credit the leaders of these fragile, fledgling democracies were pressed for even greater austerity. The response of the Reagan administration was the Baker Plan, named after the secretary of the treasury, which importuned harsh austerity measures while it piled new debts upon the old. It was like being asked to learn how not to breathe.

Early in the Alfonsín administration an attempt was made by the new government to play "debt chicken" with the over-exposed foreign banks, trying to get them to share in the losses made during the military regime or face the specter of a "debtors' cartel." For a while, the strategy seemed to work. Over time, however, the banks built up reserves against losses as they kept talking, thus shoring up their own position in the negotiations. Intermediaries such as Kissinger Associates, whose clients included the Rockefeller family's Chase Manhattan Bank, had the task of pointing out—as one executive said—"conflicts or potential conflicts that exist among the debtor nations, or to make them up where they don't exist." Meanwhile the Radicals moved slowly on needed free-market reforms, hampered by opposition from the Peronists, from businessmen grown fat on government contracts, and by their own statist notions held dear during nearly two decades in the political wilderness. Dozens of state-owned companies suffered billions of dollars in losses. Such dilations proved to be the Radicals' Achilles' heel.[37]

Dead Men's Tales

After 2,818 days it was over. The National Reorganization Process had ended. In the weeks that followed Alfonsín's inauguration, more than 200 bodies were dug up in grave sites around the country. Some were buried individually, many interred en masse. Most bore signs of violence: skulls perforated by bullet holes, skeletons missing hands, a sackful of human fragments in a dirty plastic bag. "I feel like such a fool," said one Buenos Aires businessman vacationing with his family in the Tierra del Fuego city of Ushuaia. Tears welled in his eyes as he watched a televised newscast in a hotel lobby of a search for the bodies of several children. "Just last year I was in Rome and some people there asked me about the missing. I told them they had been getting their information from the communists."[38]

For the relatives of the missing the need for psychological help was greater than at any time since the disappearances. Years of fear had given way to reliving the experience. As the bodies were unearthed, the media provided sensationalistic coverage. Some detainees had been burned alive, the reports said. Others were drugged, linked together hand and foot, and played out like a string of sausages from airplanes over the Atlantic. Pregnant women had spoons shoved up their vaginas by men with nicknames like Mengele, who then applied electric current to the fetuses.

On New Year's Eve seventy-two-year-old Alfredo Galletti, a lawyer and human rights activist whose own daughter had disappeared, jumped to his death from his fourth-story window. The sight of the bodies and the fact that most of the accused military still walked the streets as free men were too much to bear, friends said. "There are still parents who are paying dues to their children's professional associations, who are paying their membership fees in clubs and maintaining their apartments," said CELS lawyer Marcelo Parilli. "Yesterday a woman came into the office who hadn't slept for three days. She's been sitting alongside the door in her house so she'd be sure to be there when her son came home."[39]

U.S. Policy: Hedging Bets

After the Falkland/Malvinas war ended, the U.S. embassy mounted an ambitious effort to win back the generals. In June 1982, as the beleaguered military announced its plan to return power to civilians, the Reagan administration began pushing to resume arms sales—banned since 1978 as a result of rights violations—as a "good faith" gesture. Many saw the move as a sign the United States was hedging its bets on democracy and expected the military to have a future *political* role. And even though disappearances and secret executions had tapered off, it was pointed out, the architects and executioners of those policies were still in power. "If Hitler would have stopped killing Jews in 1944," noted rights activist Emilio Mignone, "it would hardly have justified the allies seeking better relations with him."[40]

Embassy deputy chief of mission John Bushnell told Mignone "how worried the military were about their safety and the possibility of acts of vengeance against their families—this at a time when Mignone and the relatives were being subjected to a campaign of intimidation." While his boss, Harry Shlaudeman, predicted a possible Alfonsín victory early on, Bushnell said that a Peronist win would provide a working-class anti-Communist bulwark in the region.[41]

Alfonsín's victory was met with apprehension and dismay by U.S. officials, particularly in the intelligence community. In *Veil: The Secret Wars of the CIA* Bob Woodward captured these policymakers' concerns, as seen through the eyes of CIA Director Casey:

> Just before the election in Argentina ... [National Intelligence Officer John] Horton had undertaken a Special National Intelligence Estimate to forecast the election. Looks like this guy Raúl Alfonsín, a center-left lawyer who heads a party called the Radical Civic Union, is going to win. ... Casey grumbled a question, and Horton said that it looked as though Alfonsín's victory was going to be good for Argentina after eight years of military dictatorship, but that, given his left-of-center position, it probably wasn't going to be so good for the United States.
>
> Casey gazed at Horton and asked, "Is he a Marxist-Leninist?"
>
> Horton wondered why that was the only question from the DCI [Director of Central Intelligence].[42]

That November Gen. Robert Schweitzer, chairman of the Inter-American Defense Board, a regional entity dominated by the United States, slipped into Argentina to meet with top military officers. The new constitutional authorities were not informed about the trip and were livid when they found out about it. The *Los Angeles Times* reported on December 30, 1983, that U.S. military attachés were "running wild" in Buenos Aires, beyond the control of the civilian staff of the embassy. The new American ambassador, Frank Ortiz, had been fired by the Carter administration as envoy to Guatemala for his coziness with the "dirty war" generals there. A U.S. "present" on the eve of Alfonsín's inauguration, lifting the arms ban, came after the new government had made it clear they did not want such a gift.[43]

Such fumbling continued well into the Alfonsín administration. The embassy scoffed at attempts by the Argentines to examine whether part of their foreign debt inheritance was "illegitimate," and an economic attaché called the discredited Martínez de Hoz, later a co-defendant in an extortion suit, a "saint." Mariano Grondona and rightist politician Alvaro Alsogaray, notorious promilitary apologists, were favored guests at embassy functions, with Alsogaray's party receiving funds from a U.S. Republican party institute.[44]

The legacy of the "dirty war" and U.S. policy toward Central America were the focus of the most bitter disputes. The new government lobbied vigorously for a negotiated approach to the conflict in Central America. In response, Ortiz launched a quiet campaign against Foreign Minister Dante Caputo, the architect of the Alfonsín policy. U.S. pressure on the Alfonsín government to march in lockstep with the Reagan administration in support of the Contras intensified palpably.[45]

Throughout 1985, both before and during the trial against the military commanders, rumors of a military coup raced through Buenos Aires' political circuits. In October, reacting to a rash of bombings by 601 army intelligence batallion officers—caught telephoning threats to grade schools—Alfonsín declared a state of emergency on the eve of parliamentary elections. (One of those named by the government as a conspirator was army Col. Pascual Guerrieri, once a key member of II Army Corps commander Gen. Galtieri's Quinta de Funes operation and, later, part of 601 chief Valín's CIA-backed Central American operation.)[46]

A month later five of the generals were convicted. Within days the U.S. chief representative to the United Nations, Gen. Vernon Walters, a former deputy director of the CIA, warned darkly of a possible resurgence of subversion in countries such as Argentina and neighboring Uruguay. "The Montoneros and the Tupamaros have not died, they've simply gone into clandestinity and now they're returning," Walters said, pointing out that, among others, Mario Firmenich was still alive. "They are still alive and we'll be hearing more about them." U.S. embassy officials denied that Walter's charge—gleefully seized upon by the Argentine right—was linked to the trials or part of an effort to throw the dispirited military a lifeline.[47]

Sequels of the Central America Connection

The legacy of the military's involvement in Central America surfaced with disquieting regularity. In late 1984 Juan Martín Ciga Correa, alias Mariano Santa María, the 601 army intelligence agent who had served as paymaster for Argentine "dirty war" operatives in Honduras, El Salvador, and Guatemala, was arrested in Mar del Plata in a stolen car. At the time of his arrest the former Milicia activist and Stefano Delle Chiaie cohort was carrying an army issue Colt .45 pistol and phony army identification credentials.[48]

That same year it was revealed that the Alfonsín government had, out of necessity, organized a small "intelligence" unit operating out of the presidential palace and a nearby office. The scandal centered around the fact that one of those recruited was Raúl Guglielminetti, a neo-Nazi and jewelry store thief who, it was later disclosed, served as Argentine army liaison with the CIA in joint operations in Central America while living in Florida. Guglielminetti was also involved, with former SIDE chief Gen. Otto Paladino and his death squad associates Aníbal Gordon and Eduardo Ruffo, in an extortive kidnapping ring. Questions arose: How did he find his way into Alfonsín's personal entourage? Who was he working for? To what purpose?[49]

Alfonsín: To Build a Democracy

"Mr. Alfonsín's first 24 months in office have been the most turbulent early term of office experienced by any of the many new Latin American presidents who have led their countries into democracy during the 1980s," reported the *New York Times's* Lydia Chavez at the end of the 1985 "dirty war" trial. "Twice, he has gone on nationwide television to warn coup plotters against conspiring to destroy his government. ... Alfonsín's greatest advantage ... is that never before in the country's life has the military been so discredited."[50]

Alfonsín had inherited a human rights and military minefield. Accountability for past crimes became a top priority. As the extent of the horror was revealed, the military remained adamant in its refusal to either judge its own in courts-martial, as the new president urged, or to admit fundamental wrongdoing in the prosecution of the "dirty war." Alfonsín, who never envisioned the prosecution of more than a handful of top brass and the most horrific rights violators, found himself carried along by a wave of civic and antimilitary fervor. Long denied justice, the human rights groups amassed huge dossiers on past crimes and presented them to the courts. What willingness the government might have tried to show in attempting a reconciliation was dashed with every new or perceived example of armed forces' perfidity. The problem became acute after an apparent assassination attempt against Alfonsín, a 1984 attempt to murder Isabel Perón and several hundred other people by planting a bomb on the airplane in which she was riding, a similar try against visiting Italian President Sandro Pertini, a rash of bombings against political party headquarters, several unsolved kidnappings, and cases in which military death squad members arrested for common crimes were found to possess reams of fake Montonero flyers. In 1987 Perón's tomb was vandalized and his hands cut off and stolen, an act widely believed to be the work of people linked to one of the intelligence services.[51]

Alfonsín's drastic military budget cuts, slashing of the number of conscripts, and transfer of broad authorities from the generals to civilians—including the transfer of internal security functions to the police—helped to demilitarize Argentina. The trials underscored the fact that the new civilian leadership would not tolerate military challenges to its authority. None of this, however, served to professionalize the armed forces, a task requiring resources and a clear definition of new responsibilities. In time an officer corps with little taste for governance when it returned to the barracks in 1983 was back in center stage in the political arena.

Under Alfonsín's leadership, torture was made a crime punishable with the same severity as murder. The architects of the military's illegal repression were jailed, as were several of the political extremists who paved the way for the "dirty war." Any potential for vengeance withered as the victims saw that the justice system was working. The military were removed from internal security tasks, and Argentina's police forces received leaders chosen from their own ranks, rather than those of the military—lifting their morale and embuing them with a new sense of professionalism. The Federal Police, once a hotbed of neo-Nazi and criminal activity, was drastically though quietly reformed. (When in late 1987 the bodies of kidnapped businessman Osvaldo Sivak and several others were discovered and a number of military and police officials arrested and charged with the murders, reform-minded Federal Police chief Juan Pirker appeared, hat in hand, on the doorstep of Sivak's home. "He told me," Sivak's widow recalled, "that he wanted to apologize in the name of the institution.") Alfonsín was alone among the leaders of the new Latin democracies to put a civilian, not a general, at the head of the Defense Ministry. A longtime military rivalry with Brazil was replaced with unprecedented economic integration. It was a time of cultural rebirth and reborn civility.[52]

There were also, Alfonsín admitted later, things that he wanted to do but could not and things he did not do but should have. An earlier effort to "democratize" the Peronist-run unions backfired, as the Radicals could not muster the necessary parliamentary support to put the reform into effect. (A series of crippling general strikes was part of the unionists' payback.) A 1987 effort to solidify working-class support for the Radicals by incorporating orthodox Peronist labor leaders into his government caused dismay and disaffection among those who believed the bosses to be undemocratic and complicit with the military. An ultimately successful effort to legalize divorce in Argentina, one of only seven countries where it was not permitted, cost substantial goodwill among the hierarchy of the Catholic church. A plan to move the federal capital from Buenos Aires to the Atlantic coast provincial town of Viedma, justified as a visionary attempt to decentralize power and modernize Argentina's ailing infrastructure, ended up being a political drag and the butt of jokes. Alfonsín was also criticized for spending a large amount of political capital trying to reform the constitution to allow for his own reelection.

The Holy Week Revolt

Alfonsín faced several factional struggles within the armed forces, mostly in the army, in the first three years of his term and responded by carrying out several purges of the military high command. Following the celebrated 1985 trials, however, the Radicals tried to put a "final stop" to prosecutions of military offenders by establishing a deadline for future legal action against members of the armed forces. The move, which Alfonsín said was designed to put a halt to "the unending suspicion" hanging over security force personnel, was bitterly criticized by the human rights organizations and large sectors of the Radical and Peronist parties, the latter in the throes of an effort to reform and modernize its appeal. In January 1987 the rights groups raced against the clock to bring more than 600 new cases, including those against five of Argentina's thirty-five serving generals and an active-duty admiral, before the courts before the deadline. The officer corps, particularly in the army, was beside itself.[53]

Following a week-long visit by Pope John Paul II, who declared "Never Again!" to a massive Palm Sunday rally in downtown Buenos Aires, Maj. Ernesto Barreiro, the chief torturer at La Perla concentration camp, holed up at an army base and refused to testify before a civilian court. Within hours officers from around the country declared their support of the protest and demanded that Alfonsín end the trials, amnesty their jailed former commanders, and purge the senior army officer corps, replacing the loyal generals with men of their choosing. For three dramatic days Alfonsín, who said Argentina's democracy "was not negotiable," rallied the country, filling the Plaza de Mayo with hundreds of thousands of people. Troops loyal to the government, however, proved unwilling to advance on their rebellious brethren.

On Easter Sunday Alfonsín went to the Campo de Mayo army base where hundreds of rebels were dug in—and were surrounded by a mob of thousands of angry citizens—to demand their surrender. Showing considerable physical courage, Alfonsín was able to force the ringleader, Lt. Col. Aldo Rico, a veteran of the Falkland/Malvinas debacle, to give up. Less than a month later, however, Alfonsin announced a further restriction on rights prosecutions of the military, with the prosecution of most officers limited to crimes of rape, robbery, theft, and the kidnapping of children. "I am perfectly aware that this law may let those who committed grave acts go free," Alfonsín admitted, "and I don't like it." The move was hailed by the the rebels as both a recognition of their demands and a concession won through revolt. Although the government responded that the concessions had been planned since earlier in the year, the public was in little mood for compromises. Alfonsín's star began to fade.[54]

There were two other armed revolts by the rebellious army officers, during the second of which several civilians were killed. The first occurred in January 1988 and was again headed by right-wing nationalist Rico. And in December Col. Mohamed Alí Seineldín, the onetime death squad leader who participated in the Bolivian "cocaine coup" and the South Atlantic campaign, returned from his post as a trainer for Panamanian Gen. Manuel Noriega's Defense Forces to carry out a third armed action against the government. Seineldín's uprising was forcefully put down by a weary army high command. The presence of U.S. Ambassador Theodore Gildred, representative of a slow, post–Iran-Contra swing to the political center by the Reagan State Department, in the Argentine parliament building at a critical time during the revolt was credited with providing dramatic and needed support for the government. Seineldín's defeat was viewed as the end of military tolerance for the barracks revolts.[55]

In early 1989 there was yet another assault on a military base, this time La Tablada army barracks just outside of Buenos Aires. Three times in the space of twenty-one months, the threat to Argentine democracy had come from officers demanding vindication for their role in the "dirty war." This time, however, those involved in the attack, in which thirty-nine people died, were leftists. The attack, which Federal Police chief Juan Pirker later said he could have suppressed "with a tear-gas brigade," was put down by army troops with a ferociousness missing during the earlier revolts by fellow officers. When the insurgents' identities and foreign connections became known, the unrepentant right—egged on by Mariano Grondona and Aníbal Vigil's *Somos* and *Gente*—had a field day. "No one," wrote the playwright Osvaldo Soriano of the guerrillas in the center-left daily *Página* 12, "had so far done so much in favor of the 'vindication' demanded by the armed forces."[56]

Among those who had died was Jorge Baños, a well-known activist and former CELS lawyer. Baños's All for the Fatherland movement suffered most of the casualties in the attack. Several of the combatants were former members of the ERP, and the leader of the assault was one of Argentina's most wanted fugitives, former ERP commander Enrique Gorriarán Merlo.

The attack on La Tablada, on the eve of Argentina's general election, created a yawning gap in public confidence and aggravated a serious economic collapse. Inflation soared to nearly 100 percent a month. Electrical brownouts and a water shortage created a sense of despair. In May food riots broke out in several major cities, including Buenos Aires. The military urged that they be called in to restore order. Devastated by events, Alfonsín nonetheless resisted. Similar disturbances a few months before in democratic Venezuela, where the military had an internal security function, had resulted in as many as 2,000 deaths. Instead, Alfonsín left the problem to the police. Although fifteen people died, few deaths were the result of police action.[57]

Like Spain's Adolfo Suárez and Soviet President Mikhail Gorbachev, Alfonsín's time in office marked a transition toward a modern democratic state but failed to provide the economic well-being most people associate with such advances. Like Moses in the Old Testament, he brought Argentina within sight of a promised land, but it was not he who was to lead them into it. On July 8, 1989, Argentine democracy took a giant step toward its consolidation. For the first time in more than sixty years a civilian, Alfonsín, placed the blue-and-white presidential sash on the shoulders of his elected successor, Peronist Carlos Saúl Menem. A prisoner of the military for five years after the 1976 coup, Menem had frequently recalled that while he was jailed he was often kept awake by the sounds of his fellow detainees being tortured during the night.[58]

Epilogue

Q: You know why there never are any military coups in the United States?
A: Because Washington doesn't have an American ambassador.
                                                    —*Common Latin American joke*

We lived many lives ... never sparing ourselves any good or evil; yet when we
had achieved, and the new world dawned, the old men came out again, and
took from us our victory, and remade it in the likeness of the former world
they knew. ... We stammered that we had worked for a new heaven, and a
new earth, and they thanked us kindly, and made their peace.
                                                    —*T. E. Lawrence*

In the late 1970s the Argentine military claimed victory in a struggle they
boasted was the opening battle of World War III. Bombast and double salaries as
"combat pay" aside, however, there was no war, only a witch-hunt whose vicious-
ness led Argentine storyteller Jorge Luis Borges to admonish puckishly that can-
nibalism cannot be ended by eating the cannibals.

In 1982 a short war with Britain showed the world that, whatever merits the Argentine generals claimed in their pursuit of unarmed workers, students, and religious activists, in a real conflict the black art of propaganda and disinformation
in the end could not hide the rout or the ease the humiliation. And throughout
the 1980s reports of brutality and murder committed by the Contras—trained by
Argentine dirty warriors at U.S. taxpayers' expense—seemed to prove the wisdom of Perón's saying: "What begins badly, ends badly."

In 1989 a group of Argentine civilian and military experts in defense issues visited the Pentagon as part of an effort by the National Democratic Institute for International Affairs (NDI), a Washington-based democratic development institute, to promote better civil-military relations in Argentina. The project was
designed to help empower civilian managers in defense and security questions, so
that they might exercise greater and more informed oversight over "the other
Argentina"—that populated by the military. The program had the explicit endorsement of President Alfonsín.

After several top-level briefings, the group stopped for lunch at a Pentagon dining room. It was still early in the thaw in U.S.-Soviet relations, and it was something of a novelty to see a knot of Red Army officers sitting down at a nearby table with their American counterparts.

The Argentines' host was Maj. Gen. Richard Goetze, the vice-director of the Pentagon's joint staff. Goetze, who had served as an air force attaché in Argentina in 1978 and 1979, turned on the charm. He mentioned the fact that his wife was born in Argentina, of Croatian parents, and told about the time he spent there. The group chuckled appreciatively at his stories. Then the laughter stopped. "You know, you wouldn't be here today if the Argentine military didn't do what it did," Goetze told his stunned guests in Spanish. "They did a good job in the antisubversive war, the trouble was *ellos no zafaron a tiempo*," he said, slipping into Buenos Aires slang, "they didn't get out of the government early enough— that was the problem."[1]

Goetze was wrong on three counts. The military had not seized power because they wanted to restore democratic rule. Nor was what they fought a war. "The problem" was not a question of timing—it was crimes against humanity, a methodology found repugnant the world over—or at least most of it. Yet Goetze's view was typical of a mind-set prevalent throughout the U.S. security establishment. Just how wrong he—and they—were, I have tried to show.

Gladiators in the Mists

In 1990 a Venetian judge investigating the detonation of a vehicle full of explosives came across a secret society whose existence was also political dynamite. Founded in the early 1950s, Gladio (the Sword) was composed of 622 members, civilian and military, who enjoyed protection from the highest levels of the Italian government. During the 1970s the military intelligence chiefs who ran Gladio were members of the P-2, including retired general and neofascist deputy Vito Miceli. Gladio's defenders suggested that the operation was designed to organize resistance to a Soviet invasion, an unlikely prospect given that hundreds of "gladiators" could not be expected to hold off the Red Army. Some saw the real threat as the possibility of an electoral victory by the Italian Communist party. Suspicions arose that the gladiators may have been involved in the fascist bombings in the 1970s, in the murder of Aldo Moro, and as part of the "strategy of tension" aimed at preventing the Communist party from being elected to government office—rather than seizing power as some fifth column force. The *New York Times* noted that "at best" Gladio

> is no more than a curious footnote to the cold war. The question is if, at worst, it could be the key to unsolved terrorism dating back two decades. ... There were long-reported links between Italian secret services and neo-Fascists. And there is the fact that the major unsolved acts of terrorism that rocked Italy in the 1970s are all pre-

sumed to be the work of people on the far right. Left-wing terrorists like the moribund Red Brigades somehow were caught and imprisoned.[2]

Roberto Cavallaro, one of those who participated in Gladio, was interviewed by the Italian newsmagazine *Panorama:*

> In answer to the question, "what was the mission of the organization?" Cavallaro said: "To engage in the covert training of groups who in the event the leftists in our country made a move, would take to the streets to create a situation so tense as to require military intervention. Our mission," he said, "was to infiltrate these groups."
> … The interviewer asked a specific question. "Are you saying that your organization infiltrated the Red Brigades?" he asked. "I had specific knowledge," Cavallaro said, "that many of the terrorists—both red and black—were acting on the basis of directives or suggestions from the secret services."[3]

Carlos Menem: To Err Is Human

As the cold war wound down, Carlos Menem sought to put Argentina on a new footing for the new world order. Throughout his presidential campaign, Menem had held out the promise of a return to Peronist orthodoxy—nationalism and statism. At the head of a heterogeneous coalition that included Montoneros and right-wing nationalists such as army rebel Seineldín, Menem vowed he would not amnesty the leaders of the military juntas convicted in 1985.

Following his inauguration, Menem confounded expectations—and jettisoned his electoral promises—by moving swiftly to privatize state enterprises and seek better relations with the United States. Both moves won wide praise in Washington. The accolades were tempered only slightly by worries about the spillover effects on Menem's free-market experiment of several public scandals within his administration. These included an alleged drug money–laundering operation run by Menem inlaws employed by the presidency, the ties to the shadowy Bank of Commerce and Credit International (BCCI) of two top Menem advisers, and a shakedown by Menem's brother-in-law of an American company doing business in Argentina. At the urging of the U.S. embassy, Menem also sought to give the military a role, albeit limited, in internal security and drug interdiction—something that had been denied to them under Alfonsín.[4]

Menem's decision to grant a blanket pardon to those tried and sentenced for their part in the "dirty war," the war in the South Atlantic, and the three military uprisings against Alfonsín created one of the greatest controversies during his early years as president. Having won office in a landslide, aligning his government with that of the United States, and signaling his intention to carry out an orthodox economic policy, there was little apparent reason or gain for Menem to bow to the highly unpopular military demand for a pardon. The unprecedented decision to try the military juntas had helped set down the basis for a return to the civility and the rule of law and marked a high point in Argentina's quest for democracy and justice. The assault on military impunity undertaken during Alfonsín's stewardship reverberated throughout the region, giving civilians a new benchmark of accountability and putting the generals as far away as El Salvador on notice that today's crimes might not be forgotten tomorrow. In a column entitled "Pardoning Mass Murder in Argentina," the *New York Times* found that the amnesty made little sense:[5]

> For no good reason, President Carlos Menem … has trashed his country's finest achievement of the last 60 years. Previous civilian authorities … courageously re-established the vital constitutional principle that all citizens, military officers included, are accountable to the rule of law. Now, in a country still prone to coup attempts, the tradition of military impunity has been restored. … Mr. Menem portrayed his action as a gesture of reconciliation, closing the book on a tragic past. Instead he has invited a repetition of the tragedy by resurrecting the idea that the military can hold itself above the law.

Jorge Videla and *Emilio Massera,* sentenced to life imprisonment in 1985, and *Roberto Viola,* sentenced to seventeen years, were all pardoned by Menem in December 1990. Videla sent Menem a letter claiming that military rule had permitted "the continuation of the republican and democratic system of government." He demanded support for all actions undertaken during the illegal repression. U.S. embassy favorite *Alvaro Alsogaray* said the generals deserved not only an amnesty but a parliamentary commendation as well. "We must give General Videla and the commanders their due," he said, "as winners of a war."[6]

José Martínez de Hoz, released from prison by Menem's pardon after being held for the extortion of an Argentine businessman while serving as economy czar, later claimed intellectual parentage of Menem's free-market reforms.[7]

Carlos Suárez Mason, the former head of the powerful I Army Corps and—like Massera and López Rega—a member of the P-2, had fled Argentina when Alfonsín was inaugurated. In January 1987 he was discovered living outside San Francisco. Deported, he faced thirty-nine counts of murder. At his trial Suárez Mason claimed that the responsibility for the repression rested with his subordinates. He, too, was pardoned by Carlos Menem.[8]

Acdel Vilas, the erstwhile "Death's General" in Tucumán, was tried for his responsibility for murders, tortures, and kidnappings while serving as second in command of the V Army Corps. "If you please, I can give you a gun so you can do whatever you want to me," Vilas told the widow of a missing Bahía Blanca municipal councilman, after offering to explain the circumstances of her husband's death. "He was in terrible shape," she said later. "Despite our surprise, we told him we were educated to respect human life, that that was not the solution we were looking for, that we only wanted justice and not vengeance." Vilas was also pardoned.[9]

Raúl Guglielminetti, the former army liaison with the CIA in Central America and mole in the Alfonsín government, was arrested in November 1991 along with nearly a dozen former security service personnel and accused of taking part in a ring responsible for the extortion and murder of Argentine businessmen in the 1970s and 1980s. He was later released.[10]

Mario Firmenich

Mario Firmenich, army 601 intelligence agent and Montonero guerrilla leader, had been apprehended in Rio de Janeiro at the request of the Alfonsín government. Extradited to Buenos Aires, he was sentenced to thirty years in prison for crimes including four counts of murder and the kidnapping of Juan and Jorge Born. Firmenich denied having taken part in the June 1975 press conference—held at a state intelligence safe house—where Jorge Born was released. While in jail, Firmenich took political science classes at a local university. Although Menem chief of staff Alberto Kohan admitted that Menem knew of Firmenich's dual identity, he was included—for balance—as a Montonero chief in the December 1990 pardon.[11]

Firmenich's cooperation with the army, well known in the U.S. intelligence community, helped the Argentine military to justify their state terrorism and the illegal seizure of power. Perhaps the most egregious example of intelligence manipulation of a guerrilla group, Firmenich's double role was, however, by no means unique in Latin America. In Uruguay, for example, union activist Héctor Amodio Pérez, one of the most important leaders of the Tupamaro guerrilla organization, worked secretly for army intelligence for several years, before the generals there used an already-exhausted leftist threat as an excuse to take power in 1973. Military rule in Uruguay, "the torture chamber of Latin America," lasted twelve years.[12]

A perhaps even more notable case was that of Brazilian José Anselmo Dos Santos, known as Cabo Anselmo. The newsmagazine *Isto E* reported that Dos Santos, a navy enlisted man who took part in a junior officers' revolt in 1964 and who later traveled to Cuba for guerrilla instruction, had been secretly responsible for the smashing of the Vanguarda Popular Revolucionaria (VPR; Popular Revolutionary Vanguard), a small cellular network waging armed struggle against the U.S.-supported military regime. In 1971, *Isto E* stated, the "guerrilla" Dos Santos became an informant for the São Paolo Department of Social and Political Order headed by CIA confidant Sergio Paranhos Fleury. According to Dos Santos's own account, "Thanks to my indications, some 100 to 200 people died," including his Paraguayan wife, Soledad Viedma.[13]

Although none of the known cases of infiltration match in cynicism and blood the cooperation extended by Firmenich to Argentine army intelligence, as in the infiltration of Italian extremist groups, serious questions arise as to the real authorship, motives, and purposes of much of the left-wing violence in Latin America for more than a decade and, to a lesser degree, in Europe. Where was the line drawn—if at all—between infiltration and instigation? Who benefited from the violence? To what purpose did these phony pied pipers of revolution help lead a generation of sometimes radicalized but largely nonviolent students, intellectuals, religious leaders, and workers to languish in torture chambers and extermination camps?

In March 1991, following his pardon, Firmenich—still playing the role of guerrilla leader—was interviewed by Spanish television. The immense majority of the missing, he said, "were Montoneros ... although a couple of *desaparecidos* might not have been involved." A "war" had existed in Argentina, and he and Videla "were scapegoats." The people, he said, "were the ones who asked for the coup, given the anarchy of the Peronist government. They supported the Videla regime socially and politically. Later, very hypocritically they said, 'I wash my hands, we didn't know anything, oh, how terrible the things they did, this man is a demon.'" Videla, Firmenich reiterated, was "a scapegoat because his dictatorship had social consensus—if not, it wouldn't have existed."[14]

On June 1, 1992, Mario Firmenich appeared for the first time on an Argentine television program. The moderator of the show was Enrique Llamas de Madariaga, a right-wing nationalist who gained international notoriety in 1981 for his blatantly anti-Semitic televised comments. ("Why is it that Jews are so greedy?" "Why are there no poor Jews?" "What are you first, Argentine or Jew?" "I don't know if there were as many Jews concerned for the victims of the earthquake in Argentina as contributed money during the Six Day War.")

Impeccably dressed in a gray suit, white shirt, and red tie, his hair groomed back in his trademark style, Firmenich claimed several times that there had been a "civil war" in Argentina, although he denied taking direct part in any armed actions after the Cámpora government took office on May 25, 1973. Although he said he accepted "political responsibility" for the Montoneros' violence, he laid the real responsibility on members of what he called the group's cellular structure. "The truth of the matter was," he said, "knowledge of each act was [limited] to those who participated in it. We called it 'strategic subordination and tactical autonomy' and it was a political measure. With absolute autonomy, the compartmentalized groups acted by themselves."

"It is not a secret to anyone that there were *fuegos cruzados* [crossfires], that there were not just two trenches. ... In some cases there was a margin of doubt about the material authorship [of specific acts of violence]." In a civil war, Firmenich added, "those not involved are those who have left the country. Everyone else takes part, some from underneath their beds, others bearing arms, but committed nonetheless."

Firmenich, who without Menem's amnesty would have been eligible for release from prison on February 13, 2014, claimed the Montoneros had made a pact with the civilian president that included Firmenich's release, part of an effort "to look forward to the future," he said. Although he was vague about much of the past, Firmenich was careful to mention the former Montonero membership of several people who had quit the organization, including Menem bête noire Horacio

Verbitsky, a highly regarded critic of government corruption and one-time intimate of Rodolfo Walsh. Verbitsky's runaway best-seller *Robo para la Corona* [Theft for the crown]—a carefully researched account of several scandals involving Menem family and friends—had already sold more than 250,000 copies. (Following publication of the book, a Menem ally in parliament, Miguel Angel Toma, accused Verbitsky of being the "intellectual author" of the 1973 murder of labor leader José Rucci. Juan Martín Romero Victorica, an ultra-right-wing federal prosecutor with ties to the military, claimed that the journalist was also involved in the 1974 killing of former Interior Minister Mor Roig. In fact, both killings were done by the minions of Social Welfare Minister López Rega.)[15]

Firmenich's appearance on television caused an uproar. "It is strange that he could remember Horacio Verbitsky's activism, but he couldn't remember who killed Rucci, Vandor or Alonso," charged former Peronist Youth leader Juan Carlos Dante Gullo. "Firmenich is a traitor, a cadaver, worse than Videla, a despicable being in every sense of the word," said Hebe de Bonafini, president of the Mothers of the Plaza de Mayo. "Everyone knows that he was on the side of the military."

The Rest of the Story

Julio Strassera, the prosecutor in the 1985 "dirty war" trials, was serving as Argentine ambassador to the UN Human Rights Commission in Geneva when the December 1990 pardons were announced. He resigned. "It is impossible for me to defend such a measure," he said. "The pardons are incompatible with the position I hold."[16]

In September 1984 *Henry Kissinger* emerged as an intermediary between the Alfonsín government and its foreign creditors. Hosting a meeting between the Argentine president and ten bankers at his Manhattan residence, Kissinger claimed, "I don't have any personal role in this, except that I am a friend of Argentina and of President Alfonsín, and of course, of the bankers." A December 1985 article in *Business Week* reported that twenty-eight U.S. and foreign multinational corporations, including David Rockefeller's Chase Manhattan, paid Kissinger a yearly retainer of between $150,000 and $250,000. In 1988 the *Washington Post* reported that he recommended at a private gathering that Israel prohibit television reporters and cameras from the occupied West Bank and that it suppress the revolts by Palestinians "as quickly as possible—overwhelmingly, brutally and rapidly." He also urged U.S. understanding and moderation with China after the slaughter of prodemocracy demonstrators there in 1989. Kissinger was a guest of honor at Menem's inauguration.[17]

Jeane Kirkpatrick frequently writes on foreign policy issues. Supporters say she had a key role in the democratization wave in Latin America that, by mid-1992 had left only the islands of Cuba and Haiti and the Republic of Peru seemingly adrift in dictatorship. During a state visit by Menem to Washington she penned an approving editorial in the *Washington Post,* underscoring his free-market reforms and pro-U.S. foreign policy.[18]

In a May 18, 1992, *Post* column entitled "Folding in the Face of Violence," Kirkpatrick heaped scorn on diplomats and international lawyers who are "misled by the likes of [Serbia's strongman] Milosevic (and the Ayatollah Khomeini and the Argentine generals). ...."

Kirkpatrick's revulsion for the Argentine military might have been taken more seriously, Holly Burkhalter, Washington director of the Human Rights Watch, noted later "if she [had] acknowledged and apologized for her indulgence of them when her views actually mattered: the years that they carried out unspeakable atrocities against the Argentine people, while she held a powerful post in the U.S. government."

About the same time *Elliott Abrams,* who replaced Patt Derian in the State Department and later became Assistant Secretary of State for Inter-American Affairs, pled guilty to lying to Congress in connection with the Iran-Contra scandal. The *Post* reported that Abrams's lobbying helped cause the Bush administration to ease sanctions against Haiti's brutal military dictatorship in early 1992.[19]

Isabel Perón was released by the military in July 1981 after serving more than six years of a seven-year, eleven-month sentence for corruption. She returned from exile in Madrid to visit Argentina several times during the Alfonsín government and is credited with playing a constructive role. Retired from politics, she spends her time in Spain and Argentina.

Mariano Grondona made use of the free press under Alfonsín to bash the new government in a way reminiscent of his anti-Illia campaign of the 1960s. An anti-Peronist commando in the 1950s, military propagandist in the 1960s, and apologist for López Rega *and* the military in the 1970s, Grondona became a visiting fellow at Harvard University after contributions for his stay were solicited from multinational corporations.[20]

José López Rega, the Rasputin of the Pampas who befriended Licio Gelli and organized Argentina's death squads, was arrested by the FBI in 1986 and extradited from Miami. Frail and sick, he died in prison in June 1989. His secrets went with him to the grave.

Licio Gelli escaped from Champs Dollon prison in Geneva, Switzerland, in August 1983. Four years later he surrendered to authorities in the same city. An Italian parliamentary commission charged that the P-2 was a subversive organization that plotted to undermine the Italian state. In testimony before the Argentine parliament Antonio Troccoli, Alfonsín's minister for law enforcement, called the P-2 "a huge criminal organization ... which was at the point of taking over the country." Convicted by a Florence court in December 1987 of having financed right-wing terrorists, three months later Gelli was extradited to Italy in a predawn police operation, apparently in fear for his life. In 1989 an appeals court overturned the convictions of Gelli and twelve others convicted for the 1980 Bologna train station bombing. The defendants included former heads of the Italian intelligence services and neo-Fascists.[21]

Stefano Delle Chiaie was arrested in March 1987 by Venezuelan police and returned to Italy to stand trial on charges that he was the mastermind of the Bologna train station bombing. His conviction, too, was later reversed by an appeals court.[22]

Enrique Haroldo Gorriarán Merlo, the ERP leader who led the attack on La Tablada army barracks during Alfonsín's government, is reported to be living in Cuba.

Jacobo Timerman returned from exile to Buenos Aires in 1984. He was compensated by the government for the illegal confiscation of his property and went on to turn the newspaper *La Razón*—a military mouthpiece since the death of Marcos Satanowsky—into a lively, informed, and *democratic* tabloid. He later wrote books critical of the dictatorships in Chile and in Cuba.[23]

Emilio Mignone, the dean of Argentina's human rights community, is still active in rights issues—and actively sought out—both in Argentina and abroad.

Carla Rutila Artés, the child kidnappped by SIDE agent Eduardo Ruffo—an aide to death squad leaders Aníbal Gordon and Raúl Guglielminetti—was recovered by the Grandmothers of the Plaza de Mayo and returned to her maternal grandmother. Although some four dozen children have been restored to the homes of their relatives, as of July 1992 more than 150 other children—either kidnapped or born in captivity—are still missing.

After a turbulent and unhappy stint as titular head of the Radical Civic Union, in 1991 *Raúl Alfonsín* resigned as leader of Argentina's largest opposition party. Like Jimmy Carter in the early 1980s, and Adolfo Suárez and Mikhail Gorbachev in the early 1990s, Alfonsín finds his most receptive audiences outside his own country. In March 1992 he was among those from Eastern Europe and Latin America who met to talk about "ways of avoiding the extremes of witch hunts and whitewashes in dealing with past political repression," the *Washington Post* reported. In an article entitled "East Europe Looks to Latin America For Cues on Repression's Aftermath," the *Post* noted that

> officials of the fledgling post-communist European democracies listened closely as ... Alfonsín told them why and how his government brought to justice the junta leaders he was elected to succeed in 1983.
>
> "Our intention," said Alfonsín, "was not so much to punish as it was to prevent, to stop what had happened from happening again, to guarantee that never again could an Argentine be taken out of his home at night and be tortured or assassinated by officials of the state apparatus."[24]

Acronyms

AAA	Triple A (Argentine Anticommunist Alliance)
AEI	aptitud especial para inteligencia (special intelligence aptitude)
AGA	Asociación Gremial de Abogados (Lawyers' Union Association)
ALN	Alianza Libertadora Nacionalista (Nationalist Liberating Alliance)
ANCLA	Agencia de Noticias Clandestina (Clandestine News Agency)
C de O	Comando de Organización (Organization Commando)
CAL	Confederación Anticomunista Latinoamericana (Latin American Anti-Communist Confederation)
CEA	Conferencia Episcopal Argentina (Argentine Episcopal Conference)
CELS	Centro de Estudios Legales y Sociales (Center for Legal and Social Studies)
CGE	Confederación General Económica (General Economic Confederation)
CGT	Confederación General del Trabajo (General Workers Confederation)
CIIR	Catholic Institute for International Relations
CNT	Convención Nacional de Trabajadores (National Workers Confederation)
CNU	Concentración Nacional Universitaria (National University Concentration)
COHA	Council on Hemispheric Affairs
CONADEP	Comisión Nacional sobre la Desaparición de Personas (National Commission on the Disappearance of Persons)
CONICET	Consejo Nacional de Investigaciones Científicas y Técnicas (National Council on Scientific and Technological Investigations)
CONINTES	Conmoción Interna del Estado (Internal Commotion of the State)
CTERA	Confederación de Trabajadores de la Enseñanza de la República Argentina (Confederation of Education Workers of the Argentine Republic)
CURS	Comité de Unificación para la Revolución Socialista (Committee for the Unification of the Socialist Revolution)
DAIA	Delegación de Asociaciones Israelitas Argentinas (Delegation of Argentine Israelite Associations)
DEA	Drug Enforcement Agency
DINA	Dirección de Información Nacional (National Information Directorate)
DOP	Departamento del Orden Político (Department of Political Order)
DS	Directivas Secretas (Secret Directives)
EAM '78	Ente Autárquico Mundial (World Cup Self-sustaining Entity)

ENC	Estrategia Nacional Contrasubversiva (National Counterinsurgency Strategy)
ERP	Ejército Revolucionario del Pueblo (People's Revolutionary Army)
ESMA	Escuela Mecánica de la Armada (Navy Mechanics School)
FAL	Fuerzas Armadas de Liberación (Liberation Armed Forces)
FAP	Fuerzas Armadas Peronistas (Peronist Armed Forces)
FAR	Fuerzas Armadas Revolucionarias (Revolutionary Armed Forces)
FOIA	Freedom of Information Act
FOTIA	Federación Obrera de Trabajadores de la Industria de Azúcar (Sugar Industry Workers Labor Federation)
FREJULI	Frente Justicialista de Liberación Nacional (Justicialist [Peronist] Front for National Liberation)
FRIP	Frente Revolucionario Indoamericano Popular (Indo-American Popular Revolutionary Front)
GOU	Grupo de Oficiales Unidos (United Officers Group)
GT	grupo de tareas (task group)
INR	Bureau of Intelligence and Research
JPA	Juventudes Políticas Argentinas (Argentine Political Youths)
JSP	Juventud Sindical Peronista (Peronist Labor Youth)
LRD	Lugares de Reunión de Detenidos (Places for the Meeting of Detainees)
MIR	Movimiento Izquierdista Revolucionario (Revolutionary Left Movement)
MON	Movimiento de Opinión Nacional (National Opinion Movement)
MOPOCO	Movimiento Popular Colorado (Colorado Popular Movement)
MSTM	Movimiento de Sacerdotes para el Tercer Mundo (Priests Movement for the Third World)
NDI	National Democratic Institute for International Affairs
NRIIA	National Republican Institute for International Affairs
NSC	National Security Council
OAS	L'Organisation de l'Armée Secrète (Secret Army Organization)
OAS	Organization of American States
OCOA	Organismo Coordinador de Operaciones Antisubversivas (Antisubversive Operations Coordinating Organ)
OCPO	Organización Comunista Poder Obrero (Worker Power Communist Organization)
OLA	Organización para la Liberación de la Argentina (Organization for the Liberation of Argentina)
OMPAM	Organización Mundial para la Asistencia Masónica (World Organization for Masonic Thought and Help)
OPS	Office of Public Safety
P-2	Propaganda Due
PO	Palabra Obrera (Workers' Word)
PRT	Partido Revolucionario de los Trabajadores (Workers Revolutionary Party)
ROE	Resistencia Obrero-Estudiantil (Worker-Student Resistance)
SES	Servicio Especial de Seguridad (Special Security Service)

SID	Servizio Informazione Difesa (Defense Information Agency)
SIDE	Secretaría de Informaciones de Estado (State Intelligence Agency)
SIE	Servicio de Inteligencia del Ejército (Army Intelligence Service)
SIN	Servicio de Informaciones Navales (Naval Information Service)
SNI	Serviço Nacional de Informações (National Information Service)
SOIN	Sindicato de Obreros de la Industria Naval (Naval Industries Workers Union)
SS	Superintendencia de Seguridad (Security Superintendency)
UCD	Unión del Centro Democrático (Union of the Democratic Center)
UCR	Unión Cívica Radical (Radical Civic Union)
UES	Unión de Estudiantes Secundarios (High School Students Union)
UNESCO	United Nations Educational, Scientific and Cultural Organization
UNS	Universidad Nacional del Sur
UNT	Universidad Nacional de Tucumán
UOM	Unión Obrera Metalúrgica (Metalworkers Union)
USAID	U.S. Agency for International Development
UTN	Universidad Tecnológica Nacional
VPR	Vanguarda Popular Revolucionaria (Popular Revolutionary Vanguard)
WACL	World Anti-Communist League

Notes

Chapter 1

1. Documents presented to the author by Strassera in 1985 showed that shortly before President Raúl Alfonsín took office the military high command issued an order that all evidence of the secret repression be destroyed. See also *Noticias*, February 23, 1992, pp. 53–54. According to testimony given to the U.S. Senate Foreign Relations Committee, Subcommittee on Terrorism, Narcotics and International Operations, on July 23, 1987, by former Argentine army intelligence agent Leandro Sánchez Reisse, days after Alfonsín's inauguration an Argentine army plane laden with secret documents was flown to Switzerland and its cargo deposited in a bank vault there. Sánchez Reisse deposition, p. 80.

2. I covered the courtroom scenes as part of my regular reporting on the 1985 trials of the nine former military junta members before the Buenos Aires federal court (hereafter, Buenos Aires federal court trial of the juntas) for *Newsweek* and the *Washington Post*.

3. *Nunca Más, Informe de la Comisión Nacional sobre la Desaparición de Personas* (Buenos Aires: EUDEBA, 1984), pp. 7–11.

4. According to Enrique H.J. Cavalini, "The Malvinas/Falkland Affair: A New Look," *International Journal of Intelligence and CounterIntelligence* 2, no. 2, pp. 207–208, by 1982 Argentina had no less than nine military-controlled intelligence services. In a nation of 27 million people, 10,000 to 12,000 agents worked mostly in internal security, with three times that number dispersed throughout Argentine society as informants.

5. Horacio Verbitsky, *La Posguerra Sucia* (Buenos Aires: Legasa, 1985) p. 82; "We're in the Third World War, we can't send people publicly to the firing squad because even the Pope would object. You're a civilian, so you don't understand," Vice Admiral Eduardo Fracassi, quoted by human rights leader Emilio F. Mignone, *Clarín*, July 16, 1985, p. 9.

6. The two guerrilla leaders were Montoneros Mario Firmenich and Roberto Quieto. Firmenich's voluntary collaboration with the army's 601 intelligence battalion was first revealed in Martin Edwin Andersen, "Dirty Secrets of the 'Dirty War,'" *Nation*, March 13, 1989. See also Andersen "Informe Especial: La conexión SIDE–Firmenich," *Expreso*, June 5 and June 12, 1987. Quieto, who was kidnapped by Argentine security forces in December 1975, was kept alive for at least sixteen months according to "The Graiver Affair," a secret State Department briefing memorandum written by U.S. diplomat William H. Luers, April 27, 1977.

7. See Martin Edwin Andersen, "Los Números de FAMUS," *El Periodista*, no. 141 (May 22–28, 1987), p. 7; for an overview of just how inflated the guerrilla threat was and of the military's desire for revenge, see Andersen, "Dirty Secrets." The former CIA station chief cited, who was interviewed by telephone in 1989, worked in Buenos Aires from 1972 to 1974; see also Rodolfo Peregrino Fernández, *Autocrítica Policial* (Buenos Aires: El Cid Editor, 1983), p. 67.

8. I found T. B. Friedman's original, uncleared memorandum in the files of the *New York Times* Buenos Aires bureau. Document on file at Centro de Estudios Legales y Sociales (hereafter, CELS), Buenos Aires.

9. Interview with President Raúl Alfonsín, in *Newsweek International* (Latin American edition), March 19, 1984. ("I think that Jimmy Carter saved lives in our country," Alfonsín said.); "Thank you, Jimmy." *Buenos Aires Herald*, October 10, 1984.

10. Alfredo Leuco and José Antonio Díaz, *El Heredero de Perón* (Buenos Aires: Planeta, 1989), p. 147.

11. For a well-presented view of the Reagan administration ties to the Argentine dirty warriors, see Cynthia Brown, ed., *With Friends Like These* (New York: Pantheon, 1985), pp. 101–108. See also Christopher Dickey, *With the Contras: A Reporter in the Wilds of Nicaragua* (New York: Simon & Schuster, 1987).

12. I was present for Corbin's testimony; *Clarín*, June 15, 1985, p. 20.

13. Letter from Córdoba morgue workers to President Jorge Rafael Videla, June 30, 1980, Comisión Nacional sobre la Desaparición de Personas (hereafter, CONADEP) file no. 0126, Córdoba.

14. Events surrounding the exhumations at San Vicente were covered by me and originally reported in a "Letter from Argentina," *Boston Phoenix*, April 10, 1984. See also Christopher Joyce and Eric Stover, *Witnesses from the Grave* (New York: Little, Brown, 1991); "Hoy habrá exhumaciones en el cementerio San Vicente," *La Voz del Interior*, March 3, 1984.

15. Moises Kijak and María Lucila Pelento, "Situaciones de Catástrofe Social," paper presented to the World Psychoanalysis Congress, Munich, August 1985, 27 pp.

16. Norberto Liwski testimony at 1985 "dirty war" trials; *Nunca Más*, pp. 27–32; interviews with Liwski (Buenos Aires, 1983–1985).

17. I witnessed the incident described.

18. On Reagan, see *Miami News*, October 20, 1978; Jeane Kirkpatrick, "Dictatorships and Double Standards," *Commentary*, November 1979; Philip Geyelin, "Human Rights Turnaround," *Washington Post*, December 12, 1980; on Abrams, see Brown, *With Friends Like These*, p. 10.

19. See Martin Edwin Andersen, "The Cost of Quiet Diplomacy," *New Republic*, March 19, 1984.

20. "Hill's biography reads like a satirical left-wing caricature of a 'yanqui imperialist.' A former vice-president of W. R. Grace and a former director of the United Fruit Company—two of the companies whose activities in Latin America have been most bitterly criticized by Latin nationalists—Hill was directly linked in testimony to the United States Senate with the planning of the coup that overthrew President Arbenz of Guatemala in 1954. He has a long-standing connection with the United States security and intelligence establishment, and his last job before being assigned to Buenos Aires was assistant secretary of defense with responsibility for international security." *Latin America*, 1973 (Christmas issue). See also Stephen Schlesinger and Stephen Kinzer, *Bitter Fruit: The Untold Story of the American Coup in Guatemala* (Garden City, N.Y.: Doubleday, Anchor, 1983), especially pp. 107, 140.

21. According to "Sam," a senior intelligence official stationed in Buenos Aires at the time, the Peronist government shielded several narcotics traffickers wanted by U.S. au-

thorities for major drug crimes. One of these, Esteban García, a Class-1 fugitive from the United States, worked in Isabel Perón's bodyguard. ("Sam," who provided me with invaluable insights for this book, would not allow his real name to be used. He responded in writing to two questionnaires I sent to him in 1987, and in November of that year he allowed a follow-up interview in Washington, D.C. Former U.S. embassy political officer Wayne Smith, who worked with "Sam" in Buenos Aires, said his credibility was excellent and he did "first rate" work in Argentina (Washington, D.C., November 1987). ("Sam's" insights are hereafter referred to as "Sam" interviews.)

22. A copy of the memorandum of conversation, written by Derian assistant (and later Reagan ambassador to Ecuador) Fred Rondon, was given to me by Patricia Derian.

23. Telephone interview with Juan de Onis, November 1985.

24. The Kissinger "green light" was originally reported in Martin Edwin Andersen, "Kissinger and the 'Dirty War,'" *Nation*, October 31, 1987.

25. De Onis confirmed, as stated in the Derian memo, that he had asked Hill about reports he had received from Argentine military sources that Kissinger had indeed given a "green light." A convincing denial by Hill, who had not yet met with Kissinger in the United States, persuaded de Onis there was nothing to the story. Other confirmations of the Hill allegations came from a senior State Department official with long experience in Argentina and a senior Argentine military intelligence official, both of whom asked not to be identified. Another, circumstantial, confirmation of Kissinger's role, comes from a comparison of the memo's rendition of the Kissinger-Guzzetti meeting to a report published in the right-wing Buenos Aires newspaper *La Nación*, on June 11, 1976, the day after the encounter. According to a cable by ANSA, the Italian news agency: "A few hours before leaving for Mexico, after a period of intense activity in Santiago, Kissinger held his longest interview with a foreign minister, that of Argentina, Admiral César Guzzetti. The meeting took place at a very early hour in the Hotel Carrera, where Kissinger was staying. Both Kissinger and his colleague spoke in their own languages, but Guzzetti demonstrated a good knowledge of English. ...The most serious part of the conversation can be synthesized into two points: a) a frank understanding by Kissinger of the current Argentine political stance; b) his promise to support the Argentine economic plan. ... During the meeting, attended by four American officials, including Deputy Secretary for Inter-American Affairs William D. Rogers, *Kissinger spoke alone with Guzzetti for a few minutes.*" (Emphasis added.) Kissinger refused to be interviewed for my *Nation* story (Andersen, "Kissinger and the 'Dirty War'") but denied Hill's account through a spokesperson. Rogers, who in the late 1970s was quoted approvingly in pro-junta advertisements prepared by the regime for use in major U.S. publications, said that he did "not specifically remember" a meeting with Guzzetti, but added: "What Henry would have said if he had had such a meeting was that human rights were embedded in our policy, for better or worse. He'd have said sympathetic things about the need for effective methods against terrorism, but without abandoning the rule of law." Andersen, "Kissinger and the 'Dirty War.'"

Chapter 2

1. V. S. Naipaul, *The Return of Eva Perón* (New York: Knopf, 1980), pp. 156–157.

2. William Ratliff and Roger Fontaine, *Changing Course: The Capitalist Revolution in Argentina* (Stanford: Stanford University–Hoover Institution, 1990), pp. 9–10.

3. Ibid., p. 7.; Richard Gillespie, *Soldiers of Perón: Argentina's Montoneros* (New York: Oxford University Press, 1982), pp. 1–2.

4. Peter G. Snow, *Political Forces in Argentina,* rev. ed. (New York: Praeger, 1979), p. 12.

5. Perón quote in *New York Times,* July 14, 1973.

6. Alain Rouquié, *Poder militar y sociedad política en la Argentina,* vol. 2, 1943–1973 (Buenos Aires: Emecé, 1983), pp. 21–27.

7. Ibid., pp. 39, 40, 49.

8. Ibid., p. 57.

9. Sábato quoted in Robert Crassweller, *Perón and the Enigmas of Argentina* (New York: Norton, 1987), p. 167.

10. Joseph Page, *Perón: A Biography* (New York: Random House, 1983), p. 239.

11. *New York Times,* November 18, 1972.

12. Eugene F. Sofer, "A New Terror Grips Argentina," *Present Tense,* Autumn 1977, p. 23.

13. Tomás Eloy Martínez, "Perón y Los Nazis," pt. 1, *El Periodista,* no. 48 (August 9–15, 1985), pp. 25–27; Scott Anderson and Jon Lee Anderson, *Inside the League* (New York: Dodd, Mead, 1986), p. 39.

14. Anderson and Anderson, *Inside the League,* pp. 38–42; see also "Mengele, the Argentine Files," *Response: Wiesenthal Center World Report* 13, no. 1 (Spring 1992), pp. 2–3.

15. Martínez, "Perón y Los Nazis," pt. 1; Agostino Rocca, a military engineer who rose under Mussolini to become the head of IRI, the Italian fascist state's industrial holding company, and who, during World War II, was the director of Turin's biggest war contractor, immigrated to Argentina in 1945 and founded the Techint Group, one of Buenos Aires' largest industrial combines. See Joel Millman, "Out of the Asylum," *Forbes,* December 23, 1991.

16. Martínez, "Perón y Los Nazis," pt. 1; on American use of ex-Nazis, see Linda Hunt, *Secret Agenda: The United States Government, Nazi Scientists and Project Paperclip, 1945 to 1990* (New York: St. Martin's, 1991).

17. Martínez, "Perón y Los Nazis," pt. 1.

18. *New York Times,* November 18, 1972.

19. Sofer, "A New Terror," p. 23; also Crassweller, *Perón,* pp. 220–221.

20. Sofer, "A New Terror," p. 23.

21. Cynthia Brown, ed., *With Friends Like These* (New York: Pantheon, 1985), p. 94; Jacob Tsur, *Cartas credenciales* (Jerusalem: Publicaciones La Semana, 1983), pp. 154–161, 227–228.

22. Martínez, "Perón y Los Nazis," pt. 1, p. 26.

23. Tomás Eloy Martínez, "Perón y Los Nazis," pt. 2, *El Periodista,* no. 49 (August 16–22, 1985), p. 25.

24. "Terrorism in Argentina: Its Role After May 25," U.S. Department of State airgram, May 16, 1973, p. 5.

25. Ratliff and Fontaine,*Changing Course,* pp. 12–13; Juan José Arregui, *La formación de la conciencia nacional* (Buenos Aires: Editorial Plus Ultra, 1973), pp. 262–264.

26. Rouquié, *Poder militar,* pp. 86–89.

27. Page, *Perón,* pp. 296–305; Rouquié, *Poder militar,* p. 97.

28. Rouquié, *Poder militar,* pp. 108–110; Page, *Perón,* pp. 306–308; Horacio Verbitsky, *La Posguerra Sucia* (Buenos Aires: Legasa, 1985), p. 303.

29. Rouquié, *Poder militar,* pp. 108–110; Page, *Perón,* pp. 309–310.

30. Page, *Perón,* p. 311.

31. Crassweller, *Perón,* pp. 278–279.

32. See Eduardo Lonardi, *Dios es justo* (Buenos Aires: Francisco A. Colombo, 1958).

33. Rouquié, *Poder militar,* pp. 116–122; Page, *Perón,* pp. 316–321.

34. J. C. Cernadas Lamadrid and Ricardo Halac, *Yo Fuí Testigo: Azules y Colorados* (Buenos Aires: Editorial Perfil, 1986), p. 25.

35. On Perón's motives, see Page, *Perón,* p. 324, and Rouquié, *Poder militar,* p. 120; Horacio de Dios, *Kelly cuenta todo* (Buenos Aires: Colección Gente, 1984), p. 92.

36. Caleb Bach, "Ernesto Sábato: A Conscious Choice of Words," *Américas* 1, no. 43 (1991); Page, *Perón,* p. 327.

37. *New York Times,* November 18, 1972.

38. Rouquié, *Poder militar,* pp. 122–128.

39. Ibid., pp. 122–127; *La Razón,* June 9, 1986; on swimming pools, interview with Argentine human rights leader Emilio Mignone. (All interviews with Mignone, who was consulted frequently by the author in Buenos Aires during the period September 1982 to October 1987, are hereafter referred to as Mignone interviews.)

40. Page, *Perón,* pp. 343–344, 371–372; *New York Times,* September 5, 1971.

41. *La Razón,* June 9, 1986.

42. Rodolfo Walsh, *Operación Masacre* (Buenos Aires: Ediciones de la Flor, 1984), p. 66.

43. Historian Félix Luna, quoted in Cernadas Lamadrid and Halac, *Azules y Colorados,* p. 34; confidential U.S. Foreign Service Dispatch, written by U.S. embassy Minister-Counselor Garret G. Ackerson, Jr., June 21, 1956. "The President at first described the revolt as 'Peronista and neo-Peronista,'" Ackerson wrote, "but subsequently he and other members of the Government have insisted on its essentially communistic nature and expressed the conviction that it had lines of direction leading to International Communism."

44. On Valle's death, see Eduardo Luis Duhalde, "Juan José Valle, A treinta años de su muerte," *Crísis,* June 1986, p. 88; *La Razón,* June 9, 1986.

45. The best account of the massacre at José León Suárez is in Walsh, *Operación Masacre;* see also Salvador Ferla, *Martires y verdugos* (Buenos Aires: private printing, 1964); *La Razon,* June 9, 1986.

46. On the phenomenon of "re-peronization," see Rouquié, *Poder militar,* pp. 140–141.

47. *New York Times,* July 18, 1970.

Chapter 3

1. "Information Report," U.S. Office of Naval Intelligence, no. 153-55, December 29, 1955.

2. José Luis de Imaz, *Los Que Mandan* (Buenos Aires: Editorial Universitaria de Buenos Aires, 1965), p. 89.

3. Alain Rouquié, *Poder militar y sociedad política en la Argentina,* vol. 2, 1943–1973 (Buenos Aires: Emecé, 1983), pp. 134–145.

4. Material in section on Satanowsky case, unless otherwise indicated, comes from Rodolfo Walsh *El Caso Satanowsky* (Buenos Aires: Ediciones de la Flor, 1986).

5. Ibid., pp. 49–57.

6. Ibid., pp. 44, 75–77, 154–155; further information on attempts on Perón's life in Horacio de Dios, *Kelly Cuenta Todo* (Buenos Aires: Colección Gente, 1984), pp. 79–87.

7. Walsh, *Satanowsky*, p. 174.

8. Rouquié, *Poder militar*, pp. 140–145.

9. Ibid., pp. 139–140.

10. Ibid., pp. 144–145.

11. Joseph Page, *Perón: A Biography* (New York: Random House, 1983), pp. 338–342.

12. Juan Corradi, *The Fitful Republic: Economy, Society and Politics in Argentina* (Boulder: Westview Press, 1985), pp. 76–77; Gary W. Wynia, *Argentina in the Postwar Era* (Albuquerque: University of New Mexico Press, 1978), pp. 83–111; Rouquié, *Poder militar*, pp. 152–156, 166–167; Robert Crassweller, *Perón and the Enigmas of Argentina* (New York: Norton, 1987), pp. 312–313.

13. Rouquié, *Poder militar*, pp. 168–169, 176; Wynia, *Argentina*, pp. 100–102; see also Roberto Carri, *Sindicatos y poder en la Argentina* (Buenos Aires: Sudestada, 1967); Julio Santucho, *Los Ultimos Guevaristas* (Buenos Aires: Puntosur, 1988), pp. 74–82; *Confirmado*, December 24, 1975; Richard Gillespie, *Soldiers of Perón: Argentina's Montoneros* (New York: Oxford University Press, 1982), pp. 23–33.

14. Page, *Perón*, pp. 367–368; Crassweller, *Perón*, pp. 312–313, 323; J. C. Cernadas Lamadrid and Ricardo Halac, *Yo Fuí Testigo: Azules y Colorados* (Buenos Aires: Editorial Perfil, 1986), pp. 44–46.

15. Rouquié, *Poder militar*, pp. 156–160; "In truth," Rouquié wrote, "'communism' did not appear to be a serious menace to Argentine society."

16. See Germán R. Teissere, "Influencia del Ejército en el Desarrollo de los Valores Materiales y Morales del Pueblo Argentino," *Revista de la Escuela Superior de Guerra*, no. 617 (January 1953), pp. 33–34; Miguel Angel Scenna, *Los Militares* (Buenos Aires: Editorial de Belgrano, 1980), pp. 13–88; Gustavo Druetta, "Del militarismo a la democracia: Críticas, autocríticas y esperanzas," *Nuevo Proyecto* 1 (1986).

17. *La Nación*, June 24, 1962.

18. Rouquié, *Poder militar*, pp. 151, 175–177; Cernadas Lamadrid and Halac, *Azules y Colorados*, pp. 53–54.

19. Rouquié, *Poder militar*, pp. 171–174; Scenna, *Los Militares*, pp. 256–261.

20. "Report to Foreign Military Attachés by Argentine Armed Forces Leaders After Frondizi Overthrow," confidential U.S. Foreign Service Dispatch, April 16, 1962.

21. Interview with former nationalist leader Guillermo Patricio Kelly (Buenos Aires, 1986); for an excellent discussion of ultra-right-wing politics in Argentina in the 1960s, in a generally uneven work, see Claudio Díaz and Antonio Zucco, *La Ultraderecha Argentina* (Buenos Aires: Editorial Contrapunto, 1987); Ted Cordova-Clauré, "Swastikas in Argentina," *Atlas World Press Review*, November 1976, p. 20; Rouquié, *Poder militar*, p. 203; Cernadas Lamadrid and Halac, *Yo Fuí Testigo: Antisemitismo* (Buenos Aires: Editorial Perfil, 1986), pp. 98–100.

22. Peter G. Snow, *Political Forces in Argentina*, rev. ed. (New York: Praeger, 1979), pp. 76–79; Scenna, *Los Militares*, pp. 272–273; Rouquié, *Poder militar*, pp. 212–214.

23. Rouquié, *Poder militar*, pp. 212–215.

24. Ibid., p. 206.

25. Cernadas Lamadrid and Halac, *Azules y Colorados,* p. 81.

26. *La Razón,* September 18, 1966.

27. Rouquié, *Poder militar,* pp. 209–210.

28. Cernadas Lamadrid and Halac, *Azules y Colorados,* pp. 92–95, 98.

29. Ibid., p. 102.

30. Rouquié, *Poder militar,* pp. 217–219; Cernadas La Madrid and Halac, *Azules y Colorados,* pp. 95, 108–109.

31. "Personnel Casualties and Equipment Losses Sustained During the Recent Navy Rebellion," confidential U.S. Department of State airgram, April 10, 1963.

Chapter 4

1. Alain Rouquié, *Poder militar y sociedad política en la Argentina,* vol. 2, 1943–1973 (Buenos Aires: Emecé, 1983), pp. 231–232; Miguel Angel Scenna, *Los Militares* (Buenos Aires: Editorial de Belgrano, 1980), pp. 287–290.

2. Gary Wynia, *Argentina in the Postwar Era* (Albuquerque: University of New Mexico Press, 1978), pp. 124–129; Rouquié, *Poder militar,* pp. 240–243.

3. Peter G. Snow, *Political Forces in Argentina,* rev. ed. (New York: Praeger, 1979), p. 94.

4. Ibid., pp. 89–92; Page, *Perón: A Biography* (New York: Random House, 1983), pp. 379, 381, 401–403; Rouquié, *Poder militar,* pp. 236–240; Wynia, *Argentina,* pp. 126–130.

5. Page, *Perón,* pp. 397–400; Robert Crassweller, *Perón and the Enigmas of Argentina* (New York: Norton, 1987), pp. 342–345; Raúl Lastiri, López Rega's son-in-law and provisional president, told U.S. embassy political officer Wayne Smith that a group of Perón's old bodyguards had come together to protect Isabel during her Argentine stay and that one was López Rega. Smith telephone interview (January 1992).

6. Rouquié, *Poder militar,* p. 244; anecdote about Timerman as xerox told to me by James Neilson, editor of the *Buenos Aires Herald* (Buenos Aires, 1985).

7. *Primera Plana,* May 31, 1966; *El Periodista,* no. 94, June 27–July 3, 1986, p. 6.

8. Rouquié, *Poder militar,* pp. 244–248; Mariano Grondona, "La dictadura," *Primera Plana,* May 31, 1966.

9. "Perspectivas-Pronósticos: Que Pasará en 1966?" *Confirmado* 1, no. 34 (December 24, 1965), pp. 14–16, quoted in Snow, *Political Forces,* pp. 72–73.

10. Crawley, *A House Divided: Argentina 1880–1980* (London: Hurst, 1984), p. 275.

11. William Ratliff and Roger Fontaine, *Changing Course: The Capitalist Revolution in Argentina* (Stanford: Stanford University–Hoover Institution, 1990), p. 15; Rouquié, *Poder militar,* pp. 254–261; Wynia, *Argentina,* pp. 166–188.

12. *Declaración de Córdoba* of the Córdoba Regional Delegation, CGT of the Argentines, March 21, 1969, pamphlet, 4 pp., cited in Rouquié, *Poder militar,* p. 284.

13. Penny Lernoux, *Cry of the People* (New York: Doubleday, 1980), pp. 160–161, 305, 342; Rouquié, *Poder militar,* pp. 259–261; Rogelio García Lupo, *Mercenarios y Monopolios en la Argentina* (Buenos Aires: Legasa, 1984), pp. 11–27; Claudio Díaz and Antonio Zucco, *La Ultraderecha Argentina* (Buenos Aires: Editorial Contrapunto, 1987), pp. 40–45; Emilio Mignone interview.

14. For an excellent review of Pope John XXIII's impact on Latin American churches, see Lernoux, *Cry,* pp. 31–80; also Richard Gillespie, *Soldiers of Perón: Argentina's Montoneros* (New York: Oxford University Press, 1982), pp. 53–56.

15. Snow, *Political Forces*, pp. 112–113; Lernoux, *Cry*, pp. 37–38;

16. *Medellín Conclusions* (Bogotá: CELAM, 1973), pp. 28–110.

17. Rouquié, *Poder militar*, p. 218; *New York Times*, March 2, 1968, and August 27, 1969.

18. García Lupo, *Mercenarios y Monopolios*, p. 168.

19. Page, *Perón*, p. 325; Rouquié, *Poder militar*, p. 122; *La Razón*, August 27, 1971.

20. García Lupo, *Mercenarios y Monopolios*, pp. 15, 20, 23.

21. *La Razón*, August 25 and August 27, 1970, and August 30, 1971; *Crónica*, August 27, 28, 29, 30, 1971; *Clarín*, August 30, 1971.

22. Próspero Germán Fernández Alvariño, *Z Argentina, El Crimen del Siglo* (Buenos Aires: private printing, 1973); *La Razón*, August 25, 1970.

23. *La Razón*, August 25, 1970, p. 8; *Buenos Aires Herald*, August 28, 1971; *La Razón*, August 30, 1971.

24. On Alvarez Saavedra's links to army intelligence, see *Final Report of the Government Commission on Human Rights*, La Rioja Province, December 1984, p. 71; *La Razón*, August 27, 1971; on friend of Castor Lorenzo, *La Razón*, August 25, 1970, and August 30, 1971; on Vago, *La Razón*, August 25, 1970, and *Buenos Aires Herald*, August 30, 1971.

25. See Stephen Schlesinger and Stephen Kinzer, *Bitter Fruit: The Untold Story of the American Coup in Guatemala* (Garden City, N.Y.: Doubleday, Anchor, 1983).

26. Magnus Linklater, Isabel Hilton, and Neal Ascherson, *The Fourth Reich: Klaus Barbie and the Neo-Fascist Connection* (London: Hodder and Stoughton, 1984), pp. 230–232.

27. See Martin Ebon, *Che: The Making of a Legend* (New York: Signet, 1969); *The Diary of Che Guevara* (New York: Bantam, 1968); Ricardo Rojo, *My Friend Che* (New York: John Day, 1968), and Crawley, *A House Divided*, pp. 291–292, 295; speechwriter was Kennedy aide Richard Goodwin, "Annals of Politics: A Footnote," *New Yorker*, May 25, 1968.

28. *Primera Plana*, no. 442, August 20, 1971, p. 39.

29. *New York Times*, May 31, 1970.

30. "Political Highlights–May 1969," confidential U.S. Department of State airgram, June 23, 1969; also see Crawley, *A House Divided*, pp. 305–309.

Chapter 5

1. Eduardo Crawley, *A House Divided: Argentina 1880–1980* (London: Hurst, 1984), pp. 309–310; Alain Rouquié, *Poder militar y sociedad política en la Argentina*, vol. 2, 1943–1973 (Buenos Aires: Emecé, 1983), pp. 273–279; Rogelio García Lupo, *Mercenarios y Monopolios en la Argentina* (Buenos Aires: Legasa, 1984); Richard Gillespie, *Soldiers of Perón: Argentina's Montoneros* (New York: Oxford University Press, 1982), pp. 61–63.

2. "Vandor Assassination and Funeral," U.S. Department of State airgram, July 21, 1969; Crawley, *A House Divided*, pp. 310; David Rock, *Argentina 1516–1982: From Spanish Colonialization to the Falklands War* (Berkeley: University of California Press, 1985), p. 351; *New York Times*, June 27 and July 2, 1969.

3. Crawley, *A House Divided*, pp. 310–312; Joseph Page, *Perón: A Biography* (New York: Random House, 1983), pp. 410–411.

4. Rock, *Argentina*, p. 355; García Lupo, *Mercenarios y Monopolios*, pp. 71–96, 199–200; Rouquié, *Poder militar*, p. 287; Page, *Perón*, p. 418; Crawley, *A House Divided*, pp. 315–317, 322–324.

5. *New York Times,* September 30, 1968.

6. Ibid., February 18, 1971; Rock, *Argentina,* p. 352–354; Crawley, *A House Divided,* pp. 325–333.

7. "Aramburu: Perspectivas," Reuters news dispatch, June 5, 1970; interview with Aramburu friend Ricardo Rojo (Buenos Aires, May 6, 1987). Rojo, who saw Aramburu shortly before his abduction, said that Aramburu believed Onganía had to be replaced because he was a "fascist." Aramburu had received Perón's support for a putsch against Onganía, Rojo recalled, promising his old nemesis a one-year truce if bars to Perón's political activity were lifted and elections were called; "ten active-duty generals," interview with Aramburu intimate Aldo Molinari (Buenos Aires, November 16, 1986; hereafter referred to as Molinari interview). Molinari, deputy Federal Police chief during the Liberating Revolution, admitted that it was Castor Lorenzo accomplice and associate of SIDE chief Quaranta, auto thief José Américo Pérez Griz, who killed Marcos Satanowsky. "A Pérez Griz, se lo escapó el tiro" (A shot got away from Pérez Griz), he said.

8. "Report to Foreign Military Attachés by Argentine Armed Forces Leaders After Frondizi Overthrow," confidential U.S. Foreign Service Dispatch, April 16, 1962, p. 9.

9. André Beaufre, *Introducción a la estrategia* (Madrid: Instituto de Estudios Políticos, 1965).

10. According to Gen. Albano Harguindeguy, who served as interior minister in the Videla government, "Our fight was related to those in Algeria and Indochina because, from 1956 on, there were French military missions here that transmitted to us their experience there," *Noticias,* February 23, 1992; Mario H. Orsolini, *La crisis del ejército* (Buenos Aires: Arayú, 1966); "Report on Conversations with General Carlos J. Rosas," U.S. Department of State airgram, July 19, 1962. See also Rosendo Fraga, *Ejército: del escarnio al poder* (1973–1976) (Buenos Aires: Planeta, 1988), p. 22; according to Rouquié, *Poder militar,* pp. 158, "Of the 60 articles published in the *Superior War School Magazine* between January 1958 and December 1962, sixteen were dedicated to anti-subversive warfare, seven of which were written by French authors." According to Argentine journalist Mario del Carril, Rosas was not without redeeming qualities. Rosas, he said, had taken the lead in putting down an April 1963 military revolt. Before that, during Frondizi's government, Rosas was kicked out of his post within twenty-four hours after lifting a long-standing proscription against Jews. Rosas died in an auto accident, del Carril added, that many suspected at the time was the result of foul play (del Carril interview, Washington, D.C., January 1992).

11. See Martin Edwin Andersen, "The Military Obstacle to Latin Democracy," *Foreign Policy,* no. 73, Winter 1988–1989, pp. 99–100.

12. Ibid., p. 100.

13. "Political-Economic Assessment," secret U.S. Department of State airgram, April 27, 1966.

14. Nelson A. Rockefeller, "Quality of Life in the Americas: Report of a Presidential Mission for the Western Hemisphere," *Department of State Bulletin,* December 8, 1969, p. 505.

15. Andersen, "Military Obstacle," pp. 100–101.

16. "Como Murió Aramburu," *La Causa Peronista,* September 3, 1974, pp. 32–34; *La Razón,* July 14, 1970; *Sunday Times,* March 28, 1971; Crawley, *A House Divided,* pp. 317–320.

17. *Clarín,* June 6, 1970, p. 16; *La Prensa,* June 4, 1971, p. 11.

18. Gillespie, *Soldiers of Perón*, p. 93.

19. Crawley, *A House Divided*, p. 320.

20. "Como Murió Aramburu," pp. 32–34; *Crónica,* August 28, 1971, p. 12; *Buenos Aires Herald,* June 5, 1971; *La Nación,* December 1, 1970; Próspero Germán Fernández Alvariño, *Z Argentina, El Crimen del Siglo* (Buenos Aires: private printing, 1973), p. 118; that Aramburu's shirt was not bloodstained was confirmed in my interview with Molinari, a close Aramburu associate (Molinari interview); *La Nación,* November 20, 1970.

21. *La Vanguardia,* August 5, 1970.

22. *Crónica,* August 28, 1971; *Clarín,* August 28, 1971; *Buenos Aires Herald,* August 28, 1971; *La Razón,* June 3, 1971, p. 10; *Clarín,* October 6, 1970; *La Prensa,* June 4, 1971, p. 11, especially "9. Elementos nazi-fascistas"; according to Molinari interview, an ultrarightist named Antonio Romano, a friend of Imaz's, was killed by Norberto Rodolfo Crocco, a young nationalist who murdered Romano as the latter prepared to go to the town of William Morris to pay off the Montoneros for their role in the abduction of Aramburu. On Romano, see Eugenio Méndez, *Aramburu: El Crimen Perfecto* (Buenos Aires: Sudamericana-Planeta, 1987), pp. 125–135. Méndez, who served as a "war" correspondent in Tucumán at a time when military clearances were needed, has himself been linked in the press to the military intelligence services; *Somos,* June 6, 1991.

23. "Views of Important Peronist Leaders," confidential memorandum of conversation with Ambassador John Davis Lodge, May 7, 1971; Fernández Alvariño, *Z Argentina;* Jorge Muñoz, *Seguidme! Vida de Alberto Villar* (Buenos Aires: Ro.Ca. Producciones, 1983), pp. 35–38; information on Villar's own investigation from Villar confidant and retired Federal Police Commissar Jorge Colotto. (Colotto was interviewed a number of times in Buenos Aires during the period June 1985 to May 1987, hereafter, cited as Colotto interviews.)

24. *Buenos Aires Herald,* December 26, 1970.

Chapter 6

1. "Peronist views of political situation," confidential U.S. embassy memorandum of conversation, October 29, 1972.

2. *New York Times,* June 9, 1970.

3. Liliana De Riz, *Retorno y Derrumbe: El Ultimo Gobierno Peronista* (Mexico City: Folios Ediciones, 1981), p. 30.

4. Ibid., pp. 30–31; "Now, during the late 1960s, faced with a military regime which seemingly ruled out all possibilities of Peronism returning to power by legal and constitutional means, direct armed action was postulated as the only effective means of toppling that regime," in Richard Gillespie, *Soldiers of Perón: Argentina's Montoneros* (New York: Oxford University Press, 1982), p. 41.

5. Seymour Hersh, "The Price of Power: Kissinger, Nixon, and Chile," *Atlantic Monthly,* December 1982; Taylor Branch and Eugene Propper, *Labyrinth* (New York: Viking Press, 1982).

6. "Spontaneous declaration" of Enrique Arancibia Clavel before Inspector Commissar Jorge Luis Santos Dell'amico, chief of the Foreign Affairs Department of the Argentine Federal Police, November 28, 1978, in Buenos Aires.

7. De Riz, *Retorno y Derrumbe,* pp. 21–22.

8. Eduardo Crawley, *A House Divided: Argentina 1880–1980* (London: Hurst, 1984), pp. 321–351; Luis Mattini, *Hombres y Mujeres del PRT-ERP* (Buenos Aires: Editorial Contrapunto, 1990), p. 84; "From 1971 on, the army took an active part in the struggle against subversive operations. At the beginning it took operational control of the police and security forces, and later began using intelligence personnel," from Rosendo Fraga, *Ejército: del escarnio al poder (1973–1976)* (Buenos Aires: Planeta, 1988), p. 23. According to reformist Federal Police chief Juan Pirker, the demoralization of the police was real. "A military man was almost always at the head of the institution, so we rarely thought about becoming chief." Pirker interview (Buenos Aires, 1987).

9. Ramón Torres Molina, "La actual etapa de las guerrillas argentinas," *Cristianismo y Revolución*, no. 29 (June 1971).

10. Mattini, *Hombres y Mujeres*, pp. 58–75, 133; Julio Santucho, *Los Ultimos Guevaristas* (Buenos Aires: Puntosur, 1988), pp. 110, 166–170; Samuel Blixen, *Conversaciones con Gorriarán Merlo* (Buenos Aires: Editorial Contrapunto, 1988), p. 113; María Seoane, *Todo o Nada* (Buenos Aires: Planeta, 1991), p. 207.

11. *Cristianismo y Revolución*, nos. 27, 28 (February, April 1971), p. 63.

12. "Carta de las FAP a los sacerdotes del Tercer Mundo," *Cristianismo y Revolución*, November 1970; Gillespie, *Soldiers of Perón*, pp. 47–88; "Summary of Terrorist Activity, September 1–November 30, 1971," secret U.S. Department of State airgram, December 20, 1971.

13. Gillespie, *Soldiers of Perón*, pp. 85, 121; Crawley, *A House Divided*, p. 326; according to Mattini, *Hombres y Mujeres*, p. 175, the real size of one ERP "regional" unit was twenty-one militants and five combatants.

14. "Los Montoneros a Perón," February 9, 1971, reprinted in *La Causa Peronista*, September 3, 1974.

15. *La Razón*, December 21, 1971, p. 10; "Perón a Los Montoneros," February 20, 1970, reprinted in *La Causa Peronista*.

16. Crawley, *A House Divided*, pp. 337–338.

17. Guillermo O'Donnell, *¿Y a mí, que me importa?* (Buenos Aires: Estudios CEDES, 1984), p. 23.

18. "Perón habla a la juventud," *Cristianismo y Revolución*, no. 29, June 1971, pp. 8–10.

19. Magnus Linklater, Isabel Hilton, and Neal Ascherson, *The Fourth Reich: Klaus Barbie and the Neo-Fascist Connection* (London: Hodder and Stoughton, 1984), pp. 211–212; Ignacio González Janzen, *La Triple-A* (Buenos Aires: Contrapunto, 1986), pp. 93–106.

20. Martin A. Lee and Kevin Coogan, "The Agca Con," *Village Voice*, December 24, 1985; Stuart Christie, *Stefano Delle Chiaie: Portrait of a Black Terrorist* (London: Refract, 1984), pp. 34–37, 66–67.

21. Lee and Coogan, "The Agca Con," p. 22.

22. Christie, *Delle Chiaie*, pp. 39–42.

23. Lee and Coogan, "The Agca Con," p. 22; Christie, *Delle Chiaie*, pp. 51–66.

24. Crawley, *A House Divided*, pp. 339–340; Gillespie, *Soldiers of Perón*, pp. 107–108; "Las Torturas," *Revista del Centro de Investigación y Acción Social* 21, no. 214 (July 1972). See also *Proceso a la Explotación y a la Represión en la Argentina* (Buenos Aires: Foro de Buenos Aires por la Vigencia de los Derechos Humanos, 1973).

25. "Summary of Terrorist Activity, May–August 31, 1971," secret U.S. Department of State airgram, September 26, 1971; "Summary of Terrorist Activity, September 1–November

30, 1971," ibid.; on Maestre's alleged involvement in death of army lieutenant Mario César Asúa, see Crawley, *A House Divided*, p. 348.

26. "Changes in Peronist Leadership," U.S. Department of State telegram, December 2, 1971; Crawley, *A House Divided*, pp. 369–370; Gillespie, *Soldiers of Perón*, pp. 119–122.

27. Crawley, *A House Divided*, p. 361.

28. Ibid., pp. 353, 361; Luis Vicens, *Loperreguismo y Justicialismo* (Buenos Aires: El Cid Editor), p. 45.

29. *New York Times*, May 25, 1972; Guido Di Tella, "La Estrategia Militar y las Torturas," and "Testimonio de Norma M. Morello," in *Revista del Centro de Investigación y Acción Social.* See also *Proceso a la Explotación y a la Represión en la Argentina*, pp. 29–31, 143–158; "La Tortura: 170 años de vergüenza argentina," *Todo es Historia*, no. 192, May 1983, pp. 9–46.

30. Fraga, *Ejército*, p. 23.

31. Gillespie, *Soldiers of Perón*, p. 111.

32. *La Nación*, April 11, 1972, pp. 1, 5, 10, 11; Crawley, *A House Divided*, pp. 355–356; Ramón Genaro Díaz Bessone, *Guerra Revolucionaria el la Argentina (1959–1978)* (Buenos Aires: Editorial Fraterna, 1986), pp. 146–151.

33. "Sánchez [is] unpopular in some political and other circles for his forceful repression of civil rights in his campaign to root out subversive elements in his zone, " in "Sánchez and Sallustro Assassinations: Part II of II," U.S. Department of State telegram, April 13, 1972; Fraga, *Ejército*, p. 22; interview with Argentine journalist Jacobo Timerman (Buenos Aires, May 1985); *La Nación*, April 11, 1972, p. 10.; Rogelio García Lupo, *Mercenarios y Monopolios en la Argentina* (Buenos Aires: Legasa, 1984), pp. 249–251.

34. "Sallustro known in business circles for sharp practices and seeking favors in government in developing FIAT into largest privately owned company in Argentina, and in labor for his heavy-handed efforts to rig company union. However, public abhorrence of violence overshadows these negative factors," in "Sánchez and Sallustro Assassinations: Part II of II"; "Sallustro Kidnap-Murder Wrap-up," U.S. Department of State airgram, April 24, 1972; on Sallustro's right-wing views, Colotto interviews.

35. "Sallustro Kidnap-Murder Wrap-up," p. 2.

36. *La Nación*, April 11, 1972, pp. 1, 5, 10, 11, 13–14; on origin of bullets that killed Sallustro, Colotto interviews and Santucho, *Los Ultimos Guevaristas*, p. 180.

37. *La Nación*, April 11, 1972, p. 12.

38. Francisco Urondo, *Trelew, La Patria Fusilada* (Buenos Aires: Editorial Contrapunto, 1988); Tomás Eloy Martínez, *La pasión según Trelew* (Buenos Aires: Granica, 1973); Mattini, *Hombres y Mujeres*, pp. 160–170; Santucho, *Los Ultimos Guevaristas*, pp. 181–186 (on Firmenich, see p. 186); Blixen, *Conversaciones*, pp. 137–163 (on Firmenich, see p. 152); *Proceso a la Explotación y a la Represión en la Argentina*, pp. 53–88.

39. *New York Times*, August 26, 1972; Colotto interviews; Blixen, *Conversaciones*, pp. 164–165.

40. *Proceso a la Explotación y a la Represión en la Argentina*, p. 80; Alfredo Leuco and José Antonio Díaz, *Los herederos de Alfonsín* (Buenos Aires: Sudamericana-Planeta, 1987), pp. 82–83.

41. *New York Times*, November 15, 1972, and May 27, 1973.

42. Joseph Page, *Perón: A Biography* (New York: Random House, 1983), p. 439; "La 'P-2' en la Argentina," *Todo es Historia*, February 1985, pp. 12, 31–32; *Somos*, July 8, 1983, pp. 80–

81; Giancarlo Elia Valori, "El Prejuicio Antimilitarista: El Papel y La Responsibilidad de las Fuerzas Armadas," *Las Bases* 1, no. 6 (January 18, 1972); the caption of a photo of Perón, his wife, and Valori in Italy identifies the latter as Perón's "spokesman in Italy," *New York Times,* November 15, 1972; see also Tomás Eloy Martínez, *La Novela de Perón* (Buenos Aires: Legasa, 1985), p. 116.

Chapter 7

1. Wayne Smith, "El Diálogo Perón-Lanusse," in José Enrique Miguens and Frederick C. Turner, eds., *Racionalidad del Peronismo* (Buenos Aires: Planeta, 1988), pp. 130–148; Eduardo Crawley, *A House Divided: Argentina 1880–1980* (London: Hurst, 1984), pp. 360–371; Horacio Verbitsky, *Ezeiza* (Buenos Aires: Editorial Contrapunto, 1985), pp. 138–139.

2. Mario Diament, "Habla Juan Manuel Abal Medina," *Siete Días* 15, no. 821 (March 8–14, 1983), p. 51.

3. Diament, "Habla Juan Manuel Abal Medina," p. 48.

4. Ignacio González Janzen, *La Triple-A* (Buenos Aires: Editorial Contrapunto, 1986), pp. 11–20; Verbitsky, *Ezeiza,* pp. 73–77.

5. Verbitsky, *Ezeiza,* pp. 23–24, 142–143.

6. Luis Vicens, *Loperreguismo y Justicialismo* (Buenos Aires: El Cid Editor), p. 48; *Las Bases* collection in my possession.

7. Diament, "Habla Juan Manuel Abal Medina," p. 51.

8. "Terrorism in Argentina: Its Role After May 25," U.S. Department of State airgram, May 16, 1973; "Summary of Extremist Activity, January 1–April 30, 1973," U.S. Department of State airgram, May 14, 1973; "Operación Poniatowski. Secuestro: Héctor Ricardo García, propietario de diario Crónica," *Liberación por la Patria Socialista,* no. 22 (July 27, 1974).

9. Vicens, *Loperreguismo,* p. 60. Information on possible authorship of the attack on the Coca-Cola executive came from "Sam," the U.S. intelligence official who monitored terrorist attacks for the embassy ("Sam" interviews).

10. Crawley, *A House Divided,* p. 379.

11. Vicens, *Loperreguismo,* p. 62.

12. "Who were the governors, for example, who received the liberated prisoners in the government houses? They are those governors who came from the so-called 'Peronist Right,' people like Julio Romero, Bittel and Sapag himself." Diament, "Habla Juan Manuel Abal Medina," p. 51; Smith, "El Diálogo Perón-Lanusse," pp. 148–149; Ramón Genaro Díaz Bessone, *Guerra Revolucionaria en la Argentina (1959–1978)* (Buenos Aires: Editorial Fraterna, 1986), pp. 167–191.

13. Crawley, *A House Divided,* p. 390; see also Julio Santucho, *Los Ultimos Guevaristas* (Buenos Aires: Puntosur, 1988), p. 195.

14. Joseph Page, *Perón: A Biography* (New York: Random House, 1983), p. 459; Vicens, *Loperreguismo,* p. 75; Colotto interviews.

15. Page, *Perón,* pp. 467–470; Robert Crassweller, *Perón and the Enigmas of Argentina* (New York: Norton, 1987), pp. 358–360.

16. Diament, "Habla Juan Manuel Abal Medina," p. 51; Verbitsky, *Ezeiza,* pp. 53–55.

17. Verbitsky, *Ezeiza,* pp. 53–69, 73–74, 84.

18. Ibid., pp. 90–112, 121–131; Crawley, *A House Divided,* p. 387.

19. Dispatch by Reuters' correspondent Ricardo Ritter, who was present at the scene; *New York Times*, June 21, 1973; Crawley, *A House Divided*, pp. 386–388; Page, *Perón*, pp. 462–464; according to U.S. labor attaché Anthony Freeman, the police "helped start the shootout at Ezeiza to get the Peronists fighting." Freeman interview (Washington, D.C., November–December 1985).

20. *La Prensa*, June 22, 1973; Verbitsky, *Ezeiza*, pp. 60, 113–116.

21. Page, *Perón*, pp. 465–466; *New York Times*, June 21, 1973.

22. Verbitsky, *Ezeiza*, p. 136; Crawley, *A House Divided*, pp. 387–388.

23. *La Nación*, September 3, 1983; *Gente*, May 25, 1981; *Somos*, September 24, 1982; *Clarín*, August 12, 1983.

24. *La Nación*, September 3, 1983.

25. Héctor Ruiz Núñez, "En el nombre de la logia: La P-2 en Argentina, pt. 1, 1973–1976," *Humor*, no. 174.

26. Ibid.

27. Héctor Ruiz Núñez, "López Rega: Esplendor y decadencia," *Humor*, no. 173; interview with Marta Rava, an official of the Fiscalía de Investigaciones Administrativas (Administrative Investigations Office; Buenos Aires, 1986); according to Colotto, López Rega was responsible for brokering Suárez Mason's continuation in the service with Perón (Colotto interviews).

28. Ruiz Núñez, "López Rega"; *Clarín*, August 12, 1983.

29. Interview with nationalist leader Guillermo Patricio Kelly (Buenos Aires, 1986); Rosendo Fraga, *Ejército: del escarnio al poder (1973–1976)* (Buenos Aires: Planeta, 1988), p. 87; according to Colotto, it was López Rega who suggested to Isabel that Massera be named naval chief (Colotto interviews). Claudio Uriarte, *Almirante Cero* (Buenos Aires: Planeta, 1992), pp. 60–64.

30. Ruiz Núñez, "López Rega"; *Panorama* (Italy), October 4, 1987, p. 64.

31. Page, *Perón*, pp. 467–470; Verbitsky, *Ezeiza*, p. 138.

32. Page, *Perón*, p. 470.

33. Verbitsky, *Ezeiza*, pp. 138–139.

34. Crawley, *A House Divided*, p. 394.

35. Ibid., p. 394; see also Alfredo Leuco and José Antonio Díaz, *Los Herederos de Alfonsín* (Buenos Aires: Sudamericana-Planeta, 1987), p. 95; another, conservative, observer who agreed that Peronism's internal strife was caused by a right-wing offensive is Fraga, *Ejército*, pp. 54, 89.

36. Confidential U.S. Department of State telegram, "Subject: Peronists Reportedly Preparing to Move Against Terrorists," June 1973; Horacio Verbitsky, *La Posguerra Sucia* (Buenos Aires: Legasa, 1985); Fraga, *Ejército*, pp. 54, 69.

37. Seymour Hersh, "The Price of Power: Kissinger, Nixon, and Chile," *Atlantic Monthly*, December 1982, p. 39.

38. Ibid.

39. Andrew Graham-Yool, *Portrait of an Exile* (London: Junction, 1981), p. 60; Enrique Pavón Pereyra, *El Diario secreto de Perón* (Buenos Aires: Sudamericana-Planeta, 1985), p. 320.

40. Page, *Perón*, p. 475; Roberto Mero, *Conversaciones con Juan Gelman* (Buenos Aires: Editorial Contrapunto, 1988), p. 93.

41. Verbitsky, *Ezeiza*, pp. 39–42; a profile by the U.S. embassy in Buenos Aires entitled "José Rucci, Unlikely Knight of Labor," July 26, 1971, called him "a second rate union leader, lacking in depth and, in the view of many observers, a political hack with style and mannerism of a Don Quixote. ... He rarely appears without his guards, which CGT staffers refer to as his 'Vandor fixation.'" Similarly, an April 30, 1973, memorandum of conversation from the Buenos Aires embassy called Rucci "quixotic, highly unpredictable and staunchly anti-American. ... [He] gave the impression of being a frightened little man."

42. Verbitsky, *Ezeiza*, pp. 39–42; González Janzen, *La Triple-A*, pp. 35–36, 46–47; Leuco and Díaz, *Alfonsín*, p. 95.

43. *La Nación*, September 27, 1973; Luis Mattini, *Hombres y Mujeres del PRT-ERP* (Buenos Aires: Editorial Contrapunto, 1990), pp. 270–271.

44. Interview of Juan Gelman by Roberto Mero, *Caras y Caretas*, no. 85 (December 1983); Richard Gillespie, *Soldiers of Perón: Argentina's Montoneros* (New York: Oxford University Press, 1982), p. 165.

45. According to "Sam," there was little doubt that the Rucci assassination was carried out by a team operating out of López Rega's Social Welfare Ministry ("Sam" interview). Among those who told me they did not believe that Rucci was killed by Montoneros were metalworkers union lawyer Fernando Torres (Buenos Aires, May 1987); former Federal Police Commissar Jorge Colotto; naval intelligence informant Carlos Durich (Buenos Aires, 1987), Peronist Youth leader Juan Carlos Dante Gullo (Buenos Aires, July 17, 1987), and Menem presidential chief of staff Alberto Kohan (La Rioja, June 11, 1985). On Durich's role as an advisor to the secret police of Nicaraguan dictator Anastasio Somoza, Jr., see Christopher Dickey, *With the Contras: A Reporter in the Wilds of Nicaragua* (New York: Simon & Schuster, 1987), p. 54.

46. Diament, "Habla Juan Manuel Abal Medina."

47. *Clarín*, October 2, 1974.

48. *Cuando la magia tomó el poder* (Buenos Aires: El Cid Editor, 1978), p. 33; González Janzen, *La Triple-A*, p. 110.

49. *New York Times*, September 30, 1973.

50. Page, *Perón*, pp. 477–478; *New York Times*, October 30, 1973.

51. "Historia negra de la P-2," *Somos*, September 24, 1982.

52. Interviews with former Triple-A gunmen; Luis Castellanos, "La historia negra de la Triple A," pt. 2, *La Semana*, 1984; "La Triple A y La P-Due," in *Todo es Historia*, p. 24; "A Too-Special Relationship? Unsettling Charges About Italy's Links to Libya," *Newsweek International*, June 2, 1986.

53. "Sam" interview.

54. *Wall Street Journal*, December 2, 1983.

55. Ibid.

56. Interview with PRT-ERP leader Luis Mattini (Buenos Aires, July 1987).

Chapter 8

1. Richard Gillespie, *Soldiers of Perón: Argentina's Montoneros* (New York: Oxford University Press, 1982), p. 126.

2. Luis Mattini, *Hombres y Mujeres del PRT-ERP* (Buenos Aires: Editorial Contrapunto, 1990), p. 276.

3. Joseph Page, *Perón: A Biography* (New York: Random House, 1983), p. 480.

4. Jorge Muñoz, *Seguidme! Vida de Alberto Villar* (Buenos Aires: Ro.Ca. Producciones, 1983), p. 64; Colotto interviews (the former Federal Police commissar was a Villar intimate and business partner).

5. Horacio Verbitsky, *Ezeiza* (Buenos Aires: Editorial Contrapunto, 1985), pp. 55–56; "Sam" interviews; Colotto interviews.

6. *Cuestionario,* March 1976; Pablo Kandel and Mario Monteverde, *Entorno y Caída* (Buenos Aires: Planeta, 1976), p. 22.

7. Kandel and Monteverde, *Entorno,* pp. 19–28; Eduardo Crawley, *A House Divided: Argentina 1880–1980* (London: Hurst, 1984), pp. 401–406.

8. *Cuando la magia tomó el poder* (Buenos Aires: El Cid Editor, 1978), p. 37, 188–189; Verbitsky, *Ezeiza,* p. 73; Ignacio González Janzen, *La Triple-A* (Buenos Aires: Editorial Contrapunto, 1986), pp. 47–49, 111, 120; Andrew Graham-Yool, *The Press in Argentina, 1973–8* (London: Writers and Scholars Educational Trust, 1979), pp. 43–44.

9. Page, *Perón,* p. 481; a U.S. Department of State airgram, "Peronist, Marxist showdown developing in Córdoba," July 1973, characterized the struggle as a "minority ortodoxo sector of Córdoba CGT is ... engaged in frontal assault on leftist legalista-independent union alliance which controls regional CGT."

10. Page, *Perón,* p. 482.

11. *Cuando la magia tomó el poder,* pp. 150–151.

12. Ibid.; *Clarín,* March 3, 1974; Page, *Perón,* p. 482.

13. "Argentina: Peronism's Fall From Power," U.S. Defense Intelligence Agency, *Intelligence Appraisal,* April 8, 1976, p. 2.

14. *Buenos Aires Herald,* March 24, 1974, p. 9; Gillespie, *Soldiers of Perón,* pp. 163–164.

15. *La Nación,* March 19, 1974, p. 4; *La Nación,* March 20, 1974, p. 8; *Buenos Aires Herald,* March 19, 1974, p. 1; *Buenos Aires Herald,* March 22, 1974, p. 7; *Buenos Aires Herald,* March 24, 1974, p. 7.

16. *Buenos Aires Herald,* March 24, 1974.

17. Crawley, *A House Divided,* p. 407.

18. Page, *Perón,* p. 488.

19. *El Descamisado,* February 12, 1974, pp. 2–3.

20. Page, *Perón,* p. 485.

21. C. M. Cerna, "Summary of Argentine Law and Practice on Terrorism," March 1976. (Declassified cable received from U.S. Department of State as a result of request under the Freedom of Information Act.)

22. *Libre* 1, no. 42 (November 30, 1984); "Summary of Argentine Law and Practice on Terrorism."

23. *Cuando la magia tomó el poder,* pp. 45–49.

24. On Mugica's life, see Jorge Vernazza, *Padre Mugica, Una vida para el pueblo* (Buenos Aires: Pequén Ediciones, 1984).

25. González Janzen, *La Triple-A,* pp. 113–114; interviews with journalist Jacobo Timerman (Buenos Aires, May 1985) and police Commissar Jorge Colotto.

26. Mario Firmenich, *El Peronista*, May 14–17, 1974.

27. Kandel and Monteverde, *Entorno*, p. 30.

28. Colotto interviews. According to Colotto, the assassin was Federal Police deputy inspector Edwin Farquarsohn, who belonged to the Triple A. Authorship of the crime has given rise to some controversy, however. In his book, *Aramburu: El Crimen Imperfecto* (Buenos Aires: Sudamericana-Planeta, 1987), p. 23, Eugenio Méndez claims Mugica was killed by the Triple A; however, in testimony in several court cases, Méndez claimed the priest was killed by the Montoneros. Similarly, in *Montoneros: Final de cuentas* (Buenos Aires: Puntosur, 1988), former Montonero Juan Gasparini says the murder was the work of the Triple A (p. 75) but quotes captured Montonero leader Antonio Nelson Latorre, believed to be the highest-ranking guerrilla to defect to the navy, as bragging in the Navy Mechanics School that "Montonero bullets killed Mugica" (p. 85). The military's account of political violence in Argentina, *El Terrorismo en la Argentina* (Buenos Aires, 1980), p. 143, states that Mugica was killed by the Triple A.

29. "Summary of Argentine Law and Practice on Terrorism": "With López Rega out of the country, a number of people with axes to grind may have gotten in to see Perón. López Rega, for example, is known to have sabotaged the idea of creating a National Security Committee. Those who favor the idea were trying to take advantage of his absence to convince Perón of its validity." Confidential U.S. Department of State telegram, June 21, 1974.

30. *Ultima Clave* 7, no. 196 (July 11, 1974), pp. 1–2; years later, one of Perón's biographers claimed that Perón died as a result of López Rega's willful neglect. Perón "was assassinated," said historian Enrique Pavón Pereyra. Pavón charged that despite the opposition of Perón's doctors, López Rega deliberately overburdened the president in an apparent effort to break his health. He also charged that López Rega threw out Perón's prescription heart medicine, *Miami Herald*, July 4, 1987.

31. Kandel and Monteverde, *Entorno*, pp. 10–13; Luis Vicens, *Loperreguismo y Justicialismo* (Buenos Aires: El Cid Editor), pp. 140–143.

32. Page, *Perón*, p. 496.

33. *Cuando la magia tomó el poder*, pp. 56–59.

34. *La Nación*, July 11, 14, 15, 1974; interviews with U.S. intelligence agent "Sam" and with former SIDE agent Carlos A. Hours (Buenos Aires, 1986). According to "Sam," curare, which stops all muscle functions, was later used during the military period before "gutting" *desaparecidos* and throwing them into the ocean from C-130 aircraft. An apparently similar attack was committed in June 1975 against Leopoldo Leonetti, editor of *Lealtad Obrera*, a magazine on trade union politics started the month before. According to Graham-Yool, *Press in Argentina*, p. 83, Leonetti "survived two attacks on his life. One was a physical attack about which there are no details; the second an overdose of some chemical, while he was in hospital recovering from the first attack."

35. U.S. intelligence agent "Sam"; Alfredo Leuco and José Antonio Díaz, *Los Herederos de Alfonsín* (Buenos Aires: Sudamericana-Planeta, 1987), p. 100; according to Montonero leader Juan Gelman, Rucci's assassination cut off working-class support for the Montoneros and that of Mor Roig deprived them of help from the middle class, Roberto Mero, *Conversaciones con Juan Gelman* (Buenos Aires: Editorial Contrapunto, 1988), p. 101; Julio Santucho, in *Los Ultimos Guevaristas* (Buenos Aires: Puntosur, 1988), p. 204, said that the PRT-ERP were the "true losers" from Mor Roig's death, and the PRT even publicly criticized it.

36. Interview with Alfonsín advisor Jorge Roulet (Buenos Aires, 1985).

37. A. J. Langguth, *Hidden Terrors: The Truth About U.S. Police Operations in Latin America* (New York: Pantheon, 1978), p. 251.

38. Ibid., pp. 124–142, 200, 242

39. Ibid., p. 242; Jack Anderson, "CIA Teaches Terrorism to Friends," *Washington Post*, October 8, 1973.

40. Rodolfo Peregrino Fernández, *Autocrítica Policial* (Buenos Aires: El Cid Editor, 1983), p. 54.

41. Ibid.

42. Interview with defense lawyer and Ortega Peña friend Eduardo Luis Duhalde (Buenos Aires, 1987); Peregrino Fernández, *Autocrítica*, pp. 12–13; *Cuando la magia tomó el poder*, pp. 59, 60–61.

43. *Cuando la magia tomó el poder*, pp. 69–70.

44. "Summary of Argentine Law and Practice on Terrorism."

45. Gillespie, *Soldiers of Perón*, p. 186.

46. *Cuando la magia tomó el poder*, pp. 128–129; Rosendo Fraga, *Ejército: del escarnio al poder (1973–1976)* (Buenos Aires: Planeta, 1988), p. 154.

47. *Cuando la magia tomó el poder;* interviews with journalist and Walsh friend Horacio Verbitsky (Buenos Aires, January 9, 1987) and with *Noticias* editor Pablo Giussani (Buenos Aires, 1986).

48. Kandel and Monteverde, *Entorno*, p. 29.

49. "La 'P-2' en la Argentina," *Todo es Historia*, February 1985, pp. 19, 33.

50. *Libre* 1, no. 42 (November 30, 1984); Vicens, *Loperreguismo*, p. 151: "It was a horrifyingly stupid provocation which only could serve to unify and harden the military."

51. "Como Murió Aramburu," *La Causa Peronista*, September 3, 1974.

52. Mero, *Conversaciones*, p. 85; Santucho, *Los Ultimos Guevaristas*, p. 210.

53. "Sam" interviews. Given the gravity of the charges, two letters from "Sam" to the author confirming Firmenich's role have been provided to Westview Press. According to "Sam," "the SIDE people were a bunch of incompetents. The 601 batallion was where the action was."

In June 1992 *Somos* published an interview with Leandro Sánchez Reisse, a civilian bookkeeper of the 601 army intelligence batallion who was involved in several extortive kidnappings of Argentine businessmen.

Sánchez Reisse denied that Firmenich worked as a member of the 601 staff but left open the possibility that the Montonero was linked to Valín. Asked whether such a connection existed, Sánchez Reisse replied: "Ah, with Valín it's possible. ... Yes, with Valín it might have. That's another story." Who controlled whom, he was asked. "I can't say," the bookkeeper responded, "but I'm convinced of one thing–they did each other favors." In Jorge Sigal and Olga Wornat, "Por que volvió Firmenich ¿Guerrillero or Servicio?" *Somos*, no. 819 (June 8, 1992).

54. *Cuando la magia tomó el poder*, pp. 68, 71–74, 110; *Buenos Aires Herald*, September 8–9, 1974.

55. Colotto interviews.

56. *La Razón*, October 1, 1986; *Tiempo* (Spain), September 9, 1983.

57. Edwin Harrington and Mónica González, *Bomba en una Calle de Palermo* (Santiago: Editorial Emisión, 1987), pp. 368–390; *Tiempo*, September 9, 1983; Taylor Branch and Eugene Propper, *Labyrinth* (New York: Viking Press), pp. 66–67.

58. *Tiempo*, September 9, 1983.

59. Hours interview.

60. "Summary of Argentine Law and Practice on Terrorism."

61. Frogman version reproduced in Eugenio Méndez, *Confesiones de un Montonero* (Buenos Aires: Sudamericana-Planeta, 1985), pp. 117–118. Méndez claims the bomb was placed under the boat; the Naval Prefecture report on the crime scene, which I examined, says the bomb was between the hull and the floorboard. Some credible sources say the "confession" is that of Alfredo Nicoletti, who, like Latorre, collaborated with the navy. Nicoletti was a frogman and reportedly participated in spectacular operations, such as the bombing of the *Santissima Trinidad* frigate in Ensenada, a failed attempt against a submarine in Mar del Plata and, perhaps, the 1977 attack on Foreign Minister Guzzetti. Nicoletti's "confession" to Méndez is widely believed to be an effort at disinformation. Suspicions, which I later confirmed were wrong, among Villar intimates that López Rega may have instigated the killing were first reported in Martin Edwin Andersen and Antonio López Crespo, "¿Quíen mató al Comisario Villar?" *Humor*, no. 182 (1986).

62. "Sam" interviews; Branch and Propper, *Labyrinth*, pp. 144–145; *La Nación*, November 10, 1974.

63. Colotto interviews.

64. Colotto interviews; Vicens, *Loperreguismo*, p. 132; Fraga, *Ejército*, p. 132.

65. *La Nación*, November 16, 1974, p. 6.

66. Rodolfo Terragno, *Contratapas* (Buenos Aires: Editorial Cuestionario, 1976), p. 83; *Cuando la magia tomó el poder*, p. 178–179; *New York Times*, December 15, 1974, p. E3; advertisement by the CGT.

67. *Carta Política*, no. 13 (December 1974), p. 13.

68. Kandel and Monteverde, *Entorno*, pp. 33–35.

69. *Cuando la magia tomó el poder*, p. 84.

70. Martin Edwin Andersen, "SIDE-Montoneros, La Conexión Secreta," *Expreso*, June 5 and June 12, 1987.

71. *Cuando la magia tomó el poder*, pp. 86, 203–208.

Chapter 9

1. *La Nación*, September 19, 1975, p. 6; Daniel Hadad, "Comandante 3-80: Jefe Militar de la 'Contra,'" *Somos*, January 14, 1987.

2. *Clarín*, February 10, 1980, pp. 2–3.

3. Testimonies about deaths of Berdina and Ignacio Maldonado, interviews with Lt. (ret.) Ernesto Urien, a military intelligence officer who served in Tucumán in 1975 (Buenos Aires, October 9, 1985), retired Federal Police Commissar Jorge Colotto (Buenos Aires, 1985), and Tucumán journalist Arturo Alvarez Sosa (San Miguel de Tucumán, October 23, 1985).

Another hint about how Berdina died is found in a 329-page book written by Gen. Acdel Vilas (hereafter, Vilas manuscript) during the height of the "dirty war" in which he describes the illegal repression he conducted in Tucumán and later in Patagonia. The military high command, which did not disagree with Vilas's "dirty war" methods, nonetheless refused to give Vilas permission to publish the work because of its open admission of practices the military regime was desperately denying occurred in Argentina. A letter sent by the soldiers' commanding officer to Berdina's parents, quoted in the Vilas manuscript, sec. 3, subheading "Tactical Plan No. 5," p. 8, noted: "The shot that got Berdina came from the guerrillas, as they were the only ones who used Amet 9mm pistols, and this being the only impact there was." If the ERP was responsible, then why the (superfluous) explanation? (A copy of the Vilas manuscript that I obtained is on file at CELS in Buenos Aires.)

According to Alvarez Sosa, Dr. Juan Carlos Picchini, a physician at the military hospital, told him of the circumstances of the lieutenant's death and Vilas's concern about what the accident meant to his own career. Alvarez Sosa said that while Picchini was working to save Berdina's life, Vilas and his personal bodyguard burst into the operating room. "Vilas implored Picchini to save Berdina's life, saying the shooting had been a terrible accident and asking how was he going to explain a death of one of his officers to his superiors. Picchini threw the general and his men out, telling Vilas that while he might be the master of the battlefield, in surgery he [Picchini] was the general." Alvarez Sosa interview. According to the Tucumán newspaper, *La Gaceta*, May 14, 1979, Picchini died in an automobile accident.

4. According to Vilas, the first head of Operativo Independencia, even as the operation began there was considerable sentiment among the military brass to let the situation get out of control as a pretext for getting rid of Isabel Perón. Vilas manuscript, p. 43; the only reporters allowed to go into the "operations zone" were those cleared by the Argentine armed forces. See Andrew Graham-Yool, *The Press in Argentina, 1973–8* (London: Writers and Scholars Educational Trust, 1979), pp. 14–17, 71; and Jimmy Burns, *The Land That Lost Its Heroes* (London: Bloomsbury, 1987), p. 39.

5. The Vilas manuscript includes army intelligence data saying that the ERP's usual strength was between 60 and 70 combatants. This number was confirmed by the author in interviews with several former ERP members, including former PRT-ERP secretary-general Luis Mattini (Buenos Aires, July 1987). Three charts compiled by Vilas in his manuscript show that the Compañía Ramón Rosa Jiménez consisted of 69 members between August and December 1974, 73 between January and May 1975, and 87 from June to December 1975. The third figure included the 11-member ERP central committee.

Vilas's numbers roughly coincide with those put forward in an eighteen-page typewritten history of the compañía put together in exile by B. R. ("Carmen") Vera, an ERP combatant and the wife of Sargento Dago, a member of the Chilean MIR and an ERP instructor in Tucumán. Vera points to severe morale and discipline problems among the guerrillas. The ERP rout at Manchalá, she wrote, was followed by "a disorderly retreat ... caused in part by the lack of combat experience shared by the comrades ... a few comrades were lost after disobeying orders, there were those who reacted individually to the attack, without obeying their commanders." She describes other problems: "The characteristics of the mountains are completely different from those of the city and many comrades had a mistaken image of what the fight in the hills was about. There were many who 'broke' after hardly reaching the mountains, others didn't even get to our camps, others who wanted to leave after three days. There were cases of comrades who were officers in the urban units, and who upon arriving broke down and others who deserted." (Manuscript obtained by me is on file at CELS.) According to ERP leader Enrique Haroldo Gorriarán Merlo, "In the year and some the guerrillas operated, there were never more than 100 insurgents," in Samuel Blixen, *Conversaciones con Gorriarán Merlo* (Buenos Aires: Editorial Contrapunto, 1988), p. 204. For propaganda purposes, the ERP claimed it fielded 300 combatants in the Tucumán mountains. Rosendo Fraga, *Ejército: del escarnio al poder (1973–1976)* (Buenos Aires: Planeta, 1988), pp. 134, 171.

A secret document dated October 28, 1975, and signed by Col. Carlos Alberto Martínez, a top intelligence official, estimated there were between 120 and 160 members of the compañía. Document on file at CELS. Gen. (ret.) Carlos Delía Larroca, who as commander of the III Army Corps was Vilas's direct superior, claimed that there were "hundreds" of well-funded guerrillas in Tucumán but that they were badly equipped and had poor logistics. "We had more problems with the national government than with subversion in the region," he said. Delía Larroca interview (Buenos Aires, September 25, 1985). An October 2, 1975, Latin-Reuter wire service dispatch by Patrick Buckley claimed that at the beginning of that year the ERP in Tucumán counted on four companies of 200 soldiers each. However, an October 23, 1976, a Latin-Reuter story by Stewart Russell said that army intelligence maintained "there were never more than 70 ERP combatants in the area."

Nevertheless, in *Cuna de la Independencia, 1816–1977: Sepulcro de la subversión, 1975–1977* (Tucumán, 1977), p. 57, an official book on Tucumán published by the army, the guerrilla unit was estimated at 280 men, with 3,000 more making up part of its clandestine apparatus, sympathizers, and forced collaborators in the province. In a five-page pamphlet written by Vilas and obtained from the archives of *La Gaceta,* the general said the compañía "had come to control the majority of the town in the zone later closed off by the army and had 350 active combatants and around 1,000 ideological subversives in its cellular support structure." Also see Daniel Frontalini and María Cristina Caiati, *El Mito de la Guerra Sucia* (Buenos Aires: Edición CELS, 1984), especially pp. 57–64, and ERP internal document reproduced in the military regime's *Terrorismo en la Argentina* (Buenos Aires: Edición Gratuita, 1980), pp. 93–94, an official apology for the generals' conduct of the "dirty war."

The military's propaganda continues to pay dividends. Bryan Hodgson, in "Argentina's New Beginning," *National Geographic,* August 1986, said the ERP "fighting unit" numbered 800. John Simpson and Jana Bennett, in a well-intentioned but misleading work, *The Disappeared: Voices from a Secret War* (London: Robson, 1985), p. 188, said 600 ERP "militants" were killed in Tucumán.

6. Several former guerrillas and state intelligence agents point out that the army knew the real size of the ERP unit, having infiltrated two agents, one by the name of Miguel Angel Lasser, into the group throughout 1975. Lasser was later killed by the ERP. His death is listed under the "general public" section of the victims of leftist terrorism listed in *Terrorismo en la Argentina,* p. 252. Another informant, Jesús ("El Oso") Ranier, reportedly sent unusable weapons to the group from Buenos Aires. B. R. Vera manuscript. Ranier is widely believed also to have blown the whistle on the Christmas Eve raid on the Domingo Viejo Bueno arsenal in suburban Buenos Aires, which resulted in a crushing defeat for the guerrillas. He was executed by the ERP in January 1976. Luis Mattini, *Hombres y Mujeres del PRT-ERP* (Buenos Aires: Editorial Contrapunto, 1990), p. 502.

7. For example, in *Terrorismo en la Argentina,* the military listed five army men—Capt. José Antonio Ramallo, Lt. César Ledesma, Sgt. Walter Hugo Gomez, and Cpls. Ricardo

Zárate and Carlos Parra—as "victims of terrorist attacks." However, in *Cuna de la Indepen-dencia*, p. 64, the propaganda effort correctly identifies the dead men as victims of an acci-dental helicopter crash on May 5, 1976. Lt. José Mundani is also listed as a terrorist victim in *Terrorismo en la Argentina*. Yet at the time of his death in 1975, the army high command said Mundani died while planting explosives in Tucumán. *La Gaceta*, August 7, 1975. And Vilas admitted that the soldier in fact died accidentally during "war games." Vilas manu-script, sec. 3, subheading "Tactical Plan No. 4," p. 10. In *Terrorismo en la Argentina*, the death of army officer Raúl García is also listed as the work of guerrillas. However, in Her-nán López Echagüe, *El Enigma del General Bussi* (Buenos Aires: Sudamericana, 1991), p. 223, García's death was correctly listed as the result of an airplane crash.

The son of police inspector Juan Sirnio testified that the latter's opposition to torture cost him his life at the hands of army captain Arturo González Naya. See Martin Edwin Andersen, "Las sucias solapas de González Naya," *Página* 12, January 21, 1988; also *Comi-sión bicameral investigadora de violaciones de derechos humanos*, anexo 2, "Homicidios," subcapítulo "Represión a personas pertenecientes a las fuerzas de Seguridad," Tucumán, 1985, pp. 26–27. Sirnio is listed as a victim of leftist terrorism in *Terrorismo en la Argentina*, p. 256. In the Montoneros' *Evita Montonera* 2, no. 13, April-May 1976, p. 17, Sirnio was listed as a victim of a leftist group "which doesn't belong to Montoneros."

Although casualties at the hands of the guerrillas were badly inflated, later efforts to identify victims of the military's repression fell far short of the real number. Although the official provincial parliamentary commission set up to investigate the missing in Tucumán received complaints about some 500 missing people, on-site interviews—particularly those in the so-called combat zone—allowed me to establish that as many as 2,000 people in Tucumán probably disappeared. Even as late as October 1985, many people, especially peasants, were either afraid to make public complaints or had accepted their losses with characteristic fatalism. Vilas claimed that 1,507 people "accused of maintaining broad con-tacts with the enemy" passed through the Escuelita camp alone between February 10 and December 18, 1975. Vilas manuscript, pt. 3, "El Desarrollo de la Operaciones," p. 11. Few survived.

8. "We know that this rural guerrilla can be contained," said one Argentine army colo-nel, "but to eradicate subversion we would have to apply the same methods we use here to the sources of the guerrilla movements, which are in the big cities." "Guerrillas in Argen-tina Battle Army in a War Without Prisoners," *New York Times*, November 11, 1975. "Dur-ing all of 1975, *Operativo Independencia* gave the army the chance to give the troops experi-ence and to compromise the force as an institution through 45-day rotation." Fraga, *Ejército*, pp. 275–276. By October 1975, "the Tucumán experience had gained relevance given the fact it was considered possible that the operations could be extended to other provinces and, as a result, was thought a similar methodology could be used." Ibid., p. 240.

9. Interviews; Antonio del Carmen Fernández, *Informe sobre el problema azucarero* (Buenos Aires: Ediciones El Combatiente, 1974). Fernández, one of the few real grass-roots union organizers attracted by the ERP, was killed on August 14, 1974, following an attack on the air transport infantry regiment in Catamarca province. Julio Santucho, *Los Ultimos Guevaristas* (Buenos Aires: Puntosur, 1988), pp. 121–126; also, unpublished manuscript by Tucumán reporter Roberto Espinoza given to me by Espinoza.

10. "Argentine Province Nears Revolt amid Poverty and Repression," *New York Times*, August 4, 1968. See also Eduardo Crawley, *A House Divided: Argentina 1880–1980* (London:

Hurst, 1984), p. 284; and *Comisión bicameral investigadora de violaciones de derechos humanos: Informe político,* Tucumán, 1985.

11. A copy of a manuscript written by Julio Santucho (hereafter, Santucho manuscript), brother of ERP leader Mario Roberto Santucho, was given to me with Santucho's permission by former PRT-ERP militant El Cabezón. Citation also occurs in Santucho, *Los Ultimos Guevaristas,* p. 107. According to ERP leader Luis Mattini, Mario Roberto Santucho also chose Tucumán because of its proximity to Bolivia, a nation whose army was not seen as the kind of threat potentially posed by that of Brazil. Mattini, *Hombres y Mujeres,* p. 315.

12. On Four Hypotheses, see Santucho, *Los Ultimos Guevaristas,* p. 115, and Mattini, *Hombres y Mujeres,* pp. 23–26; Fernández, *Informe; New York Times,* August 4, 1968.

13. Mattini, *Hombres y Mujeres,* pp. 32–39; Santucho, *Los Ultimos Guevaristas,* pp. 114–115.

14. Fernández, *Informe;* Mattini, *Hombres y Mujeres,* pp. 32–40; *New York Times,* August 4, 1968.

15. Mattini, *Hombres y Mujeres,* pp. 36, 41, 290.

16. On Santucho's personality, interviews with several former ERP combatants, including a survivor of the Tucumán campaign interviewed October 1985 in San Miguel de Tucumán. "Santucho was very unassuming and had a facility for speaking with common people, but many overestimated him," he said. "He was very influenced by the Vietnamese rural struggle, and sought almost mechanically to apply it to Tucumán." See also Mattini, *Hombres y Mujeres.* The guerrillas' capacity for self-delusion was not limited to Santucho. The ERP "needing an identity it didn't have, created images to its liking." Ibid., p. 100.

17. Santucho manuscript; Mattini said that by 1966 there was talk about launching a guerrilla movement in Tucumán, and the PRT—the ERP's parent organization—planned to do so in 1969. Mattini, *Hombres y Mujeres,* pp. 37, 47.

18. B. R. Vera manuscript, p. 16.

19. *Panorama,* June 1, 1971.

20. *Time,* January 14, 1974.

21. Santucho manuscript; Santucho, *Los Ultimos Guevaristas,* pp. 190–195. According to Mattini, the ERP—while engaged in its deadly campaign against foreign businesses—also had trouble differentiating between national and international capital. Mattini, *Hombres y Mujeres,* p. 220.

22. Vilas manuscript, 49.

23. Army Secret Order/CGE/1/23/75, Annex no. 2, February 5, 1975; forty-eight-hours rule, with thirty days to process suspects, Order no. 6/Regional Ambience/External Public.

24. Article 5 of Secret Decree no. 261, February 5, 1975, in Vilas manuscript, p. 7; *La Gaceta,* February 22, 1975.

25. Article 6 of Secret Decree no. 261, February 5, 1975, in Vilas manuscript, p. 7.

26. "Panorama Tucumano," *La Gaceta,* February 11, 1975; "Panorama Porteño," *La Gaceta,* February 13, 1975; *La Gaceta,* February 15, 1975; *La Gaceta,* February 26, 1975.

27. Acdel Vilas, *Tucumán: el hecho historico,* pamphlet from *La Gaceta* archive, copy in my possession.

28. Interviews with veteran *La Gaceta* reporters Alvarez Sosa and Cacho Garrocho (San Miguel de Tucumán, October 1985); *Comisión bicameral investigadora de violaciones de derechos humanos,* anexo 10, "Personas más nombrados," Tucumán, 1985; "twenty bodies"

told to author by retired lieutenant colonel who knew Vilas well and who later went on to help design the military policy of the Alfonsín government. Name withheld on request. Osvaldo Bayer, *Los Vengadores de la Patagonia trágica,* 4 vols. (Buenos Aires: Editorial Galerna, 1972).

29. Vilas manuscript; also see Martin Edwin Andersen and Antonio López Crespo, "La guerra sucia empezó en 1975," *El Periodista,* no. 73 (February 6, 1986), pp. 2–4.

30. Andersen and López Crespo, "La guerra sucia," pp. 2–4; Menéndez interview (October 11, 1985).

31. Interview with Gen. (ret.) José Rogelio Villareal (October 9, 1985). Villareal confirmed that López Rega was instrumental in assuring Vilas's promotion and that Salgado's plane crashed when the tip of a wing touched a tree; Fraga, *Ejército,* p. 134.

32. Interviews with Generals Villareal, former chief of staff to President (General) Videla, and Menéndez; Vilas as "mediocre man," Delía Larroca interview; Vilas was briefly a candidate for the Peronist nomination for president in 1983.

33. *New York Times,* December 25, 1975; Vilas manuscript, "Dios lo quiso," p. 8; Richard R. Valcourt, "Controlling U.S. Hired Hands," *International Journal of Intelligence and Counterintelligence* 2, no. 3, p. 166; according to Lt. Col. (ret.) José Lagomarsino (Buenos Aires, 1985), Vilas's conception of the regional troop commander having vast powers—in education, politics, economics, social welfare, and so on—came from the French experience in Algeria, where, he said, techniques were tailored to fighting in an "occupied" country; Roger Trinquier, *Guerra, Subversión, Revolución* (Buenos Aires: Ed. Rioplatense, 1975).

34. Andersen and López Crespo, "La guerra sucia," pp. 2–4.

35. Ibid., pp. 2–4; see also "Panorama Tucumana," *La Gaceta,* December 1975.

36. "We disagree with the declamatory (such as that of the French Revolution) and sensitizing humanism of certain theoreticians who, protecting those who attack society and the Fatherland, open the doors to the most aberrant crimes and affronts, unleashing barbarism upon peoples." Also: "The psychopolitical action of international communism frequently is complemented by subversive actions that in no time are converted in terrorist acts. ... Rationalist utopianism, divorced from all reality, is cold, pitiless and implacable, despite its mask of empty and theatrical sentimentalism, at once declamatory and crybabyish. Such as the liberal and rational utopianism of Rousseau and the French Revolution." Vilas manuscript, pt. 3, "La guerra," pp. 11, 13.

37. Andersen and López Crespo, "La guerra sucia," pp. 2–4.

38. *Nunca Más, Informe de la Comisión Nacional sobre la Desaparición de Personas* (Buenos Aires: EUDEBA, 1984), p. 214.

39. On torture, interview (September 1985) with Lt. (ret.) Julio Sarmiento, a member of an army special forces unit that operated in Tucumán in 1975. Sarmiento was one of thirty-three officers who were later cashiered by the military for their opposition to the "dirty war" methods being used; *New York Times,* December 25, 1975.

40. *Comisión bicameral investigadora de violaciones de derechos humanos,* anexo 1, "Metodología represiva," Tucumán, 1985.

41. Fernández, *Informe;* Alvarez Sosa interview. See also Felix Coluccio, *Diccionario de Creencias y Supersticiones (Argentinas y Americanas)* (Buenos Aires: Corregidor, 1984), pp. 190–192.

42. *Comisión bicameral investigadora de violaciones de derechos humanos,* anexo 3, "Homicidios," pp. 3–6; *La Gaceta,* April 5, 1975, and *La Gaceta,* April 6, 1975.

43. Interviews with Manuel Antonio Mercado and wife (Tucumán, October 1985).

44. "The first significant clash occurred in Manchalá. ... The second significant encounter took place in Acheral, where 14 delinquents were killed." *Cuna de la Independencia,* p. 65.

45. Mattini, *Hombres y Mujeres,* pp. 422–424; Vilas, five-page manuscript from *La Gaceta* archive, p. 3.

46. Interviews with former ERP guerrillas (San Miguel de Tucumán, October 1985, and Buenos Aires, 1985–1987); also captured ERP document, cited in *Terrorismo en la Argentina,* p. 94.

47. Claims about quantity of information on guerrillas obtained by army after clash comes from Vilas manuscript; Héctor R. Simeoni, in *¡Aniquilen al ERP! La "guerra sucia" en el monte tucumano* (Buenos Aires: Ediciones Cosmos, 1985), a pro-military history of the Tucumán campaign, p. 62; *Cuna de la Independencia,* p. 65; and Menéndez and Urien interviews.

48. B. R. Vera manuscript, pp. 5–6.

49. ERP internal document, cited in *Terrorismo en la Argentina,* p. 94; in *Cuna de la Independencia,* seven guerrilla deaths were tallied, p. 65; five-page Vilas pamphlet claimed seventeen guerrillas were killed, with no mention of army deaths; Simeoni, *Aniquilen,* p. 64, claimed no army men were killed.

50. "They didn't want to eliminate the enemy," Urien charged. "They wanted to have a latent problem as a pretext for the coup." Urien interview.

51. Interview with Federal Police official who requested anonymity; Vilas manuscript, "El Desarrollo de las Operaciones," sec. 3, subheading "Tactical Plan No. 3," p. 9.

52. B. R. Vera manuscript, p. 10; *New York Times,* November 11, 1975; Fraga, *Ejército,* p. 239; Vilas manuscript, "Tactical Plan No. 6 (Del 1 octubre hasta el 20 de diciembre)," pp. 1–5; Simeoni, *Aniquilen,* pp. 115–126.

53. *La Prensa,* August 24, 1975; *Terrorismo en la Argentina,* pp. 147–151.

54. Interview with former U.S. military attaché stationed in Buenos Aires, name withheld on request (Washington, D.C., December 1985).

55. *La Nación,* November 1, 1975, p. 5; *La Nación,* November 2, 1975.

56. Alleged pact between Vilas and Montoneros was widely rumored in Argentine army circles and was mentioned to me in Villareal interview. In refutation, see Fraga, *Ejército,* p. 242. Also, declarations of Montonero militant Alberto José Francomano to Federal Police Security Superintendency, October 17, 1975.

57. Vilas manuscript, sec. 3, subheading "Tactical Plan No. 6," p. 18.

58. *La Gaceta,* December 19, 1975; Crawley, *A House Divided,* p. 419; the Argentine public was not the only group kept in the dark about the fighting in Tucumán. In mid-1976 rank-and-file ERP members did not know the "real situation" of the compañía, still believing it was fighting the army to a "standstill," in Mattini, *Hombres y Mujeres,* p. 516.

59. *New York Times,* December 25, 1975.

Chapter 10

1. Enrique Pavón Pereyra, *El Diario Secreto de Perón* (Buenos Aires: Sudamericana-Planeta, 1985), pp. 326, 329.

2. Pablo Kandel and Mario Monteverde, *Entorno y Caída* (Buenos Aires: Planeta, 1976), p. 39.

3. Eduardo Crawley, *A House Divided: Argentina 1880–1980* (London: Hurst, 1984), pp. 415–416.

4. Interviews with "Sam," with U.S. antinarcotics personnel (Buenos Aires, 1985–1986), and with nationalist leader Guillermo Patricio Kelly (Buenos Aires, 1986); Kandel and Monteverde, *Entorno*, p. 67; former detainee Carlos Moore testimony before Brazilian Catholic church human rights organizations, São Paulo, November 15, 1980.

5. Boleslao Lewin, *Cómo fue la inmigración judía en la Argentina* (Buenos Aires: Editorial Plus Ultra, 1983); Harry Maurer, "Anti-semitism in Argentina," *Nation*, February 12, 1977.

6. Lewin, *Cómo fue.*

7. Morton Rosenthal, "The Threatened Jews of Argentina," *ADL Bulletin*, March, 1971.

8. Ted Cordova-Clauré, "Swastikas in Argentina," *Atlas World Press Review*, November 1976, pp. 20–22; Eugene F. Sofer, "A New Terror Grips Argentina," *Present Tense*, Autumn 1977, pp. 19–25; "López Rega Aims Barb at EconMin Gelbard," U.S. Department of State telegram, February 20, 1974: "Press Feb. 20 reports that at meeting between Perón and resident Arab Ambassadors Feb. 18 (seemingly called so that López Rega could report on and discuss his mission to Libya) SocWelfare Min. López Rega asserted Jewish names in Argentine Cabinet had raised difficulties in his recent negotiations with Libyans."

9. "La 'P-2' en la Argentina," *Todo es Historia*, no. 214 (February 1985), pp. 32–33; Héctor Ruiz Núñez, "López Rega: Esplendor y decadencia," *Humor*, no. 173 (May 14, 1986); *Newsweek International*, June 2, 1986.

10. Interview with leader of Jewish relief organization in Buenos Aires, name withheld on request.

11. *Somos*, July 8, 1983, pp. 81–82; *Gente*, February 7, 1974; Jimmy Burns, *The Land That Lost Its Heroes* (London: Bloomsbury, 1987), pp. 57–60; *peronista auténtico* parliamentary deputies Miguel Domingo Zavala Rodríguez and Leonardo Bettanin charged that in the deal with Kaddafi, Argentina ended up paying higher than market price per barrel of oil.

12. Ruiz Núñez, "López Rega"; Rosendo Fraga, *Ejército: del escarnio al poder (1973–1976)* (Buenos Aires: Planeta, 1988), p. 161.

13. Kandel and Monteverde, *Entorno*, p. 30; Maurer, "Anti-semitism," p. 171; *ADL Bulletin*, November 1976.

14. "Breviario de una infamia," *Cuaderno No.* 1, Comité de Lucha Contra el Racismo y demás formas de Colonialismo (eleven-page pamphlet in my possession); Andrew Graham-Yool, *The Press in Argentina, 1973–8* (London: Writers and Scholars Educational Trust, 1979), p. 77.

15. "Breviario de una infamia."

16. *ADL Bulletin*, November 1976; Maurer, "Anti-semitism"; Cordova-Clauré, "Swastikas," p. 20; "Townley made contact with members of *Milicia*, an AAA affiliate, which specialized in reprinting Nazi tracts in Spanish and promoting anti-semitism. The group coordinated its underground terrorist operations through a branch of SIDE. ... *Milicia* had earned particular distinction in the trade for stealing Ford Falcon cars to carry out kidnappings and its ideological nostalgia for Hitler and the Third Reich. It owned a publishing house, also called *Milicia*, that reprinted Nazi texts. ... *Milicia* and AAA members who

helped carry out the Prats assassination worked directly under an arm of SIDE." In John Dinges and Saul Landau, *Assassination on Embassy Row* (New York: Pantheon, 1980), pp. 140, 184, 196; "Sam" interview.

17. Graham-Yool, *Press in Argentina*, p. 97.

18. *Luchas Obreras Argentinas*, no. 7, March 1985, p. 78.

19. Ibid.; interview with metalworkers' leader Francisco Gutíerrez (Buenos Aires, 1985).

20. Interview with former Buenos Aires provincial police officer and SIDE agent Carlos A. Hours (Buenos Aires, December 1985).

21. Interview with former U.S. embassy political officer Wayne Smith (Washington, D.C., November 1985).

22. *Luchas Obreras Argentinas*, p. 54; according to *La Opinión*, March 21, 1975: "Until March 20, 1975, there was not one single conflict in the companies which make up the Villa Constitución section and ... the substantial wage increases gained were the result of talks and agreements between the parts. It also ought to be recognized that Acindar, apart from technical improvements, was the only private steel company which, in 1974, increased its production—from 137,704 to 226,480 tons."

23. *La Voz*, September 5, 1984; Rodolfo Peregrino Fernández, *Autocrítica Policial* (Buenos Aires: El Cid Editor, 1983), pp. 14–15.

24. *Luchas Obreras Argentinas*, p. 50–52; Alipio Paoletti, *Como los Nazis, como en Vietnam* (Buenos Aires: Editorial Contrapunto, 1987), pp. 43–48.

25. Liliana De Riz, *Retorno y Derrumbe: el último gobierno peronista* (Mexico City: Folios Ediciones, 1981), p. 125.

26. Alipio Paoletti, "La complicidad de Acindar, S.A.," *Madres de la Plaza de Mayo*, April 1985; *Luchas Obreras Argentinas*, p. 78.

27. "Commanding General of Army Resigns," U.S. Department of State telegram, May 14, 1975.

28. Kandel and Monteverde, *Entorno*, pp. 45–53.

29. "Argentine Administration Weakened by López Rega," *Current Foreign Relations*, U.S. Department of State, June 11, 1975.

30. *New York Times*, June 28, 1975.

31. *National Intelligence Daily*, CIA, July 2, 1975, p. 3.

32. Ibid., July 18, 1975, p. 4.

33. Kandel and Monteverde, *Entorno*, pp. 79–83; Colotto interview; *New York Times*, July 20, 1975.

34. *Crónica*, April 2, 1986, p. 4.

35. *New York Times*, July 21, 1975.

36. Martin Edwin Andersen, "SIDE-Montoneros, La Conexión Secreta," *Expreso*, June 5 and June 12, 1987; Andrew Graham-Yool, *Portrait of an Exile* (London: Junction, 1981), pp. 32–44; the military regime claimed Polisecki, "a Montonero militant, was tried and sentenced for high treason and espionage" and killed by the guerrillas. *La Nación*, May 8, 1980, p. 17.

37. Guillermo Patricio Kelly interview; Penny Lernoux, *In Banks We Trust* (Garden City, N.Y.: Doubleday, Anchor, 1984), p. 189; *La Nación*, December 2, 1976, p. 2.; *Quorum*, September 4, 1982, p. 7.

38. Dinges and Landau, *Assassination*, pp. 177, 196; Magnus Linklater, Isabel Hilton, and Neal Ascherson, *The Fourth Reich: Klaus Barbie and the Neo-Fascist Connection* (London: Hodder and Stoughton, 1984), p. 213; Scott Anderson and John Lee Anderson, *Inside the League* (New York: Dodd, Mead, 1986), pp. 6–7, 9; *Panorama* (Italy), April 19, 1987, pp. 56–57; *Ambito Financiero*, March 31, 1987; *Somos*, April 1, 1987, pp. 46–47.

39. Graham-Yool, *Portrait*, p. 65.

40. Copy of letter provided to me by the office of Argentine Federal Prosecutor Ricardo Molinas, 1986.

41. Carlos Moore testimony; Paoletti, *Como los Nazis*, pp. 201–202, 381–382; Peregrino Fernández, *Autocrítica Policial*, p. 17; *El Periodista*, no. 76 (February 21, 1986), p. 2; Fraga, *Ejército*, pp. 243–244; interview with former army officer Julio Sarmiento (Buenos Aires, 1985), who was cashiered during the military regime for his democratic beliefs; judicial declaration before Judge Carlos Oliveri by Gen. Otto Paladino, May 14, 1984, Federal Court No. 5.

42. *Clarín*, October 1, 1985, p. 14; *Clarín*, August 18, 1975; *El Periodista*, no. 44 (July 12–18), 1985, p. 8.

43. "Rightwing terrorism since López Rega," U.S. embassy cable, Buenos Aires, December 9, 1975.

44. Cited in Daniel Frontalini and María Cristina Caiati, *El Mito de la "Guerra Sucia"* (Buenos Aires: Edición CELS, 1984), p. 83.

Chapter 11

1. CIA, "Weekly Surveyor," November 15, 1975, a secret publication, from archives of Dale Van Atta and Mario Diament; Pablo Kandel and Mario Monteverde, *Entorno y Caída* (Buenos Aires: Editorial Planeta, 1976), pp. 109–121.

2. Rosendo Fraga, *Ejército: del escarnio al poder* (Buenos Aires: Planeta, 1988), pp. 234, 245.

3. Juan Gasparini, *Montoneros, Final de Cuentas* (Buenos Aires: Puntosur, 1988), p. 83; Pablo Guissani, *Montoneros, La Soberbia Armada* (Buenos Aires: Sudamericana-Planeta, 1984), p. 102; interview with former army major Ernesto Barreiro (Buenos Aires, September 29, 1987): according to Barreiro, "many of the bombs, etc., in Córdoba before the coup were 'black propaganda'—Menéndez let things go so there was a sensation of chaos"; Fraga, *Ejército*, p. 139, says that an important army sector maintained good relations with the Montoneros, if only to be able to isolate and neutralize the ERP.

4. *New York Times*, October 26, 1975.

5. *National Intelligence Daily*, CIA, October 17, 1975, from archives of Van Atta and Diament.

6. Kandel and Monteverde, *Entorno*, pp. 114–116; *La Nación*, November 6, 1975.

7. For Alfonsín's comments on situation, see *La Opinión*, January 18, 1976.

8. *La Nación*, November 14, 1975; *Clarín*, November 19, 1975; U.S. Department of State, Bureau of Intelligence and Research (hereafter, INR), "Morning Summary," November 11, 1975, and CIA "Weekly Surveyor," November 15, 1975.

9. *New York Times*, December 23, 1975.

10. *National Intelligence Daily*, November 24, 1975 (Van Atta and Diament archives).

11. New York Times, December 6, 1975; interview with former Federal Police officer Armando Luchina (Buenos Aires province, 1985).

12. Fraga, Ejército, p. 252; Kandel and Monteverde, Entorno, pp. 139–141; top secret U.S. Department of State, INR, "Morning Summary," December 23, 1975; Alfredo Leuco and José Antonio Díaz, El heredero de Perón (Buenos Aires: Planeta, 1988), p. 132.

13. Van Atta and Diament archives.

14. National Intelligence Daily, December 20, 1975 (Van Atta and Diament archives).

15. Top secret U.S. Department of State, INR, "Intelligence Summary," December 21, 1975.

16. National Intelligence Daily, December 22, 1975 (Van Atta and Diament archives).

17. New York Times, December 23, 1975.

18. "At the end of 1975 I was placed under orders of an office in the Domingo Viejo Bueno batallion. The chiefs, and my direct superiors, were Col. Eduardo Abud, Maj. Barzuk and 1st Lt. González Chipón. There an 'inter-forces group' was formed to repress subversive actions, composed of personnel from the Gendarmerie, naval prefecture, provincial police and one Federal Police official. As I had contacts with extreme right-wing groups and had belonged to them since the 1960s, I was given orders to be the 'interface,' with the purpose of handing down orders and conducting operations with the so-called 'paramilitary or parapolice groups,' all of them civilians belonging to what was called the National University Concentration (CNU), as well as conduct operations with police and military personnel and civilians belonging to the Triple-A." Declarations of Batallion 601 army intelligence agent Orestes Vaello before CONADEP, April 4, 1984.

19. Interview with former police intelligence officer Carlos Hours, who won a medal for his performance at Monte Chingolo (Buenos Aires, 1986); Luis Mattini, Hombres y Mujeres del PRT-ERP (Buenos Aires: Editorial Contrapunto, 1990), pp. 476–478; María Seoane, Todo o Nada (Buenos Aires: Planeta, 1991), pp. 276–286, claims the ERP counted on 250 combatants, a number said to be too high by ERP militants involved in the battle and unconvincing given her claim that the insurgents had 150 weapons in total (p. 281); see also Daniel Frontalini and María Cristina Caiati, El Mito de la Guerra Sucia (Buenos Aires: Edición CELS, 1984), p. 66.

20. Seoane, Todo o Nada, pp. 476–478; La Prensa, December 24, 1975.

21. Clarín, December 26, 1975; Hours interview.

22. Clarín, December 26, 1975.

23. Ibid.

24. Hours interview; Clarín, December 26, 1975.

25. La Prensa, December 26, 1975; Clarín, December 26, 1975; El Combatiente, January 14, 1976.

26. Hours interview.

27. "Informe Oficial del Comando en Jefe," Clarín, January 31, 1976. The analysis did not prevent a propaganda campaign that presented "subversion" as an overwhelming force capable of taking over the country, nor did it prevent the military from scoffing at any opinion that terrorism was a manageable police problem.

28. National Intelligence Daily, January 6, 1976 (Van Atta and Diament archives).

29. Richard Gillespie, Soldiers of Perón: Argentina's Montoneros (New York: Oxford University Press, 1982), pp. 218–221.

30. *New York Times,* January 14, 1976; Gillespie, *Soldiers of Perón,* p. 219.

31. "Sam" interview; Gillespie, *Soldiers of Perón,* pp. 217, 219–223; Juan Gasparini, *Montoneros,* pp. 138–139; according to one source close to the Montoneros, the *aspirante* (low-level guerrilla) had told police where to find guerrilla leaders Marcos Osatinsky and Juan Carlos Mendizábal in Córdoba. It was later claimed from within the organization that Quieto himself insisted on applying the death penalty.

32. Enrique Vásquez, *La Ultima: Orígen, Apogeo y Caída de la Dictadura Militar* (Buenos Aires: EUDEBA, 1985), p. 22.

33. On Lanusse's death, interview with Argentine journalist María Laura Avignolo (Buenos Aires, 1986) and with Lanusse family friends, who requested confidentiality. See also testimony of *Buenos Aires Herald* editor Robert Cox before Buenos Aires federal court, April 29, 1985, and "La Trágica Historia del General Lanusse," *La Semana,* p. 24 (my copy undated, circa 1985). According to "Sam," cases such as that of Caride de Lanusse were not unique. The Montoneros, he said, "were frequently blamed for kidnappings or political assassinations carried out by the Peronist government; however, the Federal Police were able to identify the majority of fictitious Montonero communiqués and had interrogated numerous Montonero prisoners who confirmed actual Montonero kidnappings. Additionally, the Federal Police and the various Argentine intelligence services had interrogated and tortured numerous Peronist thugs who participated in kidnappings and extortions and had been able to sort out many of these actions which were not carried out by the Montoneros." "Sam" interviews.

34. *New York Times,* October 27, 1975.

35. Jean-Pierre Bousquet, *Las locas de la Plaza de Mayo* (Buenos Aires: El Cid Editor, 1983), p. 36. Bousquet was Buenos Aires correspondent for *Agence France-Presse* from 1975 to 1980.

36. *New York Times,* March 25, 1976.

37. Identification of Alvarez Saavedra from interviews and *Comisión Provincial Derechos Humanos: Informe Final y Documentos Elaborados* vol. 1, La Rioja, 1984, p. 26; interview with Menem advisor Alberto Kohan (La Rioja, June 11, 1985).

38. José Deheza, *¿Quiénes derrocaron a Isabel Perón?* (Buenos Aires: Ediciones Cuenca del Plata, 1981), p. 172; see also Kandel and Monteverde, *Entorno.*

39. Deheza, *Quiénes derrocaron,* pp. 179–180; Vásquez, *La Ultima,* p. 24.

40. Deheza, *Quiénes derrocaron,* p. 190.

41. Vásquez, *La Ultima,* pp. 20–21; interview with Gen. (ret.) Ricardo Flouret (Buenos Aires, 1985); according to the CIA's *National Intelligence Daily,* January 16, 1976, "the impediments to military action against the President continue to diminish, but one major constraint—the potentially disruptive role of Peronist labor—remains. ... The high command balks at making a move that could bring thousands of armed workers into the streets."

42. Deheza, *Quiénes derrocaron,* p. 219.

43. *Diario del Juicio,* no. 7, July 9, 1985.

44. Deheza, *Quiénes derrocaron,* pp. 236–239.

45. Ibid., pp. 238–239.

46. Ibid., pp. 240–242.

47. Ibid., p. 245; Kandel and Monteverde, *Entorno,* pp. 209–221.

Chapter 12

1. Court documents, including letter and criminal complaint filed by his widow, Lidia Elsa Alberte, form part of Case 5007 of the Inter-American Commission on Human Rights of the Organization of American States and were provided to me by Argentine journalist Rogelio García Lupo.

2. Sarmiento quoted in Enrique Vásquez, *La Ultima: Orígen, Apogeo y Caída de la Dictadura Militar* (Buenos Aires: EUDEBA, 1985), p. 54.

3. On situation in La Plata, interview with Argentine human rights lawyer Juan Méndez (Washington, D.C., November 1985).

4. Peter Waldmann and Ernesto Garzón Valdéz, *El poder militar en la Argentina, 1976–1981* (Buenos Aires: Editorial Galerna, 1983), pp. 101–115; *Cuestionario*, May 1976; a particularly heart-rending account of the repression carried out in one factory, including a stunning admission by a member of management of corporate complicity with the military, is found in Horacio Verbitsky, "Todo Vale," *Página* 12, May 5, 1991.

5. Emilio F. Mignone, *Iglesia y Dictadura* (Buenos Aires: Ediciones del Pensamiento Nacional, 1986), p. 16.

6. *Clarín*, October 5, 1980; Waldman, *El poder militar*, pp. 106.

7. *El Periodista*, May 31–June 6, 1985.

8. Secret army orders, Intelligence Annex, DCJE 504.

9. A copy of the document was found by me in the files of the *Washington Post* Buenos Aires bureau.

10. For a misleading, but common, read on radicalization in the factories, see *New York Times*, March 24, 1976.

11. Pablo Giussani, *Montoneros: La Soberbia Armada* (Buenos Aires: Sudamericana-Planeta, 1984), p. 58; Verbitsky, "Todo Vale."

12. Alvaro Abós, *Las organizaciones sindicales y el poder militar (1976–1983)* (Buenos Aires: Centro Editor de América Latina, 1984), p. 12.

13. CONADEP files nos. 7683 and 1,638; *Siete Días,* July 11, 1985, pp. 9–10; Abós, *Las organizaciones*, p. 9.

14. Letter to Energy Secretary Guillermo O. Zubarán from former SEGBA president Juan José Taccone, July 19, 1976.

15. Abós, *Las organizaciones*, p. 23.

16. Ibid., pp. 23–24; Horacio Verbitsky, *Rodolfo Walsh y la prensa clandestina* (Buenos Aires: Ediciones de la Urraca, 1985), pp. 69–72.

17. Abós, *Las organizaciones*, p. 24.

18. Sergio Ciancaglini and Martín Granovsky, *Crónicas del Apocalipsis* (Buenos Aires: Editorial Contrapunto, 1986), p. 17; Abós, *Las organizaciones*, p. 26.

19. Abós, *Las organizaciones*.

20. "Disappearance of local power union leader: Sitrep mid-day February 18," confidential telegram from U.S. embassy in Buenos Aires to State Department.

21. "Labor Minister Replies to AFL-CIO Telegram," confidential telegram from U.S. embassy in Buenos Aires to State Department, March 7, 1978: "Sources cast suspicion particularly on navy, interpreting the action as a warning against any labor leaders who made political deals with the so-called 'populist wing' of the army."

22. Testimony of ESMA survivor Andrés Castillo, Buenos Aires federal court trial of the juntas, July 19, 1985. According to former Federal Police Commissar Jorge Colotto, the group that kidnapped Smith was headed by retired navy Lt. Alejandro ("Felipe") Spinelli (Colotto interviews). See also Alipio Paoletti, *Como los Nazis, Como en Vietnam* (Buenos Aires: Editorial Contrapunto, 1987), p. 182.

Chapter 13

1. *La Nación*, May 5, 1978.

2. Emilio F. Mignone, *Iglesia y Dictadura* (Buenos Aires: Ediciones del Pensamiento Nacional, 1986), p. 17; *Newsweek International*, September 1, 1986.

3. *Clarín*, July 15, 1975; *La Opinión*, October 12, 1976; *La Nación*, October 11, 1976; *La Nación*, May 6, 1976.

4. Ricardo Flouret interview (Buenos Aires, 1985); Penny Lernoux, "Blood Taints Church in Argentina," *National Catholic Reporter*, April 12, 1985.

5. Lernoux, "Blood Taints."

6. *National Catholic News Service*, June 19 and December 4, 1975; Mignone, *Iglesia y Dictadura*, p. 238.

7. *Excelsior* (Mexico), October 9, 1976.

8. Orestes Vaello testimony before CONADEP, May 9, 1984, Secretary Raúl Aragon presiding.

9. Report by the Catholic Institute for International Relations (hereafter, CIIR), October 18, 1976, provided to author by Penny Lernoux.

10. Ibid.

11. Ibid.; *New York Times*, July 6 and July 18, 1976; *La Voz*, July 8, 1985.

12. *El Periodista*, no. 32, April 19, 1985.

13. Testimony of Miriam Lewin de García, CONADEP, file no. 2365.

14. Penny Lernoux, *Cry of the People* (New York: Doubleday, 1980), pp. 346–347; Mignone, *Iglesia y Dictadura*, pp. 245–250.

15. Lernoux, *Cry*, p. 348.

16. ANCLA cable, Buenos Aires, September 8, 1977, in Horacio Verbitsky, *Rodolfo Walsh y la prensa clandestina* (Buenos Aires: Ediciones de la Urraca, 1985), p. 118.

17. Copies of Monsignor Angelelli's papers provided to me by his successor, La Rioja bishop Bernardo Witte (Witte interview, La Rioja, June 1985).

18. CIIR, p. 6; *Gente*, no. 963, 1984.

19. *Tablet* (Great Britain), August 14, 1976.

20. *Clarín*, June 25, 1986; *National Catholic News Service*, August 9, 1976; Mignone, *Iglesia y Dictadura*, p. 252.

21. Rodolfo Peregrino Fernández, *Autocrítica Policial* (Buenos Aires: El Cid Editor, 1983), pp. 63–66; CIIR, p. 8.

22. Testimony of José Deheza, Buenos Aires federal court trial of the juntas, 1985.

23. Testimony of Plutarco Schaller, CONADEP, file no. 4952.

24. *Clarín*, June 25, 1986; *El Periodista*, July 18–24, 1986; Mignone, *Iglesia y Dictadura*, pp. 253–256; Witte interview; according to former Federal Police Commissar Jorge Colotto, Angelelli was killed by the army intelligence service. Colotto interviews.

25. Memorandum written by human rights leader Mignone circa 1978, copy of which he gave to me; interview with Thomas Quigley, of the U.S. Catholic Conference, Washington, D.C., December 1985; Lernoux, "Blood Taints."

26. *Latinamerica Press,* June 2, 1977.

27. *Diario del Juicio,* no. 6, July 2, 1985; for a list of priests participating in the clandestine repression, see Mignone, *Iglesia y Dictadura,* pp. 30–33.

28. For more on Plaza's role in the repression, see Mignone, *Iglesia y Dictadura,* pp. 109–124.

29. Mignone, *Iglesia y Dictadura,* p. 32; Marcial Castro Castillo, *Fuerzas Armadas, Etica y Represión* (Buenos Aires: Editorial Orden Nuevo, 1976), p. 145.

Chapter 14

1. Roberto Reyna, *La Perla* (Buenos Aires: El Cid Editor, 1984), p. 52.

2. Army document DCJE 504/77.

3. Quotes are from unpublished Vilas manuscript in my possession (see Chap. 9, n. 3).

4. Ibid.

5. *La Razón,* April 29, 1976; Eric Stover, *Scientists and Human Rights in Argentina Since 1976* (Washington, D.C.: AAAS, 1981), p. 23.

6. *La Opinión,* February 7, 1978.

7. Law 21260, article 1, and Law 21380, article 5.

8. Stover, *Scientists,* pp. 15, 26.

9. Interview with CTERA president Alfredo Bravo (Buenos Aires, 1984).

10. Secret Directive of army high command, "Anexo 4—Ambito Educacional—EMGE JefIII OP-DCJE 504/77"; Enrique Vásquez, *La Ultima: Orígen, Apogeo y Caída de la Dictadura Militar* (Buenos Aires: EUDEBA, 1985), pp. 270–276; Tucumán provincial bicameral human rights commission, case no. 47-985; Bravo interview.

11. Testimony of Armando Luchina, CONADEP and Buenos Aires federal court trial of the juntas, 1985.

12. *La Razón,* October 28, 1977, p. 12.

13. Vásquez, *La Ultima.*

14. Tucumán case no. 47-985; testimony of Julio César Heredia, CONADEP, file no. 5838.

15. Vilas manuscript.

16. *New York Times,* August 5 and August 7, 1976; *Clarín,* July 13, 1985.

17. *La Voz,* May 10, 1985.

18. "La subversión en el ámbito educativo, 1977," Ministerio de Cultura y Educación, Buenos Aires, 1977.

19. A poignant overview of the case, which does not address some of the teenagers' pro-Montonero activities, is contained in María Seoane and Héctor Ruiz Núñez, *La Noche de los Lapices* (Buenos Aires: Editorial Contrapunto, 1986).

20. Testimony of Pablo Díaz, Buenos Aires federal court trial of the juntas, May 9, 1985.

21. *El Periodista,* May 17–23, 1985; Seoane and Ruiz Nuñez, *La Noche,* pp. 73, 251.

22. Díaz testimony.

23. Seoane and Ruiz Núñez, *La Noche,* pp. 196–199; confidential testimony of security force officer who participated in the kidnappings.

24. "La subversión en el ámbito educativo."

25. *La Opinión,* December 13, 1978.

26. "Anexo 4 … DCJE 504/77," pp. 5–6, signed by Viola; *Informe sobre la Situación de los Derechos Humanos en Argentina: Octubre de 1979–Octubre de 1980* (Buenos Aires: CELS, 1980).

27. Stover, *Scientists,* p. 15; *La Nación,* March 30, 1984; *Clarín,* March 31, 1984.

28. *El Periodista,* December 15–21, 1984.

Chapter 15

1. *Noticias,* February 23, 1992.

2. Daniel Frontalini and María Cristina Caiati, *El Mito de la Guerra Sucia* (Buenos Aires: Edición CELS, 1984), pp. 92–93; *Nunca Más, Informe de la Comisión Nacional sobre la Desaparición de Personas* (Buenos Aires: EUDEBA, 1984).

3. *Nunca Más,* p. 116; Alipio Paoletti, *Como los Nazis, Como en Vietnam* (Buenos Aires: Editorial Contrapunto, 1987), pp. 91–107; testimony of Néstor Cendór, CONADEP, file no. 7170, in *Nunca Más,* pp. 257, 277.

4. *El Periodista,* June 7–13, 1985.

5. *Nunca Más,* pp. 137, 166, 175, 235–238; the story about Roualdés was told to me by a retired army lieutenant colonel who strongly disagreed with "dirty war" techniques and who later served as an advisor to the Alfonsín government.

6. *Nunca Más,* p. 235.

7. Testimony sent to President Raúl Alfonsín by former prisoners Piero DiMonte, Teresa Meschiati, Liliana Callizo, and Graciela Geuna, January 15, 1984, on file at CELS, Buenos Aires.

8. DiMonte, Meschiati, Callizo, and Geuna testimony.

9. *Diario del Juicio,* no. 13, August 20, 1985.

10. *Diario del Juicio,* no. 5 (June 25, 1985); no. 6 (July 2, 1985).

11. Interviews with human rights leader Emilio Mignone and state intelligence agent Carlos Alberto ("Coco") Hours (Buenos Aires, 1986).

12. *Nunca Más,* p. 54.

13. Paoletti, *Como los Nazis,* pp. 162–163.

14. *Ultima Hora,* May 16, 1976; *Nunca Más,* pp. 182, 240–241; *Clarín,* May 29, 1985.

15. *La Razón,* May 14, 1985, p. 14; *Clarín,* May 14, 1985; Colotto interviews.

16. Testimony of Omar Eduardo Torres, CONADEP, file no. 6667; *Buenos Aires Herald,* June 8, 1985.

17. *Nunca Más,* pp. 239–241.

18. Valdéz testimony taken from notes of interview with him by CONADEP researcher Antonio López Crespo; see also *ADL Bulletin,* January 1981.

19. *Nunca Más,* pp. 78–223.

20. Paoletti, *Como los Nazis; Nunca Más;* Emilio Mignone interview (Buenos Aires, 1986).

21. Paoletti, *Como los Nazis,* pp. 91–92; *El Periodista,* no. 29 (March 29–April 4, 1985).

22. Paoletti, *Como los Nazis,* pp. 93, 101.

23. *Nunca Más,* p. 116; Paoletti, *Como los Nazis,* pp. 93–96; *El Diario del Juicio,* July 9, 1985, pp. 2–3.

24. *Nunca Más,* pp. 181–185; Paoletti, *Como los Nazis,* pp. 65–87; on transfer point of Paraguayan detainees, interview with "Sam," who saw some of them in captivity.

25. Paoletti, *Como los Nazis,* p. 69.

26. Ibid., pp. 145–150.

27. *Nunca Más,* 126–143; Paoletti, *Como los Nazis,* pp. 150–184.

28. On Club Atlético, Paoletti, *Como los Nazis,* pp. 369–372; *Clarín,* May 23, 1985; *Nunca Más,* pp. 90–92, 124.

29. On La Perla, *Nunca Más,* pp. 202–203; Paoletti, *Como los Nazis,* pp. 194–199, 209–216.

30. *Nunca Más,* pp. 62–65, 244–345; Paoletti, *Como los Nazis,* pp. 69–70.

31. *La Razón,* June 18, 1985.

32. Testimony of Pablo Díaz, CONADEP, file no. 4018.

Chapter 16

1. Juan Bosch, *El pentagonismo, sustituto del imperialismo* (Madrid: Guadiana de Publicaciones), pp. 112–113.

2. See, for example, "Guardespaldas: imagen de la Argentina," *Cuestionario,* no. 32 (December 1975), p. 17; *El Periodista,* November 15–21, 1985, p. 6.

3. Derian provided me with copy of the memo from her personal files.

4. Andrew Graham-Yool, *The Press in Argentina, 1973–8* (London: Writers and Scholars Educational Trust, 1979), pp. 117–118; interview with Adm. Horacio Zaratiegui (Buenos Aires, February 10, 1987).

5. *La Opinión,* November 9, 1976; Eduardo Varela-Cid and Luis Vicens, *Los sofistas y la prensa canalla* (Buenos Aires: El Cid Editor, 1984); Graham-Yool, *Press in Argentina,* pp. 123–124.

6. Horacio Verbitsky, *Rodolfo Walsh y la prensa clandestina, 1976–1978* (Buenos Aires: Ediciones de la Urraca), p. 6; *Noticias,* November 10, 1991.

7. Graham-Yool, *Press in Argentina,* p. 112; *La Nación,* March 17, 1984.

8. *Diario del Juicio,* July 9, 1985, p. 146.

9. Interview with *Sunday Times* correspondent María Laura Avignolo (Buenos Aires, 1984).

10. *La Voz,* July 25, 1985.

11. *Buenos Aires Herald,* July 18, 1984.

12. Interview with Guillermo O'Donnell (Buenos Aires, 1985).

13. *El Periodista,* January 11–17 and July 5–11, 1985; *Grassroots Development* 8, no. 1 (1984), pp. 39–42.

14. "Cuando vivir en Buenos Aires significa un privilegio," *Competencia,* no. 191, pp. 30–34.

15. *Humor,* no. 165 (December 1985).

Chapter 17

1. Interview with former Massera aide, Adm. Horacio Zaratiegui (Buenos Aires, February 10, 1987).

2. Enrique Vásquez, *La Ultima: Orígen, Apogeo y Caída de la Dictadura Militar* (Buenos Aires: EUDEBA, 1985), p. 28.

3. Secret Order DCJE 504/77, pp. 3–7, signed by Videla; Secret Order DCGE 405/76.

4. Vásquez, *La Ultima,* pp. 47–105; Horacio Verbitsky, *La última batalla de la Tercera Guerra Mundial* (Buenos Aires: Legasa, 1984), 40–47.

5. Vásquez, *La Ultima,* p. 69.

6. "Argentina: Junta Attacks Terrorism and Economic Problems," (secret) U.S. Department of State, INR, April 5, 1976.

7. Julio Nosigilia, *Botín de Guerra* (Buenos Aires: Cooperativa Tierra Fértil, 1985), pp. 266–287; interview with Matilde Artés Company (Buenos Aires, 1986).

8. Héctor Ruiz Núñez, "La P-2 en Argentina," *Humor,* no. 175, June 1986.

9. Héctor Ruiz Núñez, "López Rega: Esplendor y decadencia," *Humor,* no. 173, May 1986.

10. *El Periodista,* June 7–13, 1985, pp. 11–12.

11. *La Opinión,* May 8, 1976.

12. Gary W. Wynia, *Argentina in the Postwar Era* (Albuquerque: University of New Mexico Press, 1978), p. 231.

13. John Dinges and Saul Landau, *Assassination on Embassy Row* (New York: Pantheon, 1980), pp. 237–239.

14. Details of possible assassination of the future New York City mayor, which included CIA reporting on it, found in a memorandum of conversation between Patricia Derian and U.S. ambassador to Uruguay Siracusa. (Copy given to me by Derian from her personal files.) The meeting was held on March 30, 1977, at the residence of the U.S. ambassador in Buenos Aires.

15. *New York Times,* August 15, 1976.

16. "Uruguayans reported arrested," confidential memorandum from U.S. embassy in Buenos Aires to State Department, May 20, 1976.

17. Testimony of Matilde Gutiérrez Ruiz, Buenos Aires federal court trial of the juntas, July 26, 1985; interviews with Uruguayan journalist Danilo Arbilla (Montevideo, 1986) and Alfonsín advisor Jorge Roulet (Buenos Aires, 1985).

18. Mario Jaunarena, ed., *El Pueblo Vencerá* (Buenos Aires: Ediciones Fundación, 1985), pp. 325–339; "Abduction and Murder of Uruguayan Refugees Michelini and Gutierrez: Status of Ferreira," confidential cable from U.S. embassy in Buenos Aires to Secretary of State, May 25, 1976; "GOA issues statement on Michelini, et al., murders," cable from U.S. embassy, May 28, 1976; interview with Daniel Frontalini, researcher for CELS (Buenos Aires, September 1987); Martin Edwin Andersen, "Cables confidenciales, 'desclasificados' de la diplomacia de EEUU en el período en que fueron secuestrados y asesinados Michelini y G. Ruiz," *Búsqueda* (Uruguay), May 28, 1987.

19. *New York Times,* June 4, 1976; interview with Torres's widow (La Paz, July 1985); "Sam" told me that Torres's murder was part of Operation Condor; Colotto interviews.

20. *Istoé* (Brazil), June 2, 1982; Taylor Branch and Eugene Propper, *Labyrinth* (New York: Viking Press, 1982), p. 399.

21. *El Periodista,* February 7–12, 1986.

22. Alipio Paoletti, *Como los Nazis, Como en Vietnam* (Buenos Aires: Editorial Contrapunto, 1987), pp. 381–382.

23. *La Voz,* February 17, 1984; *Matchbox,* Winter 1977; testimony of Uruguayan labor activist Sergio López Burgos on file at CELS, Buenos Aires.

24. Mort Rosenblum, "Terror in Argentina," *New York Review of Books,* October 28, 1976.

25. Ramón Genaro Díaz Bessone, *Guerra Revolucionaria en la Argentina* (1959–1978) (Buenos Aires: Editorial Fraterna, 1986), p. 346.

Chapter 18

1. Interview with former ERP militant "El Cabezón" (name withheld on request).

2. On Firmenich's liaison role with ERP, see Gabriela Cociffi, "Las polémics confesiones de Firmenich: Hoy quieren volver," *Gente,* May 28, 1987; PRT-ERP leader Luis Mattini told me he suspected that Santucho had been "sold out" by Firmenich; "Sam," who later saw Santucho's body on display at a remote corner of the Campo de Mayo army base (and was told that several officers urinated on it) said, "Santucho's death was the result of Firmenich's cooperation with the army"; interview with Col. Pascual Guerrieri, who said he was part of Leonetti's patrol (Buenos Aires, 1984); also see Mattini, *Hombres y Mujeres del PRT-ERP* (Buenos Aires: Editorial Contrapunto, 1990), pp. 502–505, 516–522; and María Seoane, *Todo o Nada* (Buenos Aires: Planeta, 1991), pp. 276, 303–309; according to Argentine rights activist Juan Méndez, American Patricia Erb saw Mena in a concentration camp several weeks after he was reported to have been killed. Telephone interview (January 1992).

3. See Martin Edwin Andersen, "SIDE-Montoneros, La Conexión Secreta," *Expreso,* June 5 and June 12, 1987.

4. Julio Nosiglia, *Botín de Guerra* (Buenos Aires: Cooperativa Terra Fértil, 1985), p. 22; *La Voz,* February 21, 1984. It is interesting to note that *La Voz,* a pro-Montonero daily, claimed that Firmenich's son, Mario Javier, was born prematurely in captivity "as a result of the tortures received" by his mother upon her being abducted. Mario Firmenich, however, said the difficult birth was the result of "X-rays" administered in jail, "Los Personajes de la Historia," *Tiempo Argentino,* my copy undated. In June 1992 *Somos* quoted a former montonera activist who had lived for almost five years with María Elpidia Martínez de Firmenich after her detention in 1976. "We never, out of respect—she was [Firmenich's wife]—asked her about the circumstances of her detention and she never said anything to anybody. It always seemed strange to us that they hadn't tortured her. I always remember how they massacred the Santucho family." Jorge Sigal and Olga Wornat, "Por que volvió Firmenich ¿Guerrillero or Servicio?" *Somos,* no. 819 (June 8, 1992).

5. Andersen, "SIDE-Montoneros."

6. "Argentina: Junta Attacks Terrorism and Economic Problems," (secret) U.S. Department of State, INR, April 5, 1976.

7. Richard Gillespie, *Soldiers of Perón: Argentina's Montoneros* (New York: Oxford University Press, 1982), p. 245; *L'Espresso,* April 17, 1977.

8. Gillespie, *Soldiers of Perón,* pp. 232–238; Roberto Mero, *Conversaciones con Juan Gelman* (Buenos Aires: Editorial Contrapunto, 1988), pp. 90–93; on modified cyanide pills, interview with former ESMA detainee Carlos Muñoz (Buenos Aires, 1986).

9. Interview with "Sam" (Washington, D.C., November 1987).

10. For biographical information on Walsh, see Horacio Verbitsky, *Rodolfo Walsh y la prensa clandestina* (Buenos Aires: Ediciones de la Urraca, 1985), and Juan Sasturain, "Rodolfo Walsh: Variaciones en negro," *El Porteño,* no. 19 (July 1983), pp. 86–90; on Walsh's Montonero intelligence reports, see *Controversia,* no. 4, February 1980.

11. Verbitsky, *Rodolfo Walsh,* pp. 119–120; Gillespie, *Soldiers of Perón,* p. 246.

12. *La Prensa, La Razón,* and *La Opinión,* December 4, 1976.

13. Eduardo Crawley, *A House Divided: Argentina 1880–1980* (London: Hurst, 1984), p. 427; *La Nación,* May 16, 1984; testimony of Lila Pastoriza de Jozami, Buenos Aires federal court trial of the juntas, July 19, 1985.

Chapter 19

1. Flyer in author's possession.

2. Taylor Branch and Eugene M. Propper, *Labyrinth* (New York: Viking Press, 1982), pp. 321–323. "Sam" confirmed that Buenos Aires extortion did take place.

3. *ADL Bulletin,* November 1976; interview with police Commissar Jorge Colotto. According to Colotto, one important kidnapping ring was headed by police officer Samuel Miara, another by Interior Minister Gen. Albano Harguindeguy. Colotto also claimed that SIDE served as a virtual "extortion agency," saying that intelligence agency operatives were behind the kidnappings of the director of the Banco Londres, the president of Panificación Argentina, and a son of Argentine businessman Francisco Soldatti; the figure of 200 was also mentioned in a separate interview with former U.S. labor attaché Anthony Freeman (Washington, D.C., November–December 1985).

4. *ADL Bulletin,* November 1976.

5. Harry Maurer, "Anti-semitism in Argentina," *Nation,* February 12, 1977.

6. Enrique Vásquez, *La Ultima: Orígen, Apogeo y Caída de la Dictadura Militar* (Buenos Aires: EUDEBA, 1985), pp. 161–163.

7. Existence of Azcuenaga lodge confirmed to me by Argentine businessmen Guillermo Peña Casares and Marcelo Chavanne (Buenos Aires, 1986).

8. Interview with Gen. Rogelio Villareal, a former Videla chief of staff (Buenos Aires, October 9, 1985).

9. *La Voz,* August 11, 1983.

10. Interview with Adm. (ret.) Horacio Zaratiegui (Buenos Aires, February 10, 1987).

11. Testimony of Raúl Lisandro Cubas, CONADEP, file no. 6974; testimony of Andrés Castillo, Buenos Aires federal court trial of the juntas, July 19, 1985.

12. Testimony of Capt. Jorge F. Busico, Buenos Aires federal court trial of the juntas, July 18, 1885, and CONADEP, file no. 5013.

13. Interview with Rear Adm. (ret.) Argimiro Fernández (Buenos Aires, July 1989); Cubas testimony.

14. Eduardo Crawley, *A House Divided: Argentina 1880–1980* (London: Hurst, 1984), p. 436; Alipio Paoletti, *Como los Nazis, Como en Vietnam* (Buenos Aires: Editorial Con-

trapunto, 1987), pp. 150–154; *Nunca Más, Informe de la Comisión Nacional sobre la Desaparición de Personas* (Buenos Aires: EUDEBA, 1984), pp. 282–292; *Clarín,* July 19, 1985.

15. Interview with Federal Police officer, later promoted to rank of zonal commander.

16. *Miami Herald,* June 12, 1983; interview with Jerry Whitman (Buenos Aires, 1983).

17. Vásquez, *La Ultima,* pp. 66-68, 80–81; Horacio Verbitsky, *Rodolfo Walsh y la prensa clandestina* (Buenos Aires: Ediciones de la Urraca, 1985), pp. 77–78.

18. Verbitsky, *Rodolfo Walsh,* pp. 77–78.

19. Ibid., p. 103.

20. Interview with Patricia Derian (Alexandria, Va., November 1985); Iain Guest, *Behind the Disappearances* (Philadelphia: University of Pennsylvania Press, 1990), pp. 80–86.

21. *La Razón,* May 4, 1985.

22. *La Opinión,* November 12, 1976; Timerman did open his pages to Amnesty International, publishing a generally favorable interview of delegation leader Lord Avebury during the mission. A month later, he got into trouble by publishing a long article by a Jesuit priest about human rights. Earlier, however, he had offered himself as a witness in U.S. congressional hearings chaired by Congressman Don Fraser, in order to rebut the testimonies of exiled left-wing lawyers Lucio Garzón Maceda and Gustavo Roca. *La Opinión,* November 9, 1976.

23. Interviews with *La Prensa* publisher Máximo Gainza (Buenos Aires, April 1985) and Quijano associate Guido DiTella (Buenos Aires, July 13, 1987). DiTella later served as ambassador to Washington and foreign minister in the Carlos Menem administration.

24. See Martin Edwin Andersen, "The Military Obstacle to Latin Democracy," *Foreign Policy,* no. 73 (Winter 1988–1989), p. 104.

Chapter 20

1. *Guardian,* November 16, 1977.

2. Testimony of Emilio Mignone, Buenos Aires federal court trial of the juntas, July 15, 1985.

3. An excellent overview of Carter human rights policy is contained in Lars Schoultz, *Human Rights and United States Policy Toward Latin America* (Princeton: Princeton University Press, 1981).

4. Schoultz, *Human Rights,* pp. 257–260, 295.

5. Hipólito Solari Yrigoyen interview (Buenos Aires, 1984); on U.S. satellites, Emilio Mignone interviews and subsequent confirmation by Carter-era U.S. State Department human rights officials (Washington, November–December 1985); Carlos Delía Larroca interview (Buenos Aires, September 25, 1985).

6. Interviews with Alfredo Bravo (Buenos Aires, 1984) and Patricia Derian (Washington, D.C., November 1985) and Ernesto Barreiro (Buenos Aires, September 29, 1987); *Los Angeles Times,* November 19, 1978, sec. 8, p. 1.

7. Interview with Harris and with another U.S. diplomat, name withheld on request (Washington, D.C., November 1985).

8. Emilio Mignone interviews.

9. Interview with Mark Schneider (Washington, D.C., November 1985).

10. Interviews with Joseph Eldridge (Washington, D.C., November 1985) and Patricia Derian (Alexandria, Va., November 1985).

11. *Clarín,* July 19, 1985.

12. *Jerusalem Post,* February 5–11, 1984; interviews with U.S. diplomats (November–December 1985) and testimony of an Argentine women rescued by the Israeli effort, name withheld on request.

13. Interview with Nehemias Reznitzky (Buenos Aires, 1986); story was confirmed to me by former president Alfonsín in Washington, D.C., in 1989.

14. *El Periodista,* May 10–16 and July 12–18, 1985; *Clarín,* May 15, 1985.

15. Héctor Ruiz Núñez, "La P-2 en Argentina," *Humor,* no. 177 (July 1986); *Quorum,* September 23, 1983; *Todo es Historia,* February 1985, pp. 33–37.

16. *Todo es Historia,* February 1985, pp. 33–37.

17. Ibid., p. 35; *Somos,* July 8, 1983.

18. *CELS Boletín,* no. 6 (March 1986); interview with CELS attorney Marcelo Parrilli (Buenos Aires, 1986); Rodolfo Peregrino Fernández, *Autocrítica Policial* (Buenos Aires: El Cid Editor, 1983), p. 51; Horacio Verbitsky, *La Posguerra Sucia* (Buenos Aires: Legasa, 1985), pp. 113–119.

19. *Buenos Aires Herald,* April 21–22, 1977; *La Prensa,* April 21, 1977; Juan Gasparini, *Montoneros, Final de Cuentas* (Buenos Aires: Puntosur, 1988), p. 88.

20. *L'Espresso,* April 17, 1977.

21. *Agence France-Presse* dispatch from Lima, April 21, 1977; testimony of Graciela Daleo, CONADEP, file no. 4816; interview with Aldo Luis Molinari (Buenos Aires, November 16, 1986).

22. T. B. Friedman memorandum (cited in Chap. 1). Document in author's possession; declassified secret telegram to U.S. State Department by Ambassador Robert Hill, April 1977.

23. Anthony Haden-Guest, "The Strange Life and Stranger Death of David Graiver," *New York,* January 22, 1979.

24. T. B. Friedman memorandum; "Graiver/Timerman investigation and related, Ref: Buenos Aires 2948," secret cable from Ambassador Hill to U.S. State Department, April 1977; Juan Gasparini, *El Crimen de Graiver* (Buenos Aires: Grupo Editorial Zeta, 1990).

25. *Buenos Aires Herald,* May 18, 1977.

26. James Neilson, "The Education of Jacobo Timerman," *Books and Writers* (Great Britain), 1981.

27. Council on Hemispheric Affairs press release, May 4, 1979; "Los Judios," *Carta Política,* no. 44 (June 1977); "Sunday afternoon with the Triple A," a confidential U.S. Department of State telegram from the U.S. embassy in Buenos Aires to Washington, D.C., August 1976.

28. Derian interview (Alexandria, Va., November 1985), and interviews with U.S. embassy personnel present.

29. Memorandum given to author by Derian (November 1985) from her personal files.

30. Raúl Veiga, *Las organizaciones de derechos humanos* (Buenos Aires: Centro Editor de América Latina, 1985), pp. 41–43.

31. Enrique Vásquez, *La Ultima: Orígen, Apogeo y Caída de la Dictadura Militar* (Buenos Aires: EUDEBA, 1985), p. 130.

32. Ibid., pp. 133–135.

33. Vásquez, *La Ultima.*

34. *Clarín,* July 19, 1985.

35. *La Razón,* June 6, 1986.

36. "The Graiver Affair," U.S. Department of State briefing memorandum (secret), April 27, 1977; *La Nación,* July 23, 1977; "Terrorism—The Terrorist Organizations," *Time* Buenos Aires bureau, October 20, 1977.

37. *Ultima Clave,* August 2, 1977.

38. *Caras y Caretas,* June 1984, pp. 33, 35; *Ultima Clave,* p. 3; on Rossi's identification, interview with human rights lawyer Eduardo Duhalde (Buenos Aires, 1987).

39. *Caras y Caretas,* p. 33.

40. CONADEP, file no. 2620; *El Periodista,* May 3–9, 1985; Gasparini, *Montoneros,* p. 109.

41. Testimonies at Buenos Aires federal court trial of the juntas by Miriam Lewin de García, Lila Pastoriza de Jozami, and Andrés Castillo (July 18–20, 1985); Miguel Bonasso, *Recuerdo de la muerte* (Buenos Aires: Bruguera, 1984).

42. *Gente,* February 2, 1984; "Hombre de Massera," *La Semana* (my copy undated, circa 1985).

43. Testimony of Raúl Lisandro Cubas, CONADEP, file no. 6974; *Clarín,* July 20, 1985.

44. *Washington Post,* December 10, 1976, and October 5, 1977.

45. *Nunca Más, Informe de la Comisión Nacional sobre la Desaparición de Personas* (Buenos Aires: EUDEBA, 1984), pp. 83–84, 126–143; Bonasso, *Recuerdo de la muerte.*

46. Horacio Verbitsky, *La última batalla de la Tercera Guerra Mundial* (Buenos Aires: Legasa, 1984), pp. 48–57; Bonasso, *Recuerdo de la muerte.*

47. Jean-Pierre Bousquet, *Las locas de la Plaza de Mayo* (Buenos Aires: El Cid Editor, 1983), pp. 73–96.

48. Bousquet, *Las locas,* pp. 74–75.

49. Copy of handwritten letter by Maggio to the U.S. embassy in Buenos Aires received by me as part of a Freedom of Information Act request.

50. Bousquet, *Las locas,* p. 84; Juan Gasparini, *La Pista Suiza* (Buenos Aires: Legasa, 1986), pp. 127–139.

Chapter 21

1. February 1987 interview with Argentine army intelligence agent "Gustavo Francisco Bueno," who served under Galtieri in II Army Corps from 1976 to 1978. Tapes of Bueno testimony on file at CELS in Buenos Aires also viewed; *La Prensa,* January 16, 1987; the production of ersatz "subversive" materials in the clandestine camps was not limited to Funes. According to former La Perla detainee Graciela Geuna (CONADEP, file no. 764), "faced with the imminent strike by Córdoba's Luz y Fuerza union, the military decided to make it illegal or, as they said 'Montonero,' thus having the pretext for calling it subversive. To this end, the military at La Perla printed flyers they themselves signed 'Montoneros.' Flyers that called on the workers to strike."

2. Miguel Bonasso, *Recuerdo de la muerte* (Buenos Aires: Bruguera, 1984); Richard Gillespie, *Soldiers of Perón: Argentina's Montoneros* (New York: Oxford University Press, 1982), pp. 261–262; *New York Times,* January 29, 1978.

3. Enrique Vásquez, *La Ultima: Orígen, Apogeo y Caída de la Dictadura Militar* (Buenos Aires: EUDEBA, 1985), pp. 146–147.

4. *Washington Post,* January 27, 1978.

5. *Clarín* and *La Voz,* August 7, 1985; testimony of Silvia Agulla de Hartcourt, Buenos Aires federal court trial of the juntas, file no. 7463.

6. Interview with Larry Birns (Washington, D.C., December 4, 1985).

7. Vásquez, *La Ultima,* pp. 92–105.

8. *Testigo,* March 14, 1984; *Diario del Juicio,* December 24, 1985, p. 563.

9. *Diario del Juicio,* December 24, 1985, p. 563.

10. Eugenio Méndez, *Alte. Lacoste: ¿Quién Mató al General Actis?* (Buenos Aires: El Cid Editor, 1984); J. C. Cernadas LaMadrid and Ricardo Halac, *Yo Fuí Testigo: Los Militares y el Mundial* (Buenos Aires: Editorial Perfil, 1986), pp. 120–124, 22, 47; on Burson-Marsteller, see *Atlanta Constitution,* October 22, 1978; *Chicago Tribune,* October 4, 1978; *Wall Street Journal,* January 31, 1979.

11. *Washington Post,* June 26, 1978; J. C. Cernadas LaMadrid and Ricardo Halac, *Los Militares y el Mundial,* pp. 24, 77–79.

12. Cernadas LaMadrid and Halac, *Los Militares y el Mundial;* interview with Máximo Gainza (Buenos Aires, April 1985).

13. Cernadas LaMadrid and Halac, *Los Militares y el Mundial,* pp. 92–93.

14. Héctor Ruiz Núñez, "La P-2 en Argentina," *Humor,* no. 175 (June 1986), pp. 13–15; *Somos,* July 8, 1983.

15. Ruiz Núñez, "La P-2 en Argentina," pp. 13–15.

16. *Los Angeles Times,* November 23, 1978; *Washington Post,* October 9, 1979.

17. *Los Angeles Times,* November 23, 1978 ; Charles Maechling, Jr., "The Argentine Pariah," *Foreign Policy,* no. 45 (Winter 1981–1982), p. 76.

18. *Washington Post,* August 6, 1978.

19. *La Nación,* August 11, 1978; *Somos,* August 1978.

20. Interview with former U.S. Vice President Walter F. Mondale (Buenos Aires, April 22, 1987).

21. *Testigo,* March 14, 1984.

22. Interview with diplomat Gregorio Dupont (Buenos Aires, July 1985); *Diario del Juicio,* August 20, 1985.

23. *La Razón,* June 22, 1987; *Diario del Juicio,* December 24, 1985.

24. *Diario del Juicio,* December 17, 1985.

25. Interview with U.S. diplomats in Washington, D.C. (names withheld on request, November–December 1985).

26. *Somos,* June 8, 1979; "Spontaneous declaration" of Enrique Arancibia Clavel before Inspector Commissar Jorge Luis Santos Dell'amico, chief of the Foreign Affairs Department of the Argentine Federal Police, November 28, 1978, in Buenos Aires.

27. Arancibia Clavel declaration.

28. *Los Angeles Times,* April 22, 1979.

29. *Buenos Aires Herald,* October 11, 1979.

30. Interview with former U.S. embassy political officer Wayne Smith (Washington, D.C., December 1985).

31. *La Prensa*, October 1, 1979.

32. Interviews with Guillermo Walter Klein (Buenos Aires, 1987), Robert and Maude Cox (Buenos Aires, 1985), and *Time* special correspondent Nina Lindley (Buenos Aires, 1985). Klein maintained that the crime was investigated by the chief of homicide section of the Federal Police, although he said an effort was made not to give it publicity.

33. *Los Periodistas*, November 16, 1989; Gillespie, *Soldiers of Perón*, pp. 258–267; Roberto Mero, *Conversaciones con Juan Gelman* (Buenos Aires: Editorial Contrapunto, 1988), p. 171. "Inside the country there was nothing," said Montonero activist and poet Gelman, " … the counteroffensive caused hundreds to die, without changing a thing inside the country."

34. *Somos*, July 27, 1979; *New York Times*, July 23, 1979.

35. Council on Hemispheric Affairs press release, July 31, 1980.

36. "Asesinan en Madrid a la Sra. de Molfino," *Comisión Argentina de Derechos Humanos*, August 1980; Horacio Verbitsky, *La última batalla de la Tercera Guerra Mundial* (Buenos Aires: Legasa, 1984), pp. 71–74.

37. *Los Angeles Times*, August 31, 1980.

38. Ibid., September 21, 1980.

39. Oscar Cardoso, Ricardo Kirschbaum, and Eduardo Van Der Kooy, *Malvinas, La Trama Secreta* (Buenos Aires: Sudamericana-Planeta, 1983), p. 216; interview with army intelligence officer who participated in logistical support from Buenos Aires; testimony of former army intelligence agent Leandro Sánchez Reisse to U.S. Senate Foreign Relations Committee, Subcommittee on Terrorism, Narcotics and International Operations, July 23, 1987.

40. *Washington Post*, August 17, 1980; Verbitsky, *La última batalla*, pp. 75–76.

41. *New York Times*, August 10, 1980.

42. Ibid.; *St. Louis Post-Dispatch*, August 14, 1980; *Los Angeles Times*, August 10, 1980.

43. Verbitsky, *La última batalla*, p. 78; *Excelsior* (Mexico), April 8 and April 10, 1981; interview with former U.S. military attaché (Washington, D.C., November 1985).

44. Valín liaison confirmed to me by "Sam"; Valín's protection of Delle Chiaie confirmed by former Federal Police Commissar Jorge Colotto; interview with Delle Chiaie friend Carlos Tortora (Buenos Aires, December 1983); Magnus Linklater, Isabel Hilton, and Neal Ascherson, *The Fourth Reich: Klaus Barbie and the Neo-Fascist Connection* (London: Hodder and Stoughton, 1984), pp. 280, 288.

45. *Miami Herald*, May 29, 1983; Martin A. Lee and Kevin Coogan, "The Agca Con," *Village Voice*, December 24, 1985.

46. Linklater et al., *The Fourth Reich*, pp. 280–283, 300–301.

47. *La Nación*, September 3, 1980; *Clarín*, September 2, 1980; Scott Anderson and Jon Lee Anderson, *Inside the League* (New York: Dodd, Mead, 1986), pp. 147, 206–207.

48. "The Agca Con."

49. *La Nación*, September 3, 1980; *Clarín*, September 2, 1980; *La Prensa*, September 3, 1980.

50. "Así Maté a Somoza," *Siete Días*, July 27, 1983; *ABC Color*, September 18 and September 19, 1980.

51. Interview with retired Paraguayan army intelligence officer (Asunción, March 1989).

52. Long-standing U.S. support for the Shah, particularly the training of the SAVAK secret police, was an important factor in anti-American feeling under the Ayatollah. Jesse J.

Leaf, a former chief CIA analyst in Iran, told Seymour Hersh that the CIA's methods "were based on German torture techniques from World War II," *New York Times*, January 7, 1979.

53. Mondale interview.

54. Interviews with Alfonsín advisors Jorge Roulet and Brian Thomson (Buenos Aires, 1985 and 1986).

Chapter 22

1. Ian Guest, *Behind the Disappearances* (Philadelphia: University of Pennsylvania Press, 1990), p. 28; *Kansas City Times*, June 19, 1982.

2. Guest, *Behind the Disappearances*, pp. 501–502; Derian interview (Alexandria, Va., November 1985); *New York Times*, March 26, 1980; *Washington Post*, May 29, 1980.

3. Alexander Haig, *Caveat* (New York: Macmillan, 1984), p. 90; *New York Times*, December 8, 1991; *Clarín*, October 27, 1991; Martin Edwin Andersen interview with Carter, "Hold Up the Human-Rights Banner," *Newsweek International*, October 22, 1984.

4. Guest, *Behind the Disappearances*, pp. 276, 340; *Christian Science Monitor*, May 19, 1982.

5. Guest, *Behind the Disappearances*, pp. 279–282.

6. Ibid., pp. 283–286; Mary McGrory, "Timerman Shatters the Silence," *Washington Star*, June 14, 1981.

7. Testimony of former army intelligence agent Leandro Sánchez Reisse to U.S. Senate Foreign Relations Committee, Subcommittee on Terrorism, Narcotics and International Operations, July 23, 1987; David Corn, "The CIA and the Cocaine Coup," *Nation*, October 7, 1991; Christopher Dickey, *With the Contras: A Reporter in the Wilds of Nicaragua* (New York: Simon & Schuster, 1985), pp. 30–31, 54–55, 89–91, 113; *Washington Post*, February 23, 1992; the Argentine advisors, said former U.S. Ambassador to El Salvador Robert White, were counterinsurgency "fanatics. ... They told the Salvadoran soldiers to kill everyone, families included. The Salvadorans had to tell them, 'Look, here we're all related.'" White interview (Buenos Aires, 1986).

8. Sánchez Reisse testimony; Sam Dillon, *The Commandos* (New York: Holt, 1991), pp. 65–70; Roy Gutman, *Banana Diplomacy* (New York: Simon & Schuster, 1988); *Página 12*, July 7, 1989; Dickey, *With the Contras*, p. 112, 152.

9. Dillon, *The Commandos*, pp. 64–65, 70; *Latin America Weekly Report*, February 12, 1982. Valín "has a reputation within the force as an expert in espionage techniques"; Dickey, *With the Contras*, p. 115.

10. Dillon, *The Commandos*, pp. 64–65, 70; *New Republic*, August 5, 1985, p. 22; interview with Edgar Chamorro (Washington, D.C., 1989).

11. *New York Times*, May 25, 27–31, June 10, 17, July 17, 19, 1982.

12. *Collier's Year Book*, 1985 (New York: Macmillan, 1984), p. 83

13. *Latin America Weekly Report*, November 30, 1979; *Review of the River Plate*, January 27, 1984.

14. "Big Profits in Big Bribery," *Time*, March 16, 1981, p. 39; *Ambito Financiero*, February 8, 1982; Horacio Verbitsky, *La última batalla de la Tercera Guerra Mundial* (Buenos Aires: Legasa, 1984), pp. 112–115.

15. Jimmy Burns, *The Land That Lost Its Heroes* (London: Bloomsbury, 1987), p. 30; Guest, *Behind the Disappearances*, p. 338; *Miami Herald*, May 10, 1987.

16. On Galtieri's misperceptions, see Oscar Cardoso, Ricardo Kirschbaum, and Eduardo Van Der Kooy, *Malvinas, La Trama Secreta* (Buenos Aires: Sudamericana-Planeta, 1983); Burns, *Land*, pp. 27–48.

17. Bob Woodward, *Veil* (New York, Simon & Schuster, 1987), p. 212; *Miami Herald*, May 10, 1987.

18. Interview with María Laura Avignolo (Buenos Aires, 1984); Verbitsky, *La última batalla*, pp. 157–158, 169–183, 204–205, 208–223; *Gente*, April 29 and May 27, 1982.

19. Anaya declaration before Interforces Commission, April 22, 1983, cited in Verbitsky, *La última batalla*, pp. 167–168.

20. *Buenos Aires Herald*, May 24, 1983; *Washington Post*, October 9, 1982; Guest, *Behind the Disappearances*, p. 544; *Newsweek International*, October 25, 1982. See also Claudio Uriarte, *Almirante Cero* (Buenos Aires: Planeta, 1992), pp. 252–272.

21. *Washington Post*, October 22 and October 28, 1982; *Newsweek*, November 5, 1982; Emilio Mignone, *Iglesia y Dictadura* (Buenos Aires: Ediciones del Pensamiento Nacional, 1986), p. 73.

22. *New York Times*, June 20, September 15, and October 12, 1982.

23. *New York Times*, October 3, 1982; Máximo Gainza interview (Buenos Aires, April 1985); Massera was later quoted as saying that Gelli "helped us in the anti-subversive struggle and in promoting our image abroad." *La Voz*, August 11, 1983. See also Uriarte, *Almirante Cero*, p. 108.

24. *Washington Post*, December 2, 1982; Dickey, *With the Contras*, pp. 154, 158.

25. Dickey, *With the Contras*, pp. 115–118, 152–155; *Washington Times*, January 26, 1989; *New York Times*, February 16, 1986.

26. *Washington Post*, April 29, 1991; Martin Edwin Andersen, "Stones for Bread," *Nation*, May 14, 1983.

27. Andersen, "Stones for Bread"; *Washington Post*, May 17 and May 20, 1983.

28. In late 1982 I received confirmation from an embassy political officer that one, and possibly two, Americans were missing. Late that night the official called my home to claim he had made a mistake, telling me that if I published the story the embassy would deny it, and he would make sure there would be no future embassy cooperation with me. Although I felt I was being misled, I nevertheless did not publish the story for the lack of a second confirmation. Later James Brooke of the *Miami Herald* also got wind of the disappearances, three in all, and stories appeared in both the May 20, 1983, *Washington Post* and in the *Herald*. Guest, *Behind the Disappearances*, p. 352, cites a Shlaudeman cable to Washington confirming that "the three cases are sensitive because of possible involvement of Argentina police and military forces."

29. *Miami News*, July 7, 1983.

30. *Nation*, November 12, 1983; Martin Edwin Andersen, "Dateline Argentina: Hello Democracy," *Foreign Policy*, no. 55 (Summer 1984); *Wall Street Journal*, April 15, 1983.

31. I followed Alfonsín on several campaign stops; also, interview with Alfonsín campaign manager Bernardo Grinspun (Buenos Aires, September 1983).

32. *Washington Post*, October 19, 1983; Horacio Verbitsky, *La Posguerra Sucia* (Buenos Aires: Legasa, 1985), p. 45; I observed the coffin burning.

33. *Buenos Aires Herald,* May 4 and May 5, 1983.

34. *Newsweek,* November 14, 1983.

35. *Economist,* July 14, 1984; *La Nación,* March 17, 1984.

36. *Washington Post,* April 29, 1984; *Collier's,* p. 84.

37. Telephone conversation with Kissinger associate Alan Stoga (1984); *New York Times,* November 28, 1988; Joel Millman, "Out of the Asylum," *Forbes,* December 23, 1991.

38. I was present at the hotel in Tierra del Fuego.

39. *Nueva Presencia,* January 6, 1984; *Washington Post,* February 20, 1984.

40. Martin Edwin Andersen, "The Military Obstacle to Latin Democracy," *Foreign Policy,* no. 73 (Winter 1988–1989), p. 106; Mignone interviews.

41. Guest, *Behind the Disappearances,* pp. 351–352; Andersen, "Dateline Argentina," p. 170.

42. Woodward, *Veil,* pp. 345–346.

43. *Washington Post,* July 6, 1980; Andersen, "Military Obstacle," pp. 106–107.

44. U.S. economic attaché John Crawford canonized Martínez de Hoz in interview with me (Buenos Aires, 1984). A UCD party institute received funding from the National Republican Institute for International Affairs (NRIIA).

45. Andersen, "Military Obstacle," p. 107; *Miami Herald,* May 10, 1987; *Ambito Financiero* and *Buenos Aires Herald,* April 11, 1986; *La Razón,* April 13, 1986.

46. *Washington Post,* June 3, 1986; interview with Col. Pascual O. Guerrieri (Buenos Aires, 1984).

47. *Tiempo Argentino,* December 18, 1985.

48. *La Voz,* June 2, 1984; *La Nación,* June 2, 1984.

49. *La Voz,* July 3, 1985; *Buenos Aires Herald,* May 25, 1985.

50. *New York Times,* December 15, 1985.

51. *Buenos Aires Herald,* May 20, 1986; *Clarín,* August 31, 1985; *La Razón,* October 22, 1985; *Washington Post,* June 3, 1986; *Miami Herald* (International Edition), July 4, 1987.

52. "Argentine Jurists Shed Anonymity, Emerge as New Heroes of Democracy," *Washington Post,* May 6, 1988; Pirker story told to me by Sivak's widow, Marta, in Washington, D.C., in 1989. See also Bradley Graham, "Buenos Aires Police Show Way in Transition to Democracy," *Washington Post,* July 1, 1987.

53. *Miami Herald,* January 8, 1987; *Washington Post,* January 9, 1987; see also Horacio Verbitsky, *Civiles y Militares* (Buenos Aires: Editorial Contrapunto, 1987).

54. I covered the papal visit and the military rebellion for *Newsweek* and the *Washington Post.*

55. This was the consensus of several civilian political activists and military officers who attended a National Democratic Institute conference on civil-military relations in Argentina held in December 1988 in Santo Domingo, Dominican Republic.

56. Martin Edwin Andersen, "Dirty Secrets of the 'Dirty War,'" *Nation,* March 13, 1989.

57. Martin Edwin Andersen, ed., *Hacia una nueva relación: El papel de las fuerzas armadas en un gobierno democrático* (Buenos Aires: National Democratic Institute for International Affairs, 1990); *Los Angeles Times,* July 8, 1989.

58. *Los Angeles Times,* July 8, 1989.

Epilogue

1. I was present at the luncheon.

2. ANSA news agency dispatch from Rome, November 16, 1990; *La Repubblica*, October 30, 1990, pp. 1, 4; Daniel Singer, "The Gladiators," *Nation*, December 10, 1990; *New York Times*, November 16, 1990.

3. Quoted in *La Repubblica*, October 30, 1990, p. 3; see also *Clarín*, September 1, 1986, p. 24.

4. On corruption in Menem's government, see Horacio Verbitsky, *Robo para la corona* (Buenos Aires: Planeta, 1991); *Noticias*, June 2, 1991. According to the *Christian Science Monitor*, June 20, 1991, p. 5., "Stories abound that [U.S. Ambassador Terence] Todman pressed for the military to fight drug traffickers, though to do so would be unconstitutional."

5. *Miami Herald*, October 9, 1989; Charles Lane, "The War That Will Not End," *New Republic*, October 16, 1989. "The influential [Salvadoran] air force chief, Gen. Juan Rafael Bustillo, recently said the military must take steps 'guaranteeing officers and troop commanders that their actions will not be called into question,' as those of Argentina's dirty warriors were."

6. FBIS-LAT, December 28, 1990, p. 31; Telam, December 31, 1990.

7. *La Nación*, January 25 and February 13, 1987; Germán Sopeña, "José A. Martínez de Hoz: esta vez será distinto," *La Nación*, Fall 1991.

8. *Página* 12, April 28 and May 17, 1988.

9. *Buenos Aires Herald*, February 25, 1987, and *La Razón*, February 25, 1987.

10. *Buenos Aires Herald*, August 16, 1991; *Washington Post*, November 29, 1991, p. A42; *Noticias*, December 1, 1991, pp. 52–61.

11. Kohan made the admission to the author in Washington, D.C., several months before the pardon.

12. Since the original confirmation on Firmenich's identity by "Sam," the author has received further affirmations about his true role from a long-time lecturer at U.S. military schools and a top aide to Assistant Secretary of State for Inter-American Affairs Bernard Aronson. Both claim, in the words of the lecturer, that Firmenich's relationship "is no secret" in the U.S. intelligence community; on the strange case of Amodio Pérez, see Nelson Caula and Alberto Silva, *Alto El Fuego* (Montevideo: Monte Sexto, 1986), pp. 225–274; and Eleuterio Fernández Huidobro, *La tregua armada* (Montevideo: tea editorial), pp. 138–141.

13. *La Razón*, March 27, 1984; for role played by Fleury in the Brazilian repression, see A. J. Langguth, *Hidden Terrors: The Truth About U.S. Police Operations in Latin America* (New York: Pantheon, 1978).

14. March 17, 1991, Associated Press dispatch written by Vicente F. López in Buenos Aires; *Página* 12, March 17, 1991.

15. Jorge Sigal and Olga Wornat, "Por que volvió Firmenich ¿Guerrillero o Servicio?" *Somos*, no. 819 (June 8, 1992); "A cara de Perro: El cuadro de honor," *Somos*, December 23, 1991; "El caso Verbitsky," *Ambito Financiero*, May 22, 1992.

16. EFE (Spanish news agency) dispatch from Buenos Aires, December 30, 1990.

17. *El Bimestre* 3, no. 17 (September-October 1984), p. 43; *Business Week*, December 2, 1985; "Kissinger Said to Urge Brutal Force," *Washington Post*, March 5, 1988; I attended Menem's inauguration as a guest of the Peronist party.

18. Jeane Kirkpatrick, "Argentine Surprise," *Washington Post,* November 12, 1991.

19. "U.S. Eased [Haiti] Embargo Under Business Pressure; Abrams Pressed Jobs Issue With State Department," *Washington Post,* February 7, 1992, p. A1.

20. That contributions for Grondona's stay were solicited from multinationals, interview with U.S. banker whose name is withheld on request.

21. *La Razón,* January 19, 1987; *Clarín,* March 10, 1987; *Buenos Aires Herald,* June 7, 1987, p. 9, and September 22, 1987; *New York Times, February* 18, 1988, and August 3, 1989.

22. *New York Times,* March 30, 1987; *Ambito Financiero,* March 31, 1987; *Somos,* April 1, 1987.

23. Jacobo Timerman, *Chile* (New York: Knopf, 1987), and *Cuba* (New York: Knopf, 1990).

24. *Washington Post,* March 12, 1992, p. A24.

Bibliography

Selected Books and Articles

Abós, Alvaro. *Las organizaciones sindicales y el poder militar (1976–1983)*. Buenos Aires: Centro Editor de América Latina, 1984.

———. *La Columna Vertebral, Sindicatos y Peronismo*. Buenos Aires: Legasa, 1983.

Alfonsín, Raúl. *Inedito, una batalla contra la dictadura*. Buenos Aires: Legasa, 1986.

Andersen, Martin Edwin, ed. *Hacia una nueva relación: El papel de las Fuerzas Armadas en un gobierno democrático*. Buenos Aires: National Democratic Institute for International Affairs, 1990.

———. "Threat to Argentine Democracy." *Journal of Commerce*, April 5, 1990.

———. "Dirty Secrets of the 'Dirty War.'" *Nation*, March 13, 1989.

———. "La conexión Firmenich-ejército no es cuento de Andersen," *Crisis*, July 1989.

———. "The Military Obstacle to Latin Democracy." *Foreign Policy*, no. 73 (Winter 1988–1989), pp. 99–100.

———. "Las sucias solapas de González Naya." *Página 12*, January 21, 1988.

———. "Kissinger and the 'Dirty War.'" *Nation*, October 31, 1987.

———. "SIDE-Montoneros, La Conexión Secreta." *Expreso*, June 5 and June 12, 1987.

———. "Cables confidenciales, 'desclasificados' de la diplomacia de EEUU en el período en que fueron secuestrados y asesinados Michelini y G. Ruiz." *Búsqueda* (Uruguay), May 28, 1987.

———. "Los Números de FAMUS." *El Periodista de Buenos Aires*, no. 141 (May 22–28, 1987).

———. "Dateline Argentina: Hello, Democracy." *Foreign Policy*, no. 55 (1984).

———. "Letter from Argentina." *Boston Phoenix*, April 10, 1984.

———. "The Cost of Quiet Diplomacy." *New Republic*, March 19, 1984.

———. "Stones for Bread." *Nation*, May 14, 1983.

Andersen, Martin Edwin, and Antonio López Crespo. "La guerra sucia empezó en 1975." *El Periodista*, no. 73 (February 6, 1986), pp. 2–4.

———. "¿Quién mató al Comisario Villar?" *Humor*, no. 182 (1986).

Anderson, Jack. "CIA Teaches Terrorism to Friends." *Washington Post*, October 8, 1973.

Anderson, Scott, and Jon Lee Anderson. *Inside the League*. New York: Dodd, Mead, 1986.

Arlt, Roberto. *The Seven Madmen*. Boston: Godine, 1984.

Arriagada Herrera, Genaro. *El pensamiento político de los militares*. Santiago: Editorial Aconcagua, 1986.

———. *La política militar de Pinochet*. Santiago: Salesianos, 1985.

Asís, Jorge. *Diario de la Argentina*. Buenos Aires: Sudamericana, 1984.

Asociación de Periodistas de Buenos Aires. *Con vida los queremos.* Buenos Aires, 1986.

Bach, Caleb. "Ernesto Sábato: A Conscious Choice of Words." *Américas* 1, no. 43 (1991).

Bardini, Roberto, Miguel Bonasso, and Laura Restrepo. *Operación Principe.* Buenos Aires: Planeta, 1988.

Bayer, Osvaldo. *Los anarquistas expropriadores.* Buenos Aires: Legasa, 1986.

_____ . *Los vengadores de la Patagonia trágica.* Buenos Aires: Editorial Galerna, 1972.

Beaufre, André. *Introdución a la estrategia.* Madrid: Instituto de Estudios Políticos, 1965.

Beltrán, Virgilio R. "Political Transition in Argentina: 1982–1985." *Armed Forces and Society* 13, no. 2 (Winter 1987), pp. 215–233.

Berger, Martín. *Historia de la Logia Masonica P-2.* Buenos Aires: El Cid Editor, 1983.

Blixen, Samuel. *Conversaciones con Gorriarán Merlo.* Buenos Aires: Editorial Contrapunto, 1988.

Bonardo, Augusto. *Antología de un asco en la Argentina.* Buenos Aires: Ediciones La Gente, 1965.

Bonasso, Miguel. *Recuerdo de la muerte.* Buenos Aires: Bruguera, 1984.

Borrini, Alberto. *Como Se Hace Un Presidente.* Buenos Aires: Ediciones El Cronista Comercial, 1984.

Bosch, Juan. *El pentagonismo, sustituto del imperialismo.* Madrid: Guadiana de Publicaciones, 1968.

Bousquet, Jean-Pierre. *Las locas de la Plaza de Mayo.* Buenos Aires: El Cid Editor, 1983.

Bra, Gerardo. *El gobierno de Onganía.* Buenos Aires: Centro Editor de América Latina, 1985.

Branch, Taylor, and Eugene Propper. *Labyrinth.* New York: Viking Press, 1982.

Brocato, Carlos A. *La Argentina que quisieron.* Buenos Aires: Sudamericana-Planeta, 1985.

Brown, Cynthia. *With Friends Like These.* New York: Pantheon, 1985.

Budiansky, Stephen. "Army Pall over Argentine Science," *Nature* (September 30, 1984).

Burns, Jimmy. *The Land That Lost Its Heroes.* London: Bloomsbury, 1987.

Busquets, Julio. *El militar de carrera en España.* Barcelona: Editorial Ariel, 1984.

_____ . *Pronunciamientos y golpes de Estado en España.* Barcelona: Editorial Planeta, 1982.

Calello, Osvaldo, and Daniel Parcero. *De Vandor a Ubaldini/2.* Buenos Aires: Centro Editor de América Latina, 1984.

Camps, Ramón. *El Poder en la Sombra.* Buenos Aires: Ro.Ca. Producciones, 1983.

Cardoso, Oscar, Ricardo Kirschbaum, and Eduardo Van Der Kooy. *Malvinas, La Trama Secreta.* Buenos Aires: Sudamericana-Planeta, 1983.

Caula, Nelson, and Alberto Silva. *Alto El Fuego.* Montevideo: Monte Sexto, 1986.

Cavalini, Enrique H.J. "The Malvinas/Falkland Affair: A New Look." *International Journal of Intelligence and CounterIntelligence* 2, no. 2, pp. 207–208.

Centro de Estudios Legales y Sociales. *Terrorismo de estado, 692 responsables.* Buenos Aires: Ediciones CELS, 1986.

_____ . *Testimonio sobre el Centro Clandestino de Detención de la Escuela Mecánica de la Armada Argentina (ESMA).* Buenos Aires: Ediciones CELS, n.d.

Centro de Estudios para el Proyecto Nacional. *Los industriales argentinos: Ideología y patrones de conducta.* Buenos Aires: CEPNA, 1988.

Cernadas Lamadrid, J. C., and Ricardo Halac. *Yo Fuí Testigo: Los Militares y el Mundial.* Buenos Aires: Editorial Perfil, 1986.

————. *Yo Fuí Testigo: Antisemitismo.* Buenos Aires: Editorial Perfil, 1986.

————. *Yo Fuí Testigo: Azules y Colorados.* Buenos Aires: Editorial Perfil, 1986.

Chamorro, Edgar, with Jefferson Morley. "Confessions of a 'Contra.'" *New Republic,* August 5, 1985.

Chavez, Lydia. "Alfonsín's One-Man Show." *New York Times Magazine,* December 15, 1985.

Chelala, César. "The Argentine Military Turns on Its Own." *Nation,* February 5, 1983.

Christie, Stuart. *Stefano Delle Chiaie: Portrait of a Black Terrorist.* London: Refract, 1984.

Ciancaglini, Sergio, and Martín Granovsky. *Cronicas del apocalipsis.* Buenos Aires: Editorial Contrapunto, 1986.

Cociffi, Gabriela. "Las polémicas confesiones de Firmenich: Hoy quieren volver." *Gente,* May 28, 1987.

Coluccio, Felix. *Diccionario de Creenicias y Supersticiones (Argentinas y Americanas).* Buenos Aires: Corregidor, 1984.

Comisión Nacional sobre la Desaparición de Personas. *Nunca Más.* Buenos Aires: EUDEBA, 1984.

Constable, Pamela, and Arturo Valenzuela. *A Nation of Enemies: Chile Under Pinochet.* New York: Norton, 1991.

Contepomi, Gustavo, and Patricia Contepomi. *Sobrevivientes de La Perla.* Buenos Aires: El Cid Editor, 1984.

Cordova-Clauré, Ted. "Swastikas in Argentina." *Atlas World Press Review,* November 1976.

Corn, David. "The CIA and the Cocaine Coup." *Nation,* October 7, 1991.

Corradi, Juan E. *The Fitful Republic.* Boulder: Westview Press, 1985.

Cox, Robert. "Muzzled Journalism." *Argentine News,* April 5, 1985.

Crassweller, Robert. *Perón and the Enigmas of Argentina.* New York: Norton, 1987.

Crawford, Kathryn Lee. "Due Obedience and the Rights of Victims: Argentina's Transition to Democracy." *Human Rights Quarterly* 12 (1990), pp. 17–52.

Crawley, Eduardo. *A House Divided, Argentina 1880–1980.* London: Hurst, 1984.

Cruces, Néstor. *Hacia otro ejército posible.* Buenos Aires: Sudamericana-Planeta, 1988.

Cuando la magia tomó el poder. Buenos Aires: El Cid Editor, 1984.

de Dios, Horacio. *Kelly Cuenta Todo.* Buenos Aires: Colección Gente, 1984.

Deheza, José A. *¿Quiénes derrocaron a Isabel Perón?* Buenos Aires: Ediciones Cuenca del Plata, 1981.

De Riz, Liliana. *Retorno y Derrumbe: el último gobierno peronista.* Mexico City: Folios Ediciones, 1981.

Diament, Mario. "Habla Juan Manuel Abal Medina." *Siete Días,* March 8–14, 1983, pp. 47–55.

Diament, Mario, and Dale Van Atta. "La CIA y La Caída de Isabel Perón." *Siete Días,* May 16, 1984.

Díaz, Claudio, and Antonio Zucco. *La Ultraderecha Argentina.* Buenos Aires: Editorial Contrapunto, 1987.

Díaz Bessone, Ramón Genaro. *Guerra Revolucionaria en la Argentina (1959–1978).* Buenos Aires: Editorial Fraterna, 1986.

Dickey, Christopher. *With the Contras: A Reporter in the Wilds of Nicaragua.* New York: Simon & Schuster, 1987.

Dillon, Sam. *The Commandos.* New York: Holt, 1991.

Dinges, John, and Saul Landau. *Assassination on Embassy Row.* New York: Pantheon, 1980.

Di Tella, Guido. "La Estrategia Militar y las Torturas." *Revista del Centro de Investigación y Acción Social* 21, no. 214 (July 1972).

Duhalde, Eduardo Luis. "Juan José Valle: A treinta años de su muerte." *Crísis,* June 1986.

––––––. *El estado terrorista argentino.* Buenos Aires: Ediciones El Caballito, 1983.

Druetta, Gustavo. "Del militarismo a la democracia: Críticas, autocríticas y esperanzas," *Nuevo Proyecto* 1 (1986).

Druetta, Gustavo Adolfo, Eduardo Estévez, Ernesto López, and José Enrique Miguens. *Defensa y democracia, un debate entre civiles y militares.* Buenos Aires: Puntosur, 1990.

Ebon, Martin. *Che: The Making of a Legend.* New York: Signet, 1969.

Echagüe, Carlos. *El Socialimperialismo Ruso en la Argentina.* Buenos Aires: Ediciones Agora, 1984.

Echegaray, Fabián, and Ezequiel Raimondo. *Desencanto político, transición and democracia.* Buenos Aires: Centro Editor de América Latina, 1987.

Ejército Argentino. *El Derecho a la Libertad.* Buenos Aires: Congreso de la Nación, 1980.

Evans, Judith. "Carlos Menem: You're No Juan Perón." *International Economy,* January-February 1989, pp. 54–57.

Ferla, Salvador. *Martires y verdugos.* Buenos Aires: private printing, 1964.

Fernández, Antonio. *Informe sobre el problema azucarero.* Buenos Aires: Ediciones El Combatiente (circa 1974).

Fernández Alvariño, Próspero Germán. *Z argentina, el crimen del siglo.* Buenos Aires: private printing, 1973.

Fernández Huidobro, Eleuterio. *La tregua armada.* Montevideo: tea editorial.

Ferrer, Aldo. *Vivir con lo nuestro.* Buenos Aires: El Cid Editor, 1983.

––––––. *¿Puede Argentina pagar su deuda externa?* Buenos Aires: El Cid Editor, 1982.

Foro de Buenos Aires por la Vigencia de los Derechos Humanos. *Proceso a la explotación y a la represión en la Argentina.* Buenos Aires, 1973.

Foro de Estudios sobre La Administración de Justicia. *Definitivamente ... Nunca Más (La otra cara del informe de la CONADEP).* Buenos Aires: Fores, 1985.

Fraga, Rosendo. *Ejército: del escarnio al poder (1973–1976).* Buenos Aires: Planeta, 1988.

Frontalini, Daniel, and María Cristina Caiati. *El Mito de la Guerra Sucia.* Buenos Aires: Edición CELS, 1984.

Gabetta, Carlos. *Todos Somos Subversivos.* Buenos Aires: Bruguera, 1983.

García, César Reinaldo. *Historia de los Grupos y Partidos Políticos de la República Argentina desde 1810 a 1983.* Buenos Aires: Sainte Claire Editora, 1983.

García, Prudencio. *Ejército: presente y futuro.* Madrid: Alianza Editorial, 1975.

García Lupo, Rogelio. *Paraguay de Stroessner.* Buenos Aires: Ediciones B, 1989.

––––––. *Mercenarios y monopolios en la Argentina.* Buenos Aires: Legasa, 1984.

––––––. *Diplomacia secreta y rendición incondicional.* Buenos Aires: Legasa, 1983.

––––––. *Historia de unas Malas Relaciones.* Buenos Aires: Jorge Alvarez Editor, 1964.

García Lupo, Rogelio, Newton Carlos, and Juan Jorge Faundes. *El arsenal sudamericano de Saddam Hussein.* Buenos Aires: Grupo Editorial Zeta, 1991.

Gasparini, Juan. *El Crimen de Graiver.* Buenos Aires: Grupo Editorial Zeta, 1990.

_____ . *Montoneros, Final de Cuentas.* Buenos Aires: Puntosur, 1988.

_____ . *La Pista Suiza.* Buenos Aires: Legasa, 1986.

Gelman, Juan, and Osvaldo Bayer. *Exilio.* Buenos Aires: Legasa, 1984.

Gerschman, Rodolfo. "Indulto Controvertido." *Caretas,* January 7, 1991.

Gillespie, Richard. *Soldiers of Perón: Argentina's Montoneros.* New York: Oxford University Press, 1982.

Giussani, Pablo. "El misterio del chalet compartido." *La Razón,* November 15, 1986, p. 12.

_____ . *Montoneros, La Soberbia Armada.* Buenos Aires: Sudamericana-Planeta, 1984.

González Bermejo, Ernesto. *Las manos en el fuego.* Montevideo: Ediciones de la Banda Oriental, 1985.

González Janzen, Ignacio. *La Triple-A.* Buenos Aires: Editorial Contrapunto, 1986.

Goodwin, Richard. "Annals of Politics: A Footnote." *New Yorker,* May 25, 1968.

Gorriarán Merlo, Enrique Haroldo. *Democracia y Liberación.* Buenos Aires: Ediciones Reencuentro, 1985.

Graham, Bradley, "Buenos Aires Police Show Way in Transition to Democracy." *Washington Post,* July 1, 1987, p. A21.

Graham-Yool, Andrew. *The Press in Argentina,* 1973–8. London: Writers and Scholars Educational Trust, 1979.

_____ . *Portrait of an Exile.* London: Junction, 1981.

Grecco, Jorge, and Gustavo González. *Argentina: el ejército que tenemos.* Buenos Aires: Sudamericana, 1991.

Grondona, Mariano. "La dictadura." *Primera Plana,* May 31, 1966.

Guelar, Diego R. *El pueblo nunca se equivoca.* Buenos Aires: Sudamericana, 1988.

Guest, Iain. *Behind the Disappearances.* Philadelphia: University of Pennsylvania Press, 1990.

Guevara, Ernesto Che. *Obras Completas.* Buenos Aires: Ediciones del Plata, 1968.

Guillermoprieto, Alma. "Letter from Buenos Aires." *New Yorker,* July 15, 1991, pp. 64–78.

Gutman, Roy. *Banana Diplomacy.* New York: Simon & Schuster, 1988.

Hadad, Daniel. "Comandante 3-80: Jefe Militar de La 'Contra.'" *Somos,* January 14, 1987, pp. 4–11.

Haden-Guest, Anthony. "The Strange Life and Stranger Death of David Graiver." *New York,* January 22, 1979, pp. 47–53.

Hagelin, Ragnar. *Mi hija Dagmar.* Buenos Aires: Sudamericana-Planeta, 1984.

Haig, Alexander. *Caveat.* New York: Macmillan, 1984.

Harrington, Edwin, and Mónica González. *Bomba en una calle de Palermo.* Santiago: Editorial Emisión, 1987.

Hauberg, Clifford A. *Latin American Revolutions.* Minneapolis: Denison, 1968.

Hernández Arregui, Juan José. *La formación de la conciencia nacional.* Buenos Aires: Editorial Plus Ultra, 1973.

Hersh, Seymour. "The Price of Power: Kissinger, Nixon, and Chile." *Atlantic Monthly,* December 1982.

Hodgson, Bryan. "Argentina's New Beginning." *National Geographic,* August 1986.

Hunt, Linda. *Secret Agenda: The United States Government, Nazi Scientists and Project Paperclip, 1945 to 1990.* New York: St. Martin's, 1991.

Jaunarena, Mario, ed. *El pueblo vencerá: Discursos, entrevistas y artículos de Zelmar Michelini.* Buenos Aires: Ediciones Fundación, 1985.

Joyce, Christopher, and Eric Stover. *Witnesses from the Grave.* Boston: Little, Brown, 1991.

Kandel, Pablo, and Mario Monteverde. *Entorno y Caída.* Buenos Aires: Editorial Planeta Argentina, 1976.

Kirkpatrick, Jeane. "Argentine Surprise." *Washington Post,* November 12, 1991.

———. "Dictatorships and Double Standards." *Commentary,* November 1979.

Kornbluth, Peter. *Nicaragua: The Price of Intervention.* Washington, D.C.: Institute for Policy Studies, 1987.

Labaké, Juan Gabriel. *Carta a Los No Peronistas.* Buenos Aires: Editorial Leonardo Buschi, 1982.

Lamadrid, Alejandro F. *Política y alineamientos sindicales.* Buenos Aires: Puntosur, 1988.

Lane, Charles. "The War That Will Not End." *New Republic,* October 16, 1989.

Langguth, A. J. *Hidden Terrors: The Truth About U.S. Police Operations in Latin America.* New York: Pantheon, 1978.

Lanusse, Alejandro. *Mi testimonio.* Buenos Aires: Lasserre, 1977.

Lee, Martin A., and Kevin Coogan. "The Agca Con." *Village Voice,* December 24, 1985, pp. 19–23.

Lernoux, Penny. "Blood Taints Church in Argentina." *National Catholic Reporter,* April 12, 1985.

———. *In Banks We Trust.* Garden City, N.Y.: Doubleday, Anchor, 1984.

———. *Cry of the People.* New York: Doubleday, 1980.

Leuco, Alfredo, and José Antonio Díaz. *El Heredero de Perón.* Buenos Aires: Planeta, 1989.

———. *Los herederos de Alfonsín.* Buenos Aires: Sudamericana-Planeta, 1987.

Lewin, Boleslao. *Cómo fue la inmigración judía en la Argentina.* Buenos Aires: Editorial Plus Ultra, 1983.

Linklater, Magnus, Isabel Hilton, and Neal Ascherson. *The Fourth Reich: Klaus Barbie and the Neo-Fascist Connection.* London: Hodder and Stoughton, 1984.

Lonardi, Eduardo. *Dios es Justo.* Buenos Aires: Francisco A. Colombo, 1958.

López Echagüe, Hernán. *El Enigma del General Bussi.* Buenos Aires: Sudamericana, 1991.

Maechling, Charles, Jr. "The Argentine Pariah." *Foreign Policy,* no. 45 (Winter 1981–1982).

Mafud, Julio. *Psicología de la viveza criolla.* Buenos Aires: Distal, 1984.

Mahskin, Victor. *Operación Condor.* Buenos Aires: Editorial Cartago, 1985.

Marshall, Jonathan, Peter Dale Scott, and Jane Hunter. *The Iran-Contra Connection.* Boston: South End Press, 1987.

Martínez, Tomás Eloy. *La Novela de Perón.* Buenos Aires: Legasa, 1985.

———. "Perón y Los Nazis." *El Periodista,* no. 49 (August 16–22, 1985), p. 25.

———. *La pasión según Trelew.* Buenos Aires: Granica, 1973.

Mattini, Luis. *Hombres y Mujeres del PRT-ERP.* Buenos Aires: Editorial Contrapunto, 1990.

Maurer, Harry. "Anti-semitism in Argentina." *Nation,* February 12, 1977.

McGrory, Mary. "Timerman Shatters the Silence." *Washington Star,* June 14, 1981.

Méndez, Eugenio. *Aramburu: El Crimen Imperfecto.* Buenos Aires: Sudamericana- Planeta, 1987.

───── . *Confesiones de un Montonero.* Buenos Aires: Sudamericana-Planeta, 1985.

───── . *Alte. Lacoste: ¿Quién mató al General Actis?* Buenos Aires: El Cid Editor, 1984.

Mero, Roberto. *Conversaciones con Juan Gelman.* Buenos Aires: Editorial Contrapunto, 1988.

Mignone, Emilio F. *Iglesia y Dictadura.* Buenos Aires: Ediciones de Pensamiento Nacional, 1986.

Miguens, José Enrique. *Honor militar, conciencia moral y violencia terrorista.* Buenos Aires: Sudamericana-Planeta, 1986.

Miguens, José Enrique, and Frederick C. Turner. *Racionalidad del peronismo.* Buenos Aires: Planeta, 1988.

Millman, Joel. "Out of the Asylum." *Forbes,* December 23, 1991.

Mine, Douglas Grant. *Champions of the World.* New York: Simon & Schuster, 1988.

Mittelbach, Federico. *Informe sobre desaparecedores.* Buenos Aires: Ediciones de la Urraca, n.d.

Moneta, C. J., E. López, and A. Romero. *La reforma militar.* Buenos Aires: Legasa, 1985.

Muñoz, Jorge. *Seguidme! Vida de Alberto Villar.* Buenos Aires: Ro.Ca. Producciones, 1983.

Murmis, Miguel, and Juan Carlos Portantiero. *Estudios sobre los orígenes del peronismo.* Buenos Aires: Siglo Veintiuno Argentina Editores, 1972.

Naipaul, V. S. "Argentina Reborn?" *New York Review of Books,* February 13, 1992.

───── . "Revisiting a Cruel Country." *New York Review of Books,* January 30, 1992, pp. 13– 18.

───── . *El regreso de Eva Perón y otras crónicas.* Barcelona: Editorial Seix Barral, 1983.

Neier, Aryeh. "Argentine Jews: The Crime of Silence Revisited." *Nation,* June 13, 1981.

Neilson, James. "The Education of Jacobo Timerman." *Books and Writers,* 1981.

Nosiglia, Julio E. *Botín de guerra.* Buenos Aires: Cooperativa Tierra Fértil, 1985.

Nussbaum, Bruce. "The Big Business of Being Henry Kissinger." *Business Week,* December 2, 1985, pp. 76–80.

O'Donnell, Guillermo. *¿Y a mi, que me importa?* Buenos Aires: Estudios CEDES, 1984.

Orth, Maureen. "Charisma Argentina." *Vanity Fair,* November 1989.

Page, Diana. "Housing Groups in Argentina: Getting in on the Ground Floor." *Grassroots Development* 8, no. 1 (1984), pp. 39–42.

Page, Joseph. *Perón: A Biography.* New York: Random House, 1983.

Pandovani, Marcelle. *Vivir con el terrorismo.* Barcelona: Editorial Planeta, 1983.

Paoletti, Alipio. *Como los Nazis, Como en Vietnam.* Buenos Aires: Editorial Contrapunto, 1987.

───── . "La complicidad de Acindar, S.A.." *Madres de la Plaza de Mayo,* April 1985.

Partnoy, Alicia. *The Little School: Tales of Disappearance and Survival in Argentina.* Pittsburgh: Cleis Press, 1986.

Pascale, Graziano. *La democracia en muletas.* Montevideo: private printing, 1983.

Pavón Pereyra, Enrique. *El Diario Secreto de Perón.* Buenos Aires: Sudamericana-Planeta, 1985.

Peralta-Ramos, Monica, and Carlos H. Waisman. *From Military Rule to Liberal Democracy in Argentina*. Boulder: Westview Press, 1987.

Peregrino Fernández, Rodolfo. *Autocrítica Policial*. Buenos Aires: El Cid Editor, 1983.

Perina, Rubén, ed. *Argentina en el mundo, 1973–1987*. Buenos Aires: Grupo Editor Latinoamericano, 1988.

Perina, Rubén. *Onganía, Levingston and Lanusse: Los militares en la política argentina*. Buenos Aires: Editorial de Belgrano, 1983.

Perón, Juan. *La Hora de los Pueblos*. Buenos Aires: Ediciones PV, n.d.

Piñero Pacheco, Raúl. *La degeneración del 80*. Buenos Aires: El Cid Editor, 1981.

Potash, Robert. *El Ejército y la política en la Argentina, 1945–1962*. Buenos Aires: Sudamericana, 1980.

Ratliff, William, and Roger Fontaine. *Changing Course: The Capitalist Revolution in Argentina*. Stanford: Stanford University–Hoover Institution, 1990.

Republica Argentina. *El Terrorismo en la Argentina*. Buenos Aires: Poder Ejecutivo Nacional, 1980.

Reyna, Roberto. *La Perla*. Buenos Aires: El Cid Editor, 1984.

Rock, David. *Argentina 1516–1982: From Spanish Colonialization to the Falklands War*. Berkeley: University of California Press, 1985.

Rodríguez Lamas, Daniel. *La Revolución Libertadora*. Buenos Aires: Centro Editor de América Latina, 1985.

Rosenberg, Tina. *Children of Cain*. New York: William Morrow, 1991.

———. "Beyond Elections." *Foreign Policy*, no. 84, (Fall 1991).

Rosenblum, Mort. "Terror in Argentina." *New York Review of Books*, October 28, 1976.

Rosenthal, Morton. "The Threatened Jews of Argentina." *ADL Bulletin*, March 1971.

Rouquié, Alain. *Poder militar y sociedad política en la Argentina*, vol. 2, 1943–1973. Buenos Aires: Emecé, 1983.

Rückerl, Adalbert. *The Investigation of Nazi Crimes, 1945–1978*. Heidelberg: C. F. Müller, 1979.

Ruiz Núñez, Héctor. "La P-2 en Argentina." *Humor*, no. 175 (June 1986,) and no. 177 (July 1986).

———. "En el nombre de la logia: La P-2 en Argentina." *Humor*, no. 174 (June 1986).

———. "López Rega: Esplendor y decadencia." *Humor*, no. 173 (May 1986).

Sáenz, Dalmiro, and Sergio Joselovsky. *El Día que Mataron a Alfonsín*. Buenos Aires: Ediciones Tarso, 1986.

Sánchez Salazar, Gustavo. *Barbie, Criminal hasta el fin*. Buenos Aires: Legasa, 1987.

Santucho, Julio. *Los Ultimos Guevaristas*. Buenos Aires: Puntosur, 1988.

Santucho, Mario R. *Poder burgués, poder revolucionario*. Buenos Aires: Ediciones El Combatiente, 1974.

Scenna, Miguel Angel. *Los Militares*. Buenos Aires: Editorial de Belgrano, 1980.

Scheer, Robert. *The Diary of Che Guevara*. New York: Bantam, 1968.

Schlesinger, Stephen, and Stephen Kinzer. *Bitter Fruit: The Untold Story of the American Coup in Guatemala*. Garden City, N.Y.: Doubleday, Anchor, 1983.

Schoultz, Lars. *Human Rights and United States Policy Toward Latin America*. Princeton: Princeton University Press, 1981.

Schumacher, Edward. "Argentina and Democracy." *Foreign Affairs,* Summer 1984, pp. 1070–1095.

Senén González, Santiago. *Diez años de sindicalismo argentino.* Buenos Aires: Corregidor, 1984.

Seoane, María. *Todo o Nada.* Buenos Aires: Planeta, 1991.

Seoane, María, and Héctor Ruiz Núñez. *La Noche de los Lapices.* Buenos Aires: Editorial Contrapunto, 1986.

Serra, Alfredo. "Espionaje." *Somos,* June 8, 1979, pp. 8–13.

Siletta, Alfredo. *La secta moon.* Buenos Aires: El Cid Editor, 1985.

Simeoni, Héctor R. *¡Aniquilen al ERP! La "guerra sucia" en el monte tucumano.* Buenos Aires: Ediciones Cosmos, 1985.

Simpson, John, and Jana Bennett. *The Disappeared: Voices from a Secret War.* London: Robson, 1985.

Singer, Daniel. "The Gladiators." *Nation,* December 10, 1990, pp. 720–721.

Snow, Peter G. *Political Forces in Argentina.* Rev. ed. New York: Praeger, 1979.

Sofer, Eugene F. "A New Terror Grips Argentina." *Present Tense,* Autumn 1977, p. 23.

Solari Yrigoyen, Hipólito. *Los Años Crueles.* Buenos Aires: Bruguera, 1983.

Sopeña, Germán. "José A. Martínez de Hoz: esta vez será distinto." *La Nación,* Fall 1991.

Stein, Nancy. "U.S. Training Programs For Foreign Military Personnel: The Pentagon's Protégés," *NACLA's Latin America and Empire Report* 10, no. 1 (January 1, 1976).

Stepan, Alfred. *Rethinking Military Politics.* Princeton: Princeton University Press, 1988.

———. *The Military in Politics: Changing Patterns in Brazil.* Princeton: Princeton University Press, 1971.

Stover, Eric. *Scientists and Human Rights in Argentina Since 1976.* Washington, D.C.: American Association for the Advancement of Science, 1981.

Stover, Eric, and Elena O. Nightingale. *The Breaking of Bodies and Minds: Torture, Psychiatric Abuse, and the Health Professions.* New York: Freeman, 1985.

Szulc, Tad. *Twilight of the Tyrants.* New York: Holt, 1959.

Terragno, Rodolfo. *De Cámpora a Videla.* Buenos Aires: Peña Lillo Editor, 1981.

Tesseire, Germán. "Influencia del Ejército en el Desarrollo de los Valores Materiales y Morales del Pueblo Argentino." *Revista de la Escuela Superior de Guerra,* no. 617 (January 1953).

Thornton, Lawrence. *Imagining Argentina.* New York: Bantam, 1988.

Timerman, Jacobo. *Cuba.* New York: Knopf, 1990.

———. *Chile.* New York: Knopf, 1987.

———. *Preso sin nombre, Celda sin número.* Buenos Aires: El Cid Editor, 1982.

———. "The Bodies Counted Are Our Own." *Columbia Journalism Review,* May-June 1980, pp. 30–33.

Torres Molina, Ramón. "La actual etapa de las guerrillas argentinas." *Cristianismo y Revolución,* no. 29 (June 1971).

Trinquier, Roger. *Guerra, Subversión, Revolución.* Buenos Aires: Ed. Rioplatense, 1975.

Tsur, Jacob. *Cartas credenciales.* Jerusalem: Publicaciones La Semana, 1983.

Tusa, Ann, and John Tusa. *The Nuremberg Trial.* New York: Atheneum, 1984.

Ugarte, José Manuel. *Seguridad Interior.* Buenos Aires: Fundación Arturo Illia, 1990.

Uriarte, Claudio. *Almirante Cero*. Buenos Aires: Planeta, 1992.

Urondo, Francisco. *Trelew, La patria fusilada*. Buenos Aires: Editorial Contrapunto, 1988.

Valcourt, Richard R. "Controlling U.S. Hired Hands." *International Journal of Intelligence and Counterintelligence* 2, no. 3.

Valori, Giancarlo Elia. "El Prejuicio Antimilitarista: El Papel y La Responsibilidad de las Fuerzas Armadas." *Las Bases* 1, no. 6 (January 18, 1972).

Varas, Augusto. *Los Militares en el Poder*. Santiago: Pehuén FLACSO, 1987.

Varela-Cid, Eduardo, ed. *Los sofistas y la prensa canalla*. Buenos Aires: El Cid Editor, 1984.

Varela-Cid, Eduardo, and Luis Vicens. *La imbecilización de la mujer*. Buenos Aires: El Cid Editor, 1984.

Vásquez, Enrique. *La Ultima*. Buenos Aires: EUDEBA, 1985.

Veiga, Raúl. *Las organizaciones de derechos humanos*. Buenos Aires: Centro Editor de América Latina, 1985.

Venegas, Benjamín. "La hipótesis del doble agente." *El Periodista*, no. 232 (March 3–9, 1989), pp. 10–13.

Verbitsky, Bernardo. *Villa Miseria También Es América*. Buenos Aires: Editorial Contrapunto, 1987.

———. *Hermana y sombra*. Buenos Aires: Editorial Planeta Argentina, 1977.

Verbitsky, Horacio. *Robo para la corona*. Buenos Aires: Planeta, 1991

———. "Todo Vale." *Página* 12, May 5, 1991.

———. *La Educación Presidencial*. Buenos Aires: Puntosur, 1990.

———. *Medio siglo de proclamas militares*. Buenos Aires: Editora/12, 1987.

———. *Civiles y Militares*. Buenos Aires: Editorial Contrapunto, 1987.

———. *Ezeiza*. Buenos Aires: Editorial Contrapunto, 1985.

———. *La Posguerra Sucia*. Buenos Aires: Legasa, 1985.

———. *Rodolfo Walsh y la prensa clandestina*. Buenos Aires: Ediciones de la Urraca, 1985.

———. *La ultima batalla de la Tercera Guerra Mundial*. Buenos Aires: Legasa, 1984.

Vernazza, Jorge, ed. *Padre Mugica, una vida para el pueblo*. Buenos Aires: Pequén Ediciones, 1984.

Vicens, Luis. *Loperreguismo y Justicialismo*. Buenos Aires: El Cid Editor, n.d.

Waldmann, Peter, and Ernesto Garzón Valdéz. *El poder militar en la Argentina, 1976–1981*. Buenos Aires: Editorial Galerna, 1983.

Walsh, Rodolfo. *Caso Satanowsky*. Buenos Aires: Ediciones de la Flor, 1986.

———. *Variaciones en rojo*. Buenos Aires: Ediciones de la Flor, 1985.

———. *Operación Masacre*. Buenos Aires: Ediciones de la Flor, 1984.

———. *¿Quién Mató a Rosendo?* Buenos Aires: Ediciones de la Flor, 1984.

Wieseltier, Leon. "The Many Trials of Jacobo Timerman." *Dissent* 28, no. 4 (October 1, 1981), pp. 425–435.

Woodward, Bob. *Veil: The Secret Wars of the CIA, 1981–1987*. New York: Simon & Schuster, 1987.

Wynia, Gary W. *Argentina in the Postwar Era*. Albuquerque: University of New Mexico Press, 1978.

Periodicals and Newspapers

Argentina.

Ambito Financiero; Buenos Aires Herald; Caras y Caretas; Clarín; Confirmado; Crísis; Cristianismo y Revolución; Crónica; Cuestionario; Diario del Juicio; El Bimestre; El Descamisado; El Periodista; El Porteño; Evita Montonera; Expreso; Gente; Humor; La Causa Peronista; La Gaceta (Tucumán); La Nación; La Opinión; La Prensa; La Razón; La Semana; La Vanguardia; La Voz; Las Bases; Noticias (periodical); Noticias (newspaper); Nueva Presencia; Página 12; Panorama; Primera Plana; Review of the River Plate; Siete Días; Somos; Testigo; Tiempo Argentino; Todo es Historia.

Italy.

Corriere della Sera; L'Espresso; La Repubblica; Panorama.

United States.

ADL Bulletin; Atlanta Constitution; Business Week; Chicago Tribune; Christian Science Monitor; FBIS; Foreign Policy; Los Angeles Times; Miami Herald; National Catholic News Service; National Catholic Reporter; Newsweek; New York; Nation; New Republic; New York Times; Village Voice; Washington Post; Time; Wall Street Journal; Washington Star.

Other.

Economist; Latin American Weekly Report, and Tablet (Great Britain); Excelsior (Mexico); Búsqueda (Uruguay); Caretas (Peru); Jerusalem Post (Israel); ABC Color (Paraguay); Tiempo (Spain).

Reports

Comisión bicameral investigadora de violaciones de derechos humanos, Tucumán, 1985.

El Terrorismo en la Argentina, Buenos Aires, 1980.

Final Report of the Government Commission on Human Rights, La Rioja province, December 1984.

CONADEP, Nunca Más (Report of the Argentine National Commission on the Disappeared). Buenos Aires: Buenos Aires University Press, 1984.

Proceso a la Explotación y a la Represión en la Argentina. Buenos Aires: Foro de Buenos Aires por la Vigencia de los Derechos Humanos, 1973.

Rockefeller, Nelson A. "Quality of Life in the Americas: Report of a Presidential Mission for the Western Hemisphere." Department of State Bulletin, December 8, 1969.

About the Book and Author

In 1976 a military coup in Argentina heralded the full-scale operation of the "Dirty War." Called by the generals "the opening battle of World War III," it suggested a high-stakes fight to preserve "Western Christian civilization" against a vast army of Marxist guerrillas. But the "Dirty War" was a myth: Military intelligence services fabricated a shadowy omnipresent threat from armed leftists as a pretext for seizing power and terrorizing the civilian population. By 1983, thousands had been murdered, tortured, and disappeared.

In this gripping narrative, Martin Edwin Andersen explodes the myth, arguing persuasively that leftist guerrillas at no time represented a threat to the stability of the constitutional government. Beginning by tracing the social, economic, and political decay of a country that had been known in the early part of the century for its highly developed civil society, he then turns to the underworld of intelligence agents, military personnel, and counterinsurgency specialists who designed the "Dirty War." Giving special attention to the sectors that suffered most under military repression—the church, the universities, and factories—he documents the twisted internal security doctrines that allowed the messianic and power-hungry military to carry out its gruesome mission. The critical role of U.S. foreign policy is also analyzed, as it swung from support for the generals, to promotion of human rights, to the use of Argentine military "proxies" in Reagan's secret war in Central America.

Based on hundreds of interviews with former guerrillas, death squad members, U.S. intelligence agents, survivors of death camps, and relatives of the disappeared as well as thousands of recently declassified State Department and intelligence documents, Andersen's *Dossier Secreto* offers a powerful indictment of military rule and of the Reagan-Bush administration's involvement in one of the most sordid chapters in recent Latin American history.

Martin Edwin Andersen is a staff member of the U.S. Senate Foreign Relations Committee. He covered the 1985 "Dirty War" trials for *Newsweek* and *The Washington Post* and has also reported extensively on the military and other Latin American issues for *Foreign Policy,* the *International Herald Tribune, The Nation,* the *Economist,* and the *New Republic.*

Index

Mossad, 242, 253
Mothers of the Plaza de Mayo. *See* Madres de
la Plaza de Mayo
Movimiento de Opinión Nacional (MON),
278
Movimiento de Sacerdotes para el Tercer
Mundo (MSTM), 54–55
Movimiento Izquierdista Revolucionario
(MIR) (Bolivia), 119, 139, 225
Movimiento Popular Colorado (MOPOCO)
(Paraguay), 230
MSTM. *See* Movimiento de Sacerdotes para
el Tercer Mundo
Mugica, Padre Carlos, 110–111, 344(n28)
Mujica, Rodolfo C., 247
Mundani, José, 349(n7)
Mundo, El, 95, 109, 290
Murias, Juan de Dios, 189
Musse, Elías, 185
Mussolini, Benito, 145. *See also* Fascists
My Enemies and Yours (Hitler), 145
My New Order (Hitler), 145
Myth of the Dirty War, The (Frontalini &
Caiati), 3
Nación, La, 248, 263, 268, 269

Naftal, Alejandra, 197
Narcotics traffic, 5, 14, 142–143, 299
and Bolivia intervention, 290, 290–291,
297
U.S. fugitives, 20, 329–330(n21)
Natal Coda, Carlos, 280
National Commission on the Disappearance
of Persons. *See* Sábato Commission
National Council on Scientific and
Technological Investigations. *See*
Consejo Nacional de Investigaciones
Científicas y Técnicas
National Counterinsurgency Strategy. *See*
Estrategia Nacional Contrasubversiva
National Democratic Institute for
International Affairs (NDI), 315–316
National Information Directorate. *See*
Dirección de Información Nacional
National Information Service (Brazil). *See*
Serviço Nacional de Informaçoes
Nationalist Liberating Alliance. *See* Alianza
Libertadora Nacionalista

Nationalist Restoration Guard. *See* Guardia
Restauradora Nacionalista
National Opinion Movement. *See*
Movimiento de Opinión Nacional
National University Concentration. *See*
Concentración Nacional Universitaria
National Vanguard. *See* Avanguardia
Nazionale (Italy)
National Workers Confederation (Uruguay).
See Convención Nacional de
Trabajadores
Naval Industries Workers Union. *See*
Sindicato de Obreros de la Industria
Naval
Naval Information Service. *See* Servicio de
Informaciones Navales
Navarro, Lt. Col. Antonio, 106
Navy Mechanics School. *See* Escuela
Mecánica de la Armada
Nazis. *See* Fascists
NDI. *See* National Democratic Institute for
International Affairs
Neilson, James, 259
New Order. *See* Ordine Nuovo (Italy)
New York Times, 167
Nicaragua, 1, 287, 292, 293, 297–298, 303,
309. *See also* Central America
Nicolaides, Cristino, 211
Nicoletti, Alfredo, 346(n61)
Night of the Long Sticks, 58–59, 203
Night of the Pencils, 201–203
1955–1973 governments, 4
and Allende victory, 69–70
anti-Semitism under, 143–144
and economy, 29, 42, 48, 68, 70
Frondizi presidency, 41–45
guerrilla groups emergence, 4, 61–62, 70–
73
Illia presidency, 48–52
Lanusse regime, 75–81
Levingston regime, 68–69
Liberating Revolution (1955), 34, 36
Lonardi revolt, 32–34
military factionalism under, 13, 40–41, 45–
47
1973 elections, 82–83
Peronist resistance, 34–37, 43, 238,
332(n43), 337(n4)